Jefferson and His Time

Jefferson the Virginian
Jefferson and the Rights of Man
Jefferson and the Ordeal of Liberty
Jefferson the President: First Term, 1801–1805
Jefferson the President: Second Term, 1805–1809
The Sage of Monticello

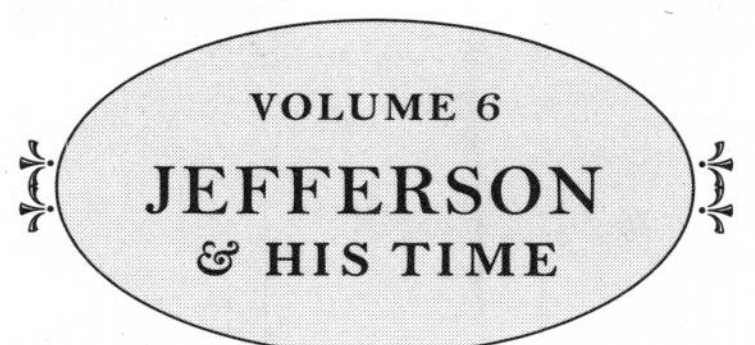

The Sage of Monticello

DUMAS MALONE

UNIVERSITY OF VIRGINIA PRESS
CHARLOTTESVILLE

This University of Virginia Press edition was made possible with the generous support of the Office of the President of the University of Virginia. Illustration research was assisted by a gift from the Institute for Advanced Studies in Culture of the University of Virginia.

University of Virginia Press

This edition published by arrangement with Little, Brown and Company (Inc.), New York, NY.
Printed in the United States of America on acid-free paper

First University of Virginia Press edition published 2005

ISBN 0-8139-2366-2 (paper)

9 8 7 6 5 4 3 2 1

The Library of Congress has cataloged the hardcover edition as follows:

Library of Congress Cataloging-in-Publication Data

Malone, Dumas, 1892–
The sage of Monticello / by Dumas Malone.— 1st University of Virginia Press ed.
p. cm. — (Jefferson and his time ; v. 6)
Originally published: Boston : Little, Brown, 1981.
Includes bibliographical references and index.
ISBN 0-8139-2360-3 (acid-free paper)
1. Jefferson, Thomas, 1743–1826. 2. Presidents—United States—Biography.
3. University of Virginia—History. 4. United States—History—War of 1812.
5. Monticello (Va.) I. Title.
E332 .M25 2005 vol. 6
[E332.6]
973.4'6'092—dc22
[B 973.4/6/0

2004030847

Frontispiece: Thomas Jefferson in 1821. Portrait by Thomas Sully. Replica of portrait painted from life at Monticello. (Courtesy of the West Point Museum Collection)

This work as a whole is for
ELISABETH GIFFORD MALONE

This volume is for
my devoted co-workers
STEVEN HAROLD HOCHMAN
and
KATHERINE MOON SARGEANT

Contents

Illustrations

Introduction

THIS book deals with the life of Thomas Jefferson between his retirement from the presidency on March 4, 1809, and his death at Monticello on July 4, 1826. It concludes the comprehensive biography entitled *Jefferson and His Time.* I began work on that in 1943, shortly after the celebration of his bicentennial, and published *Jefferson the Virginian* on his birthday five years later. In the introduction I stated that I hoped to complete the study in four volumes. By the time I wrote the next introduction I had concluded that five volumes would be required to maintain the scale of the first, and I eventually felt compelled to extend the number to six. Even so, I have left out much I would have liked to include and cannot hope to have done full justice to a virtually inexhaustible subject.

I prudently refrained from making a precise prediction of the time that would be required to complete the task. Like the construction of Monticello this work of historical biography has suffered considerable interruption. During one stretch of six or seven years I could devote practically no time to it. As a result there was a lapse of more than a decade between the appearance of Volume II in 1951 and that of Volume III in 1962. It was in the latter year that I was relieved of academic duties and entered upon the period of technical retirement during which the last three volumes of the work were written. In each of these I have made some reference to the fortunate combination of circumstances which enabled me to remain busy and productive when I might have been turned out to pasture.

This final volume covers more time than any of the others except the first and has the greatest diversity of them all. Because of the variety of Jefferson's activities and the lack of a dominant narrative thread such as was provided by public events when he was in office, I have resorted more often than hitherto to topical treatment. I hope I have been reasonably successful in avoiding excessive repetition on the one hand and imperfect synchronization on the other.

Jefferson was not strictly correct when he said that he had been continuously in public service for forty years. Actually there were a few breaks, but during almost his entire maturity he had been a public man. Again and again he had contrasted the miseries of official position with the blessings of private life. When he ferried across the Potomac on his way homeward shortly before he became sixty-six, he had no way of knowing that he would never do so again, but he was determined to remain a private citizen. Leaving affairs of state to President James Madison, whom he trusted implicitly, he avoided the very appearance of sharing the determination of public policy.

Though he claimed to be reading Tacitus and Thucydides rather than newspapers, he remained well informed about developments both at home and abroad. His correspondence provides an illuminating commentary on the main events of the time. In his private letters Jefferson spoke with candor and often with extravagance. He was frequently embarrassed by the unwarranted publication of extracts from these. On the other hand he was glad for certain letters of his to be passed around. Some of them were influential, but in general it can be said that he had slight influence on national policies during his retirement. His prestige with his contemporaries increased with the passing years, but posterity was the real beneficiary of his writings.

The blessings Jefferson expected to enjoy as a private citizen were positive as well as negative. Not only would he escape from public cares and quarrels; he would escape to his family, his farms, and his books. This he did, but the results were not in full accord with his sanguine anticipations. He knew he would face financial problems. As an ex-President of the United States he received no pension. At no time did he profit in a monetary way from his writings or his inventions. Already burdened with debt, he had only his farms to depend on. His sad financial history is recorded in considerable detail in this book. Jefferson may have lacked managerial skill, as he himself said, and his absorption in public matters had undoubtedly prevented him from giving his personal affairs the attention they deserved. But his ultimate insolvency was primarily owing to factors beyond his control.

The ex-President, who had so often complained when in office that he was deprived of family life, suffered no lack of it in retirement. His daughter Martha, with her large and growing brood, lived with him at Monticello. A couple of his grandchildren usually accompanied him on visits to Poplar Forest, his second home. He had a dozen grandchildren altogether, including Francis Eppes, the son of his deceased daughter Maria. They adored and revered the kindly patriarch and contributed greatly to his happiness. His hospitality was imposed upon by relatives, but he bore with equanimity his responsibilities as the head of the clan.

The physician who attended him in his last months said that no one could have been more amiable in domestic relations. Life at Monticello was not always tranquil, but Jefferson was at his best as a family man.

In his old age he must have been more aware of the limitations of agriculture as a means of livelihood than when he penned the rhapsody that appeared in his *Notes on Virginia*, but he continued to regard the cultivation of the soil as the most delightful of occupations. In the long run he may have found rural life less blissful than Horace and Cicero made it out to be. But he found great enjoyment in it — cultivating his garden and riding over his red hills.

In the spring of 1815 he entrusted the management of his Albemarle farms to his grandson Jeff Randolph. He did not cease to be an outdoor man at the age of seventy-two, but he may be said to have attained full stature as a bibliophile and patron of learning about this time. John Adams, reporting that the brightest young Bostonians were eager to visit the Sage of Monticello, introduced several of them to him. Pilgrimages to the shrine increased thereafter.

The Sage sold his superb library to Congress after the British burned the small one in the Capitol in Washington, but he promptly proceeded to assemble another. He now laid less emphasis on law and politics than previously and more on history and the ancient classics, which he read in the original until his dying day.

Not only did he pursue knowledge with delight and encourage others to do so; he served the cause of public enlightenment by creating institutions that were destined to endure. As a champion of individual freedom and self-government, Jefferson tended to minimize the value of institutions and even to fear them. Although a notable President in many ways, he had contributed little to the presidency as an institution. His contributions to executive procedure were not perpetuated. In his last years, however, he gave substance to his undying faith in private learning and public education in the form of a library and a university. He never claimed that he was the founder of the Library of Congress, but it was his virtual creation, and his title as father of the University of Virginia is beyond dispute.

While he himself regarded the establishment of this institution of higher learning as one of the most memorable achievements of his entire life, he failed to obtain for his state a full-bodied system of public education such as he had advocated for half a century. He was convinced that only an enlightened society was capable of genuine self-government and that no ignorant people could maintain their God-given freedom. In the numerous papers and letters he wrote on this subject he consistently championed public education at all levels, laying greatest emphasis on the elementary stage. At the same time he clearly perceived the importance of trained leadership and recognized the usefulness of knowledge. His effort to establish in his own state a temple of freedom and fount of enlightenment is described in detail in this book. I have attempted to follow the long and complicated story of the struggle step by step.

After three or four years of tedious preliminaries, the University was chartered in 1819. This turned out to be one of the most discouraging years in the history of the commonwealth and for Jefferson himself. He had told John Adams that he steered his bark with hope in the head, leaving fear astern. He never ceased to be basically optimistic and his imperturbability in the face of disaster was frequently remarked upon. But the panic of 1819, the Missouri question, and the decisions of John Marshall plunged him into the deepest depression of spirit that he had known since the time of the Alien and Sedition Acts.

He sharply criticized the oligarchic constitution of Virginia and openly advocated its democratization. Although he had no direct responsibility for the state-rights movement in his commonwealth in the 1820's, he strongly supported it in private and was induced to express approval of its principles in public. At this stage, when he had little or no influence on the course of events, he assumed a defensive posture in response to political developments and in reaction to economic trends. He deplored slavery and believed that ultimate emancipation was inevitable. On the other hand, he recognized the dangers of emancipation and denied the authority of Congress to intervene in the domestic affairs of a state. Confronted with a contradiction he could not resolve, he left this problem to another generation.

It took him and his supporters six years to make a living reality of the University that existed on paper. During this period there was little or no improvement in the economic situation in Virginia. The state, which lost its primacy in population by 1820, was clearly falling behind in influence and power in the Union. Under these circumstances Jefferson's role as a local patriot sometimes overshadowed that of Sage. He appealed to local interest in behalf of the University and expected it to be a bastion of republicanism against consolidation.

In certain religious groups he aroused fears that were destined to persist. He was not always wise or tactful, but he consistently supported religious freedom and sought academic excellence. He had to curtail his program somewhat, but the University he created was unique. There was scarcely a thing in the original institution that he did not prescribe and many of his distinctive ideas were to be long-lived. The academical village, whose beginnings I have had the pleasure of describing, is still intact. In 1976 it was voted "the proudest achievement of American architecture in the past 200 years."[1] It is a pity the author of the Declaration of Independence could not have been present to receive this accolade in person.

Many of Jefferson's contemporaries disapproved of both his buildings and his academic program. Speaking of the latter, one of his most sympathetic guests said that, while it was less impractical than he had feared, he was not sure that the institution could be successful.[2] Throughout Jefferson's career opponents and critics charged him with being an impractical theorist. In his seventy-sixth winter he told a friend that his plan for a complete system of public education in his state might be a "Utopian dream." In the twentieth century it would certainly not have been so regarded; it was merely ahead of its time. The same can be said of other projects of this forward-looking man, and the claim that he was a theorist was owing to more than his specific proposals.

Three decades after his death his granddaughter Ellen said that the main cause for the charge of impracticality against him was "his obstinate propensity to think well of mankind, of human nature, to trust largely the good sense and good feeling of the mass."[3] Much as she adored him, she did not fully share his democratic spirit. In her opinion the question whether he was right or wrong in trusting the American people as he did had not yet been answered.

It now appears that he expected citizens to be more reasonable than they are likely to be in any age. He made too little allowance for emotions and counted too much on the sufficiency of reason. In my judgment, as in that of John Adams, he underestimated the evil in unregenerate man, and time has shown that more is needed to cure the ills of mankind than the accumulation of knowledge. Having said this, I must also say that I regard his faith as the most admirable thing about him and his most enduring legacy — his faith in human beings and in the human mind. To those who exalt force and condone deception he will ever be a visionary, to be ignored or silenced. But to all who cherish freedom and abhor tyranny in any form he is an abiding symbol of the hope that springs eternal.

[1] Jefferson's design was selected in a Bicentennial poll of the American Institute of Architects (*AIA Journal*, 65 [July 1976], 91).

[2] George Ticknor to W. H. Prescott, Dec. 16, 1824 (*Life, Letters, and Journals*, I, 348).

[3] Ellen Randolph Coolidge to H. S. Randall, Feb. 13, 1856 (Letterbook, Coolidge Papers, UVA).

It has been my great privilege as a biographer to be intimately associated with this extraordinary man for many years. At the end of my long journey with him I leave him with regret and salute him with profound respect.

DUMAS MALONE

Alderman Library
University of Virginia
January, 1981

Chronology

1809

Mar. 4 TJ retires from the presidency.
11 He leaves Washington for Monticello, arriving March 15.
Apr. 19 President Madison proclaims the restoration of trade with Britain under the Erskine agreement.
Aug. 19 Non-Intercourse with Britain is resumed.
Oct. 19–23 TJ visits Richmond.
Dec. 1 He acknowledges receipt of the first volume of Hening's *Statutes at Large*.

1810

Feb. 2 The Literary Fund of Virginia is established.
July 31 TJ completes a brief for his lawyers on the New Orleans batture case.
Aug. 12 He suggests that William Duane publish Destutt de Tracy's commentary on Montesquieu.

1811

Mar. 27 Before this date, TJ becomes a great-grandfather upon the birth of John Warner Bankhead.
Apr. 6 James Monroe succeeds Robert Smith as secretary of state.
Dec. 5 Livingston *vs.* Jefferson (the batture case) is dismissed.
Toward the end of the year, TJ begins the manufacturing of cloth at Monticello.

1812

Jan. 1 John Adams renews correspondence with TJ.
Apr. 12 TJ sends William Wirt an account of Patrick Henry.
June 18 War with Great Britain is declared.

1813

Jan. 24 TJ writes John W. Eppes the first of several letters on public finance.

1814

Mar. 25	TJ is named a trustee of Albemarle Academy.
Aug.–Sept.	Thomas Mann Randolph, Jeff Randolph, and Charles Bankhead take part in the defense of Richmond.
Aug. 25	TJ assures Edward Coles that the emancipation of the slaves is inevitable but declines active leadership of the cause.
Sept. 7	He writes a letter to Peter Carr describing a scheme of public education.
21	He offers to sell his library to Congress to replace the one burned by the British on Aug. 24.

1815

Feb. 4–7	George Ticknor and Francis Gray visit Monticello.
14	About this time TJ learns of the Treaty of Ghent.
Mar. 16	Jeff Randolph is married to Jane Hollins Nicholas.
Apr. 18	About this time TJ sends his library to Washington.
June 21	Before this date, Jeff Randolph is given the management of TJ's Albemarle farms.
Sept. 18	TJ, accompanied by Francis Gilmer and the Abbé Correa, visits the Peaks of Otter.

1816

Jan. 9	TJ informs Benjamin Austin that he now supports the development of American manufacturing.
Feb. 16	He learns of the passage of the Central College bill.
March	Ellen Randolph visits Washington.
Apr. 6	TJ announces the completion of his translation of Destutt de Tracy's *Political Economy*.
July 12	He writes Samuel Kercheval about the revision of the Virginia Constitution.
Oct. 18	He is named a Visitor of Central College.

1817

Mar. 4	James Monroe is inaugurated as President.
May 5	The Board of Visitors of Central College meets for the first time.
August	TJ travels to Natural Bridge with his granddaughters.
Oct. 6	The cornerstone of the first pavilion at Central College is laid.

1818

January	TJ sums up his weather records.
Feb. 4	He writes an explanation of confidential papers he had collected while secretary of state.
22	The legislature passes a bill establishing a university.

July 30 TJ learns that the Bank of the United States is curtailing all notes, including his.
Aug. 1–4 He attends the Rockfish Gap Conference.
Aug. 7–21 He visits Warm Springs and leaves seriously ill.
Dec. 7, 9 He cancels newspaper subscriptions to all but the *Richmond Enquirer*.

1819

Jan. 25 The university bill passes, with Central College as the site.
Feb. 1 A fight takes place between Jeff Randolph and Charles Bankhead.
15 Joseph C. Cabell informs TJ of his appointment as Visitor.
Mar. 6 The McCulloch *vs.* Maryland case is decided by the Supreme Court.
29 TJ is elected Rector at the first meeting of the UVA Board of Visitors.
May He helps set up Stack's preparatory school in Charlottesville.
Aug. 5 Wilson Cary Nicholas informs TJ of his failure.
Sept. 6 TJ writes Spencer Roane about his HAMPDEN letters.
Oct. 31 He writes William Short about being an Epicurean, and afterwards completes his "Life and Morals of Jesus."
Dec. 13 Thomas Mann Randolph becomes governor of Virginia, serving three terms.

1820

Apr. 3 The Visitors accept Thomas Cooper's resignation.
22 TJ writes John Holmes about the Missouri Compromise.
Sept. 21 He instructs Francis Eppes on his trip to the University of South Carolina.
Oct. 10 Wilson Cary Nicholas dies.
Dec. 25 TJ writes to Thomas Ritchie praising John Taylor's *Construction Construed*.

1821

January Bernard Peyton succeeds Patrick Gibson as TJ's agent, and Jeff Randolph takes over the farms at Poplar Forest.
Jan. 6 TJ begins his memoirs (leaves off July 29).
31 He writes a gloomy letter to Cabell urging him to remain in the legislature.
Feb. 28 The second Missouri Compromise is approved by the Senate.
March The Greek War for Independence begins. About this time the Holy Alliance puts down Italian revolts.
April Thomas Sully visits Monticello.
June 27 TJ writes Spencer Roane enclosing a recommendation of *Construction Construed*.
Oct. 8 Edmund Bacon leaves TJ's employment.

1822

Jan. 7 TJ writes Thomas Ritchie that he will not be involved in the presidential election.
July 12 He writes William T. Barry about natural political differences among men.
Nov. 28 Francis Eppes marries Mary Elizabeth Randolph.
November TJ breaks his left arm.
December He arranges to distribute the Maverick engravings of the University of Virginia.

1823

Mar. 12 TJ orders work to begin on the Rotunda.
May 14–27 He mades his last trip to Poplar Forest.
Aug. 2 He writes Samuel Harrison Smith on the coming election.
31 The Spanish revolution is put down.
September William H. Crawford suffers a stroke.
Sept. 23 John W. Eppes dies at Millbrook.
Oct. 24 TJ writes Monroe on the momentous question of foreign relations.
Dec. 2 The Monroe Doctrine message is presented.

1824

Mar. 27 Ticknor writes a letter of introduction for Joseph Coolidge.
May Francis Walker Gilmer departs for Europe.
August TJ's recommendation of Bernard Peyton is rejected by Monroe.
September Virginia Randolph marries N. P. Trist.
Nov. 15 A dinner is given for Lafayette in the Rotunda.
Dec. 1 It becomes known that John Quincy Adams has been elected President.
December Daniel Webster and the Ticknors visit Monticello.

1825

Mar. 4 John Quincy Adams is inaugurated as President.
7 The University of Virginia opens.
May 17 Dr. Dunglison makes his first professional visit as TJ's health declines.
27 Ellen Randolph marries Joseph Coolidge.
Sept. 30–Oct. 1 Student disturbances occur.
Oct. 3–7 The Board of Visitors meets.
15 J. H. I. Browere makes a life mask of TJ.
Dec. 6 John Quincy Adams sends his first annual message to Congress.
December TJ drafts a Virginia protest.

1826

Jan. *2* The public sale of Edgehill is held.
20 TJ launches his lottery scheme.
Feb. *11* Anne Cary Bankhead dies.
17 TJ asks Madison to take care of him when he is dead.
20 The lottery bill is passed.
Mar. *16* TJ executes his will. He adds a codicil on Mar. 17.
Apr. *17* John Adams writes TJ about the visit of Jeff Randolph.
June *25* TJ writes his last letter.
July *4* TJ and John Adams die on fiftieth anniversary of the Declaration of Independence.

The Mixed Blessings of Retirement

[I]

The Return of a Native

FOR a week after the inauguration of his successor on March 4, 1809, Thomas Jefferson continued to occupy the President's House in Washington. James and Dolley Madison would have denied him nothing, but it was no real hardship for them to remain that much longer in their house on F Street. In the afternoon of inauguration day his Washington neighbors presented him with appropriate resolutions to which he made fitting response, and a couple of days later he made a graceful parting gesture to Margaret Bayard Smith, wife of the publisher of the *National Intelligencer.* That adoring lady, seeing in his cabinet a geranium he had cultivated with his own hands, had expressed the desire that, if he should not take it with him, he would leave it with her. She said she would water it with tears of regret at the departure of "the most venerated of human beings." Sending it to her, he said that this plant could hardly fail to be "proudly sensible of her fostering attentions." In parting with her he found some consolation in her promise to visit Monticello in the summer. This promise she and her husband were duly to carry out, being received "with open arms and hearts by the whole family" just as he now predicted.[1]

The retiring President had been winding up his affairs for several months. Early in the year he had obtained loans sufficient to cover the deficit he had incurred while in the highest office. This he now estimated as about $11,000. Thus he was able to settle his current accounts.[2] His trusted overseer at Monticello, Edmund Bacon, had come up to help him pack and move his things. After about two weeks, Bacon set out on the

[1] Mrs. Smith's note and TJ's reply of Mar. 6, 1809, are in *Garden Book*, pp. 382–383. The address of Washington citizens and his response are described in *Jefferson the President: Second Term*, pp. 667–668.

[2] *Ibid.*, p. 666, and, in particular, Account Book entries of Jan. 23, Mar. 10, 11, Apr. 19, 1809. His financial situation is described more fully in ch. III, below.

return trip. As he afterwards remembered, there were three wagons. Two of them, drawn by six-mule teams, were loaded with boxes. The third, a four-horse wagon, was filled with shrubbery from the nursery of Thomas Main near Washington.[3]

Thomas Jefferson Randolph — whom his grandfather called Jefferson but we must call Jeff to avoid confusion — had already gone home for a brief visit before returning to Philadelphia to continue his higher education. Toward the end of February, Charles Willson Peale, with whom he was lodging, sent the boy's grandfather a portrait of him. Peale reminded his friend that this was painted at the age of sixty-eight by one who had long neglected his art while devoting himself to the "charming study of natural history." (He seemed disposed to yield portraiture to the superior talents of his son Rembrandt.) The recipient of the portrait, who was himself nearing sixty-six, was sure it would do honor to any period of life. He described it as a treasure and took good care that it was preserved.[4]

Making a late start on March 11, two days after the departure of Bacon and the wagons, he took the Georgetown ferry for the last time and spent the night at Ravensworth, the home of Richard Fitzhugh in Fairfax County some ten miles from Washington. From his host he got for planting in his garden some peas that were already known by the name of Ravensworth and esteemed highly.[5] He did not reach Monticello until March 15, after what he described to Madison as a very fatiguing journey. The roads were excessively bad, and for eight hours he rode through one of the most disagreeable snowstorms of his experience. He caught up with the wagons at Culpeper and got home before they did.[6]

Other belongings of the ex-President were shipped by water — the expectation being that they would proceed down the Potomac to Chesapeake Bay, up the James to Richmond, and thence by smaller vessel to Milton just below Shadwell on the Rivanna. The day after he got home he learned that the vessel on which his "baggage" was shipped had gone aground in the eastern branch of the Potomac and was unable to continue its voyage. Accordingly, his things had been put aboard the *Dolphin* of York. Among these effects was a trunk containing the Indian

[3] The journey is described in Bacon's reminiscences, in H. W. Pierson, *Jefferson at Monticello* (1862), pp. 113–116, referred to hereafter as Pierson. Some allowance should be made for an old man's memory.

[4] Peale to TJ, Feb. 21, 1809 (LC); TJ to Peale, Mar. 10, 1809 (LC).

[5] The Account Book entry of Mar. 12, 1809, refers to R. Fitzhugh, while the note in *Garden Book*, p. 400, identifying the place and mentioning the peas, refers to William Fitzhugh.

[6] TJ to Madison, Mar. 17, 1809 (L. & B., XII, 266); Account Book, Mar. 14–15, 1809. Bacon's account of events in Culpeper, where he said a crowd had gathered and finally burst into TJ's private room, there to be addressed briefly by him, is rather confused (Pierson, pp. 115–116).

vocabularies, some fifty in number, that he had collected through thirty years. On the last leg of the journey, while ascending the James above Richmond, this trunk was stolen. Toward the end of May a reward for its recovery was offered by his agents in Richmond, Gibson and Jefferson. The description in the notice shows that, besides writing paper, the trunk contained a pocket telescope and a dynamometer, described as "an instrument for measuring the exertions of draught animals." To the distressed owner, his agent and cousin George Jefferson reported in June that papers from the trunk had been discovered in the James below Lynchburg. But George's personal search of the river turned up little of the contents, though the trunk and its thief were afterwards found. Only a few defaced leaves of the vocabularies were saved. In some of his comments on this irreparable loss Jefferson seemed vindictive. Later in the summer he stated with apparent satisfaction that the culprit was on trial and would doubtless be hanged.[7]

From his former secretary, Isaac Coles, he learned that the Madisons had moved into the President's House promptly but were not fortunate in their maître d'hôtel, whose insobriety was interfering with his performance of his duties. Thus reminded of his own maître d'hôtel, the former master of that house wrote a generous letter of appreciation to Etienne Lemaire, saying what he had found it impossible to say when parting with those with whom he had lived so long in Washington and by whom he had been served so well. Lemaire's whole conduct, he said, had been "so marked with good humor, industry, sobriety, and economy" as never to have given him a moment's dissatisfaction. He hoped to keep in touch with him and saluted him with "affectionate esteem." Not to be outdone, Lemaire, replying in French, said that, of all the persons he had ever worked for, Jefferson had given him the most happiness and satisfaction, for service of this master was more a pleasure than a task.[8] To another old employee of his, Joseph Dougherty, Jefferson gave what that Irish coachman described as a "noble recommendation." The two carried on animated correspondence thereafter about sheep, especially a broad-tailed ram selected from Dr. William Thornton's flock by Dougherty and designated for paternity at Monticello.[9] The affectionate relations between Jefferson and his domestic staff were

[7] Isaac A. Coles to TJ, Mar. 13, 1809 (LC); TJ to George Jefferson, May 18, 1809 (MHS); notice of reward offered by Gibson & Jefferson in Richmond *Enquirer*, May 30, 1809; George Jefferson to TJ, June 12, June 26, July 21, 1809, with enclosure (MHS); TJ to J. S. Barnes, Aug. 3, 1809 (LC); TJ to Dr. B. S. Barton, Sept. 21, 1809 (L. & B., XII, 312–313).

[8] TJ to Lemaire, Mar. 16, 1809; Lemaire to TJ, Mar. 22 (LC).

[9] Among a number of letters reference may be made to Dougherty's of Apr. 19, 1809 (LC), May 15 and 18 (*Farm Book*, pp. 118–119), and TJ's of June 26 and Aug. 25, 1809 (*ibid.*, pp. 119–120).

Monticello, View of the East Front
(Courtesy of Monticello/Thomas Jefferson Foundation, Inc.)

amply illustrated in both cases. And the parting words of his young secretary were more than perfunctory. At the end of his letter Isaac Coles had said that toward Jefferson his heart would "never cease to overflow with sentiments" to which he had "no power to give utterance."

The mansion house that Jefferson had been building and rebuilding for some forty years was now essentially finished, along with its dependencies.[10] Writing Benjamin H. Latrobe, the American whose architectural judgment he most valued and probably most feared, Jefferson observed: "My essay in Architecture has been so much subordinated to the law of convenience, and affected also by the circumstances of change in the original design, that it is liable to some unfavorable and just criticisms. But what nature has done for us is sublime and beautiful and unique."[11] Visitors to Monticello in the early years of his retirement had much to say about nature, especially in connection with the approach to the house — up an "abrupt mountain" or a "steep savage hill," through "ancient forest-trees." Jefferson himself said that his grounds were still largely in their majestic native woods with close undergrowth. On the ascent nature appeared untamed, and viewed from the summit, five hundred feet above the Rivanna, the vast panorama of forest and mountain was still little marred by the hand of man. Looking at the "spacious and splendid structure" that crowned the height, one observer said: "Here, in this wild and sequestered retirement, the eye dwells with delight on the triumph of art over nature, rendered the more impressive by the unreclaimed condition of all around."[12]

It would be nearer the truth to say that nature and art appeared here in notable conjunction, reflecting the deep feeling of Jefferson for them both. Also, his architectural creation represented a distinctive blend of the functional with the aesthetic. The connection of the service wings to the main house by covered passageways provided an excellent example of his practicality; and he manifested his modernity by filling his mansion with convenient devices and flooding it with light. Yet his orders — Doric, Ionic, Corinthian, and Attic — were designed in strict accor-

[10] The plan and its development are described in detail in *Jefferson and the Ordeal of Liberty*, chs. 14, 15. An authoritative and convenient modern account is the beautifully illustrated booklet *Monticello*, by F. D. Nichols and J. A. Bear, Jr. (1967), published by the Thomas Jefferson Memorial Foundation.

[11] TJ to B. H. Latrobe, Oct. 10, 1809 (LC, quoted in *Garden Book*, p. 416).

[12] Margaret Bayard Smith, in *A Winter in Washington* (1824), II, 261. In this work of fiction the descriptions were drawn from the author's observations, such as those she made on a visit to Monticello in the summer of 1809. Among other descriptions I have drawn on at this point are those of J. E. Caldwell, in *A Tour through the State of Virginia, in the Summer of 1808*, ed. by W. M. E. Rachal (1951), pp. 36–41, and George Ticknor, in his *Life, Letters, and Journals*, ed. by G. S. Hillard et al. (1876), I, 34–38, describing a visit of 1815.

dance with those of Palladio, while the friezes in the various rooms were adapted from the entablatures of Roman temples. His entrance hall and parlor were filled with busts and paintings. (There were too many paintings, in fact, and the entrance hall was so filled with specimens of natural history that it was already referred to as a museum.) At length he had provided for himself a habitation befitting his extraordinarily diverse and well-rounded personality. It was an expression of his love of privacy, his elevation of spirit, his sophisticated taste, his utilitarianism, his desire for self-sufficiency. The Chinese railing on the terraces was not to be installed for years, and he was to be much occupied with the grounds. Not even now was Monticello wholly complete, but to satisfy his appetite for building he had turned to Poplar Forest, though we shall not follow him to that other home quite yet.

Martha Jefferson Randolph went to Monticello several days before her father's arrival. Throughout his presidency she had made it a practice to be there, along with the children, whenever he was at home. Previously, she had returned to Edgehill after his departure but apparently she did not go back to that place, except for brief visits, after he came home to stay.[13] He had long expected that they would all live together after his retirement, and she had no thought of letting anybody else be his housekeeper. The precise position of her husband in this arrangement is not clear. Thomas Mann Randolph had his own farms to look after, but he appears to have usually had breakfast and dinner at Monticello in this period and to have slept there. A number of his slaves, brought from Edgehill, were housed on the place. The situation could not have been wholly congenial to this proud and sensitive man, but he does not seem to have fretted under it particularly.

He was now forty-one, while Martha was thirty-seven, and their children numbered eight. The eldest, Anne Cary, now eighteen, had been married in the previous fall to Charles Lewis Bankhead. Since the young couple lived at Carlton on the western slope of Jefferson's little mountain, he saw a great deal of this favorite granddaughter.[14] Her brother Jeff, whose portrait Charles Willson Peale had painted, was sixteen when he rode to the Capitol with his grandfather for the inauguration of James Madison. As expected, he returned briefly to Philadelphia for botanical lectures, but he did not go to the College of William and Mary the next

[13] *See Family Letters*, p. 384, note 2. For a map of the Monticello neighborhood, see below, p. 254.

[14] See the account of Anne and her husband by Olivia Taylor in George G. Shackelford, ed., *Collected Papers . . . of the Monticello Association* (1965), ch. V. Her troubles because of the alcoholism of her husband became acute by 1815, if not earlier.

Thomas Jefferson Randolph

Portrait by Charles Willson Peale, 1808. (Courtesy of Monticello/Thomas Jefferson Foundation, Inc.)

year as his grandfather had planned. Jefferson had become convinced of his grandson's industry and sobriety, and as time went on depended on him more and more, but it was clear that the robust lad's interests were not primarily intellectual. It was adjudged sufficient for him as a prospective planter to complete his formal education by attending the school of Louis H. Girardin in Richmond during 1809–1810.

After Jeff came four girls, ranging in age from five to twelve, all of whom went to school to their mother. The eldest, Ellen Wayles, had already shown herself to be a diligent correspondent, and she was to be Anne Cary's replacement as guardian of the flowers. Edmund Bacon said that these two girls, like their mother, had the fresh, rosy look of the Jeffersons, while most of the other children tended to be dark, like their father.[15] There were two little boys: one, born in the President's House and now aged three, was named James Madison, while the baby, still in his first year, bore the distinguished name of Benjamin Franklin. As though these were not enough, there were to be three more children, and young Francis Eppes, the son of Jefferson's lamented daughter Maria, was often at Monticello. In the winter of 1809–1810 when he was eight, he was engaged in a spirited contest with his cousin and contemporary Virginia Randolph in the art of reading.

As a father and grandfather Jefferson received the warmest of welcomes when he dismounted at Monticello. He would have been escorted to the door by a body of friends and neighbors if they had had their way. A group of citizens of Albemarle had wanted to meet him at the county line and conduct him home. They gave up the idea when informed that the precise day of his arrival was uncertain, but, before this came around, a group met at the courthouse and adopted an address in the name of all the inhabitants of the county. Since he was receiving messages from all over the Union, they could add nothing "on the score of public gratitude," they said. Referring, as so many other addresses and resolutions did, to his "voluntary relinquishment of honors and of power," they rejoiced in the restoration to them of "a friend and neighbor as exemplary in the social circle, as he is eminent at the helm of state." There was no intimation here of any sort of public failure or moral turpitude on his part. And, although these sentiments could hardly have had unanimous support in Albemarle, this affectionate address shows unmistakably that he was held in the highest honor in his own locality.

Presumably the gentlemen of the committee who had drafted the ad-

[15] Pierson, pp. 86, 88. For detailed information about the family members, see Appendix I, below.

dress bore it to Monticello and presented it in person.[16] The episode must have reminded Jefferson of the welcome he had received from his Albemarle neighbors on his return from France some twenty years before.[17] In the memorable address he made on that occasion he spoke of "the sufficiency of human reason for the care of human affairs," and of the will of the majority as "the only sure guardian of the rights of man." He urged his hearers forever to "bow down to the general reason of society." They were safe in that, he said, for although it sometimes erred, it soon returned to the right way. After observing the most philosophical phase of the French Revolution in 1789 he had been in an optimistic frame of mind. Now, receiving with "inexpressible pleasure" the cordial welcome of his local fellow citizens, he was personal rather than philosophical. He said that for the joys of affectionate association with them and the endearments of domestic life he gladly laid down "the distressing burden of power," and the measure of his happiness would be complete if his public services had received the approbation of his countrymen. In some sense he was on the defensive, though these approving neighbors had certainly not put him there. Of them he could ask with confidence, "Whose ox have I taken, or whom have I defrauded? Whom have I oppressed, or of whom have I received a bribe to blind my eyes therewith?"

An occasional visitor to Jefferson's native district asserted that he was not highly regarded by his neighbors, but the burden of testimony gives the opposite impression. Of his own attitude toward the locality which was in the deepest sense his "country" there could be no doubt whatsoever. Writing a distinguished foreign explorer and savant, now settled in Paris, he had recently said: "You have wisely located yourself in the focus of the science [knowledge] of Europe. I am held by the cords of love to my family and country, or I should certainly join you."[18] Nothing seems to have been farther from his thoughts than another trip to the vaunted scene of Europe, but he was not far from the literal truth when he said that he was burying himself in the groves of Monticello.

In late September of the year of his homecoming, shortly before Madison returned to Washington, Jefferson visited his friend and successor

[16] From the account of the episode in the Richmond *Enquirer*, Apr. 14, 1809, we learn that the citizens met at the courthouse in Charlottesville on Mar. 6 and 11. The committee consisted of William D. Meriwether (chairman of the meetings), Nimrod Bramhan, Dr. Charles Everitt, Thomas W. Maury, and Dabney Minor. Meriwether wrote TJ, Mar. 23, 1809 (LC). The *Enquirer* published both the address and TJ's reply. The latter, dated Apr. 3, is in L. & B., XII, 269–270. See also Martha to TJ, Feb. 24, 1809 (*Family Letters*, p. 384); TJ to TMR, Feb. 28 (L. & B., XII, 256–257).

[17] See *Jefferson and the Rights of Man*, pp. 246–247.

[18] To Baron Alexander von Humboldt, Mar. 6, 1809 (L. & B., XII, 263).

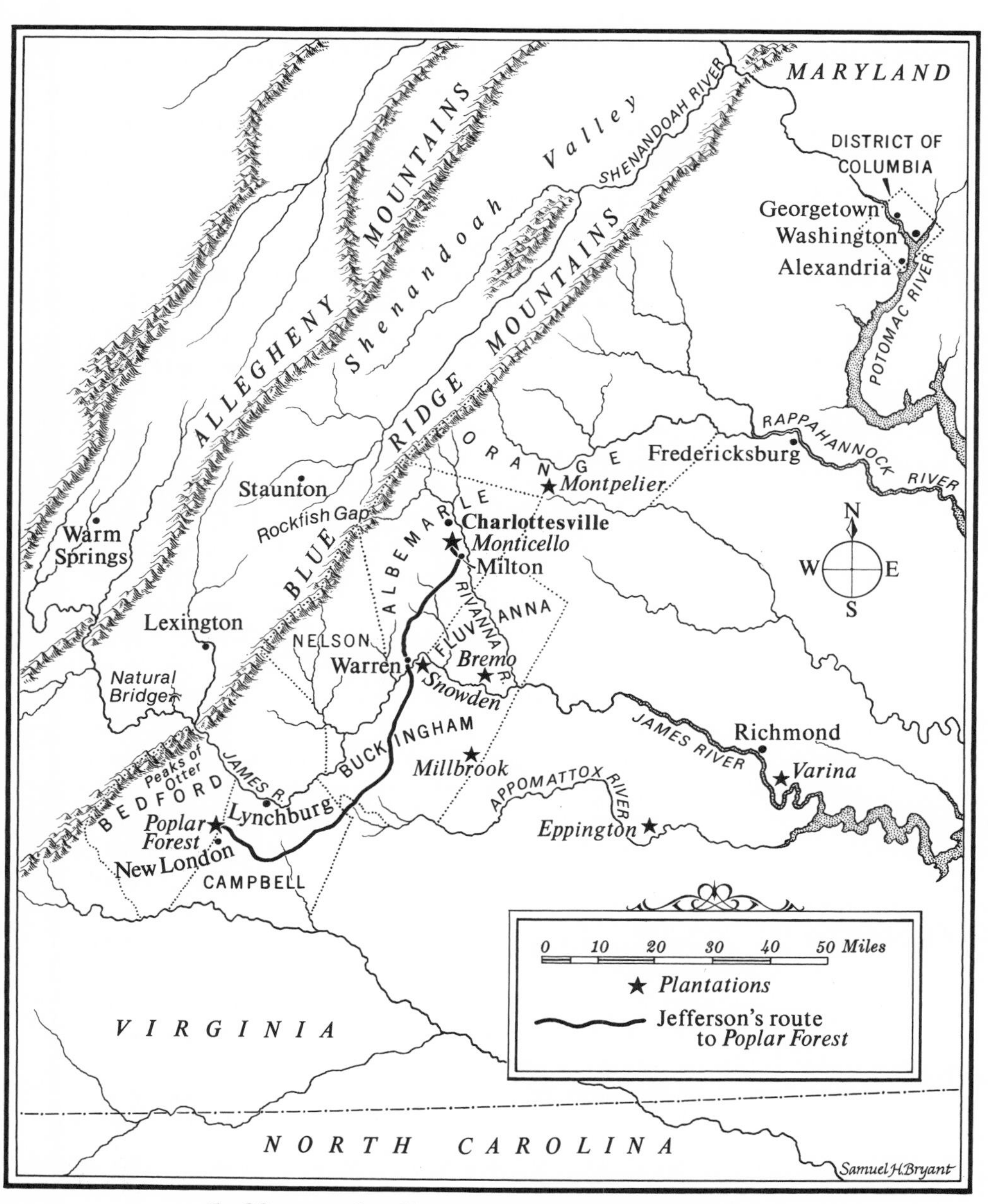

Jefferson's Country, 1809 – 1826

at Montpelier. During the rest of his life he did this almost every year, but Orange County was the closest he was to get to the capital of the Republic. Only once during the seventeen years of his retirement did he visit the capital of his own commonwealth. In the fall of this first year he went to Richmond on business, and there he received a very hearty welcome.[19] Learning of his presence, a group of citizens met at the capitol the morning after his arrival. They unanimously adopted resolutions of respect and admiration for his exalted character and of gratitude for his distinguished services. A committee was appointed to prepare an appropriate address. In his gracious reply to this he claimed no other merit than that of having contributed his best endeavors to the "establishment of those rights without which man is a degraded being." He hailed these citizens as fellow laborers in the same holy cause.

The honors paid him on this apparently unannounced visit seem to have been spontaneous. About the same time that resolutions were being adopted at the capitol, a drill muster of the 19th Regiment took place on capitol square. The officers, learning of Jefferson's arrival, invited him to dine with them at 4 P.M. that day. In due course he was escorted from the Swan Tavern with Governor John Tyler, Colonel James Monroe, and others. Among the toasts was one he offered to "the militia of the United States — the bulwark of our independence." On the next day there was a public dinner in his honor at the Eagle Tavern. A large and brilliant company were said to have attended. After Jefferson's retirement, Governor Tyler toasted him as "first in the hearts of his country."[20] If by Jefferson's country the Governor meant Virginia rather than the United States, the saying was doubtless true, and in the physical sense he was henceforth nothing but a Virginian. Until his dying day he never left the state. Late in his life he went once to Warm Springs, the westernmost point of all his travels, but he never returned to Richmond, and except for Montpelier, almost the only other place he went to was his own Poplar Forest.

He had good reason to visit the farms in Bedford County that constituted almost half of his estate, but during his presidency he was unable to make this journey of ninety miles more than once a year. According to family tradition he conceived the idea of building a house at Poplar Forest when confined for three days by rain in one of the two rooms of an overseer's cottage there.[21] The idea was natural enough in any case,

[19] Account Book, Oct. 15–31, 1809, shows that he visited Carysbrook, Clifton, and Eppington both going and coming and was in Richmond Oct. 19–23.

[20] The events of this visit, including the resolutions, address, and two dinners are described in Richmond *Enquirer*, Oct. 24, 1809.

[21] Randall, III, 341. Presumably that was where he lodged on early visits.

but he does not appear to have considered it seriously until he relinquished the purpose of building at Pantops in Albemarle County the house originally intended for his daughter Maria and John W. Eppes. This was during his first presidential term and not long after he designed Farmington for his friend and fellow horticulturist George Divers.[22] In this period he was experimenting with octagons in combination with rectangles. The plan for Poplar Forest, novel in America then and distinctive at any time, called for a regular octagon that centered on a square room lighted from above and that had porticos on the front and rear.[23] Work on the building was begun in 1806; the walls were up by the fall of 1808; and Jefferson was able to stay in the house when he visited the place a year later.[24] Plastering did not begin until two years after that, and the house that Jefferson called his retreat and designated as a legacy to his grandson Francis Eppes was long to remain unfinished. Its completion was not to require a generation, as that of Monticello did, but this was to take upwards of a dozen years.

It turned out to be an architectural gem in a harmonious setting that pleased its designer and builder. His visits to it increased in number and duration. From the second year of his retirement until he stopped traveling altogether he averaged three a year. His life there can be more fittingly described after this really became his second home; but we may note here that virtually the whole of his seventeen years of retirement was spent in the red-clay country and that, the weather permitting, he was nearly always in sight of the mountains.[25]

At the beginning of his retirement at Monticello he established a regimen from which he departed little thereafter. He continued to rise by daybreak — that is, as soon as he could make out the hands of a clock he kept beside his bed. He then recorded the temperature. Sometimes his overseer observed him walking on the terrace in the dawn's early light. Usually he started on his necessary correspondence as soon as he could, hoping to get this done by breakfast. Judging from the accounts of visitors, that meal was at nine. One wonders if he had tea or coffee when he arose. At first he seems to have managed to visit his garden and

[22] The house with later additions is now the Farmington Country Club, near Charlottesville. See the map, below, p. 254.

[23] Fiske Kimball, *Thomas Jefferson, Architect* (1916), pp. 70–72, relates the plan to TJ's studies for Farmington and to a design of Inigo Jones for a larger and more elaborate building. See also F. D. Nichols, *Thomas Jefferson's Architectural Drawings* (1961), pp. 7–8 and Plate No. 29, reproduced below, p. 295.

[24] See Hugh Chisholm to TJ, Sept. 4, 1808 (*Garden Book*, p. 377). Chisholm was a brickmason, among other things, and was dispatched from Monticello to Poplar Forest as other workmen were.

[25] His route to Poplar Forest is marked on the map, above, p. 13. For further reference to life there, see ch. XX.

shops and begin to ride about his place soon after breakfast. This he did for health and pleasure, and also to note the state of his property and crops. When his correspondence increased, with the passing months, he had to stay indoors longer, but even then he generally began his daily ride by noon.[26] On this he customarily wore a pair of overalls. By all accounts he was an uncommonly fine horseman, and in extreme old age he said that life would have been unbearable without this daily revival.[27] His ride lasted until he came in for dinner, a meal that seems to have generally begun about four in the afternoon and to have continued long. He said that he gave the time from dinner to dark to the society of neighbors and friends, and that from candlelight to early bedtime he read. When there were no special guests he may have done this in the company of members of his family, who were engaged in sewing or knitting or something else. According to some accounts, however, he customarily retired to his quarters after tea, which was served about seven.

He referred repeatedly to his beloved books and he crowded an incredible amount of reading into his last years, but during the first of them he rejoiced in his opportunity to be an outdoor man, concerned with practical affairs. "My health is perfect," he reported to General Thaddeus Kosciuszko in 1810, "and my strength considerably reinforced by the activity of the course I pursue; perhaps it is as great as usually falls to the lot of near sixty-seven years of age." (When sixty-eight he had an attack of rheumatism which reduced his walking but did not long affect his riding.) Edmund Bacon, whose acquaintance with him did not begin until Jefferson was sixty-three, thus described him: "Mr. Jefferson was six feet two and a half inches high, well proportioned, and straight as a gun-barrel. He was like a fine horse — he had no surplus flesh."[28] There were many references to his tall and slender figure, and others described it as little impaired by age, but few observers may have realized, as his overseer did, how strong he was. He had a machine for measuring strength, and very few of the men that Bacon saw try it were as strong in the arms as Thomas Mann Randolph, but Jefferson was stronger than his son-in-law. According to Margaret Bayard Smith, at the time of her visit to Monticello in August 1809, his white locks announced an age that was contradicted by his "activity, strength, health,

[26] Among the best accounts of his regimen in his early years of retirement are those he gave Thaddeus Kosciuszko, Feb. 26, 1810, and Dr. Benjamin Rush, Jan. 16, 1811 (L. & B., XII, 369–370; XIII, 1–2).

[27] Comment of Bacon (Pierson, p. 74); TJ to Wm. Short, Apr. 10, 1824, quoted in *Farm Book*, p. 87, at the beginning of a detailed account of TJ's horses.

[28] Pierson, p. 70.

enthusiasm, ardor and gaiety."[29] To Kosciuszko he wrote a few months later: "I talk of ploughs and harrows, of seeding and harvesting, with my neighbors, and of politics too if they choose, with as little reserve as the rest of my fellow citizens, and feel at length the blessing of being free to say and to do what I please without being responsible to any mortal." This was the sort of life he wanted to lead — the sort of life that had been extolled by ancient writers he knew well — Cicero and Horace and the younger Pliny. But there were practical difficulties, chiefly financial, from which there was no escape and which were eventually to bear him down. And he could not get entirely out of public affairs all at once. There were loose ends to tie up, and he could never be wholly a private man.

[29] Comment of Aug. 3, 1809, in Margaret Bayard Smith, *The First Forty Years of Washington Society*, ed. by Gaillard Hunt (1906), p. 80.

[II]

Presidential Aftermath

1809-1811

ON the eve of his retirement Jefferson said that if the country should meet misfortunes it would be "because no human wisdom could avert them."[1] There can be no more doubt of his confidence in his successor than of his relief in "shaking off the shackles of power." By this time he actually had little power left to shake off. As soon as the election of Madison was unquestionable, he had shifted to this trusted colleague all the responsibility he could, and the form that the final legislation of his presidency assumed was chiefly owing to others.[2]

In the existing state of world war the entire avoidance of misfortune was indeed beyond American wisdom. In his inaugural address Madison described the international situation as unparalleled, and the situation of his own country as full of difficulties. Neither in public nor in private did he blame his immediate predecessor, who, as he said somewhat elaborately, was now enjoying "the benedictions of a beloved country, gratefully bestowed for exalted talents zealously devoted through a long career to the advancement of its highest interest and happiness."[3] One would have great difficulty in finding anywhere in the papers of either of these longtime friends and associates any reflection on the policies or conduct of the other. The historian may properly ask, however, what sort of legacy the third President left the fourth.

For the unparalleled state of world affairs neither was responsible; and in the foreign policies that had been followed by the government it is almost impossible to distinguish between them. Madison had no apologies for a course he regarded as unexceptionable, but he recognized that

[1] TJ to Du Pont de Nemours, Mar. 2, 1809 (*J.-D. Correspondence*, p. 122).

[2] The developments during the final congressional session of his administration are treated in detail in *Jefferson the President: Second Term*. See especially chs. XXXIV–XXXVI.

[3] Madison's inaugural address is in Hunt, VIII, 47–50; quotation on p. 50.

it had not availed against "the injustice and violence of the belligerent powers." He made no specific reference to the embargo or to the modified policy of commercial restriction that was embodied in the Non-Intercourse Act as adopted at the very end of the congressional session.[4] While this measure did not mark an abandonment of the principle of economic coercion and was not hailed as a glorious victory by the anti-administration forces, it would not have been adopted in this reduced form but for the violent opposition that had been directed against the laws it superseded. On the eve of Madison's accession the government of Connecticut and the General Court of Massachusetts were defying the executive in Washington along with the embargo. While Jefferson's policies may be said to have saved the West to the Union, they had finally played into the hands of his enemies in New England and accentuated disaffection in that commercial region. The unity of the party, which he had maintained hitherto with such conspicuous success, was breached in the last half of his final congressional session by the revolt of members from the Northeast. Under these circumstances the executive branch lost the initiative that Jefferson had generally maintained. Thus his successor inherited not only a dislocated economy but a divided country and a divided government. Furthermore, it soon appeared that Madison was presiding over a divided Cabinet.

Faced with the opposition of a senatorial group that included Samuel Smith of Maryland, William Branch Giles of Virginia, and Michael Leib of Pennsylvania, he abandoned his purpose to have Albert Gallatin as secretary of state and appointed Robert Smith, brother of the Senator, to that key post, no doubt expecting to write the diplomatic dispatches himself. Gallatin remained as secretary of the treasury. Madison may be charged with weakness in yielding to this senatorial faction at the outset of his administration and may be compared unfavorably to Jefferson in his relations with Congress. Indeed, a contrast has been drawn between the Madisonian "model" of government, with its emphasis on checks and balances, and the "system" of Jefferson, which is said to have collapsed under his successor.[5] To Jefferson, who stressed political party and majority rule, has been attributed the exercise of presidential leadership with unparalleled skill and effectiveness. The reference is not to his last congressional session, however. The same senatorial faction that blocked Madison's nomination of Gallatin had rejected Jefferson's of William

[4] Act of Mar. 1, 1809, repealing the embargo and providing for non-intercourse with Great Britain and France and the opening of trade with other countries (*Annals*, 10 Cong., 2 sess., pp. 1824–1830; discussed in *Jefferson the President: Second Term*, pp. 648–649).

[5] James MacGregor Burns, *The Deadlock of Democracy* (1963), chs. 1, 2; see also pp. 265–267, 338. By the "model" of Madison is meant the one he set up in the *Federalist*, especially No. 51.

Short. Nor does it seem that, even at the time of his greatest effectiveness as a leader, he differed much from his Secretary of State in basic theory. Opposed to any sort of tyranny as he was, Jefferson adhered in principle to the division of powers and favored a limited as well as a balanced government. These doctrines served to inhibit him — not only because they were generally approved by his countrymen but also because he accepted them himself. In practice, though, he was disposed to be pragmatic. His exercise of leadership in legislative matters during much the larger part of his administration provides a striking example of this, but in deference to Congress and the doctrine of separation of powers, he kept out of sight insofar as possible. Procedure that was not formalized or even openly acknowledged could not have been expected to set a firm precedent. It may be doubted if any other President has ever employed party loyalty more effectively to procure legislation, but his party leadership was essentially personal, and from almost the beginning to almost the end it was undisputed. Madison occupied no such position of advantage. Nor did he have comparable skill in conciliating dissidents or equal ability to gain and maintain personal loyalty.

Jefferson's public image, like his physical stature, was more impressive than Madison's, but it was not that of a charismatic chieftain. Rather it was that of a friend of mankind who would ask no more of his fellows than he had to. His popularity, at least until the period of the embargo, was owing in no small part to the fact that he asked little. His domestic program was distinctly limited. He sought to maintain the freedom of his country and countrymen and to make the republican experiment a success. On the world front he was generally engaged in a holding operation; nearly always he was playing for time. His superiority to his friend and colleague in presidential leadership can be best attributed to his personality and the circumstances by which they were confronted. Although a strong President when at his best, he obviously weakened at the end; and it may be doubted if he measurably strengthened the presidential office.

From the beginning of their intimate association Jefferson had treated Madison as a peer, and he had yielded the helm to him as soon as possible. He would have been out of character if he had sought to dictate to his successor, and in fact he scrupulously avoided any suggestion of interference.[6] From their correspondence it appears that their personal relations were wholly unaffected by their change in status and that entire candor was maintained between them. During Madison's first summer

[6] Their relations were well analyzed by R. J. Honeywell in "President Jefferson and His Successor" (*A.H.R.*, XLVI, 64–75). In recent writings there has been no such over-emphasis on the former as he perceived at that time (1940).

as President he visited Jefferson at Monticello in company with Albert and Mrs. Gallatin. Unfortunately, we have no record of their private talk, but judging from their correspondence, Madison usually asked for advice only on matters carried over from Jefferson's administration or relating to it. He reported foreign affairs to his friend promptly and fully. Jefferson's comments on events were mostly meant to be encouraging.

At the outset the general impression seems to have been that the administration of Madison amounted to a continuation of Jefferson's and the initial rejection of his nomination of John Quincy Adams as minister to Russia and his forced abandonment of his plan to have Gallatin as secretary of state would lead one to suppose that the new President was as powerless at the beginning as the old President at the end. After the brief executive session of the Senate, called to consider appointments, the President was free of immediate congressional supervision until the beginning of the special session on May 22. Meanwhile, at Monticello, spending more time indoors than he liked because of the cold and backward season, Jefferson was considerably occupied with answering the many addresses and letters from Republicans that manifested their continued loyalty to him.

About a month after he got home and about a week after his sixty-sixth birthday he received highly gratifying news from Washington. He learned of the declaration of the young and friendly British minister, David Erskine, that the Orders in Council of January and November, 1807, against which his own government had so strongly protested, would be withdrawn on June 10. He also learned that, in turn, Madison had proclaimed the renewal of the commerce with Great Britain which had been proscribed.[7] One feature of the surprising Erskine agreement Jefferson regretted — the prospective sending by the British of an envoy extraordinary to negotiate a trade treaty. In his opinion they had never been known to make an equitable commercial treaty, and none could therefore be expected. Nevertheless, he rejoiced in the apparent British retreat as the triumph of the "forbearing and yet persevering system" of the American government. He told Madison that the agreement would give the country peace in his administration, and by permitting the extinguishment of the national debt would open to them "the noblest application of revenue that has ever been exhibited by any nation." No doubt the ex-President was thinking of the program of internal improvements and education he and Gallatin had had to forgo.[8]

[7] Erskine's communications of Apr. 18, 19, 1809, Madison's proclamation of the latter date, and his letter of Apr. 24 to TJ are in Hunt, VIII, 50–53. TJ commented in a letter to Madison, Apr. 27 (L. & B., XII, 274–277).

[8] See *Jefferson the President: Second Term*, pp. 553–560.

These events stimulated his imagination. While declaring that the policy of the French Emperor was so crooked as to elude conjecture, he himself engaged in a good deal of the latter — not merely with respect to the revocation of the French edicts in response to the British action, but also regarding expansion into Spanish territories and former colonies that seemed to be slipping from Napoleon's control. Besides the Floridas, his aspirations for his country as now expressed extended to Cuba. Beyond that southern outpost he would not go, but he still had hopes of including Canada in "our confederacy." Then, he said, they would have "such an empire for liberty" as had not been surveyed since the creation. And he was persuaded that "no constitution was ever before so well calculated as ours for extensive empire and self-government."[9]

The shocking news that the Erskine agreement had been repudiated by the British government reached him in early August. Such euphoria as it had created lasted not more than three months, and both he and Madison began to have doubts at least a month before that.[10] Madison had to issue another proclamation, restoring the prohibition of trade with Great Britain as required by the Non-Intercourse Act. Jefferson at Monticello, more convinced than ever of British chicanery, wrote Madison that if Bonaparte should have the wisdom to "correct his injustice" against the United States, war with Great Britain would be inevitable. While expressing continued confidence in Erskine's integrity, he spoke of the "unprincipled rascality" of Canning and described the present ministry as the most shameless that had ever disgraced England. And he sought to reassure his mortified successor by holding that both of Madison's proclamations were entirely proper under their respective circumstances.[11] The net result of these developments, according to Gallatin, was to leave the nation in a weaker condition than it had been a year earlier.[12] Thus it would seem that the Madison administration, instead of being credited with a plus mark, should have been charged with a minus, and one would have supposed that the President's credibility would have suffered. No doubt it did, but most Federalists appear to have been restrained in their early criticism. Some sharp things were said in especially pro-British papers, but in contrast to his predecessor

[9] L. & B., XII, 277. He did not allow for the increase in the slave population of the country that would result from the acquisition of Cuba. On the Floridas, see ch. VI, pp. 86–88, below.

[10] For an authoritative account of this from the British point of view, see Bradford Perkins, *Prologue to War* (1963), pp. 207–209. See TJ's comments to Madison, June 16, 1809 (Ford, IX, 255–256); Madison's to TJ, June 20 (Hunt, VIII, 60–61).

[11] TJ to Madison, Aug. 17, 1809 (L. & B., XII, 304–305, supplemented from LC). Perkins takes a much more favorable view of Canning (*Prologue to War*, pp. 210–220).

[12] Gallatin to John Montgomery, July 27, 1809 (cited, *ibid.*, p. 219).

he was not subjected to grave personal abuse. Thus far the Federalists preferred him to Jefferson.

The Erskine agreement, which seems to have been more widely and more enthusiastically hailed than the Louisiana Purchase, had been attributed in Federalist circles to the *escape* of the administration from the influence of Jefferson. One writer declared that it was owing to "fortuitous circumstances abroad, and a disposition not perverse in the new president." Said a Federalist editor: "Our only fear respecting Mr. Madison has been that he would be influenced by his predecessor."[13] Even after the repudiation of the Erskine agreement, there was a disposition in Federalist circles to absolve him from blame for the crisis. The source of the country's troubles, alleged one paper, was to be found in the eight years preceding him.[14]

Speaking of his own proceedings, Jefferson said that the "republican portion" of his fellow citizens had viewed them with indulgence. His friend Benjamin Rush congratulated him on the "auspicious issue" of *his* "free and protracted negotiations" with the British. The Richmond *Enquirer* copied from a western paper a Latin quotation which, while making him the major luminary, sought to honor both him and his successor. In translation it read: "The sun retires, but darkness does not follow." An even better expression of predominant Republican sentiment was the toast that Thomas Ritchie, editor of the *Enquirer*, gave at a Fourth of July celebration: "Thomas Jefferson and James Madison — the same in principle — the same in measures — the same in the confidence of their country."[15]

Ritchie, always a seeker after party unity, was well aware of what the Federalists were saying. So was Madison himself. Writing Jefferson about a week after the special session of Congress began, he said: "Nothing could exceed the folly of supposing that the principles and opinions manifested in our foreign discussions were not, in the main at least, common to us: unless it be the folly of supposing that such shallow hypocrisy could deceive any one."[16] In fact there *was* reason to believe that Madison was less anti-British than his predecessor and thus in a somewhat better position to negotiate. Jefferson's *Chesapeake* proclamation had been a stumbling block, and, while this was not formally disavowed, one feature of the modified policy represented by the Non-Intercourse Act

[13] *Charleston Courier* (a relatively moderate paper), May 2, 1809, quoting communication in *Baltimore Federal Gazette; Charleston Courier*, May 10, 1809, quoting *Freeman's Journal.*

[14] *Charleston Courier*, Aug. 23, 1809, quoting *Virginia Gazette;* see also Aug. 21.

[15] TJ to William Lambert, May 28, 1809 (L. & B., XII, 284); Rush to TJ, May 3, 1809 (Butterfield, II, 1003–1004); Richmond *Enquirer*, May 10, quoting *Missouri Gazette; ibid.*, July 7, containing Ritchie's toast.

[16] Madison to TJ, May 30, 1809 (Hunt, VIII, 61–62).

was that French as well as British warships were excluded from American waters. This modification he may be presumed to have acceded to, however, and Madison was entirely warranted in saying that their political enemies were seeking to make a distinction where there was no difference worthy of the name.

ii

Both Madison and Jefferson were anathema to John Randolph, erstwhile Republican turned perennial gadfly. At the beginning of the special session of Congress he introduced a resolution calling for an inquiry into the financial transactions of the government during Jefferson's two terms. The main question he raised was whether the moneys had been properly applied to the objects for which they were appropriated. But Randolph's friend Nathaniel Macon, after affirming his own belief in the propriety of investigating the money affairs of any and every administration whenever a President retired, made this observation: "I feel no hesitation in saying that the nation will never be blessed with such another Administration as the last." John Randolph, hastening to say almost the same thing with a quite different meaning, provided one of the most memorable and most unfavorable characterizations of the Jeffersonian regime:

> I do unequivocably say that I believe the country will never see such another Administration as the last; it had my hearty approbation for one half of its career — as to my opinion of the remainder of it, it has been no secret. The lean kine of Pharaoh devoured the fat kine; . . . I repeat it — never has there been any Administration which went out of office, and left the nation in a state so deplorable and calamitous as the last.[17]

In contrasting Jefferson's two terms this embittered critic did not allow for the intensification of the duel between Great Britain and France, and for the shrinkage in the options of neutrals. In calling for an inquiry into the expenditures of the recent government, furthermore, he was not attacking it at a point of particular vulnerability. It may have been less economical than it claimed to be, but it had been notably scrupulous and free of scandal. Nothing much came of this resolution. The committee made an incomplete report which was tabled.[18] The retired President does not appear to have been at all perturbed by this move, or gesture,

[17] *Annals,* 11 Cong., 1 sess., I, 69; see also pp. 63–64, 66, 68.
[18] June 27, 1809 (*ibid.,* p. 448).

of his inveterate critic, but he was disturbed by another resolution from the same hand, calling for an inquiry into prosecutions for libel in the federal courts and pointing to the libel cases in Connecticut. This caused Jefferson to write letters to Congressman Wilson Cary Nicholas and Postmaster General Gideon Granger, who had been his intermediary in this matter. As we have noted elsewhere, Jefferson's private explanation of his own connection with these abortive prosecutions for libel leaves something to be desired, but he was clearly not responsible for starting them, and the statement that Granger published in midsummer appeared to bring that controversy to a satisfactory conclusion. Not even the Connecticut Federalists entered into it with eagerness at this time.[19]

It should certainly not be supposed that Jefferson's old political foes ceased attacking him. During the first months of his retirement, while most of the Federalists were applauding Madison for his apparent diplomatic triumph, a two-volume work, entitled *Memoirs of the Hon. Thomas Jefferson*, was published in New York.[20] It was better described by one of its subtitles, for it purported to give "a view of the rise and progress of French influence and French principles" in the country. This was distinctly a High Federalist view, pro-British and anti-democratic. Following the strict party line that had been laid down in the previous decade, the author identified Jefferson with these baleful French ideas, but he gave relatively slight attention to the recent President in the first volume. In the second that gentleman was described as "weak, visionary, timorous and irresolute, destitute of fortitude, destitute of magnanimity," and he was said to have brought the country to ruin at home and disgrace abroad.[21] Jefferson does not appear to have possessed a copy of the book and may never have learned from it that his principal characteristic was duplicity. He still subscribed to the Philadelphia *Aurora*, however; and, though he claimed that he was doing little reading of newspapers, he could have seen there William Duane's comment on the work as "a satire of the American people, and disgrace to the press, and to human nature."[22]

The *National Intelligencer* responded to what it called the "clamorous abuse" of the ex-President even before Duane sought to expose the author. Samuel Harrison Smith published a series of ten articles under the

[19] There is a detailed account of these cases in *Jefferson the President: Second Term*, ch. XXI. Developments after TJ's retirement are described on pp. 388–391.

[20] Attributed to Stephen Cullen Carpenter. Right to title registered June 7, 1809.

[21] *Memoirs of the Hon. Thomas Jefferson*, II, 90.

[22] Philadelphia *Aurora*, Aug. 21, 1809. Duane, who was avidly anti-British, noted the anonymous publication Aug. 17 and referred to it a number of times thereafter. Saying that it was the work of Stephen Cullen, who had added the name Carpenter, Duane charged him with being a British pensioner.

title "Defence of Mr. Jefferson's Administration."[23] Smith blamed this abuse on the spirit of a faction: "*Professing* an unbounded respect for the present Chief Magistrate, it daringly carries the dagger to the heart of his best friend." Jefferson, who was here referred to as the Sage of Monticello, was said to need no defense, but, week by week, he received one. The successive articles dealt with practically all the controversial issues of his presidency. Smith might have made more of the Louisiana Purchase and have claimed less for the embargo than he did.

After the repudiation of the Erskine agreement, some Federalists were intimating that the difficulties confronting Madison were not of his own making. Thus one newspaper said: "Again we are inflicted with the king's evil: I mean the evil of the 'illustrious Jefferson'."[24] It is hard to determine the precise point at which Federalist praise of Madison turned to blame and he ceased being compared with Jefferson to the latter's disadvantage. Perhaps his first address to Congress marked a turning point. Disappointment was expressed that he gave no hint of a policy. Said the *Connecticut Courant:* "We are left to grope our way in the dark, without one ray of light."[25]

Of more abiding interest was a veiled attack on Jefferson, made at the very end of 1809, which escaped from the heavy-handedness that characterized virtually all other partisan attacks on him and, unlike them, gained for itself a place in literature. About Christmastime appeared *A History of New York* by Diedrich Knickerbocker — that is, Washington Irving. In this fanciful and witty work the character of William the Testy was modeled in part on Jefferson; and his administration is satirized in the account of the administration of the seventeenth-century Dutch governor Wilhelmus Kieft.[26]

The picture is inexact: William the Testy was a small man, given to violent outbursts of temper, impatient of all advice. Jefferson did not look like that, and those who knew him best would never have agreed that he was passionate and unreasonable. Unlike William the Testy, he was not enamored of metaphysics and he was too utilitarian to find enduring delight in abstractions.

Nevertheless, along with some wide misses, the young author made some palpable hits — poking fun at the Governor's "universal acquirements," his art of fighting by proclamation, his disposition to experiment in political as well as mechanical matters, his obsession with economy. Young Irving remarked that if William had been less learned he might

[23] *National Intelligencer*, July 19–Oct. 6, 1809. Smith himself was presumed to have written the articles.

[24] James Cheetham in *American Citizen*, quoted by *Charleston Courier*, Sept. 20, 1809.

[25] Quoted by *Charleston Courier*, Dec. 21, 1809.

[26] Book IV.

have been a greater governor. As for economy, Knickerbocker said: "This all-potent word, which served as his touchstone in politics, at once explains the whole system of proclamations, protests, empty threats, windmills, trumpeters, and paper war."[27] There was truth in these jests, though certainly not the whole truth, and the downfall of the prototype of William the Testy was properly attributed to the Yankees, who, in this ingenious narrative, could be regarded as either the New Englanders (with whom the New Amsterdamers were in perpetual dispute) or as the British violators of American rights.

That Jefferson was not unresponsive to humorous writing is suggested by his admiration of Laurence Sterne and his liking for *Tristram Shandy*, but there seems to be no way of knowing what he thought of this post-presidential satire on himself. He does not appear to have owned or ever to have referred to Knickerbocker's *History*.

iii

About the time of his retirement Jefferson had Samuel Harrison Smith of the *National Intelligencer* print a circular letter laying down for himself the law of never interfering with his successor or the heads of departments in any application for public office.[28] He was never quite able to live up to his resolution, but his chief departures from it were shortly before and during the War of 1812, when he was especially pressed to intervene. In the first half of Madison's first term, however, he gave significant counsel and rendered important services in connection with personnel and appointments at the highest level. In particular the reference is to James Monroe and Albert Gallatin.

Probably no one else did so much as he to prepare the way for the restoration of intimate personal and political relations between Madison and Monroe. These had been interrupted in 1808, when the frustrated ex-minister to Great Britain was set up against Madison in the presidential election by a group of dissident Republicans. The breach was grievous to Jefferson, who was always deeply concerned for party unity and was devoted to both men.[29] Soon after the ex-President got home, Monroe, who was then in the process of moving from a rented house in Richmond to his farm in Albemarle County near Monticello, dined and passed an evening there with his distinguished neighbor. Jefferson reported to Madison with particular pleasure that the latter's recent rival

[27] *History of New York*, ed. by E. T. Bowden (1964), pp. 187–188.

[28] Ford, IX, 248. An undated draft of this, addressed to Samuel H. Smith, is in the J. Henley Smith Papers (LC). Madison issued a circular of the same wording on his retirement (Hunt, VIII, 389*n.*).

[29] See *Jefferson the President: Second Term*, pp. 548–549, 551–553.

had parted company with "the junto that had got possession of him" for their own purposes. He was confident that Monroe's "strong and candid mind" would bring him to "a cordial return to his old friends."[30] Monroe's bonds with Jefferson had never been severed, and their intimacy was renewed as county neighbors. The reconciliation of Monroe and Madison was not to be effected for more than a year.

Late in the fall of 1809 the President asked Jefferson to sound out Monroe regarding his possible appointment to the governorship of the Louisiana Territory, now vacant because of the tragic death of Meriwether Lewis.[31] Jefferson rode over to Highlands (later Ash Lawn) to see Monroe, catching him the day before he was to leave for Loudoun County to look after his interests there. The ex-President reported to Madison that Monroe regarded the governorship as incompatible with the respect he owed himself. He indicated that he would have taken a place in the Cabinet if it had been offered. He was not unready to serve the public, but his main concern at present was to free himself from his financial embarrassments.

From Monroe's own account of this meeting it would appear that this hypersensitive man was offended by Jefferson's suggestions, and he was unquestionably resentful of developments in Albemarle during his absence in Loudoun. Two days after he left, announcement was made of the candidacy of Thomas Mann Randolph for the congressional seat of Wilson Cary Nicholas, who was not standing for re-election. Monroe, who had not been informed of the vacancy, believed that the timing was deliberate. He heard that Jefferson had expressed the opinion that he did not wish to be elected. He himself said that, while it would have been most difficult for him to serve, he would have agreed to do so if elected.[32] There is no evidence that Jefferson played any part in the abortive campaign of his son-in-law, who was soundly defeated by David Shepherd Garland of Amherst County.[33] And if relations between him and Monroe were somewhat strained for several weeks, he took the lead in restoring them to their old friendliness by calling at Highlands when Monroe was ill.

Meanwhile, Madison had learned from Jefferson's report that his alienated friend would have accepted and presumably would still accept an appointment to the Cabinet. In May, 1810, Monroe visited Washington,

[30] TJ to Madison, Mar. 30, 1809 (LC).

[31] Madison to TJ, Nov. 27, 1809 (MP); TJ's reply of Nov. 30 is in Ford, IX, 265–267.

[32] Monroe to Richard Brent, Feb. 25, 1810 (S.M.H., V, 108–120). In the latter part of this long letter he defended his conduct as a diplomat. While unwilling to accept any appointive office except one of the highest, he regarded election to almost any office as a vindication.

[33] Gaines, p. 70.

where he was received in a very friendly manner by the President. Writing Madison soon after Monroe returned to Albemarle, Jefferson expressed delight at the effect the visit had on his neighbor's state of mind. "There appears to be the most perfect reconciliation and cordiality established toward yourself," he said. "I think him now inclined to rejoin us with zeal. The only embarrassment will be from his late friends."[34]

Jefferson may never have been aware of the pains to which Monroe went to explain himself to his "late friends." In September he wrote to John Taylor of Caroline, one of the Old Republicans who never ceased being loyal to Jefferson and wanted Monroe to rejoin the administration. His letter was passed around as he expected, though the length of it must have been discouraging.[35] In his elaborate defense of his own official conduct he gave what amounted to a critique of the foreign policy of the government in Jefferson's second term. The rejection of the Monroe–Pinkney treaty still rankled in his breast, and he had not forgotten what he regarded as ill treatment by the administration.[36] He claimed, however, that his friendship with Jefferson had been preserved, as Jefferson himself did. And, while expressing regret for the errors of that former chief magistrate, he paid him tribute as a firm and incorruptible upholder of the rights of his country and its people.[37]

Developments in Richmond early in 1811 enabled Monroe, who was so hungry for justification, to make an honorable return to public life. The appointment of John Tyler as district court judge (which had been the subject of previous correspondence between Madison and Jefferson) was followed by his resignation from the governorship of the state and the election of Monroe in his place. Congratulating him on the governorship, Jefferson said that, while it was not a post in which much "genius" could be manifested, it was a prominent one. What most pleased him was that in elevating him the Virginia legislature bore testimony to the "fidelity" of his principles "before the Republicans of the Union generally," thus placing him back on his "antient ground."[38] His appointment by Madison as secretary of state in succession to Robert Smith followed a few months later. He wrote Jefferson that he accepted it in the hopes that his action would promote harmony, at least in their party.[39]

[34] TJ to Madison, May 25, 1810 (Ford, IX, 275). The reconciliation is described by Harry Ammon in *James Monroe* (1971), pp. 279–288.

[35] Monroe to Taylor, Sept. 10, 1810 (S.M.H., V, 121–149). See also his letter of Nov. 19 to Taylor (*ibid.*, pp. 150–158).

[36] On the rejected treaty, see *Jefferson the President: Second Term*, ch. XXII.

[37] S.M.H., V, 122–123, 131, 136.

[38] TJ to Monroe, Jan. 25, 1811 (LC), replying to Monroe's letter of Jan. 21 (S.M.H., V, 160).

[39] Monroe to TJ, Apr. 3, 1811 (*ibid.*, 184–185).

* * *

Jefferson could hardly have been unaware that the nomination of Gallatin as secretary of state had been blocked by the Smith–Giles–Leib faction in the Senate. His preference for Gallatin over Robert Smith could have been assumed long before the incompetence of the new secretary of state was signally manifested. Yet, since he wanted to be a friend to everybody — or at least to members of his own party — and persistently strove to maintain harmony within the government, he was quite in character in expressing more appreciation of his former Secretary of the Navy than that official deserved. Forwarding a letter that had come to him by mistake, Jefferson seized the opportunity to salute Smith with affection and gratitude, to remind him of the harmony and good will that had sweetened the toils of his own official family, and to express confidence that this spirit would be continued in that of Madison. With considerably more optimism than the situation warranted, he said: "I sleep with perfect composure, knowing who are watching for us."[40]

In his remote canton he may have been slow to learn of the exacerbation of the feud between Gallatin and the Smith–Giles–Leib faction. But the feeling was so strong that, when Gallatin visited Monticello with the Madisons toward the end of the summer of 1809, he told Jefferson he seriously thought of resigning.[41] Writing Gallatin a few weeks later, Jefferson said he had "reflected much and painfully on the change of dispositions" that had recently occurred in the Cabinet. Also, he said that the retirement of Gallatin would be a "public calamity." He laid first emphasis on the "extinguishment" of the national debt, regarding this as vital to the destiny of the country. (With the benefit of hindsight it may appear that this emphasis was excessive; but they had no way of anticipating the era of world peace during which the young republic was to realize so richly on its vast potentialities.) What Jefferson wanted to avoid was the cycle of debt and corruption that he perceived in England, and he believed that no other President and secretary of the treasury would ever make the reduction of the debt their major object. If Gallatin should retire before the end of Madison's administration, that would be the "most inauspicious day" ever seen by their new government. Therefore, he urged Gallatin to abandon any thought of resigning.[42] In his reply to what he described as an affectionate letter, Gallatin said that Jefferson's continued friendship and confidence more than consoled him for his recent mortifications. Sincerely attached to Madison, he voiced

[40] TJ to Robert Smith, June 10, 1809 (L. & B., XII, 287).

[41] The story of this part of Gallatin's struggle with the Smith faction, with pertinent correspondence, is in Henry Adams, *The Life of Albert Gallatin* (1879), pp. 400–411. It is covered through the year 1810 in Raymond Walters, Jr., *Albert Gallatin* (1957), ch. 18.

[42] TJ to Gallatin, Oct. 11, 1809 (Ford, IX, 264–265).

no criticism of him but admitted that his feelings had been deeply wounded.[43]

An episode that particularly troubled him and Jefferson was the publication of one of Erskine's dispatches in which Gallatin was said to have characterized Jefferson as pro-French and to have contrasted his policy with that of Madison. This occasioned the publication of a denial by Gallatin. That did not stop the outcry, and it was followed by an exchange of letters between him and Jefferson on the subject. Jefferson needed no assurance of Gallatin's loyalty. Nor did Gallatin believe that any newspaper attack would create any doubt in Jefferson's mind of the "sincerity and warmth" of his sentiments.[44] Their friendship did not waver when attacks on Gallatin continued.

Largely because of the opposition of Gallatin's enemies in the Smith–Giles–Leib faction (sometimes referred to as the "invisibles"), a bill embodying Gallatin's recommendations about commercial policy vis-à-vis the British and the French was defeated, and what is known to history as Macon's Bill Number Two was subsequently adopted. Even if not the "most disgraceful act on the American statute-book," as Henry Adams said it might well be, it was unquestionably a feeble measure.[45] Nevertheless, Jefferson's letters during the first regular congressional session of the new administration (1809–1810) imply no criticism of his successor for lack of leadership. Those to Madison himself in fact were largely devoted to the subject of Merino sheep.

The session of 1810–1811 was marked by the failure of a bill to recharter the Bank of the United States that Gallatin favored. Again the "invisibles" had defeated him. Though Jefferson himself opposed recharter, this fact did not affect his relations with Gallatin; but that frustrated official, believing that his usefulness to the administration was at an end, submitted his resignation immediately after the adjournment of Congress.[46] About this time John Randolph commented: "The Administration are now in fact aground at the pitch of high tide, and a spring tide too. Nothing, then, remains but to lighten the ship, which a dead calm has hitherto kept from going to pieces."[47] Though it sounded extravagant, the saying was all too true. During the first half of his first term, when he might have been expected to be at his strongest, Madison

[43] Gallatin to TJ, Nov. 8, 1809 (*Writings*, ed. by Henry Adams [1879], I, 464–466).

[44] Gallatin to the *National Intelligencer*, Apr. 21, 1810 (*ibid.*, pp. 475–479); TJ to Gallatin, Aug. 16, and Gallatin to TJ, Sept. 10, 1810 (Adams, *Gallatin*, pp. 418–419).

[45] Adams, *Gallatin*, p. 416. This act removed the restrictions on commerce with Great Britain and France and provided for the reimposition of these on either nation if the other, within a specified time, should withdraw its own objectionable orders or decrees.

[46] For the events and Gallatin's letter of Mar. 4, 1811, to Madison, see *ibid.*, pp. 426–435.

[47] Quoted, *ibid.*, p. 431.

controlled neither Congress nor his own household. He rose to this particular occasion, however. Declining to accept the resignation of his only strong minister, he dropped Robert Smith, who had proved disloyal as well as incompetent, and gained a superior replacement in the person of James Monroe.

Jefferson had no part in these events except for his important earlier reports on Monroe's state of mind. After being informed by Madison of the change in the Cabinet, he indicated to him his strong approval.[48] But this division among his former colleagues pained him deeply, and he wrote Gallatin and Smith claiming the privilege of neutrality and asking mutual permission to esteem all his friends, neither knowing nor asking to know the causes of their differences.[49] A little later, when Smith addressed a paper to the public in which he attacked Madison, Jefferson expressed an unfavorable view of Smith's conduct; and his former Secretary of the Navy passed out of his life at this point, while Gallatin definitely remained in it.[50]

The troubles of that harassed official were by no means over, for William Duane continued to denounce him, and under these circumstances Jefferson's relations with the passionate editor of the *Aurora* may seem surprising. As long as he was the recognized leader of the party, Jefferson, appreciating Duane's abilities and services, had borne with him patiently and had retained his loyalty. In retirement the former President carried on an extensive correspondence with him. This related chiefly to the publication by Duane of a treatise that had been sent Jefferson from France for translation and publication.[51] Because of Duane's financial difficulties, he appealed for help to the Great White Father at Monticello, expressing doubt of his ability to publish the book. In view of Duane's attacks on Gallatin, Jefferson was placed in an equivocal position. While strongly defending Gallatin to his assailant, he induced William Wirt and Peter Carr to seek aid for Duane in Virginia. Those efforts had to be abandoned when further assaults on Gallatin were coupled with violent attacks on Madison.[52] Jefferson gave the President

[48] Madison to TJ, Apr. 1, 1811 (Hunt, VIII, 136*n*.); TJ to Madison, Apr. 7, 1811 (L. & B., XVIII, 269).

[49] TJ to Gallatin, Apr. 24, 1811; to Robert Smith, Apr. 30, 1811 (*ibid.*, XIII, 45–47).

[50] TJ to Madison, July 3, 1811 (*ibid.*, p. 63). Apparently he had no later correspondence with Smith.

[51] [Destutt de Tracy], *A Commentary and Review of Montesquieu's Spirit of Laws*, printed and published by Duane in 1811. See below, ch. XIV, pp. 208–212, and TJ to Tracy, Jan. 26, 1811 (Ford, IX, 305–310).

[52] Details of this episode can be recovered from the correspondence in Ford, IX, 310–321: TJ to Duane, Mar. 28 and Apr. 30, 1811; to Wirt, Mar. 30 and May 3; to Madison, Apr. 24. See also TJ to Duane, July 25 (L. & B., XIII, 65–67). Duane to TJ, Mar. 14 and July 5, 1811, and Wirt to TJ, Apr. 17, 1811, are in LC.

a full account of his vain effort to procure financial help for Duane, asking him to show the letter to Gallatin, whom he wrote more briefly.[53] Gallatin appears to have remained silent about this episode, which actually left his affectionate relations with Jefferson unimpaired. Jefferson told Madison that he would make one last attempt to reclaim Duane "from the dominion of his passions." He afterwards learned that his letter of remonstrance had given its recipient pain.[54] Such was not his intention, and in fact he tried to help out Duane until almost the end of his own life.

This episode provides a striking example of the lengths to which Jefferson would go to retain a friend and maintain the unity of his party. The latter motive must have been predominant in this particular instance, for he was not personally intimate with Duane, and party unity was to him little short of an obsession. At this stage he virtually identified this with national unity. "For the republicans are the *nation*," he had already written Duane. "Their opponents are but a faction, weak in numbers, but powerful and profuse in the command of moneys," and backed by a foreign power (Britain). His description of them as monarchists now seems extreme, but he was championing the cause of republicanism at a time when the American Republic was even lonelier than it had been before Napoleon became emperor of France. For the union of true believers, of whom he regarded Duane as one, he would sacrifice "all minor differences of opinion."

We may discern rationalization in his identification of Republicans with republicanism. Similar claims have been made many times by partisans for their particular cause. But Jefferson's evangelical fervor suggests that he was thinking of more than political advantage. In this time of dissension among the leaders of his own group he wrote: "And when we reflect that the eyes of the virtuous all over the earth are turned with anxiety on us, as the only depositories of the sacred fire of liberty, and that our falling into anarchy would decide forever the destinies of mankind, and seal the political heresy that man is incapable of self-government, the only contest between divided friends should be who will dare farthest into the ranks of the common enemy."[55]

[53] TJ to Gallatin, Apr. 24, 1811 (L. & B., XIII, 45–46).
[54] TJ to Duane, July 25, 1811 (*ibid.*, p. 66).
[55] TJ to John Hollins, May 5, 1811 (*ibid.*, p. 58).

[III]

Assets and Liabilities

1809-1812

IN the first summer of his retirement Jefferson said that the value of his property was fifty times a debt of $4500 that might ultimately be charged against his estate.[1] We need not conclude from this that he valued his property at $225,000, nor need we try to translate this figure into its present-day equivalent, which of course would be many times that. It seems safe to say, nonetheless, that at this time — and indeed for years thereafter — he believed that his assets greatly exceeded his liabilities. The major difficulty was that of realizing on these assets. Consisting wholly of real property and chattels, they could not be quickly converted into cash in the particular economy in which he operated.

Although it would be difficult to set forth his assets in precise monetary terms, we can get a good view of his possessions at this time since he drew up a full list of his lands and slaves in 1810, about a year after his retirement.[2] The land roll of that year shows that he had slightly more than ten thousand acres. Somewhat more than half of these were in Albemarle County and fewer than half in Bedford. Also he owned Natural Bridge (157 acres) and several lots, including one in Richmond. He said that of all things he was most tenacious of land. Chiefly because of gifts to his daughters and their husbands he had a little less of it in 1810 than when he made a comparable list some fifteen years earlier.[3]

[1] TJ to John Barnes, June 15, 1809 (LC). In 1817 he placed an even greater value on his lands alone.

[2] Rolls of 1810 are in *Farm Book*, pp. 127–129. It should be noted that references to the facsimile in the Betts edn. are italicized. For editorial commentary and correspondence regarding his lands, see pp. 324–336.

[3] Land roll of 1794 (*Farm Book*, p. 32). In Albemarle, TJ gave Pantops (819¼ acres) to JWE and Maria, and sold his claim to 245 acres of John Harvie's Belmont. In Bedford, he gave 1450 acres of Poplar Forest to TMR and Martha, and sold Tullos (474 acres). The only significant addition to his property was at Milton in Albemarle (1162¼ acres). On this see Appendix II, Section A, below.

During his presidency some of his farms in Albemarle were rented. When he came home five fields of one hundred acres each below the Rivanna were leased to John H. Craven, along with the slaves residing on them, and eight fields of forty acres each at Shadwell were rented to Eli Alexander. Both tenants were obligated to follow a specified schedule of crop rotation, and the owner was to receive approximately $1000 a year in one case and about $320 in the other. Alexander was behind on his rent when Jefferson retired, and a dispute between them regarding certain additional acres that might be cleared had to be referred to arbitration. This particular tenancy was a headache to Jefferson and his rentals never proved very profitable.[4]

At this time he had about two hundred slaves, divided between Albemarle and Bedford much as his lands were. There were more domestics at Monticello than at Poplar Forest and there were a number of artisans — tradesmen Jefferson called them, though the first on the list, John Hemings, was a carpenter. One can gain a false impression from the totals, since allowance should be made for the children and the aged. A breakdown on the basis of age, from Jefferson's careful records, shows that one-third of the Negroes were ten or under. In another and smaller category were those retired from service because of age or infirmity. Notable in this group was Old Judy at Poplar Forest, aged eighty-one in 1809. Her husband, Old Will, had vanished from the scene but she remained a couple of years longer. At Monticello boys between ten and sixteen were commonly engaged in the nailery, and girls of that age were occupied in spinning.[5] Not more than a third of Jefferson's slaves were available as field hands, and at this time he actually hired a few to perform tasks beyond the capacity of his own force — such as construction work on his manufacturing mill, digging his canal, and building roads.[6] These had to be paid for in cash, once a year, but in helping construct his mill they were supposedly adding to the value of his property and to his much-needed cash income.

On his retirement from office Jefferson was still bearing a burden of pre-Revolutionary debts to British firms, as well as one dating from the

[4] See *Farm Book*, pp. 161, 171–185. The lease to Craven appears to have run through 1810, and that to Alexander until Dec. 1, 1812, although no payment after Apr. 1, 1811, seems to have been recorded in the Account Book.

[5] For an account of TJ's slaves in the 1790's, see *Jefferson and the Ordeal of Liberty*, pp. 209–212.

[6] Between 1806–1810 he hired slaves of Mrs. Mary and Miss Sarah Dangerfield of Spotsylvania County. The original agreement was for nine, but the number was slowly decreased in 1809, when he hired four from Gen. William Chamberlayne (*Farm Book*, pp. 23–33).

1790's to a Dutch financial house.[7] During his presidency he had finally relieved himself of the most pressing of his obligations — what he called "the great Wayles debt" — and he made payments on the others, but the interest that had accumulated in the years when he made no payments still left him a considerable sum to pay. What concerned him most at this time was the debt of about $11,000 that he had incurred as President.

The financial program he had worked out before coming home called for the application to this of the entire income from his Bedford lands, chiefly from tobacco but to some extent from wheat, both of which were cash crops. He estimated this income as $2500 a year, but in this period it usually came to less. He expected to live off his operations in Albemarle, but, as he told his daughter, that would require good management. Accordingly, he thought at first that, for aid on his farms, he would need to call on his Randolph son-in-law, who was perhaps at the height of his agricultural career about this time. Martha's husband had developed a system of horizontal plowing calculated to prevent erosion, and he produced excellent crops on his red-clay lands, though he was much less successful in marketing them.[8]

For reasons that are not clear Jefferson did not seek much help from his son-in-law, and in fact he does not appear to have concerned himself very much with his farms during the first months of his retirement. He took them into his own hands after Christmas, 1809, he said, and until then he devoted himself especially to his gardens. In the summer of 1810 he wrote: "My farms occupy me much, and require much to get them underway."[9] His vegetable gardens were distinctly useful but they deserve treatment, along with his flowers, elsewhere than in a chapter devoted chiefly to finances.

Precisely what the master's plantation management consisted of at this stage cannot be readily determined. Edmund Bacon, the overseer, said he received written instructions about everything, so that he always knew what to do.[10] No doubt Jefferson was diligent in farm management as in other matters, but as time went on he had to devote more and more of it to his correspondence and therefore he spent proportionately less on farming. His later references to his own management were distinctly uncomplimentary. Presumably he could have been more successful if he had concentrated his attention on it, and if the lands themselves had been better. "It was not a profitable estate," said Bacon, referring partic-

[7] These debts are described in Appendix II, Section B.

[8] On TMR at this time, see Gaines, ch. VI. He made an unsuccessful run for Congress in the winter of 1808–1809, and if anything his financial situation had worsened.

[9] TJ to S. H. Smith, Aug. 6, 1810, quoted in *Garden Book*, p. 427.

[10] Pierson, p. 44.

ularly to the part in Albemarle; "it was too uneven and hard to work." In the opinion of this competent observer, Madison's plantation was much better.

Jefferson raised some tobacco in Albemarle in later years, but at this time his only cash crop there seems to have been wheat. While he sought to approximate self-sufficiency as nearly as possible, he limited the cultivation of corn to prevent erosion and often had to buy it to feed his slaves. Among other demands for cash one of the most persistent was his account with David Higginbotham, a merchant at Milton on the Rivanna below Shadwell. Submitted annually, this included items ranging from tea and coffee to salt fish, chiefly for the slaves, and "Negro cloth" for their garments. Until Jefferson turned over all his affairs to his grandson toward the end of his life, he resorted to many and various expedients to meet this perennial obligation. Some of these will be referred to hereafter, but reference should be made first to the failure of one source of cash income on which the ex-President had been counting — namely, the rental from his manufacturing mill.

ii

He had two mills on the Shadwell side of the Rivanna, about three-fourths of a mile above the village of Milton and six miles below the village of Charlottesville. From his father he had inherited a gristmill, a canal, and a dam, but all of these were washed away in the great "fresh" of 1771, and they were not fully restored for a generation. During his first term as President a new canal was dug, at an estimated total cost of $20,000. A new gristmill was built for his own use and another dam was constructed. This had to be repaired after later floods but it seemed secure when he came home.

The manufacturing mill, which was expected to grind grain for all comers, went into operation during his second term.[11] Unlike the gristmill or toll mill, this was rented, supposedly for $1250 a year, but it was being operated badly and had brought in no rent as yet. The original arrangement had been made with Jonathan Shoemaker, who insisted on bringing in his son Isaac as a partner and left the running of the mill to him while he himself lived elsewhere. Before Jefferson got home Martha had informed him of the general opinion in the neighborhood that it would be better to get the mill back on any terms than to leave it in the hands of the Shoemakers. Shortly after his return the harassed proprie-

[11] The general account of TJ's mills, canal, and dam in *Farm Book*, pp. 341–343, is followed by extracts of letters bearing on them. They are shown on the Monticello neighborhood map, below, p. 254.

tor wrote a stern letter to Jonathan Shoemaker, as a result of which he received in midsummer a sizable payment on the rent. But this fell considerably below his expectation, and, despite later payments, Shoemaker was still about a year behind when Jefferson had been a year at home.[12]

In this staple-producing region, where cash was scarce between crops, there was much recourse to barter. Jefferson's nail business was largely on that basis.[13] But he had to pay in money for the rod and bar iron he got for his nailery from Jones and Howell in Philadelphia, and he had counted on the cash income from his mill. Disappointed in his returns from that source, he was compelled in the summer of 1809 to ask for an extension of credit from Jones and Howell. This was readily granted to him as an old customer, but he had difficulty in paying their bills in the next two or three years.[14] Before the War of 1812 caused commerce with Philadelphia to be interrupted and the operations of his nailery to be suspended, he had taken the manufacturing mill back from the Shoemakers, but it was never to bring him much of a return on his large investment in it.[15] And his operations on the little river that flowed through his lands were to involve him in difficulties and perplexities during the rest of his days.

In particular he was troubled by the activities of the Rivanna Company, created by legislative act in 1806 and designed to improve the navigation of that stream between Charlottesville and Milton. According to Jefferson, the only difficulties lay in the stretch of two and a quarter miles between Secretary's Ford and Sandy Falls — that is, the passage through the Southwest Mountains. His dam gave "a sheet of dead water" for about a mile and a half to the entrance, and his canal by-passed the remainder of the troubled waters. The problem was to get boats (bateaux) into the lower stream, and the directors, including friends and county neighbors of Jefferson's, finally decided to use his canal and build locks somewhat above his manufacturing mill. He provided the materials for these but denied that he was obligated to build them, as was claimed by the directors.

[12] Partial extracts from Martha's letter of Mar. 2, 1809, to TJ, and from his correspondence with Jonathan Shoemaker in 1809–1810, are in *Farm Book*, pp. 369–376. Shoemaker's payment of $490 on Aug. 6, 1809, already earmarked for David Higginbotham, was promptly sent that merchant. It was followed by lesser payments amounting to $571 through Mar., 1810.

[13] On the nailery, see *Jefferson and the Ordeal of Liberty*, pp. 217–220, and *Farm Book*, pp. 426–453.

[14] TJ to Jones and Howell, Aug. 10, 1809 (*Garden Book*, p. 414); extracts of correspondence of 1809–1811 in *Farm Book*, pp. 448–450.

[15] After the Shoemakers the mill was leased to TMR, who had James McKenney of Culpeper as a partner briefly, and Thomas Eston Randolph for a longer time. The latter ultimately became the sole leaser. The terms of the successive arrangements varied, payment being made at times in flour.

Beginning at least in the fall of 1810 there were differences between him and the directors, but before the outbreak of the War of 1812 these appear to have been largely worked out. One gains the impression that he was overly generous if anything. New difficulties arose in the winter of 1812–1813, when the company sought to gain legislative approval of an enlargement of its powers. Suffice it to say here that the locks worked improperly, at times causing a stoppage of the mill by depriving it of water, and that the legalities of the situation remained so unclear that Jefferson in the last decade of his life was impelled to institute a friendly suit in chancery. This was not concluded until 1819.[16]

During his first year of retirement Jefferson made no perceptible progress in reducing the deficit he had incurred while President, but, soon after he came home, he shifted his loans. Being unable to renew a private loan of $8000 which had been procured for him toward the end of his presidency, he transferred this to the Bank of Virginia in Richmond.[17] Despite later payments to this bank he was never able to extricate himself wholly from debt to it.

The story of another transaction, involving President James Madison in Washington and General Thaddeus Kosciuszko in Paris, is of particular interest. Before leaving the Capital, Jefferson negotiated a loan with the Bank of the United States. This was endorsed by Madison and by John Barnes, a factor, formerly of Philadelphia and now of Georgetown, with whom Jefferson had long dealt. Barnes was the endorser of first liability; and the old man, as Jefferson described him, was uneasy under the responsibility. Accordingly, Jefferson, after rather painful explanations of the necessities which caused him to seek the loan in the first place, asked Madison to assume the first liability.[18] No doubt this action did much to relieve the mind of Barnes, but that financier came up with a suggestion calculated to relieve the minds of all concerned. This involved General Kosciuszko and the latter's American investments, over which Jefferson had power of attorney and which were largely managed by Barnes. Certain eight per cent certificates of Kosciuszko's, totaling $4500, were on the point of being retired, and the money was to be otherwise invested at Barnes's discretion. He proposed that it be loaned

[16] Excellent overall account to Jan. 4, 1813, in TJ's letter of that date to Philip Barbour (*Farm Book*, pp. 386–393); see also Peter Minor to TJ, Nov. 15, 1813, and TJ to Minor, Nov. 18 (*ibid.*, pp. 395–398). The chancery suit is referred to in letters of TJ to Howe Peyton, Feb. 8, 1817, and J. H. Peyton to TJ, Dec. 17, 1819 (*ibid.*, pp. 400–401, 405–406).

[17] This money came from Mrs. Tabb of Amelia County, Va. See Account Book, Jan. 23, July 1, July 22, 1809, Feb. 5, 1810.

[18] TJ to Madison, May 22, 1809 (Ford, IX, 241*n.*). TJ to John S. Barnes, May 24, 1809 (LC).

General Thaddeus Kosciuszko

Engraving from a portrait by Josef Grassi. (Library of Congress, Prints and Photographs Division)

to Jefferson at eight per cent. That gentleman gladly agreed to the suggestion and retired the note in the bank in Washington.[19]

He was delighted to be rid of the obligation to the bank without inconveniencing anybody. He did not doubt that Kosciuszko would approve, since the General never intended to withdraw his capital from America and there would be no diminution in his interest. If Jefferson lived he would pay off the debt, and if he did not it would be a charge against an estate worth fifty times the amount. Along with the first remittance of interest by Barnes, Jefferson sent a long letter to Kosciuszko in the course of which he fully described this transaction. After going into embarrassing detail about his general financial situation, he said: "The proposition [of Barnes] was like a beam of light; & I was satisfied that were you on the spot to be consulted the kindness of your heart would be gratified, while receiving punctually the interest for your own subsistence, to let the principal be so disposed of for a time as to lift a friend out of distress."[20] In a letter of effusive friendliness and praise the Polish patriot expressed in French his full approval of this disposition of his funds, saying that he had complete confidence in Jefferson and asking only that the interest be paid regularly. It was remitted regularly, if not always promptly, and although the debt was not paid in four or five years as Jefferson predicted, it was paid in six or seven under circumstances which will be described hereafter.[21]

Jefferson's papers contain numerous calculations with respect to the payment of various debts, but rarely did events bear out his hopes or even his expectations. Within three years of his return home, however, he did make gratifying progress in reducing what he called his presidential debt. He was by no means over his troubles at the mill; the dam was nearly destroyed by flood in the fall of 1810.[22] He was getting most of the promised rental, but the mitigation of his financial circumstances was chiefly owing to the sale of lands on Ivy Creek in Bedford, 474 acres altogether. On April 7, 1810, he received from Samuel J. Harrison of Lynchburg the first of three annual payments, totaling $5000, and in this period he reduced his notes in the bank in Richmond by approximately that amount. Also, with the help of a good harvest he made a payment

[19] TJ to Barnes, June 15, Aug. 3, 1809 (LC). I have been unable to find the letters of Barnes to which TJ was replying.

[20] TJ to Kosciuszko, Feb. 26, 1810 (LC). A section was omitted from the letter as printed in L. & B., XII, 365–370. I am much indebted to the admirable article of Edward P. Alexander, "Jefferson and Kosciuszko: Friends of Liberty and of Man" (*Pa. Mag. of Hist.*, XCII [Jan., 1968], 87–103).

[21] Kosciuszko to TJ, Mar. 1, 1811; received July 7 (MHS). The Kosciuszko accounts, 1809–1816, are in Edgehill-Randolph Papers, UVA. For the final settlement, see below, p. 181.

[22] *Garden Book*, p. 427.

of $1000 on one of the two pre-Revolutionary debts by which he was still encumbered.[23]

His relations with the Scottish house of Henderson, McCaul & Company had been notably agreeable through a generation. He said that he had known its representative, James Lyle, longer than any other living friend. Substantial payments had been made on this debt through the years, but interest had accumulated remorselessly, and when an accounting was made in 1808 a balance of £877 was outstanding. In the fall of 1809 Jefferson visited Lyle at his house in Manchester below Richmond while on his way to that city. No doubt they enjoyed talking over old times, but Lyle may not have been entirely satisfied with their deliberations. He went to Richmond the next day, hoping to see Jefferson but found him occupied. Early in 1810 this creditor wrote his old friend, reminding him that he was "in distress for money" and that he had expected a payment. He said that he found it most disagreeable to be troubling Jefferson. That eminent debtor received the letter with "sincere affliction." For reasons into which he went at length, however, he was then utterly unable to comply.[24] He said he hoped to get rid of this debt before it destroyed him, as it probably would have done but for Lyle's patience.

The letter Lyle wrote his old friend a year later was the more appealing because of its references to his age and infirmity. Now nearly eighty-five, he besought Jefferson not only for a payment but also for aid in procuring spectacles. Jefferson promptly sent him a pair, but these proved useless. Lyle concluded that his optical ills were irremediable but gained the promise of a payment and got one a few months later.[25] The specific debt to which this payment was directed was originally one of £54 to a local merchant which had been assigned to the Scottish firm in 1775. By 1811 interest had accumulated to such an extent that Jefferson's payment of $1000 did not cover it.[26] In this case of old debt, as in others, the interest ultimately exceeded the principal. Such reductions of debt as he had made before the outbreak of the War of 1812 were largely owing to the sale of capital assets. Since he had not seriously depleted his material resources, however, he had some justification for resuming his characteristic optimism. But it remained to be seen what the weather would do to his crops and the war to his markets.

[23] Account Book, Apr. 7, June 13, 1810; Apr. 4, June 24, 1811; May 29, 1812.
[24] Lyle to TJ, Jan. 24, 1810; TJ to Lyle, Feb. 12, 1810 (MHS).
[25] Lyle to TJ, Jan. 3, Mar. 23, 1811; TJ to Lyle, Jan. 27, 1811 (*ibid.*).
[26] Lyle to TJ, Aug. 5, 1811, statement of account July 6, 1811 (*ibid.*).

[IV]

The Young Gardener

JEFFERSON believed that the particular direction his major activities took in the course of his life was owing more to circumstances than to choice. In this opinion and experience he was far from unique among human beings, but because of the extraordinary range of his interests and diversity of his talents, one cannot help wondering just what he would have done if he had really been free to choose. A couple of years after his retirement he made a suggestive statement in that regard. This was in a letter to Charles Willson Peale, the artist and museum director, who had recently left Philadelphia for a farm. To this old friend and fellow naturalist he wrote: "I have often thought that if heaven had given me choice of my position and calling, it should have been on a rich spot of earth, well watered, and near a good market for the productions of the garden. No occupation is so delightful to me as the culture of the earth, and no culture comparable to that of the garden. Such a variety of subjects, some one always coming to perfection, the failure of one thing repaired by the success of another, and instead of one harvest a continued one through the year." His little mountaintop was neither fertile nor well watered, and there was no nearby market for its produce. Under no demand except for the family table he was devoted to the garden. "But," he added, "though an old man, I am but a young gardener."[1]

This modest disclaimer did scant justice to the interest in the cultivation not merely of vegetables but also of flowers that he began to manifest, at least by the age of twenty-three. The garden book he then began to keep opened with the entry, "Purple hyacinth begins to bloom," and all the others for the year 1766 relate to flowers. In the next year he started off with a reference to the sowing of peas, and from that time

[1] TJ to C. W. Peale, Aug. 20, 1811 (L. & B., XIII, 79).

Charles Willson Peale

"The Artist in His Museum," self-portrait, 1822. (Courtesy of the Pennsylvania Academy of Fine Arts; gift of Mrs. Sarah Harrison—the Joseph Harrison, Jr., Collection)

onward vegetables and flowers were commingled in his records.[2] During his years abroad, manifesting his "zeal to promote the general good of mankind by an interchange of useful things," he instituted overseas traffic in plants as well as books, and until his dying day he was exchanging horticultural items with kindred spirits in the Old World and the New. In a list of his own services that he drew up in 1800 he included, along with the drafting of the Declaration of Independence, the sending of olive trees and upland rice to South Carolina from France. In this connection he observed: "The greatest service which can be rendered any country is to add a useful plant to its culture."[3] He perceived no conflict between utility and beauty. He admired the English most for their gardens, which he might have regarded as wasteful, and he urged young Americans to make a special point of viewing gardens when abroad, since noble ones could be so easily made in their own land. In one of the most moving of his protests against the shackles of public office he spoke of his "interest or affection in every bud that opens, in every breath that blows."[4] Rarely did he make such direct reference to his love of nature, but, as has been said, this was "so intense that his observant eye caught almost every passing change in it."[5] His joy in architecture is reflected in the saying that "putting up and pulling down" was a favorite amusement of his. Gardening supplemented architecture as an interest, and, like it, was one of the most absorbing and abiding of his life.

While his interest in plants was lifelong, that in planting necessarily varied with circumstances. Naturally it was quickened by his anticipation of his return home to stay and his expectation of the early completion of building operations at Monticello. Before the middle of his second presidential term he was dispatching fruit and shade trees, shrubs, and thorn plants, chiefly from Main's nursery near Washington. Also, he was discussing landscape gardening with William Hamilton of Philadelphia, whose grounds were the only ones in America that he regarded as comparable to those of England.[6] The thorn hedge around his orchard was only in its beginning and his hilltop was still raw when he viewed them on his spring visit two years before his retirement. At that time, besides setting out shrubs and shade trees, he laid out and planted with flowers the beds that still surround the house. The general plan for the mansion

[2] See *Thomas Jefferson's Garden Book, 1766–1824* (1944), esp. pp. 1, 4–7. Admirably annotated by E. M. Betts, this is an invaluable source, to the richness of which I cannot hope to do full justice.

[3] Ford, VII, 477; see also *Jefferson and the Ordeal of Liberty*, p. 485.

[4] To Madison, June 9, 1793 (Ford, VI, 290–291).

[5] Betts in *Garden Book*, pp. v–vi.

[6] On his activities in 1806 see *Jefferson the President: Second Term*, pp. 124–127.

and outbuildings that he had drafted a generation earlier showed rectangular beds but these existed only on paper. Those of 1807 were mostly oval though a few were round.[7] Though Jefferson personally directed these and later plantings, the actual digging was done by one of his servants, generally Wormley, while he carried a measuring line. His granddaughter Anne Cary was his enthusiastic assistant. To her he wrote that, since these beds did not provide room enough for the variety of flowers he wanted, he was planning a winding walk around the lawn on the south side, with narrow borders of flowers.[8] This was made the next year, along with a fish pond near the southeast pavilion. Also, that year the old vegetable garden was leveled.

In order to avoid excessive labor, Jefferson concluded that the garden should be in four levels and before the spring of 1808 he had instructed Edmund Bacon to that effect and had requested Thomas Mann Randolph to establish the second of these. When he came home a year later the first terrace was ready for planting. If the master's instructions were carried out, from sixty to seventy loads of manure had been dropped on it — an amount that he regarded as sufficient for the present.[9] When Margaret Bayard Smith and her husband visited Monticello in the summer of 1809, she reported that little had been done and that the chief beauty of the garden was the noble view it commanded. Before that time Jefferson had laid it off in eighteen beds or squares (later increased to twenty-four). He must have done a vast amount of planting by 1809, judging from the "Kalendar" he compiled for that year. The first in a series which, with a single interim, he continued until the last two years of his life, it lists vegetables, states when and where they were sowed, when transplanted, and when brought to table.[10] No later calendar was as long as this one; and this sowing was probably his most extensive. According to Mrs. Smith, he kept his garden seeds in a little closet. Peas and beans were in tin canisters, but all the other seeds were in "little phials," she said, "labeled and hung on little hooks," everything being in the "neatest order."[11]

He had seeds from everywhere: from county neighbors like George Divers of Farmington; from nurseryman Bernard McMahon and natu-

[7] *Garden Book*, Plate XXIII, which may be compared with Plate III. These and other flower beds were restored in 1939–1941 by the Garden Club of Virginia. (See the beautiful booklet by E. M. Betts and H. B. Perkins, *Thomas Jefferson's Flower Garden at Monticello*, 1971 edn.) Nothing was planted that he was not known to have had. Thus there is no boxwood.

[8] TJ to Anne Cary Randolph, June 7, 1807 (*Family Letters*, pp. 307–308); Plate XXIV in *Garden Book;* extract of letter of Ellen Randolph Coolidge to H. S. Randall (*ibid.*, p. 636).

[9] TJ to Bacon and to TMR, Feb. 23, 1808 (*Garden Book*, pp. 364–365; to Bacon, Dec. 26, 1808 (*ibid.*, p. 383). Actually, there were three levels in the garden as finally laid out.

[10] *Garden Book*, pp. 388–393, 395.

[11] M. B. Smith, *First Forty Years*, p. 72.

ralists William Bartram and Benjamin S. Barton in the Philadelphia district; from Thomas Main and Dr. William Thornton in that of Washington; from Justice William Johnson and General Thomas Sumter in South Carolina; from Philip Mazzei in Italy; from Lafayette's aunt, Madame de Tessé, and André Thouin, director of the Jardin des Plantes in Paris. To the latter, it may be noted, he had seeds from Lewis and Clark sent by Bernard McMahon. He made some purchases, but mostly he was engaging in two-way traffic and free exchange. No small part of his correspondence was with the botanical and horticultural enthusiasts of his age. From them he got not merely peas and beans in variety, but stones, cuttings, and seeds of trees and vines and shrubs not hitherto planted in his region — a mimosa or silk tree from Bartram, Alpine strawberries from Mazzei, the pod of an acacia and benne seed from Justice Johnson. Not all of these could have been expected to thrive in his environment and they were subject to other difficulties and dangers arising from his particular situation.

He had what he called nurseries, but these were only specially designated beds. He also had a greenhouse, but, as he himself described it, this was merely a glassed-in piazza adjoining his study. There he had hoped to have oranges, limes, mimosa, and the like for his enjoyment, but in the first winter of his retirement everything in the greenhouse froze to death. Judging from his report of the temperature in his bedroom in January, 1810 — once as low as 32½° — that fate must have nearly befallen himself.[12] Not only were his seedlings without benefit of a hothouse; they were dependent on the rains from heaven just as his grainfields were.

The water supply at Monticello was precarious. The well near the southeast pavilion was dug forty years before Jefferson ceased to be President. It had failed many times in the intervening years and was to do so thereafter. He sought to remedy the situation by means of cisterns. Following elaborate calculations made in 1808 of the number of gallons that might be expected from his roof, he built four cisterns within the next two years. These were located on the two sides of the covered ways to the east and west of the mansion. He was still trying to perfect them a decade later, and we may safely presume that they did not fulfill his expectation. His final recourse for water was to springs, of which he himself referred by name to fifteen, ten on the south side and five on the north side of the mountain.[13] In times of drought water had to be brought to the mansion from these hillside springs, and we may doubt if much of it was ever available for grass and vegetables and flowers.

[12] Betts & Perkins, pp. 25–26.

[13] *Garden Book*, Appendix II; Betts & Perkins, pp. 21–23.

The successive calendars that Jefferson drew up, from 1809 to 1824, leave no possible doubt of the vast scope of his horticultural ambitions but suggest that his reach considerably exceeded his grasp. This is especially true of the first and longest calendar, which comes to six pages in print. The sowings far outnumbered the transplantings, and, in view of the length of the list of vegetables, relatively few appear to have reached the table.[14] Obviously he was most successful with peas, beans, and other staples. Among the local gentry there was considerable rivalry with respect to the earliest production of edible peas. According to custom a dinner was given by the winner in the race, who was generally George Divers of Farmington. The story is that once, when Jefferson was ahead of everybody, he kept quiet so that this friend would enjoy success as usual.[15]

Jefferson's diet consisted mostly of fruits and vegetables, and long before he died he had from his own acres a sufficiently diverse supply of both, actual or potential. In 1811 his plan for his orchard showed that he had 384 fruit trees — peaches, apples, and cherries chiefly, along with some apricots, nectarines, quinces, plums, and pears. Among the trees he proposed to plant in seventy-one vacancies were sixteen pecan trees — spelled by him "peccans." He was unaware that they would bear no nuts in his latitude.[16] By the next year his vegetable garden was graded in three terraces — or, as he called them, platforms; and, besides an elaborate calendar, he left to posterity a plan of his planting arrangement.[17] This shows a division of his twenty-four beds into three main parts, respectively designated "Fruits," "Roots," and "Leaves." The first of these, consisting of the "upper platform," was not a section of his orchard as might have been supposed from its name, but contained peas, beans, cucumbers, tomatoes, and squashes. The "roots" on the middle terrace included carrots, beets, and onions. The third terrace, assigned chiefly to "leaves," contained lettuce and endive, celery, spinach, broccoli, cabbage, and the like. In the borders, among other things, he had strawberries and had, or hoped to have, tarragon.

Much of Jefferson's correspondence, especially that with Bernard McMahon, from whom he got so many bulbs and seeds, relates to flowers, but he kept no such records of them as he did of vegetables. Writing his granddaughter Anne Cary during one of her visits to her husband's parents, he said that, having left everything to her, he really knew nothing about the flowers. Accordingly, he suggested that she prepare a book

[14] See *Garden Book* for the years in question. It is possible that, after recording the sowings and transplantings, TJ neglected to fill in the other columns.
[15] Recounted by T. J. Randolph (Randall, III, 674).
[16] *Garden Book*, p. 468.
[17] *Ibid.*, 469.

of instructions for her sister Ellen, her designated surrogate, who had fewer cares than he.[18] This was at just the time he was assuming the personal management of his farms. Toward the end of the following summer he wrote Samuel Harrison Smith that he had made no progress that year in his works of ornament since he had been forced to attend to those of utility.[19] In the spring he had sowed larkspur and poppies in his flower borders and had planted yellow jasmine in the oval beds next to the covered ways on both sides of the house. But the manufacturing mill was more in his mind at this stage.

Perhaps the most beautiful saying of his about flowers was in a letter to his eldest granddaughter. Late in May of the year he was sixty-eight he reported to Anne Cary, who was visiting the Bankheads with his first great-grandchild, a baby boy named John:

> Nothing new has happened in our neighborhood since you left us. The houses and trees stand where they did. The flowers come forth like the belles of the day, have their short reign of beauty and splendor, and retire like them to the more interesting office of reproducing their like. The hyacinths and tulips are off the stage, the Irises are giving place to the Belladonnas, as this will to the Tuberoses &c. As your Mama has done to you, my dear Anne, as you will do to the sisters of little John, and as I shall soon and chearfully do to you all in wishing you a long, long, good-night. . . .[20]

His premonitions about himself were partially borne out a few weeks later, when he had a long attack of rheumatism. This prostrated the muscles of his back, hips, and thighs and kept him from walking. By the time he wrote Benjamin Rush in August, 1811, he was able to walk, but suffered from a pain in his hip when he did. He wrote from Poplar Forest, where he had arrived after a painful journey in a "hard-riding gig." It had been the delight of his retirement to be in constant physical activity and he deplored his inability to take exercise. His zest for gardening had suffered little or no diminution, however; the letter to Charles Willson Peale in which he extolled it was written a few days later.[21] The elaborate records of his vegetables that he kept in 1812 may reflect the fact that he was more indoors than usual, but nature smiled on him sufficiently to make that a good year, perhaps his best year as a gardener. This was the case in the realm of ornament as well as that of

[18] TJ to Anne Cary, Dec. 29, 1809 (*Family Letters*, p. 394).

[19] TJ to S. H. Smith, Aug. 6, 1810, quoted in *Garden Book*, p. 427.

[20] TJ to Anne Cary, May 26, 1811 (*Family Letters*, p. 400).

[21] TJ to Benjamin Rush, Aug. 17, 1811 (L. & B., XIII, 76); to C. W. Peale, Aug. 20 (*ibid.*, p. 79).

utility — in the realm of flowers no less than that of vegetables. In the spring he changed the planting of the borders of the winding walk behind his house so as to bring similar plants together and create better color effects.[22] The bloom of Monticello lasted from early spring till winter. Edmund Bacon said in later years that he never saw anything like it; and Ellen recalled that the moments spent by the patriarch and his flock amid the flowers were among the happiest of all their lives.[23]

In the spring of 1813 Jefferson reported to a friend that, while he could ride with sufficient comfort, he could walk no further than his garden.[24] He continued to find it easier to ride, but he did not soon cease walking to his garden. The three or four years following his retirement may perhaps be viewed as his golden age as a gardener, but he never ceased to believe that botany is one of the most valuable of sciences and association with growing plants one of life's delights. We may doubt if anybody ever said it better than he did in a letter to a learned friend when he was seventy-one:

> Botany I rank with the most valuable sciences, whether we consider its subjects as furnishing the principal subsistence of life to man and beast, delicious varieties for our tables, refreshments from our orchards, the adornments of our flower-borders, shade and perfume of our groves, materials for our buildings, or medicaments for our bodies. . . . To a country family it constitutes a great portion of their social entertainment. No country gentleman should be without what amuses every step he takes into his fields.[25]

ii

Interest in the weather was to be expected of a countryman, farmer, and horticulturist, but Jefferson's went far beyond that of his fellows, and in keeping meterological records he was an American pioneer. Systematic as he was, he might have come to the keeping of such records in any case, but as a law student in Williamsburg he may have received his original stimulus from Governor Francis Fauquier, who was an enthusiastic observer and recorder of natural phenomena.[26] His own system-

22 Betts & Perkins, p. 47, citing entry of Apr. 8, 1812, in *Garden Book*, p. 474.

23 Pierson, p. 38; Randall, III, 347.

24 To Mrs. Elizabeth Trist, May 10, 1813 (*Garden Book*, p. 501).

25 TJ to Thomas Cooper, Oct. 7, 1814 (L. & B., XIV, 201).

26 On Fauquier, see *Jefferson the Virginian*, p. 77. TJ was familiar with observations of temperature, winds, and rainfall that were made at and near Williamsburg from 1772 to 1777, as he showed by his use of them in his *Notes on Virginia* (in his answer to Query VII).

atic recording may be said to have begun in Philadelphia, where, on July 1, 1776, he made the first entry in his weather memorandum book. Though thermometers were very scarce in pre-Revolutionary America, he had acquired one by or before this time, and within a day or two he bought a relatively expensive one in the colonial metropolis. His friend and fellow observer of wind and weather, Rev. James Madison of Williamsburg (later Bishop), complained that, during the Revolution, the British robbed him of his. Jefferson reported that he was without one in the very cold winter of 1783–1784 when attending the Continental Congress in Annapolis and believed there was not one in the entire state of Maryland.[27]

Following an insistent suggestion from Jefferson, Congressman James Madison, Jr., cousin of the clergyman, was drawn into observations of the weather in Orange County, which were afterwards taken over by his father, but these meteorological coadjutors of the Squire of Monticello were handicapped by the lack of a barometer and even of a thermometer at first.[28] Jefferson's own observations do not appear to have been often limited by lack of instruments and he made them wherever he was, but the records in his Weather Memorandum Book were necessarily intermittent except when he was in one place for a considerable period.[29] They are fullest during his periods of retirement and best of all from 1810 to 1816, when they attained a degree of reliability that gratified him and has commended him to later meteorologists.

Long before he made this detailed record his travels had served to increase his satisfaction with the climate of his native region. This is well expressed in a letter he wrote his daughter Martha from Lake Champlain while he was secretary of state and on a holiday journey with Madison. Rarely did this lover of the sunshine complain of heat, but the only thing that had marred the pleasure of his trip thus far, he said, was sultry weather such as supposedly would be met with in Carolina or Georgia rather than in New York and New England. He was inclined to believe that summer heat in the North was worse than in the South while it lasted. Actually, he was never to be in New England in summer long

[27] On the meteorological activities of this member of the Madison family and TJ in the early period, see Alexander McAdie, "A Colonial Weather Service" (*Popular Science Monthly*, XLV [July, 1894], 331–337). On TJ's activities and services in this field as a whole, see E. T. Martin, *Thomas Jefferson: Scientist* (1952), ch. V.

[28] On the Madisonian collaboration, see *Papers of James Madison*, ed. by R. A. Rutland et al., VIII (1973), Appendix B, and letter of TJ to Madison, Mar. 16, 1784 (pp. 15–16), which the latter's editors describe as a virtual command.

[29] Though the Weather Memorandum Book, 1776–1820, like the Account Book, is in several volumes (LC and MHS), I have used the photostatic copy at UVA and refer to it by date only.

enough to test this opinion, but the general satisfaction with his own situation that he expressed at this time was to be maintained:

> On the whole I find nothing anywhere else in point of climate which Virginia need envy to any part of the world. Here [Lake Champlain] they are locked up in ice and snow for 6. months. Spring and autumn which make a paradise of our country are rigorous winter with them, and a tropical summer breaks on them all at once. When we consider how much climate contributes to the happiness of our condn. by the fine sensation it excites, and the productions it is the parent of, we have reason to value highly the accident of birth in such a one as that of Virginia.[30]

Half a dozen years later, writing the French traveler and scholar Volney, who had visited him at Monticello the previous June when his building operations were at a very confused stage, he described his district as the Eden of the United States.[31] Writing in early April, 1797, he spoke of his delight in the "soft genial temperature of the season, just above the want of fire, enlivened by the reanimation of birds, flowers, the fields, forests and gardens." He does not appear to have been fully aware or sufficiently appreciative of the glory of the northern autumn, but he rightly rejoiced in the long and delicious Virginia spring.

To this noted traveler he admitted some years later that people were disposed to like the sort of climate they were used to. "The Canadian," he said, "glows with delight in his sleigh and snow, the very idea of which gives me the shivers."[32] He always dreaded cold and never during his years abroad did he become reconciled to the cloudy skies of Europe. For its sunshine if for no other reason he preferred the American climate. "I think it a more cheerful one," he said. "It is our cloudless sky which has eradicated from our constitutions all disposition to hang ourselves, which we might otherwise have inherited from our English ancestors." According to his own reckoning the climate at Monticello was distinctly cheerful; he concluded that on an average five of every seven days were clear, and only one was wholly cloudy.

He kept records of the weather while President, as he did of the appearance of vegetables in the Washington market, but not until his retirement was he in position to keep a continuous meteorological diary. Not even then was he wholly stationary, for he made regular visits to Poplar Forest. On all the other days during the seven years 1810–1816, he made observations before dawn and between three and four in the

[30] TJ to Martha, May 31, 1791 (*Family Letters*, pp. 84–85).
[31] TJ to Volney, Apr. 9, 1797 (Gilbert Chinard, *Volney et l'Amérique* [1923], pp. 79–80).
[32] TJ to Volney, Feb. 8, 1805 (L. & B., XI, 63).

afternoon — that is, he noted the minimum and maximum temperature. For the days of absence he took the average of them in other years, believing that the effect on over-all averages was slight. Altogether, he made 3905 observations and for his time and circumstance attained "a good degree of exactness." He made a rough summary of his findings and from this we can ascertain the sort of weather he experienced during the early years of his retirement.[33]

He stated here, as he had in the *Notes on Virginia* and elsewhere, his belief that the climate had moderated within the memory of persons then living. Previously he had relied too much on the recollections of old men, who believed that the snow was no longer as deep as it was when they were boys, and he had no scientific warrant for dating, as he did, the beginnings of a continuous moderating trend to the time of Augustus Caesar. As President, however, he had lived through a warming period, and of the seven years covered by his record only the last — "the year without a summer" — seemed to mark a cooling trend.[34] The differences between the climate as he described it and that of the twentieth century in his part of the country, while perhaps measurable, do not appear to be worthy of special note. As reported by him the temperature ranged from 5½° to 94½° Fahrenheit and averaged 55½° for a year — from 36° in January to 75° in July. It seems to have been slightly cooler at Monticello than it was in our century in Washington or Richmond, but the difference may have been owing to the elevation of Monticello.[35] Assuming that fires were needed when the outside temperature fell below 55°, he calculated that they had these constantly for four months, and in the morning and evening for upwards of two months more. If his figures can be accepted, there was more precipitation on the little mountain than in twentieth-century Virginia, despite the fact that there were more fair days.[36] He observed, doubtless with pleasure, that the ground was covered with snow only twenty-two days in a year. He regularly noted the prevailing winds, showing in what proportion these were wet or dry.

[33] The diary and his summary are at MHS. He sent copies of the latter to Madison and Joseph C. Cabell, and, after his death, it appeared (June 24, 1829) in *Virginia Literary Museum*, a short-lived publication of the University. His grandson, T. J. Randolph, made it available. It can now be conveniently seen in *Garden Book*, Appendix I.

[34] For information about general trends I am indebted to Dr. H. E. Landsberg, formerly director of the U.S. Weather Bureau and subsequently associated with the Institute of Fluid Dynamics and Applied Mathematics, University of Maryland.

[35] Figures in the 1974 *World Almanac* for the period 1931–1960 show both Washington and Richmond to have been slightly warmer than Monticello was in the period 1810–1816, and to have had less rainfall.

[36] By a "fair" day he meant what astronomers called "observing days" (*Garden Book*, p. 625).

He dated the first blossoms of the red maple, the almond, the peach, the cherry, the lilac, the redbud, and the dogwood — the arrival of the house martin, the wood robin, and fireflies — the first appearance on the table of garden peas, artichokes, and Indian corn — the beginning of the wheat harvest and the ripening of strawberries and peaches. One of his young friends expressed astonishment that he could find time to make "such a prodigious number of observations."[37] But, quite clearly, he made them because observing nature was the thing he most liked to do.

[37]Joseph C. Cabell to TJ, Aug. 18, 1817 (Cabell, p. 78).

[V]

The Batture Controversy

1807-1814

SHORTLY after the middle of May, 1810, when Jefferson had been some fourteen months out of office, he received from the leader of the bar in Richmond a surprising letter. John Wickham had been asked by Edward Livingston of New Orleans to institute an action against the ex-President in the federal court, and Aaron Burr's former counselor was reporting that he had no choice but to do so, whether or not he would be subsequently engaged in the case. Though still uninformed of the precise nature of the suit, Jefferson appreciated the seriousness of the situation sufficiently to ask Wickham to represent him, along with the prosecutors in the Burr case, George Hay and William Wirt. Wickham's declination and his representation of Livingston were what might have been expected, as indeed were the acceptances of Hay and Wirt. To these two, Littleton W. Tazewell of Norfolk was afterwards added. Meanwhile, Jefferson learned that he was being sued for $100,000 for trespass and damages. Specifically, the action related to the eviction of Livingston from what was known as the batture in New Orleans, on orders from Jefferson while President; and, in the opinion of that gentleman and his counsel, Livingston's real concern was to strengthen his title to this property rather than to collect damages. Jefferson certainly did not ignore the personal threat, but he recognized that it was incidental to a long-standing controversy. Into the story of this we must enter, to some degree at least.[1]

Batture has been defined as "a river or sea-bed elevated to the surface."[2] In this particular case the reference was to that part of the bed of the Mississippi at New Orleans, below the levee, that was dry for about

[1] John Wickham to TJ, May 16, 1810; TJ to Wirt and Hay, May 19; Wirt to TJ, May 24; Hay to TJ, May 25; TJ to L. W. Tazewell, June 28; Tazewell to TJ, July 5 (all LC).

[2] *Oxford English Dictionary*.

half the year and covered with water during the remainder. Even more specifically, what was referred to was the batture or beach at the bend of the river opposite the suburb of Ste. Marie. This was said to have measured (in 1806) from 122 to 247 yards in breadth at low water, and was estimated by Jefferson as being worth half a million dollars.

The legal question was whether it was public or private property. From time immemorial, as Jefferson understood, it had been used by the inhabitants of New Orleans to furnish earth for streets and courtyards, to provide in the dry season a landing for boats from upstream, and, when inundated, to serve as a harbor where boats could be anchored. In his presidency claim to it was vigorously asserted by and in behalf of Jean Gravier, brother of the man who had sold the lots constituting the suburb, and whose remaining property he had acquired. These lots actually lay between Gravier's own plantation and the river, but he claimed that an alluvion had already formed before they were sold and that, in the absence of other provisions, he had title to it.[3]

After the acquisition of Louisiana, a series of confrontations ensued between Gravier and his representatives on the one hand, and the local government and the citizenry on the other. The crisis came in 1807. Previously, an enclosure that he began on the batture in 1803 had been destroyed by order of the city council, and he had sued the city of New Orleans. Edward Livingston, as his lawyer, won a judgment in his favor from the superior court of the territory in May, 1807. Having become an owner on his own account, Livingston sought soon thereafter to construct a canal and levee, but his workers were driven off.

It should be remembered that Livingston had been a thorn in the flesh of Governor William C. C. Claiborne ever since his arrival in the newly acquired province in 1804 and was viewed askance by Jefferson for that reason. Informing the President of the judgment of the territorial court against the city, the Governor said that Livingston was the real plaintiff in the case. Claiborne wrote this letter in New Orleans two days before proceedings against Aaron Burr began in Richmond, and Jefferson got it two days after he had been served with a subpoena that had been ordered by John Marshall on Burr's motion. Though the President may not have known as yet of the charge that Livingston was a Burrite, no

[3] In my effort to understand this frightfully complicated case I have been greatly aided by the account of it in George Dargo's study, *Jefferson's Louisiana: Politics and the Clash of Legal Traditions* (1975), especially ch. 4. I regard this as authoritative with respect to local developments but interpret TJ's motives somewhat differently. His own account is in L. & B., XVIII, 1–132. For the figures on the size and value of the batture, see pp. 8, 12. Estimates varied, but his were on the high side. His account can also be seen in *A.S.P.*, *Public Lands*, II (1834), 76–102. The treatment of the case by W. B. Hatcher in *Edward Livingston* (1940), ch. 8, though less than fair to TJ in my opinion, is very valuable with respect to Livingston.

doubt he heard of it and credited it before long. Meanwhile, he was informed of the opinion of Claiborne that the United States were "the legal claimants of the land in question."[4]

Shortly after the court denied the claim of the city to the batture, the Governor conferred with members of the council regarding the transfer of the claim to the federal government. No official action had been taken when Claiborne wrote Jefferson in September but a resolution was adopted soon thereafter.[5] The Governor would have been in a stronger position if he had waited for this, but no doubt he was confident of the support of the municipal authorities when he again expressed the opinion that title to the disputed land was in the United States. This he did when informing the President that in late August laborers of Livingston's had been driven off the batture by a force of citizens. He reported that the minds of the citizens were "much agitated," that opposition to Livingston was general, and that he feared bloodshed. "If the batture be reclaimed," he said, "it is feared the current of the Mississippi will in some measure change its course, which will not only prove injurious to the navigation, but may occasion degradation in the levees of the city, or those in its vicinity."[6]

During the autumn Jefferson received reports of later confrontations, along with further unfavorable comments on the man whom he had no hesitancy in regarding as the villain in this drama. "Mr. Livingston is alike feared and hated by most of the ancient inhabitants," wrote Governor Claiborne. "They dread his talents as a lawyer, and hate his views of speculation, which in the case of the batture was esteemed very generally by the Louisianians no less iniquitous, than ruinous to the welfare of the city."[7]

When Jefferson learned of this local situation in October, 1807, the foreign problems of the country were approaching a crisis. During the

[4]Claiborne to TJ, May 20, 1807, received June 17 (Clarence E. Carter, ed. *Territorial Papers of the United States*, IX [1940], 736–737). The decision was announced May 23, but the Governor was informed of it beforehand. For earlier differences between Livingston and the administration, see *Jefferson the President: First Term*, p. 358; for the charge that he was a Burrite, see Hatcher, p. 124.

[5]Dargo (ch. 4, n. 12), citing city council records, says the matter was discussed as early as May 25, 1807, that a resolution was adopted Sept. 16, and that an official request to the federal government was made Dec. 5. TJ acted before he received this.

[6]Letter of Claiborne, Sept. 3, 1807, quoted by TJ in his brief on the batture case (L. & B., XVIII, 23). This important letter, addressed to the Secretary of State and received Oct. 13, has not been discovered in the Jefferson papers or in the Archives of the U.S. (Described in summary of correspondence and documents on batture in LC). TJ's quotations from it may be assumed to be accurate, but, unfortunately, we cannot judge it as a whole.

[7]Claiborne to Secretary of State, Sept. 16, 1807, received Oct. 26. Quoted by TJ (L. & B., XVIII, 25).

next few weeks difficulties in New Orleans could hardly have been in the center of his mind. He does not appear to have referred to them often at the time. Writing about them two and a half years later, he said: "I listened to the calls of duty, imperious calls, which had I shrunk from, I should have been justly responsible for the calamities which would have followed."[8] In his judgment as pronounced later, the Governor could not have maintained the peace against "intruders on the public right" whose works would have interrupted the commerce of the entire western country and "threatened to sweep away a great city and its inhabitants, and lay the adjacent country under water."

Admittedly he did not then know as much as he did later, but he believed that he and his colleagues had amply sufficient information to justify action by the executive. From the Attorney General, Caesar A. Rodney, he received an opinion that the batture was the property of the United States, and that under an act of Congress, adopted earlier that year, the government was explicitly authorized to eject intruders from its lands. Rodney's opinion does not appear to have been based on much study, but it was accepted by Jefferson and his colleagues at a Cabinet meeting and action was unanimously agreed upon. Accordingly, the Secretary of State sent instructions to the marshal of Orleans Territory to remove any persons who had settled or taken possession of the batture fronting the suburb Ste. Marie. The Governor was authorized to use force, if necessary, in support of this action.[9] On March 1, 1808, Jefferson learned from Claiborne that the orders of the federal executive had been carried out, and six days later he referred the whole matter to Congress.[10]

Besides receiving popular approval, the actions of the federal government were supported by the executive and legislative authorities of the territory. But Jefferson could have been charged, and in fact was charged by Livingston, with disregard of local judicial authority. The territorial court had ruled that the batture belonged to Jean Gravier, who, as Jefferson put it, had already secretly conveyed to Livingston whatever right he had in it. The judgment of the court was clearly that title to the batture did *not* lie with the city, but the federal government had no part in these proceedings.

According to Jefferson, the opinion of Derbigny, attorney for the city, "first brought into view the right of the United States, and that the sen-

[8] *Ibid.*, pp. 29–30.

[9] Rodney's opinion of Oct. 24, 1807, is in *A.S.P.*, *Public Lands*, II, 12. The so-called squatter act of Mar. 3, 1807, to which he referred, is in *Annals*, 9 Cong., 2 sess., pp. 288–290, and *U.S. Statutes at Large*, II, 445. Madison's letter of Nov. 30 to Claiborne is in Dept. of State, Domestic Letters (NA).

[10] Events and message of Mar. 7, 1808, in L. & B., XVIII, 124–127.

tence of the court must of course, to them, be a mere nullity."[11] Following Derbigny, he took, and continued to maintain, the position that the "right" to it, retained by the kings of France and Spain, had been transmitted to the United States along with the province of Louisiana. He held, therefore, that as federal property it could not be questioned in this or any other court or agency, unless specific authority had been delegated to that body. Thus, as he argued, the question of title had to be referred to the federal legislature, which was at full liberty to disapprove the actions of the executive, or to set up a board of commissioners, or to make some other disposition of the matter. The measures that had been taken in the meantime were explained by him as designed to preserve the *status quo* and prevent intrusion. Livingston, holding on the other hand that his private rights had been invaded, had obtained an injunction against the United States marshal. This was disregarded by that official, who rightly followed superior authority in so doing, according to Jefferson.[12]

During a period of three years Congress proved unable or unwilling to solve the problems the President had transmitted to it.[13] Various proposals were made and debated, including the appointment of a commissioner and the reference of the question to the Supreme Court.[14] These discussions served no purpose beyond that of revealing the great variety of opinions among the legislators. Both Jefferson's son-in-law John W. Eppes and his former secretary William A. Burwell favored some provision for appeal, holding that the action of the President had been designed merely to preserve the peace and maintain things as they were until a proper legal solution could be reached.[15] They argued that this could not be reached by a territorial court since the United States was involved. The question came up every year until, on April 21, 1810, the House postponed indefinitely a bill dealing with it.[16]

The action of Jefferson was occasionally questioned by a legislator, but he himself interpreted the failure of Congress to disapprove his con-

[11] *Ibid.*, pp. 21–22. Derbigny's opinion, dated Aug. 21, 1807, is in *A.S.P.*, *Public Lands*, II, 37–43. TJ saw this in the fall. Gravier actually conveyed a claim to only part of the property.

[12] TJ denied that this territorial court was authorized to issue injunctions.

[13] The major documents, including committee reports, resolutions submitted to Congress, Livingston's "Address to the People of the United States," the arguments of P. Derbigny and P. S. Duponceau, and TJ's brief of July 31, 1810, are in *A.S.P.*, *Public Lands*, II, 5–102.

[14] In existing law there was no provision for appeals from the courts of the territories of Orleans and Mississippi. In a letter of Oct. 5, 1807, to the Secretary of State (Hist. Soc. of Delaware), Governors Claiborne and Williams urged that this situation be remedied.

[15] See, for example, speeches in debates of Apr. 21, 1808 (*Annals*, 10 Cong., 1 sess., II, 2253–2256), and June 19, 1809 (*Annals*, 11 Cong., 1 sess., I, 329–330).

[16] *Ibid.*, 2 sess., II, 1935.

duct as approval of it. There was one minor retreat by the executive branch a few months after he left office. In the autumn of 1809 the permission the district attorney had given the citizens of New Orleans to use the batture was ordered withdrawn. Jefferson himself described this as proper since it put the inhabitants "exactly on their former footing; without either permission or prohibition on the part of the National government."[17] Otherwise, Livingston's efforts appear to have been unavailing.

In the spring of 1808, after the ejection of his workmen, he came to Washington and no doubt did a good deal of lobbying with legislators, but he was unable to see Jefferson before the President left for home. He did see Madison and a printed memoir of his got into Jefferson's hands. Having passed this problem on to Congress, the chief executive unquestionably brushed Livingston off, but he read the latter's memoir with care. As a result he modified his own position regarding boundaries somewhat, but was strengthened rather than weakened in the opinion that no private grant could extend nearer the river than the high-water marks.[18] In the fall Livingston issued "An Address to the People of the United States," but he does not appear to have had much effect on public opinion in New Orleans, and the proceedings he instituted against the marshal had as yet availed him nothing.[19] He could not sue the United States, but in desperation he brought suit against the man who had ordered his ejection when in office and was now a private citizen.

ii

The case of Livingston *vs.* Jefferson did not come to trial until about a year and a half after the former President first heard of the impending suit. It was dismissed on December 5, 1811, for lack of jurisdiction.[20] That plea was suggested by George Hay in the first place and by Attorney General Rodney a little later. Saying that of all branches of the law pleading had least attracted him, Jefferson left this question to his counsel, but he undoubtedly wanted them to use any and every plea that promised to be effective.[21] While Rodney and others expressed confi-

[17] L. & B., XVIII, 127.

[18] TJ to Livingston, May 6, and Madison to TJ, May 11, 1808 (LC); TJ to Madison, May 19, 1808 (L. & B., XII, 58–59). Livingston's "Address" is in *A.S.P.*, *Public Lands*, II, 12–74, dated Oct. 21, 1808. Presumably TJ saw a briefer document.

[19] The pamphlet warfare in New Orleans and other local developments are well described by Dargo.

[20] Hay to TJ, Dec. 5, 1811 (LC); J. W. Brockenbrough, *Reports*, I, 203. I am deeply indebted to Judge Edward Dumbauld for counsel in connection with this case. He has since published his own account in *Thomas Jefferson and the Law* (1978), ch. III.

[21] TJ to Hay, Mar. 3, 1811 (LC).

dence that Livingston had no real hope of collecting damages, Jefferson was unquestionably troubled by this threat to his shaky finances, and he naturally wanted to justify his own actions.

On hearing of the suit, Governor Claiborne promptly expressed regret that Jefferson had been disturbed in his retirement by that restless and, he feared, "unprincipled man," Edward Livingston. Gallatin said that the suit against the ex-President had excited great indignation in legislative circles. He referred to Livingston as "an unprincipled and delinquent speculator."[22] The Richmond *Enquirer* condemned the procedure of Livingston and loyally supported Jefferson from the beginning. On the other hand, Hay, speaking primarily of local sentiment no doubt, took the liberty of telling his client that public approbation of his conduct was still withheld. "The subject is not understood," he said, "in fact it is *greatly misunderstood:* and it is therefore important to yourself as well as to the public interests, that the defense should be coextensive with the charge."[23] Jefferson had taken this position from the first. Therefore he quickly set out to explore the entire controversy and to provide his lawyers with full information.

To this end he corresponded extensively with President Madison and various department heads in Washington and received from them a mass of papers. The net result was a lengthy brief which he transmitted to his lawyers along with numerous supporting documents. Madison, Gallatin, and Rodney commented on drafts of this, and Governor Claiborne, on a visit to the East, went over it at Monticello. It represented weeks of laborious research and was destined to be the only book Jefferson ever published besides his *Notes on Virginia* and *Manual of Parliamentary Practice.*[24] Writing Madison of this before he had copied it and sent it to his lawyers, he said: "They desired of me to furnish them the grounds of defense. This has obliged me to study the case thoroughly, to place all the points on paper, with my own views of them & the authorities in their support. This is the more tedious as the authorities being in few hands, & being in Latin, French, & Spanish entirely, are obliged to be copied in the body of the work."[25] He was very confident of the strength of his position, saying that no clearer case had ever come before a court. As he wrote Hay, however, he would have preferred that it be tried in

[22] Claiborne to TJ, June 4, 1810 (LC); Gallatin to TJ, Sept. 10, 1810 (*Writings*, I, 488).

[23] Hay to TJ, July 15, 1810 (LC). The comment in Richmond *Enquirer*, May 18, 1810, is typical of that paper.

[24] It bears the date July 31, 1810, but includes changes and amendments that were made afterwards. Supporting documents are in LC. The titles of the tracts in Sowerby, III, 396–404, show that TJ had virtually everything that was published on this question.

[25] TJ to Madison, July 13, 1810 (LC).

a state court since he doubted if he could get a fair decision from federal judges.[26]

The comments and suggestions of Gallatin, who was himself under severe attack from William Duane and the Smith–Giles–Leib faction in this period, are of special interest for their own sake and as reflecting his devotion to Jefferson. Besides writing the ex-President at length and transmitting numerous papers, he sent an extended memorandum on the law and merits of the case. In this he strongly supported the general authority of the President to prevent encroachment on public lands and his right to do so in this particular instance despite the action of the territorial court — since, as he was convinced, Livingston had no title.[27] Jefferson explained to the Secretary of the Treasury that there was no need for him to go into the question of Livingston's title except in the public interest. He could have rested his own case, he said, on the solid ground that a public official is not responsible to a private party for honestly intended official action. While he continued to believe this to be true, the question of executive immunity was not raised at the trial. One of his lawyers regretted this, and John Adams, his predecessor in office, expressed himself with characteristic vigor on the subject: "Great God! Is a President of U.S. to be subject to a private action of every individual? This will soon introduce the axiom that a President can do no wrong, or another equally curious that a President can do no right."[28]

Jefferson was not taking his legal stand on the ground of presidential immunity or privilege, but for a time he flirted with the idea that the government (federal or local) should bear the expense of these legal proceedings. Gallatin had no doubt that Congress *ought* to defend the suit and mentioned precedents.[29] He pointed out practical difficulties, however, and Jefferson quickly abandoned the idea. When the case was finally decided, not on its merits but on the technical ground of lack of jurisdiction, he paid his counsel out of his own pocket, regarding the question as a wholly private one.[30]

[26] TJ to Hay, Aug. 1, 1810; Wirt to TJ, Aug. 9; TJ to Tazewell, Aug. 18; Tazewell to TJ, Sept. 27, 1810, disagreeing on some points (LC).

[27] Gallatin's memo is in LC; it was sent with his letter of July 14, 1810 (*Writings*, I, 479–481). TJ had already drafted his paper before he got Gallatin's specific suggestions on July 19, but he worked these in before sending it to him and Madison for approval.

[28] TJ to Gallatin, Aug. 16, 1810 (L. & B., XII, 411); Tazewell to TJ, May 15, 1812 (LC); John Adams to TJ, Feb. 10, 1812 (*A.-J. Letters*, II, 297). The question was decided in favor of executive immunity in 1896 in Spalding *vs.* Vilas (161 *U.S.*, 483).

[29] Gallatin to TJ, Sept. 10, 1810 (*Writings*, I, 487–488). The paper enclosed in this letter is in LC.

[30] He discussed the matter in a letter of Apr. 12 to Hay, who had originally said he would accept no fee (LC). TJ paid each of the three lawyers $100, which of course was a much larger sum then than now.

While asking nothing positive from Congress, he thought it desirable to guard against any legislative action that might endanger his cause. He wanted things to remain just as they were until after the trial. Accordingly, he described the situation in confidence to William Branch Giles and sent that senator a copy of the statement he had drafted for the benefit of his counsel. He hoped that Giles would peruse this despite its "revolting length" and asked that it then be sent to John W. Eppes, who would be on guard in the House.[31] To Giles, a bitter enemy of the Federalist judiciary, he said that he would have no concern whatever if his case were going before an impartial court, but that Livingston would never have brought suit in such a court.

He spoke to Giles of Livingston's "assiduities and intrigues," but he went further in an earlier letter to Gallatin, referring to the plaintiff in the case as a "spadassin" — that is, in more ordinary language, a desperado or assassin. Admitting to his trusted adviser in Washington that he was retaining, in the brief he was preparing for his lawyers, arguments that he himself regarded as inconsistent, he said that others might think differently and that against such an opponent it was lawful to use all weapons.[32]

We may surmise that the political implications of the case had made him more than ordinarily fearful. At moments in the course of this affair he gave signs of a desperation that turned out to be unwarranted. Not only so. Unguarded private expressions on his part have suggested to later critics that recommendations of his for judicial appointments at this juncture were more than coincidental.[33] At the same time that he informed Madison of the suit against him, he recommended the appointment of a judge who would probably sit on the court by which his case would be tried. And, a few weeks later, he discussed with the President and a few other associates the filling of a vacancy on the Supreme Court, to which his case might be appealed. He gave no sign that he perceived any impropriety in his own conduct, and his correspondents manifested no surprise — presumably because they believed he would have said the same things if his own case had not been pending.

[31] TJ to W. B. Giles, Nov. 12, 1810 (L. & B., XIX, 175–176).

[32] TJ to Gallatin, Sept. 27, 1810 (Ford, IX, 283*n*.). He seems to have recognized that some of the arguments he was assembling could be interpreted as supporting ownership of the batture by the municipality or territory rather than the federal government. Since the squatter law would not have applied in that case, Gallatin regarded these arguments as dangerous. TJ may have assumed that his counsel would discard them if they should see fit.

[33] Beveridge, in *Marshall*, IV, 100–107, attributes them primarily to TJ's desire to protect himself against Livingston's suit, and this interpretation has generally been accepted by other writers of a Federalist persuasion.

* * *

Two or three days before he learned of Livingston's intent from John Wickham, Jefferson received a long letter from the Governor of the commonwealth, John Tyler, saying that he would like to be appointed to the federal judiciary if a vacancy should occur. Judge Cyrus Griffin of the district of Virginia was not expected to live much longer and in fact died toward the end of the year. Jefferson described him as a cipher, as in the Burr trial he certainly was. Tyler was a Revolutionary patriot who had opposed the adoption of the Constitution of 1787 and become an ardent Republican afterwards. He was serving as a state judge when elected governor. He had frequently expressed his approbation of Jefferson's administration and had maintained with him the friendliest of relations.

Jefferson sent Madison an extract from Tyler's letter and spoke of him in terms of the highest approval. He described him as an incorruptible man, an able lawyer, and a remarkably popular governor. "It will be difficult," said Jefferson, "to find a character of firmness enough to preserve his independence on the same bench with Marshall. Tyler, I am certain, would do it." He believed that it would also be difficult to find anybody in the state who would be so generally approved. "A milk and water character in that office would be seen as a calamity," in his opinion.[34]

While the threat of Livingston's suit, of which he learned before he wrote Madison, certainly gave him reason to want a friend at court, he unquestionably believed he was acting in the public interest, and it seems safe to assume that he would have supported Tyler in any case. Writing the Governor, he said: "We have long enough suffered under the base prostitution of law to party passions in one judge, and the imbecility of another." He could have been charged with unfairness to both Marshall and Griffin, but, in view of previous utterances of his, this one is not surprising. The appointment of Tyler a few months later, which was followed by the election of Monroe to succeed him as governor, was a natural and popular one, and if he ruled in Jefferson's favor in court so did John Marshall. No counterweight to the Chief Justice was really needed in this instance. And as things turned out, the district judge had little chance to manifest independence in other matters, for he died after only two years of service.

The mutual distrust of Jefferson and Marshall was better attested on the part of the former, who may have expressed himself more freely in private letters and who certainly preserved his correspondence better.

[34] TJ to Madison, May 25, 1810 (Ford, IX, 275). Tyler wrote TJ, May 12 (LC); TJ wrote Tyler, Mar. 26 (Ford, IX, 276–277*n*.).

His opinion of the Chief Justice had not improved since his own retirement. In the fall of 1809 he reported to a sympathetic friend that he had taken up the fifth volume of Marshall's *Life of Washington* and begun to correct it.[35] He was to engage in that task intermittently in later years; and, before he died, he was to point out more clearly than he was now doing the basic difference between himself and his most enduring antagonist. That lay chiefly in their respective attitudes to political democracy. During his own presidency and that of Madison he was disposed to stress personal and partisan considerations. Thus, writing his successor, he spoke of the "rancorous hatred" that Marshall bore the government of his country as well as of the "cunning and sophistry" within which he enshrouded himself. To Governor Tyler he said that, in the hands of the Chief Justice, law was "nothing more than an ambiguous text, to be explained by his sophistry into any meaning which may subserve his personal malice." Shortly before this, in the Yazoo case, Fletcher *vs.* Peck, Marshall denied to the legislature of Georgia, on the ground of the sanctity of contracts, the constitutional right to repeal an admittedly fraudulent law. Jefferson's position with respect to this case is not clear, but he perceived in the opinion another example of the "twistifications" whereby the Chief Justice reconciled law to his "personal biases."[36]

Allowance should be made for the rhetorical excess in which Jefferson could indulge in private converse with the faithful, but it should be remembered that the federal judiciary was by no means above politics in this era, and that, in public as well as private, Federalists had denounced him as a hypocrite and demagogue. Important rulings by Marshall could be readily attributed to his partisanship, if not to his personal hostility to his distant kinsman. At any rate Jefferson charged, and for a time at least must have believed, that Livingston had brought suit in the court over which Marshall presided because of his knowledge of the Chief Justice's character.

Writing Gallatin in the early fall of 1810, the ex-President said that, while no unbiased man could doubt what the issue of the case ought to be, no one could tell what it would be. "The judge's inveteracy is profound," he asserted, "and his mind of that gloomy malignity which will never let him forego the opportunity of satiating it on a victim." Then, falling into an uncharacteristic state of gloom on his own part, he stated that only in an appeal did he see any hope of saving from disaster a fortune which in fact was already in a precarious situation. He now saw

[35] TJ to Joel Barlow, Oct. 8, 1809 (Ford, IX, 262). On his reaction to Marshall's work see *Jefferson the President: Second Term*, pp. 356–359.

[36] Quotations from letters of May 25, 26, 1810, to Madison and Tyler (Ford, IX, 275–276). On Marshall's opinion, see *Jefferson the President: First Term*, p. 456.

a prospect of improving the complexion of the highest court. "I observe old Cushing is dead," he said, referring to Justice William Cushing of Massachusetts. "At length, then, we have a chance of getting a Republican majority in the Supreme judiciary. . . . The event is a fortunate one, and so timed as to be a Godsend to me." To other former associates he referred to the event as an occasion for congratulation and rejoicing. His comments were private, but this characteristically humane and normally tactful man was manifesting very bad taste.[37]

One is reminded of the observation of a young British visitor to Monticello; Augustus J. Foster said that Jefferson's general benevolence caused him to excuse all offenses except political ones, regarding which he was "violent and vindictive."[38] This junior member of the British embassy, who visited Monticello during Jefferson's presidency, was unsympathetic to his host's democratic ideas and did not appreciate the fervor of his republicanism. Jefferson's verbal violence was directed against those he regarded as enemies of the latter. More was involved than partisanship as the term is commonly used, but the line between republicanism and the Republicans was often faint, and the issue was confused in this instance by his own injection of personal considerations. No doubt his counsel to Madison would have been the same in any case, but the episode would look better on the pages of history if the timing had been different.

Writing the President, he said, much as he had already said to Gallatin: "The nation ten years ago declared its will for a change in the principles of the administration of their affairs. They then changed the two branches depending on their will, and have steadily maintained the reformation in those branches. The third, not dependent on them [the people] has so long bid defiance to their will, erecting themselves into a political body, to correct what they deem the errors of the nation. The death of Cushing gives an opportunity of closing the reformation by a successor of unquestionable republican principles."

Madison shared these sentiments and was already looking with favor on Jefferson's first choice for the vacancy, Levi Lincoln, the former attorney general, who was widely approved in high party circles. In those days a Supreme Court justice lived and chiefly served in a particular circuit, spending only a few weeks of the year in Washington. It was recognized, therefore, that Cushing's successor must come from New England — where, unfortunately, Republican legal talent was scarce. The party had just suffered a mortifying blow in the disgrace of former

[37] TJ to Gallatin, Sept. 27, 1810; to Madison, Oct. 15; to Gideon Granger, Oct. 22 (Ford, IX, 282–288).

[38] A. J. Foster, *Jeffersonian America* (1954), p. 153.

Congressman Barnabas Bidwell, who had fled to Canada when a shortage in his accounts as county treasurer was discovered. Jefferson could think of no second choice except Gideon Granger, who was in fact an active candidate for the vacant seat but whose qualifications Madison properly doubted. The ex-President mentioned but ruled out Joseph Story, whom he viewed as a deserter in the final embargo fight and described as a pseudo-Republican and Tory.[39] He thought Story too young to be considered for the post anyway.

Jefferson's delight when informed that Madison had offered it to Lincoln turned to distress when he learned that this man of "firm republicanism and known integrity" had declined it because of failing eyesight.[40] This nomination was approved by the Senate, but that of Alexander Wolcott of Connecticut, chief organizer of the Republicans in that Federalist state, was rejected. Following wiser counsel, Madison then turned to John Quincy Adams, but that independent gentleman, in St. Petersburg at the time, preferred to remain abroad, thus assuring that his future would be in the field of diplomacy rather than law. Not until the late summer of 1811 did his decision reach Washington. A few weeks later the appointment went to young Joseph Story virtually by default. Jefferson's objections were disregarded, and the nomination was approved before Livingston's suit came up for trial.[41]

Beyond the original suggestion of Lincoln, whom Madison was already disposed to nominate, Jefferson seems to have been without influence in this matter. Apparently he accepted the appointment of Story without comment, and at the time the young Justice seems to have been wholly unaware of Jefferson's reservations about him. Several years were to pass before it became evident that Story was reinforcing Marshall and that no Republican "reformation" of the Supreme Court had occurred. Meanwhile, the federal judiciary ceased to be a threat to the ex-President personally, since Marshall, presiding over the circuit court in the Virginia district, dismissed the suit of Edward Livingston.

In his opinion, in the celebrated case of Livingston *vs.* Jefferson, the Chief Justice said at the outset that the sole question was whether the court could take cognizance of a trespass committed on lands outside the district of Virginia when the alleged trespasser resided in that district. He then announced his concurrence with his brother judge that it could not. Some months later Judge Tyler told Jefferson that during the trial

[39] See *Jefferson the President: Second Term*, pp. 645–646.

[40] TJ to Lincoln, Aug. 28, 1811 (L. & B., XIII, 81–82).

[41] The events are well described by Brant in *Madison*, V, 167–172. He stresses the independence of Madison's judgment. Gabriel Duval was confirmed at the same time as the successor to Samuel Chase.

he was suffering from a painful complaint which made it difficult for him to sit it out, but that he was determined to give an opinion.[42] He said that he had been on guard lest "the important British faction, who had enlisted on Livingston's side," might suppose that improper influence had been exerted on him in Jefferson's favor. In his opinion he complimented plaintiff's counsel (John Wickham) for ingenuity and eloquence, but said he found his argument unconvincing. Tyler recognized, as did Marshall and counsel on both sides, that at one time all actions had to be tried in the locality. By what both he and Marshall termed a legal fiction, personal actions could now be maintained wherever in the country a contract could be made, but trespass remained a local action.

According to Tyler, Marshall wanted to carry the case to the Supreme Court "by adjournment or somehow or other" but was induced to proceed to a decision, leaving the parties to appeal or not as they might choose. On the strength of this statement, presumably, it was alleged about a century later that the Chief Justice agreed with great reluctance that the circuit court had no jurisdiction. Also, it was asserted long afterwards that Marshall, in his written opinion, "gravely reflected on Jefferson's good faith in avoiding a trial on its merits."[43] Both of these appear to be over-statements, but a grudging quality can be discerned in the opinion. In a more detailed historical account than that of Tyler, Marshall pointed out how, under the common law, the principle that all actions were local had been modified in practice while maintained in form. Actions for trespass regarding land, however, were excepted.[44] By implication he regretted that this was true where only damages were demanded. He referred with apparent approval to the futile efforts of Lord Mansfield to get rid of what he regarded as merely a technical distinction. But this technical distinction was firmly established, he said, and from it he did not have the hardihood to depart.

Throughout his opinion he showed special concern to give such credit as he could to the arguments of Wickham, who was a leading anti-Jeffersonian as well as the recognized leader of the Richmond bar. One argument that specially appealed to him was that justice would wholly fail when a transgressor was held to be amenable only to the court of the district where the offense was committed but into which he himself would not go. This comment could obviously be applied to Jefferson,

[42] Tyler to TJ, May 17, 1812 (L. G. Tyler, *Letters and Times of the Tylers*, I [1884], 263–264). His opinion was published in the Richmond *Enquirer*, Dec. 19, 1811. So was Marshall's, but I am using the report of that in J. W. Brockenbrough, *Reports*, I, 206–212.

[43] Beveridge, in *Marshall*, IV, 112–116, reads into this episode considerably more than I perceive in it.

[44] Beveridge erroneously attributes to Marshall the statement that this exception, to which the defense pointed, was a legal fiction. On the contrary, Marshall applied the word "fiction" to personal suits, not to actions for trespass on land.

whom Marshall would probably have liked to see on trial in New Orleans. He said that under the law as he was now applying it there could be "a clear right without a remedy." It should be noted, however, that he did not pronounce on the validity of Livingston's title, nor enter into the fundamental question of the personal responsibility, especially financial, of the President of the United States to a private individual for his official conduct. And, ironically, this case became, despite Marshall's reservations, the leading one in the United States for the proposition that actions for trespass to real estate must be brought in the district where the land is located.[45]

It has been asserted that this case deepened Marshall's distrust of Jefferson as "dishonest and cowardly," but there seems to be no evidence that he said so. Some things in the opinion may have rankled in Jefferson's mind but he does not appear to have made any particular comment on it at the time.[46]

iii

When the suit against him was dismissed, Jefferson was in Bedford County and he did not get the news until he returned to Monticello more than three weeks later. He then wrote Hay that he owed it not only to himself but to the public to lay the case before them, since they would otherwise remain uninformed of the justice of his position, and the impression produced by Livingston's "squalling as if his throat had been cut" would be uncorrected.[47] He would enter the arena of public debate with the utmost reluctance, he said. Not only had his temperamental aversion to controversy increased with age and retirement; he was too weary of the subject to revise his paper and put it in more popular form. He believed that most readers would find it "unnecessarily erudite and pedantic." A special problem was presented by the long quotations from foreign languages — French, Spanish, Latin, and even Greek — which, to the best of his knowledge, only one press in the country was competent to print.

Accordingly, he sent to Ezra Sargeant in New York the manuscript he had written in his own clear hand.[48] Besides ordering copies for distribution by himself, chiefly to members of Congress and officials of the executive branch, he authorized the printing of others for sale, if desired. But he wanted no copyright taken out and informed Sargeant that this

[45] Statement of Judge Dumbauld in letter of May 13, 1974.

[46] The references are to allegations of Beveridge.

[47] TJ to Hay, Dec. 28, 1811 (LC).

[48] Sargeant printed the American edn. of the *Edinburgh Review*. TJ wrote him Feb. 3, 1812 (L. & B., XIII, 131–133).

dry legal argument was not at all suited to popular reading. Before the end of March, 1812, he began distributing copies of the piece, which for convenience we call the *Proceedings.* He reported, soon after war with Great Britain was declared, that he had only one copy left.[49]

His account was received with enthusiasm by his friends and supporters. The Richmond *Enquirer* gave it favorable advance notice in the fall of 1810, reporting that he had exhausted every point in the case in a sketch which was "a brilliant monument of his acuteness, his legal erudition and his extensive researches."[50] William Wirt, the most oratorical of his counselors, as well as the one with whom he was on the most affectionate terms, described his exposition as the "best piece of Grecian architecture" he had ever seen. He wondered how its author could have effected such union of "lightness and solidity, or beauty and power."[51] On the other hand, Tazewell was critical of the arrangement and believed that more concentration was needed to follow the argument than was to be expected of most people. He was confident, however, that attentive readers would be convinced, as he himself had been, though decidedly against the claim of the United States in the first place.[52] One old friend of Jefferson's, Mrs. Elizabeth Trist, who had long known Edward Livingston and thought him in many ways amiable though imprudent, had been disposed to feel sorry for him. Jefferson sent her a copy of his paper, with translations of the more "outlandish passages," and by this she was, or claimed to be, convinced that he was in the right, as he had expected she would be.[53]

Jefferson showed no compassion for Edward Livingston. He told the latter's brother Robert, to whom somewhat surprisingly he sent a copy of his pamphlet along with a letter chiefly devoted to agricultural matters, that they were confronted with an "abstract question of right," and he appears never to have questioned his own rectitude at any stage of this controversy.[54] There was ground for charging him with self-righteousness, and it need not be supposed that his conduct in this conflict

[49] The full title is *The Proceedings of the Government of the United States, in Maintaining the Public Right to the Beach of the Missisipi, adjacent to New Orleans, against the Intrusion of Edward Livingston.* He sent copies to Madison for the executive offices, and to the secretaries of the Senate and House, Mar. 26, 1812. Extracts of correspondence regarding the distribution of the work, and a list of persons to whom copies were sent, Apr. 14–June 23, 1812, are printed in Sowerby, III, 406–412. The printing cost him $151.50 (Account Book, Mar. 29, June 17, 1812).

[50] Richmond *Enquirer*, Oct. 16, 1810.

[51] Wirt to TJ, Apr. 15, 1812 (Sowerby, III, 407).

[52] Tazewell to TJ, May 15, 1812 (*ibid.*, 408–409).

[53] Elizabeth Trist to TJ, Mar. 24, 1812; TJ to E. Trist, May 10; E. Trist to TJ, June 7 (all MHS).

[54] TJ to R. R. Livingston, Apr. 20, 1812 (MHS).

was unaffected by political considerations — such, for example, as the desire to support Claiborne. But there need be no doubt of the genuineness of his concern for what he regarded as the rights of the public. He could be stern indeed when he believed the larger interest to be challenged by a lesser. For Livingston, whom he regarded as a speculator, ruthlessly pursuing private gain, he had no more sympathy than he had had for profiteers under the embargo.

Though he went into great detail about the title to this disputed land, he never seems to have harbored any doubt that it was public property. Toward the end of his paper he said that he claimed no exemption from mistake, but that public officials were not answerable in their purses to private persons for honest errors of judgment. They might indeed be punished for malicious or corrupt conduct, but, as he insisted in a rather shrill peroration, there had been no malice or corruption on his side in this affair. He denied that there had been a combination of public functionaries to oppress the plaintiff in the case but said it was not to be believed that they should have been "playing pushpin with judges and lawyers, while Livingston was working double tides to drown the city."[55] He argued that Livingston was taking dangerous and unlawful liberties with the river when, on his own authority, he sought to erect works on its beach. That aggressive gentleman could claim, in turn, that Jefferson was greatly exaggerating the dangers and taking the popular side for political reasons. Also, seizing derisively on the indiscreet remark about playing pushpin, he could charge the former President with disregard of the law and disrespect of the courts.

Following the ejection of his workmen in 1808, Livingston instituted in the federal court a suit against the United States marshal which was destined to pursue a long and tortuous course — rather like that of the river itself, in fact. About six months after he filed suit against Jefferson in Richmond, judgment in his favor was entered in the district court in New Orleans and the hapless marshal was instructed to put him in quiet possession of the disputed property.[56] But a stay was granted a few days later, and the proceedings dragged on more than a year and a half after the case against Jefferson was dismissed in Richmond. Late in the summer of 1813, he learned from Governor Claiborne that the district judge had ruled that the dispossessing of Livingston on Jefferson's order was illegal.[57] This was by no means the end of litigation over the batture, which appears to have lasted in one form or another through the rest of

[55] L. & B., XVIII, 132.

[56] Oct. 15, 1810 (extract from court records, courtesy of Judge Edward Dumbauld and Nelson B. Jones, clerk, U.S. Dist. Court, New Orleans).

[57] W. C. C. Claiborne to TJ, Aug. 14, 1813 (LC).

Jefferson's lifetime, but, as it relates to him, the story need not be carried beyond 1814, when he was seventy-one and very weary of this business.[58] No opinions of the court discussing the issues of the case as decided in 1813 have been discovered, and there appears to be no evidence that his arguments as set forth in the pamphlet he had caused to be printed the previous year were employed by the defense counsel in New Orleans. But they were again made available to the public when reprinted in 1814, along with an answer to them by Livingston, in the *American Law Journal*.[59] Thus a retired statesman who loathed controversy confronted a formidable adversary in cold print.

Since his own arguments have already been sketched in this narrative, we concern ourselves here briefly with Livingston's.[60] His paper was considerably longer than the one he was answering, and it was primarily designed to influence public sentiment, whereas Jefferson's was prepared for the benefit of his lawyers and, except perhaps for its final passage, was not aimed at a popular audience. Yet Livingston, chiding Jefferson for not proceeding through the courts as he himself had done, attributed his executive action in this affair to his craving for popularity. Livingston claimed that there had been no talk of ownership of the batture by the United States government until after the territorial court had ruled in his favor. And, although there were lands like his at every bend of the river, his were singled out because of their convenience for public use, and their seizure was popular for that reason.[61]

Livingston charged the former President with acting on the basis of insufficient information and questioned his authority to seize what in Livingston's mind was undoubtedly private property. He asserted that the actions of the executive represented unconstitutional defiance of the principle of the separation of powers. He claimed that Jefferson was trying to shield himself behind the Cabinet, which he was turning into a star chamber. In his concluding remarks this critic stated that Jefferson should not be reproached for his failure to understand the nature of Liv-

[58] The publicity given the batture case occasioned a successful attempt of the French heirs of Bernard Gravier to defend rights that Jean Gravier had disregarded. In 1819 they were awarded three-quarters of the batture. Thus Livingston got only a portion of it (F. P. Burns, "The Graviers and the Faubourg Ste. Marie" in *La. Hist. Quart.*, XXII [Apr., 1939], 407–408, 413–415). In the course of time, however, he got enough to discharge his debt to the government.

[59] By John E. Hall in *American Law Journal*, vol. V (Baltimore, 1814). Hall to TJ, Nov. 15, 1813 (LC); TJ to Hall, Dec. 31, 1813 (LC). The "Proceedings" in L. & B., XVIII, seems to be based on this text.

[60] For a convenient summary of TJ arguments, see *ibid.*, pp. 113–116. The main text of Livingston's answer is in *American Law Journal*, V, 113–289.

[61] Note that Jefferson did not speak of the seizure of private property, but rather of guarding public property against intrusion.

ingston's title, but that his action without adequate knowledge was surprising, while his resort to force was astonishing and his talk of conscious rectitude amazing. The explanation of all this Livingston found in Jefferson's "inordinate passion for popularity."[62]

Even though it be admitted that Jefferson as President would not have acted as he did in this matter without assurance of popular support, the insufficiency of Livingston's explanation should be obvious to anyone aware of Jefferson's characteristic concern for the public good — in disregard of private gain if need be. His support of the "ancient inhabitants" against an American newcomer need not be attributed wholly, or even primarily, to personal and political considerations. Some recognition must surely be given his humane sentiments.[63] But the charge of hasty and high-handed action cannot be so readily disallowed.

In this extraordinarily complicated case it is difficult indeed to determine where the right lay and how serious the situation was, but, in the effort to safeguard what Jefferson believed to be an imperiled public interest, he resorted to an uncharacteristic exercise of authority. Furthermore, his subsequent defense of his actions bordered at times on desperation. He does not appear at his best in this affair.

The editor of the *American Law Journal* lavished praise on Livingston's paper as "one of the most able and masterly performances that ever came from the pen of a lawyer or scholar in any country" and as an enduring "model of judicial eloquence and argument."[64] But Hall was an intense Federalist, to whom no doubt the denigration of the archenemy of his party was very pleasing. Hence his exaggeration no more deserves literal acceptance than does that of William Wirt on the other side. Livingston's paper may have been the more appealing of the two to most people, but judgment for or against the former President was based primarily on political considerations.

[62]*American Law Journal*, V, 289. Dargo charges TJ with clinging to Derbigny's position after it had been refuted by P. S. Duponceau, continuing to emphasize French law when in his opinion Spanish law was in effect (see especially p. 217, n. 118). He recognizes, however, that the question is difficult and that opinions still differ to some extent.

[63]I do not enter into the conflict of legal traditions — those of the civil and the common law — which is described by Dargo. TJ never seems to have referred to the batture controversy in these terms.

[64]*American Law Journal*, V, iv.

War and Peace

[VI]

Patriotism at Home

1810-1812

ABOUT two weeks before Jefferson learned that Edward Livingston was instituting a suit against him, the measure known as Macon's Bill Number Two was signed by his successor in Washington.[1] The measure marked a further retreat from the restrictive system in that it repealed the Non-Intercourse Act; but it provided that if either the British or the French should withdraw their objectionable edicts, the restrictions of the Non-Intercourse Act would be reimposed on the other. Since the French afterwards pretended to do that, this feeble measure became a link in the chain of events leading directly to the War of 1812, but the country remained at peace for a couple of years longer.

The ex-President had no responsibility for what turned out to be a fateful law and he seems to have made no particular reference to it. He was not concerning himself much with congressional actions in this period. For months he was bogged down in the batture controversy, and at this same time he was deeply involved at Monticello with sheep as well as with vegetables and flowers. He did not go as far as Dr. William Thornton, who said he himself was "sheepishly inclined," but in the breeding of these animals he found a welcome outlet for his patriotism. Cultivating self-sufficiency was one way to defy the Old World and support American independence. In the last throes of the embargo he wrote Lafayette that this very trying measure had one happy result: it had set them all on domestic manufacture. He predicted that as a consequence their future demands on England would be reduced by half. He raised sheep partly for food, but at this stage he did so chiefly for the wool that

[1] For comments on the passage of the bill by the House see Madison to TJ, Apr. 23, 1810 (Hunt, VIII, 95).

could be turned into garments for his family and his people, as he called his slaves.[2]

During the first few years of his retirement his interest in sheep raising may even have approached that in gardening; and, although he had several varieties of sheep, he said most about merinos at first. He had had some of them for years but doubted if they were full-blooded. One of the memorable personal episodes of the prewar period was his acquisition of certified members of this prized Spanish breed. In February, 1810, the American consul at Lisbon, William Jarvis, shipped by the *Diana* for Alexandria, Virginia, nine merino rams and four ewes. These had been obtained by him after much exertion and were "warranted of the best blood in Spain." He designated a pair as a gift to Jefferson and another pair for Madison. They arrived in May.[3] Toward the end of the summer Bacon fetched Jefferson's pair from Montpelier, where they had been pasturing, and then or later he got two more ewes. Time was to show that he hoped far too much from their offspring, but his plans, as outlined in letters to Madison and others, strikingly reveal both his patriotism and his benevolence.[4]

He told Madison he was disgusted with the "scandalous extortions" lately practiced on innocent farmers in the sale of merinos. The seven rams that had accompanied his and Madison's on the *Diana* had sold for more than $500 each at public auction and would have commanded twice that at New York or Boston.[5] To Dr. Thornton he had previously said: "I have not been satisfied with that kind of patriotism the strongest feature of which is to enrich the patriot himself." He would take no profit from this gift, he told Jarvis. He made and Madison acceded to a proposal that all the full-blooded males they could raise should be given to the various counties of the state, beginning with those contiguous to their own.[6] His former coachman, Joseph Dougherty, was so impressed with this plan that he asked if he could publish a portion of the letter in which his old employer briefly described it. Jefferson flatly refused, saying that he was unwilling to seem as avaricious of praise as some other people were of money. Critical eyes may perceive self-righteousness in

[2] For a general account of his sheep raising see *Farm Book*, pp. 111–113; for extracts of letters on the subject, 1809–1813, including that to Lafayette, Feb. 24, 1809, see *ibid.*, pp. 117–141.

[3] William Jarvis to TJ, Jan. 20, Feb. 19, 1810; J. H. Hooe to TJ, May 4, 1810; Joseph Dougherty to TJ, May 5, 1810; TJ to J. H. Hooe, May 10, 1810 (*ibid.*, pp. 125–128).

[4] Well described in his letter of May 13, 1810, to Madison (L. & B., XII, 389–391). See also letters to Joseph Dougherty and to William Thornton, May 24, and to William Jarvis, Dec. 5, 1810 (*Farm Book*, pp. 130–132, 135).

[5] William Thornton to TJ, June 8, 1810 (*ibid.*, p. 133).

[6] Like others at this time, TJ held that four crossings would give a pure breed. On this basis he figured that in about seven years a ram could be supplied every county in Virginia. After that full-blooded ewes could be distributed.

his references to his own motives, but throughout his long life on the land he made it a practice to pass on to other farmers the benefits of any improvements he had made. He described this as a duty but in it he found one of his greatest pleasures.

He might have been unable to carry out his grandiose plan in any case, but the fact is that his merinos did not breed as rapidly as he expected. One of his ewes died of the scab and the others produced no ewe lambs. At the end of a couple of years he had a few blooded rams along with many male half-breeds (which he gave away generously), but still had only two full-blooded ewes. He might have gained a better sexual distribution if he had had the counsel of Dr. Thornton a little earlier. That "sheepish" gentleman believed that if the ram were put to the ewes in the increase of the moon the offspring would tend to be male; if in the decrease of the moon, female. Having made a similar observation in the case of horses, he was inclined to believe that "all animals are lunatics in love."[7]

Not only did the shepherd-gardener of Monticello have an insufficiency of blooded sheep for the Virginia counties. It also appeared that the farmers did not want them. On Christmas Day, 1812, he wrote Joseph Dougherty that the "merino fever" had entirely subsided in his locality, since these sheep produced less wool than those already possessed by the farmers, and this was too fine for the coarse cloth manufactured in the neighborhood. Half a dozen years later he sent a friend in the Shenandoah Valley a merino ram, born of his imported stock, and in this he still took pride.[8] He continued to keep sheep of several breeds after the crisis of war was long past, but they never again bulked as large in his mind as during the years when he regarded the raising of them as an act of patriotism.

In the postscript of a letter he wrote Pierre Samuel du Pont de Nemours on the eve of his retirement, Jefferson asked that friend to bring a couple of "true-bred" shepherd dogs with him on his next visit to America.[9] The visit was delayed for six years, but considerably before it occurred he possessed a "genuine race" of shepherd dogs. The first of these were selected for him in France by the Marquis de Lafayette. He gave a good many away, but in 1813 he said he had four pairs at different places, where he suffered no other dog to go.[10] He described these

[7] Thornton to TJ, June 18, 1812 (*ibid.*, pp. 138–139).

[8] Letters, June 18, 1812–Aug. 15, 1813, from William Thornton, to E. I. du Pont, and to Joseph Dougherty; to Archibald Stuart, May 28, 1818 (*ibid.*, pp. 138–141).

[9] TJ to P.S. du Pont de Nemours, Mar. 2, 1809 (*J.-D. Correspondence*, p. 123).

[10] TJ to Harry Innes, Sept. 18, 1813 (*Farm Book*, p. 140); also TJ to Joseph Dougherty, June 27, 1810 (*ibid.*, p. 134).

animals as "the most watchful and faithful of all servants," and he regarded them as not only the best farm dogs but also the best house dogs he had ever seen. It is not likely, however, that they had the run of the house at either Monticello or Poplar Forest. Apparently this would not have been according to the custom then prevailing in the society of that region, and if anybody in Albemarle County then valued dogs as household pets Jefferson certainly did not.

Viewing the canine tribe as a whole with a strictly utilitarian eye, he passed harsh judgment on it for wastefulness and destructiveness. At the height of the "merino fever" one of his fellow planters, reminding him of the necessity of guarding valuable sheep against the ravages of dogs, sought his support of a law to control them. Peter Minor would have liked to diminish a race of animals he regarded as a nuisance at best and as a curse when in a state of madness. Jefferson said he fully shared this feeling and would really like to exterminate the race. "I consider them as the most afflicting of all the follies for which men tax themselves," said he in a burst of indignation. More realistically he favored a law requiring every dog to wear an identifying collar and making owners responsible for their dogs' mischief.[11] The danger from uncontrolled dogs was undoubtedly great. Jefferson had a paling fence around his garden and a thorn hedge around his orchard, but the rail fences that separated most of his fields offered his flocks little protection from canine destroyers. So aware was he of this peril and so concerned to get enough wool to provide clothing for his slaves that he once instructed Bacon to have all the Negroes' dogs killed.[12] This drastic order was carried out, and except for a couple of dogs allowed the overseer, there may have been only shepherd dogs at Monticello during Jefferson's retirement. Even they had to be attached to a master, he said. If, because of hunger or neglect, they should prowl by themselves they would become the most destructive of marauders because of their sagacity. His dogs, beginning with a thoroughly trained bitch that Lafayette got for him, appear to have been dutiful — guarding the sheep, going for the cows in the evening, and driving the ducks, turkeys, and chickens to their respective houses. They were in great demand from his friends and he was constantly giving pairs of them away.

Early in 1812 Jefferson wrote Dr. William Thornton that in his part of the country they were busily engaged in the household manufacture

[11]Peter Minor to TJ, Sept. 17, 1811; TJ to Minor, Sept. 24 (ibid., pp. 137–138).

[12]TJ to Bacon, Dec. 26, 1808 (*Garden Book*, p. 383); Bacon to TJ, Dec. 29 (UVA). The menace of dogs was referred to, Dec. 27, in the Richmond *Enquirer*.

of clothing.[13] Several times he said that to clothe his family and "people" he needed every year two thousand yards of linen, cotton, and woolen. All the fine and most of the middling cloth had to be procured elsewhere. It was only coarse cloth that he and his fellow farmers could hope to supply from their establishments. He raised very little flax, believing that it injured the soil, and he was too far north for cotton, the material he most needed. It came to Richmond from points farther south and was brought to Albemarle County on bateaux by way of the James and the Rivanna. He estimated that a sheep per person was sufficient for woolen clothing and may be presumed to have generally had that many. For years some spinning and weaving had been done at Monticello by means of the spinning wheel and the handloom, but there was much more of it just before and during the War of 1812, when imported cloth was scarce or unavailable.

Toward the end of the summer of 1811, Jefferson acquired a spinning jenny and a loom with a flying shuttle and made an arrangement for the training of servants of his, women and girls, in spinning and weaving. This was with a man named William Maclure, who moved to the neighborhood from North Carolina under an engagement to give such instruction. Jefferson supplied him with a house and provided food for his family during a period of more than two years. Apparently a common manufacturing room was set up, some distance away from Monticello; and, after a period of learning, the servants came home to that place or to Poplar Forest.[14] The master kept a close eye on their progress. After getting his first spinning jenny from Maclure, who made them, Jefferson, always on the lookout for improved machines, acquired several more elaborate ones. He made extensive preliminary inquiries about these and entered into considerable discussion of them, but in the end he contented himself with the simpler machine, which his workmen could repair and even construct.[15] In June, 1814, he said that he and his son-in-law had four jennies at work, one of forty spindles and three of twenty-four. Somewhat later he spoke of having two common looms

[13] Jan. 14, 1812. This topic is treated in *Farm Book*, pp. 464–465; pertinent extracts from letters, 1811–1818, pp. 463–493.

[14] TJ to Maclure, Sept. 10, 1811; Oct. 16, 1813; and letter of commendation (*ibid.*, pp. 468–469, 484–486). See also comments in his letter of Mar. 5, 1813, to Jeremiah Goodman, his overseer at Poplar Forest, referring to particular women and to a "spinning house" there (*ibid.*, p. 483). At Monticello the "weaver's cottage" still stands, though it now serves a very different purpose.

[15] The particular reference is to the machine of Oliver Barrett and Ebenezer Herrick. He also bought a "hand carding engine for cotton" (bill of Dec. 12, 1812, in *Farm Book*, p. 481).

with flying shuttles and said he produced the required two thousand yards of cloth. In this operation he had to employ only a few women and children who could do little on the farm.[16] He seems to have run up no balance sheet, and, although he originally estimated the cost of the machines as small, he may have spent too much on them before he got through. Upon its face, however, this was a sensible undertaking and it brought considerable satisfaction to this advocate of economic self-sufficiency.

Shortly after the American consul at Lisbon, William Jarvis, dispatched the shipment of merino sheep to America, he retired from his post and was succeeded by George Jefferson, who had long been Thomas Jefferson's factor in Richmond. As we have previously observed, the ex-President was never able to live up fully to his self-denying resolution regarding appointments. As President he had refrained from appointing relations to his office, but as a private citizen he felt free to exert himself in behalf of his second cousin. The appointment is also worthy of note in that it caused the first citizen of Albemarle to deal henceforth with Patrick Gibson, of the firm of Gibson and Jefferson. The name of the junior member disappeared from the correspondence of the firm's most distinguished client for another reason. After serving in Lisbon for about a year, George Jefferson embarked for home in a state of derangement and took his own life shortly before reaching the shore of Virginia.[17]

Besides genuine sorrow, this event brought some embarrassment to his kinsmen at Monticello. The merchant in Milton from whom Jefferson bought so much and to whom he was always in debt, concluded that he would like the post. David Higginbotham's eminent customer saw no choice but to recommend this neighbor and friend, whom he esteemed highly as a country merchant but believed to be unsuited to the office abroad. In this dilemma he wrote two letters to his friend the President. The first contained no falsehood, he said, but for the whole truth a second was needed. He asked that the latter be kept in Madison's private papers, for he was "unwilling to make a public record of it in the case of so good a man."

A few months after he arrived at this tactful solution of an embarrassing problem, he arranged an ingenious triangular deal whereby the merchant acquired the property of William Short, then known as Indian

[16] TJ to William Thornton, June 9, 1814; to James Maury, June 16, 1815 (*ibid.*, pp. 486, 490). He discussed the cost of looms in several letters (*ibid.*, pp. 487–490).

[17] George Jefferson to TJ, Mar. 8, 1811 (MHS); TJ to George Jefferson, Mar. 11 (photostat, UVA, courtesy of Mrs. Virginius Dabney); Fontaine Maury to TJ, July 18, 29, 1812, reporting the events (Mo. Hist. Soc.).

Camp (later Morven), in return for the cancellation of Jefferson's account to August 1, 1812. On his part Jefferson gave Short his bonds to the amount of $10,000. This transaction, which seems to have been regarded at the time as mutually beneficial, fixed Higginbotham even more firmly in Albemarle County, and it did no injury to Short, who was paid off in less than three years. It was of only temporary benefit to Jefferson, who could not escape from the old round of credit and was in debt to this good merchant on the day he died.[18]

Though his honest judgment prevented him from backing the application of an unqualified friend and neighbor, he supported in good conscience the candidacy of David B. Warden for the consulship at Paris. This was over the opposition of John Armstrong, recent minister to France. A man of learning, Warden was already a correspondent of Jefferson's, for whom he had performed various commissions during previous service in Paris. After a visit of his to Monticello that lasted ten days but does not seem to have wearied his host, Jefferson wrote a lengthy letter about him to Madison, who proceeded to appoint him despite Armstrong's objections. Warden lost the post a few years later but remained in Paris. He corresponded fruitfully with Jefferson until nearly the end of the latter's life, transmitting letters of his to European friends and performing literary commissions for him.[19]

ii

Though Madison reported international developments to Jefferson promptly and candidly, he did not ask his predecessor's counsel about the conduct of foreign affairs, and the former President, regarding himself as *hors de combat*, rarely offered a suggestion. From his letters to various people, however, his judgment of the situation during the months immediately preceding the War of 1812 can be readily ascertained. He continued to claim that the basic reason for the failure of his own administration to solve the country's international problems was attributable to the unexampled world situation. Writing his former Attorney General about a year after he left office, he said: "At any other period, the even-handed justice we have observed towards all nations . . . would have preserved our peace, and secured the unqualified confidence of all other nations in our faith and probity. But the hurricane

[18] Two letters of TJ to Madison, Aug. 10, 1812 (LC); a fuller account of the deal for Indian Camp is in Appendix II, Section C.

[19] TJ to Madison, Dec. 8, 1810 (L. & B., XIX, 177–178); Madison to TJ, Mar. 18, 1811 (Hunt, VIII, 135); letters of TJ to Warden, in "Some Jefferson Letters," ed. by Sigmund Diamond, in *Miss. Valley Hist. Rev.*, XXVIII (Sept. 1941), 225–242. The latter reveal much about TJ's cultural interests, international relations, and his views on a variety of subjects.

which is now blasting the world, physical and moral, has prostrated all the mounds of reason as well as right."[20] No doubt he over-stated the degree of righteousness that obtained in international affairs in peacetime, but he certainly had ground for believing that in the heat of this conflict governments had become deaf to appeals to both morality and reason. They recognized no law but force and, in their madness, could even be blind to self-interest. This situation had imposed virtually insuperable difficulties on his young country as it sought to proceed about its commercial affairs, but to his mind these were slight in comparison with the troubles in the Old World. Such scenes of "tumult and outrage" had never before existed, he said. "Every government but one on the continent of Europe demolished, a conqueror roaming over the earth with havoc and destruction, a pirate spreading misery and ruin over the face of the ocean. Indeed, my friend, ours is a bed of roses. And the system of government which shall keep us afloat amidst the wreck of the world, will be immortalized in history."[21]

As he told John W. Eppes, he was far from believing that the reputation of Americans would be tarnished by their having kept out of "the mad contests of the rest of the world." On the contrary, he held that the preservation of their country "tranquil and prosperous," while every one on the other side of the Atlantic was prostrated, would place Americans "high in the scale of wisdom." He asked his son-in-law: "Which of them [the countries of Europe] have better preserved their honor? Has Spain, has Portugal, Italy, Switzerland, Holland, Prussia, Austria, the other German powers, Sweden, Denmark, or even Russia? And would we accept of the infamy of France or England in exchange for our honest reputation, or of the result of their enormities, despotism to the one and bankruptcy and prostration to the other, in exchange for the prosperity, the freedom and independence which we have preserved safely through the wreck?"[22] To General Kosciuszko he wrote a little earlier: "It would have been perfect Quixotism in us to have encountered these Bedlamites, to have undertaken the redress of all wrongs against a world avowedly rejecting all regard to right. . . . Peace then has been our principle, peace is our interest, and peace has saved to the world the only plant of free and rational government now existing in it."[23]

It was fortunate for America, as he had observed, that the Mammoth could not swim or the Leviathan operate on land. If Americans would stay out of their way, the predatory powers could not get at them. "Our

[20] TJ to C. A. Rodney, Feb. 10, 1810 (Ford, IX, 271).

[21] TJ to Dr. Walter Jones, Mar. 5, 1810 (Ford, IX, 274).

[22] TJ to JWE, Sept. 29, 1811 (L. & B., XIII, 93). It should be noted that Great Britain was suffering from a depression at this time.

[23] TJ to Kosciuszko (*ibid.*, pp. 41–42).

business certainly was to be still," he said. Though the embargo of his second term had a coercive as well as a protective purpose, it was a notable manifestation of the policy of stillness. Not wholly without reason did his political foes in New England charge him with indifference to the commercial interest, for it was this, more than anything else, that drew his country into the vortex. As an advocate of economic self-sufficiency he had modified his views of manufacturing since he wrote the *Notes on Virginia*, but he had not ceased to set higher store on the values of an agricultural than on those of a commercial society. One reason for his distrust of the British, though certainly not the only one, was that they were a nation of merchants — a modern Carthage to which a Punic faith could be imputed. "Money," he said, "and not morality, is the principle of commerce and commercial nations."[24] During his second term he had engaged in private controversy with one of his own supporters, who described merchants as a "swinish multitude" and opposed all efforts to protect foreign commerce, holding that these inevitably led to war. Though Jefferson, while President, may have wished he could dispense with the carrying trade, as a responsible executive he took the position that the government was obligated to protect commerce like any other lawful enterprise and that if it always turned the other cheek its citizens would be victimized by other nations.[25] He denied Quakerism as well as Quixotism. They were the Scylla and Charybdis between which this classicist had had to steer.

Also, the government must steer between the British and the French if it would maintain neutrality. The main difference he perceived between them was that the sea lords had much the greater power to inflict injury on his country. If he ever deserved to be called pro-French, as he habitually was by political enemies in his heyday and has been by some historians until our day, this was certainly not toward the end of his presidency or soon afterwards. In his eyes Napoleon was "the first and chiefest apostle of the desolation of men and morals," and his death might remove the "scourge of the land." But how were freedom and order to be restored to the sea? Britannia ruled the waves, and in his opinion her concern went far beyond the defeat of the French Emperor. She wanted to control the seas absolutely in her own commercial interest, exacting tribute from all others who would venture on them. He was convinced that the policies she sought to justify on grounds of desperation were to no small degree motivated by avarice. For this reason he was more fearful of the continuance of the British threat than of the French, which might be expected to vanish with Napoleon. He had

[24] TJ to Gov. John Langdon of New Hampshire, Mar. 5, 1810 (L. & B., XII, 376).

[25] For correspondence of 1806, see my *Public Life of Thomas Cooper*, pp. 190–191.

fleeting hopes of the modification of British policy after the death of George III, of which he learned in the early fall of 1811, but at this stage he minimized the power of the King. And, while certainly not absolving particular ministers from blame, he was disposed to attribute their actions to the dominant spirit of commerce. He had a high opinion of the character of the English as individuals, but he intensely disliked and strongly distrusted their government. So, also, did he distrust those Federalists whom he called Anglomen and described as monocrats.[26]

Believing as he did that France, while lacking comparable power to inflict damage on his country, had kept pace with England in "inquity of purpose," he had no desire to aid her and her tyrannical emperor. After war was finally declared he observed that Americans had been spared many years of it by the difficulty of selecting a foe between the two contesting powers.[27] One of the merits of the embargo of his administration was that it maintained the form of neutrality, and he never ceased believing that it constituted the best means — perhaps the only means — whereby the rights of his country could be peaceably safeguarded. More afterwards than at the time, seemingly, he regretted its abandonment. In the second summer of his retirement he wrote his former Secretary of War: "The federalists . . . by forcing us from the embargo, inflicted a wound on our interests which can never be cured." Referring to the repeal as a "fatal measure," he said: "This is the immediate parent of all our present evils, and has reduced us to a low standing in the eyes of the world."[28] He said repeatedly that he himself agreed to the abandonment of the embargo because the opposition to it threatened the Union. To one such statement he made this addition: "But from that moment, I have seen no system which could keep us entirely aloof from these agents of destruction."[29] He over-rated the merits of the embargo, but he was far from unrealistic in believing, after its abandonment, that his countrymen were left with no choice but that between war and submission.

Though characteristically defensive and negative in his attitude toward the powers and affairs of Europe, Jefferson continued to be positive and

[26] TJ's letters to New Englanders of his own political persuasion are full of comments on the British and the "Anglomen." See in particular his letter to Gov. Langdon, Mar. 5, 1810 (L. & B., XII, 373–379). His reference to American monarchists seem less extreme than they once did in view of descriptions of the presidency in the 1970's as a sort of republican monarchy. His comments on the insecurity of a government under a parliamentary system also have contemporary relevance (1974).

[27] TJ to Kosciuszko, June 25, 1812 (Ford, IX, 361).

[28] TJ to Henry Dearborn, July 16, 1810 (Ford, IX, 277).

[29] TJ to Dr. Walter Jones, Mar. 5, 1810 (Ford, IX, 274). He expressed continued belief in the embargo on the last Christmas of his life in a letter to W. B. Giles, Dec. 25, 1825 (Ford, X, 656).

aggressive as an advocate of American territorial expansion. He was not directly responsible for the actions of Madison with respect to West Florida, but these were in full accord with his policy. In mid-October, 1810, Madison informed him that the revolt in the Baton Rouge district against Spanish rule had confronted the executive with a problem. He believed that the government might fairly take possession of the country to the Perdido River since, in his opinion, it already belonged to the United States.[30] Such had been the claim of the administration ever since it acquired Louisiana. The question of rightfulness, therefore, was not one that he saw any need to raise with Jefferson. But Spain had never conceded that the province of Louisiana extended to the Perdido, and Madison wondered if the physical occupation of the disputed territory would not also be viewed with disfavor by England and France and lead to conflict with all three countries. He put these fears behind him soon thereafter, when he received a direct request from the revolters that the Baton Rouge district be incorporated in the United States. On October 27, 1810, he made it known by proclamation that orders had gone forth to possess the country to the Perdido.[31]

Jefferson's hearty approval of this action could have been taken for granted by anyone familiar with his persistent efforts to establish this territorial claim. A few weeks after the congressional session began, he sent John W. Eppes, at that Congressman's request, the paper on the boundaries that he had drawn in 1803 and that represented the official American position. He now expressed the hope that Congress would authorize the President to seize East Florida and thus forestall the British, who would otherwise occupy St. Augustine and Pensacola, claiming to act in the name of Spain. That was the compelling reason for the contemplated action, but he also believed it could be justified as a reprisal for indemnities due from and acknowledged by Spain.[32] Congress granted this authority to Madison without much ado, but Eppes appears to have played no particular part in the proceedings, and, for reasons we need not go into here, Madison did not pursue the matter.[33] Thus Jefferson's prediction that the militia of Georgia could take over East Flor-

[30] Madison to TJ, Oct. 19, 1810 (Hunt, VIII, 110). The Perdido bounds the present state of Florida on the west.

[31] Hunt, VIII, 112–114. The events are described in Brant, V, ch. XII. Actually, the Americans did not seize Mobile until 1813.

[32] TJ to JWE, Jan. 5, 1811 (Ford, IX, 289–291). On TJ's memoir of Sept. 7, 1803, see *Jefferson the President: First Term*, p. 309. Eppes had recently informed Jefferson of his sale of Eppington and removal to Millbrook in Buckingham County. This was in the district of John Randolph, against whom he ran for Congress unsuccessfully in 1811 and successfully in 1813.

[33] TJ's hopes were further expressed in a letter of Mar. 8, 1811, to Madison (L. & B., XIII, 22).

ida in a fortnight was not tested. He had to wait eight more years for the acquisition of this coveted peninsula.

After the enactment of Macon's Bill Number Two (May 1, 1810), to which Jefferson made no particular reference, the next important event was the issuance of a letter by the French foreign minister, the Duc de Cadore, announcing that the Berlin and Milan decrees would cease to be effective against the United States on November 1, 1810. According to this communication, the French understood that the English would "revoke their orders in council and renounce the new principles of blockade, which they have wished to establish," or that the United States, conformably with the Act of May 1, 1810, would "cause their rights to be respected by the English."[34] On hearing reports of the letter, Jefferson congratulated his successor on the "revocation" of the French decrees. He rejoiced, he said, that one power had got out of the way and left them a clear field with the other. Madison hastened to inform him that there was still uncertainty about the French action, but expressed the hope that they would have but one contest on their hands at a time. In fact, the French promise was equivocal and other actions of theirs tended to neutralize it, but Madison decided to use it as a bargaining weapon. Accordingly, on November 2, 1810, in a proclamation, he announced that the French, having ceased to violate American commercial rights, were henceforth free from that law's restrictions.[35] According to the law, non-intercourse had to be reimposed on the British in three months if they did not take action comparable to that now officially attributed to the French. This they did not do during the life of Madison's first Congress (the eleventh). The measure, introduced by John W. Eppes and adopted at the very end of the session, imposed non-importation rather than non-intercourse on Great Britain, but it constituted another link in the chain of events that led to war.[36] On his return to Albemarle from a journey of five weeks in Bedford County, Jefferson congratulated Madison on the close of his "campaign," saying that, while it had not conquered all of his difficulties, it had given him time to consider and provide for them.[37] The ex-President did not hint that his successor had been gullible.

[34]Cadore to Armstrong, Aug. 5, 1810 (*A.S.P.F.R.*, III, 387). This was first reported to Madison by William Pinkney in England on the basis of newspaper accounts.

[35]TJ to Madison, Oct. 15, 1810 (Ford, IX, 282); Madison to TJ, Oct. 19, 1810 (Hunt, VIII, 109); proclamation of Nov. 2 (*A.S.P.F.R.*, III, 392). The Cadore letter of Aug. 5, 1810, and Madison's decision with respect to it, are discussed by Perkins, pp. 245–252, and by Brant, V, 194–197, and ch. XIV.

[36]Approved Mar. 2, 1811 (*Annals*, 11 Cong., 3 sess., pp. 1338–1339).

[37]TJ to Madison, Mar. 8, 1811 (L. & B., XIII, 22).

* * *

War with the British was not officially proclaimed for another year, but William Pinkney, the American minister, having concluded that friendship with them was impossible as long as the existing government remained in power, brought his mission to a close the last day of February, 1811. At just the time in the summer that he got home, a newly designated and personally agreeable British minister arrived in America. From the outset Jefferson foresaw the failure of the mission of Augustus J. Foster, and if he had seen the young envoy's instructions he would have found ample support for his expectations. As he had supposed and the high American officials soon found out, British obduracy was not owing solely to justifiable doubts of the French revocation of the Berlin and Milan decrees as affecting the United States. In truth they were determined to maintain the Orders in Council until they themselves were freed from the restrictions of the Continental System. And, at this time, they showed a disposition to tighten their policy rather than to moderate it.[38]

Under these circumstances, the settlement of the *Chesapeake* affair, which was effected in the fall, evoked slight response from the government or the public.[39] Jefferson seems to have made no reference to it at the time, but no doubt he regarded the belated acceptance of the American contentions as a vindication of his own patience after the outrage. He was unquestionably glad that he had not permitted this to become an immediate occasion of war, as he believed he could have easily done.

A couple of months after Foster arrived, Jefferson said to a correspondent in the West Indies that the British, by their actions against American vessels, were already waging war, and that "it would be folly in us to let that war be all on one side only."[40] In this letter to a British colonial, and in a long and affectionate one in the spring to his old schoolmate James Maury, who lived in England, he insisted that he had no personal hostility to that country and no liking for imperial France. "The object of both is the same," he said, "to draw to themselves the power, the wealth and the resources of other nations. We resist the enterprises of England first because they first come vitally home to us. And our feelings repel the logic of bearing the lash of George the III for fear of that of Bonaparte at some future day." To his boyhood friend he said that the world would surely acquit the American government of having

[38] TJ's anticipatory comment is in his letter of May 5, 1811, to John Hollins (L. & B., XIII, 58). Foster's instructions are in *I.B.M.*, pp. 310 ff. They are discussed (*Prologue to War*, pp. 276–279) by Perkins, who sees naked selfishness in them.

[39] *I.B.M.*, pp. 318–319; *A.S.P.F.R.*, III, 499–500; Perkins, *Prologue to War*, pp. 354–355.

[40] TJ to Clement Caine in St. Kitts, Sept. 16, 1811 (Ford, IX, 330).

sought war. Indeed, he believed that there had been no previous instance of a nation's bearing so much.[41]

Some latter-day critics have not regarded the patience of Jefferson and Madison as a virtue, and some have laid the major responsibility for the war on them.[42] Both may be blamable for having sought "absolute right" with inadequate means, but the high British officials appear to have been equally rigid. And we may doubt if any means that were actually available to the American leaders would have been sufficient to deter the sea lords from their ruthless course. Neither Jefferson nor Madison provided sufficient leadership of public opinion, but a major share of responsibility for the psychological unpreparedness of the citizenry must be borne by the opposition. At the end of the congressional session of 1810–1811, John W. Eppes thus described it to his father-in-law: "United by no fixed principles or objects & destitute of every thing like American feeling, so detestable a minority never existed in any country."[43] Allowance must be made for partisanship and exaggeration on both sides, but the Hyperfederalists (as John Adams called them) undoubtedly contributed greatly to the British impression of American weakness, cowardice, and disunion.[44]

Precise assessment of responsibility for this conflict is impossible, but a major share of blame must surely be placed on those who were in the best position to prevent it. Jefferson was not as critical of himself as latter-day historians may think he should have been, and he and his successor made tactical mistakes, but the British government left no real alternative between submission and war. And it can certainly be argued that the High Federalists, who to all practical purposes advocated the former and who did their utmost to defeat the most serious effort to find an alternative, contributed more to national disunity and loss of self-respect than Jefferson and Madison did. Foster, the young British envoy, reported that, in the opinion of Henry Clay and his friends — who were to be known afterwards as War Hawks — war was "as necessary to America as a duel is to a young officer to prevent his being bullied and elbowed in society."[45] Being a critic of dueling, Jefferson might not have relished this figure of speech, but he resented contemptuousness and arrogance as he did few qualities, and he had sought full independence for

[41] TJ to James Maury, Apr. 25, 1812 (Ford, IX, 348–351). See also TJ to Kosciuszko, June 12, 1812 (*ibid.*, 361).

[42] See, for example, the summary of Perkins (*Prologue to War*, pp. 436–437).

[43] JWE to TJ, Mar. 20, 1811 (UVA).

[44] Writing TJ, Mar. 10, 1812, Gallatin said war was inevitable and blamed on domestic faction the failure of the effort to preserve peace (*Writings*, I, 517). He probably had Republican dissidents as well as Federalists in mind.

[45] Foster, *Jeffersonian America*, p. 14.

his country throughout his public life. In his mind, considerably before 1812, the question had resolved itself into the maintenance of what he had proclaimed in 1776. Freedom was again at stake.

He was speaking for himself as well as his neighbors when he wrote Madison at the beginning of spring: "Every body in this quarter expects the declaration of war as soon as the season will permit the entrance of militia into Canada, & altho' peace may be their personal interest and wish, they would I think disapprove of its longer continuance under the wrongs inflicted and unredressed by England."[46]

[46] TJ to Madison, Mar. 26, 1812 (LC).

Dr. Benjamin Rush

Painted and engraved by William Haines, 1805. (Library of Congress, Prints and Photographs Division)

[VII]

Renewing Old Friendship

THE reconciliation of the two ex-Presidents of the United States, some six months before the War of 1812 began, was an event of the utmost importance in the personal history of both of them. Dr. Benjamin Rush, without whom it might never have come about, was convinced that it was also of the first importance to the country. A fellow signer of the Declaration of Independence, the kindly Philadelphian, though closer to Jefferson politically than to John Adams, was actually more intimate with the latter. He was devoted to both men, however, and the suspension of communication between them, which had lasted more than a decade, was painful to him on both personal and public grounds. His successful efforts to bring it to an end constitute an engrossing story.[1]

These efforts began in the autumn after Jefferson's retirement. At that time Rush, with no little audacity, recounted to Adams an alleged dream of his. After reviewing the past relations between these two champions of independence who later became rivals, he described the restoration of cordiality between them, saying that the initiative in this was taken by Adams. That old patriot, while certainly not fooled, did not seem to be offended. Denying that this was history, though it was actually that in part, he said it might be prophecy. But he was obviously unwilling to do anything as yet toward its fulfillment.

Some fifteen months later, in the course of a long letter to Jefferson, Rush urged upon him the revival of correspondence with his old friend, claiming that an advance on his part would surely be welcomed by Adams. "Tottering over the grave," said Rush, "he now leans wholly upon the shoulders of his old Revolutionary friends. The patriots gener-

[1] It has been told with authority by L. H. Butterfield in "The Dream of Benjamin Rush: The Reconciliation of John Adams and Thomas Jefferson" (*Yale Review*, XL [Dec., 1950], 297–319).

ated by the funding system, &c., are all his enemies." Rush was reminding Jefferson not only of Adams's comradeship in the struggle for independence but also of his continuing share in the enmity of Hamilton's followers.[2] Nothing was said here about the repudiation of Adams, along with his son John Quincy, by New England Federalists because of the latter's support of Jefferson's foreign policy while in the Senate, but Jefferson could not have been unaware of these developments. Also, he must have known that John Adams had defended him in print against accusations of the Hyperfederalists.[3] In truth, there were few differences between him and his predecessor regarding the issues of the day, and he believed that political disagreement should not affect personal relations anyway. He had the same good opinion of John Adams that he had always had, he said, but was well aware of that gentleman's envious and suspicious nature. One could never be sure that he would not repulse an advance. A further reason for his own unwillingness to make one was his memory of the rebuff he had received from Mrs. Adams, supposedly with her husband's acquiescence, in their ill-fated correspondence after the death of his daughter Maria. He sent copies of the letters between Abigail Adams and himself to Rush so that the Doctor could form his own judgment of them.[4]

While recognizing that Jefferson had grounds for hesitation Rush refused to be discouraged, and in the summer of 1811 events played into his hand. John and Edward Coles of Albemarle County, with whom Jefferson had often talked about the past, chanced to visit John Adams at Quincy, and from them their host learned somewhat incidentally of his successful rival's particular concern not to wound his feelings after his defeat for re-election. Adams responded impulsively, according to his nature. "I always loved Jefferson," he said, "and still love him." Informed of this by the Coles brothers, Jefferson, loosening the tight rein he generally kept on his emotions, told Rush that this was enough for him.[5] He would gladly express his unchanged affection as soon as an "apposite occasion" should occur, he said, but he hoped that if one should present itself first to Adams that he would avail himself of it. That testy but

[2] Rush to TJ, Jan. 2, 1811 (Butterfield, II, 1076).

[3] As, for example, in his communication to the *Boston Patriot*, May 29, 1809, copied in the Richmond *Enquirer*, July 7. He said that accusations against TJ of "blind devotion to France, of hostility to England, of hatred to commerce, of partiality and duplicity in his late negotiations with the belligerent powers" were without foundation.

[4] TJ to Rush, Jan. 16, 1811 (Ford, IX, 294–299). For an account of the correspondence with Abigail Adams, see *Jefferson the President: First Term*, pp. 422–424.

[5] TJ to Rush, Dec. 5, 1811, reporting Adams's affirmation (Ford, IX, 299–301*n*.). Edward Coles gave H. S. Randall a detailed account of the visit to Adams, May 11, 1857 (Randall, III, 639–640).

playful veteran, learning of developments from Rush, kept the solicitous intermediary on tenterhooks a while longer, but on New Year's Day of his seventy-seventh year he reopened a dialogue which was to enrich the rest of his life and that of his correspondent, and the record of which was to prove a priceless gift to posterity.[6]

In making the first move for reconciliation Adams was in character, for he was the more spontaneous of the two. It is not surprising that he made something of a joke of his advances, and perhaps Jefferson was in character in not immediately perceiving it. Aware of his interest in domestic manufacture, Adams sent him "two pieces of homespun lately produced in this quarter by one who was honoured in his youth with some of your attention and much of your kindness." He was referring to two volumes of his son's *Lectures on Rhetoric and Oratory*, published a couple of years earlier, which did not reach Jefferson until after he had replied to this letter. He should have recognized the reference to his own association with John Quincy Adams long ago in Paris, but in his haste to respond he took the word "homespun" literally and began his own letter with a paragraph describing the domestic manufacturing in his own neighborhood. Its recipient was pleased with this report, as he was with the speedy transmission of Jefferson's letter (seven or eight days), and when that gentleman discovered his mistake he paid deserved tribute to the learning and literary craftsmanship of the younger Adams.

At the outset the two veterans brought each other up to date about their health. Jefferson, who was approaching sixty-nine, reported that he was on horseback three or four hours every day but found a mile too far to walk. Adams, already seventy-six, said he sometimes walked three or four miles a day but had a complaint that "nothing but the ground" (that is, death) could cure. This was the palsy, "a kind of paralytic affection of the nerves" that caused his hand to tremble, rendering writing difficult and good writing impossible. Nevertheless, in the course of the next few years he wrote much more often than Jefferson. He appears on the whole, and especially at first, to have gained more pleasure from their renewed friendship than his correspondent did. The older, the lonelier, and the less occupied of the two, he seems to have had more need of it. It was precious to them both, however, and well deserves its renown. At this point some comments on the basis of this historic friendship appear to be in order.

[6] A number of their letters were published in various editions of their writings, but the full richness of the correspondence was revealed only with the publication of the whole of it, along with that of Abigail Adams with TJ, in *The Adams-Jefferson Letters*, ed. by L. J. Cappon (2 vols., 1959 — referred to as *A.-J. Letters*). The part of the correspondence dealt with here is in Vol. II, beginning on p. 290, but I am citing the letters by date only. I do not attempt to reproduce Adams's capitalization.

* * *

The first and perhaps the most important thing to be said about it is that it was deeply rooted in a past of which they both were immensely proud. Rush addressed them as "fellow laborers in erecting the great fabric of American independence," and in his first letter Jefferson echoed these words. Then, resorting to a nautical metaphor as he often did despite his relative unfamiliarity with the sea, he said: "Laboring always at the same oar, . . . we rode through the storm with heart and hand, and made a happy port." As he could not have failed to perceive, Adams had long and deeply resented what he regarded as the disproportionate credit given Franklin and Washington for the success of this voyage. Jefferson's most memorable contribution was made at its beginning, when he was unquestionably in the same boat with Adams. They had served together on the committee from which a memorable document emerged, but, as a matter of fact, his former colleague had recently disparaged this. Only six months before they resumed correspondence, Adams, in political isolation at Quincy, made the following observation to their mutual friend in Philadelphia: "The Declaration of Independence I always considered as a theatrical show. Jefferson ran away with the stage effect of that . . . and all the glory of it."[7]

This was in a letter that Adams himself described as ill-natured and that contained references to a number of other people who in his opinion had gained more fame than they deserved. Fortunately, Jefferson did not see this reference to himself, but if he had done so he might have made allowance for Adams's wounded pride, as Rush did, and for his proneness to intemperance in speech. Jefferson's pride in the authorship of the noble pronouncement with which the history of the nation began might have been assumed, but the part he played in its adoption and promulgation was undramatic and his subsequent references to it were becomingly modest. Employing their respective talents, he and Adams had supplemented each other well. What the skilled literary craftsman from Virginia wrote was staunchly and successfully supported in crucial debate by the forceful delegate from Massachusetts. The former always looked back on this as the most memorable occasion in his public life, and he never forgot his fellow members of the class of 1776. In the first of his letters to Adams in 1812 he lamented that so few of the signers of the Declaration were left. Among them, for services at the birth of the Republic, he always placed Adams first, as that patriot surely knew. He

[7] Adams to Rush, June 21, 1811 (*The Spur of Fame: Dialogues of John Adams and Benjamin Rush, 1805–1813*, ed. by J. A. Schutz and Douglass Adair [1966], p. 182); see also his letter of Sept. 30, 1805 (*ibid.*, p. 43).

liked Jefferson for that reason and, according to his own report, soon loved him for himself.

Speaking years afterwards of their association in the Continental Congress, he said that the young Virginian soon seized upon his heart.[8] One reason for this he suggested in a letter to Jefferson in which he spoke of "that friendly warmth that is natural and habitual to you."[9] Friendly warmth did generally characterize Jefferson in personal relations, after his first stiffness wore off, but it was not often attributed to Adams. The blunt Yankee antagonized people and never enjoyed wide personal popularity. He was demonstrative to his few real friends, however, giving freer rein to his words and emotions than Jefferson did. Benjamin Rush's wife said that her husband and Adams corresponded "like two young girls about their sweethearts." Throughout his correspondence with Jefferson, Adams used affectionate language, but he seems to have had an even warmer place in his heart for Rush. The death of the good Doctor, a little more than a year after he brought the two ex-Presidents together, was a blow to both of them, though presumably a greater one to Adams. Quite clearly, he had a higher personal regard for Jefferson than for any other of his major contemporaries. Of the two, Jefferson was more restrained in expressing both his likes and dislikes, and if tactfulness was not natural to him it had become habitual. He had always recognized Adams's honesty, courage, and patriotism, and as a result of observation arrived at what he regarded as "a just estimate of his virtues and passions." Jefferson was one of the few who perceived amiability beneath his colleague's prickly exterior. Shortly before Adams returned to America from England, Jefferson, in France, predicted that Madison would love him after coming to know him — as, apparently, Madison never did.[10]

The friendship that was rooted in common loyalty to the class and cause of 1776 was cemented in the next decade when both of these laborers for independence, representing their young country abroad and seeing eye to eye in official matters, shared the disappointments of their missions. It was during this period that the widower from Virginia entered the Adams family circle. He was described by Abigail at this stage as "one of the choice ones of earth," and her husband afterwards said that in Paris their son John appeared to be almost as much Jefferson's boy as his. Later, when the minister to France visited the minister to England, the two American envoys shared a snub from King George III

[8] See *Jefferson the Virginian*, p. 203.
[9] July 9, 1813 (*A.-J. Letters*, II, 351).
[10] TJ to Madison, Jan. 30, 1787 (Boyd, XI, 95).

and toured the English countryside together. Later still, Mrs. Adams with the utmost tenderness, harbored little Polly Jefferson on her way to join her father in Paris.[11]

Early in his retirement, when still in a depressed state of mind, Adams said in a private letter (which was published a score of years later, much to his dismay) that when abroad he met Jefferson seldom except on business and that, although they generally agreed, there was "no very close intimacy" between them.[12] Replying to Rush's report of his dream some five years later, after Jefferson himself had retired, Adams said that there had never been "the smallest interruption" of their personal friendship. He then offered some gratuitous information which Rush wisely refrained from passing on. "You should remember that Jefferson was but a boy to me," he said, adding incorrectly that he himself was ten years older instead of seven and a half. An extraordinary statement followed: "I am bold to say I was his preceptor in politics and taught him everything that has been good and solid in his whole political conduct."[13] The younger man may have erred somewhat on the side of deference, but this claim would have surprised him greatly, and he might have been annoyed by Adams's account of their meeting in Holland, shortly before he returned to America: "I then *instructed* him in the situation of all *my* [that is, American] money matters before I left Europe."[14] Such braggadocio suggested that the septuagenarian had not grown up, but he spoke truly when he said that in France they had lived in "the most perfect friendship and harmony."

They were in essential agreement regarding the time when they began to disagree. According to Adams, this was when his former colleague returned from France, full of unwarranted confidence in the revolution then under way in that country. He prided himself afterwards on having proved the better prophet with respect to the course of this revolution. In truth, even at this early stage, Jefferson's confidence in it was less than complete, and his relative optimism was a reflection of temperament, just as Adams's pessimism was. He dated the beginnings of their divergence from his perception of Adams's hankering after the trappings of monarchy when Vice President. Learning of the miniature tempest in which that newly installed official had involved himself as an advocate of pomp and ceremony, Jefferson repeated to Madison the characterization of him by Franklin as always an honest man, often a great one, and

[11] *Jefferson and the Rights of Man*, pp. 7, 13–14, 55, 60–61, 135–136.

[12] Adams to William Cunningham, Jan. 16, 1804 (*Correspondence between the Hon. John Adams . . . and the Late Wm. Cunningham* [1823], p. 9). On later developments, see *A.-J. Letters*, II, 555, 600, n. 77.

[13] Adams to Rush, Oct. 25, 1809 (*Spur of Fame*, pp. 158–159).

[14] Italics added.

Abigail Adams (Mrs. John Adams)
Engraving from a portrait by Gilbert Stuart. (Library of Congress, Prints and Photographs Division)

sometimes absolutely mad. While Jefferson probably continued to believe that Adams was out of his mind at this stage, he modified the latter part of the quotation when writing Benjamin Rush a score of years later, saying merely that Adams was "sometimes incorrect and precipitate in his judgments."[15] He had writings of the Vice President in mind when he referred to "political heresies" that had sprung up among his countrymen, and to no less a personage than George Washington he spoke of Adams's "apostasy to hereditary monarchy and nobility." That Revolutionary patriot stoutly denied the charge of faithlessness to republicanism, and Jefferson's rhetoric now appears to have been over-blown. But his verbal extravagance was generally confined to private utterances, and he rarely equaled Adams in indiscretion.

Years after these events, it was aptly said of the latter: "He was *terribly* open, earnest, and direct, and could not keep his mouth shut."[16] Throughout his life he delighted in playing the hose of common sense on the follies and sentimentalities of mankind, and he did not hesitate to voice his grave reservations about democracy — which was direct democracy as he used the term. In his judgment of human beings he may actually have been less severe than he sounded, but he certainly had less faith in them than Jefferson did. In this respect as in others the two men supplemented each other.

A renewal of the intimacy they had enjoyed abroad was hardly to be expected after they returned home. They became contrasting images in the minds of their countrymen during Washington's first term — one as a champion, and the other as a supposed critic, of the rights of man. Nevertheless, their personal relations remained surprisingly good upon the surface until they were set up as rivals for the presidency. On the eve and during the first stage of their reconciliation the grievances that had accumulated after 1796 were kept out of sight. The emphasis was not on past differences but on present agreement. In the dangers of 1812 they were fellow patriots, as they had been in those of 1776. In his first letter Jefferson recalled a succession of external dangers that the young Republic had weathered, and Adams responded by listing domestic characters of whom they both had good reason to disapprove. "The Union is still to me an object of as much anxiety as ever independence was," he said, adding that he had sacrificed his popularity in New England to this.[17] Not only had he condemned those he regarded as dis-

[15] On Adams and titles, see *Jefferson and the Rights of Man*, pp. 259–261, and TJ to Madison, July 29, 1789 (Boyd, XV, 315–316). On the modification of the saying, see TJ to Rush, Dec. 25, 1811 (Ford, IX, 300*n.*).

[16] Theodore Parker, *Historic Americans* (Boston, 1871 edn.), p. 210.

[17] Adams to TJ, Feb. 3, 1812.

unionists, like Senators Timothy Pickering of Massachusetts and James Hillhouse of Connecticut; also, he had long opposed the pro-British faction in his section. But, as he believed, the national government by its embargoes and other actions restricting commerce and, most of all, by its opposition to naval power, had continually played into the hands of these people.[18]

While avoiding reference to past rivalry and personal grievances, Adams made it entirely clear at the start that he had not agreed with Jefferson and Madison in "measures of administration." He recognized that they had a perfect right to their opinions and that final judgment on these must be left to posterity. He was confident, however, that posterity would agree with him in his objection to the repeal of excise taxes and of the judiciary act, and to the neglect of the navy. But he had no more doubt of the integrity of these successors of his than he did of that of George Washington, and in basic foreign policy he, like his son, was much closer to them than to those whom he designated as Hyperfederalists. He believed these Anglophiles to be at heart enemies of an American navy. "Their *summum bonum*," he said to his friend Dr. Benjamin Waterhouse, was "a war with France, an alliance with England, and a dependence on the British navy for the protection of their commerce." He sounded more pro-French than Jefferson. "France is the natural ally of the U.S. if we must have any ally," he said. "We ought not to war with her, but in the last necessity. . . . I have never varied one moment from this opinion, nor departed from this principle in practice for thirty-seven years."[19]

While generally disapproving of Jefferson's domestic policies, Adams staunchly supported him in one highly controversial matter. In the spring of 1812 he received at Quincy what was described by the sender as a "piece of homespun." Like the one that had been previously received at Monticello, this consisted, not of wool, but of print and paper. It was a copy of Jefferson's pamphlet on the batture. Adams, who was already aware of this controversy and had a distinctly unfavorable impression of Edward Livingston, promptly observed: "Neddy is a naughty lad as well as a saucy one." He was indignant at the suit against a former President for an official act, and he praised the production with extravagance comparable to that of William Wirt. "It is as masterly a pamphlet as ever I have read," he said, "and every way worthy of the mind that composed and the pen which committed it to writing. There is witt and fancy and delicate touches of satyr enough in it to make it entertaining while the

[18] Adams to TJ, May 3, 1812.

[19] Adams to Benjamin Waterhouse, Mar. 14, 1813 (*Statesman and Friend: Correspondence of John Adams with Benjamin Waterhouse*, ed. by W. C. Ford [1927], pp. 92–93).

profusion of learning, the close reasoning and accurate criticism must have required a patience of investigation that at your age is very uncommon."[20]

In one of his later letters Adams said that he had been writing "by fits and starts for fifty or sixty years without ever correcting or revising anything."[21] But, while characteristically imprecise and diffuse, his letters were also characteristically spontaneous. Jefferson's were better organized, as his life was, and he was more careful to keep the correspondence in safe channels, especially at first. Responding to some of the queries in the rambling letters from Quincy, he largely confined his early replies to Indian folklore and early American history. He avoided all reference to embargoes and other restrictive measures of which his correspondent disapproved but took occasion early in the war to congratulate his predecessor on the successes of the little American navy. These, he said, "must be more gratifying to you than to most men, as having been the early and consistent advocate of wooden walls." He claimed that if he himself had differed from Adams regarding a navy, this was not on the principle but on the time. No other praise could have pleased the elder of the two retired statesmen more, and in his reply he credited the younger, as secretary of state, with advocating the use of sea power against the Barbary pirates — a policy which he believed Hamilton to have opposed.[22]

As things turned out, the compliment to the Father of the United States Navy arrived at a time when he needed mollification. A few days before he received it, somebody put into his hands a book that contained, in an appendix, two letters from Jefferson when President to Dr. Joseph Priestley and a letter of Priestley's in which he was quoted.[23] Adams promptly asked Jefferson if he had seen the book and, after giving the dates of the letters, announced that in due course he would have much to say on the subject they dealt with. Before he got a reply from Monticello he made known in other letters that, in his opinion, certain things Jefferson had said to Dr. Priestley needed to be explained. One of these was that Adams, in an answer to an address made to him as President, had denied the possibility of any real advance in science — that is, in knowledge. Another was that the Alien Act (believed by some to have been aimed at Priestley) was a libel on legislation.

He disclaimed the sentiment about human knowledge that was attrib-

[20] Adams to TJ, May 3, 1812; see also May 1, 1812, and TJ's of Apr. 20.

[21] Adams to TJ, May 29, 1818.

[22] TJ to Adams, May 27, 1813; Adams to TJ, June 11, 1813. He seems to have been wrong about Hamilton. For a discussion of TJ's attitude toward the navy, see *Jefferson the President: Second Term*, ch. XXVII.

[23] Thomas Belsham, *Memoirs of the late Reverend Theophilus Lindsey* (London, 1812).

uted to him, declaring it to be totally incongruous with the principles he had held for threescore years. He was certainly no foe to learning and inquiry, but a few days later he admitted that in a sense he held to the opinion that there was nothing new under the sun. The lesson of history, as he claimed to see it, was that, despite waves of reform and revolution, things were essentially unchanged and unimproved — especially in the realm of government. As for the Alien Act, he claimed that, since Jefferson had signed the measure as Vice President, he shared responsibility for it. That was absurd, since Jefferson's action was a mere formality, but the statement of Adams that the law was never executed was factually correct.[24]

The letter to which Adams made particular reference was written by Jefferson shortly after his inauguration. Since he had genuine regard for Priestley, a liberal clergyman and an eminent chemist who had been a favorite target of the Federalists ever since he came to America from England, the effusiveness of his letter is explicable.[25] But its references to bigotry in politics as well as in religion, and its tone of exultation at the triumph of reason and progress, could hardly have failed to offend the former President. Adams resented religious obscurantism and intolerance much as his successor did, and he could not have been expected to agree that the accession of his rival had marked the end of a storm and the dawn of a brighter day. At other times Jefferson expressed his undying faith in the American experiment in self-government, but never more than on this occasion did he glory in the distinctiveness he perceived in it. Thus he said: "We can no longer say there is nothing new under the sun. For this whole chapter in the history of man is new." The affirmation was to be echoed through the generations and to quicken the faith of very many of his countrymen. Though notably patriotic, Adams was not so disposed to distinguish the American experience from that of the rest of mankind. He could hardly have been expected to rejoice in the "mighty wave of public opinion" that had rolled over the country and washed him out of office.

While announcing that he meant to discuss these questions with the utmost candor, he continued to employ expressions of affection. Thus he said: "You may expect many more expostulations from one who has loved and esteemed you for eight and thirty years." Expostulation was characteristic of this vain and contentious man. He dearly loved to argue and may perhaps be said never to have ceased being a lawyer. His correspondent, on the other hand, abhorred personal controversy, hated to hurt other people's feelings, and expressed his own feelings more

[24] Adams's comments as reflected here are drawn from his letters of May 29, June 10, 14, 1813.

[25] TJ to Priestley, Mar. 21, 1801 (Ford, VIII, 21–23).

strongly in private than he permitted himself to do in public. While notable for his insistence that full information be made available about public matters, he always sought to guard the sanctity of private correspondence. Accordingly, he regarded the publication of his letters to Priestley as a gross abuse of confidence. They had vanished from his memory, he said, but since he had kept copies of them, he was able to look them up.

Jefferson sought to soften his criticism of Adams's pessimistic remark about the advance of knowledge.[26] It did not represent Adams's deliberate opinion, he said, but was "an expression lent to the prejudices" of his political friends. This was a shrewd observation, but there were some philosophical differences between the two men on this point, though these may have been less pronounced than those between the two parties. Nothing was more characteristic of Jefferson than his belief in the improvability of the human mind and the limitless progress of human knowledge. Adams, who prided himself on his realism, was considerably more skeptical.

Probably anticipating that Adams would be offended by his comment about the Alien Act, he said that, while only posterity could decide whether or not he had accurately portrayed the character of the time, there could be no doubt of the sensations excited by the terrorism of that day. "None can conceive who did not witness them," he said, "and they were felt by one party only." In assessing blame for the terrorism he distinguished between Adams and the extreme Federalists, as he had always done, and declared that he would enter into no political discussions. He never descended to particulars, but after he got more of Adams's expostulations he dispatched a little disquisition on political parties in response.

Paying subtle compliment to the learning of his correspondent by opening his letter with a quotation in Greek (a language in which Adams claimed he had grown rusty), he stated emphatically that he had no intention of entering into "the forest of opinions, discussions and contentions" which had occurred in their day.[27] "The summum bonum with me is now truly Epicurean," he said, "ease of body and tranquility of mind; and to these I wish to consign my remaining days." Judging from his actions, he was certainly not consigning his days to idleness, but he was obviously avoiding controversy and trying to pitch this dialogue on as high a plane as possible. He did not deny differences between himself and Adams and between their parties, but he set these in the framework of human history and human nature. Thus he said:

[26] TJ to Adams, June 15, 1813.
[27] TJ to Adams, June 27, 1813.

> Men have differed in opinion, and been divided into parties by these opinions, from the first origin of societies; and in all governments where they have been permitted freely to think and to speak. The same political parties which now agitate the U.S. have existed thro' all time. Whether the power of the people, or that of the aristoi [aristocrats] should prevail, were questions which kept the states of Greece and Rome in eternal convulsion, as they now schismatize every people whose minds and mouths are not shut up by the gag of a despot. And in fact the terms of whig and tory belong to natural as well as to civil history. They denote the temper and constitution of mind of different individuals.

He was describing parties in terms of principles without regard to organization or spoils and seemed to be disregarding the factor of self-interest in the conduct of individuals, but, as he implied, the differences between him and Adams could be considerably explained in terms of temperament and personality.

In seeking to apply his thesis to their respective careers he also indulged in over-simplification. He said that the issue on which he and Adams first diverged was that of the relative strength of the more popular branch of the government (Congress, especially the House of Representatives) and the more permanent branches (the President, the Senate, and presumably the judiciary). Such a line could have been drawn between the two parties that arose, but, at least from the time of his own governorship of Virginia, he had been fearful of legislative dominance. It may be doubted that Adams, even in his most vainglorious phases as an executive ever ceased to favor a balanced government, and he well described his present position in a letter that he had already written but that had not yet reached Monticello. "Checks and ballances, Jefferson, however you and your party may have ridiculed them, are our only security, for the progress of mind, as well as the security of body."[28] It would seem that each had misinterpreted the position of the other at the beginning of their rivalry. There was a recognizable difference between their attitudes toward popular government and toward people generally, however, and Jefferson certainly did not exaggerate the bitterness and indecency that had marked the conflict between the parties which set them up as rivals. While he always denied that this was a personal conflict and generally claimed that he had avoided all public participation in it, he admitted that he had sometimes given unguarded expression to his feelings in private — as he correctly supposed that Adams had done. He made it abundantly clear that he did not want to revive the memories of those feelings, or to renew these old discussions.

[28] June 25, 1813.

On the road this letter crossed one in which Adams told him not to be alarmed by the publication of his letters to Priestley and joined him in deploring the gross abuse of his confidence.[29] He said that they did the writer no dishonor, and he claimed that he cared not a farthing for his own reputation. But, while saying that he held it "a bubble, a gossamer, that idles in the wanton summers air," he left no doubt that he valued Jefferson's approbation and understanding. A few weeks later he said: "You and I ought not to die before we have explained ourselves to each other." He did a good deal of explaining and expostulating before he got the letter in which Jefferson drew the line between parties. Jefferson had referred to terrorism directed against the Republicans. Adams, in response, recalled a number of instances of terrorism directed against the Federalists. Far from describing parties in terms of principle, he did so in terms of the loaves and fishes they feared to lose or sought to gain. In this respect he saw no real choice between them.[30] While Jefferson was in an elevated seat at Monticello, Adams believed himself to be down to earth at Quincy.

He never wholly ceased being contentious and at times he sought to draw his correspondent into an argument in which that less belligerent gentleman would not engage. But they had plenty to talk about without entering into controversy that was best forgotten. Engaging in discussion rather than debate, until the end of their days they dealt with broader topics and more enduring themes. Refusing to be gladiators, they conversed as sages.

The re-established friendship between the two veterans had survived a major test; and, in midsummer of 1813, the wife of the elder, whose bitterness had outlasted his, gave the reconciliation her blessing by sending her regards to the younger in a postcript to one of her husband's letters. That gave Jefferson a good excuse to write her, as he did rather stiffly.[31] He had not learned as yet of the death of her daughter and namesake, but before long she wrote him about this more fully than her husband did.[32] To this letter he made no direct reply, and he told her husband he was remaining silent on that subject.[33] He knew the depth of their affliction, he said, but had learned that the only medicine for grief is time and silence. He did not mention the name of their daughter and did not need to remind them that he too had lost one. Effusiveness in deeply personal matters was not in his nature, but his old friends at Quincy could not doubt that his tie with them was stronger than ever.

[29] Adams to TJ, June 25, 1813.
[30] Adams to TJ, June 30, 1813.
[31] P.S. to Adams's letter of July 15, 1813; TJ to Abigail Adams, Aug. 22, 1813.
[32] Abigail Adams to TJ, Sept. 20, 1813.
[33] TJ to Adams, Oct. 12, 1813.

[VIII]

The Impact of War

JEFFERSON told John Adams that he had abandoned newspapers for Tacitus and Thucydides, Euclid and Newton, and he was duly congratulated on the exchange. But, while his opinion of the press remained highly critical, he certainly did not dispense with newspapers during the war years. He had not lost interest in public affairs. Far from being in political isolation, he was in intimate contact with Madison and Monroe, and received from headquarters firsthand reports on the course of events. If any word of criticism of his successor ever crossed his lips there appears to be no record of it. In private, however, he spoke with devastating candor of the conduct of others and freely expressed himself regarding developments.

His support of the war was unqualified and unreserved. It has often been described as an unnecessary war, and it probably would not have occurred if there had been a transatlantic cable. Before it was declared, the assassination of the British prime minister, Spencer Percival, had removed the official most committed to a strong anti-American policy; and the suspension of the Orders in Council had actually been announced in Parliament. In Jefferson's opinion, earlier action of this sort might have prevented war, but more was needed to make peace. "The sword once drawn, full justice must be done," he said. Claiming that a thousand ships had been taken and six thousand seamen impressed, he held that Canada would serve as indemnification for these. Also, it would be the best obtainable security against the Indians, who, as he never doubted, were incited against the Americans by the British in Canada. If, in addition to the cession of this territory, the impressment question should be settled, he would be for "peace with England, and then for war with France."[1]

[1] TJ to Robert Wright, Aug. 8, 1812 (L. & B., XIII, 184–185). He expressed similar sentiments in other letters at the time.

James Madison

Portrait by Joseph Wood, 1817. (Courtesy of the Virginia Historical Society, Richmond)

Such prognostications may be cited as illustrations of the disparity between national aims and available means that marked this conflict.[2] The sanguineness of Jefferson's nature often induced in him a mood of over-confidence, and at times his patriotic exaggeration rivaled that of the War Hawks. But as President he had generally been more realistic about military matters than his own partisans in the legislative branch, and they were more blamable for the military inadequacy of the country than he was.[3] Early in 1812 he expressed to Madison some doubt whether, in case of war, Congress could be counted on to do its proper part. The trouble he foresaw was that a body containing a hundred lawyers would be unable to restrain its loquacity.[4] (He never ceased being critical of the contentious profession to which he once belonged.) At the outset of the conflict he seems to have had few qualms about the military outlook. He admitted to a less optimistic observer that they faced inevitable difficulties in a country where the young had never seen military service, where the old were past it, and where the elements of tactics were unknown. Disasters might be expected but for the weakness of the enemy and their consequent inability to exploit American errors. Apparently he was unaware that in the governor of Upper Canada, Major General Isaac Brock, the enemy had a military commander of unusual competence, and he certainly did not anticipate the magnitude of American errors. At any rate, in the summer of 1812, he made a fatuous prediction: "The acquisition of Canada this year, as far as the neighborhood of Quebec, will be a mere matter of marching, and will give us experience for the attack on Halifax the next, and the final expulsion of England from the American continent."[5] Within two weeks of this utterance General William Hull surrendered to the British at Detroit and the incompetence of American military leadership soon became shockingly manifest.

Early in the year Madison had appointed as the senior major general Jefferson's old secretary of war, Henry Dearborn, in whose character, patriotism, and loyalty to the party he had complete confidence and whom he congratulated with entire sincerity. James Wilkinson was no longer the ranking officer, though that tattered warrior survived another court-martial in the winter before the war began. In the course of this, rumors connecting Jefferson's name with certain of Wilkinson's alleged misdeeds occasioned the ex-President to make in private what is perhaps the best statement of his attitude toward that highly controversial officer.

[2] See the astute comments by R. F. Weigley in *The American Way of War: A History of U.S. Military Strategy and Policy* (New York: Macmillan, 1973), pp. 46–55.

[3] See *Jefferson the President: Second Term*, ch. XXVIII.

[4] TJ to Madison, Feb. 19, 1812 (Ford, IX, 337).

[5] To William Duane, Aug. 4, 1812 (Ford, IX, 366).

Writing James Monroe, he said: "I have ever and carefully restrained myself from the expression of any opinion respecting General Wilkinson, except in the case of Burr's conspiracy, wherein, after he got over his first agitations, we [he and Dearborn] believed his decision firm, and his conduct zealous for the defeat of the conspiracy, and although injudicious, yet meriting, from sound intentions, the support of the nation. As to the rest of his life, I have left it to his friends and his enemies, to whom it furnishes matter enough for disputation."[6] Madison wrote him that, after a month, he had not yet got through the voluminous materials in this case.[7] In the end Madison saw no choice but to approve the acquittal of Wilkinson, but the restoration of his sword to this embattled veteran was not to prove advantageous to the country.

There was no little irony in these developments, for Dearborn, while secretary of war, had shown favoritism to Wilkinson that, if not improper, was certainly unwise. Now sixty-one, he lacked the vigor that his new position required, and events were to prove him deficient in military wisdom. He was specifically assigned the section of the Canadian border from the Niagara River to New England and was expected to lead the attack on Montreal. Modern critics are generally agreed that other actions should have been subordinated to this one, but in the summer of 1812 Dearborn spent precious weeks in New England, seeking to expedite recruiting and to induce reluctant Federalist governors to call out the militia. Toward the end of the summer Madison wrote Jefferson that the "seditious opposition" in Massachusetts and Connecticut had "clogged the wheels of the war." As a pronounced partisan, Dearborn was hardly the best person to combat this and he spent too much time in his vain efforts to do so. Thus it came about that the first attack on Canada was launched from Detroit.[8]

William Hull, who had done brave and honorable military service during the Revolution, had been appointed governor of Michigan Territory by Jefferson in 1805. In the spring of 1812 he was induced to accept appointment as brigadier general and commander of the troops designed to protect that territory. Responsibility for the unwise plan to attack Canada from Detroit without having gained naval control of Lake Erie must be shared by the Secretary of War and the President. Furthermore, the expected demonstration in the Niagara region did not take place and the British were thus enabled to concentrate their forces in the endangered sector. Surrender at the time was not inevitable, however, and Hull was afterwards convicted by court-martial on counts of cowardice

[6] TJ to Monroe, Jan 11, 1812 (Ford, IX, 332), replying to letter of Jan 6 (S.M.H., V, 197–198). For earlier comments see *Jefferson the President: Second Term*, pp. 276–278.

[7] Madison to TJ, Feb. 7, 1812 (Hunt, VIII, 176–177).

[8] Madison to TJ, Aug. 17, 1812 (*ibid.*, 210–211).

and neglect of duty. Jefferson had charged him with "detestable treason," but he was acquitted of that.

Jefferson's harsh comment, which may be attributed to excess of patriotic zeal or excess of loyalty to the administration, was made in a letter to William Duane, who was much more disposed to be critical of the government and who believed that it would be greatly bolstered by Jefferson's presence in it. Late in September he reported with approval the rumor that the ex-President had agreed to serve as secretary of state during the present crisis and that Monroe would become secretary of war in place of William Eustis. Said Duane: "The effects of Hull's surrender are not to be imagined — and some great and decided act of the Executive appears to be essential in order to turn the current of public feeling."[9] The need could not be doubted, but there was no sufficient reason to believe that Jefferson could meet it or that there was any likelihood of his being asked to do so. His reply is of special interest, however, as an expression of his judgment of the major actors in this affair and also of himself.

Now six months short of seventy, he said that the "hand of age" was upon him — adding that every year was marked by the departure of faculties. "The last year it was the sight, this it is the hearing, the next something else will be going, until all is gone." Before he left Washington he was conscious of the decay of his hearing, he said; this had become disastrous and he believed that his mind had weakened. Meanwhile, he had good health and was perfectly resigned to the immutable and universal laws of decay.

Recognizing no responsibility on the part of Madison for the disaster at Detroit, he blamed this on the "treachery" of Hull. He declined to condemn Secretary William Eustis for it but obviously was uncertain of his competence. That official's knowledge of military matters had been picked up during service as an army surgeon in the Revolution, and the major reason for his appointment by Madison appears to have been the desire to maintain geographical balance in the administration. He was a loyal Republican from New England. Jefferson said he had known him only "as a pleasant gentleman in society" and doubted his ability, when "translated from a colloquial circle," to direct the extensive operations of war.

Monroe afterwards reminded Jefferson of a conference between them in the summer of 1812, when they agreed that Eustis would have to be replaced. Monroe left no doubt of his own willingness, not to say eagerness, to assume military responsibilities.[10] Jefferson fully agreed with

[9]Duane to TJ, Sept. 20, 1812 (LC). TJ replied Oct. 1 (Ford, IX, 367–369).
[10]Monroe to TJ, June 7, 1813 (S.M.H., V, 260).

Duane regarding his competence and expressed confidence that Madison would make any changes that might be needed, saying that he might be making them now. That supposition was premature, but toward the end of the fall Eustis resigned and Monroe served temporarily as his successor while continuing as secretary of state.

By that time the situation on the Canadian border had worsened, except for the death of Brock. Following the attack on Queenston by General Stephen Van Rensselaer in October, a thousand men surrendered; and, after the failure of an attempt to cross the Niagara River in November, the army of General Alexander Smyth dissolved. Jefferson viewed these failures with indignation and pronounced severe judgment on these commanders. He expected Van Rensselaer to be broken "for cowardice and incapacity."[11] That officer, who, like Hull, had assumed command reluctantly, resigned his commission. Jefferson had some responsibility for Smyth, whom he had commissioned as colonel in the regular army in his second term. Sending Madison a paper highly critical of Smyth that he had received, he duly acknowledged that he had been greatly deceived as to his character.[12] Smyth was shortly legislated out of the army. Dearborn's inadequacy was not fully manifested until the spring campaign of 1813, and Jefferson may be presumed to have shared Gallatin's opinion that he had done all in his power. Meanwhile, from Lieutenant Colonel Isaac Coles, he had received a firsthand report of the chaos in the Niagara sector. Writing after the disaster at Queenston, Jefferson's former secretary said that nothing seemed to have been provided, that they did not know whether they would winter in Canada or in heaven, and that there was inconceivable irregularity and disorder in every branch of the service. He expected nothing but disasters until the army should be organized and disciplined in all parts.[13]

Early in 1813, Madison appointed John Armstrong secretary of war. The former minister to France had been highly critical of the Virginia leaders and was no favorite of theirs, but he had supported Madison for the presidency in 1812 and was now a brigadier general. In naming him Madison was doubtless proceeding on the assumption that he must appoint a northerner of political prominence. In view of Jefferson's reservations about Armstrong his congratulations to him seem rather too warm, but he was disposed to support all of his successor's actions with unquestioning loyalty and he undoubtedly regarded the New Yorker as

[11] TJ to Madison, Nov. 6, 1812 (Ford, IX, 370).
[12] TJ to Madison, Feb. 8, 1813 (L. & B., XIII, 218–219).
[13] Isaac Coles to TJ, Oct. 24, 1812 (*Papers*, *MHS*, pp. 174–176); also, Jan. 8, 1813 (LC).

a great improvement on Eustis.[14] Commenting on military leadership, he said: "It is unfortunate that heaven has not set its stamp on the forehead of those whom it has qualified for military achievement, that it has left us to draw for them in a lottery of so many blanks to a prize, and where the blank is to be manifested only by the public misfortunes." Later events were to cast serious doubt on Armstrong's own qualifications, but to him belongs the credit for promoting Andrew Jackson, Jacob Brown, and Winfield Scott.

Jefferson seems to have made no reference to the potential value of the academy at West Point in training military commanders as well as engineers, but the events of the war deepened his conviction that the militia system must be reformed, and led him to advocate universal military training. Writing Monroe, who was envious of Armstrong and whom Jefferson continued to prefer on military as well as on personal and political grounds, he attributed the delay in recruiting to the happiness of the people at home. There was all the more necessity, therefore, to oblige every citizen to be a soldier. Such was the case with the Greeks and Romans, and must be in every free state. "We must train and classify the whole of our male citizens and make military instruction a regular part of collegiate education. We can never be safe till this is done."[15] Toward the end of the war he expressed the same ideas even more forcibly. He then attributed the military misfortunes of the country to the failure to classify the militia and to bring it under greater national control.[16]

ii

Jefferson's comments on military affairs were marked by good sense and showed that, despite his excess of confidence at the outset, he was more realistic and more forward-looking than the congressional majority, as he had been during his own presidency. He discussed these affairs most fully with Monroe, who unbosomed himself to his old friend and to whom Jefferson was less reluctant to make suggestions than to Madison. Writing Monroe, he said the unwarranted charges that he intermeddled in the executive councils, and the "indecent expressions" of hope

[14] TJ to Armstrong, Feb. 8, 1813 (L. & B., XIII, 220–222). The occasion of this letter was the transmission of the private communication criticizing General Alexander Smyth to which we have previously referred.

[15] TJ to Monroe, June 18, 1813 (L. & B., XIII, 261).

[16] TJ to Monroe, Oct. 16, 1814; to W. H. Crawford, Feb. 11, 1815 (Ford, IX, 492, 502–503). See *Jefferson the President: Second Term*, p. 514.

that his successor would pursue *his* principles, made it improper for him to hazard advice to Madison. Also, he was conscious that his views must be imperfect because of the incompleteness of his information.[17]

His comments on naval matters did, in fact, reflect the inadequacy of his information, and in this connection he made some impracticable suggestions. Thus he advocated the keeping of the frigates together in a body in a safe place from which they could easily sally forth. But, as Monroe reported, the naval officers were convinced that if the frigates were stationed in some port, like New York, the British would immediately block it up and harass the coast at will. This reasoning was fully accepted by the Squire of Monticello, who repeatedly expressed his pride and gratification at "the brilliant achievements of our little navy."[18]

To the President he made a suggestion with a view to breaking the blockade of Chesapeake Bay that was bottling up the wheat of Maryland and Virginia. In this instance his own interests and those of his neighbors were involved. Early in the spring of 1813 he had between four and five hundred barrels of unsold flour in Richmond. Thomas Mann Randolph, who raised crops so much better than he marketed them, was worse off. He had withheld 2650 barrels of flour from the market in the expectation of benefiting from the rise in price.[19] When his hopes were disappointed that the British vessels would depart from Lynnhaven Bay after the equinoctial storms, Jefferson expressed the opinion that they could be effectively assailed by gunboats stationed there. Recognizing, however, that these would be vulnerable to land attack, he suggested the building of a canal, six or eight miles in length, to the Elizabeth River. This would serve as an avenue of escape. In reply, while speaking respectfully of gunboats, Madison said that the Bay could be effectively blockaded by cruisers outside the Capes, beyond the reach of the gunboats.[20]

Since this episode was not publicized, it may be presumed to have occasioned Jefferson only slight embarrassment. Such was certainly not the case with another episode a little later. Toward the end of 1813 a Federalist paper in Philadelphia printed an extract from a private letter of his, written a couple of months earlier. In this he voiced his detesta-

[17] TJ to Monroe, May 30, 1813 (L. & B., XIII, 250–253). Monroe's letter of June 7, 1813 (S.M.H., V, 259–268), which was unusually long because of his inability to write TJ during the congressional session, exemplified the fullness and frankness of his communications.

[18] He made this suggestion in his letter of May 30, 1813, to Monroe, who replied to it June 16 (S.M.H., V, 268–270). See also TJ to Monroe, June 18 (L. & B., XIII, 262).

[19] TJ to S. J. Harrison, Apr. 3, 1813, and to John Barnes, Apr. 23 (*Farm Book*, pp. 212–213; Gaines, pp. 83–84).

[20] TJ to Madison, May 21, 1813 (Ford, IX, 381–384); Madison to TJ, June 6 (MP).

tion of Napoleon, describing him as "the unprincipled tyrant who is deluging the Continent of Europe with blood." At the same time the ex-President expressed his gratification at the recent disasters of the unprincipled French Emperor in Russia and the successes of "the virtuous Alexander."[21] From this extract alone it would seem that, at a time when his own country was at war with the British, he was siding with them against their inveterate foe, and his strong language was particularly disturbing to members of his own party who retained pro-French sentiments. One of these, his old landlord in Philadelphia, Thomas Leiper, wrote him in dismay, saying that he hoped the quotation was a forgery. Similar incredulity was expressed by a contributor to the Richmond *Enquirer*, which had promptly reprinted the extract. Its authenticity was quickly confirmed by the newspaper that had first printed it, as it was early in the new year by Jefferson, who in a private letter explained just what had happened.[22]

The quotation was from a letter of his replying to one from Dr. George Logan, a Quaker. This former supporter of his had once gained favor in Republican circles, and reprobation in Federalist, for his efforts to prevent war with France. A doctrinaire pacifist now seeking to end the war with Great Britain, he besought Jefferson to ask Madison to "come forward with just and honorable proposals for peace." He was entirely confident that these would be accepted. Instead of brushing him off as a visionary, Jefferson wrote him a long account of Anglo-American relations, leaving no doubt of his own conviction that the object of procuring a just peace would be "best promoted by a vigorous and unanimous prosecution of the war."[23] As he explained to Leiper, the references to Napoleon, while indisputable, were incidental. They were being quoted wholly out of context by a former friend who had become a "bigoted partisan of England, and malcontent of his own government." This breach of confidence had caused the former President to be dragged into the newspapers when he had hoped to pass the evening of his life in tranquillity, undisturbed by their peltings and passions.

Apart from his extreme distaste for public controversy there were patriotic considerations which would probably have been sufficient in themselves to deter him from making a public reply. Any answer from him, he said, would have involved an avowal and might have embar-

[21] *Poulson's American Daily Advertiser*, Dec. 6, 1813, quoting from a letter of TJ's to a gentleman in Pennsylvania, Oct. 3, 1813. On TJ's relations with and admiration for Tsar Alexander I, see *Jefferson the President: Second Term*, ch. XXIV.

[22] *Poulson's*, Dec. 11, 1813; Richmond *Enquirer*, Dec. 11, 1813, and communication signed "Common Sense," Dec. 13; Thos. Leiper to TJ, Dec. 9, 1813 (LC); TJ to Leiper, Jan. 1, 1814 (Ford, IX, 443–446).

[23] Logan to TJ, Sept. 18, 1813 (LC); TJ to Logan, Oct. 3, 1813 (Ford, IX, 421–423).

rassed the administration in the event of a French protest.[24] He said afterwards that the French minister did lodge an informal complaint, and that he had thought it incumbent on him to explain to a member of the government that this was a partial and unauthorized publication. He explained himself fully to Thomas Leiper, authorizing him to pass the word on to their friends, but he said nothing at the time to the man who had abused his confidence. Logan, seemingly oblivious of his infidelity, and believing no doubt that the sacred cause of peace fully justified his action, wrote Jefferson again in behalf of peace.[25] Presumably that aggrieved gentleman thought that further argument would be wasted on this correspondent and that the wise course was to give him nothing further to reveal. Apparently he did not know that Timothy Pickering had discussed the extract with Logan, referring to its author as "the arch hypocrite." A couple of years later, after peace had been attained, he told Logan that this publication had produced more complaints from his best friends and had called for more explanation than any other transaction of his life. He may have been exaggerating, but by that time he had further ground for indignation since Logan had betrayed his confidence again.[26] Late in the summer of 1815, he sent Jefferson an extract about the emperor Napoleon. Replying to this after some weeks, Jefferson referred to the Tsar, to the prospective peace settlement in Europe, and to the British and Napoleon. It was not a notably severe letter, but Jefferson was appalled when it appeared in a newspaper. He became aware of this when he was just on the point of answering another letter which Logan had had the effrontery to write him.[27]

In a letter of his own which was evoked by these circumstances Jefferson not only rebuked Logan for his betrayal of confidence, but drew a distinction between private and public communications of which would-be interpreters of his vast correspondence should be aware.[28] He said that anyone entering the arena of public controversy must weigh every sentiment or fact, every sentence and syllable and be ready to defend them in debate. But the situation was quite different in private correspondence. "We are careless, incorrect, in haste, perhaps under some transient excitement, and we hazard things without reflection, because without consequence in the bosom of a friend." He did less than justice to the thousands of personal letters he wrote during his long life, but a

[24] Unprinted postscript in letter of Jan. 1, 1814, to Leiper (LC).

[25] Logan to TJ, Dec. 9, 1813 (LC).

[26] Timothy Pickering to Logan, Jan. 29, 1814 (Frances A. Logan, ed., *Memoir of Dr. George Logan . . . with Selections from His Correspondence* [Philadelphia, 1899], pp. 191–192); also Feb. 24, 1816 (*ibid.*, pp. 192–202).

[27] Logan to TJ, Apr. 27, 1816 (LC). TJ's letter of Oct. 13, 1815, which Logan gave to the press, is in L. & B., XIV, 354–355, under the incorrect date of Oct. 15.

[28] TJ to Logan, May 14, 1816 (Ford, X, 26–27).

fair number of them, including some that were destined to be widely quoted, reflected the attitude he described, being couched in more extravagant language than he would have used in public or after reflection. In retrospect he regarded his censure of Napoleon as very just, but when torn from its context, it gave an erroneous impression; and in any case it was not meant to be published and should not have been without his permission. In a later letter, replying to Logan's assertion of good intentions, he said he did not question these, but that he was insisting on the sanctity of private correspondence. As for the slanders of his political enemies, he said: "I never wished them to be answered, but by the tenor of my life, half a century of which has been on a theatre at which the public have been spectators, and competent judges of its merit. . . . I should have fancied myself half guilty had I condescended to put pen to paper in refutation of their [his enemies'] falsehoods, or drawn to them respect by any notice from myself."[29] This was, in fact, his consistent policy with respect to scandalmongers, and no doubt he would have recommended its employment in any age.

iii

From the time that war became imminent Jefferson was subjected to pressure from friends and acquaintances who wanted to get into military service as officers, and even from persons he did not know. He claimed that he declined most solicitations, but it was hard for him to refuse to transmit applications.[30] Writing Madison shortly before the declaration of war, he distinguished between communication and solicitation and transmitted with virtually no comment letters that had come to him. He was always sensitive and always scrupulous regarding relatives — of whom he had an embarrassingly large number. In one case of the sort, while giving the applicant a letter to the Secretary of War which truthfully described the good points of this relative, he wrote Madison in confidence about a couple of bad ones he was aware of — namely, that the applicant was a zealous Federalist and a quarrelsome fellow.[31] Occasionally he went out of his way to commend a friend, as he did to the Secretary of War in the instance of Robert Carter Nicholas, without that officer's solicitation.[32] After hostilities had ended he told Monroe he had capitulated all too often to the importunities of friends, acquaintances, and even strangers, and in that very letter he mentioned the desire of a friend for a commission for his son.[33] His activities of this sort had been

[29] TJ to Logan, June 20, 1816 (*ibid.*, 27*n*.).
[30] For his earlier resolution on this subject, see above, p. 27.
[31] TJ to Madison, May 2, 1812 (LC); May 25, 30, 1812 (Ford, IX, 353–354).
[32] TJ to John Armstrong, Feb. 21, 1813 (Ford, XX, 381).
[33] TJ to Monroe, Jan. 21, 1815 (LC).

laborious to him and, as he believed, "embarrassing and unpleasant to the government." But neither Madison nor Monroe appears to have thought so, and there is no reason to suppose that his actions were injurious to the country.

He had nothing to do with the appointment of Thomas Mann Randolph as a colonel in the United States Army. His son-in-law, already a lieutenant colonel in the Virginia militia, was recommended by Congressman William A. Burwell and commissioned by President Madison on March 3, 1813. Writing an old friend a couple of months later, Jefferson said: "Mr. Randolph has been seized with the military fever. He expects to be called to his regiment this month. He will be a great loss to his family, and no man in the world a greater one to his affairs."[34] Actually, the call did not come until late summer, but in the meantime Colonel Randolph was engaged in recruiting, since the 20th Regiment of Infantry, to which he was assigned, was far below authorized strength. On August 11 he was ordered to Sackets Harbor on Lake Ontario and during the fall he served under General James Wilkinson on the Canadian border.[35]

The state of his affairs at this time was enough to disturb his father-in-law, who could now walk no farther than the garden and who at this stage was under-rating his own durability, if not his strength. The 2650 barrels of flour Randolph had kept from the market remained unsold and, just before he departed, he told his father-in-law that he intended to give up the lease of the manufacturing mill. What actually happened was that his son took over the management in his absence. A satisfactory performance was expected of Jeff by his grandfather, but that elderly gentleman admitted in the fall that there had been discouragements.[36]

The Colonel was at home on leave before Christmas. The expedition down the St. Lawrence that started in November met reverses and the attack on Montreal was called off. He endured hardships without complaint, saw some fighting, and in general conducted himself well, but he had no stomach for winter quarters. Nor had he any taste for the recruiting, which he was asked to resume before the winter was over. His intimation that, rather than engage in it, he would resign his commission was accepted as a resignation. This was in February, 1814. He got out of the army with what now appears to have been surprising ease, and he did not return to military service until summer, when, as an officer of

[34] TJ to Mrs. Elizabeth Trist, May 10, 1813 (*Glimpses of the Past: Correspondence of Thomas Jefferson* [1936], p. 120).

[35] Gaines, pp. 83–89.

[36] TJ to Youen Garden, a former employee, Aug. 20, 1813; to TMR, Nov. 14 (*Farm Book*, pp. 394–395).

the militia, he was called to the defense of Richmond against the threat of British invasion.[37]

The Monticello family was well represented in the military service in the darkest period of the war. Toward the end of August, 1814, Jefferson reported that all of the young men of his area were "thronging to the standard of their country." His son-in-law and grandson had already set out and his grandson-in-law was doing so. In a letter to a colonel of the militia that was borne by young Charles Bankhead, the former President also made the following statement: "If I were able either to walk or ride I would join them."[38] Irrespective of his temporary inability to ride, at seventy-one he was warranted in identifying himself with the "silver greys" who must remain at home, but such an expression of personal belligerency was unusual in this inveterate civilian. No doubt it reflected his desperation at this time of grave danger. With the cessation of hostilities in Europe, Wellington's veterans had been released for service in America. The force invading the country from Canada by way of Lake Champlain constituted much the greater peril, but the contingent under Major General Robert Ross that landed on the shore of Chesapeake Bay imposed a threat, not only on Washington, but on the whole of that region. Fearing for Richmond, the Governor of Virginia had called out the militia.

Thomas Mann Randolph, who had retained his old rank of lieutenant colonel in the militia, might not qualify as a young man now that he was nearing forty-six, but he had by no means recovered from his military fever. His assignment would have been important if the British had actually moved against Richmond. He was placed in command of a mobile force of some six hundred men and assigned the task of guarding the approaches to the city.[39] He had the capacity to win the devotion of his men, whose hardships he shared, and to inspire them with military ardor, but he had no taste for administration and owed his personal popularity in considerable part to the laxity of his discipline. His son Jeff served as a private in an artillery company commanded by Captain William Wirt. Writing his grandfather from Richmond after he had heard of the sack of Washington, he said: "God forbid that I should have been last to come forward in defence of my country, for which I should always be proud to sacrifice my life." A little later, encamped in King and

[37] Gaines, pp. 89–93. Meanwhile, he served as collector of federal revenue in his congressional district.

[38] TJ to Col. Charles Yancey, Aug. 29, 1814 (LC), replying to a letter of Aug. 22 (LC). TJ asked Yancey to do what he could for Bankhead, who was going as a volunteer.

[39] There is an excellent account of this episode in TMR's military career in Gaines, pp. 93–100.

Queen County near the headwaters of the York River — up which it was thought the British might come — he reported that the troops lacked everything necessary for the support of an army, though admirably supplied with ticks and mosquitoes. Toward the end of September, weary of waiting for the invaders, he took off for home, as did Francis Walker Gilmer, the Carr brothers, and presumably Charles Bankhead.[40] Lieutenant Colonel Randolph stayed a little longer, but this phase of his military career, like the earlier one, ended in frustration. He returned home to find that crops were bad and taxes rising.

Jefferson had probably learned of the humiliating happenings in Washington before he heard from his grandson about affairs on the Richmond front. Three days after the British entered the Federal City his favorite paper, the *Enquirer*, reported that the Capitol and the President's House were in ruins.[41] He may be presumed to have read this account, and a few days later he received in a private letter a firsthand report of the battle of Bladensburg, which immediately preceded the fall of the city.[42] "Sad arrangements," said this writer, "sad doings indeed, treachery I think, cowardice I saw, the Maryland militia won't fight. No Va. soldiers in this battle."

Before he got the letter Jefferson could have read in the *Enquirer* about events in Alexandria, then in the District of Columbia, events which caused that patriotic paper to thank God that "this degraded town" was no longer a part of Virginia.[43] Following the surrender of Fort Warburton on the Potomac below Alexandria, a delegation was dispatched to ask terms from the invaders and capitulation "at discretion" ensued. Said the indignant *Enquirer:* "We would scorn to live in the same state with men who would stoop to kiss the foot of a British officer, and throw themselves upon his discretion." This paper suggested that these men had been contaminated by British influence. In fact Alexandria, a commercial town, was strongly Federalist in spirit. Ironically, its present mayor, Charles Simms, was believed to have initiated an unfounded charge against Jefferson which had hounded that gentleman throughout his subsequent career. In 1796 Simms asserted that Jefferson, as governor of Virginia during the Revolution, had displayed cowardice in the face of British invasion.[44] This appeared to be a clear case of the pot's calling the kettle black.

[40] TJR to TJ, Aug. 31, Sept. 9, 1814 (*Family Letters*, pp. 406–408); William Wirt to his wife, Sept. 26, 1814 (J. P. Kennedy, *Memoirs of the Life of William Wirt*, I [1850], 337).

[41] Richmond *Enquirer*, Aug. 27, 1814.

[42] J. W. Wallace from Fauquier, Va., to TJ, Aug. 29, 1814; received Sept. 9 (LC). Wallace also wrote TJ from Dumfries, Sept. 7, and from Aquia, Sept. 13 (LC).

[43] Richmond *Enquirer*, Aug. 31, 1814; other accounts Sept. 3, 7, 14.

[44] See *Jefferson and the Ordeal of Liberty*, pp. 279–280. I am assuming that the Charles Simms of 1814 was the same man.

Jefferson seems to have made no reference to the parallel but his remembrance of past personal attacks and his awareness of present political alignments could hardly have lessened his patriotic indignation. Responding to a dolorous letter from John W. Eppes, he expressed himself with a vehemence such as he generally displayed only against those he regarded as traitors to the country or to the sacred cause of republicanism. He hoped the law would lay hold on Simms and company, "if it could lay hold on anything after the experiment on Burr." He believed that Congress could punish Alexandria "by repealing the law which made it a town, by discontinuing it as a port of entry or clearance, and perhaps by suppressing its banks." He said he did not expect anything of the sort to happen, but he was certainly blowing off steam with extreme violence. And, at a time when the prospects of his country were at their blackest, this congenital optimist pointed to a weakness in its government, perhaps a fatal one, which he may indeed have previously perceived but which he did not normally emphasize. "No government can be maintained without the principle of fear as well as of duty," he said. "Good men will obey the last, but bad ones the former only."[45]

Within a couple of weeks some good news reached Monticello. The invaders were repelled at Fort McHenry, below Baltimore, and Francis Scott Key's verses about the star-spangled banner were printed in the *Enquirer* toward the end of September, though Jefferson is not known to have referred to them.[46] Details of a more important success, that of Thomas Macdonough on Lake Champlain, leading to the abandonment of the invasion by that route, were slow in coming through, but Jefferson congratulated Madison on this "countervailing event" when writing him a month after the British entered Washington.[47] For the late events at Bladensburg and the ravage of the capital he laid no blame whatever on the chief executive, whose goodness and wisdom he never questioned. He said every sensible person knew that a President could only issue orders and must leave the execution of them to others. He believed that probably the same thing would have happened if George Washington had been in Madison's place.

He discussed the matter of responsibility for the disaster more fully at a later time, after he had received Monroe's version of events. He then said: "I never doubted that the plans of the President were wise and sufficient." And, although he mentioned no names in his letter of sympathy to his successor, he afterwards attributed the failure to the "insubordinate temper" of Armstrong, the Secretary of War, and to the

[45] TJ to JWE, Sept. 9, 1814 (Ford, IX, 484), replying to a despondent letter of Sept. 7 (LC).

[46] Richmond *Enquirer*, Sept. 28, 1816; report that Baltimore was saved, Sept. 17.

[47] TJ to Madison, Sept. 24, 1814 (LC).

"indecision" of General William Henry Winder, the hapless commander at Bladensburg.[48] While historians are still arguing about these matters, according to their custom, few are so charitable to Madison with respect to his choice and direction of his subordinates.

In the grim autumn of 1814, Jefferson's indignation was chiefly directed against the British. He wrote Monroe that the events in Washington "disgrace our enemies much more than us." That is, he deplored their brutal destructiveness. When he learned that the negotiations at Ghent were on the point of breaking down, he said that the British had changed the whole character of the conflict and that Americans must now prepare for "interminable war."[49] They must put their house in order "by providing men and money to indefinite extent."[50]

The war years were bad ones for Jefferson as a farmer. In the summer of 1813 he wrote Madison that he had the poorest wheat harvest he had ever seen. There had been only one rain to wet the ground since April, and he expected to carry to his barn not more than a third of a normal crop. His gardens were totally burned up, and it was possible to jump across the Rivanna at places. He had some hopes of his corn, but the rain did not come soon enough. He wrote his brother Randolph in August that instead of seven to eight hundred barrels of corn he would make about thirty. He would have to send his stock to Bedford to winter. He was now describing the drought as the worst one since 1755.[51]

That same summer, when Jefferson's fields were so parched, there was a real estate boom in Richmond. Of this he took advantage on behalf of Philip Mazzei, now in Italy, whose American affairs had been left in his hands much as had those of Kosciuszko. He sold two lots belonging to Mazzei for more than $6000, which he said was six times what his friend originally paid for them. Since he was unable to send this money abroad during the war, he was faced with the problem of reinvesting it. Being highly distrustful of the banks, he was unwilling to put it into bank stock and did not want to tie it up in long-range government securities. Therefore, he retained it as a temporary loan to himself on which interest would be duly paid. No exception to this temporary disposition of what was in fact a windfall was taken by Mazzei and his heirs. After the war

[48] TJ to Monroe, Jan. 1, 1815 (Ford, IX, 496), replying to Monroe's letter of Dec. 21, 1814 (S.M.H., V, 303–306). TJ believed that he was voicing the prevalent opinion in Virginia.

[49] TJ to Monroe, Sept. 24, 1814 (Ford, IX, 488–489); Monroe to TJ, Oct. 10, informing him of developments at Ghent (S.M.H., V, 299–300); TJ to Monroe, Oct. 16 (Ford, IX, 492).

[50] For his suggestions on public finance, see ch. X, below.

[51] TJ to Madison, July 13, 1813 (*Garden Book*, p. 502); TJ to Randolph Jefferson, Aug. 8, 1813 (*Thomas Jefferson and His Unknown Brother Randolph*, ed. by Bernard Mayo [1942], p. 84).

the latter, who distrusted the financial management of the elderly Florentine, preferred that the principal be kept out of his faltering hands for a while longer. The embarrassing developments of later years need not concern us yet.[52] Suffice it to say here that in an abnormal time Jefferson eased his immediate difficulties by incurring another debt on the assumption that things would surely get better.

They did not get better. In 1814 he again had a short crop of wheat, and because of the British blockade he and his neighbors had great difficulty marketing what little they had. Actually wheat was being eaten by laborers and horses because the price had fallen below that of corn.[53] That was still the case in the fall and winter following the British raid on Washington. Writing his friend Mrs. Elizabeth Trist the day after Christmas, Jefferson said, however, that things were not quite as bad as they seemed: "We are feeding our horses with our wheat," he said, "and looking at the taxes coming on us as an approaching wave in a storm; still I think we shall live as long, eat as much, and drink as much, as if the wave had already glided under the ship. Somehow or other these things find their way out as they come in, and so I suppose they will now."[54]

Such optimism was characteristic of him, but by this time in fact he had reason to believe that his fortunes, as well as those of the country, would soon improve. Not until the summer of 1815 did he receive from Benjamin H. Latrobe a detailed account of the destruction at the Capitol, but from the first reports he had learned that the congressional library had been burned. He immediately seized on the opportunity to offer his own magnificent collection of books as a replacement and he was to be occupied for many months in the transaction that ensued. By means of it he became to all practical purposes the founder of one of the world's greatest libraries and at the same time he gained from the sale a measure of financial relief. That story deserves treatment by itself.[55] By Christmas he had learned from Monroe that, far from being given up, the negotiations at Ghent were nearing completion. He had to wait several months to find out what the terms of peace really were, and the affairs of Europe remained in uncertain state for some time thereafter. News reached Monticello slowly, but sooner or later Jefferson commented extensively on the era that was passing and the significance of these historic events.

[52] This episode and its consequences are more fully described in Appendix II, Section D.

[53] TJ to Madison, Mar. 10, 1814 (*Garden Book*, pp. 525–526).

[54] TJ to Mrs. Elizabeth Trist, Dec. 26, 1814 (*ibid.*, p. 526).

[55] See ch. XII.

[IX]

The Meaning of the Peace

EARLY in December, 1814, Jefferson learned from Monroe that peace negotiations had been resumed at Ghent and few difficulties remained.[1] The British were still trying to retain territory in Maine of which they had gained possession. They had not yet yielded to the insistence of the Americans that the *status quo ante bellum* be restored. Impressment was no longer an issue, however, since that question had been laid aside. This news was most unwelcome to Jefferson, who never ceased believing that impressment was a major cause of the war, and who said repeatedly in the next few months that the settlement could be no more than a truce as long as this question remained. He counted on the suspension of the practice of impressment while the European nations were at peace, but on the basis of past experience he had little reason to expect them to continue so. Monroe's report could not have failed to bring him temporary relief, but it was not exhilarating. News of the glorious victory of Andrew Jackson at New Orleans, which reached him two months later, should have been, but he was said to have received this with seeming indifference.[2]

At the time, he had as visitors two young Bostonians, George Ticknor and Francis C. Gray, who had brought letters of introduction from John Adams. Their memorable visit, which signalized in some sense the national recognition of the ex-President as the Sage of Monticello, will be described more fully hereafter in another connection. Ticknor, regaling his father with fascinating comments on the host and household, reported two incidents in which Jefferson manifested surprising imperturbability. One morning, on returning from his daily ride, he stated quietly to his son-in-law that his dam had been carried away the night before. From his manner his young guest supposed this to be a matter

[1] Monroe to TJ, Nov. 30, 1814 (S.M.H., V, 300–301).

[2] He got the news about Feb. 4, 1815. The battle occurred on Jan. 8.

of small concern, but Ticknor was informed afterwards that $30,000 would be required to repair the damage.[3]

The other incident occurred the night before the departure of the two Bostonians. After they had gone to bed young Randolph brought from Charlottesville the astounding news of the British defeat at New Orleans. Presumably the report created considerable excitement in the household, but into this Jefferson did not enter. Declining to open his door, he said he would wait till morning, and at breakfast time next day he had not yet seen the newspaper account.

It would appear that the septuagenarian had learned to maintain his equanimity under virtually any circumstance, but as a mill owner he was undoubtedly distressed by what had happened on the Rivanna, and as an ardent patriot he was unquestionably glad to learn that the Mississippi was still flowing unhampered to the sea. If the British had captured and retained New Orleans, as according to Ticknor he had believed they would, his long effort to keep the Father of Waters open would have been nullified. In due course he manifested great pride in the deeds of his countrymen. Within a few weeks, when writing his friend Kosciuszko in Paris, he spoke exultantly of the "brilliant transactions" at New Orleans and seemed almost to gloat over the British casualties. Soon thereafter, in a letter to Francis Gray, he congratulated this recent visitor on the peace and more especially on the "éclat" with which the war ended.[4]

News of the treaty of peace arrived about ten days after that of Jackson's victory, and a round of congratulations followed. It now appeared that the Republic had emerged from the conflict without loss. This relatively favorable outcome was attributed by many to Divine Providence, but some of those who wrote the ex-President recognized human agency. Said one of them: "Next to that Good Being who has kindly guided this great people to their present happy state, I feel an emotion of gratitude to Mr. Jefferson which I have not language to express."[5] The old patriot had had little to do with the war but he shared the euphoria that followed the peace and on his own part did a good deal of boasting. He went to particular pains to describe developments in letters to friends abroad with whom his correspondence had been interrupted during the war. Some of these letters were very slow in reaching their destination, and others seem never to have been received by the persons for whom

[3] George to Elisha Ticknor, Feb. 7, 1815 (*Life, Letters, and Journals*, pp. 34–38, reprinted in F. C. Rosenberger, ed., *Jefferson Reader* [1953], pp. 84–85). Gray referred to the same episode (*ibid.*, p. 80). See also Pierson, p. 62.

[4] TJ to Kosciuszko, Mar. 1, 1815 (MHS); to Francis C. Gray, Mar. 4, 1815 (L. & B., XIV, 270). He used the word "éclat" in other letters, apparently liking it.

[5] Josiah Meigs to TJ, Feb. 16, 1815 (LC).

they were intended. They are no less significant, however, as expressions of his judgment.[6]

While he had by no means banished his fears of future conflict with the British and at this time was urging the reform of the militia system and the regularization of the finances of the country, the recent events of the war had increased his confidence in the prowess and loyalty of his countrymen. To the Marquis de Lafayette he wrote that Americans had so clearly established their superiority over their recent enemies at sea with equal force that the British did not allow their frigates to cruise alone. Not only could they be beaten on their own element, ship for ship. He wrote General Kosciuszko that recent military actions had proved that, when well commanded, both American regulars and militiamen were superior to British regulars. Dismissing late events in Washington and disregarding the British presence in New England during the last months of the war, he asserted that, if it had gone on, American standards could have been planted on the walls of Quebec in one campaign, and on those of Halifax in another. Characteristically seeking to present American affairs in the best possible light to friends abroad, he did not admit that the conflict had really ended in a draw.

He could hardly have avoided reference to the dissatisfaction that had been manifested by pro-British New Englanders throughout the war and most recently in the Hartford Convention. He minimized that gathering, as at this stage he well might, since the "ambassadors" from it arrived in Washington with their demands when the country was exulting in victory and peace. Furthermore, he sincerely believed in the loyalty of the overwhelming majority of his countrymen. He thus expressed himself to Lafayette: "The cement of the Union is in the heartblood of every American. I do not believe there is on earth a government established on so immovable a basis."[7] He spoke of Marats, Dantons, and Robespierres in Massachusetts who were seeking to "anarchise" their country, but he was confident that even in that state anyone attempting to raise the "standard of separation" would be quickly put down by a mass uprising. And he reported that the incendiaries had not been able to make themselves even a subject of conversation but had been treated with "silent contempt."[8]

In a letter introducing to Jefferson one of the young visitors from Bos-

[6] Special mention should be made of his letter of Feb. 14, 1815, to Lafayette (*Letters of Lafayette and Jefferson*, ed. by Gilbert Chinard [1929], pp. 367–375), which was not received for more than two years; and that of Mar. 1, 1815, to Gen. Kosciuszko (MHS), which seems never to have been received.

[7] *Letters of Lafayette and Jefferson*, p. 371.

[8] It is not clear whether he was referring specifically to the Hartford Convention or to those he supposed to have been its most extreme members.

ton, shortly before the Hartford Convention began, John Adams had said: "If he can explain to you the incomprehensible Politicks of New England, he can do more than I shall or can pretend to do." And, when Henry Dearborn congratulated his old chief on the peace, he expressed extreme mortification as a citizen of Massachusetts at the conduct of his state.[9] Jefferson was not disposed to discuss unpleasant topics with Adams, but he addressed himself to the erring sister in his reply to his old secretary of war:

> Oh, Massachusetts! how have I lamented the degradation of your apostasy! Massachusetts, with whom I went with pride in 1776, whose vote was my vote on every public question, and whose principles were then the standard of whatever was free or fearless.[10]

As he noted, that was when she was under the counsels of John and Samuel Adams, and he predicted that she would be as nothing among the states under her present leaders. But if she should again "buckle on the republican harness," she would be received as a sister and her wanderings would be blamed on the "parricides" and "venal traitors" who had temporarily conducted her affairs.

The sincerity of the veteran's patriotic indignation cannot be doubted, but he had fallen into the sort of rhetorical excess that he allowed himself in private among the faithful, and his exhortation smacked of the self-righteousness he deplored in his New England foes. No doubt it would have excited a passionate reaction if it had been publicized, as fortunately it was not. But in his chiding of Massachusetts he probably reflected the predominant sentiments of his own region. Continuing, he said:

> Let us look forward, then, to the act of repentance, . . . and if her humiliation can just give her modesty enough to suppose that her Southern brethren are somewhat on a par with her in wisdom, in information, in patriotism, in bravery, and even in honesty, although not in psalm-singing, she will more justly estimate her own relative momentum in the Union. With her ancient principles, she would really be great, if she did not think herself the whole.

There was to be no such reconciliation between Massachusetts and Virginia as that between Adams and Jefferson. The two commonwealths arrived at no comparable understanding before the two old men died, and the grievances of commercial New Englanders against Jefferson were

[9] Adams to TJ, Dec. 11, 1814; Dearborn to TJ, Feb. 27, 1815 (LC).
[10] TJ to Dearborn, Mar. 17, 1815 (L. & B., XIV, 288).

George Ticknor

Portrait by Thomas Sully, ca. 1831. (Courtesy of the Hood Museum of Art, Dartmouth College, Hanover, NH; gift of Constance V. R. White, Nathaniel T. Dexter, Philip Dexter, and Mary Ann Streeter)

not soon to be forgotten. But the High Federalists, who most disliked him, were now discredited; and before long, even in New England, the image of the recent President was to be obscured, though certainly not obliterated, by that of the living Sage. John Adams used the term when he introduced George Ticknor — saying that the most exalted of the young geniuses of Boston wanted to see him and his house and his books. Between the Sage of Monticello and New England's intelligentsia there was, and has never ceased to be, a kinship of the mind.

Jefferson claimed that the great "revolutions" that occurred in the world after he left office had left him undisturbed. Writing his former attorney general, Caesar A. Rodney, he said: "To me they have been like the howlings of the winter storm over the battlements, while warm in my bed."[11] His mind had certainly not been dominated by world affairs, but he made comments on them that are not without interest to posterity. These were not always timely, for his knowledge lagged behind events in Europe. Viewing the distant scene from Monticello shortly before the spring equinox in 1815, he told Rodney: "The unprincipled tyrant of the land is fallen, his power reduced to its original nothingness." In fact, Napoleon had returned from Elba by this time and was to enter Paris four days later. Jefferson's comments on that conquerer were subject to temporary revision. But events were not to invalidate his observation that the "tyrant of the ocean," whom he regarded as equally unprincipled with the dethroned Emperor, was still stalking in power over the deep.

He had lost none of his distrust of the British government, but in the mood of euphoria that was induced by the advent of peace he expressed the hope that American relations with the mother country would change. In the same letter he said: "There is not a nation on the globe with whom I have more earnestly wished a friendly intercourse on equal conditions." Far from being personally hostile to the British, as had been often charged, he would sacrifice more to be friends with them than with any other people. "They can do us, as enemies, more harm than any other nation," he continued, "and in peace and in war, they have more means of disturbing us internally." In part his words anticipated those he addressed to the President of the United States in 1823, shortly before the pronouncement of the Monroe Doctrine.[12] At this stage he held that Americans must remain on guard. As he presently told Secretary of State Monroe, he believed that the first impressment of an American

[11] TJ to C. A. Rodney, Mar. 16, 1815 (*ibid.*, 284–287).

[12] For his famous letter of Oct. 24, 1823, to Monroe, see Ford, X, 277.

should be regarded as a declaration of war.[13] He would hold out the hand of friendship only on the basis of equality, he said. Not that he was seeking to match British power on the sea; he did not speak of that and no doubt still regarded it as an impossibility. What he did speak of again and again was the attainment of a greater degree of economic self-sufficiency. It was for that reason that he was laying so much stress on the development of manufacturing.[14] While he had no thought of abandoning Old World culture, he was personally resolved to use only articles of domestic manufacture when these were available.

He had long regarded the New England Anglophiles as subservient to Great Britain in spirit, whereas he himself had sought to maintain full independence and to attain a status of equality. On that basis he believed that friendship between the two countries would be mutually beneficial. Nowhere did he voice his hopes better than in his letters to James Maury, the former schoolmate now living in England.[15] They had scanned Virgil together nearly threescore years before. Inviting this old friend to look forward through a period of that length, he predicted that the United States would then have a population of eighty millions. His estimate was too high but he was abundantly warranted in pointing out that friendship with his rapidly growing country would be increasingly important to the British. He ended one of his letters to this boyhood companion with a moving passage:

> No one feels more indignation than myself when reflecting on the insults and injuries of that country to this. But the interests of both require that these should be left to history, and in the meantime be smothered in the living mind. I have indeed little personal concern in it. Time is drawing her curtain on me. But I should make my bow with more satisfaction, if I had more hope of seeing our countries shake hands together cordially.[16]

Full cordiality was to be slow in coming, but the basic causes of his own anti-British sentiment were destined to disappear before he made his final bow.

[13] TJ to Monroe, July 15, 1815 (LC).

[14] See ch. X, below, for a discussion of this.

[15] TJ to James Maury, June 15, 16, 1815 (L. & B., XIV, 311–319). On their early association, see *Jefferson the Virginian*, p. 42.

[16] L. & B., XIV, 315. Though his letters to Maury were relatively hopeful, he said much in them about the impressment question and the continued hostility of the British government.

* * *

Never was he to lose his affection for France. In the autobiography he began to write when seventy-seven he said that, like others who had traveled there, he would rather live in France than in any other country except his own.[17] As respected the public interest, however, he could now view that humbled nation with relative indifference, since the United States had nothing either to fear or to hope from it. He had long had a low opinion of its government, and when he learned from the newspapers that Napoleon had abdicated he described the fallen Emperor to John Adams as the Attila of the age, a ruthless destroyer whose thirst for human blood seemed unquenchable. Regarding him as merely a military man, Jefferson said: "Bonaparte was a lion in the field only. In civil life a cold-blooded, calculating, unprincipled usurper, without a virtue, no statesman, knowing nothing of commerce, political economy, or civil government, and supplying ignorance by bold presumption."[18] Before the end of his days, on the basis of fuller information, he revised his opinion of Napoleon's intelligence, but he never ceased to regard him as a monster.[19]

Several months after his utterance to Adams about Attila, he received from Lafayette a detailed account of developments and thus was enabled to peer behind the scene in France.[20] The Marquis also reported the severance of some of his old friend's personal ties with the French. Their beloved Madame de Tessé, with whom Jefferson had corresponded through so many years on horticultural subjects, did not live long enough to receive the last token of his remembrance — that is, his last letter — and her husband had vanished from the scene shortly before she did. Lafayette did not bemoan the departure of Napoleon to Elba, but was rather less severe in his judgment of the fallen chieftain than Jefferson was, probably because he understood the love of military glory better than that inveterate civilian did. He said that Napoleon's "strong powers and singular genius" were "disharmonised by the folly of his ambition, the immorality of his mind," and by the madness which is "developed by the love and success of despotism." While Lafayette spoke highly of Tsar Alexander, whom Jefferson still admired, and of the King of Prussia, he would have preferred that the overthrow of Napoleon had been due to domestic revolt rather than foreign invasion, and he had no liking for the restored Bourbons. Neither had his American

[17] Ford, I, 148–149.

[18] TJ to Adams, July 5, 1814; see also Adams to TJ, July 16.

[19] TJ to Adams, Feb. 25, 1823.

[20] Lafayette to TJ, Aug. 14, 1814; received Dec. 9 (*Letters of Lafayette and Jefferson*, pp. 340–347). The excessive capitalization is not followed here.

correspondent, but that distant observer was disposed to be reassuring.[21]

Though congenitally sanguine, Jefferson indulged in no facile optimism in his reply to Lafayette. In fact, he took occasion to castigate the "closet politicians, unpractised in the knowledge of man" who had pressed self-government too fast and too far in the French Revolution. For the limited monarchy they had already gained, and with which both he and Lafayette believed at the time they should have been content, they exchanged "the unprincipled and bloody tyranny of Robespierre, and the equally unprincipled and maniac tyranny of Bonaparte." Never perhaps did this champion of human freedom state more clearly that liberty is a dubious blessing to any people unprepared for it. He doubted if the French would be ready for a "full measure of liberty" for another generation. Knowledge must advance among them, and they must become habituated to "an independent security of person and property" before they could really estimate the value of freedom and the necessity of preserving it. He summed up the history of many other revolutions besides the French when he said: "Instead of that liberty which takes root and growth in the progress of reason, if recovered by mere force or accident, it becomes, with an unprepared people, a tyranny still, of the many, the few or the one."[22]

In a letter to another old French friend, Pierre Samuel du Pont de Nemours, about the same time, he stated that the essentials of a free government were freedom of religion and of the press, trial by jury, habeas corpus, and a representative legislature.[23] Louis XVIII had not promised that much, but Jefferson hoped that, under pressure from the patriots, the restored monarch would permit them "a temperate degree of freedom and security." If this should not prove to be the case he feared a "relapse into discontents" which might enable Bonaparte to return. When things came out just that way, Du Pont, who as secretary of the provisional government had signed the decree of deposition, did not await the former Emperor's return. Hurriedly leaving France, he joined his family at the Eleutherian Mills near Wilmington, Delaware. He missed Jefferson's relatively encouraging letter, but he soon got another, welcoming him to America and commiserating with him on the

[21] TJ to Lafayette, Feb. 14, 1815 (*ibid.*, pp. 367–373). This letter, in which TJ expressed himself so fully about recent events, did not reach Lafayette for more than two years (judging from Lafayette's letter to TJ dated Apr. 25, 1817). It was borne by George Ticknor, who was to go direct to Paris, but because of a change of plans went to London instead, and then on to Göttingen. In neither place could he find a safe way of sending the letter to Paris. Lafayette said that since the letter was written "two Revolutions and two Dynasties had successively reigned in France."

[22] *Ibid.*, p. 367.

[23] TJ to Du Pont, Feb. 28, 1815 (*J.-D. Correspondence*, pp. 150–153).

reinstitution of military despotism in France.[24] Du Pont did not go back and, during the next two years, he and Jefferson corresponded at length about education, political economy, political democracy, and other matters, but they did not meet. He never reported to his old friend the details of his last days in France, and Jefferson had to wait until almost the end of 1815 for further information from Lafayette.

At one time after Bonaparte's return from Elba, Jefferson viewed the former conqueror of Europe with somewhat less execration than usual, saying that he had changed places with his foes. The allies were now parceling out territories in their own interest, just as he had done, while he was defending the independence of his own country against invasion and appeared to have popular support.[25] Not only did he arouse patriotic ardor; as Lafayette was to report, he had availed himself of the follies of the restored Bourbons "to reappear as a representative of the Revolution."[26] Lafayette clearly recognized, however, that the Corsican employed the language of revolution for purposes of his own. Jefferson's mature judgment, as expressed to the Marquis, was that the loss of Waterloo was the salvation of France — for, if Bonaparte had been victorious, he would have riveted a military despotism on the necks of his countrymen.[27] The French were not ready for full self-government as yet, and there was some real hope of gain under the Bourbons. This judgment was welcome to Lafayette, whose patriotic pride had been sorely wounded by national defeat, but who made a creed of the Declaration of the Rights of Man and the Citizen and believed that most of his countrymen still did.[28]

In the autumn after Waterloo he wrote Jefferson that his eleventh grandchild, the son of George, had received, along with the family name of Gilbert, "the friendly name of Thomas."[29] Jefferson did not return this particular compliment. Even if he had not been running out of grandsons, he would have had difficulty in choosing from among Lafayette's many names. His letters were less affectionate, more restrained than those of his distant correspondent, but he was sending just the sort of comments and counsel Lafayette needed.

His judgment, as expressed to Lafayette, that the "closet politicians" of the French Revolution bore a heavy share of responsibility for the

[24] TJ to Du Pont, May 15, 1815; Du Pont to TJ, May 26 (*ibid.*, pp. 154–161). Du Pont's wife joined him afterwards.

[25] TJ to Adams, Aug. 10, 1815.

[26] To TJ, Oct. 10, 1815, received Dec. 16 (*Letters of Lafayette and Jefferson*, p. 375).

[27] May 17, 1816 (*ibid.*, p. 383).

[28] Lafayette to TJ, Dec. 10, 1817 (*ibid.*, p. 391).

[29] Lafayette to TJ, Oct. 10, 1815 (*ibid.*, p. 376).

failure of his hopes, and that the tyranny of Robespierre was as reprehensible as that of Napoleon, was fully shared by John Adams, who had long since expressed himself vehemently on the subject. In the months after Waterloo, in his correspondence with his fellow alumnus of the class of 1776, Adams reasserted in memorable phrase his implacable hostility to any and every form of despotism. Along with the passionate love of liberty that he avowed and Jefferson did not question, he was still manifesting grave skepticism about human beings and their progress. He took the position that the rights of mankind were as unattainable as human perfection. So he said in one letter to his generally optimistic friend, but in the next one he claimed that the eighteenth century, during which they had spent most of their lives, had a relatively good record. Despite its errors and vices, it has been "the most honorable to human nature" of all that had passed. "Knowledge and virtue were increased and diffused," he said, "arts, sciences useful to men, ameliorating their condition, were improved more than in any former period."[30] The question he propounded was whether the nineteenth would provide a contrast by extinguishing "all the lights of its predecessor." Current developments, including the proceedings of the Congress of Vienna, seemed to point in that direction. "The priests are at their old work again," he said. "The Protestants are denounced and another St. Bartholomew's day threatened."[31] Adams manifested no sympathy whatever with the counter-revolutionary spirit that now dominated the counsels of the Old World. A private letter in which he criticized the optimism of early supporters of the French Revolution had recently been referred to in public without his consent. While he properly resented the invasion of privacy and told Jefferson so, he undoubtedly prided himself on the accuracy of his prophecy.[32]

Jefferson fully supported Adams in the defense of personal privacy, and in his reply frankly admitted that Adams had been the better prophet. He also made memorable comments on the period of history they had lived through, and on the era that had ended. He fully agreed about the eighteenth century. During it, he said, "the sciences and arts, manners and morals, advanced to a higher degree than the world had ever before seen."[33] Surveying developments since the era of the Borgias, when in his opinion national morality was reduced to the "lowest point of depravity," he observed that the arts and sciences gradually ad-

[30] Adams to TJ, Nov. 23, 1815; see also Aug. 24, 1815.

[31] It should be noted that TJ's anticlericalism was directed more against the Protestant than the Catholic clergy, since it was with them that he was in more direct conflict.

[32] The reference was to a letter to the Rev. Richard Price that had recently been described in a memoir of that ardent believer in the Revolution.

[33] TJ to Adams, Jan. 11, 1816.

vanced through the sixteenth, seventeenth, and eighteenth centuries, "softening and correcting the manners and morals of man." Also, by "illuminating public opinion," they created a censor before which even the most exalted must tremble. He believed that in the greater European nations, morality came to occupy "an honorable chapter in the political code." He clearly had international affairs in mind, for he referred to the partition of Poland as a wound to the honor of the eighteenth century, but he regarded England and France as blamable in this only in their aloofness. Accordingly, he found it hard to understand how and why these nations, "so great, so dignified, so distinguished by science and the arts . . . threw off suddenly and openly all the restraints of morality, all sensation to character, and unblushingly avowed and acted on the principle that power was right."

He was disposed to date the change from the declaration of Pillnitz between the terrified monarchs of Austria and Prussia, which led to the first coalition against the French. That is, he attributed the decline he had perceived in international morality to the clash between revolutionary and counter-revolutionary forces. What he himself had favored while in France could be better described as reformation than revolution. His fervor for the cause of the French had reached its highest pitch thereafter, when it was threatened from without and, as he then believed, American liberties were imperiled with it. He now blamed the French for conduct as cruel and repressive as that of their foes. He did not believe that the light from the West — originally from his own country — was wholly extinguished. The spread of the idea of representative government throughout Europe gave him hope for the future.

This judicious and candid letter was described by Adams as "one of the most consolatory" he ever received.[34] So far as world affairs were concerned, past and present, there appeared to be no difference of any consequence between them, but in seeking to explain "the apostacy from national rectitude," which he also had observed, he was disposed to lay large blame on human nature. Thus he said that while he believed there were such things as reason and conscience, these seemed to be no match for "human passion, human imagination and human enthusiasm." He fully agreed, however, that the despotic governments of Europe had feared the fires being kindled under them and he included with the civil rulers the priests of all nations. Never before, he said, had priests and politicians "so suddenly and so unanimously concurred in re-establishing darkness and ignorance, superstition and dogmatism." He also pointed out that under the prevalent morality of patriotism nations regarded

[34] Adams to TJ, Feb. 2, 1816.

themselves as above the law. "We must come to the principles of Jesus," he said. "But when will all men and all nations do as they would be done by?" He was quite willing for those who cherished hopes of human perfectability to continue to do so — provided they did not engage mankind in crusades or French revolutions. In explanation of the actions of European nations on the principle that might makes right, his comment was that "power always thinks it has a great Soul . . . and that it is doing God service, when it is violating all his laws." In modern terms he was saying that man has a vast capacity for rationalization, and he reminded his friend that power must never be trusted without a check. Jefferson did not need to be told that and, in fact, he revealed in this elevated dialogue no significant difference from Adams except in his more favorable view of human nature.

He had by no means abandoned his belief in human improvability or his faith in knowledge. The remaining years of his life were to prove his most memorable as an apostle of enlightenment and a patron of learning. Before considering him as such, however, we should view him in another and less influential role. During the war and soon afterwards this characteristically hopeful man appeared at his most fearful in the realm of what he called political economy.

[X]

The Political Economy of a Country Gentleman

THE national issue on which Jefferson spent most time and thought during the latter half of the war was the financing of the conflict. He could not keep his mind off the subject, he said, and his lengthy communications about it represent an extraordinary output of intellectual energy on his part — the largest, seemingly, since he prepared his brief in the batture controversy. He presented his ideas most fully to his son-in-law, John W. Eppes, who had defeated John Randolph in the congressional election and who not only occupied the latter's old seat in the House, during the sessions of 1813–1815, but also served as chairman of the Ways and Means Committee. There would have been no need for the former President to present his fiscal ideas to Albert Gallatin, who was thoroughly familiar with them, but that veteran, harassed by his foes within the party, had left the country on a diplomatic mission and was destined never to resume the headship of the Treasury. During the summer and fall of 1813 his old department was administered by the Secretary of the Navy, William Jones.

In the first of three letters that Jefferson wrote Eppes about public finance in this period he said: "Our government has not, as yet, begun to act on the rule of loans and taxation going hand in hand."[1] In his opinion, a tax should be laid that would be sufficient not only to pay the annual interest on a loan but also to provide for its redemption in a given term. His overriding concern was to avoid *permanent* national debt, his fear of which amounted to an obsession, and against it he evoked the "principle" he had asserted shortly after his return from France a quarter of a century before. In a letter to Madison he then said: "The earth belongs always to the living generation."[2]

[1] TJ to JWE, June 24, 1813 (Ford, IX, 388–395, quotation on p. 391).

[2] TJ to Madison, Sept. 6, 1789, mailed Jan. 7, 1790 (Boyd, XV, 392–397; edit. note 384–391).

It has been averred that this "concept of political relativism" was the only important addition to Jefferson's thought during his years abroad.[3] There can be no doubt of his adherence to it throughout the rest of his life, but his applications of it varied somewhat. The most important of these was that laws and constitutions could not, in right, be perpetual but were subject to periodic revision. In the present instance he applied the principle to the question of public debt, denying the right of one generation to burden another beyond the "natural" limit of its powers. This limit, he claimed, was the additional time that adult members of society might be expected to live from any particular moment. On the average, according to the best European statistics available to him, he figured that they would survive about nineteen years. Accordingly, he held that every debt should be limited to such a period at the outside.

He did not want Congress to make a formal declaration of the principle he was now pronouncing. He stated here that they should not enter into abstractions and at various times he said that he himself did not like these, but rarely was he so theoretical as in this discussion. When the "principle" was first presented to Madison, that cogent thinker, while readily agreeing that the interests of the living are paramount, described his friend's applications as unrealistic for the most part.[4] Generations cannot be defined with such arithmetical precision and there is an inescapable continuity in human affairs. Madison pointed out that posterity inherits benefits along with debts, and Jefferson heartily agreed that all future generations would be beneficiaries of the American Revolution. However, he never got over his obsession regarding debt.[5] No doubt this reflected, in the private sector, his painful personal experience in the debt-ridden society of Virginia; and, in the public, his observation of the fiscal difficulties of the British and the French, which he regarded as a major cause of their involvement in war and revolution. He believed that "the modern theory of the perpetuation of debt" had "drenched the earth with blood, and crushed its inhabitants with burdens ever accumulating." Therefore, he urged that provision be made for the payment of any and every public debt within nineteen years, though he afterwards accepted twenty as a round figure.

Recognizing that loanable funds were limited and that the legislators would soon be scraping the bottom of the barrel, he favored the issuance of treasury notes to meet the immediate problem of financing the war. These should be redeemable in a specified period and bear interest in the first instance, though not necessarily thereafter. He believed they would

[3] *Ibid.*, p. 384.

[4] Madison to TJ, Feb. 4, 1790 (Boyd, XVI, 146–154 with edit. note).

[5] For an admirable discussion of their dialogue on this subject, see Adrienne Koch, *Jefferson and Madison: The Great Collaboration* (1950), ch. 4.

be more acceptable than the bank bills then in circulation. He was convinced that the authority to issue circulating paper should rest with Congress alone, and he optimistically predicted that on request the southern and western states would deny themselves the right to delegate that authority to banks. Like John Adams he was very skeptical of these institutions as then conducted, and he specially objected to their issuance of what amounted to paper money.

Writing from Washington, Congressman Eppes asserted that only a "rigid adherence" to such principles as were stated in Jefferson's letter would secure them against the evil of a "permanent debt."[6] At this session of Congress, though taxes were increased, a loan was authorized without provision for its systematic curtailment. Eppes said that at the next session they must provide for its payment in fifteen years — an action they did not then take. Regarding himself as little versed in political economy and recognizing Jefferson as an unfailing fount of enlightenment, he expressed the hope that, before his own legislative duties were resumed, this learned gentleman would outline his system. "By executing such a task," said the Congressman, "you will add one more essential benefit to the long list of important services already registered in the hearts of your countrymen."

Jefferson's lengthy response to this must have taxed the patience and comprehension of his correspondent.[7] He made it on one of his visits to Poplar Forest, where he had no books or papers bearing on the subject but had more leisure than at Monticello. In this long letter he not only repeated arguments he had already made but also provided Eppes with a formula that the Committee on Ways and Means might apply to any loan. Assuming that provision must be made both for annual interest and for full liquidation in twenty years, he worked out an equation in which only the rate of interest and the amount of the loan were variables. If the former was 7½ per cent and the latter a million dollars, an annual tax of $100,000, or one tenth of the amount of the loan, would be required. He drew up a table on this basis, showing the state of the declining principal year by year. In other calculations he allowed for the increase in population and consequent increase in taxes, arriving at even more gratifying results.

No doubt he beguiled many hours at Poplar Forest with these delightful mathematical exercises, and his policy looked good on paper. But government officials were faced with immediate problems not susceptible of theoretical solution. As Eppes had observed, it was difficult at this stage to devise taxes that were both equitable and adequate. Jefferson

[6] JWE to TJ, July 21, 1813 (LC).

[7] TJ to JWE, Sept. 11, 1813 (Ford, IX, 395*n*.–403*n*.).

himself recognized that it would probably be impossible to float loans sufficient to meet the extraordinary expenses of war. In fact, opponents of the war, especially in New England, were little disposed to lend the government money, and the agricultural districts never had much to lend. He continued to advocate reliance on treasury notes if need be and reaffirmed his opposition to bank paper.

He made two drafts of what he regarded as an important communication and authorized Eppes to make such use of it as he might see fit — without involving him, however, in any public controversy.[8] Since the charter of the Bank of the United States had expired in 1811 and had not been renewed, all the banks were state banks, but he did not trust them any more for that reason. James Monroe must have had them in mind when he wrote Jefferson that the country was "now at the mercy of monied institutions, who have got the circulating medium into their hands." Monroe, who was in Albemarle County in the early fall, saw the letter to Eppes or something like it. Returning his neighbor's "remarks on finance," he said he preferred Jefferson's plan to those of others but doubted that it could be put into operation because of "the ascendency gained by the existing institutions, and the opposition they would be sure to make to its introduction in the radical form proposed."[9] The "radical" element in the proposal was the denial to banks of the authority to issue circulating paper and the vesting of this solely in the federal government.

Before the legislators reassembled in Washington he wrote an even longer letter to Eppes about public finances. This was occasioned by a proposal of which he had been informed, to charter another Bank of the United States.[10] On the strength of the discussion a couple of years earlier, when it was decided *not* to recharter the existing institution, he believed there was general agreement that Congress lacked the constitutional authority to incorporate a bank.[11] Since he had taken that position from the first, his statement here that he wished Congress had that power "exclusively" sounds equivocal. At the moment he may have dreaded the existing state banks more than he did a national bank, but he strongly objected to the present proposal to create one. Since nothing came of this, his arguments against its specific provisions need not concern us. The letter is most significant as manifesting his conviction that coin is much to be preferred to paper money as a circulating medium. Also, it reflects his horror of debt and fear of inflation.

[8] The two drafts are in LC.

[9] Monroe to TJ, Oct. 1, 1813 (S.M.H., V, 273–274).

[10] TJ to JWE, Nov. 6, 1813 (Ford, IX, 403*n.*–417*n.*; L. & B., XIII, 404–432); TJ to Thomas Law, Nov. 1, 1813 (Ford, IX, 433).

[11] On his disagreement with Hamilton on this point and his opposition to the first bank, see *Jefferson and the Rights of Man*, ch. XX.

Written at Monticello, where he had access to his unrivaled collection of books, the letter showed an acquaintance with current writings on political economy that relatively few of his American contemporaries could match. Though he did not always agree with Adam Smith (as in the matter of paper money), he had long been familiar with the *Wealth of Nations*. He was also familiar with Jean-Baptiste Say's *Traité d'Economie Politique*, which was not yet available in English translation. He described this treatise as "shorter, clearer, and sounder" than the prolix work of Smith.[12] He had also drawn on his memory of Continental currency, but he perceived a difference between the paper emissions of the old Congress and those of present banks. "The object of the former," he said, "was a holy one; for if ever there was a holy war, it was that which saved our liberties and gave us independence. The object of the latter is to enrich swindlers at the expense of the honest and industrious part of the nation." To the speculative spirit he was implacable, and he was convinced that there was too much money in circulation. At this moment he had little expectation that this would be curbed. Instead he predicted that the "overbearing clamor of merchants, speculators, and projectors" would drive all before them until, as in the Mississippi bubble, the citizens would be "overtaken by the crush of this baseless fabric."[13]

The letters to Eppes do not constitute a systematic treatise. They have the *ad hoc* quality that is so characteristic of his writings, and he himself said that, viewed as a whole, they were devoid of order. But, better perhaps than anything else, they reflect his economic thinking in the period of war. Early in 1814 he sent copies of them to a member of the Virginia Senate, Joseph C. Cabell, for that young gentleman's own perusal. He had no objection to the circulation of his ideas and arguments but did not want his own name to be used in any way. "I am too desirous of tranquility," he said, "to bring such a nest of hornets on me as the fraternities of banking companies, and this infatuation of banks is a torrent which it would be folly to get into the way of. I see that it must take its course, until actual ruin shall awaken us from its delusions."[14]

A native and resident of what is now Nelson County, Cabell, who

[12] He owned a copy of the 3rd edn. of Smith's *An Inquiry into the Nature and Causes of the Wealth of Nations* (3 vols., London, 1784), and a first edn. of Say's *Traité d'Economie Politique* (Paris, 1803). Sowerby gives comments of his on these works under the respective titles.

[13] Quotations from Ford, IX, 416*n*.

[14] TJ to J. C. Cabell, Jan. 17, 1814 (L. & B., XIV, 68). While many of his letters to Cabell are in L. & B. and Ford, their extensive correspondence can be better viewed in *Early History of the University of Virginia, as Contained in the Letters of Thomas Jefferson and Joseph C. Cabell*, ed. by N. F. Cabell (Richmond, 1856). This invaluable collection is referred to as Cabell. The reference here is to pp. 13–16.

was to be Jefferson's chief coadjutor in establishing the University of Virginia, was a man of parts who had spent some years in Europe. To his economic education the older man had already contributed. He had called Cabell's attention to the writings of Thomas Cooper, describing these as the best by an American in this field, and had recently lent him his own copy of Say's treatise. Much of their correspondence at this stage related to the Rivanna Company and pending legislation with respect to it. The bill called for a charter extending to 1840 — twenty-seven years. Jefferson agreed to the term but told Cabell that it was seven years longer than the legislature really had the right to make it. He was applying the principle that no generation had the right to bind another beyond its own lifetime.[15] Cabell's expression of interest in this occasioned Jefferson to send him the correspondence with Eppes. The letters took longer to digest than their recipient had expected. He read them three times, as almost anybody trying to understand them would have had to, and copied a number of passages for his own use. Also, after extracting a promise that the author's name would not be divulged, he showed them to William Cabell Rives, Judge St. George Tucker, Thomas Ritchie, and John H. Cocke.[16] These were kindred spirits with whom educational activity could be safely carried on. Meanwhile, Jefferson had to hold in abeyance his hopes that "good old Virginia" would set an example to the rest of the country by beginning to reduce the quantity of bank bills.

Fears predominated in his mind, and, as occasion offered during the spring and summer of 1814, he voiced them to his fellow Virginians, Madison and Monroe. To the President he said with wry humor that the excess of bank paper should facilitate the government's next loan: there was so much of this "trash" afloat that large holders would want to get rid of it. He believed that the "whole system must blow up" before the year was out.[17] Though at Montpelier briefly in May, Madison was unable to visit Monticello, and apparently he saw no need as yet to comment seriously on his predecessor's views of public finance.

Late in the summer Monroe said to Jefferson: "Your idea had much weight on my mind, but so wedded were our financiers to the plan in operation that it was impossible to make any impression on them in favor of any other."[18] Presumably he meant that the financiers were indifferent to the idea of making specific provision for interest on loans and for their systematic retirement, and undisposed to dispense wholly with

[15] TJ to Cabell, Nov. 7, 1813 (Cabell, p. 9). On the Rivanna Co., see above, pp. 38–39.
[16] Cabell to TJ, Nov. 29, 1813; Mar. 6, 1814 (Cabell, pp. 11, 24).
[17] TJ to Madison, Feb. 16, 1814 (Ford, IX, 453).
[18] Monroe to TJ, July 29, 1814 (S.M.H., V, 288–289).

bank bills. However, he believed that the situation was now more favorable to the "arrangement" contemplated by Jefferson and said he would be happy to promote it. He asked that a copy of his friend's "thoughts" be sent him so that he might read it again. Shortly after his letter reached Monticello, the British invaded Washington, set fire to the Capitol, and threw the financial as well as the military affairs of the government into chaos.

The military situation considerably improved in the next few months, but, as has been aptly said, the summer and fall of 1814 "marked the lowest ebb in the financial history of the United States."[19] The disaster in Washington and the threat to Baltimore brought about a run on the banks which was followed by their suspension of specie payments except in New England. Time was to show that the banks themselves did not suffer. They continued in business, passing out their own paper and often making handsome profits. But bank notes depreciated — considerably more in Jefferson's country than in the Northeast — while tax collections were alarmingly interfered with and the federal government had great difficulty in meeting its ordinary running expenses. One of its critics, summing things up, taunted it as being "without money, without credit, and destitute of the means of defending the country."[20]

The Commonwealth of Virginia was also in financial straits, as Jefferson found out from his young friend Cabell if he was not aware of it already. He was well aware of the efforts to guard Richmond against the British since his son-in-law, his grandson, and his grandson-in-law were involved in these. He knew that they and the other militiamen were supposed to be paid and no doubt perceived a connection between the inadequacy of supplies about which his grandson had complained and the financial difficulties of the state. He may have heard from Cabell for the first time of the suspension of specie payments by the two Richmond banks that had reluctantly agreed to lend it money. He spoke of these institutions as bankrupt and believed that they were done for.[21] Time was to show that he had under-estimated the vitality of the banks and over-estimated the depreciation of their paper. Their notes did not fall to the value of oak leaves, as he predicted, though he could have claimed that their relative acceptability was owing to the lack of other and sounder currency. His unheeded recommendation was that the state meet its immediate needs by issuing due bills or certificates of indebtedness, levying a tax sufficient for their redemption in ten years.

[19] H. L. Coles, *The War of 1812* (1965), p. 238.

[20] Bray Hammond, *Banks and Politics in America* (1957), pp. 227–230; quotation, p. 230.

[21] TJ to Cabell, Sept. 17, 23, 1814 (Cabell, pp. 24–27, 27–30).

Cabell, who was looking forward to the meeting of the General Assembly, sought counsel about the financial problems of the state rather than about those of the federal government, but Jefferson could not refrain from discussing the latter. Regarding bank notes as intrinsically undesirable and assuming that they would greatly depreciate, he believed that Congress should act immediately to replace them with treasury notes. He spoke of a "competent" and a "wholesome" circulation and expected its reduction once the abnormal demands of war were over. Presumably he thought that this should be carried out just as in the case of debt, and quite clearly this old-fashioned country gentleman was much more insistent than most that all the obligations of the government should be firmly anchored to taxation.

He sent Monroe a copy of his letter to Cabell, and on the same day he wrote Madison for the first time since the debacle in Washington.[22] Being chiefly concerned to express sympathy and confidence, he referred to fiscal problems only incidentally in this letter. Saying that his writings on the subject were too long for the busy President to read, he referred that harassed official to Monroe for an outline of his views. Madison, who was already aware of the general character of these, was obviously dubious of them, on practical grounds at least. He had always had reservations about the "principle" that one generation has no right to bind another, and, whereas Jefferson found the British experience with paper money alarming, Madison was impressed that so much of it had been kept afloat with little or no depreciation.[23] In this crisis he was not of a mind to take drastic action. A little later he said: "I cannot but think that a domestic capital existing under various shapes . . . may not still be obtained on terms tho' hard, not intolerable, and that it will not be long before the money market abroad will not be entirely shut against us."[24] This statement was made after the receipt of a letter in which Jefferson had presented his views in considerable detail.[25]

Monroe approved of Jefferson's ideas. He was convinced that the government, "having better credit than any bank, or than all the banks together," could issue paper that would circulate throughout the country without the aid of the banks and on terms much more favorable to the public.[26] A couple of months later, when the military and diplomatic situations had very considerably improved but the state of the finances

[22] TJ to Monroe, Sept. 24, 1814 (Ford, IX, 488–489); TJ to Madison, Sept. 24, 1814 (L. & B., XIV, 194–196).

[23] Madison to TJ, Oct. 10, 1814 (Hunt, VIII, 313–316).

[24] Madison to TJ, Oct. 23, 1814 (*ibid.*, 314*n.*).

[25] TJ to Madison, Oct. 15, 1814 (Ford, IX, 489–492).

[26] Monroe to TJ, Oct. 10, 1814 (S.M.H., V, 299).

was still deplorable, he said: "My opinion always was that a paper medium supported by taxes, to be funded at proper times would answer the public exigencies, with a great saving to the Treasury." He believed that, with some modifications, Jefferson's plan seemed admirably suitable, but by that time the country had a new secretary of the treasury who had submitted another plan. Alexander J. Dallas of Pennsylvania, who had been opposed by the same faction that had virtually driven Gallatin from office, was nonetheless confirmed October 6. Monroe had promptly put into the new Secretary's hands Jefferson's remarks on public finance and reported that he thought highly of them. Dallas had already communicated to Congress a plan that included the rechartering of the Bank of the United States. Speaking for himself, Monroe said: "I have been willing to adopt almost any plan, rather than encounter the risk of the overthrow of our whole system, which has been so obvious and imminent."[27]

Some fifteen months passed before the second Bank of the United States was chartered (April 10, 1816). At that time John W. Eppes was no longer in Congress; and, in the interim, Jefferson appears to have refrained from specific comment on the successive recommendations of the Secretary of the Treasury. He continued to inveigh against the "bank mania" (which can perhaps be best described as mania for easy credit) and to urge in his own state the gradual reduction of the bank notes.[28] This recommendation came to naught, however, as in fact he expected. By this time he was manifesting more concern and more hopefulness about the actions of the General Assembly in educational than in fiscal matters.[29]

In the fall of 1815 James Monroe, the chief supporter of Jefferson's financial "plan" among high federal officials, said that it represented the only alternative to a national bank.[30] But he did not suggest the possibility of its adoption and he returned the papers describing it. Jefferson was not disposed to criticize any action of Madison's government, but neither was he disposed to dismiss his constitutional objections to the Bank of the United States. He does not seem to have recognized the potential value of this institution in exercising restraint on the loose banking and the currency inflation that he so strongly opposed. Since it was actually under private control despite public representation among its directors, he believed that in authorizing it to issue paper money the

[27] Monroe to TJ, Dec. 21, 1814 (*ibid.*, 305).

[28] See, for example, his letter of Jan. 6, 1816, to Col. Charles Yancey, delegate to the General Assembly from Albemarle (Ford, X, 1–4).

[29] His activities had begun with respect to Central College, from which the University of Virginia developed. See below, p. 248.

[30] Monroe to TJ, Sept. 23, 1815 (LC).

government was surrendering its own function. His own "plan," calling for the entire suppression of bank paper and its replacement by treasury notes, anchored to taxation, was described at the time as radical. It was unquestionably drastic and may have been quite impracticable, but, when viewed in retrospect, his reaction to the economic problems of his day can better be designated as conservative.

ii

The term "agrarian" has often been applied to this country gentleman who viewed scientific progress with confidence but who voiced so many fears in economic matters. No single term fits one who held in balance a mass of apparent contradictions.[31] Care should be taken not to align him with the agrarians of the late nineteenth century in the United States, for their ideas and aims in the financial sphere were actually antithetical to his. They wanted more currency and more credit, not less. Only in the sense that he spoke for the "people," especially the country people, and was opposed to the "interests" was he a forerunner of the Populists. But he was and always remained a countryman, rooted in the soil; and, although less rhapsodic than when he wrote his *Notes on Virginia,* he still believed that agriculture offered more freedom and happiness than any other form of activity. "It is the manners and spirit of a people which preserve a republic in vigor," he had said in his *Notes on Virginia*, and he had described the mobs of great cities as sores on the body politic.[32] This was in the brief section on manufactures, which, in the light of later observation, he would have liked to revise, though actually he never did.

Toward the end of his first term as President he said: "As yet our manufacturers [that is, the workers] are as much at their ease, as independent and moral as our agricultural inhabitants, and they will continue so as long as there are vacant lands for them to resort to; because whenever it shall be attempted by the other classes to reduce them to the minimum of subsistence, they will quit their trades and go to laboring the earth."[33] If he had not banished all his fears of the ill effects of industrial employment on human beings, rarely did he voice them in later years, and as we have seen, he believed that the development of

[31] Over-all treatments worthy of special note are: Joseph Dorfman, "Thomas Jefferson: Commercial Agrarian Democrat," in *The Economic Mind in American Civilization, 1606–1865* (1946), I, 433–447; W. D. Grampp, "A Re-examination of Jeffersonian Economics," in M. D. Peterson, ed., *Thomas Jefferson, A Profile* (1967), pp. 135–163 (article originally published in 1946).

[32] *Notes on Virginia*, Peden edn., p. 165.

[33] TJ to J. Lithgow, Jan. 4, 1805 (L. & B., XI, 55, wrongly addressed; LC).

manufacturing during the period when imports from Europe were shut off, was in the national interest. Shortly after his retirement from the presidency, when speaking of the effect of the embargo laws in turning the minds of citizens and legislators to "the establishment of useful manufactures," he described this as an "inestimable advantage" to the country. The observation was in a reply to an address from a group of his supporters in Pennsylvania in which he gave one of the clearest descriptions of the sort of balanced economy he had come to favor. To these well-wishers he said: "They [the embargo laws] will have hastened the day when an equilibrium between the occupations of agriculture, manufactures, and commerce shall simplify our foreign concerns to the exchange only of that surplus which we cannot consume for those articles of reasonable comfort or convenience which we cannot produce."[34]

Observation of the conflict into which his country had been drawn in 1812 served to strengthen his conviction that "to be independent for the comforts of life Americans must fabricate these for themselves." A year after the war ended he said: "We must now place the manufacturer by the side of the agriculturist."[35] The manufacturing that he had personally observed and especially encouraged since his retirement was domestic in the full sense, being done at home, but apparently he was not deploring factories at this stage. Perhaps he now regarded them as a necessary evil. At any rate he approved of the moderate protective tariff of 1816. While convinced that his countrymen must fabricate enough to meet their own needs, he was uncertain how much further they should go. The question whether they should devote their surplus labor to manufacturing or to agriculture could be settled later in the light of the existing situation, he said: "for in so complicated a science as political economy, no one axiom can be laid down as wise and expedient for all times and circumstances."[36] In this wise utterance he spoke as a relativist, not a doctrinaire, but we may doubt that he would ever have wanted American industry to go far beyond self-sufficiency.

The same international circumstances that had caused him to welcome or at least tolerate industrial development had engendered in him, it would seem, a reaction against foreign commerce — some of it anyway. Despite his early wish that all Americans could be husbandmen, he had long since recognized that many of them had a marked taste for navigation, and as a diplomat abroad and secretary of state at home he had devoted a large, perhaps a disproportionately large, amount of time and

[34] TJ to the Democratic Republican Delegates from the Townships of Washington County in Pennsylvania, Mar. 31, 1809 (L. & B., XVI, 356).

[35] TJ to Benjamin Austin, Jan. 9, 1816 (Ford, X, 10).

[36] Ford, X, 10.

effort to the promotion and protection of foreign trade.[37] In his first inaugural address he had referred to commerce as the handmaid of agriculture, and during the latter part of his presidency he was beset with the problem of protecting the ships and seamen of his country. He had no doubt that the War of 1812 was waged in their behalf, and he resented what he regarded as the selfish and unpatriotic attitude of certain mercantile groups toward it.

Writing the American minister in Paris, William H. Crawford, a year and a half after the inglorious conflict ended, he said that the "commercial dashers" had already cost the country more lives and dollars than they and all their commerce were worth.[38] In this letter to a future secretary of the treasury he said that it might be advantageous to the country as a whole for Americans to carry their surplus products to foreign markets. "But," he added, "it does not follow, that with a territory so boundless, it is the interest of the whole to become a mere city of London, to carry on the business of one half the world at the expense of eternal war with the other half. The agricultural capacities of our country constitute its distinguishing feature; and the adapting our policy and pursuits to that, is more likely to make us a numerous and happy people, than the mimicry of an Amsterdam, a Hamburgh, or a city of London." Distinguishing between "licentious commerce and gambling speculations for a few, with eternal war for the many" on the one hand, and, on the other, "restricted commerce, peace, and steady occupations for all," he obviously identified anti-administration groups in New England with the former. He was undoubtedly thinking of the threats of disunionists in that commercial region when he said: "I would rather the States would withdraw, which are for unlimited commerce and war, and confederate with those alone which are for peace and agriculture." To this startling declaration he added the assertion that "no earthly consideration" could induce him to consent to such a debt as England had contracted by her "wars of commerce."

Time was to show that these particular fears were unwarranted. The dangers of involvement in war and debt in behalf of commercial interests and the carrying trade, which had been so great during so much of his public life, were to be remote for decades to come. In the light of actual developments the picture he painted seems highly unrealistic. It would appear that in important respects he was not reading the economic signs aright. But he viewed the economic scene as a humanitarian who was seeking to promote the welfare and happiness of the great body of his

[37] See the admirable article "Thomas Jefferson and Commercial Policy, 1783–1793" by Merrill D. Peterson in *Thomas Jefferson, A Profile*.

[38] TJ to W. H. Crawford, June 20, 1816 (Ford, X, 34–37).

fellow citizens. As an old man he was still concerned that his country should be a land of opportunity, not for the favored few, but for the many. Thus he wrote to Crawford: "A government regulating itself by what is wise and just for the many, uninfluenced by the local and selfish views of the few who direct their affairs, has not been seen, perhaps, on earth. Or if it existed, for a moment, at the birth of ours, it would not be easy to fix the term of its continuance." Still, he believed that it existed in his country to a greater degree than anywhere else and he prayed for its growth and continuance.

To him, predominantly, property was real property, and the forms of economic activity that he valued most were those that were unquestionably productive. Since this lover of the woods and fields was fascinated by machines, it need not surprise us that at length he should have set manufacturing beside agriculture, though he thought of the latter as a way of life, not merely as a form of economic enterprise, and never ceased to prefer it to all others. As a classicist, however, he must have perceived that Attica offered advantages that were lacking in Boeotia; and, toward the end of his life, he stated that in his own country civilization reached its height in the seaport towns and was constantly moving thence to the westward.[39] But of all forms of economic activity he was least at home in finance and banking, which were and still are especially associated with urban life.

He was intensely suspicious of the "paper system" that Hamilton had set up — as was his friend John Adams — and he deplored the speculative spirit he connected with it. Hamilton could not have been justly blamed for the loose banking of the second decade of the nineteenth century, but his title as the major American prophet of the new order had been strengthened by the great changes in the economy. By the same token Jefferson and John Adams and John Taylor of Caroline had been made to appear old-fashioned. As has been well said, these changes "were shaking to pieces the simpler economy of the 18th century America and undercutting the moralities that had subsisted among a people who were mostly agrarian."[40]

In Albemarle County there was still recourse to barter. Jefferson had generally been paid for his nails in produce, and at times the rent for his mill was paid in flour. He had lived in a world of things, where there had been a shortage of money. His region actually stood to gain from the growth of a monetary system. But the confusion and uncertainties of the times greatly disturbed him, and he was thoroughly unsympathetic to the speculative spirit. In part, no doubt, his reaction was that of an

[39] TJ to William Ludlow, Sept. 6, 1824 (L. & B., XVI, 75).

[40] Hammond, *Banks and Politics*, p. 274; see also the admirable comments on pp. 275–276.

old man disturbed by the rapidity of change, but perhaps it can be best explained on moral grounds.

Believing as he did that the earth belongs always to the living generation, he recognized the inevitability of change in any vital society and was certainly no foe to material progress. But his own conduct had been marked by unusual patience — notably in his building operations — and he tended to take the long view of things. He attributed timelessness to no human institution but he perceived it in moral principles and human values. The values and standards of conduct that had been associated through the centuries with agricultural society were not destined to crumble immediately, and nowhere in the Republic perhaps were they to linger longer than in the region where he lived. But they were imperiled by the more competitive, more ruthless, more impersonal spirit of a new age of business enterprise. The country was not without business leaders who maintained the old traditions, but, as a noted historian of banking has observed, "the majority were green, brash, and irresponsible."[41] The circulation of bank paper beyond the actual store of specie was incomprehensible to many besides Jefferson and Adams, including most bankers, very few of whom had read Adam Smith. The distinction between right and wrong was hard to draw, and the old moralities did not seem to apply to corporations as they had to individuals. Far from being sympathetic to the aggressive spirit of business enterprise, which manifested itself in this period of monetary and moral confusion, and which was to be so characteristic of American life thereafter, Jefferson spoke with dismay of "speculators, projectors, and commercial gamblers" who, we may assume, did not heed him if they heard him. He was destined to have very slight influence on his countrymen in the economic sphere.

[41] *Ibid.*, p. 274.

Light and Learning

Martha Jefferson Randolph

Portrait by Thomas Sully. (Courtesy of Monticello/Thomas Jefferson Foundation, Inc.)

[XI]

The Monticello Circle

WHEN Jefferson retired as President, three of his sisters and his only brother were still living.[1] They were Martha, Lucy, and the twins, Anna Scott and Randolph, who were twelve years younger than he. Of these the one closest to him was Martha, the widow of his boyhood friend Dabney Carr and three years his junior. When able, she spent much of her time at Monticello. So also did her three sons, Peter, Samuel, and Dabney, and two of her three daughters, Polly and Jane Barbara (Mrs. Wilson Cary).[2] Midway in his own sixty-ninth year, her elder brother wrote her younger: "Our worthy sister Carr has at length yielded to the wasting complaint which has for two or three years been gaining upon her."[3] At Monticello she joined the first occupant of the graveyard, her husband, whom her brother had caused to be buried there thirty-eight years before. Thus, so far as mortals could judge, she was to remain forever in the family circle.

Little is known of Jefferson's relations with his sister Lucy, who was younger than Martha but died a year sooner. She had married her first cousin, Charles Lilburne Lewis, and until 1807, when she moved to Kentucky, she lived at Monteagle in Albemarle County. Despite propinquity and the closeness of the relationship, there appears to have been little contact between her family and her elder brother. She died in Kentucky about a year after he came home to stay. About a year and a half

[1] His sister Mary, two years older than he, who was married to John Bolling, died during his first term as President (Anne Cary Randolph to TJ, Jan. 21, 1804, *Family Letters*, p. 254). For a list of the children of Peter Jefferson and Jane Randolph see *Jefferson the Virginian*, p. 430.

[2] The third daughter, Lucy (Mrs. Richard Terrell), lived in Kentucky. For more on the family see Elizabeth Dabney Coleman, "The Carrs of Albemarle" (M.A. thesis, UVA, 1944), and Ellen Randolph Coolidge to Henry S. Randall, July 10, 1853 (Letterbook, Coolidge Papers, UVA).

[3] TJ to Randolph Jefferson, Sept. 6, 1811 (Mayo, *TJ and Randolph*, p. 19). For full cite, see n. 6 below.

after that her son Lilburne, with the concurrence of another son Isham, murdered a slave named George. We can only conjecture how soon Jefferson learned of this sensational episode and how much he knew of its aftermath. No doubt he was informed of the indictment and suicide of his nephew Lilburne Lewis, and of the flight of Isham, but he seems to have left no reference to these nephews, whose dark deeds contrasted so sharply with his luminous career. He may possibly have acceded to the request of their sisters for financial aid, but quite clearly these relations were remote from the Monticello circle.[4]

Jefferson's youngest sister, Anna Scott, whose marriage to Hastings Marks had occurred while he was in France, was a special object of his solicitude throughout his last years. No doubt her visits grew longer during his retirement, and after the death of her husband in 1811, she became a resident at Monticello. In a letter Martha Randolph wrote her father shortly before his retirement, she described Aunt Marks as an excellent creature, but implied that she was not a forceful personality. "The servants have no sort of respect for her and take just what they please before her face," said her niece. She appears to have been a gentle person and to have been in feeble health by the time she came to Monticello to stay, but she outlived all the rest of Peter Jefferson's children, dying two years and four days after her eminent brother (July 8, 1828).[5]

The contrast between her twin brother Randolph and their brother Thomas may be said to exemplify the natural inequality of men, since the opportunities of the two were not dissimilar. Randolph's teachers did not come up to James Maury, William Small, and George Wythe, but, like Thomas, he went to the College of William and Mary after having been privately taught. Therefore, one cannot help being surprised at the disregard of grammar that he exhibited in his letters to his brother, who made a fine art of writing.[6] Randolph said "would of" instead of "would have"; "have wrote" and "have rode"; "tech" for "touch"; and was entirely colloquial when not ungrammatical. His brother's slave Isaac is reported to have said that he was "a mighty simple man; used to come

[4]Lucy Jefferson Lewis died May 26, 1810 (Martha C. Lewis and others, Livingston, Ky., to TJ, Sept. 17, 1810, UVA). The murder occurred on Dec. 15, 1811. Lilburne was indicted Mar. 18, 1812, and committed suicide Apr. 10. Isham fled in May. This episode is the subject of Robert Penn Warren's powerful poem *Brother to Dragons*. Boynton Merrill, Jr., recounts the rise and fall of the Lewis family in *Jefferson's Nephews: A Frontier Tragedy* (1976).

[5]Martha to TJ, Mar. 2, 1809 (*Family Letters*, p. 388); Cornelia Jefferson Randolph to Mrs. Joseph Coolidge, Jr., July 6–8, 1828 (Coolidge Papers, UVA).

[6]Twenty-eight letters between them, 1807–1815, were published in 1942 by the McGregor Library, UVA, under the title, *Thomas Jefferson and His Unknown Brother Randolph*, with an admirable introduction by the editor, Bernard Mayo. Unless otherwise indicated, the letters referred to by date in the present account are from that collection.

out among black people, play the fiddle, and dance half the night; hadn't much more sense than Isaac."[7] This uncomplimentary appraisal need not be taken at face value. Captain Jefferson, as Randolph was called, was a reputable and probably a popular man. But Nature unquestionably distributed talents most unevenly in this family.

Randolph Jefferson's inheritance, including the plantation Snowden in Buckingham County, across from Scott's Ferry on the James, was roughly comparable to that of his brother in Albemarle. Thomas, while attesting to Randolph's extreme "kindness of temper," described him as "not possessing skill for the judicious management of his affairs."[8] But he lived simply as a country squire and appears to have run into no serious financial difficulty until the last years of his life. Despite the disparity between them, the attitude of Thomas toward Randolph was in no sense patronizing but was consistently considerate and affectionate. They addressed each other, not by given name, but as "Dear Brother," signing themselves respectively Th: and Rh: Jefferson. They exchanged visits and did services for each other, those performed by the elder being much the more numerous. He had Randolph purchase clover seed for him and seek carp for his fishpond. He lent Randolph the harness for a gig, had his watch repaired in Richmond, sent him vegetable seeds and agricultural suggestions, gave him at least one shepherd dog and also a spinning jenny. At his suggestion, a girl was sent from Snowden to Monticello to learn how to run the machine.

In May, 1808, when President Jefferson was at home briefly, he wrote a will for his brother, who was then a widower with five sons and a daughter. This will, which was duly attested, was left in his hands. According to him, he was consulted by Randolph on all matters of importance, with one conspicuous exception: the latter's marriage to Mitchie B. Pryor of Buckingham, which probably occurred later in 1808 or in 1809. Her brother-in-law referred to her in letters as "my sister" and sent her a book on gardening to help her cultivate the flower seeds she had received from his daughter. She was invited to visit Monticello but it is uncertain whether she ever did. Jefferson saw her at Snowden on his visits there in May and September, 1813, the last he made. During the first of these, she complained of her husband's financial management and besought her brother-in-law to ask him to let her have a greater share in it — a thing that gentleman did not do.

After his remarriage, Randolph denied reports that he had made a settlement on his second wife involving most of his estate. He said that

[7] Isaac Jefferson, *Memoirs of a Monticello Slave. As Dictated to Charles Campbell*, ed. by R. W. Logan (1951), p. 35.

[8] Deposition of Sept. 15, 1815 (see n. 10, below).

her dower rights would be sufficient, and Thomas understood that the will in his hands continued to represent his brother's wishes. He saw no special signs of extravagance on his last visits to Snowden, but Randolph afterwards complained that his wife was running up bills at Scott's Ferry that he could not meet, and he informed his brother in the spring of 1815 that he had sold some of his best lands in order to pay his debts.[9] His health, already bad, became precarious in the summer, and in early August Jefferson learned from a nephew that Randolph had signed another will which he did not really understand but which was obviously to his wife's advantage. By this account, Randolph wished to revoke this and asked his brother to come to see him. Accordingly, Thomas drew an instrument revoking the new will and restoring the old one, but could not set out immediately. He had just dispatched his sister Marks to Randolph's bedside and had to await the return of his horses. He left home on August 7, 1815, and, on his arrival at Scott's Ferry, learned of his brother's death that very day.

The new will was promptly challenged by the five sons of the first marriage, who were supported by a lengthy deposition from their uncle. He said that his amiable brother was easily influenced but believed that if he had been himself he would never have signed the paper. His views were set forth in a document that is notable for its legal precision and beauty of form, but which failed to convince the court.[10]

On the occasion of his visit to Snowden in May, 1813, he had become better acquainted with the youngest of his brother's sons by the latter's first marriage, Lilburne Jefferson, and had suggested that he come to Monticello for a spell and engage in a course of reading under his direction. It is not clear whether anything came of this, but after Randolph's death, Lilburne was invited to make his home at Monticello. He did not accept the offer, but in his grateful reply he reported that Snowden was to be rented out and that the widow had moved to her brother's. She had not been gone two days when the house caught fire and burned to the ground.[11]

The central figure in Thomas Jefferson's personal life, and in the establishment at Monticello, was his daughter Martha. Upon her fell the heavy burden of domestic management. Meanwhile, she continued to bear children. To the eight who were living when her father came home for good she added three thereafter. A son, born in 1810, was named Meriwether Lewis in memory of the noted and lamented explorer. A

[9] Randolph Jefferson to TJ, Apr. 2, 1815.

[10] Deposition of Sept. 15, 1815 (Carr–Cary Papers, UVA). My account of this episode is largely based on this document.

[11] James L. Jefferson to TJ, Feb. 18, 1816 (UVA).

girl, born in 1814, was named Septimia Anne because she was the seventh daughter. The last of the flock, George Wythe Randolph, born in 1818, need not enter into this narrative as yet. Five of the six oldest children were girls, who appear to have received all their formal schooling in the home — at the hands of their mother and of their grandfather.

There can be no possible doubt that they were fortunate in both their teachers, for Martha, who looked so much like her father, was a remarkable woman. An Albemarle neighbor had this to say about her:

> Mrs. Randolph is decidedly the most accomplished woman I have ever known: her person tall, large, loosely made, and awkward; but her actions and manners are graceful, easy, and engaging, her face not what would be esteemed beautiful, but her features are flexible and playful, and agreeable. An expression of intelligence always animates her countenance; a turn for the ludicrous, a sweet & variable voice, the contraction of the muscles about the eyes when she speaks, vast and various information, frankness and eloquence far above what I have ever met with in any other person of her sex, give a charm to her manners and conversation such as I never have found in those of any other. Her exemplary life, devotion to the instruction of her children, and everything in her history conspires to make her one of the most interesting persons of the age.[12]

This language may sound extravagant, but there is abundant contemporary testimony to her accomplishments, her strength of character, and her amiable personality. One of her daughters was afterwards to say that she had the sunshine of heaven in her nature, and she generally bore her heavy burdens with cheerful equanimity. For one thing she put up with an erratic husband, whose financial situation continued to deteriorate. In 1810 he sold the lands in Bedford County which had constituted her dowry, and his affairs fell into great confusion during the war years. Soon thereafter she was confronted with something even more painful. The personal affairs of the eldest and perhaps the prettiest of her daughters reached a crisis.

As we have seen, Anne Cary shared her grandfather's love of flowers.[13] She must have looked like one when she was married to Charles L. Bankhead at seventeen. Her grandfather once remarked to her that the belles of the garden could not blossom always, but he could hardly have anticipated that her reign of beauty would be so troubled and that he himself would outlast her.[14] It is uncertain just when her skies began

[12] "The Autobiography of Peachy R. Gilmer," in R. B. Davis, *Francis Walker Gilmer* (1939), p. 373.

[13] See above, p. 46.

[14] TJ to Anne, May 26, 1811 (*Family Letters*, pp. 400–401); see above p. 49.

Anne Cary Bankhead

Portrait by James W. Ford, 1823. (Courtesy of Monticello/Thomas Jefferson Foundation, Inc.)

to cloud over, but unquestionably they were very dark in 1815, when she was twenty-four. In the spring of that year, in order to provide for their debts, the young couple had to deed Carlton, along with its slaves, stock, and buildings, to Dr. John Bankhead, Thomas Mann Randolph, and another as trustees. In effect their fathers assumed their debts. After these were paid the property was to be used for the benefit of the family, but the young husband was deprived of all management of it. Jefferson drew the deed of trust, and he himself deeded to the trustees two tracts of land, adjoining Carlton and totaling about one hundred acres, for the benefit of his granddaughter. This property also was to be wholly out of her husband's control.[15]

Whether the financial troubles of Charles Bankhead were owing to his alcoholism or his alcoholism was occasioned or accentuated by them is an unanswerable question, but quite clearly he was now regarded as a medical case. For a time he was in his parents' home in Caroline County under the care of his father, who was a physician. He seemed restored to normality on his return to Albemarle, but fell back into drunken ways and treated his young wife with cruelty. An incident at Monticello, when she fled to her mother's room to escape him, provided the occasion for a long letter from Jefferson to Dr. John Bankhead, which is one of the important sources of our knowledge of this tragic situation.[16] Jefferson's conclusion was that Charles could be kept sober and his family safe only under his father's roof. It should be noted that Jefferson did not recommend that Anne leave her husband. While he certainly did not want her to be endangered, he characteristically counseled the patient endurance of inescapable domestic ills.

He had expressed himself to that effect almost a score of years earlier when commenting on the habitual intoxication of John Bolling, husband of his elder sister Mary. "Of all calamities this is the greatest," he said. From his daughter Maria, who had been visiting her aunt, he had learned that Bolling was behaving better toward his wife than hitherto, and she seems to have been in no physical danger. Writing his daughter, who had been only a few months married to John W. Eppes, he expressed the wish that his sister would bear the misconduct of her husband more patiently. "When we see ourselves in a situation which must be endured and gone through, it is best to make up our minds to it. Meet it with firmness and accomodate every thing to it the best way practicable. This lessens the evil, while fretting and fuming only serves

[15] Deed of trust of Apr. 1, 1815, and indenture of that date in Carlton Papers, UVA.

[16] TJ to Dr. John Bankhead, Oct. 28, 1815 (Carr–Cary Papers, UVA). Partly copied in G. G. Shackelford, ed., *Collected Papers . . . of the Monticello Association*, pp. 73–74.

to increase our own torment." He undoubtedly wished his recently wedded daughter to heed his exhortation. "Harmony in the marriage state is the very first object to be aimed at," he said. "Nothing can preserve affections uninterrupted but a firm resolution never to differ in will and a determination in each to consider the love of the other as of more value than any object whatever on which a wish has been fixed."[17] To him the marriage tie was indissoluble and he expected wives to be dutiful. Time was to show that his granddaughter was to suffer grievously from her loyalty to his teaching.

It would appear that Charles Bankhead was for a considerable time under his father's care after Jefferson wrote to the Doctor. Upon his return to Albemarle he "stood his ground firmly" until on a trip to Charlottesville on court day "his resolution gave way." He was brought to Monticello in a drunken condition and kept in bed for a couple of days. He escaped to Charlottesville, however, and returned in what Jefferson described as a state of mental aberration. That temperate gentleman reluctantly told the painful story to his friend Dr. Bankhead, asking him to advise them what to do.[18]

Apparently Charles was induced to make another visit home, but on his return about a month later he resumed his drunken ways. So Martha reported to her father, then at Poplar Forest, saying that Charles had thrown away all respect for Dr. Bankhead, who was in utter despair and said that but for Anne and the children he never wished to see his son's face again. Martha herself, showing a lack of charity for her son-in-law, suggested that a keeper should be hired to keep him from mischief and that he be permitted to drink himself to death.[19] There seems to be no clear record of just what happened in the Bankhead household during the next two or three years, but Charles was very much alive and capable of great mischief at the end of that period, as we shall see hereafter.[20]

The relations between Jefferson and his eldest grandson and namesake, which had always been close, became increasingly so after the war. Some years earlier, when the boy was at school in Philadelphia, his mother said that she saw enough of the Randolph character in him to have some uneasiness about him.[21] Apparently she was thinking particularly of the sort of temper and jealousy her temperamental husband sometimes displayed. Time was to show that Jeff admired his father

[17] TJ to Maria, Jan. 7, 1798, replying to her letter of Dec. 8, 1797 (*Family Letters*, pp. 149–153).

[18] TJ to Dr. John Bankhead, Oct. 14, 16, 1816 (Carr–Cary Papers, UVA).

[19] Martha to TJ, Nov. 20, 1816 (*Family Letters*, 417).

[20] See below, pp. 298–300.

[21] Martha to TJ, Nov. 18, 1808 (*Family Letters*, p. 360).

considerably less than his grandfather. He did not emulate the latter in intellectual pursuits, but in practical matters he was a mainstay throughout that learned gentleman's last years.

About six weeks after he brought to Monticello from Charlottesville the news of the American victory at New Orleans he was married at Warren in Albemarle County (March 16, 1815) to Jane Hollins Nicholas, daughter of Wilson Cary Nicholas, who was then Governor of the state. He was twenty-two and she seventeen at the time. Though the political and personal relations between his grandfather and Nicholas had long been close, and his mother and sisters must have had ample forewarning of this event since he and Jane had been engaged for two years, they had some doubts about her at first. These were quickly dispelled, however, and the young couple entered upon what was to prove a long, fruitful, and happy marriage. For a couple of years they lived at Monticello in the dome room, which, though light and spacious, could hardly have been intended for such domestic uses. Presumably they were still there when the first of their thirteen children was born.[22]

Before the summer of their first year, Jeff had assumed the management of his grandfather's farm in Albemarle, and after a time he and his family lived at Tufton, where they had fewer stairs to climb than at Monticello. It may be that the reliance of Jefferson on his grandson was regarded by Thomas Mann Randolph as a reflection on him and thus contributed to his disquietude, but he had troubles enough of his own and Jefferson had wisely picked not only a younger but also a steadier man to lean on.[23] In his great size Jeff Randolph was said to have been like Peter Jefferson. Whether or not he came up to his great-grandfather in effectiveness he surpassed his own father in that respect, and he unquestionably served his grandfather with affectionate devotion.

Next in age after Jeff among the grandchildren was Ellen Wayles, the belle of the family in this period and at all times a highly articulate member of it. There was much coming and going in the household and, as the eldest of the unmarried girls, she did more visiting than her sisters. In the spring of 1814, when a few months past seventeen, she made a visit of several weeks to her father's sister Mary (Mrs. David Meade Randolph) in Richmond. Her letters to her mother do not state whether her aunt was still conducting the boarding-house she had set up five or six years earlier after her insolvent husband fled to England.[24] A major

[22] Margaret Smith Randolph, born Mar. 7, 1816.

[23] Gaines, p. 103. Good account of Jane Nicholas and T. J. Randolph in Shackelford, ed., *Collected Papers . . . of the Monticello Association*, ch. VI. Unpublished doctor's dissertation on T. J. Randolph by J. C. Vance, 1957 (UVA).

[24] On the troubles of TMR's sister, see *Jefferson the President: Second Term*, p. 528. Ellen's letters of Mar. 30, Apr. 28, 1814, to her mother are in the Coolidge Collection, UVA.

purpose of this trip was to get dresses made, but she was caught in a social whirl, and this attractive and vivacious girl by no means escaped masculine admiration.

In the winter and spring of 1816 she made a trip which began in Richmond and extended to Washington, Baltimore, and Philadelphia. Accompanied by her sister-in-law Jane to Richmond, she again stayed with Aunt Randolph and attended to dressmaking business. In Washington she was received by Mrs. Madison with open arms and for a couple of months she was a guest at the White House. She received much attention from old friends of her grandfather and from the young gentlemen of the Capital, but she reported to her mother that Washington could boast of few "first rate beaux." The most agreeable and attractive man she met was married, so she could not see much of him.[25]

Among the people Ellen met in Washington were a number from Philadelphia, including members of the family of the Secretary of the Treasury, Alexander J. Dallas, and toward the end of March she decided to extend her journey to that city. This she would hardly have done if she had not received a letter from her grandfather in which he said that, having sold his tobacco, he was replenishing her *moyens de jouissance* to the amount of a hundred dollars. In a letter to her mother she criticized herself at length for her extravagance while they were in financial trouble, and she wondered what Papa would think. She was assured that Grandpapa would approve her plan to extend her journey and avail herself more fully of her opportunities. She was not aware that he renewed a note in the Bank of Virginia in Richmond two days after he wrote her.[26]

In Philadelphia as in Washington she received much attention from her grandfather's old friends. She sought out the places where he had lived as secretary of state and Vice President; and once, when she and the daughter of the Secretary of the Treasury were being serenaded, the band struck up "Jefferson's March." On her way back she visited her sister-in-law's aunt in Baltimore and was then visited by several grandees, she said. In May she found the heat hard to bear and was weary of city life. She wanted Jeff to come for her, as presumably he did.[27]

[25] Ellen to her mother from Richmond, Jan. 5, 1816; from Washington, Jan. 22, 31; Feb. 2, 7, 17; to her sister Virginia from Washington, Feb. 28 (UVA). These letters are detailed, colorful, and at times critical.

[26] TJ to Ellen, Mar. 14, 1816, and Ellen to TJ, Mar. 19 (*Family Letters*, pp. 412–414); Ellen to her mother, Mar., 1816 (UVA); Account Book, Mar. 16, 1816.

[27] Letters to her mother in Apr. and May, 1816 (UVA).

ii

The spacious house on the little mountain did more than provide shelter for the large family to which this eager girl belonged, and for the relatives who found a haven there or happened to drop in. It also provided gracious hospitality for visitors who came out of curiosity or as pilgrims to a shrine. They became a heavy burden long before the master died, but they served to enlarge the Monticello circle and some of them greatly enriched its life.

Among the latter during and just after the war was a scientist of international reputation, who referred to his first visit as a pilgrimage. It was afterwards said of the Portuguese botanist, the Abbé Correa de Serra, that he belonged to every philosophical society on earth and knew every distinguished man alive. He came to the United States shortly before the War of 1812 began, bearing numerous and impressive letters of introduction, and promptly announced his arrival to Jefferson. Not until the summer of 1813 did he get to Monticello but he spent more than a month on that visit and came so regularly thereafter that one of the rooms was designated as the Abbé Correa's room. It may be doubted if any other visitor ever brought more pleasure and stimulation to this host and this circle.[28]

Born in Portugal, whence his father was forced to flee because he had displeased the Holy Office, Correa was educated in Italy. There he took Holy Orders — possibly as a shield for his scientific work. In his maturity he lived for a time in his native land and received many honors there; he spent some years in England and came to America after long residence in Paris. The world of plants, on which his interest centered, was one in which his host was especially at home, and he was a man of universal knowledge after Jefferson's own heart. He bore highly commendatory letters of introduction from Lafayette, Du Pont de Nemours, Alexander von Humboldt, and André Thouin, director of the Jardin des Plantes. Writing Dr. Caspar Wistar, his successor as president of the American Philosophical Society, of which Correa had been promptly elected a member, Jefferson said that his visitor had fully lived up to expectations. He described his recent guest as the "best digest of science in books, men, and things that I have ever met with, and with these the most amiable and engaging character."[29]

[28] I am much indebted to the admirable account by Richard Beale Davis, "The Abbé Correa in America, 1812–1820" (*Transactions of the Am. Philos. Soc.*, new series, vol. 45, pt. 2, 1955, pp. 87–197). This consists of a narrative with appended letters. The room at Monticello — on the right as one enters — is marked as that of the Abbé on the plan in *Domestic Life*, p. 334.

[29] TJ to Wistar, Aug. 17, 1813 (quoted by Davis, "Abbé Correa," p. 99); see also Correa to TJ, Mar. 6, 1812; and TJ to Correa, Apr. 17, 1812 (*ibid.*, pp. 123–124).

Apparently it was from the time of Correa's second visit, in the fall of 1814, that the room at Monticello was designated as his. At this time he met and made an ardent disciple of Francis Walker Gilmer, son of Jefferson's old friend Dr. George Gilmer of Pen Park, and his later collaborator in assembling the first faculty of the University of Virginia. This brilliant young man, who made an avocation of botany, accompanied Correa back to Philadelphia. He described that learned gentleman as "the most extraordinary man now living, or who, perhaps, ever lived."[30] Correa and Gilmer visited Monticello together in the summer of 1815 and accompanied their host to Poplar Forest. The trio took the elevation of the Peaks of Otter, explored these heights for botanical subjects, and visited Natural Bridge, which Gilmer afterwards described for the benefit of the American Philosophical Society. Correa and his enthusiastic young protégé then proceeded on a tour of the southern country, armed with letters of introduction from their recent host. To the Governor of Georgia Jefferson described Correa as the most learned man he had ever met in any country, and Gilmer as a young man of such promise that he could look forward to any position he desired. "At home in every science," he said, "botany is their favorite."[31]

Returning to Monticello from Poplar Forest later than had been expected, he missed a visit from Correa and Du Pont de Nemours. The mishap may be attributed to the difficulties of communication in those days and perhaps to the absentmindedness of elderly gentlemen. Du Pont lingered several days after Correa had left and might have stayed even longer if his son, who had accompanied him and served as his interpreter, had not felt compelled to return to his business. The distinguished Frenchman had not seen Jefferson since his return to America and was destined not to do so before his death a couple of years later.[32] Meanwhile, they continued to correspond. Correa made other visits to Monticello, though he was not as free for botanical expeditions after he became the Portuguese minister to the United States in 1816.

Shortly before Christmas in 1814, John Adams wrote his friend Jefferson that the "most exalted" of the young geniuses in Boston were ambitious "to see Monticello, its Library, and its Sage." He had given letters of introduction to three of them. Edward Everett, the most celebrated, had to turn back from Washington; but Francis Calley Gray and

[30] F. W. to P. R. Gilmer, Nov. 3, 1814 (*ibid.*, p. 101).

[31] TJ to Gov. John Milledge, Sept. 22, 1815 (*ibid.*, p. 102).

[32] Du Pont de Nemours to TJ, Dec. 10, 20, 1815; TJ to Du Pont, Dec. 31 (*J.-D. Correspondence*, pp. 164–175).

George Ticknor arrived at Monticello early in February, 1815.[33] This visit lasted only three days, though the host urged that it be extended and seems to have expected his guests to remain a week. Despite its brevity it was significant because of the quality and the origins of these young literati. As New Englanders of Federalist upbringing they might have been expected to find the political atmosphere at Monticello uncongenial, but as men of cultivation and lovers of learning they were quite at home. Fortunately they left relatively full accounts of what they saw and heard.

Both of them were impressed with the wildness of the approach to Monticello. Ticknor spoke of the "steep, savage hill" and Gray of the noble forest of oaks from which it emerged. They said little about architecture, a subject to which they appear to have been relatively indiffer-

[33] Adams to TJ, Dec. 14, 1814; see also Dec. 11. Accounts of their visit can be conveniently seen in F. C. Rosenberger, ed., *Jefferson Reader* (1953), pp. 76–85. It is referred to in ch. IX, pp. 124–125, above.

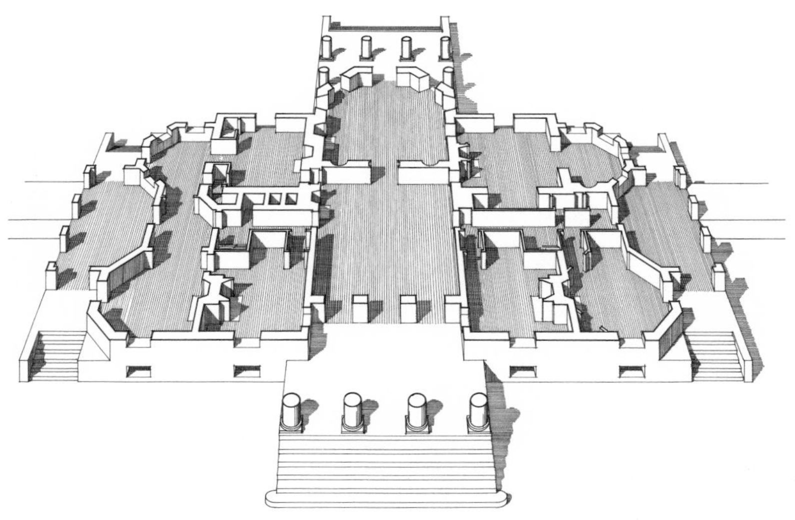

Monticello: Projection, First Floor

(Courtesy of Monticello/Thomas Jefferson Foundation, Inc.)

ent, but they left to posterity fascinating glimpses of the interior of the house. They found the entrance hall to be a veritable museum of natural history; one of them left a rather non-committal description of the paintings, saying that the best were in the lofty drawing room; and they both made highly appreciative comments on the books.[34] Of greatest interest, however, is what they said about their host and the household.

Ticknor's expression of surprise that Jefferson was a tall man reminds us that in their prephotographic age relatively few Americans ever had a full-length view of the third President of the United States. While Ticknor regarded Jefferson's taste in clothes as rather capricious and surprising, he perceived "dignity in his appearance, and ease and grace in his manners." Gray described him in greater detail:

> He is quite tall, six feet, one or two inches, face streaked and speckled with red, light gray eyes, white hair, dressed in shoes of very thin soft leather with pointed toes and heels ascending in a peak behind, with very short quarters, gray worsted stockings, corduroy small clothes, blue waistcoat and coat, of stiff thick cloth made of the wool of his own merinos and badly manufactured, the buttons of his coat and small clothes of horn, and an under waistcoat flannel bound with red velvet. His figure bony, long and with broad shoulders, a true Virginian.[35]

The two young men, who had spent the night in the village of Charlottesville, arrived at Monticello by hack one rainy Saturday morning. Mr. Jefferson promptly sent for their baggage and spent most of the forenoon talking with them. Dinner was at four. A toddy was offered them, according to Virginia custom, but was declined by them and never offered thereafter. They had beer and cider at dinner, and wine after the cloth was removed. Speaking of this occasion and of the members of the family who gathered around the board, Ticknor said he had seldom met a pleasanter party. The host led the conversation, but, somewhat to the surprise of the guests, the feminine members of the family joined in it freely, however high it might be. The ladies left at about six but returned within an hour with the tea tray. More talking ensued until they retired at about half past ten.

The gentlemen found fires in their bedrooms when they got there. Presumably they did not rise at dawn, like their host, and certainly they did not light their own fires as he did his. A servant attended to that before they arose. Meanwhile, Mr. Jefferson was working on his correspondence. At eight or soon after, a warning bell sounded and at nine

[34] See below, pp. 173–174.

[35] Rosenberger, ed., *Jefferson Reader*, pp. 77–78.

the family and guests assembled for breakfast, which was undoubtedly a robust meal. The regimen varied somewhat on Sundays, when there was rather more time for talk, but these observers were impressed with the regularity of the household. Mr. Jefferson took his daily ride; his daughter retired to the classroom with the children; and the others proceeded briskly about their particular affairs.

Learning that Ticknor was planning to study in Europe, Jefferson offered him letters of introduction to such of his old friends as remained. Until the end of his days, he maintained intellectual companionship with this scholar, who was destined to be a distinguished professor at Harvard after his fruitful years abroad. To their correspondence, especially as it bears on linguistics and educational matters, we shall recur. Meanwhile, it seems sufficient to say that his visitor, while regarding his host as somewhat "notional," recognized him not merely as a perfect gentleman in his own house but as an extraordinary character.[36]

About a year after these young visitors left Monticello, John Adams wrote his friend there what he described as a very frivolous letter. In this he asked if Jefferson would be willing to live his seventy years over again. In his reply Jefferson, who was actually nearing seventy-three, said emphatically that he would. He believed this world to be a good one on the whole, "framed on a principle of benevolence," and dealing out more pleasure than pain. He recognized that there were differences of opinion on this point, differences not unrelated to temperament, and he made here one of the most famous and one of the most revealing of his characterizations of himself. "My temperament is sanguine," he said. "I steer my bark with Hope in the head, leaving Fear astern. My hopes indeed sometimes fail; but not oftener than the forebodings of the gloomy."[37] In the happiest life there were convulsions, as he acknowledged; and there was grief, the purpose of which he said he could not understand. He must have been thinking of the untimely loss of his wife and his daughter. It was in his family chiefly that he had found joy to offset the pain of public life. Once, while Vice President, he wrote his daughter Martha that her letters were like "gleams of light to cheer a dreary scene where envy, hatred, malice, revenge, and all the worst passions of man" were marshaled. One evening at her fireside, he said, was worth more than ages in the political atmosphere of Philadelphia. Presumably he found the political air of Washington somewhat more salu-

[36] In the chapter on Ticknor in *Literary Pioneers* (1935), O. W. Long describes his association with TJ, giving numerous extracts from their correspondence. I am much indebted to this study.

[37] TJ to Adams, Apr. 8, 1816, replying to a letter of Mar. 2.

brious when he went there as chief executive, but early in his presidency he wrote his other daughter that only in the love of one's family was "heartfelt happiness" to be found.[38]

He had sedulously avoided public controversy since he left office and was remote from it when he wrote this self-revealing letter to John Adams in 1816. The Monticello family was by no means free of trouble, but joy and hope seem to have been clearly in the ascendant over fear and sorrow at this time. Charles Bankhead appears to have been out of sight; Jeff Randolph and his wife Jane had just become proud parents; and Ellen was proceeding on her tour of visits, aided and abetted by her grandfather. He may have supposed his finances to be in a better state than they actually were when he sent her a hundred dollars, but seemingly they had improved. He was not entirely free from the management of his affairs, but his grandson had relieved him of many of them. As he told John Adams, his optimism was temperamental, and, as he had so often told his daughters, he found his happiness in the family circle, but his outside activities at this stage could hardly have failed to contribute to it.

He had entered a period of creative public service such as he was especially qualified to perform. Central in this was the arduous and far from painless but richly rewarding task of establishing a university; but the Sage of Monticello furthered learning and promoted civilization in many other ways. For one thing he enriched and illuminated history by his letters. Also, he served the public far more than himself by the sale to Congress of the library he had spent a lifetime in assembling. The transaction occurred in the winter of 1814–1815 and has already been mentioned but it deserves another look.

[38] TJ to Martha, Feb. 8, 1798; to Maria, Oct. 1, 1801 (*Family Letters*, pp. 155, 210).

[XII]

Books in Transit: The Library of Congress*

AS his servant Isaac observed, Old Master had an abundance of books and was always looking things up in them.[1] When Jefferson was an eager young student in Williamsburg, books had begun to unlock for him the vast treasure house of human knowledge, and the process of acquisition into which he then entered was to cease only with his life. In his rural canton he had only his own library to rely on, and the loss of his first collection by fire at Shadwell when he was twenty-seven was a heavy blow. That library consisted mostly of lawbooks, but George Wythe had commended to him the works of classical writers as well as those of legal luminaries, and these must have been well represented in his first collection as they were to be in his last. He estimated the monetary value of his lost books as £200, and for a young lawyer in that era his collection was doubtless a creditable one. Within a dozen years, however, he had replaced it many times over.

When he was nearing forty he had 2640 volumes, according to his own report. Besides becoming a regular purchaser from dealers, he had acquired the libraries of Richard Bland and Peyton Randolph, senior statesmen of the province who were distant kinsmen of his. His collection of Virginia laws was already notable, and he had procured writings of other sorts from private libraries, such as those of the Reverend Samuel Henley of the College of William and Mary and William Byrd of Westover. By March 6, 1783, he had made a catalogue of his library, following a system of classification based upon the faculties of the mind as set forth by Francis Bacon. One of the most systematic of men, he was in character as a cataloguer, and in arranging his books he may have

*This chapter was published separately by the Library of Congress in 1977 under the title *Thomas Jefferson and the Library of Congress.*

[1] Isaac Jefferson, *Memoirs of a Monticello Slave*, p. 22.

found solace for the death of his wife, which had occurred about six months earlier.[2]

This was just about the time his mansion was completed in its first form — a form it was to retain for another decade, until the master began the remodeling that was to last virtually until his retirement from the presidency. In the first house the library was in the room on the second floor just above the parlor. This fitted the collection snugly but not uncomfortably until that was swollen by a flood of books from France.

For three decades Jefferson continued to add titles to the catalogue of 1783, though he occasionally neglected to list something he had bought. He eagerly availed himself of the marts of the Old World during his ministry in France and maintained for the rest of his life close contact with booksellers, both at home and abroad. He may be described not improperly as a compulsive buyer, but he was generally a careful one. He had a keen eye for bindings but made no point of first editions. He designated himself as a bibliomaniac and his tastes were catholic. While in Paris he bought for himself, as for his friend Madison, books that were "old and curious or new and useful."[3] To him books were tools; they were storehouses of knowledge and wisdom to which his curious mind could repair; they were friends to turn to, as to his red fields and his beloved family.

During the long years when he was rebuilding his house his books must have been out of sight for part of the time, and we may doubt if any considerable number of his countrymen were really aware of the size and scope of his library. Also, we may wonder just where he found room for it when the house was done and he was at home to stay. He did not know precisely how many volumes he had then, but he figured in 1815 that they took up 855.39 square feet of wall space and that the cases occupied 676 cubic feet altogether.[4] To find that much wall space in his personal wing of the house one must include virtually the whole of it except for his chamber. His cabinet, which was separated from the

[2] This catalogue, a bound volume originally consisting of blank pages on which TJ wrote, is in MHS. It is referred to briefly in *Jefferson the Virginian*, pp. 401–402. The doctoral dissertation of W. H. Peden, "Thomas Jefferson, Book-Collector" (UVA, 1947), deals with all of TJ's libraries. The monumental compilation by E. Millicent Sowerby, *Catalogue of the Library of Thomas Jefferson*, 5 vols. (1952–1959), treats in extraordinary detail the one he sold to Congress (referred to as Sowerby).

[3] See *Jefferson and the Rights of Man*, p. 87. In "Thomas Jefferson and His Library," E. M. Sowerby, while recognizing TJ as a bibliomaniac, denies him the title of bibliophile (Bibliographical Soc. of America, *Papers*, L [1956], 217). This of course is largely a matter of definition, but quite clearly he was more concerned about the contents of books than he was for show.

[4] The figures are in his observations on the transportation of his library (LC, 36168; W. D. Johnston, *Hist. of the Library of Congress* [1904], I, 99).

chamber by his bed, seems to have been lined with books, and, besides filling all the wall space in what is now known as the book room and in the passageway to it, they must have overflowed into what was afterwards called Martha Randolph's sitting room.[5]

Margaret Bayard Smith, on a visit to Monticello in 1809, was honored by the invitation to see what she called her host's sanctum sanctorum, but she admitted disappointment at the appearance of the library. With its "numerous arches and divisions" it was less impressive, she said, than it would have been in one large room.[6] As the front hall was a veritable museum, the eastern end of the house must have been a forest of bookcases. Jefferson does not appear to have said so, but there is little doubt that his library had considerably outgrown its quarters.

Although he guarded these rooms jealously, he had permitted a trusted young friend to use the library in his absence and he was characteristically generous with his books.[7] There was probably no time when some of them were not loaned out. It is impossible to determine just when he reached the conclusion that such a collection should be in public rather than private hands, but toward the end of his first presidential term he said that if a university should be established in his state on a worthy plan, he would leave his books to that institution.[8] Hope of a university was deferred, however, and in the meantime he must have concluded that his financial circumstances would not permit him to be that generous. Before the fall of 1814 he was already thinking of offering his books to Congress in his will—that is, of offering that body the option of acquiring his library at their own price. Circumstances occasioned him to do this sooner.

The financial relief that he gained as a result was temporary, but, through the institution to which he committed his cherished books, this Apostle of Enlightenment made a lasting as well as a highly distinctive contribution both to his own country and to civilization. He never claimed that he founded the Library of Congress, but the institution that emerged from the ashes after the war was virtually his creation.

When the government of the young Republic moved from Philadelphia to the wilderness village of Washington, a special collection of books for the use of the senators and representatives became a necessity. One

[5] The total wall space thus arrived at would have been only barely adequate. Some books that were in a closet in 1806 may have still been there in 1815.

[6] Smith, *First Forty Years of Washington Society*, pp. 71–72.

[7] He granted this privilege to James Ogilvie, who had a school in Milton. His letter of Jan. 31, 1806 (Ford, VIII, 417–419) contains much information about the arrangement of his books.

[8] TJ to L. W. Tazewell, Jan. 5, 1805 (UVA). See *Jefferson the President: Second Term*, p. 22.

was started in 1800, toward the end of John Adams's presidency, and the little library got under way during that of Jefferson with the benefit of his counsel on acquisitions.[9] The collection consisted of perhaps three thousand volumes when the British invaders destroyed it in the late summer of 1814. Learning of this action from the newspapers, Jefferson described it as the triumph of vandalism over knowledge itself. He promptly offered to sell to Congress his own library, which turned out to be more than twice the size of the one that was lost. The moment seemed opportune, not merely because he needed the money (a consideration he did not mention) but also because Congress could not easily replace its losses by shipments from Europe while the war was still going on, and probably could acquire no such a collection as his anyway.

These things and more he said in a letter to Samuel Harrison Smith, former publisher of the *National Intelligencer* and now commissioner of revenue, asking that old friend to pass the offer on to the chairman of the Joint Committee on the Library, of whose identity he himself was not aware. He intended this letter to be made public, as it was, and with it he sent a catalogue of his collection as he supposed it then stood.[10] In a covering letter, admitting some anxiety, he asked Smith to inform him of the intentions of the committee as soon as he could form a conjecture regarding them. Three days later, in letters dealing chiefly with other matters, he informed his friends the President and the Secretary of State what he had done.[11]

Joseph Milligan, a bookseller in Georgetown with whom Jefferson was accustomed to do business, was also in his confidence. Apparently Milligan had made a recent visit to Monticello and had discussed this prospective transaction with his host at that time. After doing so with Monroe in Washington, presumably on his own initiative, he reported back to Monticello that Jefferson's "truly magnanimous" offer would be very acceptable. Milligan offered to arrange the books without charge but did not want the post of librarian.[12]

The prospects of Jefferson's truly magnanimous proposal were far from unclouded. His offer was not formally accepted for four months, and at times its fate hung by a hair. The Joint Committee on the Library

[9] Johnston, *Lib. of Congress*, especially pp. 23–37.

[10] This catalogue has not been discovered, but presumably it corresponded in the first place to the catalogue now in MHS. TJ made a copy of this in 1812 and added titles as late as 1814. See Sowerby, I, ix.

[11] Both of TJ's letters to S. H. Smith, Sept. 21, 1814, are in LC. The public letter is in Ford, IX, 485–488; L. & B., XIV, 190–194; and elsewhere. TJ to Madison, Sept. 24, 1814 (L. & B., XIV, 176); to Monroe, Sept. 24 (Ford, IX, 488–489).

[12] Joseph Milligan to TJ, Sept. 24, 1814 (LC). It seems unlikely that he could have seen TJ's letter of Sept. 21 to S. H. Smith by this time and internal evidence suggests that he had not.

acted expeditiously and appears to have been favorably disposed at all times. The chairman, Senator Robert H. Goldsborough of Maryland, submitted to the Senate on October 7 a resolution authorizing the committee to make a contract with Jefferson for the purchase of his library and this was adopted without dissent on October 10. In the House the resolution encountered some difficulty, and it was amended on October 19 so as to require congressional ratification of any agreement that should be reached. This requirement, in which the Senate concurred the next day, seemed neither unnatural nor improper, but it meant that the sale would be delayed and might be prevented.[13]

Hardly any of the members of Congress had ever seen the library at Monticello, and most of those who were aware of its existence probably had no real idea of what it contained. But Jefferson's letter to Smith, the catalogue made by his own hand that he sent with it, and an alphabetical list of authors that he dispatched a little later — all these were open to the perusal of the representatives during the nine days that the Senate resolution of October 10 was pending in the House.[14] The titles and names had to be left to speak for themselves in diverse tongues, but in his letter Jefferson spoke of and for the collection as a whole.

He sought to demonstrate its distinctiveness by describing his extraordinary efforts in its behalf while abroad. For months he haunted the shops of Paris, looking particularly for books relating to the New World; and he had standing orders for such works with booksellers in other major centers of the Old World. He believed that no comparable collection, relating to America, would ever be made, since it was highly unlikely that "the same opportunities, the same time, industry, perseverance and expense, with some knowledge of the bibliography of the subject" would happen to concur.[15] So far as he and his contemporaries could anticipate the future, this was not an unreasonable conjecture, and his claims for his collection of Americana have been conceded by experts from that day to this.

They were strongly supported that winter by one of his knowledgeable young visitors from Boston. Francis C. Gray described it as "without a question the most valuable in the world." His companion, George Ticknor, who afterwards helped Jefferson so much in the replacement of classical works, made a different and more amusing comment on the library at this time. It seemed to him that "the most curious single specimen — or, at least, the most characteristic of the man and expressive of

[13] Discussions, with votes and texts of resolutions, Oct. 11–20, 1814 (*Annals*, 13 Cong., 3 sess., pp. 23–26, 29–30); Johnston, pp. 72–78.

[14] TJ to Smith, Oct. 11, 1814, sending alphabetical list (LC).

[15] Ford, IX, 486.

his hatred of royalty" was a collection of memoirs which he had recently had bound in six volumes as *The Book of Kings*. The satisfaction he took in these "documents of regal scandal" may doubtless be attributed to the fervid republicanism of this collector of Americana.[16]

Unquestionably a pioneer in that field, he had picked up many a choice item abroad — such, for example, as Theodor de Bry's *The Great or American Voyages*, Parts I–XI, in Latin (1590–1619), which he acquired in Amsterdam for twelve guineas, and *Purchas his Pilgrimage* (second edition, 1614), which he seems to have procured in London at the bargain price of four shillings.[17] His classification of the latter work under American geography suggests where his interest lay. But he had books on exploration in French, Spanish, Portuguese, and Italian, and he could hardly have expected the interest of many of his countrymen in the subject to extend that far.

He said he had been equally diligent in procuring books that bore on the public affairs of his country. Accordingly, he claimed that his library extended particularly to whatever concerned the American statesman, being especially full in parliamentary and diplomatic matters. His claim was well founded. There were far more volumes in the section dealing with politics and commerce than in any other — 1309 altogether. But his was a general, not a specialized professional, library. It was created in the spirit of eighteenth-century universalism, as indeed were those of other gentlemen of Virginia like Peyton Randolph. But he had distinctive interests, and his collection ranged far beyond theirs in comprehensiveness. There could not fail to be books in it that some legislator would see no need for. Yet he was entirely unwilling for his library to be divided. He would have preferred to keep some of the books, but he made no point of that and he specifically stipulated that Congress must take the whole of it or none at all. "I do not know," he said, "that it contains any branch of science [knowledge] which Congress would wish to exclude from their collection; there is, in fact, no subject to which a member of Congress may not have occasion to refer."[18] That was an effective observation to make to the legislators themselves, but quite clearly he envisaged an institution covering the entire field of human knowledge and designed to serve learning as well as legislation.

[16] For details about the work, see Sowerby, I, 181–182. The comments of Gray and Ticknor can be conveniently seen in Rosenberger, ed., *Jefferson Reader*, pp. 80, 83.

[17] These titles can be seen on adjoining pages in Sowerby, IV, 166–167. In "Some Notes Concerning Thomas Jefferson's Libraries" (*W. & M.*, July, 1944, p. 272), W. H. Peden describes TJ as a trail-blazer, especially in the field of Americana and philology. For suggestive comments, see E. M. Sowerby, "Thomas Jefferson and His Library," and F. R. Goff, "Jefferson the Book Collector" (*Quart. Journal of the Lib. of Congress*, XXIX [Jan. 1972].

[18] Ford, IX, 487.

ii

The response to the ex-President's offer by the various members of Congress was a more accurate reflection of their politics than their learning. In the House of Representatives, Federalist graduates of Yale, Brown, Columbia, and Harvard took the lead in opposing the Senate resolution, and hardly a member of their party in Congress favored the purchase at any stage.[19] Some Republicans joined their political rivals in support of amendments to the Senate resolution that were designed to defeat its purpose. One would have authorized the joint committee to negotiate for a library without specifying this one. Another called for the selection of suitable books from Jefferson's collection, implying that it contained unsuitable works and disregarding his statement that it might not be divided. Still another stipulated that the cost should not exceed $25,000, which in fact it did not do.

In this time of financial stringency at the end of the war some objection to the purchase on grounds of economy was to be expected, and the claim that Congress did not really need all of those books was not surprising. But one can scarcely justify the objections of supposedly enlightened men to this collection because it contained the writings of Voltaire, Rousseau, and John Locke. The comment of a Washington correspondent of a Boston paper reflected this attitude: "The grand library of Mr. Jefferson will undoubtedly be purchased with all its finery and philosophical nonsense."[20]

This was after the House had defeated all of the crippling amendments and had adopted one calling for congressional ratification of any agreement the joint committee should enter into. Though introduced by the chief Federalist spokesman against the purchase at this stage, Thomas J. Oakley of New York, it could not have been objected to on principle by any member of the legislative body that was supposed to hold the purse strings. From the point of view of the opposition, no doubt, this was a delaying action, but the committee was authorized to proceed with negotiations for this particular library as a whole. Federalist diehards in the Senate registered their disapproval, but they were overwhelmed by a 3 to 1 margin.[21]

Since the joint committee was already on record as favoring the purchase, the main problem now before them was that of determining the

[19] D. C. Mearns, in *The Story Up to Now: The Library of Congress, 1800–1946* (1947), pp. 18–20, points out the academic connections of the chief debaters.

[20] *Boston Gazette*, Oct. 27, 1814, quoted by Johnston, p. 78.

[21] The various resolutions with the votes on all of them are in Johnston, pp. 72–78, in virtually the language of the *Annals*.

price. Jefferson had taken the position in the beginning that this should be set by Congress, not by him, and had expressed his willingness to accept payment in such form and at such time or times as would be most convenient to the government. He had supposed that some person or persons would be sent to Monticello to value his library. He was willing to be bound by any estimate arrived at in this way or in any other that the representatives of the government should prescribe. Furthermore, he recognized that this estimate might be rejected by either the committee or by Congress. But the committee seemingly embarrassed by its responsibility, pressed Smith for a proposition.

Jefferson, who was trying to be entirely passive in this matter, had no desire to present one and was in no position to make an estimate anyway, he said, since he did not have the catalogue. Accordingly, he passed the problem on to Milligan. He asked that obliging man to make an accurate count of the books listed, distinguishing between them as to size, and to report the figures to Smith, who could use them as the basis of an estimate. The rate per volume was actually suggested by Milligan, who was busily engaged in counting the titles while Jefferson was on a fortnight's visit to Poplar Forest. When that gentleman returned to Monticello in mid-November he learned that he owned some 6500 volumes which were worth more than $24,000 on the scale of valuation that the bookseller was following: namely, ten dollars for a folio, six for a quarto, three for an octavo, and one for a duodecimo. He was entirely willing to accept this figure as a maximum.[22]

As reported to Congress the number of volumes was 6487 and the value was $23,950.[23] From Jefferson's point of view, the language of the committee was unfortunate, though he does not appear ever to have said so. There was no reference to the appraisal by a competent outsider, which had actually been made. Furthermore, the statement that "precise terms" had been received from Jefferson's "agent" tended to make him seem less passive and less generous in the matter of valuation than he really was.[24]

No one at that time could have been expected to anticipate the great monetary value that would be attached to such a collection a century and

[22]This story is told more fully in the letters of Smith to TJ, Oct. 21, 1814; TJ to Milligan, Oct. 29; TJ to Smith, Oct. 29; Milligan to TJ, Nov. 16 (Johnston, pp. 80–84); TJ to Milligan, Nov. 24 (LC). TJ still had the catalogue now in MHS. Because of its interlineations and insertions, however, it would have been very difficult to use. He afterwards expressed great need of the "fair copy."

[23]Miss Sowerby says she was never able to determine whether the figures used in this transaction referred to the number of titles or the number of volumes ("Thomas Jefferson and His Library," p. 214). I am assuming that the references are to volumes.

[24]Johnston, pp. 84–85.

a half later.[25] Contemporary judgments sharply reflected political and personal attitudes. While the original resolution was pending in the House, Jefferson's proposal was ridiculed in a Federalist paper as an attempt, which might well be emulated by other elderly gentlemen, to turn useless books into cash. Before Congress took final action the ex-President's sheep-raising friend, Dr. William Thornton, advised members of that body to offer him $50,000 without further ado. Subsequently, a friendly commentator went so far as to assert that Parliament would have gladly given £50,000 for such a collection. Another supporter of the sale contented himself with the declaration that the library was worth twice what was asked for it. He was indulging in speculation, to be sure, but there appears to be merit in the claim that the government was offered a bargain.[26] To booklovers of a later day the most meritorious of all contemporary comments perhaps was the observation of a correspondent of the *National Intelligencer* that valuation of such a library was "absurd and impossible." Saying that he knew it well, he described it as unique — a library which "for its selection, rarity and intrinsic value, is beyond all price."[27]

About ten days after Milligan suggested to Jefferson what the approximate price should be, the joint committee got around to considering it. They quickly accepted the bookseller's final calculation and on December 3, 1814, a bill authorizing the purchase of the library was passed by the Senate without debate. The House did not act on it until January 26, 1815, and the bill was not approved until the thirtieth. During this interval Jefferson heard nothing from Smith, but he does not appear to have been perturbed. Milligan wrote him that ten wagons would be enough to transport the books, and before he received word that Congress would buy them he was talking of his desire to arrange them.[28] Apparently he did not realize how precarious the situation in the House of Representatives really was.

The offer which Milligan thought so generous, and which Jefferson regarded as timely, barely escaped rejection. A motion by Joseph Lewis, a Federalist congressman from his own state, that consideration of the bill should be indefinitely postponed was defeated by only four votes.

[25] In 1971, Frederick R. Goff, chief of the Rare Book Division, Library of Congress, stated that fifteen years earlier he submitted eleven titles from TJ's library to booksellers for appraisal, and that the value assigned this group approximated the amount paid for the entire collection in 1815 ("Jefferson the Book-Collector," p. 35).

[26] Johnston, pp. 89–95.

[27] *Daily National Intelligencer*, Nov. 16, 1815, quoted by Johnston, p. 91. This correspondent looked up some prices in English catalogues, anyway.

[28] Milligan to TJ, Dec. 14, 1814 (LC); TJ to Smith, Jan. 30, 1815 (LC).

Another, that it be postponed to March 4, was defeated by only six. Almost as much support was given a more humiliating motion by Cyrus King of Massachusetts. This would have authorized the joint committee, on receipt of the library Jefferson had spent so many years in collecting, to select from it the books that were suitable and to sell the rest. The final vote on the bill authorizing the purchase of the collection as a whole was 81 to 71.[29]

A modern analyst of this vote has observed that, instead of being regarded as "a triumph of the children of light over the powers of darkness," it should be recognized as a narrow victory of the administration over the opposition.[30] It is uncertain just what Madison and Monroe did to further this legislation, if indeed they were in position to do anything much at this juncture, but their support of it may be assumed; and the record shows that the Federalists opposed it, almost to a man. Among those voting in the negative were Timothy Pickering, of whom partisan bigotry was to be expected, and Daniel Webster, who had not yet emerged as a champion of nationalism but was still in a provincial stage. In no section was the opposition so great as in New England, and the bitterest of all the speakers seems to have been Cyrus King. According to the unsympathetic report in the *National Intelligencer*, he said he was "opposed to a general dissemination of that infidel philosophy" and the principles of a man who had inflicted more injury on the country than anybody else except Mr. Madison. The books for which money was to be put into Mr. Jefferson's pocket were described by this well-educated spokesman of High Federalism as "good, bad, and indifferent, old, new, and worthless, in languages which many can not read, and most ought not." The whole transaction was in "true Jeffersonian, Madisonian philosophy, to bankrupt the Treasury, beggar the people, and disgrace the nation."[31]

Although it may be presumed that the Federalists would have opposed the bill under almost any circumstances, the arguments against it appealed to a considerable number of Republicans. Among the fifteen members of the majority who voted in the negative was the veteran Nathaniel Macon, a sincere advocate of economy in all fields. By this time the legislators knew that the prospect of successful negotiations at Ghent had improved, but news of neither the treaty of peace nor Jackson's vic-

[29]Jan. 26, 1815 (*Annals*, 13 Cong., 3 sess., pp. 1105–1106). The measure was approved Jan. 30 (*Daily National Intelligencer*, Feb. 4).

[30]Mearns, p. 24. This historian of the Library of Congress tabulates and analyzes the votes, pp. 21–25. He designates members of the party of the administration as Democrats, whereas I am continuing to call them Republicans.

[31]Quoted by Johnston, p. 86. The debate was more favorably reported from the Federalist side by the *New York Evening Post*, Jan. 31, 1815 (*ibid.*, pp. 87–88).

tory at New Orleans had yet reached Washington. The financial problems of the country were far from solution — a fact of which no one was more aware than Jefferson. It could certainly be argued sincerely that, at such a time, money was needed for other things much more than for what then seemed a big library. The large vote for postponement of this question is far from inexplicable. But, as viewed by posterity, the basic question was that of the character of the library.

The legislators could not have proceeded indefinitely without books, but if this particular collection had not been offered and accepted, we may wonder if Congress would soon, or ever, have set up one of comparable scope. This was a general, not a narrowly professional, library and, by acquiring it, Congress laid the foundations of a great national institution, destined to rank with the Bibliothèque Nationale and the British Museum. Most of the legislators may have continued to think of it as their own particular possession, but it could and did serve a larger clientele and a wider purpose. Their final vote may have been determined primarily by political considerations, and we cannot ascertain the number who shared Jefferson's vision; but the legislators well deserve the gratitude of posterity for what they brought about.

iii

On February 5, 1815, nearly five months after he offered his library to Congress, Jefferson learned of the official approval of the purchase and received a copy of the bill.[32] This was during the brief visit of George Ticknor and Francis Gray, when he was also informed of the victory at New Orleans and became aware of the destruction of his milldam by flood.[33] He seemed imperturbable in the midst of these important events and appears to have drawn up no private balance sheet of loss and gain. Payment for his library was to be made to the full amount in treasury notes, but he declined to receive it as yet. When asked just how he wanted these notes made out, he replied that they should not be made out at all until the books had been or were ready to be delivered. They had to be arranged and that was a task that he alone could perform. It would require him to be on his legs the whole time, he said, and he did not know how long they would hold out. He thought perhaps the work could be done in a fortnight but hoped the people in Washington would be patient.[34] In fact they were in no hurry. Nearly a month elapsed before Congress passed a supplementary measure, authorizing the Pres-

[32] Smith to TJ, Jan. 30, 1815, received Feb. 5 (LC).
[33] See above, ch. IX, pp. 124–125.
[34] Smith to TJ, Feb. 15, 1815; TJ to Smith, Feb. 27 (LC).

ident to select a suitable chamber for the library and to provide for its transportation. Smith reported a recommendation of Madison that the actual removal be delayed until May.[35]

In their arrangement Jefferson's books followed the order of his catalogue.[36] When seeking information he sometimes had a score of them around him, as his servant Isaac had observed. Mrs. Smith reported that he had several hundred of his favorites in his cabinet, and no doubt these came from various sections. It is hard to believe that this exceedingly systematic man ever let his books get into serious disarray or was often unable to lay hands on one he wanted, but he had not reviewed the entire collection for a score of years. He was now seeking to put it in perfect order, and for this he needed his catalogue.

He did not get that back until the middle of March, but he probably did some "arranging" while waiting for it, and in the meantime he sought to retrieve books that had been borrowed from him. Among these were several he had loaned Madison during his own presidency. Suspecting that they were somewhere in the Department of State, he asked Milligan to inquire about them there. The compiler of the statutes of Virginia, William Waller Hening, was allowed to keep some of the volumes of the laws until he was through with them.[37] Among other delinquent borrowers were Dr. Benjamin S. Barton of Philadelphia, who had a botanical work, and George Hay of Richmond, who had a legal treatise.

He had supposed that somebody would be sent to check his books against the catalogue and was prepared to make appropriate financial adjustment for the deficiencies that were to be expected. Milligan came in due course to supervise the packing, but he himself appears to have done all the checking. He was pleased to discover after a rigorous review that the losses were more than offset by accessions that were not recorded in the catalogue from which Milligan had made his estimate. Accordingly, he concluded that he was giving good measure.

The books were to be shipped in the pine cases they already occupied. Generally a case was about nine feet high and consisted of three tiers of shelves with backs. These shelves were of varying depth to accommodate folios and quartos, octavos, and duodecimos as was required. Since the tiers could be separated from one another (and perhaps the shelves could be), the bookcases could be turned into packing cases when their fronts

[35] Act of Mar. 3, 1815, in *Daily National Intelligencer*, Mar. 8, 1815; Smith to TJ, Mar. 11 (LC). Most of the important documents are printed in Johnston's admirable account of the removal (pp. 97–104).

[36] See TJ to James Ogilvie, Jan. 31, 1806 (Ford, VIII, 417–419).

[37] TJ wrote to George Watterston, Jan. 3, 1816 (LC) that one volume was still in Hening's hands. His correspondence with Hening, Mar. 11–Apr. 25, 1815 (LC), is of special interest in this connection.

were covered with boards.[38] The covers were being prepared by workmen at Monticello, but Milligan was asked to bring paper parings to guard against jolting and sheets of paper to put between every two volumes. Books with fine bindings had to be specially wrapped, but every volume could be left in its proper place. Accordingly, all that needed to be done on arrival in Washington would be to set up the cases and remove the boards and paper.

A few days after his seventy-second birthday Jefferson wrote the Secretary of the Treasury that the books were now ready for delivery and that their removal had actually begun. Therefore, he was now ready to receive payment. He asked that $4870 be sent John Barnes in Georgetown (to cover his debt to Kosciuszko), $10,500 be sent to William Short, and the balance to him personally. The treasury notes had depreciated slightly, but Short had signified his entire willingness to accept them at par value in full payment of the debt to him. Jefferson thus freed himself of the two obligations that troubled him most, and out of the rest of the payment he met others that were less pressing.[39]

Presumably, Milligan was then at Monticello, packing the books. Weeks earlier, Joseph Dougherty, Jefferson's old coachman, had expressed his interest in their transportation. Smith and Madison arranged with him to supervise this at five dollars a day, though he claimed that little more than his expenses would be covered. Learning of Jefferson's plan to leave for Poplar Forest as soon as the books were packed, Dougherty was afraid he would miss seeing his old employer, but that gentleman remained at Monticello until the last and tenth wagon had set out. About the same time he learned that seven wagons had crossed the Rappahannock at Fredericksburg, but not until midsummer, after he had made a trip to Poplar Forest, did he receive a report of the arrival of all the wagons in Washington. By that time Milligan had unpacked the books and found them entirely uninjured.[40] The room provided for them was large enough, he believed. There was more space for the library at the Capital than at Monticello, and it could perform a larger service there. When reporting to Smith the pending departure of the last portion of his library, Jefferson said: "It is the choicest collection of books in the United States, and I hope it will not be without some general effect on the literature of our country."

[38] TJ described this ingenious plan in some observations on the transportation of his library, enclosed in his letter of Feb. 27, 1815, to Smith, and in his letter of Mar. 28 to Milligan (LC; Johnston pp. 99, 103). The bookcases that were installed at Monticello about a century and a half later were designed from these descriptions.

[39] TJ to A. J. Dallas, Apr. 18, 1815 (Ford, IX, 514–515); TJ's receipt to Treasury, Apr. 23 (LC); Account Book entries of Apr. 29, May 9, and soon thereafter; William Short to TJ, Mar. 11, 1815 (*Papers, MHS*, 227–230).

[40] TJ to Samuel H. Smith, May 8, 1815 (LC); Milligan to TJ, May 6, July 31 (LC).

* * *

With the books Jefferson sent the catalogue which had guided him in their arrangement. He might have done this even if the person who was to have charge of them had not requested it. Formerly, the clerk of the House of Representatives had served as part-time librarian, but a full-time position had been recently created and to this George Watterston had been appointed. Toward the end of April, somewhat apologetically, he asked Jefferson's advice about arrangement. In his reply Jefferson dealt chiefly with practical matters rather than with theoretical considerations, but he cast much light on his catalogue and on himself as a cataloguer.[41]

Two methods of classification offered themselves, he said — the alphabetical and that by subject. Finding the former unsatisfactory, he had adopted the latter, while recognizing that it presented difficulties. A library shelved in strict alphabetical order, by authors or by titles, would indeed present a "medley" to the mind, as he observed. And anyone who has had access to the stacks of a modern library can recognize the convenience of having books on a particular subject close together. A recent librarian, who attached that designation to Jefferson, observed that he had "a perfect passion for the systematic and orderly arrangement of data so as to make it most readily available for actual use."[42] Being concerned for the accessibility as well as the systematic arrangement of books, he had supplemented his subject catalogue with an alphabetical list of authors' names with references to the numbered labels he had pasted on his books.

He saved Watterston a vast amount of time and labor, but he presented that librarian with a *fait accompli.* One reason why his general system was continued until almost the end of the century doubtless was that successive librarians of Congress did not know how to get out of it. He made no attempt to justify it on principle at this stage. He contented himself with saying that he took the basis of distribution from "Lord Bacon's table of science, modifying it to the changes in scientific pursuits which have taken place since his time, and to the greater or less extent of reading in the science which I proposed to myself."

His "system" of classification was based on the division of the faculties of the mind into memory, reason, and imagination, and the corresponding division of human knowledge into history, philosophy and the fine arts. Toward the end of his life he said that the "origination of this

[41] Watterston's letter of Apr. 26, 1815, and TJ's answer of May 7 can both be seen in Johnston, pp. 141–145.

[42] Randolph G. Adams, in *Three Americanists* (1939), p. 72. The title of ch. III of this work is "Thomas Jefferson, Librarian."

division" was actually with the Abbé de Charron. Nonetheless he himself appears to have derived the idea from Bacon, whom he listed with Sir Isaac Newton and John Locke in his trinity of immortals. The table that was presented by him was even closer to that of Jean d'Alembert, who elaborated somewhat on Bacon's in the middle of the eighteenth century.[43]

He used the terminology of his own era, not that of ours. As we have seen, to him the word "science" meant knowledge, and what we now call science was designated by him as natural history or natural philosophy. Like Bacon and d'Alembert, he placed civil and natural history in the same division and listed physics and astronomy under philosophy. He went considerably beyond these predecessors in the number of subdivisions and arranged them somewhat differently. One of the most distinctive of his additions was "gardening," which he classified among the fine arts and placed just after architecture. Unlike earlier classifiers, he was using his table as a guide in the arrangement of his books. Accordingly, he assigned a chapter number to each subdivision. Ancient history was number 1, botany was 13, geography 29, music 32; and there were 44 chapters altogether.

His classification was not a complete innovation. The most recent catalogue of the congressional library (1812), following that of the Library Company of Philadelphia, was based on Bacon–d'Alembert tabulations of knowledge.[44] Jefferson's classification was much more extensive, however, and it marked a notable advance in what came to be called library science. It received some criticism at the time on theoretical grounds, and it unquestionably reflected its author's personal tastes and interests. He himself recognized that he had a disproportionate number of subdivisions in the field of law, and his classification of religion under the head of jurisprudence strikes one as downright capricious.[45] In the printed catalogue of 1815, Watterston, seeking to provide a useful guide, arranged the titles alphabetically within the chapters. This was a depar-

[43] TJ's table can be seen in the front matter of Sowerby, I. He referred to Charron's *La Sagesse* (1601) in his letter of Mar. 24, 1824, to Judge A. B. Woodward (L. & B., XVI, 17). Apparently he was relying on his memory, for he incorrectly dated Bacon's *Advancement of Learning* (1605). The table of d'Alembert, to which he did not refer here and may have forgotten, appeared in *Discours Préliminaire de l'Encyclopédie* (1751). It is printed along with those of Bacon and TJ by Leo E. LaMontagne in *American Library Classification, with Special Reference to the Library of Congress* (1961), pp. 36–39. Ch. II of this authoritative work deals with TJ as a classifier.

[44] LaMontagne, p. 45, listing eighteen classes. He is uncertain whether this was chiefly owing to the part-time librarian, Patrick Magruder, or to Samuel Latham Mitchill, a member of the library committee. The latter, who knew TJ well over a long period, might have picked up the idea from him.

[45] His system was criticized at the time by A. B. Woodward, who advanced his own scheme of universal knowledge. See LaMontagne, pp. 40–43, and TJ's letter to Woodward, Mar. 24, 1824 (L. & B., XVI, 17–20).

ture from Jefferson's own unprinted catalogue, a departure he did not like, but there was no important change in his classification until after his death. In 1830 new subdivisions were added, as they continued to be until the end of the century, when an entirely new classification was adopted.[46]

If, somehow, he could be informed of later developments, he would probably be surprised that his basic system was not superseded sooner. He himself modified it in connection with the library of the University of Virginia, grouping subjects according to professorships. He was no rigid theorist in the world of books, if indeed he was in any field, and he fully recognized the inevitability of change in human affairs. A scheme of classification that sufficed for a library of sixty-five hundred volumes could not have been expected to meet the needs of 750,000. Not even he expected the vast proliferation of knowledge during the rest of the nineteenth century, not to mention that of the twentieth.

Fortunately, he did not know that most of the books he sold the government would be destroyed by fire in 1851. A couple of thousand of them remain in the Library of Congress as cherished treasures. If they could be identified in no other way, they can be from his characteristic bookmark. Before the signature "I" (there was then no "J"), he wrote the letter "T," and after the signature "T" he wrote the letter "J." On the shelves of one of the world's largest libraries these old books of his are a tiny fraction, but in some sense he may be said to have put his stamp on the entire collection. His catalogue may now seem archaic, but, as has been suggested, he might well be termed the Father of American Librarianship.[47] Few wonders of the modern world would delight him more than the card catalogue, and in any great library he would soon make himself at home.

[46] Developments are described by LaMontagne in ch. III.

[47] Adams, *Three Americanists*, p. 95.

[XIII]

The Ways of a Humanist

I CANNOT live without books," wrote Jefferson to John Adams about a month after the tenth and last wagonload from his library set out for Washington.[1] Most of that month he had spent on a visit to Poplar Forest, where he still had a small non-professional collection, but before he left Monticello he must have set up at least one bookcase in place of the score or more that had crowded his quarters. If the books for which he paid $187 to Thomas Mann Randolph did not fill it, no doubt some that he had ordered from Milligan had been received by this time. He had already made specific plans for purchases abroad in which the services of George Ticknor were included.[2]

He was trying to replace his "literary treasures" only in part. Fewer books would suffice, he said, "when amusement, and not use," was his sole future object. In the ensuing decade he was to build up a library of about a thousand volumes. Within these limits it was a comprehensive collection in which no important branch of knowledge was unrepresented.[3] In its proportion, it differed considerably from the library that was sold to Congress. For example, there was a relative decrease in works of law, politics, and economics. Obviously he had less use for these than formerly. Yet we need not believe that he now wanted books wholly for amusement, as the term is generally understood. Among those in the vanished library that he was most anxious to replace were mathematical works. He had about thirty of them in the library of his

[1] TJ to Adams, June 10, 1815. All the correspondence between these two men is in *A.-J. Letters*, and the references in this chapter are to the dates only.

[2] Account Book, May 10, 1815, showing payment of $187 to T. M. Randolph for books; July 5, showing remittance of $550 to John Vaughan for purchases abroad. He wrote Vaughan about his plans on Mar. 1 (LC). Orders to Milligan are referred to in their correspondence.

[3] A catalogue of this library was printed in Washington in 1829 for the purposes of an auction. This was copied from a manuscript in his handwriting now in LC. I have used a facsimile of a copy in the Clements Library, Ann Arbor, Mich.

old age. No doubt he found enjoyment in them since mathematics was a favorite subject with him, but he made practical use of the books of tables and must have valued others for their utility. What, on the other hand, did he think of books that are commonly read for pleasure rather than information — that is, works of the imagination, prose and poetry?

The term fiction does not appear in any of the catalogues of his own libraries, but he had a good deal to say about it in connection with a book list he drew up at the age of twenty-eight. A few months before his marriage he prepared for his prospective brother-in-law, Robert Skipwith, a catalogue of a general collection of books for a private gentleman.[4] In his self-conscious letter this serious-minded young man justified fiction on moral grounds. Its "entertainments" were not merely pleasant but useful, he said, for "everything is useful that contributes to fix us in the principles and practice of virtue." He observed that the villainous murder of Duncan excited just as much horror in the mind of the reader of *Macbeth* as if that had been a sober work of history. And he believed that a sense of filial piety was more strongly impressed upon the mind by *King Lear* than by "all the dry volumes of ethics and divinity that ever were written".

Besides the two Shakespearean tragedies he cited *A Sentimental Journey*, which continued to be a favorite of his, at least until he went to France more than a decade later. In the whimsies of Laurence Sterne he found not only entertainment but moral value.[5] The modern reader may have more difficulty in perceiving this and doubtless will be less disposed to look for it, but he cannot fail to be impressed with Jefferson's broad acquaintance with the literature of his mother country before he became deeply involved in affairs of state. He seems to have included in this book list every important English author from Chaucer to Goldsmith.

It need not be assumed that he had read all of the works he cited at this early age, but, far from confining himself to legal treatises and what he called "the learned lumber of Greece and Rome," he had kept himself abreast of the literature of his era. Despite his increased involvement in public affairs, he continued to do so at least until the eve of the French Revolution, when he was in his forties. In Paris, besides widening his acquaintance with French literature, he drafted a paper he entitled "Thoughts on English Prosody." This seems never to have been dispatched to the Marquis de Chastellux, for whom it was intended, and it appeared in print only in the twentieth century, when it could not have

[4] TJ to Robert Skipwith, Aug. 3, 1771, with catalogue (Boyd, I, 76–81). His early literary tastes are described in *Jefferson the Virginian*, pp. 104–105.

[5] Boyd, in a footnote (I, 81), says that fiction was similarly defended by English critics of the time and regards the catalogue as more noteworthy, perhaps, for its up-to-the-minute character.

been expected to have any scholarly impact. It tells us a good deal, though, about his literary interests.[6]

During the visit of the learned Chastellux to Monticello toward the close of the American Revolution, he and his host had discussed the measure of English verse.[7] Jefferson had then taken the position, which was in fact Dr. Samuel Johnson's, that it depended on quantity as did Greek and Latin verse — "on long and short syllables arranged in regular feet." Chastellux disagreed at the time, as he may be assumed to have done when the discussion was renewed in France. Turning the subject over in his mind during daily walks in the Bois de Boulogne, Jefferson determined to present his views in writing. As his study proceeded, however, he came to the conclusion that the measure of English verse was determined, not by quantity but by accent.

Presumably, his plan to communicate his essay to Chastellux was interrupted by the accident which resulted in the dislocation of his right wrist.[8] With his left hand he drafted a rather stilted letter in which he said: "Error is the stuff of which the web of life is woven; and he who lives longest and wisest is only able to wear out the more of it." If he had the benefit of twentieth-century scholarship, he might conclude that he had attributed somewhat too much regularity to English verse.[9] But this essay leaves us in no doubt of his wide knowledge of it and genuine interest in it in his own time. He quoted, often at length, from Milton, Pope, Shenstone, Gray, Collins, Swift, Young, Cunningham, Addison, and Hopkins, as well as from Homer, Theocritus, and Horace.

Perhaps the French Revolution marked a turning point in his reading as it did in human history. In what he afterwards called belles-lettres he seems never to have emerged from the eighteenth century and to have entered the nineteenth. A few months after he became President he spoke of the decline of his interest in poetry. "In early life I was fond of it, and easily pleased," he said. "But as age and cares advanced, the powers of fancy have declined. Every year seems to have plucked a feather from her wing till she can no longer waft one to those sublime heights to which it is necessary to accompany a poet. So much has my

[6] The paper is printed in L. & B., XVIII, 415–451, from LC. In the note on the covering letter to the Marquis de Chastellux, the editor of the *Jefferson Papers* describes the uncertainties in this episode and provides the most acceptable conjecture about what happened (Boyd, X, 498–499).

[7] The visit is described in *Jefferson the Virginian*, pp. 391–393.

[8] Sept. 18, 1786. See *Jefferson and the Rights of Man*, p. 73. Chastellux died in 1788.

[9] Paul Fussell, Jr., describing TJ as an "absolute stress-regularist," says that his essay "would hardly do credit to a school-boy's literary sensibility" (*Theory of Prosody in Eighteenth-Century England* [1954], pp. 29–30). This judgment I regard as hypercritical and unfair. Of course Jefferson was an amateur, but he must be judged in the setting of his own time, and, in my amateurish opinion, he was not an absolutist with respect to poetry or anything else except the rights of man.

relish for poetry deserted me that I cannot read even Virgil with pleasure."[10]

Actually, his own language was far from prosaic and his lack of relish for the poetry of the ancients was not permanent. He read Virgil to some extent in old age and never lost his taste for Homer. He occasionally quoted an eighteenth-century English poem to John and Abigail Adams, but the name of William Wordsworth appears in none of the later catalogues of this nature lover. Nor did this early admirer of Laurence Sterne recommend to his granddaughters the romances of Walter Scott, which they seem to have read with avidity.[11]

He came to view contemporary literary trends with disquietude. In the last decade of his life he deplored the "inordinate passion" of the day for novels. "When this poison infects the mind," he said, "it destroys its tone and revolts it against wholesome reading. Reason and fact, plain and unadorned, are rejected. Nothing can gain attention unless dressed in all the figments of fancy, and nothing so bedecked comes amiss. The result is a bloated imagination, sickly judgment, and disgust towards all the real business of life."[12] While he regarded most novels as trash, he recognized that a few, such as the writings of Maria Edgeworth, inculcated principles of sound morality. He warned against over-indulgence in poetry, but regarded some of it as useful in forming taste and style. As he admitted, "Pope, Dryden, Thompson, Shakespeare, and of the French, Molière, Racine, the Corneilles, may be read with pleasure and improvement."

In the system of classification followed in the catalogue of the library of his last years, a distinction is made between ancient and modern history, but not between ancient and modern literature. It is difficult to measure the decline of his interest in the latter. Among the few books he listed under the heading "Romance" are *Don Quixote* in Spanish and Boccaccio's *Decameron* in Italian, but there is nothing in English. *Paradise Lost* was on his poetry shelf along with the *Iliad* and the *Odyssey*. He appears to have spent considerably less time on Shakespeare than on the great Greek dramatists. He was well supplied with grammars and dictionaries, and maintained his interest in language. Years earlier he had criticized Dr. Samuel Johnson for that lexicographer's ignorance of northern languages and relative disregard of Anglo-Saxon, as compared with Greek

[10] TJ to John D. Burk, June 21, 1801 (Ford, VIII, 65).

[11] As is suggested in a letter of Apr. 28, 1822, from Virginia Randolph to Nicholas Trist (Trist Papers, LC).

[12] TJ to Nathaniel Burwell, Mar. 14, 1818 (Ford, X, 104–105). He was replying to a letter of inquiry about female education and said other things of interest which we cannot go into here.

and Latin, in the origin of words.[13] However, he regarded the learned Doctor as the best English etymologist, and the Dictionary was on one of his first lists of desiderata in 1815.

He sent this list to George Ticknor, whom he described to John Adams as the best "bibliograph" he had encountered. When that young scholar went abroad shortly after his visit to Monticello, he bore letters of introduction from his recent host to Lafayette, Du Pont de Nemours, Jean-Baptiste Say, and others. In his turn he expected to perform purchasing commissions for Jefferson on the Continent. As things turned out, his trip to Paris was long postponed and for many months his correspondence with Jefferson was conducted from Göttingen. For all that gentleman's recognition of the importance of northern languages, his linguistic knowledge did not extend to German, and Ticknor's discussion of the state of German literature introduced him to a relatively unknown field. There is no reason to believe that Goethe ever meant anything to him, and this fascinating correspondence is chiefly significant in its bearing on his works in the classics, which actually provided his major literary "amusement" in old age.[14]

When Ticknor and Gray were at Monticello the latter observed that their host's collection of the ancient classics was complete with respect to authors, but "very careless in the editions."[15] Ticknor, who was enormously impressed with the scholarship of the Germans, urged upon Jefferson the superiority of their editions of the classics to many of those he had requested. In reply, Jefferson, who was characteristically modest in all matters of scholarship, stated that he had no more knowledge of editions than he had picked up in Paris thirty years before, and authorized his young friend to exercise his own judgment in this regard. He reminded Ticknor, however, of his continued dislike of folios and quartos, which were so fatiguing to the "nerveless hand" of a septuagenarian. "I value explanatory notes," he added; "but verbal criticisms and various readings, not much."[16] Ticknor's arrival in Paris, where Jefferson had supposed he would perform most of his functions as a purchasing agent, was long delayed, but he bought classical works during his stay at Göttingen. Since the explanatory notes were in Latin, Jefferson could read them.

[13] TJ to Sir Herbert Craft, Oct. 30, 1798 (L. & B., XVIII, 361–364). This letter is followed by his essay on Anglo-Saxon, which he is sending (pp. 365–411).

[14] O. W. Long describes Ticknor's relations with TJ at this stage and gives lengthy extracts from their letters in *Literary Pioneers*, pp. 7–10, 17–25. For an early book list from TJ, see p. 228, note 23.

[15] Rosenberger, ed., *Jefferson Reader*, p. 79.

[16] TJ to Ticknor, Feb. 8, 1816 (Long, p. 21).

ii

From his catalogue we can ascertain the number of books in the library of his last years and can note that it was weighted on the side of classical antiquity. The extent of his reading cannot be measured with precision, and he complained that he had fallen far behind John Adams in this respect. When Jefferson was nearing seventy-four his more elderly friend in Quincy reported boastfully that in the past year he had read forty-three volumes, eleven of them quartos. Jefferson's response, that half a dozen octavos were as many as he could find time for, was doubtless an understatement. During the morning hours and from dinner to darkness he was "drudging at the writing table," he said, and had to do all his reading by candlelight.[17] The burden of his correspondence was indeed heavy, and he told Adams a year later that his repugnance to writing was becoming "more deadly and insuperable" every day and every hour. By contrast he had a "canine appetite for reading" that he was indulging. "I see in it a relief against the taedium senectutis," he said, "a lamp to lighten my path through the dreary wilderness of time before me, whose bourne I see not."[18]

He probably exaggerated the tedium of old age, but in his retirement he undoubtedly found renewed delight in reading — especially Greek and Roman writings "in the beauties of their originals."[19] During his presidency he stated that he never read translations, but, since he had a good many of them, it would doubtless be more correct to say that he much preferred to read originals. He was at home in French, Italian, and Spanish, and stressed their importance, but he regarded Greek as the finest of human languages. He said that Homer must ever remain the first of poets until a language "equally ductile and copious shall again be spoken."[20]

He was much interested in the pronunciation of classical Greek, and had made special efforts to ascertain this in Paris, where he learned the pronunciation of modern Greek from persons who spoke it. Though he accepted this as something of a guide, he fully recognized that, since sound is "more fugitive than the written letter," there must have been very considerable change after so long a time. He did not really hope

[17] TJ to Adams, Jan. 11, 1817.

[18] TJ to Adams, May 17, 1818.

[19] Quotation from his letter to John Brazier, Aug. 24, 1819 (L. & B., XV, 207–211), containing one of his fullest discussions of the value of the classics. Among many treatments of this topic I am specially indebted to Louis B. Wright, "Thomas Jefferson and the Classics" (from *Proceedings of the Am. Philos. Soc.*, vol. 87, Nov., 1943), and to Karl Lehmann, *Thomas Jefferson, American Humanist* (2nd impression, 1965).

[20] TJ to John Waldo, Aug. 16, 1813 (L. & B., XIII, 341; cited by Sowerby, IV, 412).

Monticello: Jefferson's Study
(Courtesy of Robert C. Lautman/Thomas Jefferson Foundation, Inc.)

ever to recapture the voices of Homer and Demosthenes, but he never ceased to regard Greek as a notably euphonious language. He quoted it frequently to John Adams, though in letters to persons of lesser learning he generally contented himself with Latin.[21]

He accepted the Italian pronunciation of Latin and seems to have harbored little doubt of its authenticity. In the last year of his life he bemoaned the necessity of admitting "shameful Latinists" to the classical school (department) of the University of Virginia, being specially disturbed by the pronunciation they brought with them. Thus he said: "We must rid ourselves of this Connecticut Latin, of this barbarous confusion of long and short syllables, which renders doubtful whether we are listening to a reader of Cherokee, Shawnee, Iroquois, or what."[22]

He appears to have said much less about Latin as a language than about Greek, but, while something of a stickler about its pronunciation, he was not one about its grammar. Outside the realm of poetry his favorite among the Roman writers was Tacitus, of whom he said: "It is by boldly neglecting the rigorisms of grammar that Tacitus has made himself the strongest writer in the world. The Hypercritics call him barbarous; but I should be sorry to exchange his barbarisms for their wire-drawn purisms. Some of his sentences are as strong as language can make them. Had he scrupulously filled up the whole of their syntax, they would have been merely common."[23] He was nearing eighty when he said this. A decade earlier he had made a similar observation: "Fill up all the ellipses and syllepses of Tacitus, Sallust, Livy, etc., and the elegance and force of their sententious brevity are extinguished."[24]

It may be noted by way of analogy that if he was a strict constructionist with respect to the American Constitution he was certainly not one with regard to English grammar. When President, he asked Madison to read and revise his first annual message to Congress, saying: "Where strictness of grammar does not weaken expression, it should be attended to in complaisance to the purists of New England. But where by small grammatical negligences, the energy of an idea is condensed, or a word stands for a sentence, I hold grammatical rigor in contempt."[25] More than a score of years later, after acknowledging a translation of a Greek grammar that Edward Everett had sent him and discussing certain questions that it raised, he told this learned young New Englander that he

[21] The appearance of a pamphlet on the pronunciation of Greek occasioned him to discuss the subject with Adams, Mar. 11, 1819, with John Brazier, Aug. 24, 1819, and with others.

[22] To W. B. Giles, Dec. 26, 1825 (Ford, X, 357).

[23] TJ to Edward Everett, Feb. 24, 1823 (L. & B., XV, 414–415).

[24] To John Waldo, Aug. 16, 1813 (L. & B., XIII, 339).

[25] TJ to Madison, Nov. 12, 1801 (Ford, VIII, 108*n.*–109*n.*)

was not "an adept in the metaphysical speculations of Grammar," nor "a friend to a scrupulous purism of style." Instead he readily sacrificed "the niceties of syntax to euphony and strength." He then made the comment on Tacitus we have already quoted and gave an English sample. Instead of saying "Resistance *against* tyrants," the saying was "Resistance *to* tyrants is obedience to God," which he regarded as much stronger.[26]

He was quoting the motto on his own seal and extending his essential philosophy to the realm of language. There, as elsewhere, he advocated a maximum of freedom and opposed the tyranny, actual or potential, of the schoolmasters. These he tended to locate in New England for reasons that were doubtless to some extent political.[27] Since his day the dangers of grammatical purism have become increasingly remote, and the adjectives "ductile" and "copious" which he used in describing Greek, can be more aptly applied to English than to any other living language. He might issue very different warnings if he were here now and, in view of the increased hospitality of a later age to new words, he would probably not need to defend the neologisms for which political enemies sought to ridicule him. One gains no sense of grammatical licentiousness from his own writings, but, characteristically, this accomplished linguist recognized that, like government, language was made for man, not man for language, and his classicism was the more vital because it was not pedantic.

In one of the fullest statements he ever made about the values of classical learning, he said in the first place that the Greek and Latin languages offered "models of pure taste in writing."[28] To them he credited "the rational and chaste style" of writing in the nations familiar with them. "Without these models," he said, "we should probably have continued the inflated style of our northern ancestors, or the hyperbolical and vague one of the East."

It is most unlikely that this man of diverse tastes and universal spirit ever set up for himself a specific literary model. Like everybody else he learned to write by writing, of which he did far more than most people who did not make a business of it. The clarity, force, and grace that marked nearly all of it was a reflection of his own mind and personality. The style was the man and is equally unsusceptible of complete or precise analysis. But he was of course affected by what he read, and the words we have quoted leave no doubt of the qualities he himself valued

[26] TJ to Edward Everett, Feb. 24, 1823 (L. & B., XV, 414–415).

[27] His attitude is admirably described by Robert L. Kellogg in "Language and Culture in America" (*South Atlantic Bulletin*, XLI [Jan. 1976], 3–8).

[28] TJ to John Brazier, Aug. 24, 1819 (L. & B., XV, 208).

in classical writings. Comments on particular authors appear from time to time in his letters, but rarely does he commend or condemn one of them for form alone. Cicero may be cited as a doubtful case. Jefferson, who approved of his character and republican principles, admired his letters but not his long speeches. To his own son-in-law in Congress he wrote: "I doubt if there is a man in the world who can now read one of his orations through but as a piece of task-work."[29] If that was contrary to the judgment of most classicists then and thereafter, it was in full accord with that of many a schoolboy.

A second value of classical learning, as perceived by the Sage of Monticello, lay in the sheer pleasure to be derived from reading Greek and Latin works in the beauty of the originals.[30] Several times he said that he prized this "luxury" more than any other his father had placed within his reach. Such a dialogue with antiquity as he carried on was not for everybody, as he recognized, but it was no mere luxury when he began it in his youth, and one may doubt if it was when he resumed it in full form in later life. At seventy-six he said: "When the decays of age have enfeebled the useful energies of the mind, the classic pages fill up the vacuum of *ennui*, and become sweet composers to that rest of the grave into which we are all sooner or later to descend." He also observed that there were stores of real knowledge in these writings — "to wit, in history, ethics, arithmetic, geometry, astronomy, natural history, etc." On this vast storehouse he was constantly drawing, and, without entering into all these categories, we should say something about what he found.

Jefferson read ancient history with avidity and talked about the great Greek and Roman figures with more familiarity than most educated Americans of today speak of him and John Adams. He drew on ancient as well as modern political experience to enrich his own.[31] But he set little value on the classical writings on government that were readily accessible on his bookshelves. Shortly before he sold his library to Congress he tried to read Plato's *Republic* on a visit to Poplar Forest. On his return to Monticello he wrote John Adams that it was the "heaviest task-work" he ever went through. Of the renowned author he said: "His foggy mind is forever pursuing the semblances of objects, which, half seen thro' a mist, can be defined in neither form or substance."[32] While he spoke of Plato's "unintelligible jargon," he referred also to his "elegant

[29] TJ to J. W. Eppes, Jan. 17, 1810 (L. & B., XII, 343). See comment of Gilbert Chinard in *Literary Bible of Thomas Jefferson: His Commonplace Book* (1928), p. 14.

[30] His statement to that effect and the quotations in this paragraph are from his letter to John Brazier.

[31] His attitude toward history is discussed more fully in the next chapter.

[32] TJ to Adams, July 5, 1814.

diction," attributing to this in part the philosopher's escape from oblivion. Jefferson believed that a more important reason for this "escape" was the incorporation of Plato's "whimsies" into what he himself called "artificial Christianity" — thus obscuring the real teachings of Jesus. His dislike of Plato was not owing primarily to that philosopher's political writings, though his comments on them reflect his own emphasis on rationality and his distaste for philosophical systems of any kind.

The basic reason for his indifference to Greek works on government is well expressed in a response of his to an inquiry about a recent edition of Aristotle's *Politics*. This noted work he dismissed from consideration on the ground that it was now outmoded. Of the Greeks he said: "They had just ideas of the value of personal liberty, but none at all of the structure of government best calculated to preserve it." They knew no medium between a pure or direct democracy, which was practicable only within a town, and aristocracy or tyranny that was independent of the people. The idea of a representative government, which could be exercised over territory of any extent, did not occur to them. "The full experiment of a government democratical, but representative, was and is still reserved for us," he said. He believed that the introduction of the representative principle had rendered virtually useless everything that had been previously written on the subject of government.[33]

He presented his own views at greater length but to much the same effect in a letter written when he was eighty. He had just received a couple of books by ancient Greek authors from a Greek patriot who was deeply involved in his country's struggle against the Turks.[34] In his letter of thanks, Jefferson observed that he and his fellows should avail themselves of their rich heritage of knowledge but could not return to a government like that of Athens or Sparta. He emphasized the principle of representation and, in response to his correspondent's request, described in detail the American application of it in federal and state governments.

He did not doubt that in the matter of organization and procedure his country had provided an example for all others that might seek self-government. In presenting this, however, he paid tribute to Homer and Demosthenes and "the splendid constellation of sages and heroes" to whom his generation was, and all future races of mankind would be, indebted. They provided "the lights which originally led ourselves out of Gothic darkness," he said. They were the first of civilized nations to present "examples of what man should be."[35]

[33] TJ to I. H. Tiffany, Aug. 6, 1816 (L. & B., XV, 65–66).

[34] TJ to A. Coray, Oct. 31, 1823 (L. & B., XV, 480–490), replying to a letter of July 10. Coray, who had met TJ in Paris, was an editor of classical works.

[35] *Ibid.*, p. 481.

As he did not look to the Greeks for examples of what government should be, neither did he look to the Romans. He did not disown the great figures of the Roman republic, whose names were so often invoked by American patriots in the Revolutionary era. The Roman statesman he talked most about was Cicero. Expressing to John Adams his surprise that "foggy-minded" Plato should have been eulogized by Cicero, he described the latter as "able, learned, laborious and practised in the business of the world."[36] At this time he also described Cicero as the first master of style in the world. He said, however, that the orator lacked the "dense logic" of Demosthenes, and he later characterized him as "diffuse, vapid, rhetorical, but enchanting."[37] Those reservations did not apply to Cicero's principles, which Jefferson never ceased to admire. In another letter to Adams he pointed out the limitations of the statesmanship of this defender of the Roman Republic, and of the political inadequacy of the Republic itself.

His comments grew out of his recent reading of Cicero's letters. Of these he said: "They certainly breathe the purest effusions of an exalted patriot, while the parricide Caesar is left in odious contrast."[38] But he was under no illusions about the government that Caesar subverted and Cicero wanted to restore. It was not good government, for the Romans had never had that. He wondered what Cicero, Cato, and Brutus could have done if they had had the power to do what they wanted to do. "They had no ideas of government themselves but of their degenerate Senate," he said. He was convinced that no government could remain good except under control of the people, and saw no hope of this when they were as "demoralized and depraved" as the Roman people then were. Unlike the Americans, they were not prepared for self-government; they never had been free and enlightened. Apart from the civic virtues of individuals that marked the Roman Republic at its best, he saw in it little or nothing to emulate.

Since his republicanism amounted to a passion, he could not have been expected to approve of empire as a form of government. He had profound respect for the law of the Romans and was enormously indebted to them in architecture. He was well aware of the splendor of the Roman empire and of its historic services in extending the bounds of civilization and in preserving this against encircling barbarians. But the mission of Rome as described by Virgil was in no sense a parallel to the

[36] TJ to Adams, July 5, 1814.

[37] L. & B., XV, 219. TJ's attitude toward Cicero's style was equivocal. See comment on his oratory (p. 194).

[38] TJ to Adams, Dec. 10, 1819.

mission of America as perceived by Jefferson.[39] His mind could not consent to the rule over other peoples against their will, and the imposition of law by force. Though he was a territorial expansionist, the only sort of empire he favored was an empire for liberty, and the only sort of government he wanted his country to exemplify was self-government.

As a practical man he valued what he called the "good sense" of the Romans and he admired their physical achievements. He even credited them with some good emperors. But the historic characters he most admired were not rulers or builders of states but Francis Bacon, Isaac Newton, and John Locke, whom he regarded as the major seers and prophets of the Enlightenment. Accordingly, one would have expected him to find his chief ancient favorites among those who did most to free the mind and extend knowledge. He had little liking, however, for the most noted of classical philosophers.

He abominated Plato not only as an obscurantist but also as a system maker. He largely disregarded Aristotle and disliked all philosophical systems because of their rigidity. They tended to become ends in themselves and imposed limitations on the freedom of the mind, just as theological dogma did. Whether he himself can be properly designated as a philosopher is essentially a question of semantics, but he was certainly no system builder, and this lover of books never doubted that he lived in the world of concrete reality.

To John Adams he wrote: "I am not fond of reading what is merely abstract, and unapplied immediately to some useful service." A few years later he said to this favorite correspondent: "I have a prejudice against what they call Metaphysicks because they pretend to fathom deeper than the human line extends." In still another letter he described his own more modest course: "When I meet with a proposition beyond finite comprehension, I abandon it as I do a weight which human strength cannot lift, and I think ignorance in these cases is truly the softest pillow on which I can lay my head."[40] Thus, his favored reading was in books that bore more directly on human conduct. He sought counsel, not from the metaphysicians, but from the Greek and Roman moralists.

At the age of seventy-six he told his old secretary William Short that he was an Epicurean, thus seeming to associate himself with a particular system of moral philosophy. He hastened to add that the doctrines of

[39] See *Aeneid*, end of Book VI, especially lines 851–853. Since TJ was very fond of Virgil he must have read this passage, referring to the reign of Augustus.

[40] TJ to Adams, Oct. 14, 1816, Feb. 21, 1820, Mar. 14, 1820.

Epicurus had been much misrepresented. As understood by him they were in no sense a cloak for sensuality or any form of self-indulgence.[41] In almost the same breath he expressed his appreciation of Epictetus, and his own life was marked by self-discipline such as is commonly associated with Stoicism. As has been well said, he did not distinguish sharply between the two rival systems but used them as "complementary techniques in the realization of the good life."[42]

According to the syllabus of the doctrines of Epicurus that he drew up for the benefit of Short, happiness is the aim of life, and virtue is the foundation of happiness. It is asserted here that tranquillity of mind (which Jefferson often spoke of as his major objective in old age) can be produced by avoidance of desire and fear, the chief diseases of the mind. To him this was not a negative philosophy. Activity, which is described as agreeable motion, is recognized as a means to happiness. It is one that he ceaselessly employed.

He picked up clues to the attainment of the good life from other ancient writers. In his student notebook he copied from Horace a famous injunction: "*Carpe diem, quam minimum credula postero.*"[43] The copying of these words does not necessarily mean that he accepted this advice, but in personal matters he was disposed to put the future out of his mind and make the most of the present. A gourmet and a connoisseur, he could be correctly termed an epicure. He was no foe of human pleasure, and that was one of his reasons for calling himself an Epicurean rather than a Stoic. But he kept himself under very strict control. While generally tolerant of human frailty and less didactic as an old man than earlier, he never ceased to couple the good life with self-mastery.

About a year after he sold his library to Congress, he received from a distant schoolmaster a request for a piece of his handwriting. This was to be in Latin for translation by the students of Fryeburg Academy in Maine. Since he had probably not been able to replace many of his classical works as yet, he may have gone back to his old student notebook for the passage from Horace that he sent. We quote it as translated by another hand:

[41] TJ to William Short, Oct. 31, 1819, with syllabus of doctrines of Epicurus (L. & B., XV, 219–224). That moralist himself, speaking of the misinterpretations of his doctrines, said that the pleasure he advocated should not be identified with that of the libertines, but with "freedom from bodily harm and mental agitation" (quoted in *Hellenistic Philosophy*, ed. by Herman Shapiro and Edwin M. Curley [New York, 1965], pp. 8–9).

[42] Adrienne Koch, *Philosophy of Thomas Jefferson* (1943), p. 4. This work contains (pp. 2–8) an admirable discussion of TJ's attitude toward Epicureanism and Stoicism.

[43] Chinard, *Literary Bible*, pp. 118–119, with translation by the editor: "Enjoy the day and put as little trust as possible in the morrow."

Now what man is free? The wise man who rules himself, afraid neither of poverty, death or prison; who has enough strength to check his passions and scorn honors; who is self sufficient; who offers to external accident no hold and whom chance cannot catch unaware.[44]

To students of that day this friendly septuagenarian commended a "moral morsel" that he had discovered half a century earlier and still esteemed. In the meantime he had come to perceive limitations in the moralists of Greece and Rome. As he averred to Dr. Benjamin Rush during his first presidential term, their precepts relating to self-control and the attainment of tranquillity were admirable, but they were deficient with respect to one's duties to others. The circle of their benevolence was too restricted. By this time he had perceived in the ethics of Jesus a fullness and a sublimity never attained by a classical moralist. Until the end of his days he was anticlerical and antidoctrinal but he regarded himself as a Christian.[45] For ideals of human relationships and universal benevolence he looked higher than Epicurus and Epictetus, Horace and Cicero, but for what he learned from them and their compatriots about the good life and the way to pursue it he was always profoundly grateful.

[44] Chinard, *Literary Bible*, pp. 120–121; TJ to Amos J. Cook, Jan. 21, 1816 (L. & B., XIV, 403–406), replying to a letter of Dec. 18, 1815 (MHS). Cook sent a copy of verses, distinctly pessimistic in character, that he had received from John Adams. In his reply TJ said they reminded him of a passage in the Book of Ecclesiastes, which he quoted before proceeding in a more cheerful manner. Thus the replies of the two men suggest their differences in temperament and philosophy.

[45] He compared the ethics of Jesus with those of the classical philosophers in a syllabus he sent Dr. Rush, Apr. 21, 1803 (see Ford, VIII, 223–228, and *Jefferson the President: First Term*, pp. 201–205). For further comments on TJ's religion, see below, pp. 490–491.

[XIV]

The Uses of History

JEFFERSON sought to maintain balance in his library, as in his life, but history may have been somewhat over-represented on his shelves.[1] History bulked large on the lists of books he drew up at various times for others, and the subject was generally favored in his own reading. This great and enduring interest in the past may seem surprising in one who in his own time was notably present-minded. "The earth belongs always to the living generation," he said; and no one was more concerned than he that this generation should not be hampered by the dead hand of the past. He himself read historical works in half a dozen languages and he was thoroughly informed of modern developments, but in his later years he said repeatedly that he preferred to read about the ancients. He sounded as though he wanted to get rid even of them when, as a septuagenarian, he told John Adams that he liked "the dreams of the future better than the history of the past."[2]

By this statement he may be presumed to have meant that he expected the future to be better than what had gone before. He preferred the hopes of tomorrow to the disappointments of yesterday. But he was certainly not dismissing the record of the past from consideration. Assiduous study of it through half a century had enormously enriched his life while broadening his experience and would continue to do so until the end. He might have said about travel in time what he did say about travel in space: namely, that it makes one wiser but not happier. He never went so far as to say with Gibbon that history is "little more than

[1] In this chapter, the term "history" is applied to civil history, as distinguished from natural. In the catalogue of the Monticello library of 1815–1826, there are more titles in this subdivision than in any other; and in the catalogue of the library he sold Congress the number is second only to that in the subdivision of politics and commerce. The history books in his successive libraries are listed by H. Trevor Colbourn in *The Lamp of Experience* (1965), pp. 217–222.

[2] TJ to Adams, Aug. 1, 1816 (*A.-J. Letters*, II, 485).

the register of the crimes, follies, and misfortunes of mankind,"[3] but he recognized, especially in his later years, that it enlarged the reader's knowledge of evil. The evil deeds of which he himself was most aware were those of rulers. He preferred the history of the ancients to that of the recent past, he said, because their Catilines and Caligulas had already received condemnation at the hands of Livy, Sallust, and Tacitus, while that of the Georges and Napoleon at the bar of history was still to come.[4]

He said this during the War of 1812. Half a century earlier, when he was a student in Williamsburg, the old definition of history as "philosophy teaching by example" was still widely accepted, and throughout his life he found examples of private virtue in both the recent and the distant past. When he was chief of state, however, he did not expect to find in recorded experience, especially that of other countries, much positive guidance in matters of public policy. To a young inquirer he wrote: "History, in general, only informs us what bad government is."[5] He believed that, if truly reported, history would show him and his contemporaries what to avoid and oppose, *not* what to seek and do.

Bonaparte had not yet appeared on the public stage and the American rebels were still battling King George III when the author of the Declaration of Independence observed that power could be perverted to tyranny in any government. In his now-famous but long-disregarded bill for the more general diffusion of knowledge he pointed out the most effectual means of preventing this:

> to illuminate, as far as practicable, the minds of the people at large, and more especially to give them knowledge of those facts, which history exhibiteth, that, possessed thereby of the experience of other ages and countries, they may be enabled to know ambition under all its shapes, and prompt to exert their natural powers to defeat its purposes.[6]

He wanted schoolchildren to become acquainted with history — Grecian, Roman, English, and American — in the first stage of the educational system he was proposing.[7] Whatever may be thought of the feasibility or pedagogical wisdom of this particular proposal, it evinces his belief that the people generally should be informed in history for their

[3] *Decline and Fall of the Roman Empire* (New York: Modern Library, 1932), I, 69.

[4] TJ to William Duane, Apr. 4, 1813 (L. & B., XIII, 230).

[5] TJ to John Norvell, June 14, 1807 (Ford, IX, 72).

[6] Bill of 1779 (Boyd, II, 526–527).

[7] The subjects to be taught in the lowest schools are described in Sec. VI of his bill. One gains the impression that the children were to do much if not most of their earliest reading in history books.

own protection. He never ceased to emphasize the preventive value of historical knowledge in public matters, and at an early stage in his career he found support for his most cherished convictions in the generally discouraging history of his mother country.

From his days as a student of law he was steeped in English history and from it he drew copiously before he wrote the Declaration of Independence, when warning his fellow colonials of tyranny, actual or potential, and asserting the rights of Englishmen. In his vigorous pamphlet, *A Summary View of the Rights of British America* (1774), he justified the rights on grounds of history rather than philosophy. He drew a parallel between the American settlers and the Anglo-Saxons, who of their own accord emigrated from the German forests to Britain and, living there under laws of their own making, enjoyed notable freedom until the Normans forced on them alien rule and feudal institutions. Accepting as history what has come to be called the Saxon myth, as did his fellow patriots generally, he found in it not only examples of tyranny to put Americans on their guard, but also of liberty and democracy that deserved emulation and offered encouragement.[8]

It should not be supposed that he became a champion of individual freedom and self-government *because of* what he read and believed about the Saxons, or that his democratic faith was dependent on the correctness of this particular view of early English history. He believed that the rights of man — inherent, universal, and inalienable — were written in the book of Nature. To be sure, this was the assumption of a man of faith, but he regarded himself as an empiricist, not a theorist, and in all fields of life and learning he set great value on experience. What he saw in the "happy state" of the Saxons strengthened his convictions and provided him with patriotic ammunition at a time he greatly needed it.

After the winning of independence he had little need to rely on a parallel between the Anglo-Saxons and the American colonists — or, indeed, on any political analogy — since he came more and more to regard the American experiment as unique, but until his dying day he associated the Saxons and the Normans, respectively, with the Whigs and Tories.

At times he employed these party labels virtually as generic terms. On several occasions he expressed the belief that such parties, under one name or another, had existed since the beginning of government and that

[8] For a full treatment of this theme, see Colbourn, *Lamp of Experience*, especially ch. VIII, which is devoted to Jefferson. The historical circumstances of the *Summary View* are described in *Jefferson the Virginian*, ch. XIV.

their differences were seated in human nature itself. Early in his presidency he made the following observations to one of his supporters:

> As the division between whig and tory is founded in the nature of men, the weakly and nerveless, the rich and the corrupt seeing more safety and accessibility in a strong executive; the healthy, firm and virtuous feeling confidence in their physical and moral resources, and willing to part with only so much power as is necessary for their good government, and therefore to retain the rest in the hands of the many, the division will substantially be into whig and tory, as in England, formerly.[9]

As stated here, the chief difference between contending parties lies in the attitudes of human beings to governmental power, especially that of the executive, on the one hand, and to individual freedom on the other. Irrespective of his own exercise of executive authority when bearing the responsibilities of office, there can be no doubt that he was by temperament a Whig, as he understood the term.

He expressed himself somewhat differently and more moderately to John Adams when he was in private life and their friendship had been resumed. He again said that the same question had divided parties from their beginnings and would continue to do so. To this he added the observation that "every one takes his side in favor of the many, or of the few, according to his constitution, and the circumstances in which he is placed."[10]

As a general explanation of political alignments in the countries he knew best this statement can hardly be improved upon, but he was rarely so fatalistic and not always as tolerant of differences of political opinion as in this letter to an old friend and onetime opponent whom he was anxious not to alienate. In judging his own countrymen he could be harsh on opinions that seemed to him to fall outside the bounds of republicanism, that smacked in any way of monarchism. While he could do nothing about Toryism in England except complain, he intensely disliked it and he was not without fear that Americans would be infected with its spirit. Despite what he said about human nature, he had not ceased to believe that people are influenced in their opinions by the books they read, and in his later years he was much concerned with books and the education of the young. Several times in this period he

[9] TJ to Joel Barlow, May 3, 1802 (Ford, VIII, 150). See also TJ to Lafayette, Nov. 4, 1823 (Ford, X, 281); to Henry Lee, Aug. 10, 1824 (*ibid.*, 317–318).

[10] TJ to Adams, June 27, 1813 (*A.-J. Letters*, II, 337).

expressed strong disapproval of a work that presented in classic form the Tory view of English history. Furthermore, he vainly sought to promote what he regarded as a salutary corrective.

In his student days, soon after the first edition of David Hume's *History of England* appeared, Jefferson read that work with much enthusiasm.[11] He never ceased to admire its literary form, and half a century later he recalled that only after much time, research, and reflection was he able to free himself from the "poison" it had instilled in his mind. This he stated when discussing it with William Duane, publisher of the *Aurora*, in the second year of his retirement. At this time he asserted that Hume, beginning his historical writing with the Stuarts, became their apologist and defended their "enormities."[12] According to Jefferson, he went back to the Tudors to support his position, causing their arbitrary arts to appear as "genuine samples of the constitutional power of the crown." Continuing to write backwards, Hume presented the Saxons and Normans from the same "perverted view."

After the War of 1812, complaining to John Adams of what this single book had done "to sap the free principles of the English constitution," Jefferson compared its Scottish author to an American portrait painter who saw only the ugly features of his subject. "So," he said, "Hume has consecrated, in his fascinating style, all the arbitrary proceedings of the English kings, as true evidences of the constitution, and glided over its whig principles as the unfounded pretensions of factious demagogues. He even boasts, in his life written by himself, that of the numerous alterations suggested by the readers of his work, he had never adopted one proposed by a whig."[13]

Hume's work was unquestionably marred by many factual errors and distortions. As Jefferson became increasingly aware of them he might have been expected to deplore them, since he was notable for his insistence on accuracy in matters of scholarship. But he had not yet come to the point of regarding historical writings as ends in themselves, irrespective of what they portray.[14] He viewed them as no detached Olympian, but

[11] Hume's *History* was published in 1754–1759. TJ's first copy of this work may have been destroyed by the fire at Shadwell in 1770. The eight-volume set he sold Congress in 1815 appeared in 1790–1791 (Sowerby, I, 156–157).

[12] TJ to William Duane, Aug. 12, 1810 (L. & B., XII, 405–406).

[13] TJ to Adams, Nov. 25, 1816 (*A.-J. Letters*, II, 498–499). The portrait painter to whom he was referring was Joseph Wright, one of whose portraits of George Washington he possessed. It is now in the Massachusetts Historical Society. In this the General's nose is very large.

[14] On this general topic, see T. P. Peardon, *The Transition in English Historical Writing, 1760–1830* (New York, 1933); G. H. Nadel, "Philosophy of History before Historicism" in *Studies in the Philosophy of History* (New York, 1965), pp. 49–73.

as a passionate partisan of republicanism, by contrast with monarchism, and he would have equated republicanism with Americanism if he had used the latter term. He was convinced that republicanism had roots in the English past; and, whatever may be said about the Saxons, it undoubtedly drew sustenance from the seventeenth century, when Commonwealth men defied the Crown. Recognizing that English history was an important part of the American heritage and would continue to be read, he believed that Hume's one-sided account required an antidote. In his opinion, however, no satisfactory general history was available. He continued to prefer one that had originally appeared in French, but even in English this long work was not suitable for common use.[15] Accordingly, he recommended a work in which Hume's *History* was both abbreviated and "republicanized."

Early in his second presidential term he acquired, through a London bookseller, a work by John Baxter entitled *A New and Impartial History of England.*[16] Commending it some months later to John Norvell, a young Kentuckian who had inquired about books and newspapers, he said that the author had "performed a good operation" on Hume.[17] He described the "operation" in his reply to Norvell and rather more fully in a letter to William Duane three years later, when he was in retirement. He then said that Baxter had corrected the misrepresentations in Hume's text, "supplied the truths he suppressed," and given the rest of the work in Hume's "own words." Jefferson noted that relatively little interpolation was necessary to make this a "sound history," and that in bulk it had been reduced by half. A fitting title for it, in his opinion, would have been: "Hume's history of England abridged and rendered faithful to fact and principle." He did not bother to read much of Baxter's continuation of the narrative to 1801 and was unimpressed with that writer's style. He said that the book was unpopular in England because of its republicanism and probably had not gone beyond one edition, as in fact it had not. He doubted if there was a copy of it in the United States besides his own but expressed the hope that it would be reprinted here.[18]

In his prompt reply Duane reported that he himself had a copy of the work, which in fact he had acquired at Jefferson's earlier suggestion, and

[15] Paul de Rapin Thoyras, *Historie d'Angleterre* (10 vols., 1727). The English edn. of a few years later was standard until Hume's *History* appeared.

[16] The work was published *circa* 1796–1801. TJ's copy was received Nov. 12, 1805, and bound in 1806. The note in Sowerby, I, 174–179, contains this and other interesting information.

[17] TJ to Norvell, June 14, 1807 (Ford, IX, 72). Later in this letter appears his well-known statement about abuses of freedom of the press. (See *Jefferson the President: Second Term*, pp. 384–385.)

[18] TJ to Duane, Aug. 12, 1810 (L. & B., XII, 406–407). See also excerpts from Duane to TJ, Aug. 17, 1810 (Sowerby, I, 176).

said that he proposed to reprint it. He never got around to doing so, though he carried out another enterprise that was proposed by Jefferson at the same time.[19] The idea of reprinting that work appears to have lain dormant in Jefferson's mind for eight years after he first suggested it. By that time he was without the book since his copy was in the library he sold to Congress. He remembered it well enough to describe it to another Philadelphia publisher, Mathew Carey, late in 1818, when again seeking an antidote to the "poison" in Hume's engrossing *History*.[20]

To Carey he said that there were two ways to counteract the baneful influence of that author. The better one would be to publish his text entire, and, in parallel columns or notes, to confront "its disguises, its misrepresentations, its concealments, its sophisms, and ironies" with antidotes of truth from honest authors. He regarded this procedure as impracticable since it would produce too large a work and would require more learning than was available. The other method was the one Baxter used. In turn, Mathew Carey said the reprinting of Baxter's work was impracticable. In fact he could not find a copy of it, and, despite his repeated efforts to do so, Jefferson seems never to have replaced the one he had sold the government.[21]

In the last year of his life he recommended this book along with others for reading in history at the University of Virginia, commenting on it much as he had done earlier. It is not listed in the first catalogue of that institution and may be presumed to have been unprocurable.[22] Strong support of the charge that Hume's work was full of errors was given in a book by another Whig partisan, George Brodie, that appeared in England a few years before the opening of the University.[23] Jefferson recommended that this be read along with Hume, but he believed that, before sensitive students were exposed to the blandishments of the latter, they should read Baxter's work. Thus he stuck to it to the end.

"The Baxter episode," which consisted on Jefferson's part of comments and recommendations in some half-dozen letters over a score of years, reflects no credit on him, except perhaps in demonstrating his persistent championship of republicanism. At best, his actions were awkward and ill-judged. But, in view of his great services to sound learning in this period, the importance of this episode can be easily exaggerated.

[19] The publication of a translation of a commentary by Destutt de Tracy on Montesquieu's *Spirit of Laws*. See below, 208–212.

[20] TJ to Mathew Carey, Nov. 22, 1818 (Sowerby, I, 176–178).

[21] Carey to TJ, Jan. 18, 1819, June 30, 1821 (Sowerby, I, 178).

[22] TJ to G. W. Lewis, Oct. 25, 1825 (L. & B., XVI, 128).

[23] George A. Brodie, *History of the British Empire from the Accession of Charles I to the Restoration*, 2 vols. (London, 1822, 1826).

It should certainly be considered in the light of the times.[24] In the eighteenth and early nineteenth centuries there was no such regard for the integrity of literary and historical works as among scholars of later generations. Plagiarism was so common that it occasioned little or no surprise. In the formal writings of John Adams, for example, there are numerous passages from other writers that are undistinguished by quotation marks. Edmund Randolph, who wrote his history of Virginia a generation later, stated that he had drawn on that of William Stith, but he inserted passages without specific indication that they were not his own.[25] While Jefferson, like most of us, sometimes used the words of another without acknowledgment, he never engaged in such extensive borrowings from the writings of others. But he could not have been expected to transcend the prevalent standards of his own day in everything and he was least likely to do so when politics and government were involved.

In his championship of republicanism he often sounded like a political dogmatist, but he advised students to read widely. He continued to believe that truth will overcome error if left free to combat it. And, on pragmatic grounds if on no other, this passionate patriot felt himself fully warranted in combatting doctrine he regarded as incompatible with the American venture in self-government. In his effort to counteract the antirepublicanism he perceived in another famous work, he pursued a wiser course than in the Baxter episode. He served the cause of learning as well as that of self-government by facilitating the publication of an able commentary on Montesquieu's *Spirit of Laws.* The distinguished author was not named, however, and the public did not know that the original manuscript, in French, was supplied by the Sage of Monticello.[26]

[24] TJ has been sharply criticized by scholars viewing the episode from the vantage point of the twentieth century. Arthur Bestor in his sympathetic article in *Three Presidents and Their Books* (1955), p. 19, describes this as "one of his very few lapses — perhaps his only lapse — from strict scholarly integrity." Leonard Levy, in *Jefferson and Civil Liberties* (1963), pp. 144–147, makes much of the episode as exemplifying the inconsistency, even the insincerity, which he attributes to TJ as a libertarian. Trevor Colbourn, in *Lamp of Experience*, pp. 178–179, raises no question of impropriety.

[25] Zoltán Haraszti says that Charles Francis Adams, in editing his grandfather's *Works*, inserted some quotation marks but by no means all that were needed (*John Adams and the Prophets of Progress* [Cambridge, Mass., 1952], pp. 46–47). See also Peter Shaw, *Character of John Adams* (Chapel Hill, 1976), p. 234; introduction by Arthur H. Shaffer to Edmund Randolph's *History of Virginia* (Charlottesville, 1970), p. vii, and Randolph's note on p. 23.

[26] *A Commentary and Review of Montesquieu's Spirit of Laws* (Philadelphia, 1811), printed by William Duane.

ii

This publishing episode, which was also an incident in international friendship, had its beginning late in the summer following Jefferson's retirement from the presidency. He then received a letter from Lafayette, forewarning him of one that he got a few weeks later, along with a manuscript, from Senator Destutt de Tracy.[27] The latter was a liberal French nobleman, whose daughter had married a son of Lafayette's. Though Jefferson does not appear to have consorted with him while in France, they had engaged in some correspondence and recognized themselves as kindred spirits. During his second presidential term he had received parts of the work on ideology for which Tracy is most renowned, but he said he would be unable to read them at the time and appears not to have done so until considerably after his retirement. Though he then spoke of the *Idéologie* most approvingly, he probably never got through the whole of it since he did not care much for abstractions.[28]

The unsolicited work that was now entrusted to him may have been of more intrinsic appeal, and the immediate circumstances could not have failed to excite his sympathy. The author did not dare publish the work in Napoleonic France, and he enjoined Jefferson to conceal his identity during his lifetime. Tracy's purpose, as stated by Lafayette, was to have his manuscript translated into English and published in the only republican country in the world as the work of an American. He had some hope that it would return to the Old World one day and be retranslated into French for the benefit of his own countrymen. The question of immediate procedure was referred to Jefferson for decision. Tracy expressed diffidence in submitting his work to the man in the universe whom he respected most and whose approbation he most coveted; but Lafayette, though also deferential, had no real doubt that his illustrious American friend would like it. So Jefferson did, with only slight reservations, but he was slow in doing anything about it.

Almost a year passed before he commended the work to William Duane, along with that of Baxter. Apparently he was less disturbed by Montesquieu than by Hume at the moment. He described the *Spirit of Laws* as "a book of paradoxes, having indeed much of truth and sound

[27] The two letters, both dated June 12, 1809, were received respectively on Aug. 3 and Sept. 28. See *Letters of Lafayette and Jefferson*, ed. by G. Chinard, pp. 287–288, and Chinard's *Jefferson et les Idéologues* (1925), pp. 43–45. The fullest account of this episode is in ch. II of the latter work (referred to hereafter as *Idéologues*), which contains most of the pertinent correspondence. See also Sowerby, III, 3–11; Koch, *The Philosophy of Thomas Jefferson*, ch. XVI.

[28] TJ to Tracy, Feb. 21, 1806 (*Idéologues*, p. 41); TJ to John Adams, Oct. 14, 1816 (*A.-J. Letters*, II, 491).

principles, but abounding also in inconsistencies, apocryphal facts, and false principles." Tracy, devoting a chapter to each of the books into which Montesquieu's work was divided, supported it in some cases and sought to refute it in others. Jefferson never doubted the compatibility of Tracy's views with republicanism, which he himself described as "the true principle of Government." He had not read the entire work when he first wrote Duane about it, but he sent, as a sample, a chapter of it that he himself had translated. A month later, reporting that he had finished it, he described it as "the most valuable political work of the present age."[29]

At this time he sent the entire manuscript to Duane, who needed business and was in a receptive state of mind. The publisher procured a translation and during the fall he sent this in successive packets to Monticello. The learned gentleman there made some minor corrections in it but because the original manuscript was not returned with it, he was unable to compare them. Though never entirely satisfied with the translation, he afterwards told the author that it was substantially correct. He concluded, however, that it was not sufficiently idiomatic to pass as the original work of a native American. Accordingly, he introduced the author differently in the "brief proem" he drafted and sent Duane to appear at the beginning of "our book." Written in the first person as though by the author himself, this introduction described him as a native of France and former supporter of its revolution, now living in the United States, whither he had fled from "the tyrannies" of the monster Robespierre. The real author's original desire had not been fulfilled precisely, but he was protected from the wrath of Napóleon at any rate.[30]

Not until he had gone over the last of the translation and drafted a foreword did Jefferson write Lafayette and Tracy about the manuscript the latter had dispatched to him a year and a half before.[31] Finding a safe conveyance for his letters took months longer, with the result that they did not start their perilous transatlantic voyage until the late summer of 1811.

Along with a printed copy of the book, which Jefferson received from Duane just in the nick of time, they were entrusted to David B. Warden, who was considerably indebted to the ex-President for his appointment as American consul at Paris. The book was actually sent to Lafayette for

[29] TJ to Duane, Aug. 12, 1810; Sept. 16, 1810 (L. & B., XII, 407–408, 413; *Idéologues*, pp. 54–55, 59).

[30] TJ's letter of Jan. 18, 1811, and the "proem" enclosed in it are in *Idéologues*, pp. 63–64. See also TJ to Duane, Oct. 29, 1810 (*ibid.*, p. 61), Nov. 13, 1810 (L. & B., XII, 132–134) and various extracts from their correspondence about this book in Sowerby, III, 3–11.

[31] TJ to Lafayette, Jan. 20, 1811 (*Letters of Lafayette and Jefferson*, pp. 321–333); TJ to Tracy, Jan. 26, 1811 (*Idéologues*, pp. 74–79).

delivery by him to Tracy, and presumably Warden did not know who the author was. He reported, however, that the Senator was well pleased with the book.[32]

The effusive praise of Tracy's work in the long letter from Monticello more than made up for months of silence. He was so gratified by the outcome of this venture in international cooperation that he entrusted Jefferson with another manuscript of his. This was a treatise on political economy which Jefferson himself translated in due course and eventually caused to be published.[33] But, disregarding that work and that transaction for the present, we return briefly to the commentary on Montesquieu and its fortunes.

Jefferson afterwards said that he ordered ten copies of the book for presentation to friends abroad but that, finding his plan impracticable, he distributed them in the various American states. He did manage to get a couple of copies to Lafayette, and Warden had one of these at a relatively early date. Du Pont de Nemours, who was still in France, borrowed this and was reported to have begun translating it into French. Writing Jefferson he said that it was undoubtedly the work of a great man of state, and he attributed its authorship to Jefferson himself. The latter, without giving Tracy away, denied the charge, saying that such a work was far beyond his qualifications.[34]

Several years later, after Napoleon had been exiled for good, and when Tracy's connection with the book may be presumed to have become an open secret, Jefferson referred to it in a letter to Du Pont, who was now in America to stay.[35] He gave a brief account of his connection with the American edition of the work and said that the French manuscript was still in his possession. He hoped the original would be published and so it was, anonymously, the next year at Liège.[36] Jefferson

[32] TJ to Lafayette, July 10, 1811 (LC); TJ to Warden, July 10, 1811 (LC); Warden to TJ, July 24, 1811 (LC); Dec. 10, 1811 (LC). Joel Barlow, the American minister to France, made the crossing at the same time on the *Essex* and also performed commissions for TJ.

[33] *A Treatise on Political Economy* by the Count Destutt [de] Tracy (Georgetown, D.C., published by Joseph Milligan, 1817). See below, 305–307.

[34] Warden to TJ, Nov. 1, 1812 (Sowerby, III, 9); TJ to Du Pont, Nov. 29, 1813 (*J.-D. Correspondence*, p. 145), replying specifically to Du Pont's letter of Jan. 25, 1812 (G. Chinard, ed., *The Correspondence of Jefferson & Du Pont de Nemours* [1931], pp. 179–193). While promising to send Du Pont a copy of the book if he could get hold of one, TJ appears to have been trying to brush off his query, devoting himself after the first paragraph to other matters dealt with in various letters of Du Pont.

[35] TJ to Du Pont, Aug. 13, 1816 (*J.-D. Correspondence*, pp. 187–188). On the Montesquieu episode, see, besides the works of Chinard previously cited, Ambrose Saricks, *Pierre Samuel du Pont de Nemours* (1965), pp. 325–327.

[36] Presumably these printings were from a copy Tracy had retained, since Jefferson never returned the one he had. Not until 1819 was there an edition bearing Tracy's name. Sowerby, III, 11; Tracy to TJ, Apr. 11, 1818, and Mar. 15, 1823 (*Idéologues*, pp. 180–212). There was no second American edition, though Duane appears to have lost no money on the first one. He gave TJ a favorable report Feb. 14, 1813 (Sowerby, III, 9).

caused the book to be used as a textbook at the College of William and Mary and he never ceased to praise it and its author. Its impact on American opinion cannot be precisely measured and may have been small. But from this minor episode we can learn much about Jefferson.

His activities reflected his abiding concern for the diffusion of what he regarded as sound principles of government. Although Tracy assumed the mantle of neutrality when describing forms of government, there could be no doubt where his own sympathies lay. He and Jefferson were fully agreed that tyranny is wrong and that the sovereignty of the people is right. In applying these "principles," however, the Frenchman was the more theoretical of the two. The American availed himself more of past experience: he made fuller use of history.

To reduce the danger of tyranny, Tracy recommended a plural rather than a single executive. On no other point did Jefferson express such strong disagreement with his correspondent. However attractive a plural executive might be in theory, he said, it had failed in practice — most notably in the French Directory. That failure he attributed, not to external circumstances, but to the inescapable facts of human nature. He believed that in any executive group without a recognized head jealousy and dissension were inevitable. The rival American experiment with a single executive, which had been conducted during what he described as the "most tempestuous times" ever presented by human history, was regarded by him as a distinct success.[37] His highly favorable judgment on the institution of the presidency, and the declaration of this unauthoritative man that authority must center somewhere, are significant. Even more notable is his recognition that, in the conduct of public affairs, theory must yield to experience.

Though he does not appear ever to have said so, he and Tracy were not fully agreed on the mechanism and operations of political democracy. He himself rarely used the term "democracy," preferring "republicanism." Tracy's favorite expression, on the other hand, was "representative democracy." Jefferson laid great emphasis on representation, of which the ancients knew nothing and of which Montesquieu was said by Tracy to have been unaware.[38] (It seems incredible that Montesquieu could have known nothing of representation, but he appears to have ignored it.) Jefferson was conscious of the limitations of direct democracy, "participatory" in modern parlance, but he allowed it a more extensive function than Tracy did.[39]

[37] A large part of his letter of Jan. 26, 1811, to Tracy (*Idéologues*, pp. 74–79) is devoted to this topic. It appears to be the only one on which he strongly expressed disagreement with Tracy.

[38] *Commentary*, p. 19.

[39] Koch, *Philosophy of Thomas Jefferson*, pp. 149–161.

While impatient with abstractions and averse to systems of philosophy, he placed a high value on human experience, and the political experience most valued by him was that of his own country. He was wholly in character when striving to preserve its records and aiding writers who sought to tell its unique story. And, as patron and promoter, he made significant contributions to American history.

[XV]

Keeping the Record Straight

WHILE he never ceased to take political doctrine into account when evaluating historical writings, Jefferson maintained a deep respect for facts. He clearly perceived the danger that fable could pass for history, and in the last decade of his life he observed to John Adams that "genuine history" was rare.[1] He did not set up a goal of complete objectivity as a later school of professional historians was to do, and when commenting on political foes he was often injudicious. He was generally less so than they were, however, and in matters of scholarship he was characteristically fair-minded. Recognizing that both sides of controversial questions should be presented, he expressed regret that our knowledge of Carthaginian history was derived solely from the Romans.[2]

When he designated history as a science he merely meant that it was a branch of learning — not that it was characterized by the precision of mathematics or the orderliness that might be perceived in nature. But the spirit in which he approached the subject was akin to that of a modern scholar. He took it with the utmost seriousness. To an admirer who told him in his old age that he should be writing history he made this reply: "While in public life I had not time, and now that I am retired, I am past the time. To write history requires a whole life of observation, of inquiry, of labor and correction. Its materials are not to be found among the ruins of a decayed memory."[3] The statement about the requirements of the craft is one of which its present-day practitioners will cordially approve.

Jefferson never abandoned the didactic theory of history which was so prevalent in his student days, or came to regard history as merely a subject sufficient unto itself regardless of its teachings. If he came to

[1] TJ to Adams, Sept. 8, 1817 (*A.-J. Letters*, II, 520). See also TJ to William Wirt, Aug. 14, 1814 (Ford, IX, 471).

[2] TJ to Adams, May 5, 1817 (*ibid.*, 513).

[3] TJ to Dr. J. B. Stuart, May 10, 1817 (L. & B., XV, 113).

believe that ancient and English history offered little beyond warnings, he found ground for hope in the record of the American experience, and he regarded the preservation and presentation of this as matters of great concern.[4]

A grateful writer whom he had assisted, John Daly Burk, aptly described him as the guardian and patron of the history of Virginia. At the time he was President of the United States, and he was also hailed by this writer as the first and most useful citizen of the Republic.[5] Before that time he had assembled his extraordinary collection of Americana and could have been accurately designated as the guardian and patron of American history as a whole. Although this maker of history did not write books about it, he helped others to do so.

He was eighty years old when he wrote to a fellow Virginian that it was "the duty of every good citizen to use all the opportunities which occur to him, for preserving documents relating to the history of our country."[6] Declaring that he himself had not been amiss while he had "youth, health, and opportunity," he spoke particularly of his collection of the laws of Virginia, which he began to assemble early in his career.[7] His period of greatest activity as a collector of Virginiana and Americana appears to have ended with his return from France, but he never lost interest in historical documents, and by the last decade of the eighteenth century this patriotic antiquarian had manifested great concern for their publication.

When secretary of state he wrote an encouraging letter to Ebenezer Hazard, who was committing to the press a collection of American state papers. Regarding historical records of this sort, he said:

> Time and accident are committing daily havoc on the originals deposited in our public offices. The late war has done the work of centuries in this business. The lost cannot be recovered; but let us save what remains: not by vaults and locks which fence them from the public eye and use, in consigning them to the waste of time, but by such a multiplication of copies, as shall place them beyond the reach of accident."[8]

[4] See George H. Nadel, "Philosophy of History before Historicism," *Studies in the Philosophy of History*, pp. 50–53.

[5] In the dedication of Burk's *History of Virginia*, vol. I (1804). See *Jefferson the President: Second Term*, pp. 23–24, for TJ's relations with Burk.

[6] TJ to Hugh P. Taylor, Oct. 4, 1823 (L. & B., XV, 473), replying to an inquiry regarding materials relating to Indian antiquities.

[7] See *Jefferson the Virginian*, p. 286.

[8] TJ to Hazard, Feb. 18, 1791 (Boyd, XIX, 287). He had a copy of vol. I of Hazard's *Historical Collections* (Philadelphia, 1792). Apparently he did not have a copy of vol. II, which related to the New England Confederation, but his sympathy with this pioneer collector and editor in his later difficulties may be safely assumed.

Jefferson did not make his unrivaled collection of the laws of Virginia for purposes of private gratification. His only object, he said, was to save those that were not already lost in the hope that some day they would be published.[9] He had to wait a long time for the realization of his hope, but in the autumn following his retirement from the presidency he received a book that brought him great satisfaction. This was the first volume of the *Statutes at Large; Being a Collection of All the Laws of Virginia, from the First Session of the Legislature in the Year 1619*. In a foreword the editor, William Waller Hening, stated that only by the "pious care" of private individuals had these records been preserved, and that he was chiefly indebted to the recent President of the United States for the materials in this volume.[10] Hening was the first person to avail himself fully of Jefferson's collection of ancient laws, but the legislature of the commonwealth had been informed of it more than a decade earlier and it had been subsequently utilized to some extent by courts and writers.

In 1795, when the former secretary of state was in temporary retirement at Monticello, the General Assembly appointed a committee to collect and publish the laws of Virginia that related to lands. George Wythe, who was a member of the committee along with John Marshall, wrote his favorite pupil about making use of his collection.[11] Jefferson sent Wythe for examination all the printed laws in his possession but did not send those in manuscript, believing that they would not withstand transportation. He was so fearful that some of them would crumble into dust he sewed them up in oilcloth. Being convinced that the only sure way to preserve them would be to multiply them in printed copies, he urged the publication of all the laws ever passed by the legislatures of Virginia that could now be found. He offered to oversee the copying of his manuscripts if the work could be done no farther away than Milton or Charlottesville. He said that he had already spent more time familiarizing himself with these manuscripts than anyone else was likely to do, and no reader of his long letter to Wythe could fail to be impressed with the extraordinary zeal, industry, and patience he had displayed in making and preserving his collection.[12]

The recipient of this letter valued it both for the information it contained about the laws that were extant, and for Jefferson's exhortation

[9] TJ to W. W. Hening, Jan. 14, 1807 (L. & B., XI, 138).

[10] The work, covering the years 1619–1792, was published in 13 volumes (1809–1823). Extracts from the correspondence of Jefferson and Hening are in Sowerby, II, 255–261.

[11] Wythe to TJ, Jan. 1, 1796, cited by Edward Dumbauld in "A Manuscript from Monticello: Jefferson's Library in Legal History" (*Am. Bar Assoc. Jour.*, XXXVIII [May, 1952], 446). The episode is well described in this article.

[12] TJ to Wythe, Jan. 16, 1796 (Ford, VII, 52–55). The catalogue of TJ's collection which accompanied this letter is in LC. See also *Jefferson and the Ordeal of Liberty*, pp. 253–254.

that these precious records of the past be printed and made widely accessible. He caused the letter itself to be printed and distributed to the members of the General Assembly. The idea of a partial publication was abandoned by that body, but the one proposed by Jefferson was more than the legislators were ready to undertake. Among other things that may have discouraged them was his calculation that it would take a clerk upwards of a year to copy his manuscripts, and that considerable further time would be required for their editing. The seed he sowed lay dormant for a decade and in the meantime his library came to be regarded by the courts as a repository of public records. A copy of a legislative act from his collection was as acceptable as the original.[13]

His concern for the preservation of precious public records was matched by his desire that they be used. Early in his second presidential term he made his volumes of printed laws available, under careful safeguard, to John Daly Burk, who was writing a history of Virginia.[14] He was still in office and the manuscripts about which he had written George Wythe were still stored at Monticello when he learned that William Waller Hening, a former resident of Albemarle County who was now clerk of the chancery court in Richmond, was thinking of printing the statutes and desired his help. On being informed that the legislature had authorized the publication of all the extant laws, Jefferson promptly said he would be pleased to allow the free use of his collection and invited Hening to visit him in the spring of 1808.[15]

The two men had already been in correspondence about the copying of the manuscripts. Apparently dissatisfied with one copyist who was suggested, Jefferson said that some collating was necessary and that the work was beyond the capacity of an ordinary scribe. He said that he himself would have to direct it when at home and that presumably the copyist would have to live at Monticello. But Hening must have convinced him that the manuscripts were safe in his hands. They were entrusted to Hening, at any rate — eight volumes of them altogether, with some unbound papers. Hening also obtained the volumes of printed laws afterwards. The materials he got from Jefferson extended to the year 1772, and were more extensive and important than those from any other individual.[16]

[13] Dumbauld brings this out in his article describing in particular (pp. 389–391) a case decided in 1808, Pallas *vs.* Hill, in which a copy of an old law was provided by TJ on request and proved decisive.

[14] See *Jefferson the President: Second Term*, pp. 23–24. The dedication of the first volume of Burk's work to TJ is referred to above, p. 214. For the later story, see below, pp. 218 ff.

[15] Hening to TJ, Dec. 26, 1806; Feb. 7, 1808; TJ to Hening, Feb. 26, 1808 (Sowerby, II, 256–258).

[16] TJ to Hening, Feb. 27, 1807, June 7, 1808; Hening to TJ, Apr. 23, 1809 (*ibid.*, 257–258).

Acknowledging the first volume of this compilation, Jefferson said that his opinion of its importance could be inferred from the trouble and expense he had gone to in his early life to collect and preserve these old laws, and that Hening's compilation was just what he had long regarded as a desideratum for their country. A dozen years later, when the work was approaching completion, he described it as "a most invaluable collection, for which posterity must be forever thankful."[17] He seems to have taken greater pride in the help he gave Hening than in anything he did for any of the other writers and collectors who sought his aid. And the contributions to the history of his native region that he made indirectly in the *Statutes at Large* may be regarded as his greatest after the publication of his *Notes on Virginia*.

He would have liked to retain the collection of laws on which he had spent so much time and money, but it was included in the library Congress purchased as a whole in 1815. He ran into some difficulty in the effort to get everything back from Hening at the desired time. The editor asked if he might keep one volume until he could finish with it and Jefferson finally permitted him to do so, saying that he would apologize to Congress for his delay in delivering it.[18] When rounding up his manuscripts he learned from Hening that one was missing and that another, long believed by him to have been lost, had been found.

The latter, dealing with the assembly of 1645, had belonged in the first place to Sir John Randolph and was transmitted to his son Peyton, from whose estate Jefferson acquired it. Before he went to France, he loaned it to Peyton's son Edmund Randolph and that gentleman, apparently believing it to be his own, made it available to Hening. The latter eventually discovered that it belonged to Jefferson, and so stated in a letter to him and in a note in the second edition of his work. The other manuscript, containing acts of 1623–1624, was returned to Jefferson years later after surprising peregrinations. Writing Hening in 1820, Jefferson said that it had been found in the papers of Littleton W. Tazewell ten years earlier by an acquaintance who had carried it to the West, and, noting Jefferson's handwriting on it, had left it for him when he himself was again in Virginia.[19]

[17] TJ to Hening, Dec. 1, 1809 (*ibid.*, 260); May 8, 1822 (LC).

[18] TJ to Hening, Mar. 11, 1815; Hening to TJ, Mar. 15; TJ to Hening, Mar. 25 (LC).

[19] TJ to Hening, Apr. 15, 25, 1815 (LC); Sept. 30, 1820 (Sowerby, II, 237–238); *Statutes at Large*, I (2nd ed., 1823), 298.

ii

John Daly Burk, after publishing three volumes of his projected history of Virginia, had the misfortune to be killed in a duel in 1808. The disappearance of the valuable collection of Virginia newspapers that Jefferson had loaned him provided an illustration of the perils of generosity and trustfulness, but the owner recovered it soon enough to include it in the library he sold to Congress, along with his extensive files of papers from other parts of the Republic. Meanwhile he was engaged in helpful correspondence with Skelton Jones of Richmond, who sought to carry on Burk's history.[20] Jefferson does not appear to have entrusted this writer with any rare volumes, but he gave him a good deal of information and loaned him a hundred dollars in order that he might continue to pursue "literary matters."[21] Jones, who was reputed to be reckless and had killed a man in a duel, was himself the victim of one in 1812. The literary task he left unfinished was carried on by Louis H. Girardin, who published the fourth volume in 1816. He carried the story from 1775 through the surrender of Cornwallis. This proved to be the last of the series, although Burk had planned to go farther. The work was based on materials in the library at Monticello.

During the years 1813–1815, before that library, including its collection of Virginiana, was transferred to Washington, Girardin lived in Albemarle County near Shadwell and conducted a school at his home, Glenmore.[22] A well-born and well-educated Frenchman who had changed his name when he fled to America during the revolution in France, he taught modern languages for a time at the College of William and Mary and afterwards had a school in Richmond. This was attended briefly by Jeff Randolph. He was just the sort of man Jefferson might have been expected to welcome. Besides lending Girardin books and giving him access to the collection at Monticello, Jefferson read his manuscript and gave him his counsel. In a prefatory note in the published work the author referred to the "happy circumstance" of his propinquity to Jefferson, and he dedicated the fourth volume of the history to him as Burk had the first. The man of learning who had already been designated as the guardian and patron of Virginia history was described by Girardin in these words:

[20] TJ informed Jones that the newspapers loaned to Burk were missing (July 28, 1809, L. & B., XII, 297–303). He asked his agent, George Jefferson, to assist him in their recovery (Oct. 29, 1810, LC), but his replies of Dec. 10 and Dec. 17 (listed in the index of correspondence) are not extant. The newspapers are listed in the catalogue of the library sold to Congress (Sowerby, I, 267–268). Fillmore Norfleet gives a brief account of Jones in *Saint-Mémin in Virginia: Portraits and Biographies* (Richmond, 1942), p. 179. In succession to his brother Meriwether, he published the Richmond *Examiner* unsuccessfully in 1803–1804.

[21] Jones to TJ, Jan. 15, 1811, and TJ to Jones, Mar. 4, 1811 (LC).

[22] The best account of him that I have seen is that of Norfleet in *Saint-Mémin in Virginia*, pp. 166–167.

> The obliging neighbour, the warm, kind, Indulgent Friend, as well as the active Patriot, the Able Statesman, and the Liberal Philosopher.

The description was apt, but we may properly ask if Girardin was unduly influenced by his generous neighbor who, as a statesman, had been personally involved in many of the events referred to in the book.

If his own words are to be believed, Jefferson sought no personal glorification at the hands of historians whom he helped. Skelton Jones, originally intending to include biographical information in his continuation of Burk's work, sent a set of questions to a number of persons who had participated in the American Revolution. The reply of John Adams was destined to enliven the pages of history but Jefferson declined to make one, saying that nothing could be more repugnant to his feelings than to write the story of his life. He said that he, like others, had been connected with the great events that happened to mark the era in which they lived, but that credit for these did not belong to anyone in particular, since all of them had done their parts.[23] While claiming no special credit for himself, he believed that the service of his state in the Revolution had been under-rated and that a "patriotic historian" could set that record straight. He made no effort to disguise his local pride, but in itself his remark was not injudicious and in this instance his judgment was essentially correct.

Half a dozen years later he said that Girardin would make him happiest by "a rigorous suppression of all friendly partialities."[24] In view of the favors he did this author he could hardly have expected him to be impartial, but he recognized and often said that the actions of any man must speak for themselves. His major concern, as he himself expressed it, was to keep the record straight and he continued to believe that there could be no "true history" without supporting documents. One that Girardin published in the appendix of his book was his host's diary of Arnold's raid in 1780–1781. This bore directly on Jefferson's conduct as war governor of his state, which had been so sharply, and to his mind so unjustly, criticized by his political foes. Shortly before he made his books and papers accessible to Girardin, the question was raised anew by General Henry (Lighthorse Harry) Lee in that bitter enemy's *Memoirs of the War in the Southern Department* (1812). Following the appearance of this partisan work, Jefferson seems to have gone over his papers relating to this phase of the war and he called Girardin's attention to his own

[23] TJ to Jones, July 28, 1809 (L. & B., XII, 302). The queries of Aug. 1808 are in LC; Jefferson did not receive them until June 29, 1809. Adams's reply of Mar. 11, 1809, is in his *Works*, IX, 610–613.

[24] Mar. 27, 1815 (L. & B., XIV, 295).

diary and correspondence.[25] Whatever may be said of his governorship on balance, he had unquestionably been the victim of inaccurate reporting and the correction of this was a service to "true history" as well as a benefit to his reputation. Because of his extreme aversion to personal controversy, he sought to remain invisible and as a rule he was more patient than John Adams. That old friend was disposed to seek immediate vindication, while Jefferson generally was content to leave things to the judgment of posterity.

The charges against him as war governor rankled in his mind until his dying day, but they had long since ceased to be a novelty. At this stage he seems to have been more disturbed by observations, previously unknown to him, on an episode in the governorship of Patrick Henry. Not until he read Girardin's manuscript did he know what Edmund Randolph and Judge St. George Tucker had said about the case of Josiah Philips, although the quotations from them must have come from books in his own library. As a rule he made only minor corrections in the drafts submitted to him, but he told Girardin that in this instance he did what he had never done before and hoped he would never do again. He struck out the quotations from these two contemporaries of his and revised the account of the case according to his own recollection of it.[26]

Josiah Philips of Princess Anne County, whom Jefferson described as "a man of daring and ferocious disposition," was the leader of a band that spread terror and destruction in the southern counties during the early years of the War for Independence. Retiring into the Dismal Swamp he repeatedly baffled those who sought to apprehend him. Matters reached a crisis in the spring of 1778. Governor Patrick Henry, acting by authority of the council of state, had previously issued a proclamation outlawing Philips. Militia were called out and a reward was offered for his apprehension dead or alive. When the militia proved ineffective, the situation was so desperate that Colonel John Wilson recommended to the Governor that families cooperating with the outlaws be removed from the area. Jefferson recollected attending a conference called by the Governor at which it was determined that a bill of attainder should be enacted against Philips. It may be, however, that the Gover-

[25] See Boyd, IV, 256–278, for comments on this and related documents. We need not reopen the highly controversial question of his conduct as war governor at a time of British invasion, which has been discussed at length in the other volumes of the present work. (See *Jefferson the Virginian*, pp. 301–369; *Jefferson and the Ordeal of Liberty*, pp. 279–283; *Jefferson the President: First Term*, p. 220; *Jefferson the President: Second Term*, pp. 15–17.

[26] TJ to Girardin, Mar. 12, 1815 (L. & B., XIV, 271–278). I discuss the case in *Jefferson the Virginian*, pp. 293–294. Boyd in an excellent note (IV, 191–193) describes the later controversies surrounding Jefferson's actions. Much of the following is based on his account.

nor merely referred to the General Assembly the question of the removal and that the legislative leaders decided instead on a bill of attainder. Jefferson, as chairman of the appropriate committee, drafted and presented one to the House of Delegates. He said it was adopted without dissent and duly became law. According to its terms, Philips would be judged guilty of treason if he did not give himself up for trial within a month. Actually, he was apprehended before the date at which the attainder would have become effective. He was tried under the common law, convicted of robbery (a capital offense), and hanged. Jefferson was uncertain whether the prisoner was charged with robbery or murder, but he had no doubt whatever that Philips was an utter villain who got what he richly deserved. Jefferson believed that this was what the vast majority of Virginians thought at the time. But the criticism he was now seeking to counter did not bear on the merits of the case but centered on the question of procedure — that is, on the bill of attainder itself.

According to the Virginia Declaration of Rights no man should be condemned without a hearing. Bills of attainder, which had been instruments of tyranny in England, were still legal in America in 1778 but were forbidden in Jefferson's own proposals for a state constitution in 1783 and in the Constitution of the United States in 1787.

It was in the Virginia ratifying convention of 1787 that Edmund Randolph condemned the actions of the state government in the case of Josiah Philips. Jefferson, who was in France during the sessions of the convention, was unaware of the incident until he was informed a quarter of a century later by William Wirt, who was writing a biography of Patrick Henry, that the former governor had been severely censured by Randolph. Apparently without looking up the speech, Jefferson assured Wirt that the censure was undeserved.[27]

He did not take the censure so lightly on reading the quotation in Girardin's manuscript some months later, when he realized that it was also directed against him and recognized how severe it was. In the heat of debate Edmund Randolph used very strong language. There had been a shocking violation of human rights in this case, he said. So horrid was it, indeed, that if ever there should be a repetition he would be disposed to emigrate. Jefferson was amazed that the memory of Randolph, who was attorney general at the time, should have been so bad. Randolph asserted that the government had acted on inadequate information and gave the impression that the attainder had actually gone into effect. He referred to no conference, and, although he did not mention Jefferson by name, he left no doubt of his identity and imputed to him a great if

[27] Wirt to TJ, July 27, 1814, in LC; TJ to Wirt, Aug. 14, 1814 (Ford, IX, 465–472).

William Wirt

Engraving by C. B. J. F. de Saint-Mémin, 1807–1808. (Courtesy of the Smithsonian Institution, National Portrait Gallery; gift of Mr. and Mrs. Paul Mellon)

not a major share of blame. In his own statement to Girardin, Jefferson, besides pointing out errors in Edmund Randolph's account of these events, might have laid more emphasis on the fact that they occurred in wartime and might have said that bills of attainder were employed by other states during this conflict.[28] He did not put it quite that way, however. He did not regard the bill as a regrettable aberration but defended it as a wise action and went to surprising lengths in claiming that in extreme circumstances bills of attainder are justifiable. This was in response to the comments of St. George Tucker in his edition of Blackstone. Jefferson had a copy of the work but until now apparently had not examined this portion closely. Tucker's condemnation of bills of attainder was unqualified. One of his sentences must have been particularly unpalatable to Jefferson, who championed both law and freedom: "They supply the want of legal forms, legal evidence, and every other barrier which the laws provide against tyranny and injustice in ordinary cases."[29] Jefferson, like other countrymen of his, had previously concluded that the dangers of this instrument were so great that its use should be forbidden altogether. In defending it now he laid himself open to the charge of inconsistency.

Soon after he wrote his letter to Girardin, Jefferson sent extensive excerpts from it to William Wirt and he referred to the Philips case several times in later correspondence with Patrick Henry's biographer. On reflection he was more convinced than ever that the action of the state government was wise under the existing circumstances, but he urged Wirt to inquire into the matter further. In the text of his biography Wirt told the story essentially as Jefferson had done and he printed the letter from Colonel Wilson advocating the removal of the families cooperating with Philips. Wirt said, however, that his readers must pass judgment for themselves on the conduct of the government. Not only did Jefferson grant Wirt permission to quote him; he asked that the errors of Randolph and Tucker be pointed out in a special note. As a result, the lengthy excerpt from his letter to Girardin appeared in an appendix.[30] Thus his unfortunate and unnecessary comments on bills of attainder were made public in a work that had far wider circulation than Girardin's history. In his own day his theoretical inconsistency does not appear to have marred his reputation as a champion of human rights, but, in his under-

[28] Merrill Peterson comments on the widespread use of bills of attainder in other states (*Thomas Jefferson and the New Nation* [1970], p. 132).

[29] Tucker, ed., *Blackstone*, I (1803), Appendix, pp. 292–293.

[30] TJ to Wirt, May 12, 1815 (Ford, IX, 472); Aug. 5, 1815 (*ibid.*, 474); Oct. 8, 1816 (*ibid.*, X, 63). Wirt, *Henry*, pp. 216–224; Appendix, pp. ix–xii.

standable effort to show that in this instance these had not been violated, he over-reached himself.[31]

iii

"Who shall write the history of the American Revolution? Who can write it? Who will ever be able to write it?" John Adams hurled these questions at Jefferson a few weeks after that comrade of 1776 had sought to correct the account of a remote episode in the War for Independence. The sessions of Congress between 1775 and 1783 were all secret, said Adams; speeches were extemporaneous, unrecorded, and imperfectly remembered. As he observed, essential source materials were lacking. In reply to Adams's rhetorical questions Jefferson said that nobody could write a history of their revolution beyond a mere account of its external events. To the best of his knowledge the members of Congress did not even make notes, and in his opinion the true character of their revolution would remain forever unknown.[32] Actually, he himself in the summer of 1776 took brief minutes of debates in the Continental Congress. These were subsequently incorporated in his autobiography, though they were not published in his lifetime.[33] Elsewhere he expressed the wish that more public men would take notes of the transactions in which they were engaged, and he informed Adams with pride of the extensive ones taken by Madison in the Federal Convention of 1787.

In a letter that was destined to be quoted frequently by historical scholars of later generations, Adams, distinguishing between the Revolution and the War for Independence, said that the former occurred in the minds and hearts of the people between 1760 and 1775, before a drop of blood was shed at Lexington.[34] For the understanding of this, he wisely said that the records of all thirteen of the colonies must be studied, along with the pamphlets and newspapers of the times. He also set high value on private letters, as Jefferson did, and he correctly predicted that many of them would eventually emerge from hiding.

Jefferson's views of the desiderata of Revolutionary scholarship were essentially the same as those of Adams, and, as was virtually inevitable in those times, his own contribution to it lay chiefly in the field of Vir-

[31] Peterson attributes Jefferson's reversal on bills of attainder not to a change of principle but to an inability on his part to admit a mistake (*TJ and the New Nation*, p. 292). However, as I have remarked before, Jefferson could be harsh toward traitors, and his justification of extreme measures was not out of character.

[32] Adams to TJ and Thomas McKean, July 30, 1815; TJ to Adams, Aug. 10, 1815 (*A.-J. Letters*, II, 451–453).

[33] Boyd, I, 299–329.

[34] Adams to TJ, Aug. 24, 1815 (*A.-J. Letters*, II, 455).

ginia history. He by no means neglected the period of the war, but the year 1760, when, according to Adams the most crucial period began, had no little significance in his own history. That was the year in which he entered college, and, as he told William Wirt, he met Patrick Henry on his way to Williamsburg. That was one of many things he told Henry's biographer; and their extensive correspondence, besides being of unusual interest in itself, reveals much about him and his standards.

In the first summer of his second presidential term Jefferson had received from Wirt a deferential letter about a projected biography of Patrick Henry. The young lawyer, who had married a daughter of Jefferson's old friend Dr. George Gilmer, had resided in Albemarle County for several years but had moved to Richmond after her death in 1799. No doubt he had been at Monticello at some time and he was certainly intimate with Dabney and Peter Carr. He gave them as references in his letter, though he did not need to do so. Their uncle was quite willing to trust him and disposed to help him if and when his circumstances would permit.[35]

Wirt believed that Henry's life and example offered "fine lessons," that both his faults and virtues would be instructive, and stated that he was determined not to be a panegyrist. Fully approving of that attitude, Jefferson proceeded to characterize his former associate in a memorable passage:

> He was certainly the man who gave the first impulse to the ball of revolution. Were I to give his character in general terms, it would be of mixed aspect. I think he was the best humored man in society I almost ever knew, and the greatest orator that ever lived. He had a consummate knowledge of the human heart, which directing the efforts of his eloquence enabled him to attain a degree of popularity with the people at large never perhaps equalled. His judgement in other matters was inaccurate; in matters of law it was not worth a copper: he was avaritious & rotten hearted. His two great passions were the love of money & of fame: but when these came into competition the former predominated.[36]

Wirt had promised not to abuse the President's confidence, and Jefferson was prone to indulge in exaggeration in private letters to persons he trusted. The extravagance of his praise and the harshness of his censure in this instance may be thus explained. But, even though over-colored, this balanced statement reflected his reasoned judgment.

[35] Wirt to TJ, July 23, 1805 (UVA). Joseph C. Robert, "William Wirt, Virginian," *Va. Mag.*, LXXX (Oct., 1972), 396–398.

[36] TJ to Wirt, Aug. 4, 1805 (UVA).

More than four years passed before Wirt renewed his request that Jefferson draw on his memory for anecdotes of Patrick Henry. In the meantime, Wirt had commended himself to Jefferson and gained bright laurels for oratory as one of the lawyers for the prosecution in the Burr trial. Also, he had made numerous inquiries about the subject of his projected biography, with results that he found disturbing. So warm were the prejudices of Henry's admirers and detractors that he had wondered if the subject were not too ticklish to handle. He was not abandoning it, however, being convinced that Patrick Henry provided "a good text for a discourse on rhetoric, patriotism, and morals." Since he had never seen or heard him, Wirt was seeking light on "his peculiarities of character as a man, a patriot, and an orator." By this time he appears to have become less concerned to provide a good likeness than to offer an example worthy of imitation, but such was not the case with the Sage on the mountain.[37]

Jefferson had already expressed to Wirt his appreciation of the Revolutionary services and his admiration for the oratory of Patrick Henry, but he had no thought of presenting him as a model character. His judgment could hardly have failed to be affected to some degree by his belief that his predecessor as governor of Virginia was considerably to blame for the unfair criticism of his own conduct in that office, and that he regarded Henry in his later years as a defector from the sacred cause of republicanism. But he wanted the memoir that he began promptly to draw up for the benefit of Henry's biographer to be correct in all matters of fact. He kept it more than a year after he wrote it, hoping to add to it something about Henry's "ravenous avarice," but, as he told Wirt, he gave up the idea because his information on that point was secondhand. He said that the biographer must seek from others better testimony than he could offer and must follow his own judgment regarding its use. No doubt Jefferson continued to believe that the backwoods lawyer loved money excessively, but he frankly recognized that he could not prove it.

He also recognized that he had had no personal contact with Henry after 1783, when he himself entered upon a period of national and international service. His specific contribution to Wirt's biography, therefore, lay within a period of somewhat less than a quarter of a century (1759–1783). Since his memoir is discussed in detail in *Jefferson the Virginian*, we need not enter into it here except to say that American historical literature has been enriched by Jefferson's account of Henry at the beginning and at the height of his meteoric career.[38]

[37] Wirt to TJ, Jan. 15, 1810; TJ to Wirt, Mar. 25, 1810 (LC).

[38] See *Jefferson the Virginian*, pp. 89–96, and what is better, the memoir itself in Ford, IX, 339*n*.-345*n*., enclosed with TJ to Wirt, Apr. 12, 1812 (*ibid.*, 338–341).

He sent his paper on Henry to Wirt the day before he became sixty-nine, which was several weeks before the War of 1812 began. During the next four years he responded to numerous inquiries from the prospective biographer, who, as we may note in passing, represented him in the batture case and other legal matters. In the midst of these troubles Wirt told Dabney Carr that he had pestered Jefferson so much that he was ashamed to do so further.[39] He did not cease to question that friend's uncle, however, and in the summer of 1816 he asked him to read the entire manuscript. Jefferson got this in batches and made comments on it that were always polite and generally encouraging. An unfavorable one that is of special interest related to the alleged claim of Patrick Henry that he read Livy every year. Jefferson protested that no one who knew the man could believe that he ever read any book twice — that, indeed, he rarely got through a book once. While recognizing the orator's indolence, Wirt retained this passage, citing the person who said he heard the claim from Henry himself. While Jefferson rejected it and did not hesitate to depict Henry as a man lacking in polite learning, he was not being patronizing when he said that Henry drew human rights from "a purer source — the feelings of his own breast."[40]

Wirt said that he sent volleys of letters over the state in his effort to inform himself about a man who had left hardly any records and he was indebted to many persons besides Jefferson. But he drew extensively on the latter's memoir and numerous letters, quoting him many times in the text. In general it may be said that he accepted everything that was favorable to Henry. He could hardly have been expected to describe Henry as "rotten hearted," and one may doubt that Jefferson himself would have done so in print. Wirt does not appear to have ignored unfavorable comments, but he undoubtedly toned them down.

While describing his difficulties wittily in a letter to Dabney Carr (who was a judge), Wirt spoke of the problem of "stating facts with rigid precision, not one jot more or less than the truth." He then exclaimed: "What the deuce does a lawyer have to do with truth!" After he got the facts accurately, he said, he was faced with the task of narrating them happily, and that was like trying to run when tied in a bag.[41] There is no reason to suppose that Jefferson ever saw this vivid letter, but he recognized the problem, and, while encouraging and well-mannered, he criticized the book on both factual and stylistic grounds. Before he read Wirt's manuscript he thus expressed himself to another: "A fair and honest narrative of the bad is a voucher for the truth of the

[39] Wirt to Carr, Aug. 20, 1815 (Kennedy, *Wirt*, I, 346).

[40] Wirt to TJ, Aug. 10, 1816 (LC); TJ to Wirt, Sept. 4, 1816 (Ford, X, 54–60). Wirt and TJ exchanged ten letters between August and November, 1816.

[41] Wirt to Judge Dabney Carr, Aug. 20, 1815 (Kennedy, *Wirt*, I, 344).

good."[42] The brief biographical sketches that he himself wrote on request from time to time are notably well balanced and are the more convincing because he portrays faults as well as virtues.[43] To his mind, Wirt had followed no such prescription in the effort to insure credibility. Although Wirt admitted to Dabney Carr that he perceived "ugly traits" in Henry's character, he gave little place to what Jefferson called "animadversions." This friendly critic said: "You have certainly practiced vigorously the precept of '*de mortuis nil nisi bonum.*' This presents a very difficult question — whether one only or both sides of the medal shall be presented. It constitutes, perhaps, the distinction between panegyric and history."[44] There can be little doubt that Jefferson placed this work in the former category. Wirt certainly thought he did. But he said that the work would be useful to the public and honorable to the author. It would bring pleasure to its readers; and no one who started it would be able to lay it down.

When questioned about style, he candidly admitted that to his mind some passages were "too flowery for the sober taste of history." They would appeal to the young, he said, but would be better liked by the old if some of their excrescences were removed. It would appear that the classicist was speaking to the romanticist. He expressed admiration for Wirt's "rich and captivating" style and said that too little pruning would be better than too much. But Wirt told Francis Walker Gilmer that the Honorable Thomas, while giving him extravagant encouragement, had challenged almost all his favorite passages.[45]

The work which its author modestly entitled *Sketches of the Life of Patrick Henry* was published in 1817. In thanking Jefferson for his help, Wirt referred to his customary kindness and candor. In due course that learned and patriotic gentleman warmly congratulated the author, saying that the popular reception of the book and Wirt's appointment as attorney general of the United States had brought him much gratification. Though the work was and long continued to be a great literary success, it received sharp criticism on historical grounds and in some of this Jefferson was implicated. His assertion, which Wirt quoted, that Henry had set the ball of revolution rolling, excited heated protest in New England, notably from John Adams. His friend Dr. Benjamin Waterhouse reported this to their mutual friend Jefferson. Harking back to the struggle over writs of assistance, Adams championed the claim of James Otis

[42] TJ to Mathew Carey, June 19, 1813 (L. & B., XIII, 264).

[43] A number of these sketches, including TJ's remarkable appraisal of Washington, are grouped in *The Complete Jefferson*, ed. by S. K. Padover (1943), pp. 890–928.

[44] TJ to Wirt, Nov. 12, 1816 (Ford, X, 61*n.*–62*n.*).

[45] TJ to Wirt, Sept. 29, 1816 (Ford, X, 62*n.*); Wirt to F. W. Gilmer, Jan. 26, 1817 (Kennedy, II, 15).

to primacy. He observed that Jefferson was a mere college boy at the time, too intent on his studies to pay much attention to happenings in Massachusetts. He "probably knew more of the eclipses of Jupiter's satellites than he did of what was passing in Boston." Jefferson was well aware that there were major grievances in Massachusetts sooner than in Virginia, and that serious conflict with the British government occurred in Adams's province earlier than in his own. It might have been assumed, he said, that primacy was claimed for Patrick Henry in Virginia rather than in the colonies as a whole. It may be assumed also that when Jefferson described the unparalleled popularity of the orator, he was thinking of his own province and state.[46]

John Adams, who was never noted for patience, vented his intense local patriotism in an indignant public letter. Jefferson was informed of this by Thomas Ritchie of the *Richmond Enquirer*, who did not want Virginia to be divested of any laurels to which she was entitled and wondered what if anything he should do. Jefferson sent the highly respected journalist an excerpt of his own letter to Dr. Waterhouse and took the position that public controversy on this subject would be futile and unwise. He himself would enter into none. In saying that a state, like an individual, should not praise itself, he was being somewhat inconsistent. He had told Girardin that Virginia deserved more credit than she had received for her military services in the Revolution. But he knew that questions of priority often boil down to questions of semantics. Also, he regretted the reputation for bragging that Americans had acquired and knew that the prominence of his state in national affairs was resented in other parts of the country — mostly, perhaps, in New England.[47]

Toward the end of his life Jefferson made to two New Englanders a more unfavorable comment on the biography than any he is known ever to have made to Wirt. To Daniel Webster and George Ticknor he is reported to have said: "It is a poor book, written in bad taste, & gives so imperfect an idea of Patrick Henry, that it seems intended to show off the writer, more than the subject of the work." Years later Jefferson's granddaughter told his biographer that this quotation gave an incorrect impression of his attitude toward the book and, in particular, toward Wirt.[48]

It would have been unlike him to cast aspersions on Wirt's motives or taste, but his dissatisfaction with the use of the materials he had pro-

[46] Benjamin Waterhouse to TJ, Feb. 26, 1818 (LC), with quotes from Adams to Waterhouse; TJ to Waterhouse, Mar. 3, 1818 (Ford, X, 102–104); Adams to Wirt, Jan. 5, 1818 (Kennedy, II, 43–44).

[47] Ritchie to TJ, Mar. 13, 1818 (LC); TJ to Ritchie, Mar. 20, 1818.

[48] "Notes of Mr. Jefferson's Conversation 1824 at Monticello," in the *Papers of Daniel Webster, Correspondence*, I, 373. Ellen Wayles Coolidge to Henry Randall, 1857 (Randall, III, 506–508).

vided seems to have increased with the passing years. Speaking of Wirt and his book, a perceptive modern historian has said: "For him Henry's limitations became his strengths."[49] According to this view, Wirt wove these limitations into a legend of a natural leader who lacked learning and cultivation but did not need them. Such an interpretation was quite unacceptable to Jefferson. While he had great respect for native genius and recognized that it might appear almost anywhere in human society, he had no thought that it was sufficient in itself. He feared ignorance as he did tyranny, prized knowledge as he did freedom, and, at just this time, was setting up an institution of higher learning in which he expected future leaders to be trained.

[49] William R. Taylor, *Cavalier and Yankee: The Old South and American National Character* (1961), p. 84. A chapter of this is devoted to Wirt (pp. 67–94) and includes an excellent discussion of the Henry biography.

Genesis of a University

[XVI]

Educational Aspirations

1779-1814

IN the first major phase of his career Jefferson gained enduring fame as a champion of freedom. In the final phase, when in nominal retirement, he rendered his most memorable public services as an advocate of enlightenment. Circumstances differed in the two periods, as did some of his immediate objectives, but his long-range purposes were unchanged. To the venerable Sage as to the bold Revolutionary patriot, freedom and knowledge were inseparable. In the early morning of the Republic he had launched a crusade against ignorance as well as against tyranny. Besides his famous bill for establishing religious freedom, he drafted one for "the more general diffusion of knowledge."

If this bill had been enacted, along with one also drafted by him that would have transformed the College of William and Mary, his commonwealth would have had a system of public education extending from primary schools to a potential university.[1] His program was too much for the General Assembly. In 1796 that body provided for the establishment of primary schools on local initiative, but the truncated measure of that year proved to be virtually a dead letter, and the reluctance of the gentry to tax themselves for the benefit of the children of the poor was unabated. At the turn of the century, however, Jefferson believed that there was some sentiment for the creation of an institution of higher learning.

[1] An additional bill would have established a public library dedicated to the "researches of the learned and curious." The bills were included in the report of the committee on the revisal of the laws of Virginia, presented to the General Assembly in 1779 (Boyd, II, 526–553). They are described and discussed in *Jefferson the Virginian*, pp. 274–285. For sound treatments of TJ's educational work as a whole see Roy J. Honeywell, *The Educational Work of Thomas Jefferson* (1931), and James B. Conant, *Thomas Jefferson and the Development of American Public Education* (1963). These books are referred to hereafter by their authors' names.

He did not regard the top of the educational pyramid as the best place to begin. If there had to be a choice, he held that public elementary schools should come first. But, if he could not get all that he sought, he was disposed to accept what he could get. Believing that schools to teach reading, writing, and arithmetic to the children of the land would undoubtedly be established some day, he turned his mind to education at its highest level. He no longer aspired to transform the College of William and Mary. That historic institution was eking out a precarious existence in a remote and, to his way of thinking, unhealthy part of the growing state. He had in mind an establishment in a more central location and a more salubrious climate — a fresh creation that would be adapted to the needs of the living generation.

Shortly before and during his presidency, successive governors of Virginia, beginning with James Monroe, called attention to its educational needs and referred specifically to a university. The chances of getting one turned out to be more remote than Jefferson may have supposed, but, believing that a plan was now needed, he set out to assemble materials from which one could be constructed. In 1800 he consulted Dr. Joseph Priestley, the eminent English chemist and Unitarian clergyman who was ending his days in Pennsylvania, and Du Pont de Nemours, the noted French philosopher, who at this time was in Delaware. In his letters to these learned friends he disclosed the advanced ideas about the character and functions of a modern university that he himself held.[2] In particular he asked them what subjects should be taught and how these should be grouped. The question was one that he was as competent to answer as they were, for he had surveyed the entire field of knowledge when cataloguing his library. He finally concluded that this was a topic on which no two men agreed, but he welcomed suggestions, and during his first presidential term he sought them from the universities of Geneva and Edinburgh and the Institute of France.

There was considerable interest in a university in the General Assembly in 1805 and a bill for one was proposed the next year. Nothing came of it, however, and Jefferson's correspondence at this time is chiefly significant for what it reveals of his own ideas.[3] These extended to the procedure to be followed in the legislature in setting up a university, and

[2] TJ to Priestley, Jan. 18, 27, 1800 (Ford, VII, 407–409, 413–415); TJ to Du Pont, Apr. 12, 1800 (*J.-D. Correspondence*, pp. 8–9). In the present connection these letters are of greater interest than the replies. The correspondence is described in *Jefferson and the Ordeal of Liberty*, pp. 450–451.

[3] TJ to Littleton W. Tazewell, Jan. 5, 1805 (UVA). It was in this letter that TJ said he would leave his library to the University (see *Jefferson the President: Second Term*, p. 22). On the bill proposed in the Assembly, see Richmond *Enquirer*, Jan. 16, 1806.

the make-up and duties of its governors; but we are most concerned here with his aspirations for the university itself.

Although the needs of his beloved state were central in Jefferson's thought, the institution he was planning was to be neither provincial nor traditional. In speaking of its plan to Littleton W. Tazewell, he used the adjectives "broad," "liberal," "advanced," and "modern." All "sciences" — that is, all branches of learning — would fall within the province of this university, and the subjects should be taught, he said, "in the highest degree to which the human mind has carried them." Nevertheless, selection was both necessary and desirable. "Science is progressive," he wrote Tazewell. "What was useful two centuries ago is now become useless." He would discard some subjects that were still being generally taught and would replace them with others that were now more valuable.

It should be noted that he conceived of utility in broad and comprehensive terms. He never held that man could live by bread alone. To him anything that benefited human beings in spirit or body was useful. But he viewed learning with a discriminating eye and was in the vanguard of his generation in academic thinking. Indeed, he said that Oxford, Cambridge, and the Sorbonne were from a century and a half to two centuries out of date. He hoped to attract some of the "first characters of science" in Europe to the modern university he was planning and wanted it to set the pace in both hemispheres.

By the time he retired from public office he had arrived at the basic plan for the housing of the community of scholars which he was afterwards to elaborate and perfect. He wrote Tazewell that a university should be a village, not a big building. There should be houses for each of the professors with students' rooms between them, connected by a covered passageway and fronting on a court. Thus he foreshadowed his architectural masterpiece as well as the institution that would, as he hoped, crown an educational system.

President Jefferson became the founder of a national institution of learning when he established (1802) a corps of engineers at West Point as a military academy. It was essentially a school of engineering in his day, and the "sciences" taught there fully met the tests of utility that were applied by this lover of mathematics who had surveyed his own lands.[4] During his presidency he gave encouragement and advice to Joel Barlow, who was designing a system of national education culminating in a university. He appears to have influenced Barlow very little and the poet's elaborate plan may have called for more centralization than he favored, but in his sixth annual message he recommended that Congress

[4] See *Jefferson the President: Second Term*, pp. 510–511.

take steps toward the establishment of a national university. Believing that a constitutional amendment was required, he suggested that the process of procuring one be begun.[5]

The worsening of the international situation provided an explanation of the failure of Congress to act in this matter during the remainder of Jefferson's administration, but we may doubt if it would have done so in any case. He seems to have been undisposed to press matters. Writing Barlow, he said:

> There is a snail-paced gait for the advance of new ideas on the general mind, under which we must acquiesce. A forty years' experience of popular assemblies has taught me, that you must give them time for every step you take. If too hard pushed, they baulk, and the machine retrogrades.[6]

This apostle of enlightenment who was so aware of public apathy tended to take the long view of social progress; and, being temperamentally sanguine, he was characteristically patient. With notable patience he combined extraordinary tenacity in the pursuit of major goals. As a foe of ignorance and a friend of learning he was to manifest both qualities during the rest of his long and useful life.

For some five years after his return to Virginia as a private citizen, Jefferson did little to quicken the snail-paced gait of the commonwealth in matters educational. He was sedulously avoiding political controversy of any sort and scrupulously refraining from actions that might be interpreted as interfering with the prerogatives of those charged with the conduct of the state government. Accordingly, he tried to keep out of sight — especially out of sight of contentious legislators.

Throughout the first quarter of the nineteenth century the governors of the state were generally friendly to education. All of them may have consulted Jefferson, and John Tyler certainly did. There is no record of their conversations when the ex-President visited him in Richmond in the fall of 1809, but soon thereafter Tyler described the educational backwardness of the state in a strongly worded message to the General Assembly. That body responded by creating the Literary Fund. The Act of February 2, 1810, provided that all escheats, confiscations, fines (except militia fines), penalties, forfeitures, and derelict personal property accruing to the state be appropriated for the encouragement of

[5] See message of Dec. 2, 1806 (Ford, VIII, 494); Honeywell, pp. 61–64.
[6] TJ to Barlow, Dec. 10, 1807 (Ford, IX, 169).

learning.[7] A year later, provision was made for the administration of the fund, and the Act of February 12 stipulated that when a sufficient sum had been acquired, schools for the poor should be set up in all the counties of the state.[8] Jefferson was aware only of the Act of 1810, when in May of that year the Governor asked him to put on paper his thoughts on education.

He seems to have wholly refrained from adverse comment on the Literary Fund, but obviously it fell far short of his aspirations. Replying to a letter from Tyler, he told the Governor what he really wanted. At heart he had two measures, he said, without which no republic would maintain itself "in strength." The first of them could hardly have surprised his correspondent. It would provide for general education such as he had long advocated. The second would cause the counties to be divided into hundreds, which would be of such size that every child would be in reach of a central school.

These hundreds, which he described more fully elsewhere and generally called wards, were to have officials of their own and were to constitute in effect little republics. They were to represent the first stage in self-government, as the free primary schools were to represent the first stage in public education.[9] His emphasis on the hundreds as political entities may be attributed in part to the impression he had gained of the New England town meetings, which had shaken the very foundations of his government at the time of the embargo.[10] With respect to education, however, he was saying essentially what he had said thirty years before in the portion of his bill for the more general diffusion of knowledge, which dealt with the primary schools. He was still putting first things first.

He never ceased believing that the enlightenment of the people generally was a matter of supreme importance, but he was well aware that a democratic society was also faced with another task that he did not hesitate to designate as noble — training its future leaders. He had asserted that the earth always belongs to the living generation, but he clearly recognized that every generation must render its youths fit to govern the next.

[7] *Supplement, Containing the Acts of the General Assembly* . . . (Richmond, Samuel Pleasants, 1812), pp. 48–49. An account of the development of the Literary Fund is in William A. Maddox, *The Free School Idea in Virginia Before the Civil War* (1918), pp. 42–62. However, this study is not wholly free of error.

[8] "An Act to Provide for the Education of the Poor," *Supplement, Containing the Acts of the General Assembly* (1812), pp. 67–68. I make no attempt here to cover all later changes in this fund.

[9] TJ to Gov. John Tyler, May 26, 1810 (Ford, IX, 277–278), replying to a letter of May 12.

[10] See *Jefferson the President: Second Term*, pp. 608–611, 613.

Soon after he wrote Tyler, he expressed himself to that effect in his response to a request for his assistance to a projected college in East Tennessee.[11] In this letter he recommended the same sort of architectural plan that he had described briefly to Tazewell five years before and now used the expression "academical village." He had no real reason to design one until after he became a trustee of Albemarle Academy four years later, and during most of the intervening period he was occupied in other than educational matters — the batture controversy, for example.

In 1813, he was engaged in a dialogue with John Adams, which is fascinating in itself and which illustrates both his social and his educational philosophy. Adams introduced the subject of aristocracy with a Greek quotation and pursued it in six letters, displaying impressive learning and employing fervid rhetoric.[12] Philosophers equate the "aristoi" with the wise and the good, Adams said. But, manifesting the realism on which he prided himself, he observed that through the ages aristocracy in practice had always been associated with birth, wealth, and beauty. Among the "pillars" of aristocracy he also included genius and virtue but said that these were incapable of contending with any one of the other three. He went to great lengths in support of his position, laying special emphasis on the importance of good birth — in human beings as in domestic animals. The idea of the well-born was no prejudice, he said. It was in the constitution of human nature by ordinance of God. Philosophers and politicians might "nibble and quibble," but they could never get rid of it. All they could do would be to control it. He said less about wealth, which he described as another monster to be subdued, but made a strong case for beauty, especially feminine beauty, as a factor in human affairs. "Millions of examples might be quoted from history sacred and profane," he said. Among recent aristocrats of beauty he mentioned Mesdames Du Barry and Pompadour and made much of Lady Hamilton.

Jefferson did not take up Adams's arguments one by one, and we cannot hope to do justice here to Adams's doctrine of aristocracy as set forth in his vigorous, colorful, and ill-organized letters. Jefferson, who made a point of stressing what they had in common, did not fail to do so now,

[11] TJ to trustees for the lottery of East Tennessee College, May 6, 1810 (L. & B., XII, 386–388).

[12] Adams's first two letters to TJ on aristocracy (Aug. 14, Sept. 2, 1813) are essentially philosophical, while the final four (Sept. 15, Nov. 12, Nov. 15, Dec. 19) are essentially illustrative. The series is divided by TJ's reply and statement of Oct. 28, 1813, and closes with his letter of Jan. 24, 1814. All may be read in the *A.-J. Letters.* The original quotation was from Theognis of the sixth century B.C. Adams added his own translation for TJ to compare with a Latin translation by Grotius and judge which was truest to the meaning of the original.

but there were differences. Accordingly, this member of the gentry of the proud Virginia commonwealth, who had been privileged from his birth, set forth his views of aristocracy, true and false, in one of the most memorable of his letters.[13] To his loquacious friend he said:

> I agree with you that there is a natural aristocracy among men. The grounds of this are virtue and talents. . . .[14] There is also an artificial aristocracy founded on wealth and birth, without either virtue or talents; . . . The natural aristocracy I consider as the most precious gift of nature for the instruction, the trusts and government of society. . . . May we not even say that that government is the best which provides most effectually for a pure selection of these natural aristoi into the offices of government? The artificial aristocracy is a mischievous ingredient in government, and provision should be made to prevent its ascendancy.

He himself relied on the citizens to separate the wheat from the chaff. "In general," he said, "they will elect the wise and good." Of this Adams was distinctly skeptical. Also, he attributed to the great families an influence which Jefferson found surprising in the case of New England and unacceptable in that of Virginia. He reminded Adams of the laws, fathered by himself, by means of which his commonwealth got rid of entails and primogeniture. Thus, he claimed, the ax was laid at "the root of the 'pseudo-aristocracy.' " He over-emphasized the effect of these measures and may have exaggerated the unpopularity of the great families.[15] It should be noted, however, that, while committed to furthering economic freedom and equality of opportunity, he was no enemy to wealth as such. The position he took here was that in the management of human affairs — especially public affairs — merit and character should be preferred.

He told his argumentative correspondent in Massachusetts that, if his bill for the more general diffusion of knowledge had been passed, it would have completed the work begun by the actions against entails and primogeniture. The description he gave of it in this letter need not be repeated here, but reference should be made to one of the distinctive features of the measure: the selective principle embodied in it. Only in the primary grades was education to be free to all comers, but youths of special promise were to be chosen periodically from the mass for education at public expense in the grammar school and the university. As a

[13] TJ to Adams, Oct. 28, 1813.

[14] *A.-J. Letters*, p. 388. Adams had not said this in as many words but in his letter of Nov. 15 he accepted this statement, while interpreting it somewhat differently.

[15] On the abolition of entails and primogeniture, see *Jefferson the Virginian*, pp. 247–260.

result of these provisions, Jefferson said, "Worth and genius would thus have been sought out from every condition of life, and completely prepared by education for defeating the competition of wealth and birth for public trusts." This longtime champion of equal rights had sought to further equality of opportunity by removing artificial barriers and special privileges. But his egalitarianism did not blind him to the differences in individual potentialities, nor did his democratic spirit reconcile him to the rule of mediocrity. He told his correspondent that the schooling of the mass of the people for which his bill made provision would not only enable them to defend themselves against oppression; it would also "qualify" them to elect "true aristoi" to the offices of government.

Although John Adams was not noted for his tact, he refrained from critical comment on the plan of education of which Jefferson hoped so much and to which he clung so tenaciously. Adams said, however, that he was equally impressed with the stupidity and credulity that the populace had displayed throughout history and with the cupidity and cruelty of the rulers of mankind. Accordingly, he was more dubious than his optimistic friend of the ultimate triumph of wisdom and goodness. In a long, colorful, chaotic letter he made some fun of the simple faith which in fact was one of the things that endeared Jefferson to him. Also, he argued vigorously about terminology. He observed that talents are very diverse and claimed that the talented in almost any field should be designated as "natural" aristocrats. To him aristocracy was "artificial" only when it had the support of law. Notwithstanding his qualifications, definitions, and expostulations, he declared that he saw no disagreement between himself and Jefferson. He avowed his detestation of hereditary privilege, and in the course of his letter spoke of the aristocracy created by the banking system in language that was little short of contemptuous.[16]

Jefferson, resuming his usual policy of avoiding contention, left Adams's arguments unanswered. He knew that the honest old patriot valued character and wisdom as he did and fully agreed with him that the public servants should be well educated.[17]

[16] I find Adams's letter of Nov. 15 almost impossible to summarize. Regarding some of it as improper for any of the feminine members of his family to see, he did not have it copied by one of them as was his custom and asked TJ to return it to him.

[17] In TJ's letter of Jan. 24, 1814, which closed this dialogue, he returned to the question of the influence of prominent families in New England, attributing it, as he had done earlier, to the alliance between church and state.

XVII

From Academy to College

1814-1816

IN the spring of 1814, several months after the dialogue about aristocracy ended and shortly before Jefferson's seventy-first birthday, five men who were meeting in a tavern in Charlottesville nominated him to serve as a trustee of Albemarle Academy. Although it had been chartered a decade earlier, the institution existed only on paper; and the surviving members of the original Board of Trustees, including Peter Carr, were trying to breathe life into it. According to a long-lived story, Peter's uncle, chancing to be riding by, was observed and invited to participate in the deliberations. However, it is hard to believe that Jefferson became connected with the enterprise by accident. We may reasonably suppose that this tireless champion of education at all levels was well informed of the local situation and that, if he was present at the meeting, he had been properly invited in advance.[1]

He did not attend all the later meetings of the Board, and he probably tried to avoid the appearance of dominating it, especially at first. Nevertheless, he recognized the opportunity to promote the educational purposes that had long been in his mind. Before the legislature met, toward the end of the year, he had gained the support of his colleagues for recommendations that they could hardly have anticipated in the spring. The available records leave us in some doubt regarding the means he employed to bring about this result.[2] He may be safely presumed to

[1] This story seems to have been first told by John B. Minor in 1870 ("Historical Sketches of Virginia — University of Virginia," pt. I, *The Old Dominion,* IV [Mar., 1870], 150). Philip Alexander Bruce repeated it but corrected obvious errors in Minor's version (*History of the University of Virginia* [1920], I, 121). TJ was nominated for the Board at its reorganization meeting on Mar. 25, 1814, but his attendance is not recorded until the second meeting on Apr. 5 (minutes in Cabell, Appendix A, pp. 379–380).

[2] Minutes and documents in *ibid.*, Appendices A–D, pp. 379–393, supplemented by records in TJ Papers, UVA.

have had from the beginning the full cooperation of Peter Carr, who was elected president of the Board at its second meeting. He could draw on the large store of good will that he had accumulated in his own county through the years, and his prestige assured him of a respectful hearing. Also, he had a clear-purposed goal and vastly superior knowledge. Few of his new colleagues may have suspected what they were in for when they sought to avail themselves of his wisdom and experience, but, if not wholly convinced, they were overwhelmed by the papers he drafted. At the outset most of his fellow trustees probably envisioned an academy largely devoted to the teaching of the classics, such as existed in fair number in the state. There was considerable sentiment in the community for the location of the school in the stone tavern where the meeting was held. The purchase of it would have been advantageous to its genial and popular proprietor, Triplett Estes. Jefferson could not be content with an institution of such restricted scope in such limited quarters.[3]

A couple of months before he first met with the trustees he wrote Thomas Cooper of the possible establishment in his vicinity of an institution which could offer that man of learning a worthy place.[4] Then on the faculty of Carlisle College, Cooper, of whose diverse scholarship and anticlerical spirit Jefferson highly approved, was looking for a position. He would not have fitted into what Jefferson termed a petty academy, and quite clearly the Sage had something much better in mind. To Cooper he afterwards said: "Caesar and Virgil, and a few books of Euclid, do not really contain the sum of all human knowledge."[5] He made a similar observation to John Adams in the first summer of his trusteeship.[6] He then said that from these academies young men emerged "with just taste enough of learning to be alienated from industrious pursuits, and not enough to do service in the ranks of science." His heart was set on an institution where all the useful branches of human knowledge should be taught in the highest degree, and in the summer of 1814 he continued to ask learned friends what these branches were and how they should be grouped. As stated to Cooper, his objective was "to bring the whole circle of useful science [knowledge] under the direction of the

[3]Without authorization by the trustees a petition signed by 147 citizens of Albemarle was sent to the legislature asking permission for a lottery to raise money to purchase Estes's property for the Academy. The conflict with TJ's proposals was pointed out and the petitioners' request was rejected (TJ to Col. Charles Yancey, Oct. 15, 1815, LC; Joseph C. Cabell to TJ, Feb. 21, 1816, Cabell, p. 59 and note p. xxiv).

[4]TJ to Cooper, Jan. 16, 1814 (L. & B., XIV, 59–60).

[5]TJ to Cooper, Oct. 7, 1814 (*ibid.*, p. 200).

[6]TJ to Adams, July 5, 1814 (*A.-J. Letters*, II, 434).

smallest number of professors possible, and that our means may be so frugally employed as to effect the greatest possible good."[7]

Jefferson's letter to Cooper was concerned solely with a university. "We are about to make an effort for the introduction of this institution," he said. By then he had almost certainly devised the plan to transform the projected academy into a college and to translate the college into the university of his dreams. But he had to take one step at a time, and the goal he hoped ultimately to reach was the establishment of a state-wide system of public education that would provide instruction at all levels. This he made entirely clear in a letter he addressed to Peter Carr for the benefit of the Albemarle trustees.[8] He had promised these country gentlemen to prepare a plan for the academy or college to be established in the neighborhood, but he gave them a great deal more. Unquestionably he was trying to put this local project in the setting of his full educational plan.

The program he was proposing would have seemed ambitious long after his day.[9] On reading the lengthy lists of "sciences" that he recommended, one can but wonder what subjects he left out on the ground of uselessness. He summarized his plan of distribution as follows:

First or Elementary Grade in the Ward Schools:
Reading, Writing, Arithmetic, Geography.

Second or General Grade:
1. Language and History, ancient and modern.
2. Mathematics, viz: Mathematics pure, Physico-Mathematics, Physics, Chemistry, Anatomy, Theory of Medicine, Zoology, Botany and Mineralogy.
3. Philosophy, viz: Ideology, and Ethics, Law of Nature and Nations, Government, Political Economy.

Third or Professional Grades:
Theology and Ecclesiastical History; Law, Municipal and Foreign; Practice of Medicine; Materia Medica and Pharmacy; Surgery; Architecture, Military and Naval, and Projectiles; Technical Philosophy; Rural Economy; Fine Arts.

[7] TJ to Cooper, Aug. 25, 1814 (L. & B., XIV, 173–174). Along with Adams and Cooper, he consulted Casper Wistar, Aug. 25, 1815 (LC), asking particularly about courses at the University of Philadelphia.

[8] TJ to Carr, Sept. 7, 1814. This letter, which afterwards became a famous document in American educational history, may be seen in L. & B., XIX, 211–221, in Honeywell, pp. 222–227, and elsewhere.

[9] One of the novel features was a provision for a technical school, offering free nightly lectures for the benefit of craftsmen of almost every sort.

His initial plan for the projected college in his county embraced the sciences of the "general" grade.[10] It called for four professors and a corresponding division of the subjects of instruction into four rather than three groups (as indicated in the distribution plan). He afterwards learned that he was proposing a more advanced program than the one in effect at the University of Pennsylvania, which he regarded as the most celebrated seminary in the nation.[11]

Jefferson drafted his ambitious proposals in one of the grimmest periods of the war. In August British troops had sacked Washington and were believed to endanger Richmond. All the eligible males in his own family were guarding the approaches to the capital of the commonwealth. As he himself reported, the only men left in Albemarle were the "silver grays." He included himself in that category, deploring his inability to walk and at this juncture even to ride.[12] He may have exaggerated his own debility, but the reason he gave Peter Carr for making him the depository of his ideas was that he might be unable to attend the meetings of the trustees. His nephew, the president of the Board, did not return to Albemarle with Jeff Randolph and other militiamen until the end of September, and Jefferson probably delayed the delivery of his long and formidable letter until after that. At some time, perhaps at the same time, he sent Carr a copy of a letter of his to Thomas Cooper which he seems to have regarded as a supplement to his major communication.[13] In the letter to Carr he had listed medical theory and theology as subjects of instruction, but to Cooper he said that the one was the "charlatanerie" of the body and the other that of the mind. This private letter would hardly have strengthened his tactical position, but apparently few people ever became aware of it.[14]

Just when Jefferson's "plan" was presented to the trustees of Albemarle Academy is still a matter of uncertainty. A meeting was scheduled for the third Friday in November, and one may have occurred then, but no record of it seems to have been preserved.[15] Jefferson's handwriting

[10] Honeywell observes with sagacity (p. 41) that he was assigning to institutions of the second grade subjects that he had proposed in 1779 to give to William and Mary.

[11] Wistar to TJ, Apr. 27, 1815 (LC).

[12] See ch. VIII, pp. 119–120, above.

[13] TJ to Cabell, Jan. 5, 1815 (Cabell, pp. 36–37). The letter was TJ to Cooper, Oct. 7, 1814 (L. & B., XIV, 199–202). On Sept. 10 he sent Cooper a copy of his letter of Sept. 7 to Carr (*ibid.*, pp. 179–180). Cooper commented on subjects of instruction Sept. 22 (LC).

[14] It contains a passage on botany which should certainly be cherished by all devotees of that science (see ch. IV, p. 50, above).

[15] Minutes of meeting of Aug. 19, 1814 (Cabell, p. 383). This was the last recorded meeting.

was notably legible, but we may doubt if all of the trustees got through his entire letter to Peter Carr. And we need not suppose that they all agreed with the whole of his educational philosophy. At some time before the end of the year, however, a majority of them must have agreed to a petition to the legislature that he had drafted in their behalf, along with a bill showing what they wanted of that body.[16]

Some months earlier he had been named to a committee, along with Peter Carr and Thomas Mann Randolph, who had become a member of the Board, to petition the legislature for the proceeds of the sale of the glebe lands in Fredericksville and St. Anne's parishes.[17] The present petition also asked for a grant from the dividend of the Literary Fund.[18] More noteworthy in the light of later events was the request that the name of Albemarle Academy be changed to Central College. This was in full accord with Jefferson's hopes for an institution on a more advanced plane in his own locality that could be turned into a university. Since he had previously said that, to be effective, a governing board should be small, his hand may be seen in the recommendation that the members of this one should be reduced from eighteen to six.

Another request, for which he must have been directly responsible, showed unmistakably that he had lost none of his concern for the enlightenment of the people generally. To the petition and bill relating to the establishment of a college he attached a rider, as it may be called, that dealt with elementary schools. That is, the legislature was asked to authorize the Visitors of Central College to initiate proceedings for the establishment of primary schools in Albemarle County. By the act of 1796 this authority had been vested in the county court, and the attempt to take it from that body was destined to meet insuperable objections. Jefferson's willingness to run these risks and to disregard prescribed procedure was a measure of his determination.

He regarded the cost of these elementary schools as trivial in comparison with the cost of ignorance. But, realizing that crops had been bad and times were hard, he modified his proposals of 1779 significantly to mollify reluctant taxpayers. Instead of offering free schools for all without distinction, as he undoubtedly preferred, he now proposed that those who could afford to pay should be required to do so. The cost of tuition to the wealthy need be no more than they would otherwise pay to pri-

[16] The petition is in Cabell, pp. 390–391. The bill printed there (pp. 391–393) is the version passed by the legislature. TJ's copy of his original bill is at UVA with the legislature's alterations underscored by him.

[17] Meeting of Apr. 15 (Cabell, p. 381). The law provided that with the consent of the electorate, they might be used for schools.

[18] This was to be proportionate to the county's share of the contributions to the fund from the entire state.

Joseph C. Cabell
(Courtesy of the University of Virginia Library, Prints File, Special Collections)

vate tutors, and, in his opinion, the poor were not sufficiently numerous to impose much of a burden.[19]

The petition of the trustees of Albemarle Academy was not presented to the legislature at the session of 1814–1815. Jefferson did not know what had become of it and the other papers he had drafted. He left these with Peter Carr, who was expected to see that they were properly presented in Richmond, but Carr's illness and death prevented him from doing so.[20] About a month before Carr died (in February, 1815), Jefferson voiced his uncertainties to Joseph C. Cabell, whose senatorial district included Albemarle County, and sent that legislator his own copies of the papers.[21] He probably did not consult his nephew at this time because of the latter's illness. In any case he now turned to the man who was henceforth to be in effect his legislative agent in educational matters. Jefferson had previously corresponded with Cabell at length regarding public finance and regarded him as one of the most promising young men in Virginia.[22]

The Senator could report little about the missing papers. Apparently they were sent to David Watson of Louisa County, instead of to one of the delegates from Albemarle. Colonel Charles Yancey, who represented Jefferson's county, saw the petition and recognized the handwriting. He said afterwards that it was not presented because of its late arrival.[23] In truth, the circumstances were not propitious and the delay was probably fortunate. Meanwhile, Cabell had materials on which to ponder. He had read the papers several times, he said, but meant to read them again shortly before the next session of the General Assembly. Even to this highly intelligent man they were not easy reading, but he was fully informed of Jefferson's ideas and purposes when a more opportune time arrived.

During the spring of 1815 the Sage himself was busily engaged in preparing to send to Washington the library he had sold to Congress. Absorption in this task doubtless served to lessen the sorrow caused by the untimely death of the son of his sister Martha and the dearest friend of his youth. Peter Carr, whom he had regarded and treated as a son, had not fully realized upon his promise, but this highly agreeable man

[19] In these papers TJ made no reference to one of the most notable of his earlier educational proposals — the selective principle. This called for the education of youths of demonstrated promise at public expense in schools of intermediate grade and the university. He recurred to this a couple of years later. (See above, ch. XVI.)

[20] TJ to John Wood, Aug. 5, 1815 (LC).

[21] TJ to Cabell, Jan. 5, 1815 (Cabell, pp. 36–38).

[22] For their correspondence about finance, see above, ch. X, pp. 141–142. TJ rated him with William Cabell Rives and Francis Walker Gilmer as a future statesman.

[23] Cabell to TJ, Mar. 5, 1815 (Cabell, pp. 38–40); Yancey to TJ, Sept. 26, 1815 (LC).

was a favorite in the Monticello circle and his death was a great loss to it.[24]

From Jefferson's remarks in the summer of 1815 one might have supposed that his own hopes of a college had grown dim when his nephew's light went out. To one who was looking for a position he wrote that, since the bill was not yet passed and they lacked both funds and buildings, there was no immediate prospect of "the employment of talents, however eminent and however desired."[25] Nevertheless, the veteran had not lost his resiliency. During the next legislative session, in the course of a long letter to Colonel Yancey, he said: "I recommend to your patronage our Central College. I look to it as a germ from which a great tree may spread itself."[26] No single metaphor could fully convey his hopes and fears, but he was undoubtedly thinking of general enlightenment, and not of this particular institution only. In the same letter he said: "If a nation expects to be ignorant and free, in a state of civilization, it expects what never was and never will be."[27]

Yancey had told Jefferson that he would support the educational bill, and presumably he did so in the House of Delegates, where it was passed after the provision for a grant from the Literary Fund had been stricken from it.[28] As Cabell reported, however, that delegate from Albemarle did not like the proposed transfer of authority to the Visitors of Central College with respect to the setting up of elementary schools in the county.[29] After consulting the Governor and other sympathetic friends, Cabell concluded that this questionable provision would have to be omitted. So it was left out of the bill as passed by the Senate.

Cabell had told his correspondent that there was strong sentiment for the establishment of a state-wide system of elementary education. Jefferson could not set himself against that. He clearly recognized that the state must participate in education; he advocated public not private schools. But he insisted on decentralization in their administration and in government for the same reason.[30] His confidence in the ability of the local citizens to manage the elementary schools was inseparable from his belief in the capacity of his countrymen for self-government. He said

[24] TJ to Dabney Carr, Jan. 19, 1816 (L. & B., XIV, 401); and William Wirt to Dabney Carr, Aug. 20, 1815 (Kennedy, *William Wirt*, I, 347).

[25] John Wood to TJ, July 18, 1815; TJ to Wood, Aug. 5 (LC). Writing for himself and Thomas Cooper, Wood was inquiring about the prospects for their employment in TJ's neighborhood.

[26] TJ to Yancey, Jan. 6, 1816 (Ford, X, 2).

[27] *Ibid.*, p. 4.

[28] Jan. 15, 1816.

[29] The correspondence between Cabell and TJ in Jan. and Feb., 1816, from which the legislative history can be reconstructed, is in Cabell, pp. 43–61.

[30] See TJ to Cabell, Feb. 2, 1816 (Cabell, p. 54). For discussion of TJ's fears of governmental centralization in his old age, see ch. XXIV.

that as Cato ended every speech with the exhortation "*Carthago delenda est*," he would end every opinion with the injunction "Divide the counties into wards." His injunction was to prove wholly vain, and in the present instance all he and his colleagues got was a permit to create a college if they could.[31]

Two other actions of the legislature were significant. The surplus of the federal debt to the state for expenditures during the war was added to the Literary Fund.[32] Also, the officials of the fund were asked to report to the next session of the legislature on a desirable system of public education from primary schools to university. Cabell had caused Jefferson's letter to Peter Carr to be published, and he attributed to it much influence in creating sentiment for these measures. He believed that it would have "a very happy effect on the interests of science in this state."[33] Cabell had told Jefferson that he was trying "to prevent this game from being easily taken out of the hands of those who are entitled to it."[34] Other statements of his clearly identify those into whose hands he feared the game might fall. Opposition to Central College and to Jefferson's plans for it was to be expected from the Scotch–Irish of Staunton, who wanted to make that little city the capital of the state as well as the site of the University, and from the Presbyterians of Lexington, seat of Washington College, which would be the "bantling of the Federalists."[35]

These references struck a responsive chord in Jefferson. He regarded the Shenandoah Valley as the "Tory" district of the state and had a special aversion to Presbyterians, whom he associated with their fellow Calvinists in New England. He had good reason to dislike the established clergy of New England, but his fear of their designs bordered on the obsessive. At just this time he charged them with plans to evangelize and catechize the South, going as far as to warn Thomas Ritchie of the *Enquirer* to be on guard against them.[36] He believed that in his own state the natural allies of these ancient foes of his, whom he also regarded as hostile to the freedom of the mind, were the Presbyterians. There may

[31] Cabell wrote Jefferson Feb. 14, 1816, that the Central College bill had passed the legislature (Cabell, p. 56).

[32] *Richmond Enquirer* (Mar. 2, 1816) estimated that ultimately the Literary Fund would gain nearly a million dollars by this act.

[33] Quotation from letter of Feb. 21 (Cabell, p. 60).

[34] Cabell to TJ, Jan. 24, 1816 (*ibid.*, p. 51).

[35] Cabell to TJ, Feb. 26, 1816 (Cabell Papers, UVA). The printed version of this letter (Cabell, pp. 60–61) is somewhat expurgated.

[36] TJ to Ritchie, Jan. 21, 1816 (L. & B., XIV, 406–407), enclosing a passage about this he had struck out of a letter to a stranger (TJ to H. B. Spafford, Jan. 10, 1816, LC), but the details of which he thought should be made known. Ritchie printed this anonymously in the *Enquirer*, Jan. 27.

have been a spark of fanaticism in his own heterodoxy, and his fears of this particular group in Virginia were exaggerated, but the lines of future conflict were unquestionably being drawn on grounds of geography, politics, and religion. While Jefferson can hardly be said to have been tolerant of Federalists and Presbyterians, he was far from intolerant of Westerners as such. He was advocating constitutional changes in representation and suffrage which would have been advantageous to the Virginians beyond the Blue Ridge.[37]

Governor Wilson Cary Nicholas was very slow in appointing the Visitors of Central College — perhaps because he had been assigned a more arduous task which required attention first. As president of the Literary Fund, he was obligated to report to the next legislature an educational program for the state, and he appears to have sought the counsel of his friend Jefferson before turning to anybody else.[38] The act creating the college stipulated that there be six members on the Board of Visitors, whereas there had been three times that many trustees of Albemarle Academy. Some of the latter may have resented their displacement. Such was not the case with a group of them who met after the legislative session of 1815–1816 ended and drew up a slate of desirable appointees. While admitting that they had no authority to make recommendations, they submitted to the Governor the following list: Mr. Madison, Mr. Monroe, Mr. Jefferson, Mr. David Watson of Louisa County, General John H. Cocke of Fluvanna, and Mr. Cabell of Nelson.[39] Jefferson afterwards described the three latter as eminent residents of "circumjacent counties." Nicholas was informed that the first two persons on the list had been suggested by the third and had assured him that they would accept appointment. Similar assurance had been received from Watson, and there was no doubt about the two others. Besides being a distinguished group it promised to be an effective board, and the Governor accepted the recommendations in their entirety.

The appointment of all these men may have been confidently anticipated, but Jefferson did not get his notice of appointment until the last day of October, when he was at Poplar Forest. Cabell did not receive his until the middle of the next legislative session, and there was no meeting of the Visitors until the following spring.

[37] TJ to Samuel Kercheval, July 12, 1816 (Ford, X, 37–45).

[38] TJ replied Apr. 2, 1816 (L. & B., XIV, 451–455) to a letter of Mar. 22 (LC). He reminded Nicholas of his letter to Peter Carr and sent him extracts of other letters bearing on the subject.

[39] Frank Carr to Gov. Nicholas, Mar. 25, 1816, in *Calendar of Va. State Papers*, X, 437–438.

[XVIII]

The Start of an Academical Village

1816-1817

JEFFERSON was still at Poplar Forest, planting bulbs in his flower garden, when the turbulent legislative session of 1816–1817 began. He did not get back to Monticello until about a week after the report of the president and directors of the Literary Fund was presented.[1] Presumably he saw this in the *Enquirer*, though no comment of his on it seems to have been recorded. He could hardly have failed to approve of the comprehensive system of public education that was recommended since this was in essential accord with his own proposals. However, he favored other means for its support.

He had consistently held that elementary education should be locally supported and locally controlled. The president and directors of the Literary Fund had proceeded on the assumption that the monetary needs of this system could not be met by funds extracted directly from the people. According to their report, reliance must be placed on the Literary Fund. But the fund was being called upon to bear more than could be expected of it.[2] Recognizing that in no case would financial resources be unlimited, they recommended that primary schools be established first, that intermediate schools should follow, and that the university should be last. Jefferson had no quarrel with these priorities, but he had by no means abandoned his hope that a full system of education could be established.

[1] He got back Dec. 11, 1816. The report was presented Dec. 5 and printed in the *Richmond Enquirer* Dec. 10.

[2] The president and directors recommended that it be augmented by using it as capital for a new system of state banks. Enough 6 per cent stock would be created to increase the fund to $2,000,000. This proposal was presented Dec. 12 (*Richmond Enquirer*, Dec. 14). TJ probably agreed with the delegate who said that linking the holy cause of education with banks would be a "sacrilegious touch" (Mr. Blackburn, Jan. 6, 1818, quoted in the *Enquirer*, Jan. 16).

Speaking of the legislators at the end of the session, Thomas Ritchie said in the *Enquirer:* "Let the truth be told: they have spent a great deal of time in doing very little good. . . . They have attempted to do many things which finally ended in smoke."[3] There was considerable discussion of educational matters after the receipt of the Governor's report, but nobody knew at the end of the session whether a general system of public education would be established, or just what would be done about a university.

Jefferson could have followed the course of events as reported in the *Enquirer*, but he had relatively little correspondence with Cabell during these weeks and, so far as the record shows, he made no comment at the time on any of the specific educational proposals that were acted on. The most important of these was the bill of Delegate Charles F. Mercer, which passed the House near the end of the session but was defeated in the Senate by a tie vote.[4] This would have created a board of public instruction with large powers and would have authorized a full system of public education to be supported by the Literary Fund. Primary schools were to be established first, as the Governor had recommended and as Jefferson had consistently urged. Provision would be made for numerous academies, including a few for girls. Four new colleges were also to be established, including one below the James to be named Jefferson. Central College was not mentioned, but the three existing collegiate institutions might be incorporated in the system. Finally, a university was to be established.

Ritchie described the plan as "magnificent but impracticable," and when Jefferson finally saw the text of the bill he objected to it on the ground of inadequate financial provisions.[5] It had originally contained a stipulation that the university be located in the Shenandoah Valley, but that provision was stricken out in the House, and its narrow rejection by the Senate must be otherwise explained. Actually, the bill had passed the House by a small vote very late in the session after many delegates had gone home and was regarded by others besides the editor of the *Enquirer* as hasty legislation on which final action was wisely deferred.[6]

In this period of Virginia history, while aversion to taxation was general, political alignments tended to be sectional. The Mercer bill was

[3] *Richmond Enquirer*, Feb. 28, 1817.

[4] The bill as introduced into the House was published by Mercer in *A Discourse on Popular Education* (Princeton, 1826). The bill as passed by the House, and with the amendments proposed in the Senate, can be seen in *Sundry Documents on the Subject of a System of Public Education for the State of Virginia* (Richmond, 1817). For Jefferson's later comments on this bill, see below, pp. 267–268.

[5] TJ to J. C. Cabell, Oct. 24, 1817 (Cabell, p. 83).

[6] *Richmond Enquirer*, Feb. 18, 20, 1817.

ardently supported by Westerners, and it was defeated in the Senate, where Tidewater was over-represented to a greater degree than in the House of Delegates. The delaying action in the upper chamber may have indicated that there was less concern there for the education of the people than in the lower and may have reflected more concern for a university, but there is no evidence that Jefferson had any responsibility for these events. At the time he appears not to have known what was going on.[7] Having reached no decision regarding educational policy, the legislators sought to facilitate discussion of this question by ordering the printing of important documents bearing on it. Included among these were the Mercer bill, Jefferson's bill of 1779 for the more general diffusion of knowledge, and his letter to Peter Carr.[8]

ii

At the end of the legislative session of 1816–1817 the status of Central College was unchanged from what it had been a year earlier except that the projected institution now had a duly commissioned Board of Visitors. Jefferson had avoided involvement in legislative matters, but from this time he was the prime mover in the affairs of the college on the local scene. He was eager to get started and to proceed with all possible speed so that a good showing could be made to the next General Assembly. If a university was to be established, he wanted it to be at Central College.

Recognizing that he would have to take the initiative, he issued a call for a meeting of the Visitors, but despite his eagerness he delayed the meeting in the hope that it could be attended by Madison, whose presidential term ended on March 4. The retiring President was detained in Washington longer than Jefferson expected, however, and his successor, James Monroe, could not leave the capital as yet. Since David Watson was kept at home in Louisa County by illness, only Thomas Jefferson, Joseph C. Cabell, and John H. Cocke were present at the first meeting on April 8, 1817. They were an effective trio, as time was to demonstrate, but they did not constitute a majority. Accordingly, their actions had to be approved at a regular meeting.[9]

[7] The account of the legislative session of 1816–1817 in Maddox, *Free School Idea in Virginia Before the Civil War*, pp. 57–62, 64–72, is confusing and gives what I regard as an incorrect impression of TJ's personal involvement in this conflict and his attitude to Mercer. In his generally admirable study, Conant (pp. 30–32) follows Maddox and blames the "Jeffersonians" for the defeat of the Mercer bill. Specifically, he states that Cabell, after failing to fix the site of the proposed University in Charlottesville, lent his influence to defeat the proposal. But the Senate Journal for Feb. 20, 1817, shows that Cabell did not attempt such an amendment and, in fact, voted for the bill.

[8] Jefferson saw the Mercer bill for the first time in the pamphlet which Cabell sent him in the fall of 1817. TJ to Cabell, Oct. 24, 1817 (Cabell, p. 83). See below, ch. XIX.

[9] TJ to Madison, Apr. 13, 1817; also Feb. 8, Mar. 10 (LC).

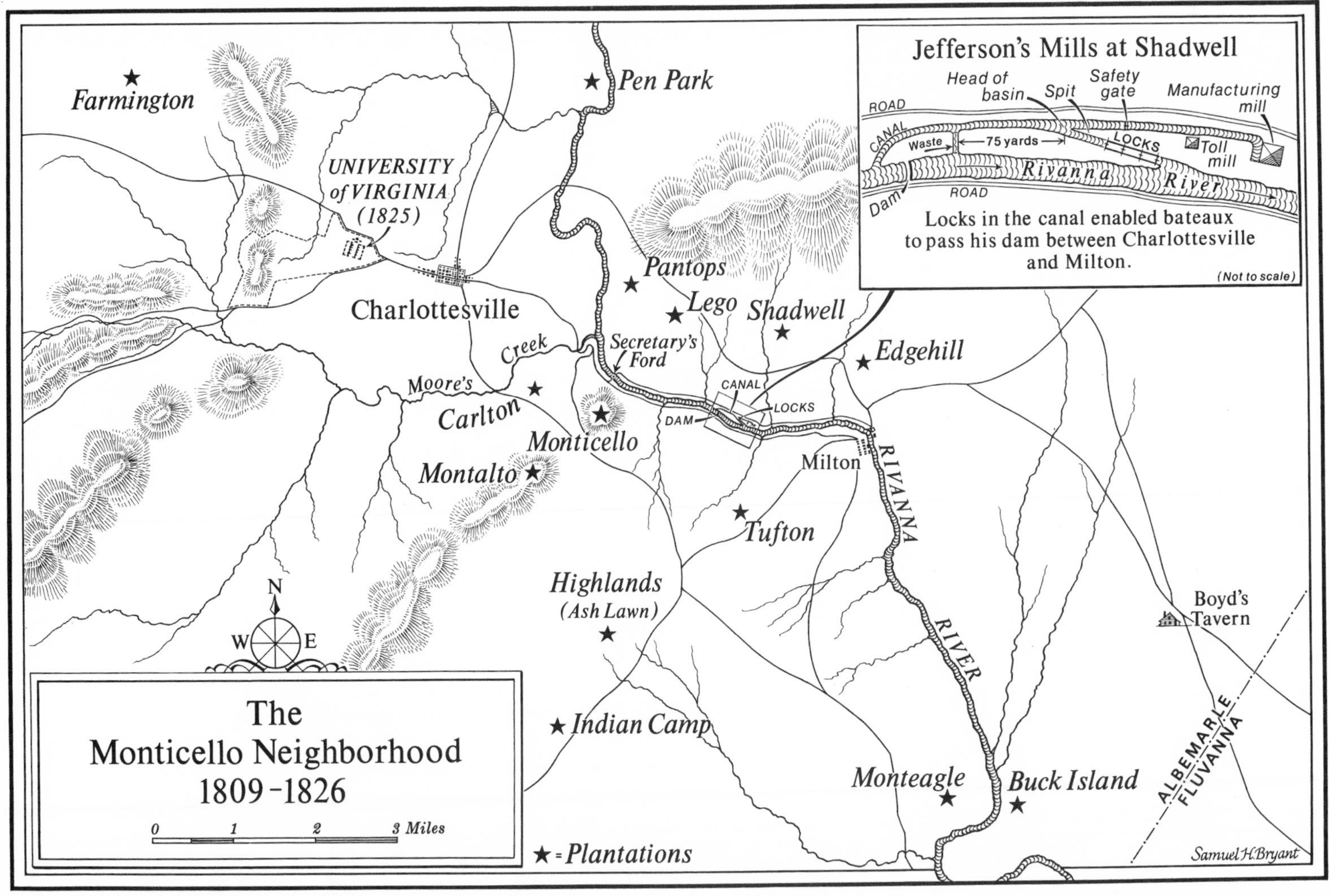

The Monticello Neighborhood
1809-1826
0 1 2 3 Miles
N W E
★ = Plantations
Jefferson's Mills at Shadwell
Head of basin
Spit
Safety gate
Manufacturing mill
ROAD
CANAL
Waste
75 yards
LOCKS
Toll mill
Rivanna River
Dam
ROAD
Locks in the canal enabled bateaux to pass his dam between Charlottesville and Milton.
(Not to scale)
Farmington
Pen Park
UNIVERSITY of VIRGINIA (1825)
Charlottesville
Pantops
Lego
Shadwell
Edgehill
Secretary's Ford
Moore's Creek
Carlton
Monticello
Montalto
CANAL
LOCKS
DAM
Milton
RIVANNA RIVER
Tufton
Highlands (Ash Lawn)
Indian Camp
Monteagle
Buck Island
Boyd's Tavern
ALBEMARLE
FLUVANNA
Samuel H. Bryant

The most important of these actions was the selection of a building site for the College. After viewing several bodies of land near Charlottesville, they chose a site a mile west of the village. This was on land which formerly belonged to Monroe and was now the property of John M. Perry. According to local tradition, Jefferson really preferred land owned by John Kelly, who, disliking him for political reasons, said he would see him "at the devil" before selling it to him at any price. As the story goes, Jefferson, on hearing of this, said that Kelly was a fool, but that if they could not get the best site, they would have to content themselves with the best site they could get.[10] He is known to have stated that he preferred the one they got, but it presented a number of practical difficulties, as he found out when he made a survey in midsummer.[11]

The first regular meeting of the Visitors occurred on May 5, 1817, about a month after the informal one. Jefferson was anxious that it should be impressive and strengthen the position of Central College as a potential university. Being already assured of the attendance of Madison, he brought great pressure to bear on Monroe. He was well aware of the publicity value of the President's attendance.[12] Monroe was able to be present, but neither Cabell nor Watson could be there. General Cocke completed the quartet that constituted a quorum.

The meeting took place in Charlottesville on court day, when the streets of the village were more crowded than usual. Those who did not actually cast eyes on the dignitaries could not have failed to learn of their presence. The occasion received considerable attention from the press. The *Richmond Enquirer* commented:

> On the 5th of this month, three men were seen together at Charlottesville (county of Albemarle), each of whom alone is calculated to attract the eager gaze of their Fellow Citizens — We mean, Thomas Jefferson, James Madison, and James Monroe. . . . They have been friends for years, and are as sincere friends at this moment. . . . The appearance of three such men together at a village where the citizens of the county had met to attend their court, is an event, which for its singularity, deserves the notice of a passing paragraph.[13]

[10] TJ's grandson, G. W. Randolph, to Dr. J. L. Cabell, Feb. 27, 1856, saying that Alexander Garrett told him the story many times (Cabell Papers, UVA). Kelly's land included a ridge on the approximate line of Preston Ave., which is to the northeast of the University grounds.

[11] TJ to James Dinsmore, June 25, 1817 (UVA).

[12] TJ to Monroe, Apr. 13, 1817 (LC); Monroe to TJ, Apr. 23 (S.M.H., VI, 22–23).

13. *Richmond Enquirer*, May 13, 1817; copied in *National Intelligencer*, Washington, May 26. On May 23, the *Enquirer* printed extracts from a letter describing the meeting. This appears to have been written by an insider, but it does not sound quite like TJ.

The association of the three members of the Virginia Dynasty in this educational enterprise greatly impressed John Adams, who learned of it from his correspondent at Monticello. "From such a noble triumvirate," he said, "the world will expect something very great and very new." To his encomium, however, he added a grim prophecy: namely, that if there should be anything "quite original, and very excellent" in the institution, deeply rooted prejudices would prevent it from lasting long. It might be accepted at first but would not always have "three such colossal reputations to support it."[14] Jefferson undoubtedly wished to create an institution that was "very excellent," and as planned by him, this embodied much that would be regarded by his contemporaries as "quite original." As usual, he was disposed to take a less fearful view of the distant future than his friend Adams. But he was convinced that the circumstances required the Visitors to proceed promptly on a positive course.

From the minutes he himself kept we can learn what he and his colleagues did at their first regular meeting. They confirmed the choice of a site for the College, which had been made in April, and authorized the purchase of some two hundred acres of land. The Visitors also authorized the erection of a building in accordance with this plan. The cost of the purchase (about fifteen hundred dollars) could be met from the proceeds of the sale of the glebe lands in the county, which amounted to somewhat more than three thousand dollars. The newly appointed proctor, Alexander Garrett, was instructed to procure these funds.[15] He was also instructed to draw up a subscription paper, providing for annual payments in four installments if desired. It became known later that the four Visitors, beginning with Jefferson, subscribed a thousand dollars each at this time. Cocke took the liberty of doing the same for Cabell. Jefferson put a good deal of personal effort into the subscription campaign during the course of the summer, but before that he entered upon the more congenial task of providing a fitting habitation for this seminary of learning.[16]

The idea of an academical village had been in his mind for more than a decade, and he had made a tentative sketch of one a couple of years before he picked a site for Central College. The minutes of the meeting of the Visitors at which this site was approved contain the following impersonal statement:

[14] Adams to TJ, May 26, 1817, replying to a letter of May 5 (*A.-J. Letters*, pp. 513, 518).

[15] Garrett was also acting treasurer and was later appointed treasurer after resigning as proctor.

[16] J. H. Cocke to Cabell, May 15, 1817 (Cabell Papers, UVA); *Richmond Enquirer*, July 19, 1817, naming chief contributors. In view of the state of his finances we may question whether TJ could really afford to be this generous. On this, see below, pp. 301–303.

> On view of a plan presented to the trustees of Albemarle Academy for erecting a distinct pavilion or building for each separate professorship, and for arranging these around a square, each pavilion containing a schoolroom and two apartments for the accommodation of the professor, with other reasonable conveniences, the Board determines that one of those pavilions shall now be erected.[17]

The Visitors also determined that, as soon as sufficient funds were available, adjacent dormitories should be built, as in the plan — not more than ten on each side.

The essential and most distinctive feature of Jefferson's design was thus approved — the professorial pavilion, designed for both educational and residential purposes, with student rooms joined to it by a covered passageway for "dry communications." This house and these adjacent rooms were to constitute a residential and academic unit which could be multiplied as circumstances might require. In the theoretical plan he showed his colleagues, Jefferson had grouped nine of these units around an open-ended square, thus allowing for future expansion.[18] At his suggestion, no doubt, the Visitors determined that two parallel lines of indefinite length be drawn on the building site and that the authorized pavilion be set on one of these. The location of these lines was not specified, nor was the distance between them.

On June 23, 1817, Alexander Garrett, proctor of the College, purchased for it from John M. Perry two parcels of land. These were not contiguous and the larger tract need not concern us here. The smaller parcel, which consisted of 43.75 acres, was to be the site of the institution of learning.[19] Jefferson had seen this tract of land twice before its purchase was approved by the Visitors, and he may have looked at it again before he surveyed it and laid out the grounds on July 18, but his earliest plans for an academical village were unrelated to this site. Not only was this true of the drawing he showed his colleagues on May 5, but of the sketch he sent William Thornton a few days later and one that

[17] May 5, 1817. Printed minutes in Cabell, pp. 394–395.

[18] William B. O'Neal, *Pictorial History of the Univ. of Va.*, 2nd edn. (1976), p. 12.

[19] The larger tract of 153 acres, containing most of Observatory Mountain, was joined to the grounds of the University of Virginia by a further purchase in 1825. On Aug. 7, 1817, Jesse Garth gave the college, in lieu of a subscription, 6.25 acres that adjoined the site on the north. There were no further acquisitions prior to the chartering of the University in 1819. All of these transactions are described in a memorandum prepared by Kendon L. Stubbs for C. Waller Barrett, Mar. 1, 1973. A plat drawn by TJ shows the successive acquisitions, their areas, costs, and dates (both UVA).

he sent Benjamin H. Latrobe in June.[20] According to the first of these, the distance between the two wings of the open-ended quadrangle was more than 250 yards, and he wrote Latrobe six weeks later that it was 700 to 800 feet. As he found out in due course, however, this site was unsuited to such a grouping of buildings. The tract acquired from Perry consisted of a ridge, sloping from north to south and capable of being leveled to a width of only 200 feet.[21] All that he could preserve of the open-ended square was the open end.

Jefferson appears to have had no existing or historic model in mind when he set out to design an academical village. Instead, it seems that the overall plan he finally carried into effect was arrived at stage by stage and step by step as circumstances required. The germinal concept — the juxtaposition of pavilion and dormitories, of professor and pupils, the linking of learning and domesticity — this idea or cluster of ideas was clearly his own. Latrobe, who had long been dissatisfied with what he called "the usual barrack arrangement" in colleges, described Jefferson's general plan as "entirely novel."[22] In seeking to implement his novel idea Jefferson could draw upon the rich body of architectural knowledge he had accumulated and the extensive practical experience as a builder gained in the course of his long and incessantly active life.[23]

At the inception of this undertaking, which was destined to be his most ambitious as an architect and builder, he took more counsel than was customary with him in such matters. He sought suggestions from Dr. William Thornton, who may be described in architectural terms as a gentleman amateur, and from Latrobe, who was unquestionably a professional.[24] This was before he had measured the site and adjusted his general plan to what he called "the law of the ground."[25] Though

[20] TJ to Thornton, May 9, 1817 (photoengraving after p. 396 in L. & B., XVII), and TJ to Latrobe, June 12, 1817 (LC, and in Fiske Kimball, *Thomas Jefferson, Architect*, pp. 187–188 without illustration).

[21] He so stated to Latrobe, Aug. 3, 1817 (*ibid.*, p. 190). The tract extended roughly from the present McCormick Rd. to Hospital Dr. The grounds west of McCormick Rd. were acquired later.

[22] Latrobe to TJ, June 17, 1817 (*ibid.*, p. 188).

[23] For architectural details it is well known that TJ relied heavily on books, as is demonstrated in William B. O'Neal, *Jefferson's Fine Arts Library: His Selections for the University of Virginia Together with His Own Architectural Books* (Charlottesville, 1976). Mary N. Woods has noted that the Royal Hospital at Stonehouse near Plymouth, England, as pictured in a book owned by TJ — John Howard, *State of Prisons in England and Wales* (1784) — bears a resemblance to TJ's overall plan. She discusses this in her seminar paper "Thomas Jefferson's Library and Sources of the Plan for the University of Virginia." Louis XVI's château at Marly is another possible influence, as was first suggested by Fiske Kimball. Frederick D. Nichols has pursued this suggestion (Nichols, introduction to Kimball, p. ix, and Kimball, p. 80).

[24] Kimball discusses their correspondence (pp. 75–80).

[25] To Latrobe, Aug. 3, 1817 (*ibid.*, p. 190).

some confusion resulted from the timing, he got useful suggestions from both men. It should be noted that these ideas, like those he got out of books, passed through his own mind and had his stamp upon them when they emerged from his drawing board.

Toward the end of the American Revolution a French visitor had described Jefferson as the first American to turn to the fine arts to learn how to shelter himself from the weather.[26] His architecture was both functional and artistic. In his earliest sketches the covered passageway was supported by square brick piers, much like those on the service wings at Monticello; but he promptly accepted Thornton's suggestion that they be round columns. Also, his first plans showed pavilions that were all alike. When writing Thornton a few days after the meeting of the Visitors, however, he said that the pavilions should be "models of taste and good architecture, and of a variety of appearance, no two alike, so as to serve as specimens for the Architectural lecturer."[27] He asked Thornton for suggestions for the fronts of these buildings, saying that a few slight sketches would serve.

Jefferson agreed with this adviser that the pavilions should allow more living quarters for professors.[28] After all, the faculty could not consist wholly of celibates and childless couples. Latrobe also argued for more living space for professors, and at the fall meeting of the Visitors it was determined that they might have four rooms instead of two.[29]

When surveying the college site on July 18, he staked out three terraces which he called squares, although each one was 200 by 255 feet. On each of these he located two pavilions, one on the west and one on the east. The first pavilion was to be in the center of the western border of the middle terrace. This was the point of immediate interest, but, in view of later developments, there was another that deserves special mention. In the pocket notebook in which the operations of this day were recorded, he drew a diagram of the grounds. In the center of the northern square he marked a point at which "some principal building" was destined to stand.[30] Thus Jefferson at this early stage anticipated an edifice that would complete his plan and crown his architectural creation.

A couple of weeks after he made this survey, he received a letter from Latrobe, who still thought that an open-ended quadrangle of considerable breadth was being planned. Latrobe suggested for the longest side

[26] Chastellux; see *Jefferson the Virginian*, p. 392.

[27] TJ to Thornton, May 9, 1817, quoted by Kimball, p. 75.

[28] Thornton to TJ, May 27, 1817 (LC).

[29] Latrobe to TJ, July 24, 1817 (Kimball, pp. 189–190). Minutes of the Visitors, Oct. 7, 1817 (Cabell, p. 397).

[30] A page from his Specifications Book dated July 18, 1817, and headed "Operations at and for the College" (UVA). Reproduced as Plate 13 in William A. Lambeth and Warren H. Manning, *Jefferson as an Architect and a Designer of Landscapes* (Boston, 1913).

Jefferson's Drawing Desk
(Courtesy of Robert C. Lautman/Thomas Jefferson Foundation, Inc.)

of this a "center building" which should exemplify architecture at its best. He enclosed a sketch showing a structure with a dome. In his prompt reply Jefferson described the general plan on which he was actually proceeding and explained how the lay of the land had caused him to adopt it.

Although only one pavilion had been authorized as yet, Jefferson was talking of the early construction of two others and had at least half a dozen in mind, along with the adjacent dormitories. These buildings had to be given priority, and, as he duly recognized, the ultimate size and form of his academical village depended on circumstances. The north end would be left open, he said; but to this announcement he added what proved to be a prophecy — namely, that if the legislature should establish a university, the empty space might be filled with "something of the grand kind." Not until six years had passed, however, was construction begun on the Rotunda, and Latrobe never saw the noble building which both Jefferson and he hopefully anticipated.[31]

Latrobe, who, without Jefferson's knowledge, had gone to the trouble of drawing a plan for the long side of the projected quadrangle, was obviously piqued when he learned that he had been laboring under a misapprehension. When informed by Jefferson of the character of the site and the intended disposition of the future buildings, he candidly stated that he regarded the situation as most unfortunate. As grouped on this ridge, all the apartments must necessarily face east and west. That exposure or "aspect" was undesirable in both winter and summer, as Jefferson did not deny. He claimed that he was overcoming this disadvantage by giving the pavilions more flank than front, and by leaving a gap between each of these and its adjacent dormitories, thus assuring the main room a southern exposure. He admitted that he could do little for the dormitories except by means of Venetian blinds and the covered passageways, but he consoled himself with the thought that the students would not be in their rooms much in the daytime anyway.[32]

iii

The day after he surveyed the grounds, Jefferson invited General Cocke to go with him and see what was done and doing there. "Our squares are laid off," he said; "the brick-yard begun, and the leveling

[31] Latrobe to TJ, July 24, 1817 (Kimball, pp. 189–190 and sketch reproduced in Figure 213), received Aug. 2; TJ to Latrobe, Aug. 3, 1817 (LC, printed without sketches in Kimball, pp. 190–191). The fact that TJ had thought of placing a "principal building" near the later location of the Rotunda before he received Latrobe's suggestion seems to have been generally overlooked or disregarded. Latrobe's drawing may have caused him to think of the Pantheon. See below, p. 394.

[32] Latrobe to TJ, Aug. 12, 1817 (Kimball, p. 191); TJ to Latrobe, Aug. 24 (*ibid.*).

will be begun in the course of the week."[33] About a week later Cocke arrived from Bremo, bringing Cabell with him, and after viewing the grounds, the trio proceeded to Montpelier for a meeting of the Visitors on July 28. Jefferson, who had been planning to visit Madison anyway, suggested this meeting.[34] Since subscriptions had exceeded anticipations, there was good reason to proceed with building operations. Also, after approving Jefferson's plan for the first pavilion, the Board took a step toward the appointment of the first professor. This action proved to be premature and can be better described hereafter.

Writing John Adams about six weeks after this meeting, Jefferson said that all of the administrative work of the College fell on him as the only resident Board member.[35] In fact, he spent much of the summer at Poplar Forest, where he was at the moment, but he was busily occupied when in Albemarle and kept in touch with operations when away. On the last day of August he expressed pleasure that the bricks were in "such forwardness" and requested that he be informed of developments once a week.[36] The bricks were being made on the spot, as they had been at Monticello. Impressed by the beautiful brickwork at Lynchburg, he had engaged masons from there to come up later and begin the first pavilion.[37] For the capitals of the columns a stone-cutter from Italy would be needed, and, following the instruction of the Board, he was already trying to procure one.[38]

He had arranged in April with James Dinsmore, who had served him so long and well at Monticello as a carpenter, to superintend the construction of all the College buildings. In midsummer, however, he wrote this skilled workman that John Perry had been willing to sell his land only on the condition that he be given the carpentry in the first building. Dinsmore was to have all the others.[39] But neither carpenter nor stone-cutter was to be needed in 1817, and for more than a year and a half the architect was to remain uncertain whether he was supervising the construction of a village or a hamlet.

[33] TJ to J. H. Cocke, July 19, 1817 (LC).

[34] TJ wrote Madison on July 23, 1817 (LC). The minutes of the meeting of July 28 (UVA) are not in his handwriting. They are printed in Cabell, p. 396.

[35] TJ to Adams, Sept. 8, 1817 (*A.-J. Letters*, p. 519).

[36] TJ to Hugh Chisholm, Aug. 31, 1817 (UVA).

[37] TJ to Latrobe, July 16, 1817 (Kimball, p. 189).

[38] TJ to Thomas Appleton, Aug. 1, 1817 (LC).

[39] TJ to Dinsmore, Apr. 13, 1817; Dinsmore to TJ, Apr. 22; TJ to Dinsmore, June 25 (all UVA). William B. O'Neal in *The Mag. of Albemarle County History* has published three useful articles on the construction of the University ("The Workmen at the University of Virginia, 1817–1826, with Notes and Documents," XVII, 5–48; "Michele and Giacomo Raggi at the University of Virginia: with Notes and Documents," XVIII, 5–31; and with Frederick D. Nichols, "An Architectural History of the First University Pavilion," XV, 36–43).

Shortly before the midsummer meeting of the Visitors, there appeared in the *Enquirer* the statement that the College "is extending its funds with the most brilliant success."[40] Later in the summer Jefferson said that about $30,000 had been promised by citizens of Albemarle alone.[41] Presumably subscribers affixed their names to papers passed from hand to hand. The degree of Jefferson's personal participation in this county campaign may have been small, but its success was undoubtedly due in large part to his prestige and example. He was not averse to appealing to local interest.[42] He confidently expected the College to serve a wider constituency, however, and joined his colleagues in seeking wider support for it.

At the meeting at Montpelier he appears to have been allotted certain names of people outside the county, and before he set out for Poplar Forest he wrote virtually identical letters to a number of prominent men whom he could address as friends.[43] In this communication he gave an excellent account of the affairs and prospects of the College. "The plan of this institution had nothing local in view," he said. "It is calculated for the wants, and the use of the whole state." Such was undoubtedly the case; but the larger public was not readily convinced, and the response of the rest of the state to the appeal for subscriptions never approximated that of Albemarle County.[44]

The Visitors, encouraged by the success of the campaign for subscriptions, had resolved that "application be made" to the Reverend Dr. Samuel Knox of Baltimore to accept the professorship of languages and belles-lettres.[45] We may wonder why Jefferson's mind should have turned to a Presbyterian clergyman. The explanation seems to be that Knox, besides being a man of considerable distinction, had views regarding the separation of church and state that were similar to Jefferson's and was also a pioneer advocate of a comprehensive system of public education. The great library at Monticello had contained writings of his, including an anonymous pamphlet in which Jefferson's religion was defended. Though it was designed to aid him in the campaign of 1800, he

[40] July 19, 1817.

[41] TJ to Thomas Cooper, Sept. 1, 1817 (UVA).

[42] In a letter of June 28, 1817 (MHS) he said to Craven Peyton that the establishment of the College in their neighborhood would make it the central object of the state.

[43] Three copies of these letters of Aug. 4, 1817, are at UVA. He addressed seven men, including James Pleasants, John W. Eppes, and William B. Giles. He hoped that they would take charge of the subscription papers in their respective localities.

[44] An admirer of Jefferson's letter of Aug. 4 caused it to be printed in a Petersburg newspaper but said that few subscriptions could be expected from that district (Archibald Thweatt to TJ, Sept. 27, UVA). In a letter of Sept. 10, 1817, to Cabell, TJ referred to the difficulty of eradicating the idea that this was merely a local institution (Cabell, p. 80).

[45] Minutes of meeting of July 28, 1817 (*ibid.*, p. 396).

did not learn of its authorship until a decade later. Mutual admiration was then expressed in an exchange of letters between the two men.[46]

Before the summer of 1817 ended Jefferson was informed by a correspondent in Baltimore that Knox had "retired with a competency from the business of instructing youths."[47] The report of Knox's retirement turned out to be premature, but no offer was ever made him in behalf of Central College. It was also reported that he was a man of violent temper. This Scotsman would have brought considerable learning to the young institution, but he might have been a disturber of the peace.

If Jefferson was trying to be conciliatory, he now took the wrong direction. He turned to Thomas Cooper, whom he regarded as a paragon of learning, but who was also an inveterate controversialist and might have been expected to offend the orthodox of all hues. Shortly after he learned that Knox was unavailable, Jefferson brought Cooper up to date regarding developments. He asked his help in the search for a professor of languages to occupy the pavilion which was expected to be in readiness in the spring. They would have two more pavilions a year later, he said, and would establish two more professorships. He also said that they had in mind to offer Cooper that of zoology, chemistry, botany, mineralogy, and anatomy. Law was added to this formidable list in order to increase his income.[48]

Not until their fall meeting a month later did the Board of Visitors formally authorize the construction of two more pavilions and approve the proposals to Cooper. The salary of $1000 was to be supplemented by $20 for each student under his instruction (tuition was set for $60 per annum and lodging at $15). Provision was also made for the expense of moving Cooper's minerals and apparatus, and for the rental or ultimate purchase of these. Meanwhile, he was urged to visit Monticello, as in fact he afterwards did.[49]

Early in September an unsigned communication about Central College appeared in the *Enquirer*. Ostensibly from Warm Springs, it had actually been written by Jefferson and dispatched from Poplar Forest.[50] Rarely in the course of his long career had he shown concern for favorable pub-

[46] Knox to TJ, Jan. 22, 1810 (Sowerby, IV, 326–327); TJ to Knox, Feb. 12, 1811 (L. & B., XII, 361). The pamphlet, *A Vindication of the Religion of Mr. Jefferson* . . . , presumably appeared in the newspapers before it was printed along with the *Notes on Virginia* in 1801.

[47] John Patterson to TJ, Aug. 11, 1817 (HEH), received Aug. 23. Knox, who was then principal of Baltimore College, actually continued to teach for some years. See the sketch in the *D.A.B.*

[48] TJ to Cooper, Sept. 1, 1817 (UVA).

[49] Minutes of the Visitors, Oct. 7, 8, 1817 (Cabell, pp. 396–399).

[50] *Richmond Enquirer*, Sept. 5, 1817, sent by TJ to Thomas Ritchie, Aug. 28, (LC).

licity to such a degree as he did for this cherished project. On this occasion he wrote what amounted to a progress report, and it may have been the more impressive because his name was not attached to it. His name did appear in the laudatory note with which the editor introduced the article. Thomas Ritchie said that he looked to Central College with hope as the "future nursery of Science and of Liberty"; and, referring to Jefferson as the chief founder, said that, having contested for liberty in his youth, he was contending in old age for the means to perpetuate it.

The laying of the cornerstone of the first pavilion on October 6, 1817, received less publicity than the first meeting of the Board of Visitors in May, although the same trio of presidential dignitaries was in attendance. The *Enquirer* stated in its brief account that the stone was laid "with all the ceremony and solemnity due to such an occasion."[51] President Monroe officiated, the other five Visitors were present, the local fraternity of Freemasons participated, and a large crowd attended. According to Edmund Bacon, the "old, turned-out field" was filled with carriages and people.[52] From the references in the minutes of the meeting of the Visitors next day it would appear that there was still terracing and leveling to be done. Jefferson had already used the term "lawn," which was destined to endure, but as applied to this old field it was and would long continue to be a misnomer.

The pavilion whose walls were beginning to emerge from the raw red earth was to be numbered seven when it acquired a full complement of companions and years later was to be turned into a faculty club.[53] Jefferson's plans called for a Doric portico in the upper story, supported by an arcade in the first story. This strongly reflected but did not exactly follow suggestions made by Thornton. The pavilion was to have two front doors, one for the students to use in entering and leaving the classroom, the other to serve as an entrance to the professor's quarters. Likewise, there were to be two "necessaries" (privies). Planned at first to be up against the house, they were afterwards placed in the garden.[54]

A few days after the meeting of the Visitors, Jefferson told Latrobe that the fronts of the two pavilions just approved would be taken from those suggested by him in the drawing that had recently been received. These were to be also on the west side and would later be numbered

[51] Oct. 10, 1817.

[52] Pierson, p. 20.

[53] The Colonnade Club of the University of Virginia. As finally erected, there were ten pavilions numbered from north to south, with odd numbers on the west and even numbers on the east. Thus, number seven is next to the last on the west.

[54] Kimball, p. 76; and Frederick D. Nichols, note on TJ's plan in *The Eye of Thomas Jefferson*, W. H. Adams, ed. (1976), p. 287. The catalogue of this bicentennial exhibition at the National Gallery is a most useful reference for TJ and the arts.

respectively three and five. They were not to be started that year, but it may be noted here that their porticos were to have columns extending the height of both stories, which would break the line of the covered passageway.[55] He afterwards designated the columns and capitals of these two pavilions as the Corinthian and Ionic of Palladio. Having sold to Congress all his copies of the works of that master, he borrowed one from Madison that fall and no doubt referred to it frequently when making his own drawings.[56] He may not have turned to the drawing board until winter had shut him in. Toward the end of October he told Cabell that the operations of the College gave him more employment than he was equal to.[57] He said that the dilatoriness of the workmen required him to be at the site of building operations every other day. To his great disappointment the walls of the first house in this projected village were only one story high in mid-November, when they were covered over to await the coming of spring.

When he complained of being over-burdened, no doubt he was thinking of paperwork as well as the supervision of construction, and at this time he appears to have been more impressed than previously with the difficulty of assembling an eminent faculty. Cooper was holding off and Jefferson was wondering if they would not have to go abroad for professors of languages and mathematics. Again and again he said that they would never be content with mediocrity. Several times he said he wished the College could have a Ticknor as professor of languages, and to this learned and sympathetic young friend he described his hopes and fears with notable impressiveness.

Other expressions of his in this period show that he had by no means lost his belief in representative government. As a champion of both general and higher education, however, he recognized that the "ordinary character" of the legislators imposed limitations. Unfortunately, they did not realize that "knowledge is power, that knowledge is safety, and that knowledge is happiness."[58] No doubt it meant all that to him and, in his opinion, might mean that to any individual. But what he was stressing was the value of education to his commonwealth. In the autumn of 1817 he drafted bills that would have made provision for public education at all levels. Also, for the benefit of the General Assembly he prepared a report on Central College.

[55] Kimball, pp. 76–77. Since Latrobe's drawing has not been preserved, we cannot surely know how closely Jefferson followed his suggestions.

[56] TJ to Madison, Nov. 15, 1817 (LC): Madison to TJ, Nov. 29 (LC).

[57] TJ to Cabell, Oct. 24, 1817 (Cabell, pp. 84–85).

[58] TJ to Ticknor, Nov. 25, 1817 (Ford, X, 96). I have modified the spelling, changing "knolege" to "knowledge."

[XIX]

Winning a Charter

1817-1819

ABOUT a month before President James Monroe laid the cornerstone of the first building of Central College, ex-President Jefferson sent Joseph C. Cabell the draft of a bill for the establishment of elementary schools throughout Virginia. He had promised it to this colleague and state senator, perhaps at the midsummer meeting of the Visitors, and he prepared it at Poplar Forest, where he had more leisure than in Albemarle. He said that he had sought to avoid the "verbose and intricate style" of modern statutes but was willing for his bill to be corrected to the taste of his fellow lawyers. Accordingly, he authorized Cabell to make every other word a "said" or an "aforesaid," and to repeat everything so many times that only lawyers could untwist the diction.[1]

A few weeks later Cabell asked him for bills for academies and a university. In response he transmitted from Monticello a comprehensive bill for a state system of elementary, intermediate, and higher education.[2] He said that writing was slow and painful because of his stiffening wrist and that he had a deadly aversion to the writing table. Nonetheless, with the aid of no secretary but his polygraph, he produced a paper which now fills almost eleven pages in an octavo volume, and the legibility of his manuscript shows that his skill as a penman had been maintained.

As he told Cabell, his willingness to endure such a task had been aroused by his first serious perusal of the bill drawn by Charles F. Mercer. This was included in the pamphlet ordered by the last legislature.[3] He believed that unless something less extravagant could be devised their

[1] This draft, which TJ enclosed with his letter of Sept. 9, 1817, to Cabell (Cabell, pp. 79–80), can be conveniently seen in *Complete Jefferson*, ed. by Padover, pp. 1072–1076.

[2] Cabell to TJ, Oct. 14, 1817 (Cabell, p. 82); TJ to Cabell, Oct. 24 (*ibid.*, p. 84). The earlier bill for elementary schools was included with minor changes in this comprehensive bill. As revised by TJ, the latter is at UVA and is printed in Honeywell, pp. 233–243.

[3] For the bill and pamphlet, see above, pp. 252–253.

"whole undertaking" must fail. The primary schools alone, under that plan, would require all the available funds, he said, and since the colleges would need an equal amount, a university "would never come into question." He was not objecting to the priorities but calling attention to the inadequacy of the means proposed for the support of this elaborate system of schools. He still believed that elementary schools could be supported locally and that the Literary Fund should be reserved for colleges and what he always called "an" university. Nevertheless, he recognized the necessity of devising an over-all plan that was more economical than this one.

He described the bill he sent Cabell as being in substance his bill of 1779, "accommodated to the circumstances of this, instead of that day."[4] For example, he incorporated the Literary Fund into his system and transformed its governing group into a "Board of Public Instruction." To this he assigned ultimate authority over the institutions of secondary and higher learning.[5] On the elementary level, he envisioned a countryside dotted with log-cabin schoolhouses built by the local citizenry. Each would have a schoolmaster, part of whose pay might be in kind. In this bill he made no provision for tuition, as he had sometimes done in the past, but proposed three years of free schooling for rich and poor alike, as in 1779. Accordingly, there would have to be some local taxation, but he did not think it would amount to much. Tuition was to be charged in college and university, but in the final section of this bill he sought "to avail the Commonwealth of those talents and virtues which nature has sown as liberally among the poor as [among the] rich." As in 1779, he provided for the education at public expense of poor youths of notable promise. In modern lingo, he would have set up scholarships based on merit.[6]

On the intermediate level, he now proposed that there be nine colleges and designated their districts, specifying that the first of them should be named for his beloved mentor George Wythe.[7] The colleges, while an improvement on the classical academies, were to be small in size and limited in scope. Each was to have two professors — one for languages and one for other subjects. In the beginning of the part of his bill that was devoted to the university, he provided alternative wordings which

[4] TJ to Correa da Serra, Nov. 25, 1817 (L. & B., XV, 156).

[5] While this plan was in a sense less democratic, it was also far simpler to put into operation than either TJ's earlier plan or Mercer's bill. See Honeywell (pp. 19, 26–53) for a generally sound comparison of TJ's plans.

[6] For a highly favorable comment on this provision see Conant, pp. 15–16.

[7] In 1779 he had proposed twenty "grammar" schools. The Mercer bill provided for forty-eight academies for boys and three for girls, four new colleges, and incorporation into the system of three existing colleges.

Cabell was to choose between in the light of circumstances. One called for the establishment of a university in a central and healthful part of the state, while the other specified that the choice should fall on Albemarle County and Central College. He described the scope of the institution much as he had done elsewhere, saying that it should have no more than ten professors. In this carefully drawn bill he provided in specific detail for the organization and government of the university, as he did also for the colleges and elementary schools. Speaking to Cabell of his bill, he said:

> Take it and make of it what you can, if worth anything. . . . I meddle no more with it. There is a time to retire from labor and that time has come with me. It is a duty as well as the strongest of my desires to relinquish to younger hands the government of our bark and resign myself as I do willingly to their care.[8]

During the long legislative struggle over public education he sought to keep out of sight, but inevitably he was identified in the public mind with the issue that was closest to his heart. No other in his entire career seems to have evoked more emotional expressions of concern on his part. This concern was not merely, nor even primarily, for the college which was under his particular charge and which he hoped would develop into a university, but for the system as a whole.

It was several weeks after this letter to Cabell that he complained to Ticknor of the legislators' insufficient faith in knowledge. He was even more plaintive in a letter to his botanical friend Correa that same day. After describing his general plan, he said: "Mine, after all may be an Utopian dream, but being innocent, I have thought I might indulge in it until I go to the land of dreams, and sleep there with the dreamers of all past and future times."[9] It would be difficult to match these words elsewhere in his voluminous correspondence. He regarded himself as no visionary, and he contended that his plan was practicable — as, to his mind, the Mercer bill clearly was not.

His hopes had revived somewhat by the time he wrote Cabell a week before Christmas. To that young legislator he said:

> Pray drop me a line when any vote is passed which furnishes an indication of the success or failure of the general plan. I have only

[8] Oct. 24, 1817 (Cabell, p. 84).

[9] TJ to Correa, Nov. 25, 1817 (L. & B., XV, 155–157). The letter of the same date to Ticknor is quoted on p. 266, above.

> this single anxiety in the world. It is a bantling of forty years' birth and nursing, and if I can once see it on its legs, I will sing with sincerity and pleasure my *nunc dimittas.*[10]

These moving words were written at Poplar Forest in mid-December. Their author was back at Monticello in time to have Christmas dinner there, and about a week later he learned from Cabell what had happened to the "general plan" thus far.[11] After consulting "friends of learning" in Richmond, Cabell reported a mixed reaction. He said there was virtual unanimity regarding the "propriety" of having a university, and pretty general concurrence regarding the desirability of colleges, along with differences of opinion about their number and location. He found that there was "great contrariety" of opinion regarding the practicability and expediency of primary schools.

At first Cabell showed Jefferson's bill to only a select few, but when the report got out that he had such a document, he decided to send a copy of it to the chairman of the committee on schools and colleges in the lower House. On the advice of friends who had read it, he left some things out. Among these were all the references to ministers and religion. Judge Spencer Roane, one of the "friends of learning" who commented on Jefferson's bill, regarded these provisions as unnecessary and almost certain to give offense. Thomas Ritchie agreed with him.[12] Cabell was still talking about the hostility of the Presbyterians to Jefferson, but they were not alone in regarding him as an infidel. Though he was not one, his anticlericalism was almost as obsessive as his antimonarchism and, unlike the latter, had come to be a political liability. Therefore, his friends showed political wisdom in seeking to prevent him from flaunting it.

Also omitted was a provision requiring literacy for citizenship. In explanation of this provision he said he would be reluctant to impose compulsory school attendance. He believed, however, that society could rightfully disfranchise those who failed to avail themselves of free elementary education.[13] Judge Roane was certainly not the only one who regarded the provision as too rigorous. Cabell also left out the sections referring specifically to Central College. He made no change in the sections dealing with the local financing of the primary schools, though

[10] TJ to Cabell, Dec. 18, 1817 (Cabell, p. 88).

[11] Cabell to TJ, Dec. 29, 1817, with enclosures (*ibid.*, pp. 90–98).

[12] TJ had specified that ministers of the gospel should not be Visitors and that there be no sectarian teaching or religious exercises. Notes from Roane and Ritchie on TJ's bill are in the Cabell papers, UVA.

[13] TJ had attached an explanatory note to this provision (Cabell, p. 97). See also TJ to Du Pont, Apr. 24, 1816 (*J.-D. Correspondence*, pp. 185–186).

practically nobody regarded these as acceptable. Indeed, it could be said that this legislature would have approved no plan of public education that required taxation.

In his covering letter to the committee chairman Cabell quoted the moving words in which Jefferson said he willingly relinquished public affairs to younger men. And Cabell was careful not to claim too much for the bill the veteran had drafted.[14]

The Visitors of Central College were not required to report their doings to the legislature, but they had decided to do so. If the specific suggestion did not come from Jefferson, it was in full accord with his desire to identify the projected institution closely with the commonwealth. He had caused the appointment of its Visitors to be vested in the Governor and had consistently emphasized its public and general character.

In the report that he took upon himself to draft late in the year he gave a favorable account of developments. Including subscriptions, actual and expected, financial assets amounted to between $46,000 and $47,000. He did not fail to point out that even for a college more would be required. He was too optimistic in his anticipation of contributions and the beginning of operations, but his carefully drafted paper was on the whole judicious and restrained. Also, it was deferential. The Visitors declared that they would gladly transfer to the state all the property and rights of Central College if the legislature in its wisdom should decide to establish a university and choose this as its site.[15]

Jefferson circulated his draft among his colleagues. From Madison he received minor suggestions. He signed for Monroe, who had approved a previous draft, but all the others signed for themselves.[16] Cabell promptly presented the report to the Governor, who transmitted it to the legislature, and 250 copies of it were ordered to be printed. Cabell believed that it could not fail to help the cause of the college but gave a discouraging account of its reception in the House of Delegates. He said it was recognized as an able paper that bore great names but that it had had no discernible effect on the feelings and opinions of the members.[17]

[14] Cabell to Scott, Dec. 13, 1817 (Cabell, pp. 94–96).

[15] For the report, which is dated Jan. 6, 1818, see *ibid.*, pp. 400–404.

[16] Monroe was delayed in returning the report by TJ's request that he show it to Charles F. Mercer, who was now in Congress. Despite their differences regarding an educational system, TJ said he respected Mercer's "liberal views" and wanted to be considered as "merely a cooperator with him." TJ to Monroe, Dec. 13, 1817 (UVA): Monroe to TJ, Dec. 23 (S.M.H., VI, 46); TJ to Madison, Dec. 30 (UVA); Madison to TJ, Jan. 1, 1818 (MP); TJ to Madison, Jan. 2 (LC).

[17] Cabell to TJ, Jan. 22, 1818 (Cabell, p. 108).

* * *

On the first day of the new year there appeared in the *Enquirer* the beginning of a series of essays attacking the idea of a system of public education. They were aimed chiefly at the Mercer bill, but they contained pointed references to Jefferson. These verbose essays continued through the legislative session in what must have seemed an interminable procession, and we may doubt if he ever waded through all of them. Thomas Ritchie, who published them despite his obvious dislike of them, said that they were marked by "broadness of raillery" without the saving grace of wit. Though anonymous, they were quickly recognized as the work of William Branch Giles. That pugnacious former congressman and senator was one of the most noted obstructionists in the Republican party, but hitherto he had been more loyal to Jefferson than to anybody else.[18]

Giles now designated the former head of his party as the "prince of philosophers" and spoke repeatedly of Jefferson's learning in a sarcastic tone. He observed that the most brilliant and most improved minds often indulged in the "greatest and most unaccountable eccentricities." He suggested that Jefferson, who had been long abstracted from practical affairs and engaged in "delicious contemplations," might be unaware of the difficulty of putting theories into effect and warned Virginians to be on guard against his airy fancies. This heavy-handed and wearisome harangue may be regarded as demagogic and anti-intellectual. Soon after it began Cabell said it had little influence, and reaction might have been expected against such excess. But the elaborate list of subjects of instruction in Jefferson's letter to Peter Carr lent itself to ridicule. Many of his terms were not in common use, as Giles observed, and no doubt there were many ordinary people who questioned the applicability of this learning to the human condition.

The "prince of philosophers" appears to have brushed off the aspersions of Giles without comment. He was visibly disturbed, however, by Cabell's reports from the seat of government. This trusted correspondent gave him a very unfavorable account of the House of Delegates, stating repeatedly that there was little likelihood of the establishment of a full system of public education. According to Cabell, the "friends of learning" who had been shown the bill regarded the method of financing the

[18] Altogether, nine essays and a supplement appeared in the *Enquirer*, Jan. 1–Feb. 21, 1818, under the heading, "Doubts concerning the Merits of the Proposed System of Education . . . by a Constituent." Cabell wrote TJ about them Jan. 5 (Cabell, p. 100). The quotations below are from the Jan. 1 essay. Ironically, TJ had solicited a subscription to Central College from Giles, addressing him as a friend.

elementary schools as unacceptable. In mid-January Jefferson sought to demonstrate that this plan was in fact economical.[19] He seemed to be pronouncing his own valedictory as crusader, when he said to Cabell:

> A system of general instruction, which shall reach every description of our citizens, from the richest to the poorest, as it was the earliest, so will it be the latest, of all the public concerns in which I shall permit myself to take an interest.

He added that he was not tenacious of a particular plan, believing that any one adopted could be subsequently adjusted to human needs. Therefore he urged the adoption of a system of public education in any form and did not doubt that for this "inestimable boon" the citizenry would be profoundly and eternally grateful.

Cabell promptly got a copy of this letter into the hands of Chairman Scott of the committee on schools and colleges in the House of Delegates and circulated the original among other members of the legislature. He did not believe that Jefferson's general plan, or any other for a full system of education, would be adopted. Nor did he now have much hope that something would be gained for Central College. He kept talking about the low quality of the legislative body and the desirability of inducing more enlightened men to stand for election to it.[20]

Deeply disappointed by the bill that finally emerged from Scott's committee in the House, Cabell persuaded Samuel Taylor, a delegate from Chesterfield County, to propose Jefferson's bill as a substitute.[21] A motion that 500 copies of it be printed was defeated, and to Cabell's horror there was some opposition to printing any at all, but 250 were ordered. Cabell believed that, even though the likelihood of the adoption of Jefferson's specific proposals was slight, the publicizing of his ideas was highly desirable. Therefore, after consulting with friends but without waiting to ask Jefferson's consent, he took it upon himself to publish the letter in which Jefferson had sought to demonstrate the practicability of his proposals and had spoken so plaintively of his long crusade for public education.[22]

This appeared in the *Enquirer* on February 10, 1818, after a lengthy synopsis of the bill that was to be voted on the next day, and which in

[19] TJ to Cabell, Jan. 14, 1818 (Cabell, pp. 102–106). He suggested as a possible compromise that two-thirds of the Literary Fund be assigned to elementary schools, and only a meager third be appropriated to colleges and universities.

[20] Cabell to TJ, Jan. 22, 1818 (*ibid.*, pp. 108–110).

[21] Cabell to TJ, Jan. 23, Feb. 1, 1818 (*ibid.*, pp. 111–113).

[22] Cabell to TJ, Feb. 6, 10, 1818 (*ibid.*, pp. 116–121). TJ expressed his approval, Feb. 16 (*ibid.*, p. 124).

fact also was Jefferson's, though his name was not attached to it. Thomas Ritchie was doing what he could for it.[23] His help was of no avail, however. As Cabell regretfully informed the Sage of Monticello, his bill received very few votes. No action was taken in behalf of either general or higher education. Instead, a motion was passed for an appropriation of $45,000 from the Literary Fund for the education of the children of the poor.[24]

Writing Cabell a few days later, Jefferson, far from indulging in recrimination, was disposed to blame himself for "meddling." He expressed the opinion that he had done more harm than good. They must turn to the affairs of the College, their particular charge, he said, and do what they could on its own scanty funds.[25] This was perhaps the darkest hour of his educational crusade, but the skies brightened soon thereafter. Cabell reported in his next letter (February 20) that the bill had been favorably amended in the Senate and was expected to be approved by the House, as it soon was.[26]

In a private memorandum Cabell afterwards stated somewhat more fully what actually happened. When the bill reached the Senate, it was referred to a committee of three, of whom he was one. For a time he favored an amendment providing for both colleges and a university but was persuaded to drop the former because the question of their number and location would inevitably involve the legislators in divisive debate. The committee finally recommended an amendment providing for the establishment of a university and an annual appropriation of $15,000 to it after its site had been determined by law.[27] The Senate adopted this by a large majority, and it was approved by the House with a proviso designed to safeguard future appropriations for the education of the poor.[28] Refraining from any comment on the inadequacy of the measure, Jefferson congratulated Cabell on having gained something for education.[29]

[23] *Richmond Enquirer*, Feb. 10, 1818.

[24] Cabell to TJ, Feb. 13, 1818 (Cabell, p. 122); *Richmond Enquirer*, Feb. 17.

[25] TJ to Cabell, Feb. 16, 1818 (Cabell, p. 124).

[26] *Ibid.*, pp. 125–126.

[27] "Explanatory Note" in Cabell papers (UVA).

[28] The House acted on Feb. 21, 1818, and Cabell wrote TJ next day (Cabell, p. 127). The act can be conveniently seen in Cabell, pp. 427–432. The measure set up what amounted to a system of scholarships for elementary school based wholly on need and created local boards to administer this. Time was to show that needy parents were not especially eager to apply for what could be regarded as charity, and in educational matters Jefferson sought to avoid such a distinction between rich and poor as was made here.

[29] TJ to Cabell, Feb. 26, 1818 (*ibid.*, p. 128).

ii

To aid the legislature in choosing a suitable location for the University and making plans for it, provision was made for a commission of twenty-four members, representing the various senatorial districts of the state. This was to be appointed by the Governor and meet at Rockfish Gap in the Blue Ridge on August 1. It was authorized only to make recommendations to the General Assembly, and the law explicitly stated that the University should "in all things, at all times, be subject to the control of the Legislature."[30]

Believing that Governor James P. Preston would be amenable to suggestions, Cabell asked Jefferson if he would serve on this important commission. In his reply Jefferson said he believed that his presence on it would do the cause of the University more harm than good. He recognized that the welfare of the institution would ultimately depend on the will of the legislature and could afford to lose no votes in that body. He had learned from Cabell that much of the opposition to Central College arose from hostility to him. "There are fanatics both in religion and politics," he said, "who, without knowing me personally, have long been taught to consider me as a raw head and bloody bones."[31] Therefore, he felt that Cabell would be more effective than he on the commission and urged his appointment for their district. He had not declined to serve, however, and the friends whom Cabell consulted must have over-ruled Jefferson's objections. In March the Governor, who did not know him personally but was well disposed toward him, appointed him to the commission along with President Madison, Judge Spencer Roane, and other men who were notable in the state or their own localities.[32]

Cabell, in one of his gloomiest moments, had stated that the character and conduct of the House of Delegates was "despicable."[33] His fears persisted after the session ended. He said that even though the commission should recommend Central College, the action of the next legislature would be uncertain. Therefore he continued to urge that discreet efforts be made to get able and virtuous men into the Assembly. Jefferson advised Francis Walker Gilmer to seek election to it, which that

[30] These words were repeated in the act of 1819 by which the University of Virginia was created.

[31] Feb. 26, 1818 (Cabell, p. 128). Cabell had stated that there was opposition to TJ even in his own county. To TJ, Feb. 13, 1818 (UVA).

[32] List in *Enquirer*, March 20, 1818; Cabell to TJ, March 11 (Cabell, p. 129), saying he was referring to a group of friends the question of TJ's appointment.

[33] Feb. 13, 1818 (UVA). This was omitted from the published text of this letter (Cabell, p. 123).

promising young man did not do, and he manifested needless concern lest John Randolph should do so.[34]

Leaving to chance nothing that was foreseeable, Jefferson prepared for the Rockfish Gap "campaign" with the utmost care. Indeed, he may be said to have won it before it opened, for the report that the commission adopted was drafted by him in advance. Toward the end of June, on the eve of his departure for Poplar Forest, he sent his draft to Madison.[35] He stated that he had sought to adapt it to the House of Delegates. In the hope of winning the support of the wavering members he threw in ideas on the benefits of education. Thus he said, among other things, that nothing more than education advances "the prosperity, the power and the happiness of a nation."[36] He also told Madison that he could not fail to speak of the desirability of establishing a general system of primary and secondary schools. He was battling for more than Central College.

He had no reason to doubt that most if not all of his fellow commissioners would subscribe to his general philosophy and accept his views about the character of the University. The only real question at issue would be that of its location, and the only known rivals to Central College were Staunton and Lexington, the seat of Washington College. Lexington had more to offer in lands and buildings than the institution in Albemarle could match, but the latter had the geographical advantage suggested by its name. Besides availing himself of census returns, Jefferson had Alexander Garrett procure statistical material from the various counties of the state. With these figures in hand he sought to demonstrate by means of a map that the site near Charlottesville was nearer the center of white population than either of the others that had been proposed.[37] He submitted his tables to Madison, along with the text, and this colleague appears to have made no significant changes.

In the year 1818 the first day of August fell on Saturday. Because of the roughness of the roads, Jefferson, who was now seventy-five, chose to make the journey of thirty miles to Rockfish Gap on horseback, though not all in one day. Accompanied by Madison, he proceeded on Thursday to Farmington, where bed and dinner were provided by his close friend and rival gardener George Divers. (Shortly before he left Monticello he received bad financial news from Richmond, but there

[34] TJ to Gilmer, Apr. 10, 1818 (LC); J. C. Cabell to J. H. Cocke, Mar. 31, 1818 (Cabell Papers, UVA).

[35] TJ to Madison, June 28, 1818 (LC). See also TJ to Madison, Apr. 11 (*ibid.*).

[36] From what appears to be TJ's second draft of the Report of the Rockfish Gap Commission (UVA).

[37] George Wythe Randolph to James L. Cabell, Feb. 27, 1856 (Cabell Papers, UVA).

appears to be no record of his having mentioned it to his companion, his host, or his fellow commissioners.)[38] He did not divide his journey into two equal parts, for twenty-three miles remained, but he seems to have covered them without incident. Ahead of him by some hours went his baggage, including a mattress and trestles, which he preferred to a bed in hot weather. In a letter to the proprietor or manager of the tavern he said that if he could get a room by himself he would regard it as a great indulgence. Since there were forty rooms in the tavern, it seems likely that his wish was granted.[39]

The fact that this historic meeting was held in a gap in the Blue Ridge is significant because sectionalism was such an important ingredient of politics in Virginia at the time, and this lovely range of mountains was generally regarded as the dividing line between the eastern and western sections of the state. The former was over-represented on the commission as it was in the upper chamber of the legislature, since one member was appointed from each senatorial district. Cabell believed that this would be to the advantage of the cause of Central College, but Jefferson deplored the inequities in the system of representation and sought to avoid the appearance of localism in his own argument.

He dealt here with a group of men whose ability and character clearly warranted no such complaint as Cabell had directed against the members of the House of Delegates. In the parlance of a later generation this was a "blue-ribbon" commission. Besides two ex-Presidents of the Republic, it contained a former governor and the chief judicial officer of the state, along with a couple of other judges. Jefferson was unanimously elected president of the body and he got from it precisely what he wanted, but the result was not owing to aggressive procedure. After the meeting, one of the commissioners told Cabell that the presiding officer's conduct was marked by great forbearance and moderation. He said that Jefferson "did not even intimate a wish at any time or in any shape except when his name was called and his vote given."[40] It would have been unlike him to speak out of turn, and on the chief point at issue he had a map to speak for him. This has been described as a blunderbuss that was fired with devastating effect after the claims of Staunton and Lexington had been presented.[41]

[38] He described the arrangements for the trip to Madison in his letter of June 28. Madison wrote his wife from Monticello on the morning of their journey, July 30, 1818 (Chicago Hist. Soc.). For financial developments at this stage, see below, pp. 304–305.

[39] TJ to Mr. Barnet, July 30, 1818 (LC); TJ to Archibald Stuart, May 28, 1818 (Mo. Hist. Soc.).

[40] J. G. Jackson to Cabell, Dec. 13, 1818 (Cabell Papers, UVA).

[41] Bruce, I, 218. The basis of this account is the letter of G. W. Randolph to J. L. Cabell, Feb. 27, 1856 (Cabell Papers, UVA), in which he repeats the story of Alexander Garrett.

No vote on a site was taken on Saturday, the first day of the meeting, but a committee of six was elected to draw up a report on all the other matters the commission had been instructed to consider. Jefferson's name was the first on the list and that of Madison followed. They had been expected to bring something with them, and the other four committeemen had Saturday night and Sunday to examine the report that had been drafted in advance.[42] On Monday a vote was taken on the question of the site. Staunton got two votes and Lexington three, while Central College got the remaining sixteen.[43] After the vote had been incorporated and minor amendments approved, the report was unanimously adopted.

The recommendations regarding the buildings, subjects of instruction, and organization of the University were essentially the same as those Jefferson had previously made and thus require no description here. He now spoke of "hotels" where the students would be fed, and he referred to a central building as a possibility, but he had not yet designed either the Ranges or the Rotunda. The report recommended ten professorships, among which the field of useful knowledge was to be divided. In his effort to cover the whole of this he assigned to the prospective professors more subjects than they could really be expected to teach. He recognized that in due course adjustment would have to be made to practical necessity.[44]

Two fair copies of the report were made — one for each branch of the General Assembly — and on Tuesday they were signed by each of the twenty-one commissioners. Then, on motion of Judge Spencer Roane, seconded by General James Breckenridge, a final resolution was adopted. In this, thanks were expressed to Thomas Jefferson, Esq., for the "ability, impartiality, and dignity" with which he had presided over the meeting. That gentleman, in turn, thanked his fellows for the harmonious spirit they had displayed and voiced confidence in the future of their beloved state under the sort of leadership they provided.[45]

[42] Archibald Stuart to TJ, May 30, 1818 (MHS).

[43] The names of those voting for each site were given in an account of the proceedings in the *Richmond Enquirer*, Aug. 11, 1818. The best edition of the official *Proceedings and Report of the Commissioners for the University of Virginia* is in the *Manual of the Board of Visitors of the University of Virginia, 1975* (Charlottesville, 1975), pp. 41–77. This includes an introduction by John Cook Wyllie, pp. 31–36.

[44] The report contains a precise description of the conditional offer by Lexington of land, buildings, and funds as well as a description of the offer from Central College. TJ had gone to great pains to get the consent of the subscribers and had caused a deed of conveyance to the state to be drawn and recorded. He said that this had not been done by the promoters of the Lexington site but could be if desired.

[45] The wording of TJ's final remarks as given on a paper from his own files (UVA) differs slightly from that in the excellent account of the meeting in *Richmond Enquirer*, Aug. 11, 1818. I have followed the former.

* * *

After the adjournment of this distinguished body the late presiding officer proceeded into the Shenandoah Valley to Staunton. There he was the guest of Judge Archibald Stuart, who had voted for that place as a site for the University. Jefferson then rode to Warm Springs in the company of General Breckenridge, who had supported the claims of Lexington. He said later that this companion of the road had served as the mentor he needed on his return to society after a long absence from it.[46] The journey took him to the westernmost point in all his travels, and he spent three weeks in the lovely Warm Springs Valley. Though he enjoyed the company of Breckenridge and Colonel William Alston (father-in-law of Aaron Burr's lamented daughter, Theodosia) as long as they were there, on the whole he found life boring.[47] Apparently he had not brought enough to read, and obviously he did not have enough to do.

He had made the trip in the hope that the baths would help his rheumatism, and this they seem to have done, but he blamed them for the great trouble that befell him toward the end of his stay. In the third week of his visit he wrote his daughter: "I do not know what may be the effect of this course of bathing on my constitution; but I am under great threats that it will work its effect through a system of boils."[48] These were on his seat, he said, and, as a traveler far from home, he was faced with a grave problem. He managed to get successive rides in wheeled vehicles, but according to his own account, the journey over rough roads reduced him to the lowest level of debility.[49]

For several weeks he wrote letters when in a reclining position, and for several months he did not mount a horse. He believed that this agonizing experience undermined his health, and rumors spread that his death was near. A report to that effect was published in a New York paper. This was denied by Ritchie in mid-November, and by that time Jefferson appears to have assumed a normal posture when writing letters.[50] Madison, who rode over from Montpelier in December to see how he was, found that he had resumed riding on horseback.[51]

During the fall season his personal supervision of building operations on the grounds of Central College must have been largely if not wholly

[46] TJ to Martha, Aug. 4, 7, 1818 (*Family Letters*, pp. 423–424); TJ to Breckinridge, Oct. 6 (LC).

[47] TJ to Martha, Aug. 14, 1818 (*Family Letters*, p. 425).

[48] TJ to Martha, Aug. 21, 1818 (*ibid.*, p. 426). Several times thereafter, when describing his condition, he said he was suffering from an imposthume (abscess) and eruptions. Presumably he had what we now call a staphylococcus infection. He could have picked this up in the baths.

[49] TJ to Francis Eppes, Sept. 1, 1818 (*ibid.*, pp. 426–427); TJ to William Alston, Oct. 6 (LC).

[50] *Richmond Enquirer*, Nov. 17, 1818.

[51] Madison to Monroe, Dec. 11, 1818 (Monroe Papers, LC).

suspended. He described to several men of learning his hopes and aspirations for the faculty of the future University, but nothing came of his advances, and at this stage he could do little more than engage in wishful thinking.[52]

iii

Toward the end of November Jefferson sent to the speakers of the Senate and the House of Delegates the two fair copies of the report which had been signed by the twenty-one members of the Rockfish Gap Commission.[53] Cabell was in ill health at this crucial time but was determined to stick to his legislative post until the question of the University site had been answered to his satisfaction. He said that the report was read in both chambers and that its ability and value were universally recognized. Besides printing many copies on order of the legislature, Ritchie published it in full in six and a half columns of the *Enquirer*. In his introductory note the sympathetic editor expressed great pride in presenting to the public an essay which, in his opinion, would do honor to any nation in any age. He attributed the document to the "ever-luminous pen" of Thomas Jefferson. At the beginning of the legislative session Cabell, while recognizing the uncertainties in the situation, reported to the penman at Monticello that "all that I can now positively affirm is, that the clouds seem to be scattering, and the prospect to smile."[54]

The optimism of this zealous senator was short-lived. He soon informed Jefferson that the western opponents of Central College were active, that its eastern supporters were apathetic, and that a goodly number of the legislators wanted no university at all. In the committee of the House of Delegates to which the recommendations of the Rockfish Gap Commission were referred, the adherents of Lexington sought to have a bill reported without designation of a site. The vote on this question was a tie until the chairman broke it in favor of Central College. This was a close call, and things got a good deal worse before they got better. Cabell afterwards said that in the week between Christmas and New Year's Day the success of the University bill was despaired of.[55]

[52] TJ to George Ticknor, Oct. 25, 1818; TJ to Nathaniel Bowditch, Oct. 26; TJ to Dr. Kain, Nov. 11 (LC). TJ had learned earlier that Thomas Cooper had failed to receive the appointment he desired in Philadelphia and was thus in position to carry out his engagement.

[53] The one to the Speaker of the Senate was sent to Cabell for delivery. TJ to Cabell, Nov. 20, 1818 (Cabell, p. 136).

[54] Cabell to TJ, Dec. 8, 1818 (*ibid.*, pp. 137–138). *Richmond Enquirer*, Dec. 10. A copy of the report got to Boston, where it was discussed at length in the *North American Review* in June, 1820. TJ commented on this review in his letter of Aug. 15, 1820, to John Adams.

[55] Cabell to TJ, Dec. 14, 17, 24, 1818; Jan. 7, 1819 (Cabell, pp. 138–144, 146–149).

Jefferson, who claimed that he was in revolt against letter writing, answered relatively few of the lengthy communications he received from his diligent correspondent. He replied to a request for further explanation of his procedure in locating the center of white population, and no doubt Cabell drew on this in his own effort to meet the objections of westerners.[56] Cabell caused some strong letters to be written and published in the *Enquirer* but concluded that the action of the General Assembly would not be determined by well-reasoned argument. Writing from Richmond to the apostle of reasonableness at Monticello he said: "The liberal and enlightened views of great statesmen pass over our heads unheeded like the spheres above. When we assemble here, an eastern and western feeling supercedes all other considerations."[57] He reported that, accordingly, he had determined to meet the opposition on their own ground.

Against the western sectionalists he set out to arouse the more numerous easterners to a sense of their own rights and interests and to induce the "friends of learning" to exert their powers. Before the beginning of the debate on the University bill in the House of Delegates (January 12, 1819), a countermovement had set in, and Cabell expressed confidence that they would be victorious over "the enemy beyond the mountain." Having spent his nights in "watchful reflection" and his days in "ceaseless activity," this tireless champion of Central College was more responsible for the change in sentiment than anybody else.

Cabell may have over-emphasized his difficulties somewhat, but Jefferson recognized that these were very great. Writing John Adams on January 19, he stated that they were on tiptoe at Monticello in hourly expectation of a report of the action of the Assembly. This zealous advocate of self-government rarely voiced criticism of the legislative branch, but he said that this body of men was "a good piece of a century" behind the age. He undoubtedly thought that Virginia was backward in educational matters, and he was far from certain that it would not continue so. To his learned friend in Massachusetts he said: "We have to contend with so many biases, personal, local, fanatical, financial, etc., that we cannot foresee in what their combinations will result."[58] Actually, the crucial vote had already been taken, though he had not yet heard of the favorable outcome.

At four o'clock in the afternoon of the day before he wrote Adams, Cabell addressed to him a letter which began as follows: "Grateful, truly

[56] TJ to Cabell, Jan. 1, 1819 (*ibid.*, pp. 145–146). Earlier, Cabell had TJ's computations published in the *Enquirer* (Dec. 17, 1818).

[57] Cabell to TJ, Jan. 7, 1819 (Cabell, pp. 146–149).

[58] TJ to Adams, Jan. 19, 1819.

grateful, is it to my heart, to be able to announce to you the result of this day's proceedings in the House of Delegates."[59] Minor amendments had been defeated on previous days, and on this day the main one was disposed of. A motion to strike the name of Central College from the bill was defeated by a vote of 114 to 69. This was a more decisive victory than the supporters of that institution had expected.

The debate had been divisive as well as spirited, but a western delegate made an eloquent plea for harmony after the vote was taken. Briscoe G. Baldwin of Staunton announced that he would support the measure he had vainly sought to amend and urged his fellow westerners to dismiss all local feeling and give full support to the University. It was reported that most of the delegates were reduced to tears by the speech, and that this magnanimity on the part of a "defeated adversary" excited general admiration. His plea appears to have had no inconsiderable effect. When the bill came up for final action, it was passed without debate by a vote of 143 to 28.[60]

Cabell steered the measure through the Senate, although he was suffering from internal bleeding and at times had to leave his post. A motion in that chamber to strike the name of Central College from the bill was defeated (January 25) by a vote of 16 to 7. It then passed by a vote of 22 to 1.[61] In the letters of congratulations that Jefferson received at this time he was hailed as the founder of the University of Virginia, and at a later date he proudly designated himself as its father. With due allowance for the imprecision of biological analogies, Joseph C. Cabell may be said to have served as midwife at the birth of the infant and to have been an ever-solicitous uncle thereafter.[62]

While rejoicing in their victory, Jefferson was well aware that it was at best a limited one, and he thought of it not as an end but as a beginning. The annual grant to the new institution was still only $15,000, and he quickly recognized that his full plan would require much more than that. The University of Virginia existed only on paper, and he was destined to spend nearly all of his remaining days in the effort to make it a living reality.[63]

[59] Cabell to TJ, Jan. 18, 1819 (Cabell, p. 149). The events of the day are described in *Richmond Enquirer*, Jan. 19, 1819.

[60] Cabell to TJ, Jan. 18, 1819 (Cabell, pp. 149–152); *Richmond Enquirer*, Jan. 21, reporting on the session of Jan. 19.

[61] Cabell to TJ, Jan. 21, 25, 1819 (Cabell, pp. 152–153). The act is printed (*ibid.*, pp. 447–450).

[62] Among the letters of congratulation special mention may be made of those from W. C. Rives, Jan. 20, 1819, and W. C. Nicholas, Jan. 25 (LC).

[63] He said much the same things in his letters of Jan. 28, 1819, to Cabell (Cabell, p. 154); to W. C. Rives (LC); and to W. C. Nicholas (LC). The difficulties he faced will be referred to when the story of the University is resumed.

The Cares of a Septuagenarian

[XX]

The Solicitous Grandfather

JEFFERSON was seventy-two years old in the spring of 1815 when he turned over the management of his farms in Albemarle to his eldest grandson. He retained control of operations at Poplar Forest and was not completely free of business responsibilities at Monticello, but Jeff Randolph relieved him of many cares and much anxiety. About a year after he put his stalwart grandson in charge of the Albemarle farms he said that nothing else was needed to render them adequate to all his wants and to put his mind at perfect ease. He made this over-optimistic statement to John W. Eppes when claiming the privilege of meeting the educational expenses of young Francis. "I consider all my grandchildren as if they were my children, and want nothing but for them," he said.[1]

At this time he had eleven grandchildren altogether. A couple of years later his prolific daughter Martha rounded out a dozen by giving birth to a baby boy, but she still had fewer sons than daughters.[2] Except for Jeff, all of the sons were small, and, although their grandfather undoubtedly found pleasure in all of them, the older girls entered into his life to a greater extent than did the little boys. To the girls he was generous beyond his means, but he did not need to pay for their formal schooling, since they were taught by their mother. Ellen and Cornelia pursued their studies at Poplar Forest when accompanying their grandfather on visits there and were undoubtedly encouraged by him. The person with whose education he was most concerned in his seventies, however, was Francis Eppes, who was next to the oldest of his grandsons. In point of age this boy's turn had come, and, as the only surviving child of Jefferson's daughter Maria, he was an object of his grandfather's special solicitude.

Francis, who was not yet three when his mother died, was in his eighth year when his grandfather retired from the presidency. He was at Monticello the next two winters, while his father, who was a member of

[1] TJ to JWE, Apr. 30, 1816 (HEH).

[2] For detailed information about the family, see Appendix I, below.

Congress and had remarried, was in Washington. According to his grandfather the boy endeared himself to everybody by his excellent disposition and affectionate nature. Jefferson's highly favorable reports were made not only to John W. Eppes, with whom he had maintained intimacy, but also to Francis's grandmother, who was the half sister of his own long-lost and ever-lamented wife. Writing Elizabeth Wayles Eppes early in 1810, he said: "Forty years of pure friendship have in my feelings identified yourself and family with my own, and certainly there is no portion of my life on which I look back with such heartfelt satisfaction as that during which ourselves and families were the most intimately associated."[3] The grandson whom he shared with her was cherished for his own sake, but he was also a living link with a treasured past.

To his great sorrow the good lady at Eppington did not survive the spring. On receiving word of the death of one of the last of his early and most beloved friends, he compared himself to the trunk of a tree from which all the limbs had fallen. With this striking figure of speech he coupled a sagacious observation: "Thus it is that nature, by depriving us of our friends and faculties one by one, prepares us for our own exit with the less regret."[4] He never ceased to bemoan the loss of old friends, but, turning to the young, he seized upon the recompense that nature had beneficently provided. Faith in youth was an essential ingredient of his philosophy.

Several months after his mother's death John W. Eppes sold his interest in Eppington and removed to Millbrook in Buckingham County. This move took him out of the congressional district he was representing into that of John Randolph, whom he unsuccessfully opposed at the next election, despite the confident predictions of Jefferson.[5] Two years later he retrieved the defeat and occupied the former seat of that redoubtable orator for a term (1813–1815). As chairman of the Ways and Means Committee he received lengthy communications about public finance from his erstwhile father-in-law.[6] In the interim he spent his winters in Buckingham County rather than in Washington, and his son Francis does not appear to have been at Monticello.

Relations between Jefferson and the boy's father became somewhat strained in this period. The two men were in disagreement regarding Francis's future property. Included in this was the land at Pantops, originally bequeathed by Jefferson when hoping that Maria and her husband would make a home there. Eppes retained only a life interest in the

[3] TJ to Mrs. Elizabeth Wayles Eppes, Jan. 9, 1810 (HEH), sending her a letter from Francis. He sent others to the boy's father and stepmother.

[4] TJ to Archibald Thweatt, son-in-law of Mrs. Eppes, June 14, 1810 (*ibid.*).

[5] TJ to JWE, Mar. 24, 1811 (*ibid.*).

[6] See above, ch. X, pp. 137–138.

property after Maria's death, and the report that he wanted to sell it was received with considerable concern by its donor. Jefferson did not want these fields, which he could so easily look down upon, to pass from the family. He asked that he be given the refusal of the tract at the same price that would be expected of another.[7]

It would have been exceedingly difficult for him to finance such a purchase, and he soon had a better idea. Before the summer of 1812 was over he proposed that the land at Pantops be exchanged for a comparable tract at Poplar Forest, where he was finishing a house that he intended to give to Francis one day.[8] This appears to have been a practicable as well as a generous proposal. Nevertheless, Jefferson said in the spring of 1813 that the further the negotiations proceeded, the wider the gap between him and Eppes became.[9] There was more open land in the tract at Pantops than in the one at Poplar Forest. Jefferson expected to have clearing done at the latter place. But he was taken aback by the proposal that the disparity be corrected by the immediate addition of the house to the designated parcel at Poplar Forest. Eppes over-reached himself in making his proposal, but he was annoyed that the land at Pantops had not been conveyed to him in fee simple in the first place, as the legacy of Jefferson's wife had been conveyed to him.

Eppes even claimed that Thomas Mann Randolph had been better treated by Jefferson than he had.[10] The reference was to financial, not social, relationship. While both sons-in-law were living in the President's House, Congressman Randolph had complained that their father-in-law preferred Congressman Eppes to him. Jefferson may have preferred the company of the more genial and less gloomy of the two, but if his generosity to them was not even-handed, this was wholly because of differences in circumstances.

Nothing came of the negotiations about Pantops, but in 1817 Jeff Randolph bought some eight hundred acres there for about $11,000 and kept the land in the family until nearly the end of his grandfather's life. The sale was made in behalf of Francis and was contingent on his approval at twenty-one. This was given in due course.[11] Between 1812 and 1819 John W. Eppes did not visit Monticello. He believed it better for the

[7] TJ to JWE, June 3, 5, 1812, in Norma B. Cuthbert, "Poplar Forest: Jefferson's Legacy to His Grandson," *Huntington Library Quarterly*, VI (May, 1943), 340–342.

[8] TJ to JWE, Sept. 18, 1812 (*ibid.*, pp. 342–345).

[9] TJ to JWE, Apr. 18, 1813 (*ibid.*, pp. 345–347).

[10] JWE to TJ, May 25, 1813 (UVA). The reference seems to have been to the unrestricted sale by Randolph of lands constituting Martha's dowry.

[11] TJ, Opinion on the will of JWE, 1823 (UVA); Indenture of TJR and JWE, May 1, 1817, Albemarle County Deed Book, vol. 20, pp. 411–412; Indenture of TJR, JWE and FWE, Dec. 13, 1822, *ibid.*, vol. 23, p. 253; Indenture of TJR and James Leitch, Dec. 1, 1825, *ibid.*, vol. 26, p. 93 (microfilm, UVA).

harmony of the family to avoid meeting with Thomas Mann Randolph. Jefferson visited Millbrook and carried on an extensive correspondence with its owner, recognizing no diminution in their mutual affection.[12] Much of their correspondence related to Francis, and, while Jefferson generally maintained his rights and exercised his privileges as a grandfather, things did not always go smoothly.

When he returned home in May, 1813, from a visit to Poplar Forest he received information which he wished he had had sooner. Awaiting him was a letter in big childish script, to which the following printed version cannot do justice:

> Dear Grand Papa
> I wish to see you very much. I am Sorry that you wont Write to me. This letter will make twice I have wrote to you and if you dont answer this letter I Shant write to you any more. I have got trough my latin Gramer and I am going trough again. I enclose a leter in this from My Cousin Wale Baker. Give my love to all of the family.
> Believe me to remain with the filial love your most affectionate Grand Son,
> Francis Eppes[13]

This epistle was written in Lynchburg, which was only a few miles from Poplar Forest. Jefferson had recently passed near the place, not knowing that the boy was in school there. At the time he gave no sign of annoyance that he had been left in ignorance of Francis's proximity, and, despite the dire threats in his grandson's letter, he does not appear to have written him until he himself was again in Bedford County. He then sent horses to Lynchburg with an invitation for Francis and his cousin to make him a weekend visit. Finding that the boy had gone back to Millbrook to see his father, who had not yet set out for Washington, the disappointed grandfather then requested of Eppes that permission be granted Francis to visit him at Poplar Forest whenever he was there.[14] Afterwards, in November, the two boys visited him on the horses he had sent to Lynchburg. They did so again the following spring.[15]

12 JWE to TJ, July 10, 1809 (MHS). After serving in the House of Representatives, 1813–1815, Eppes was in the U.S. Senate until 1819, when he retired because of bad health.

13 Apr. 11, 1813 (UVA; printed in *Family Letters*, p. 402). Wayles Baker was TJ's grandnephew.

14 TJ to Francis, Aug. 28, 1813 (*ibid.*, p. 403); TJ to JWE, Sept. 11, 1813 (Ford, IX, 402–403).

15 TJ to Francis, Nov. 26, 1813 (*Family Letters*, pp. 403–404); TJ to Martha, June 6, 1814 (*ibid.*, p. 405).

Writing Eppes in the summer of 1814, when the Congressman was at home from Washington, Jefferson described in some detail the progress he was making on the "excellent house" he was building at Poplar Forest. The interior was nearly done, he said, and a service wing, similar to those at Monticello, had just been added. The present value of this house was at least $10,000, as he believed, and would be more before he finished with it. Since he was clearing the adjacent lands more rapidly than he originally intended, Francis would have three hundred open acres when he came of age. Thus his grandson would be "comfortably and handsomely fixed" in a district of the state second to none in soil, climate, and accessibility to market.[16]

When Jefferson visited Poplar Forest in the spring of 1815, Francis was at school in Lynchburg. On his return he brought the boy with him, although the term was not quite over. Since he did not have time to secure parental authorization, he sought to justify his action on educational grounds. Writing Eppes in Washington he said: "French is become the most indispensable part of modern education."[17] He argued that Francis, whose education up to this point had been largely in Latin, could study French to great advantage at Monticello. His daughter Martha spoke French like a native, he said; and her children had picked up her accent. He believed that after a few months in such a favorable atmosphere, Francis would be able to continue the study of French on his own.

Eppes gave his consent to what was in fact a *fait accompli;* and, besides spending the summer of 1815 at Monticello, Francis spent the next winter there. To all practical purposes Jefferson had assumed the direction of his education and now claimed the right to pay for it. He had already made an advance payment for the expense of a term at the New London Academy, which was located three miles from Poplar Forest.[18]

To Francis, who was now reported to be able to read French for his amusement, Jefferson sent a Greek grammar, suggesting that the boy amuse himself by learning the alphabet before taking up the study at the Academy. Besides this suggestion the letter contained moral exhortations such as had been addressed to Peter Carr a generation earlier and more recently to Jeff Randolph. He advised the young freely with regard to conduct as well as learning. Along with the importance of Latin, Greek, and French, he stressed that of honesty, disinterestedness, and good humor.

The maxims he commended would doubtless have been approved by

[16] TJ to JWE, July 16, 1814 (Cuthbert, "Poplar Forest," pp. 348–349).
[17] TJ to JWE, June 1, 1815 (HEH).
[18] TJ to JWE, Apr. 30, 1816 (*ibid.*).

the moral philosophers of classical antiquity and were in full accord with Christian ethics. The following injunction reflects an emphasis which, while not unique, was especially distinctive: "Above all things, and at all times, practice yourself in good humor. This, of all human qualities, is the most amiable and endearing to society."[19] His moralism was tempered by his habitual good humor, as Francis must have found out by now. And the boy probably did not need to be told that his grandfather regarded the esteem of one's fellows as a major factor in the attainment of happiness.

After a term in the New London Academy, Francis spent another winter at Monticello, where he had the advantage of instruction in Spanish by his cousin Ellen. According to her grandfather, her accent was better than his own.[20] He was not directly responsible for all the subsequent peregrinations of his grandson, but by the spring of 1816 he was fully recognized as the boy's mentor. If Francis was not a permanent member of the circle at Monticello, he was entirely at home there, and at the family outpost at Poplar Forest he was welcomed as heir apparent.[21]

ii

In this decade Jefferson made three trips a year to his farms in Bedford County on an average. The original purpose of his visits, and always a major one, was to look after his agricultural affairs, but as time went on he became increasingly involved in building operations. He never entirely finished these, and apparently it was not until seven years after his retirement that he regarded the house as suitable for feminine occupancy. Having spent years at Monticello while construction was going on, he should have felt at home in an unfinished house, but he complained of the loneliness of this one. Writing Martha in 1811 when kept indoors by rain, he said that for days he had seen only servants and felt like a state prisoner.[22]

Jeff Randolph often accompanied him on visits to Bedford County and as construction proceeded, workmen were brought from Monticello. In

[19] TJ to Francis, May 21, 1816 (*Family Letters*, pp. 414–415).

[20] TJ to JWE, Mar. 30, 1816 (LC).

[21] Francis was at school in Richmond one year and at Georgetown College another, while his father was in the U.S. Senate. The delay in the opening of Central College prevented his attending that institution, and he was back at the New London Academy for a time. Correspondence between TJ and Francis is in *Family Letters*. Much correspondence between TJ and JWE is in Cuthbert, "Poplar Forest," and in "Some Family Letters of Thomas Jefferson," ed. by W. M. Cary, *Scribner's Magazine*, XXXVI (Nov., 1904), 573–586.

[22] TJ to Martha, Feb. 24, 1811 (*Family Letters*, p. 400).

the late summer of 1815, the report spread among the local residents that he was preparing a place for Napoleon, who had recently been defeated at Waterloo.[23] A year later he was accompanied by Martha and two of her daughters (Virginia and Mary). She could rarely be spared from Monticello, but a pattern had been set. Thereafter, he customarily brought a couple of his granddaughters with him, and by this time the house at Poplar Forest may be said to have become a home.

He was not free from all care at this place. He was confronted with marketing problems and had to meet crises that resulted from the excesses of Mother Nature. In the spring of 1816, six months after he spoke so confidently of his prospects to John W. Eppes, he wrote Albert Gallatin in France that Americans had never before experienced such a spell of cold and drought.[24] In what came to be known as the year without a summer Virginia fared somewhat better than her northern sisters, but the crop of wheat and tobacco at Poplar Forest, on which he relied so much for cash, fell far below expectations. Not until 1821 did he turn over such problems to his eldest grandson, but in the meantime the octagonal house in Bedford County served as a sanctuary where he could brush off his mundane troubles more easily than at Monticello and was subject to no such interruptions by guests and visitors as he suffered there.

The spacious house in Albemarle County was the rallying point for a large family connection. Long and frequent visits by relatives were customary in that society, but the recognized head of this clan had more than his share of them. His granddaughter Ellen reported two extreme cases of the abuse of his generous hospitality. One of her aunts was said to have made annual visits of from six to eight weeks to Monticello with children and horses, until the last year of Jefferson's life. Ultimately she had six children, but it is uncertain whether they were ever all there at the same time. Another aunt, on arriving with two of her own and two stepchildren from Spain, where her husband was in the consular service, made one visit of ten months and another of six. During the first of these she bore a child.[25]

Jefferson's regimen may have been little affected by relatives who stayed too long. His own quarters at Monticello were sacrosanct, and the guest rooms on the first floor appear to have been reserved for such

[23] TJ to Martha, Aug. 31, 1815 (*ibid.*, p. 410).

[24] TJ to Gallatin, Sept. 8, 1816 (Ford, X, 64).

[25] Ellen Randolph Coolidge to H. S. Randall, Feb. 13, 1856 (Letter Book, pp. 47–49, Coolidge Papers, UVA), referring to her Aunt Cary (Virginia Randolph) and her Aunt Hackley (Harriet Randolph). Both were younger sisters of T. M. Randolph who were long dependent on him. Their presumption may seem somewhat less for that reason. Ellen dates the second episode in 1810–1811.

guests as the Abbé Correa, James Madison, and the Visitors of Central College. When not out of doors the numerous children were upstairs. He was probably much more disturbed by what his granddaughter called "disagreeable intrusions." Just when they became embarrassingly frequent is uncertain, but presumably this was after the coming of peace in 1815. A succession of vehicles filled with inquisitive people gained the top of the little mountain while Martha was at Poplar Forest with her father in September, 1816. Ellen, who had been left in charge of the establishment, described the visitors vividly, if not always charitably, in a letter to her mother.[26] Many of them were fashionably dressed and bore letters of introduction, but they were motivated chiefly by curiosity and came at all hours. Ellen was shocked by the bad manners of some of them and rejoiced that her grandfather was spared these "indelicate and improper visits."

On her first visit to Poplar Forest, a few weeks later, Ellen observed that her grandfather received calls from gentlemen of the neighborhood, but these appear to have been less numerous than those she and her sister Cornelia had from the local ladies. (She described the latter much more fully to her mother, at any rate.) As time went on, Jefferson had occasional house guests, but this much less commodious house continued to be a more private place than Monticello.[27]

The journey between the mansion in Albemarle County and the retreat in Bedford, which the Randolph girls made so often with their grandfather, usually took three days. The distance, as measured by an odometer attached to a wheel of his carriage, was ninety-three miles. Jefferson had acquired an improved instrument during his second term as President. It recorded fractions of a mile in what he called dimes and cents, ringing a bell when it reached the hundred mark. He approved of this application of the decimal system and appears to have found the sound encouraging on what must have often been a tedious journey.[28] The route he habitually took was perhaps twenty miles longer than that by the Old Lynchburg Road (from Charlottesville) but was less steeply

26 Sept. 27, 1816 (UVA).

27 Details of life at Poplar Forest can be gleaned from the contemporary letters of the girls, beginning with Ellen's to her mother in Nov., 1816 (UVA), and Cornelia's to her sister Virginia, Oct. 25, 1816 (Trist, UNC). TJ's letters to Martha (*Family Letters*) are much less gossipy. Years later Ellen gave a reminiscent account to H. S. Randall, as in her letter of Feb. 18, 1856 (Randall, III, 342–344). Omitted sections are in her Letter Book, p. 51 (UVA).

28 For a good general account of the odometer and TJ's experience with it, see Edwin T. Martin, *Thomas Jefferson: Scientist* (1952), pp. 90–93. Among the tables of mileage drawn up by TJ is one covering the route from Monticello to Poplar Forest with the distances between intermediate points (UVA).

graded and better adapted to the vehicular traffic and horsepower of his era.

In his seventies he usually made the trip in a carriage that had been built by his own artisans at Monticello and was listed as a landau. Vehicles of this style had a hood that rolled backward and forward, and two seats facing each other. According to Edmund Bacon, Jefferson's carriage was drawn by four horses, each pair being guided by a postilion. Burwell, the principal servant, rode behind or beside the carriage on a fifth horse.[29] This equipage was followed at a distance by a wagon or cart, drawn by mules and containing baggage and supplies.

Of the two nights on the road, the first was usually spent at Warren, the home of Wilson Cary Nicholas, on the James. During the first day's journey, therefore, they rolled through the lovely countryside of Albemarle. After crossing the river by ferry, they proceeded through the less hilly county of Buckingham, past the site where Appomattox Courthouse was afterwards to stand, through Campbell Courthouse, and thence by one or the other of alternate routes south of Lynchburg. For meals and lodging they stopped at taverns, where Jefferson was a familiar figure and is said to have been called "the Squire." Sometimes (most likely on the second day) they had a cold meal by the roadside. On these occasions Grandpapa is said to have sliced the ham and chicken and to have poured out the wine and water in proper mixture.[30]

The octagonal house at which they arrived was one story high in front, and, because of the slope of the ground, two stories high in the rear, where a veranda overlooked a terrace. Jefferson never completed the lower floor, and all the bedrooms were not finished when his granddaughters first arrived. Eventually the house became very comfortable, by all accounts, and it attained a certain elegance, but its furnishings were unpretentious.

Life here doubtless varied somewhat as the granddaughters themselves did, but it was marked by the regularity which was so characteristic of its owner. On their first visit Ellen and Cornelia resumed the studies they had been carrying on at Monticello. Jefferson himself usually spent the morning with his polygraph and papers in the living room, from which French doors opened on the veranda. As at Monticello, he rode about his farms before dinner, which was at three. After that he sometimes took a nap. He walked with his granddaughters in the twilight, chatted with them over the teacups, and kept company with some favorite author before retiring.

[29] Bacon's undated account is in Pierson, pp. 56–59. He names five horses, saying that they were trained for riding as well as carriage use.

[30] General accounts of these journeys by Ellen and Virginia can be conveniently seen in Randall, III, 342–344. The route is indicated on the map, p. 13, above.

* * *

In a note to Martha late in the summer of 1817, Jefferson said that he had nothing to report from Poplar Forest since the sun, moon, and stars moved as they did at Monticello, and rains fell at the two places in the same way. In fact, he had just returned from an expedition to Natural Bridge, which his granddaughters Ellen and Cornelia had found very exciting, and the account of which he left to them.[31]

According to Ellen, the expedition was a chapter of accidents. One that occurred on the first day was described in some detail by Cornelia to her sister Virginia. A wheel horse, Bremo by name, fell halfway through a rotten bridge. Fortunately, no serious injury was incurred, and, after the bewildered Bremo had been extricated, the party proceeded to a log cabin in a clearing at the foot of the mountain. Here they left the carriage and crossed the Blue Ridge on horseback. The single room of the cabin housed an entire family — three generations to be exact. In Cornelia's eyes they were shockingly uncivilized. On this trip these two well-bred girls were exposed to a ruder society, as well as to wilder scenery than anything they were accustomed to and felt that they were in another world. Their grandfather, who was entitled Colonel by one of the uncouth old men in the log cabin, may have had it in mind to broaden their social as well as their physical horizon.

The rest of the journey was less fully reported than the first day, but both girls described the circumstances as unfavorable. Cornelia raved over the scenery but described their lodging house as "polluted." The sheets on the bed were so dirty that she slept on top of the covers. On crossing the Blue Ridge and coming into cooler air, Ellen caught a cold which settled upon her face, causing her such pain that she spent most of the night walking around the room. Their grandfather said he had a good room, but, according to Cornelia, he shared it with two or three other men. On her return, Ellen reported to her mother the "wonder and delight" she experienced when she caught sight of Natural Bridge. Echoing her grandfather, she described it as "the most sublime of Nature's works." The girls shared their grandfather's admiration for this scenic wonder, but they were less appreciative of the fierce independence of the American frontiersmen. No doubt they picked up their books with some relief on returning to the regimen at Poplar Forest.

Writing to Martha a few weeks after they got back, Jefferson said that Ellen and Cornelia were the "severest students" he ever met with; they emerged from their room only to come to meals.[32] He gladly discussed

[31] TJ to Martha, Aug. 18, 1817 (*Family Letters*, p. 418). Cornelia to Virginia Randolph, Aug. 17, 19, 30, 1817 (Trist Papers, UNC), and Ellen to her mother, Aug. 18 (UVA).

[32] TJ to Martha, Aug. 31, 1817 (*Family Letters*, p. 419).

View at Poplar Forest
(Library of Congress, Historic American Buildings Survey)

their studies and reading with them but did not try to be their mentor, as in the case of their cousin Francis Eppes. In fact, he denied ever having made female education a subject of "systematic consideration." In reply to an inquirer, he said he had thought little about it except in connection with his own daughters.[33] He had caused them to receive a "solid education" because they, as members of a rural society, would probably have to teach their daughters and might even have to educate their sons. This explanation, besides being unsatisfactory to later feminists, did less than justice to his concern for his motherless girls. He undoubtedly wanted them to exercise their intelligence and acquire knowledge for their own sakes and not merely for the benefit of their progeny.

With the aid of Martha and one of her daughters (presumably Ellen), Jefferson drew up a list of books upon which they had based their course of reading.[34] This impressive list actually differs little from those he so often compiled for the benefit of male youths. He made one apparent concession to femininity by excluding works of technology, and presumably he did not expect young ladies to venture far into mathematics and natural philosophy. Many of the titles are in French, which he regarded as basic in all modern education and which Martha was especially competent to teach. Ancient classics are listed here in English translation. He may not have expected his granddaughters to read Homer and Horace for pleasure in the original, but Ellen and Cornelia studied Latin and Greek assiduously. The reading list ranged through the whole of modern English and French literature, but, as we have previously observed, Jefferson was highly critical of contemporary fiction and warned his granddaughters against addiction to it.[35] He recommended many books of history, including works on their own state.

Jefferson was less didactic toward his granddaughters than he had been toward his daughters before their marriages, and less moralistic than to his grandsons. He held that in feminine education some attention should be paid to "the ornaments . . . and the amusements of life." He spoke particularly of dancing, drawing, and music. The first he regarded as a necessary accomplishment, though of short use; he approved of the French rule that no lady should dance after marriage. Drawing he described as "an innocent and engaging amusement, often useful." Cornelia

[33] TJ to Nathaniel Burwell, Mar. 14, 1818 (Ford, X, 104–106), enclosing a list of readings.

[34] This list in his own writing is attached to his letter of Mar. 14, 1818, to Nathaniel Burwell (LC) but does not appear in the printed version of this letter in Ford and L. & B. It contains eighty-three titles, representing a considerably larger number of volumes. Multi-volume works, such as those of Shakespeare, are designated by a single title.

[35] See above, p. 188.

Cornelia Jefferson Randolph
Terra cotta bust by William John Coffee, ca. 1820. (Courtesy of Monticello/Thomas Jefferson Foundation, Inc.)

pursued this pleasing occupation at Poplar Forest, though at the outset her strict schedule permitted her to do so only on Sunday.[36] In due course she made architectural drawings for her grandfather, who undoubtedly recognized her talent and encouraged it. Music, which was a lifelong delight to Jefferson, was described by him as invaluable to anyone who had an ear for it. By this time the musical activity of this former violinist appears to have been largely confined to humming, but his daughter shared his taste, as did at least two of his older granddaughters — Ellen and, most particularly, Virginia. He provided them with musical scores along with books and urged them to practice as well as to study.

For all his emphasis on industry and good conduct Jefferson wanted his granddaughters to enjoy themselves, and he loved to give them presents. His gifts were numerous and some of them had considerable intrinsic value. He gave Virginia a guitar that cost $30, and to Ellen's delight presented her with an elegant watch that cost $135. His gifts were notable for their appropriateness and timing. Years after his death Ellen wrote: "Our grandfather seemed to read our hearts, to see our invisible wishes, to be our good genius, to wave the fairy wand, to brighten our young lives by his goodness and his gifts."[37] These presents may have been somewhat embarrassing to Thomas Mann Randolph, who was in no position to do as much and who could hardly have failed to perceive that his father-in-law was possessive as well as generous. In any event, the girls found their grandfather's kindness and thoughtfulness invincible. He respected them as persons, talking with them about their affairs, honoring their youthful opinions. Ellen, who seems to have accompanied him most often to Poplar Forest and may have talked with him more than any of her sisters, wrote thus in her own middle age: "Such was the influence of his affectionate, cheerful temper, that his grandchildren were as much at their ease with him, as if they had not loved and honored and revered him more than any other earthly being."[38]

iii

By the time the legislature had determined the site of the University of Virginia the chief advocate of that location was a great-grandfather several times over. He had gained the distinction in the first place through Anne Cary, the eldest and most ill-fated of Martha's children.

[36] Cornelia to Virginia, Aug. 30, 1817 (Trist, UNC).
[37] Randall, III, 349.
[38] *Ibid.*, 343.

She and her several small children were now living precariously at Carlton on the west side of Monticello Mountain with her handsome alcoholic husband, Charles Bankhead. Her brother Jeff and his wife Jane had recently presented to the world a third daughter. After they left their original quarters in the dome room they occupied a farmhouse across the Rivanna, but Jefferson did not like for his indispensable grandson to be that inaccessible. Therefore, as he reported to a family connection on the last day of January, 1819, a house was being prepared for Jeff and his family at Tufton, which was below the Rivanna and only a mile away.[39]

In Charlottesville a day later Jeff and his brother-in-law, Charles Bankhead, engaged in a street fight in which blood flowed freely and Jeff was seriously wounded. Charles is said to have been a man of violent temper even when sober, and he was unquestionably abusive and dangerous when in a drunken state. Long years later Ellen stated that he had committed the unpardonable offense of striking Burwell. That trusted servant was reported to have refused to turn over the keys of the wine closet at Monticello. Another story or possible variant of this one is that Charles mistook Thomas Mann Randolph for Burwell, cursed him, and was promptly felled by a poker. In later life Jeff Randolph held that story to have been exaggerated. This powerful young man usually kept himself under control, but he is said to have been infuriated by an abusive letter that his wife had received from Bankhead.[40]

The details of the encounter in Charlottesville on court day (February 1, 1819) are confused and incomplete, but both men seem to have anticipated something of the sort. Jeff was carrying a riding whip and Charles was armed with several knives. They met in front of Leitch's store and may be presumed to have exchanged hot words. Whether the flourishing of the whip or the brandishing of the knife came first in point of time is uncertain, and they may have been virtually simultaneous. When backing away from the onrushing blade, Jeff tripped and fell. Doubling up his whip, he gave Charles a heavy blow across the face with the butt. His assailant grappled with him on the ground, stabbing him in the hip and left arm. Jeff bled profusely and was carried into the store in a seriously weakened state. Fortunately, several doctors quickly appeared and in due course Charles's face was also attended to. He was promptly brought before court and required to post bail.

Jefferson had been in town earlier in the day but had returned to

[39] TJ to John Patterson, Jan. 31, 1818 (LC). See map, above, p. 254.

[40] Ellen to H. S. Randall, Mar. 13, 1856 (Letter Book, p. 57, UVA); Bacon, in Pierson, p. 94; Gaines, p. 108; Joseph C. Vance, "Knives, Whips and Randolph on the Court House Law," *Magazine of Albermarle County History*, XV (1955–1956), 28–29.

Monticello, and there he received the news after sunset. Ordering his horse, he rode the four miles to Charlottesville in the darkness. He is said to have wept at his grandson's bedside. He sent a litter with eight servants to take the wounded man to Monticello, but Jeff remained in the store a couple of days and then was removed to the home of Alexander Garrett. For a time there was doubt about whether he would regain the use of his arm. In a few weeks he was again on horseback, but he was to bear the scars from this encounter to the end of his life.

Several days after the affair Bankhead wrote a letter to Jefferson, whom he claimed to have always venerated. He asserted that his opponent had been the aggressor and that he himself had acted only to avoid being horse-whipped.[41] He did not submit his case to the judgment of his fellows. He failed to appear on his recognizance, having left the county, and the general assumption was that he would not return lest he be apprehended. He was never again to imperil his brother-in-law but was an ever-present danger to his wife. As Jefferson told Wilson Cary Nicholas, she was so attached to her husband that she could not be persuaded to leave him and live at Monticello.[42] In Jefferson's opinion the proper place for Bankhead was the penitentiary — for the safety of others and his own reformation. He observed, however, that the execution of the law in their society was so lenient that citizens were "left in a state of nature to save their own lives" by taking those of others. He cast no blame on his grandson, but this champion of human liberty had no sympathy with the tolerance of violence among his countrymen in that age.

[41] Bankhead to TJ, received Feb. 7, 1819 (LC).

[42] TJ to W. C. Nicholas, Mar. 8, 1819, replying to a letter of Feb. 28 (both LC). By this time, if not earlier, TJ must have concluded that she was not obligated to remain with her husband. See above, ch. XI, pp. 159–160.

XXI

The Harassments of Debt

1817-1822

THE sale of his library to Congress enabled Jefferson to reduce his burden of debt by more than half.[1] He was still heavily obligated, however, and his hopes for relief depended ultimately on his plantations. At the time of the coming of peace in 1815 these were not in good condition, but by turning over the management of his Albemarle farms to Jeff Randolph, and by hiring a new overseer, Joel Yancey, for his Bedford estates, he thought he would improve his prospects.[2] Still he was at the mercy of the weather. Produce prices rose extraordinarily during the next two years, but his crops suffered from severe drought, and he was obliged to purchase corn at an excessive price to feed his slaves. In the spring of 1817 one of his mules, weakened by hunger, died on the way from Poplar Forest to Monticello, and, according to his own account, his animals in Albemarle were on the verge of starvation because of the lack of forage.[3]

Early in the year Jefferson's financial difficulties had been compounded by the unfavorable outcome of an arbitration. This arose from his purchase of a portion of the Milton lands from the heirs of Bennett Henderson. The sale of fields belonging to heirs who were under age at the time had been ruled invalid, and Jefferson was ordered to make immediate payment of close to $800 for rent. To retain the fields he had to repurchase them for $1600. Craven Peyton, who had acted for him in this business, offered him an emergency loan, and a couple of months

[1] For details, see above, ch. XII, p. 181.

[2] TJ to William P. Newby, June 21, 1815 (LC).

[3] TJ to Martha Jefferson Randolph, Aug. 31, 1815 (*Family Letters*, p. 410); TJ to Patrick Gibson, Nov. 22, 1816 (LC); TJ to Joel Yancey, Mar. 19, 1817 (MHS); TJ to Patrick Gibson, Apr. 17, 1817 (MHS).

later Jefferson reported he would be able to cover that amount by the sale of a less desirably located parcel of land.[4]

Unfortunately, this did not end his need for cash. A few days after his seventy-fourth birthday he wrote Patrick Gibson, his agent in Richmond, that unless a bank loan could be procured he would be "much distressed." It was required for a promised payment on a debt of long standing. This was to the house of Van Staphorst in Amsterdam, now represented by Leroy and Bayard of New York. As contracted in the 1790's, it was for approximately $2000; but, when refinanced in 1816, it amounted with interest to more than $6000.[5] This account provides a striking example of the way Jefferson was eaten up by interest, and he was specially embarrassed because he had so long neglected it. He had agreed to pay it off in three annual installments to begin in May, 1817.

In due course the Bank of Virginia discounted a sixty-day note, signed by Jefferson and endorsed by Gibson. Much to the relief of the former, the promised payment to Leroy and Bayard was made, although it was slightly delayed. He also had to pay them interest, as he did to the bank. Therefore, he really needed more money than he had borrowed.[6] Furthermore, he learned that this note could not be renewed. Following Gibson's advice, he approached Wilson Cary Nicholas, president of the newly opened Richmond branch of the Bank of the United States, and through him secured a loan of $3000 from that institution with assurances that it would be renewed.[7]

When explaining the Van Staphorst debt somewhat apologetically to Gibson, Jefferson said that he could have made ends meet that year but for the necessary payment to Leroy and Bayard on that old account.[8] In adverse circumstances he was pursuing the makeshift policy of meeting an inescapable obligation by assuming another which promised to be less pressing. He actually increased his total indebtedness by his transactions with banks during the spring and summer. Nonetheless, with undiminished generosity he subscribed $1000 to Central College at the first meet-

[4] TJ to Craven Peyton, Feb. 6, Apr. 15, 1817 (MHS). Because of other demands he actually had to defer payment to Peyton. On the Milton lands, see Appendix II, Section A.

[5] TJ to Patrick Gibson, Apr. 17, 26, 1817 (MHS).

[6] Account Book, May 24, 25, 1817, noting renewal of old loan and procurement of new one. TJ to Leroy & Bayard, May 25, 1817 (LC). The payment was for $2083 with interest, totaling $2260.

[7] TJ to W. C. Nicholas, June 10, 1817 (LC); Nicholas to TJ, June 16 (LC). Account Book entry of July 2, 1817, noting renewal of "standing" note of $2000 at the Bank of Virginia, and new loan of $3000 from the Bank of the U.S.

[8] TJ to Gibson, Apr. 26, 1817 (MHS). He did not refer to his even older mercantile debt to James Lyle, on which interest continued to accumulate. Nor did he mention the Mazzei debt, on which in fact he did pay the interest. He was scrupulous abut this and cherished the hope of reducing the principal the next year. See Appendix II, Section B.

ing of the Board of Visitors. He appears to have been his usual cheerful self when visiting Natural Bridge in August with his granddaughters, and when witnessing the laying of the cornerstone of the first pavilion of his academical village in October.

During the fall of 1817 and the ensuing winter, while he was chiefly occupied with educational matters, his notes were duly renewed. Despite the complete failure of his wheat crop in Bedford caused by the Hessian fly, he managed to pay the interest, but he saw clearly that the income from his farms would not enable him to make the second annual payment to Leroy and Bayard in May. Well in advance of that date, he turned again to Wilson Cary Nicholas.[9] Through the influence of this friend he got a second loan of $3000 from the Bank of the United States. Driven by necessity, he continued the costly policy of paying one debt by incurring a greater. Also, he became obligated further to Nicholas, who of his own accord endorsed the note.[10]

A few weeks later Nicholas asked his *quid pro quo*, though he did not put it just that way. While at Poplar Forest on the last day of April, Jefferson received the request that he endorse two of that helpful friend's notes, each for $10,000.[11] He was told that his endorsement would be needed for a year at the longest, and that Nicholas's estate was worth at least $350,000. Though he was urged not to comply with the request if in any doubt, he was actually confronted with the notes and placed in an exceedingly difficult situation. Besides being president of the bank, Nicholas, as the father-in-law of Jeff Randolph, was virtually a member of the family whose trustworthiness could hardly be questioned.

Nicholas was obviously engaged in financial transactions of considerable magnitude, but he tried to minimize the significance of his request. Thus he said: "You will do me the justice to believe that this request would not be made but under the most entire confidence that you can never suffer the slightest inconvenience from complying with it." In his prompt reply Jefferson said that the only possible reason for hesitation on his part was his desire "to leave as clear a state of things as possible" at the close of his life. This, however, must yield to the desire to render a service to Nicholas.[12] Thomas Mann Randolph, who suffered much from endorsing notes for his friends, said afterwards that his father-in-law had made it a rule not to do so. With the benefit of hindsight Jefferson himself said that he was reluctant in this instance.[13] That debt-

[9] TJ to W. C. Nicholas, Mar. 26, 1818 (LC).

[10] W. C. Nicholas to TJ, Mar. 30, 1818 (LC).

[11] Nicholas to TJ, Apr. 19, 1818, received Apr. 30 (LC).

[12] TJ to Nicholas, May 1, 1818 (LC).

[13] TMR to Nicholas Trist, Aug. 15, 1819 (Trist Papers, LC); TJ to Patrick Gibson, Aug. 11, 1819 (MHS).

ridden gentleman may have been more hesitant than he seemed, but apparently he saw no choice but to accept Nicholas's assurances at face value.

As spring passed into summer he viewed his own prospects with increased confidence. The second payment to Leroy and Bayard was made in May; his notes at the banks were renewed without question in June; and in midsummer he wrote hopefully to Gibson about his wheat.[14] The crop in Bedford would be less than mediocre, he said, but that in Albemarle would be good. If prices were favorable, he believed he could make the third and final payment to the New York firm in the next year from the proceeds of his farms and could then begin to pay off his debts to the banks. He was short of cash, however. In anticipation of his trip to Rockfish Gap, where the commission charged with recommending a site for the University of Virginia was to meet on August 1, he borrowed $100 from James Leitch, the Charlottesville merchant with whom he was now doing considerable business.[15]

He made this journey in the company of James Madison according to plan, but just before they set out he got news from Patrick Gibson that was as startling as it was unexpected. It was contained in a printed notice from the Bank of the United States, which announced that after the first Wednesday in August a curtailment of twelve and a half per cent would be required on all notes when presented for renewal. Gibson anticipated that the requirement would cause much distress in the state, and in fact it marked the beginning of the policy of restricting credit, after a period of excess, which brought on the panic of 1819. The message of the moment was that a note of Jefferson's for $3000 could be renewed for only $2625.[16] In the letter he wrote to Gibson just before setting out with Madison, he said: "That notification is really like a clap of thunder to me, for God knows I have no means in this world of raising money on so sudden a call." All he could do in these distressing circumstances was to sign a blank note and send it to Jeff Randolph for endorsement and transmission, along with the request that Gibson do the best he could for him.[17] Since he went to Staunton and Warm Springs after the meeting at Rockfish Gap, he had no communication with Gibson for more than six weeks. During that period he appears to have kept his financial troubles entirely to himself. They do not seem to have diminished his effectiveness as a commissioner and could not be blamed for the boils with which he was afflicted at Warm Springs, but they must have contributed to his unhappiness on that unfortunate visit.

[14] Account Book, May 12, June 11, 1818; TJ to Gibson, July 20, 1818 (LC).

[15] TJ to James Leitch, July 28, 1818 (LC).

[16] Gibson to TJ, July 27, 1818, received July 30 (MHS).

[17] TJ to Gibson, July 30, 1818 (MHS).

On returning to Monticello he wrote Gibson before he was able to sit up, saying that his grandson had sent fifty barrels of flour in August and would send that many more. However, Jefferson was troubled by the low level of the river, which made shipping uncertain.[18] The price of flour fell sharply between shipments, signaling the decline which was to accentuate the woes of debt-ridden farmers. The only good news from Richmond was that Jefferson's two notes at the Bank of the United States could be renewed in their original amount. Gibson said he would curtail one of his own to meet the requirement.

At this time Jefferson was saying that his health was shattered. Nicholas, writing from Warren, expressed sympathy for that gentleman in his continued indisposition. Along with his good wishes he sent two notes to be endorsed, since his own loan of $20,000 had to be renewed.[19] Being unable to resume his daily ride until nearly the end of the year, Jefferson had more time than usual to reflect on his precarious financial situation and the economic state of the country. He seemed more concerned about the latter than the former and in fact faced no immediate crisis in the autumn of 1818. He had been well treated by the lords of finance in Richmond and had no personal complaint against them. He perceived the gathering storm, however, and blamed it chiefly on the banking system.

ii

Jefferson was largely responsible for the appearance, late in 1818, of *A Treatise on Political Economy* by Destutt de Tracy. He had received the manuscript of this work from its author in 1812, after he had caused Tracy's commentary on Montesquieu to be published, and he had been occupied with it intermittently during later years.[20] His efforts in connection with this work provide an admirable illustration of his industry, zeal, and patience as a promoter of learning. He conducted protracted and frustrating negotiations with printers and spent about five hours a day for a period of two or three months revising the translation and providing an introduction.[21] Afterwards he corrected the proof.

He now had a special reason for wanting to make available this work on political economy. To the author he said: "There is no branch of science on which information is more wanted here, and, under the want

[18] TJ to Gibson, Sept. 10, 1818 (MHS).

[19] Gibson to TJ, Sept. 14, 1818 (MHS); Nicholas to TJ, Sept. 14, (LC).

[20] The best account of TJ's role in publishing this book and much correspondence relating to it is in Gilbert Chinard, *Jefferson et les Idéologues*, pp. 97–188. On the *Commentary on Montesquieu*, see above, ch. XIV.

[21] TJ to Tracy, Aug. 3, 1816, in Chinard, *Idéologues*, pp. 159–161.

of which, we are suffering more."[22] These words were written before the national economy plunged sharply downward. Apart from the effects of drought, the chief financial ills the country was then enduring were occasioned by inflation. The speculative boom that had marked the post-war period had not yet ended, though Jefferson expected the bubble to burst. He was thoroughly unsympathetic to this speculation and blamed it mostly on the money lenders.

He originally stipulated that his name should not appear in print as the sponsor of Tracy's work.[23] By the fall of 1818, the financial situation of the country had worsened, and for that reason or some other he changed his mind. For publication in the book he wrote a letter that acknowledged his connection with it. He said: "The merit of this work will, I hope, place it in the hands of every reader in our country. By diffusing sound principles of political economy it will protect the public industry from the parasite institutions now consuming it."[24] By the "public industry" he meant the aggregate of the labors of private individuals. He was more explicit in a letter to Albert Gallatin, then in France as American minister, to whom he sent a copy of the book for transmission to Tracy. Speaking of the "parasite institutions" of banks to the former Secretary of the Treasury, he said: "The flood with which they are deluging us of nominal money has placed us completely without any certain measure of value, and by interpolating a false measure, is deceiving and ruining multitudes of our citizens."[25] The "nominal money" to which Jefferson referred consisted of the notes, issued by banks, which fulfilled the role of a paper currency at this time in American history. These were promissory notes which had been emitted to amounts far beyond the specie in the vaults necessary to redeem them. Jefferson condemned not only this practice but the theory behind it.[26]

During his long period of public service, Jefferson had been a close observer of financial affairs at home and abroad. Furthermore, he was familiar with the literature of the young science of political economy. He paid his respects to Adam Smith and Jean Baptiste Say in the introduction he wrote to Destutt de Tracy's treatise.[27] That work, as described by him there and elsewhere, was essentially a condensation of

[22] TJ to Tracy, May 15, 1817 (*ibid.*, pp. 170–171).

[23] TJ to Joseph Milligan, Apr. 6, 1816 (*ibid.*, p. 145).

[24] TJ to Milligan, Oct. 25, 1818 (L. & B., XIX, 263).

[25] TJ to Gallatin, Nov. 24, 1818 (Ford, X, 116).

[26] This topic is discussed in ch. X, above. Bray Hammond in *Banks and Politics in America* provides an excellent account of the banking practices which so disturbed TJ. While Hammond agrees that they were unsound, his analysis of the situation is different from TJ's.

[27] Called the "Prospectus," pp. iii–vii. The complete treatise is given in facsimile in John M. Dorsey, *Psychology of Political Science* (1973).

writings of his predecessors. It was commended by Jefferson chiefly on the grounds of brevity and lucidity. He referred to it as a manual, as an elementary textbook by means of which the leaders of the future could receive economic enlightenment.[28] Of more immediate significance was the treatment of money and banking. Jefferson especially approved of this. Tracy held that there was no real money but gold and silver, that depreciation of the currency was a form of theft, and that the institution of banking was attended with grave dangers.

John Adams was in full agreement with these views. The New Englander wrote his friend at Monticello that this book was "a magazine of gunpowder under all our mercantile institutions." He seems to have been as unsympathetic to postwar economic speculation as his agricultural friend in Virginia was. He attributed his own unpopularity in no small part to his "heretical" opposition to banks. Actually, these were more conservatively conducted in New England than in the South and West. A better designation than heretic can be found for him and Jefferson; in that age these two religious liberals could have been aptly described as economic fundamentalists.[29]

About six months after Tracy's treatise appeared, its sponsor expressed himself to the American minister in Great Britain with respect to the rapidly deteriorating economic situation. To Richard Rush, son of his old friend Benjamin, he said: "The enormous abuses of the banking system are not only prostrating our commerce, but producing a revolution of property, which without more wisdom than we possess, will be much greater than were produced by the Revolutionary paper. That too had the merit of purchasing our liberties, while the present trash has only furnished aliment to usurers and swindlers."[30] He asserted that the banks were doing business with capital that was three-fourths fictitious, and that they had loaned this to speculative operations from which there would be inevitable losses. In his opinion these losses would have to be made up at the expense of the holders of real property.

He made no reference here to the speculation in western lands, which was rampant after the War of 1812. He himself was not involved in this and had no sympathy with it or any other form of gambling. It is now

[28] TJ to Tracy, Dec. 26, 1820 (Ford, X, 174). The book achieved no such currency and popularity as TJ had hoped for. Despite his recommendation of it, the works of Adam Smith and Say were the first textbooks in political economy at the University of Virginia, and Say's *Treatise* was the most popular in the South until the Civil War. Tipton R. Snavely, *George Tucker as Political Economist* (1964), pp. 15, 23.

[29] Their fascinating correspondence regarding Tracy's book is in *A.-J. Letters*, II, 491–492, 531–540. Adams was particularly pleased with Tracy's ch. 6, "Of Money." With his consent TJ sent his letter of Mar. 2, 1819, to the publisher for purposes of promotion. TJ to Joseph Milligan, Apr. 13, 1819 (LC).

[30] June 22, 1819 (Ford, X, 133–134).

clear, however, that he had not been sufficiently cautious in the conduct of his own affairs. He was not responsible for drought or flood, but in constructing a costly milldam and canal, in purchasing the Henderson lands, and in his building operations at Monticello and Poplar Forest, he had over-reached himself. He made no mention of his personal difficulties in this letter to Rush. It would have been uncharacteristic of him to do so, but he must have been thinking of himself as well as of his country neighbors when he described the basic problem as he saw it. This was to find a way for the owners of real property "to back out of their entanglements by degrees." He feared that this would not happen because of the lack of knowledge of political economy. The eyes of the citizens were not yet open to the true cause of their troubles — the banking system.

iii

In the interval between the publication of Tracy's treatise and the writing of Jefferson's despondent letter to Richard Rush, his own financial troubles multiplied. In the first month of 1819 he learned that the General Assembly had approved the recommendation of the Rockfish Gap Commission regarding the location of the University of Virginia. Later news from Richmond was much less pleasing, and the year turned out to be the gloomiest in his financial history thus far.

In February he was informed by Patrick Gibson that additional curtailments of his bank loans would be required and that the price of flour had fallen further.[31] Both of these items of news were most unwelcome, but, of the two, the latter should have been the more alarming. The worldwide decline in the market price of wheat and tobacco upset Jefferson's calculations, which were too sanguine in the first place and imperiled his financial structure at its base. While this depression lasted he would have a hard time meeting current expenses, much less reducing the old debt. He gained the consent of Leroy and Bayard to the postponement till 1820 of the third and final payment to them on the understanding that he would pay the interest when due in May.[32] Because of his reduced income from sales of produce and payments of interest on bank loans, he fell into serious arrears in his account with Gibson. He told that patient friend and agent that he was resolved to sell lands sufficient to pay off all his debts, and he went to considerable pains to make known his willingness to sell.[33] Unfortunately, he found that land

[31] Gibson to TJ, Feb. 18, 1819 (MHS).
[32] TJ to Leroy & Bayard, Feb. 21, 1819; Leroy & Bayard to TJ, Feb. 27 (LC).
[33] TJ to Gibson, Feb. 22, 1819; to Joel Yancey, Feb. 22, 1819 (MHS).

prices had plummeted along with those of produce, and that there was little disposition to buy land at any price.[34]

He seems to have had no doubt that his capital assets would enable him to meet his difficulties when the storm abated, but he could not realize on them at the moment. The *modus vivendi* at which he arrived in these desperate circumstances was to borrow more money. His ability to do so at a time of enforced reduction of bank loans is surprising. It is ironical that this severe critic of banks should have had such recourse to them, but there was nowhere else to go for cash. His credit in his own country was owing in part, no doubt, to the high esteem in which his character was held, and in part perhaps to ignorance of his precarious financial situation. It was also due in no small degree to the friendly interest of Wilson Cary Nicholas.

Jefferson saw no choice but to accept the suggestion of this helpful man that he get around the requirement of curtailment at one bank by taking out a loan at another. This loan had to cover the deficit in his account with Gibson and other inescapable obligations. As a result of these maneuvers, Jefferson had five loans in three Richmond banks in midsummer. The most recent was for $3000 at the Farmers Bank, of which Philip Norborne Nicholas, brother of Wilson Cary, was president. The note was endorsed by the latter. In the course of the year Jefferson's debt to the banks had increased by approximately that amount.[35] He had paid the interest on the debt to Philip Mazzei's heirs, as well as to Leroy and Bayard, and the second installment of his subscription to the University of Virginia. However, he was far behind in his account with James Leitch, the merchant in Charlottesville, and was still obligated to others.

His situation was by no means unusual. Debt was the rule rather than the exception in this society, and Gibson said that since he had been in business there had never been such a serious lack of money.[36] Shortage of cash was no new experience for Jefferson, but we may doubt if this landholder had ever been more painfully conscious of it than now. "To owe what I cannot pay is a constant torment," he said.[37] In a letter he got a few days later, Wilson Cary Nicholas observed that no man could say what should be done to alleviate the woes of the country.[38] Along with this discouraging observation he sent two fresh notes of his own for $10,000. Jefferson endorsed these without complaint. A few weeks later he wrote Nicholas that "the sudden suspension of all demand for either

[34] TJ to Gibson, Apr. 22, 1819 (MHS).

[35] Gibson reported the five loans, totaling $10,950, in a letter to June 10, 1819 (MHS).

[36] Gibson to TJ, May 8, 1819 (MHS).

[37] TJ to Joel Yancey, May 25, 1819 (MHS).

[38] Nicholas to TJ, June 1, 1819 (LC).

produce or property" had caused such distress in the country as he had never before seen.[39] He was aware of the crash of the great fortune of Samuel Smith, a citizen and merchant of the first importance in Baltimore, who was the brother-in-law of Nicholas.[40]

When Jefferson set out for Poplar Forest in July, he seems to have had no personal forebodings. He actually forgot to renew one of his notes, and Gibson had to substitute one of his own for it.[41] The situation in Bedford was dreary. There had been serious sickness among the Negroes, who had been ill treated by a quack.[42] After the wheat crop had been badly damaged by hail, weeks of drought ensued.[43] Furthermore, Jefferson himself was experiencing one of his worst attacks of rheumatism. Such were the circumstances when he received an alarming letter from Richmond. "It is with the greatest pain and mortification," wrote Wilson Cary Nicholas, "I communicate to you that I was obliged to suffer a protest the day before yesterday." He said that he had not feared this until a few days earlier and had done everything possible to prevent it. He had turned over all his property to trustees and believed there would be a surplus. He recognized that he was under the strongest obligation to safeguard Jefferson but thought it impossible that his endorser would be adversely affected by this disaster. "If I am the cause of your being uneasy or being put to inconvenience," he said, "I shall never forgive myself."[44]

In his reply, far from indulging in recrimination, Jefferson manifested deep sympathy for Nicholas and put the best possible face on his own perilous situation. "A call on me to the amount of my endorsements for you would indeed close my course by a catastrophe I had never contemplated," he said, "but the comfort which supports me is the entire confidence I repose in your friendship to find some means of warding off this desperate calamity."[45] On that same day he wrote Gibson, who seems to have had no previous knowledge of his endorsement of Nicholas's note. A year earlier Jefferson had described a notice from the Bank of the United States as a clap of thunder. He repeated the expression now but gave slight outward sign of perturbation in this crisis. Gibson

[39] TJ to Nicholas, July 2, 1819 (LC).

[40] The failure of Smith affected the future of Robert Carter Nicholas, son of Wilson Cary, who asked TJ's influence to procure a federal appointment for him. W. C. Nicholas to TJ, June 28, 1819 (LC).

[41] TJ to Gibson, July 28, 1819 (MHS).

[42] Joel Yancey to TJ, July 1, 1819 (MHS).

[43] TJ to T. M. Randolph, Aug. 9, 1819 (LC).

[44] W. C. Nicholas to TJ, Aug. 5, 1819, received Aug. 9 (LC).

[45] TJ to Nicholas, Aug. 11, 1819 (LC).

had little to suggest and may have been somewhat impatient with his trustful client.[46]

Before he left Poplar Forest Jefferson wrote President Monroe in behalf of Nicholas, saying that the former governor and his family had not a penny with which to buy bread and that he would probably accept almost any appointment.[47] Writing Nicholas, he said: "Your misfortunes are sufficient to humble us all, and to extort the involuntary exclamation of, 'Lord, what are we?' "[48] He stopped at Warren on his way back to Monticello and went to the utmost pains to show that his friendship with Nicholas was unbroken. In another letter he said: "I know well how apt we are to be deluded by our own calculations, and to be innocently led into error by them."[49] He received successive assurances from Nicholas and on several occasions during the fall expressed entire confidence that he himself would not suffer from his downfall. Others were less tolerant and less confident. Patrick Gibson and Bernard Peyton, Jeff Randolph's agent, were minor victims of this failure, having endorsed notes for Nicholas. Gibson reported that the debts of that gentleman, amounting to more than $200,000, would completely sweep away his property, and Peyton saw no hope of recovering his own loss.[50]

Jefferson could not believe that all was lost and continued to suppose that he would be a preferred creditor. However, he was reminded by the bank of his liability and informed that he would have to provide more security. For this reason, he deeded a tract of land in Bedford to Jeff Randolph in trust and had his grandson as endorser. The bank was considerate in deferring payment of the principal. Bonds were signed, calling for the payment of his in two, three, and four years. Thus the evil day was postponed for a time.[51]

As a result of what he was pleased to call the misfortune of Nicholas, Jefferson's liabilities were greatly increased at just the time his assets were declining. Before the year was out he said that a farm could be sold for no more than a year's rental. He claimed that he was safe in Nicholas's hands, that he was assured he could not be called on for a dollar, but in fact a sword of Damocles was hanging over his head.[52] If, in his

[46] TJ to Gibson, Aug. 11, 1819; Gibson to TJ, Aug. 27 (MHS).

[47] TJ to Monroe, Aug. 17, 1819 (LC).

[48] TJ to Nicholas, Aug. 17, 1819 (LC).

[49] TJ to Nicholas, Aug. 24, 1819 (LC).

[50] Gibson to TJ, Aug. 27, 1819; Peyton to TJ, Sept. 9 (MHS).

[51] The arrangements are described in the following letters: J. B. Dandridge to TJ, Aug. 19, 1819 (MHS); TJ to Joseph Marx, Aug. 24 (LC); Marx to TJ, Sept. 2 (LC); TJ to Joel Yancey, Dec. 4 (MHS). The deed of trust of Sept. 15 is at UVA.

[52] TJ to Gibson, Sept. 10, 1819 (MHS).

philosophy, the *summum bonum* was to be unpained in body and untroubled in mind, as he said in a letter to William Short, this was not a good year to attain it.[53] He told John Adams that he had three long and dangerous attacks of rheumatism in 1819. He said nothing to this ancient friend about his personal financial difficulties, though he continued to be highly articulate about the ills of the time. Toward the end of the year he said that the paper bubble had burst, just as they and all other reasoning men had expected.[54] He now hoped that the legislature would do something to reduce the consequences of the disaster and prevent its repetition. About this time he sent his young friend William Cabell Rives, a member of the General Assembly, a plan he himself had drafted.[55]

Jefferson did not carry the doctrine of laissez-faire to the point of believing that this situation should be left to remedy itself. He held that the troubles of his country were produced first by the flood and then by the ebb of bank paper and blamed government for having allowed this to be issued. He said that never before had any nation "abandoned to the avarice and jugglings of private individuals to regulate, according to their own interests, the quantum of circulating medium for the nation." The plan that he sent Rives, after having talked with him about it at Monticello, related to Virginia only. He instructed the young legislator to keep his name wholly out of it and seems to have expected little to come of his proposal. He advocated the gradual reduction of the circulating medium to what he called a standard level — namely, that "which a metallic medium will always find for itself." As for bank paper he would eliminate this completely and interdict it for all time. Besides seeking to make the deflationary process gradual, he favored stay laws that would permit debtors to meet their obligations gradually.

Jefferson's anonymous "plan" had no legislative result, and the distress of his region was not alleviated.[56] Though he himself had been granted a reprieve on the notes of Nicholas, this did not lighten his other burdens. During most of the fall and winter he was unable to ship his flour down the Rivanna to Richmond because the little river was frozen.[57] Flour sold for very little when it got there. He stated that two years of abysmally low prices had brought him to the verge of bankruptcy. In

[53] For a fuller account of his letter of Oct. 31, 1819, to Short (Ford, X, 143–146), see ch. XIII, above, pp. 197–198.

[54] TJ to Adams, Nov. 7, 1819. (*A.-J. Letters*, II, 546–547).

[55] TJ to W. C. Rives, Nov. 28, 1819 (Ford, X, 150–151).

[56] For the Virginia debate on debtor relief, see Murray N. Rothbard, *The Panic of 1819: Reactions and Policies* (1962), pp. 35–38, 137–140.

[57] TJ to Gibson, Jan. 16, 1820 (LC).

the spring of 1820, writing from Monticello to Joel Yancey at Poplar Forest, he said: "Never were such hard times seen as we have here now. Not a dollar is passing from one to another."[58] He could not collect the rent for his mill, nor pay his own bills to the merchants in Charlottesville, Milton, and Lynchburg who supplied his household and provided clothing for his "people." When writing a friend whose personal loan he could not repay, the only thing he could think to say was: "Forgive us our trespasses as we forgive those who trespass against us."[59] He told Yancey that he was determined not to engage for anything he could do without.

He believed that most people were accepting the situation philosophically, but not everybody was exercising forbearance. A zealous insurance agent caused him to receive a court summons for an unpaid premium. This led to an unusually indignant letter on his part and profuse apologies from the president of the company.[60] It was difficult to maintain customary civilities in such times. Early in the year, when Patrick Gibson was ill, someone in his office expressed uncertainty about his ability to honor Jefferson's over-drafts. Explaining this months later when he first heard of it, Gibson spoke plaintively of his own situation. "The truth is that too great a confidence in mankind has deprived me of all my means and prevents my making even the trifling temporary advances generally required."[61] This kindly man had endorsed too many notes, including one of Wilson Cary Nicholas. About this time Jefferson relieved him of the responsibility for one of his by having Jeff Randolph endorse it.[62] Another had been signed by Bernard Peyton, Jeff's agent, who was getting more of the family business now.

Toward the middle of the year John W. Eppes came to the aid of the hard-pressed head of the clan. Needing laborers to clear a considerable body of land, he offered to exchange bank stock for slaves from Poplar Forest, and to return them to Francis at that place after a couple of years. Though reluctant to sell slaves, Jefferson agreed to a proposal that would keep them at Poplar Forest and in the family. By this deal he was loaned $4000 to be repaid in slaves who would go with the Bedford estate to Francis.[63] In midsummer he sold Pouncy's, a detached parcel of land in Albemarle, to Dr. Charles Everett. This transaction netted him $5000. By realizing to this extent on capital assets he was able to meet

[58] TJ to Yancey, Apr. 22, 1820; see also Mar. 16 (MHS).

[59] TJ to Peyton, Mar. 8, 1820 (MHS). He wrote similar letters to other creditors.

[60] TJ to Samuel Greenhow, Apr. 21, 1820; James Rawlings to TJ, May 4, 1820 (MHS).

[61] Gibson to TJ, July 17, 1820, replying to a letter of May 22, 1820 (LC).

[62] TJ to Gibson, July 14, 1820 (LC).

[63] J. W. Eppes to TJ, June 12, 1820; TJ to Eppes, June 30, July 29 (*Scribner's Magazine*, XXXVI, 579–585). Account Book, Oct. 18, 1820.

pressing current obligations.[64] He could do no more than that, however, and he soon had to give up all hope of aid from Wilson Cary Nicholas.

When the leaves were turning in the woods, Nicholas died at Tufton (October 10, 1820). It is uncertain whether he was living with his daughter and her husband or was merely visiting them, but it is significant that he ended his days in this family circle and was buried in the graveyard at Monticello. Toward the end of Jefferson's own life, when he was unquestionably on the brink of financial disaster, he said that he had received the coup de grâce from the hand of this longtime friend, but, according to family tradition, he would allow no word in discredit of Nicholas to be spoken in his presence. Some of the stories about his magnanimity are almost too good to be true, but, if he harbored resentment against the man who had signally failed to fulfill his promises, Jefferson was highly successful in concealing it. Loyalty to old friends was one of his most notable characteristics, and he could hardly have forgotten what this one had done for him. Furthermore, he undoubtedly wanted to shield his granddaughter-in-law and maintain family solidarity. Besides treating her father with complete respect as long as he lived, Jefferson continued to give him the benefit of the doubt, attributing his failures primarily to unavoidable circumstances.[65]

For several years after the death of Nicholas, Jefferson remained hopeful that he could realize something from his estate. Meanwhile, though not compelled to reduce the principal of the debt of $20,000, he had to pay interest on it. Therefore, he still had great need for ready cash.[66] The price of wheat improved slightly in the spring of 1821, but the most encouraging event in Jefferson's financial history that year was the transfer of the management of his affairs in Bedford County to Jeff Randolph. His grandson had had considerable success in restoring the lands and increasing the yields of the farms in Albemarle. Jefferson, who became seventy-eight that spring, said that his age had rendered him incompetent to manage a plantation.[67] Joel Yancey was persuaded to continue his services at Poplar Forest until fall, but Jefferson's affairs had entered into a fresh phase. Bernard Peyton took over the tasks that had been

[64] Account Book, July 13, 1820, shows the first payment. TJ wrote Everett, July 21 (MHS), sending a copy of patent and plat.

[65] He used the expression "*coup de grâce*," in a letter to Madison, Feb. 17, 1826 (Ford, X, 377). See Randall, III, 533–535, for family stories about TJ's magnanimity. One of the harshest comments on the financial activities of Nicholas is that of Edmund Bacon in Pierson, p. 126.

[66] The story of this obligation is resumed on p. 448, below.

[67] TJ to Yancey, Jan. 4, 1821 (MHS).

performed for Jefferson so long and faithfully by Patrick Gibson, who was now broken in health and depressed in fortune.[68] The year was also marked by the retirement of the overseer at Monticello, Edmund Bacon, who adored Jefferson but was no admirer of Thomas Mann Randolph and appears to have been somewhat jealous of Jeff.[69] There was sadness in these changes and departures, but age had given way to youth, as Jefferson said it always must, and his own health had recovered.

He was by no means free from difficulty. Because of the breaking of its main shaft and other troubles at his mill, it was out of operation much of the year 1821.[70] Further curtailments were required by the banks, and in the next year or two he had to borrow more money. He did not improve his basic position in 1821 and 1822 and may have lost some ground. But his personal responsibility was lessened. After he forgot to renew a note, Bernard Peyton got a power of attorney from him.[71] He had to keep on juggling loans, and the sword of Damocles still hung over him, but not until almost the end of his life was he faced with an overwhelming financial crisis.

[68] TJ to Gibson, Jan. 27, 1821 (LC).
[69] See Bacon's recollections in Pierson.
[70] TJ to Gibson, Jan. 27, 1821 (LC); TJ to Yancey, Aug. 15, 1821 (MHS).
[71] TJ to B. Peyton, July 6, 1821 (MHS).

XXII

The Hopes and Fears of a Slaveholder

IN one of the last letters he ever wrote, Jefferson said that the subject of slavery was one on which he did not permit himself to express an opinion except when "time, place, and occasion" could give it "some favorable effect."[1] He added that his sentiments had been before the public for forty years. He must have been referring primarily to what he said in his *Notes on Virginia*, which appeared during his ministry in France. After his return to America in 1789, he seems never again to have expressed himself publicly on the subject of domestic slavery. Throughout the rest of his life he responded candidly to private inquiries about his views, and he elaborated on them somewhat in private letters. They remained essentially unchanged, but nowhere were they so vividly presented as in the book he published and the letters he wrote to men of learning while in the Old World.[2]

He deplored the institution of slavery as unjust to its victims and injurious to the characters of its ostensible beneficiaries. The lurid picture he drew in the *Notes* of a raging master and hapless slave could hardly have been matched in later abolitionist literature.[3] A few years after his retirement it was criticized by John Taylor of Caroline as extravagant and atypical.[4] However, he did not disown it, nor did he try to tone it down.

His moral indignation was never more strikingly displayed than in certain comments he made when in Paris to the editor of the *Encyclopédie Méthodique:*

> What a stupendous, what an incomprehensible machine is man! Who can endure toil, famine, stripes, imprisonment or death itself

[1] TJ to James Heaton of Middletown, Ohio, May 20, 1826 (LC).

[2] For TJ's views on slavery as expressed in his *Notes on Virginia* and for the circumstances under which that work was prepared and published, see *Jefferson the Virginian*, pp. 263–269, 373–377, and *Jefferson and the Rights of Man*, pp. 94–98, 104–106, 505–506.

[3] *Notes on Virginia*, ed. by Peden, pp. 162–163.

[4] *Arator* (1813), pp. 68–74.

> in vindication of his own liberty, and the next moment . . . inflict on his fellow men a bondage, one hour of which is fraught with more misery than ages of that which he rose in rebellion to oppose.[5]

Judging from other words of his, he did not believe that his own slaves were in constant misery, but the contradiction that he observed in human nature and in his native society deeply troubled him as a rational and humane being. He clearly perceived that this contradiction could be resolved only by the abolition of legalized slavery.

He was one of the first Americans to propose a specific plan of emancipation. He said he devised it when engaged in the revision of the laws of Virginia during the American Revolution. The plan called for the freeing of all slaves born in his state after a specified date, for their training in useful pursuits under public authority, and for their removal to another locality on reaching maturity. The time did not seem ripe to present the plan to the legislature, nor did anything come of his draft of a constitution for Virginia (1783), containing a provision for the emancipation of slaves born after 1800. Both of these proposals appeared in print in his *Notes on Virginia.*[6]

As designed by Jefferson, emancipation was to be a gradual process and, under his plan, the freed slaves were to go through a long period of preparation for economic independence and self-support. The wisdom of this provision could hardly have been questioned, whatever might have been said about its feasibility. He himself thought that someone would probably ask why he proposed that the emancipated blacks be ultimately deported instead of being incorporated into the state. This generally optimistic man did not believe that the whites and blacks could live together peaceably on the basis of equality. In a memorable passage in his *Notes on Virginia*, he said:

> Deep rooted prejudices entertained by the whites; ten thousand recollections, by the blacks, of the injuries they have sustained; new provocations; the real distinctions which nature has made; and many other circumstances, will divide us into parties, and produce convulsions which will probably never end but in the extermination of the one or the other race.[7]

[5] TJ to Jean Nicholas Démeunier, June 26, 1786 (Boyd, X, 63). This powerful passage was incorporated without attribution in the article *"Etats-Unis."* In 1829 the passage was published in TJ's *Memoirs* and soon after that was made use of by William Lloyd Garrison (Nov. 6, 1830). See *Letters of William Lloyd Garrison*, ed. by Walter M. Merrill (1971), I, 112.

[6] *Notes*, ed. by Peden, pp. 137–138, 214.

[7] *Ibid.*, p. 138.

He may never again have spoken so strongly about racial conflict, but he never lost his fear of it. And he spoke for himself as well as for his society when he said: "This unfortunate difference of color and perhaps of faculty is a powerful obstacle to the emancipation of these people." He was well aware of the obstacle which most people probably regarded as the main one — the financial interest of slave-owners. The statement he made to Dr. Richard Price while in France, that the contest in Virginia would be between justice and avarice, was an over-simplification, as other comments of his clearly show.[8] In his early years of service in the House of Burgesses, however, he had gained impressions of complacent self-interest that remained vivid in his memory. Speaking years later of the attitude of planters of the pre-Revolutionary generation toward their slaves, he said:

> Nursed and educated in the daily habit of seeing the degraded condition, both bodily and mental, of those unfortunate beings, . . . few minds had yet doubted but that they were as legitimate subjects of property as their horses and cattle.[9]

He resented the designation of these unfortunate human beings as property. He did not even like to call them slaves. When referring to those in his own possession, he generally spoke of them as servants or as his "people."

Until the end of his life he claimed that he would gladly bear the financial loss from emancipation if a practicable plan could be adopted.[10] Since he was never put to the test, his dismissal of financial considerations as unworthy may be regarded by latter-day critics as an empty gesture, but it was an indication of his scale of values. No doubt he was viewed by many of his fellows as a dreamer. At any rate, he realized that planters who grew up in colonial Virginia took slavery as a matter of course. Such hopes as he had of relieving his state of the moral stigma of slavery lay with the rising generation, whose members had imbibed or should have imbibed the spirit of freedom with their mothers' milk. As things turned out, they were as apathetic as their fathers and more fearful.

In later years Jefferson said that if he had remained in the service of his state the problem of slavery would have been a major object of his attention.[11] What the results might have been we can only guess, but judging from his own report of what happened before and after he went

[8] TJ to Price, Aug. 7, 1785 (Boyd, VIII, 357).
[9] TJ to Edward Coles, Aug. 25, 1814 (Ford, IX, 477), slightly corrected from original.
[10] See, for instance, TJ to John Holmes, Apr. 22, 1820 (Ford, X, 157).
[11] TJ to David Barrow, May 1, 1815 (Ford, IX, 515).

to France, he might have expected severe rebuffs. Actually, his public service was on the federal level until his retirement from the presidency in 1809, while domestic slavery was regarded by virtually everybody as solely subject to state authority. It was not a national issue when he became secretary of state, and his public silence on the question afterwards should not be surprising.

Jefferson never ceased to believe that the condition of mankind would progressively improve with the growth and spread of knowledge. He was keenly sensitive to public opinion and was notably patient as well as persistent in the pursuit of goals. The purpose of all government, as he saw it, was to secure human rights, and throughout life he sought to broaden the concept of humanity. As a public servant, however, he had to devote himself to the business at hand — most importantly, the completion and preservation of American independence, along with the maintenance of true republicanism. As a party chieftain he was faced with the task of unifying his followers, and as President with that of holding the nation together.

When in France he went to considerable pains to point out the obstacles to emancipation in his own country. These by no means disappeared in the score of years after his return to America. Although early in 1805 he observed that slavery was becoming undesirable on economic grounds, slaves actually constituted a larger percentage of the total population of Virginia in this decade than at any other in Jefferson's lifetime.[12] The Gabriel revolt early in his administration proved abortive, but the revolution in St. Domingo was unquestionably successful. The massacre of the whites and mulattoes by the triumphant blacks bore out Jefferson's direful forebodings of racial conflict.

Added to the fear occasioned in his state by this revolution was a growing distrust of free blacks. Their numbers had increased since the passage of the liberal manumission law of 1782. Stories of their idleness and corruption could easily have been exaggerated, but these were not confined to the slave states. Near the end of Jefferson's days, the editor of the *North American Review* in Boston referred to "the living pestilence of a free black population."[13] In 1806 the General Assembly of Virginia had tried to avoid this by amending the manumission law of 1782. Henceforth an emancipated slave was required to leave the state within a year.[14]

[12] TJ to W. A. Burwell, Jan. 28, 1805, quoted in *Jefferson the President: Second Term*, p. 542. Population statistics are in L. C. Gray, *History of Agriculture*, p. 656.

[13] Jared Sparks, *North American Review*, vol. XVIII, new series, vol. IX, Boston, 1824, p. 61. See also George M. Fredrickson, *The Black Image in the White Mind: The Debate on Afro-American Character and Destiny, 1817–1914* (1971), pp. 3–6.

[14] See Hening, XI, 39–40, for the Act of 1782; for the Act of Jan. 25, 1806, see Samuel Shepherd, *Statutes at Large of Virginia* (1836), III, 251–253. Nothing was said in the latter about exceptions, but in specific cases they were made by legislative action.

As President, Jefferson followed a policy of non-involvement in state and local affairs, believing that his intervention would be resented and that his advocacy of a particular cause or measure might do it more harm than good. His private letters show that he regarded the abolition of slavery as inevitable, but he had no hope that peaceful emancipation would be effected or even begun in any southern state in the near future. Midway in his presidency he frankly described the policy he had imposed on himself in these circumstances. He told a Quaker abolitionist that he had "most carefully avoided every public action or manifestation" on the subject of slavery. He added that if an occasion should arise when he "could speak with decisive effect," he would do his duty.[15]

As the responsible head of the Republic, he was probably wise in avoiding futile gesticulation, and he availed himself of one opportunity to act decisively. As the time neared when the legal importation of slaves could be terminated, he recommended that Congress put an end to this long-continued violation of the rights of the "unoffending inhabitants" of Africa. A law was passed, but neither he nor anybody else made much of it in that time of world war.[16]

ii

Abolition did not become a live issue during the years immediately following Jefferson's retirement from public office, when he was personally directing agricultural operations at Monticello and trying to straighten out his tangled financial affairs. As in the past, he received occasional letters relating to slavery. In the last summer of the war (1814), he had one from a fellow Virginian on the question that he himself had refrained from discussing in public. The writer was Edward Coles of Albemarle County, then in his late twenties, who was now secretary to President Madison, as his elder brother Isaac had been to Jefferson.[17]

In a deferential letter his young friend urged the former President to devise and promote a plan for the general emancipation of the slaves in their state. To perform this difficult task Jefferson was pre-eminently qualified, he said, because of that patriot's avowed principles and conspicuous services to the cause of human rights. He believed that the author of the Declaration of Independence could do more than anybody else to bring the "hallowed principles" of this document into full effect.

[15] TJ to George Logan, May 11, 1805 (Ford, VIII, 352).

[16] See *Jefferson the President: Second Term*, pp. 541–547.

[17] Edward Coles to TJ, July 31, 1814 (*Papers, MHS*, pp. 200–202). Coles played a significant role in the reconciliation of TJ and John Adams. See above, p. 94.

Coles urged Jefferson not to be deterred by fear of failure, saying that the influence of his example would be even greater after death than in life, and that he would be on the side of emancipation in future conflict. Speaking for himself, Coles, who had recently inherited a score of slaves, said he found the system so repugnant that he was determined to leave the state. He said nothing about taking slaves with him, giving the impression, unwittingly no doubt, that he was abandoning them along with his land, his relatives, and his neighbors.

When Jefferson replied to this letter, about three weeks after he got it, he did not know that the British were sacking Washington. He did know that all the young men in his family had gone to the defense of Richmond, and at seventy-one he was feeling old.[18] Under the confused circumstances of the time his answer was slow in reaching Coles, but before the end of another month the young man learned that his own letter had been read with "peculiar pleasure." Its sentiments did honor to both the head and the heart of its writer, said Jefferson. He himself regarded it as shameful that Virginians had made no effort whatsoever to rid themselves of their condition of "moral and political reprobation." (Apparently he did not think that his own proposals should be described as "efforts." They had resulted in no action and could be considered as no more than an expression of personal opinion.) Early in his public career he had concluded that nothing could be expected of masters of slaves who had attained the fullness of age in the period of colonial subservience. Furthermore, on the basis of his own experience he could testify that anyone seeking to alleviate the conditions of the slaves would probably be considered an enemy of his society. Despairing of the old, he had placed his hopes on the young, but they in turn had disappointed him. His statement that only the voice of Coles had broken the silence may not have been literally true, but there could be no doubt of the general apathy.

An element of fatalism marks Jefferson's attitude toward emancipation. In his letter he said that only time would show whether it would be brought about by the "generous energy" of their own minds or by the "bloody process" of St. Domingo. When asking him to devise a plan, Coles made no mention of the one described in the *Notes on Virginia*. Still believing that this offered the most expedient method of relieving their commonwealth of the burden of slavery, Jefferson summarized it for the benefit of his idealistic young friend. It was a rational plan, designed to transform the economy of the state by the gradual replacement of black slaves with free white workmen. But its practicality was open to serious

[18] TJ wrote Coles, Aug. 25, 1814 (Ford, IX, 477–479). The invasion and burning of Washington was on Aug. 24–25. See above, p. 119, for the departure of the young men.

question, and public support for it would certainly have been hard to gain.

Coles had made his request at a particularly unpropitious moment in Jefferson's personal history and in that of the Republic, but the orderly transformation of their society according to Jefferson's ideas would have been a slow operation under the most favorable circumstances. He asserted that it was no task for an old man to assume. Priam should not be asked to buckle on the armor of Hector, he said. Coles had referred to the possibility that Jefferson might fail in his own lifetime, but the old warrior did not go so far as to remind Coles of young Hector's fate before the walls of Troy. Instead he invited him to remain in Virginia and become a "missionary" of the principles he professed. Speaking of his own slaves, he said:

> My opinion has ever been that, until more can be done for them, we should endeavor with those whom fortune has thrown on our hands, to feed and clothe them well, protect them from all ill usage, require such reasonable labor only as is performed voluntarily by freemen, & be led by no repugnancies to abdicate them, and our duties to them. The laws do not permit us to turn them loose, if that were for their good: and to commute them for other property is to commit them to those whose usage of them we cannot control.[19]

Coles appreciated Jefferson's desire to retain him as a neighbor and was not offended by the intimation that he was trying to escape his responsibilities to the state and to his own slaves. In his reply to Jefferson's letter he said he would gladly remain in Virginia if he thought he could do anything at all to promote the cause of general emancipation.[20] He assured his solicitous correspondent that he was not planning to abandon his slaves. He expected to take them with him to the territory northwest of the Ohio River where they could live in freedom. (This he did five years later.) He had chosen the only sure way of escape for himself and for them from the system into which they had all been born. If he had decided to remain in Albemarle County, he could not have manumitted his slaves and employed them for wages because they would have been required by law to leave the state within a year.

His claim that he could do nothing for general emancipation in Virginia suggests that Coles regarded the prospects of the cause as bleak, and no doubt he was correct in believing that only a recognized leader

[19] Ford, IX, 479.

[20] Coles to TJ, Sept. 26, 1814 (E. B. Washburne, *Sketch of Edward Coles* [1882], reprinted in Clarence W. Alvord, ed., *Governor Edward Coles* [1920], pp. 28–30).

could hope to arouse Virginia society from its apathy. Jefferson said that at his age he had only prayers to contribute. Like many other elderly people he may have talked too much about his age and infirmity. But he had other reasons for declining to follow the suggestion of Coles. His personal finances were in a precarious state, and after forty years of public service he was determined to be a private man.

Despite his belief that, as a rightful cause, emancipation was sure to triumph eventually, it was a forlorn cause in their state at that time. We may properly ask just what he could have done to advance it. Judging from his suggestions to Coles as a prospective "missionary," the situation called for a long educational campaign, and there is no reason to believe that he thought himself capable of doing anything decisive. The predictable outcome of any crusade for abolition in Virginia was failure and opprobrium for those engaged in it. Virginians were less fearful of abolitionists than they afterwards became, but opponents of the slavery system were actually faced with a choice between exile, martyrdom, and quiescence.

Edward Coles, who was a bachelor, chose exile. The ex-President, who was more deeply rooted in their native soil and had far greater personal responsibilities, chose quiescence. His aversion to slavery may have been less known to his fellow Virginians than he claimed, but, judging from the private letters he received during the rest of his life, it was widely recognized in the nation. At this time, when the cause of abolition was so feeble, his interest in it may have been described not improperly as theoretical. In view of the immediate circumstances and his total record, however, he does not deserve the censure he has received from some modern historians of the antislavery movement. One of the best of them has said: "The exchange with Edward Coles dramatized Jefferson's fundamental commitment to his 'country' as well as his extraordinary capacity to sound like an enlightened reformer while upholding the interests of the planter class."[21]

Though Jefferson was unquestionably committed to his state and concerned for its welfare, he never sought to promote the interests of the planters as a class. He prided himself on the blows against the landed aristocracy that he struck during the American Revolution, and he consistently tried to increase the opportunities and advance the interests of small, independent farmers. Though he had a healthy respect for real property, he believed that the best and happiest society was one where inequalities of conditions were not great.

[21] David Brion Davis, *The Problem of Slavery in the Age of Revolution, 1770–1823*, p. 182. TJ did not learn of the plans of Coles until he got the latter's second letter.

At just this time he said that in the United States the wealthy knew nothing of luxury in the European sense.[22] They had only somewhat more of the comforts of life than the workers who provided them. He was not comparing his state with any other in the Union, but he claimed that even the enslaved blacks were "better fed . . . , warmer clothed, and labored less than the journeymen or day-laborers of England." Also, unlike the wretched poor of England, they were secure from want as long as they lived. It was true that they were subject to physical coercion, but so were British soldiers and seamen. The latter had also been brought into subjection by force — that is, by the press gang. He said he did not condone wrong committed by Americans against Africans because of those committed by Englishmen against their own kind, but we may be sure that many of his countrymen did. Also, these private reflections may have constituted a form of self-justification, even though he did not admit it. While he prized industry, he disliked severity. That there was less of this on his farms than on others we cannot say, but he is reputed to have been a kindly master, and there can be no doubt of his solicitude for his "people." He was sure that, with rare exceptions, they were wholly unprepared for self-government and he liked to think that for the present they were safe and relatively comfortable.

Jefferson never ceased to urge the necessity of a "practicable" plan of emancipation and to say that he knew of none better than his own. As an advocate of self-government he not only insisted that the slaves be prepared for it. He assumed that the consent of the owners must be gained. He was proposing no compensation and seems to have been relying entirely on moral suasion to overcome the "obstacles of self-interest" in the minds of the masters. He recognized that this would require much time and patience, but he sounded a note of hope in many a private letter on the subject. Considering the circumstances, that persistent hope is as noteworthy as his desire to maintain silence in public.[23]

He told William Short that his repugnance to the "political pen" was insuperable.[24] His former secretary wanted him to protest against the "foul traffic" in slaves which was being openly carried on, especially by certain "scoundrels" from Rhode Island. Jefferson's record of opposition to the foreign slave trade was clear and consistent, but Short said that some people were unaware of it and thought that a public communication from him might be helpful. He had entered his seventy-fourth year several months before he received this suggestion. When rejecting it he

[22] TJ to Thomas Cooper, Sept. 10, 1814 (L. & B., XIV, 182–184). If his granddaughter Ellen is to be believed, life at Monticello was far from luxurious.

[23] See, for example, TJ to David Barrow, May 1, 1815 (Ford, IX, 515).

[24] TJ to Short, Aug. 10, 1816 (LC), replying to a letter of July 18 (*Papers*, *MHS*, pp. 258–261).

asserted that the problem could be safely left to his juniors and that it was their responsibility anyway. "The concerns of each generation are their own care," he said. Until the end of his days, however, his juniors continued to seek his opinion and they often published his private letters.

A few weeks after Jefferson replied to Short, his name was evoked and his words were employed to promote the colonization movement. In the House of Delegates of Virginia in December, 1816, Charles F. Mercer obtained a resolution calling on the federal government to secure territory outside the United States as a refuge for free blacks. In support of this resolution Mercer produced hitherto unpublished correspondence of 1801–1802 between President Jefferson and Governor Monroe regarding the possible establishment of a settlement for deported blacks. In this correspondence the inquiries that Jefferson made at the request of the legislature were reported.[25]

At almost the same time that these events occurred in Richmond, the American Colonization Society was being independently organized in Washington by Dr. Robert Finley of New Jersey, a Presbyterian minister. On January 1, 1817, officers of the society were elected. Jefferson seems never to have specifically endorsed this organization, but an earlier letter of his (January 21, 1811), supporting colonization, was published in the *Richmond Enquirer* on April 11, 1817. When the national society met on its first anniversary, Henry Clay introduced the letter into the records as evidence of Jefferson's support of the cause. At the same meeting, Mercer introduced the Monroe–Jefferson correspondence. All of this was published in the society's *First Annual Report.*[26]

Early in 1817 Jefferson privately expressed approval of the proposal to establish a refuge for free blacks on the coast of Africa, which was made at this time and carried into effect five years later. But his own hopes went far beyond this. In his mid-seventies, while somewhat encouraged, he saw no sign that a practicable plan of general emancipation would be adopted in his day.[27]

As Jefferson foresaw, he was doomed to spend the rest of his life in a society that was based on slave labor, but his friend Edward Coles finally managed to escape from it. This was about four and a half years after he informed the older man of his intention to emigrate from Vir-

[25] P. J. Staudenraus, *African Colonization Movement, 1816–1865* (1961), p. 31. For a reference to the correspondence, see *Jefferson the President: First Term*, pp. 252–253.

[26] Staudenraus, *African Colonization*, p. 48.

[27] TJ to Dr. Thomas Humphreys, Feb. 8, 1817 (Ford, X, 77).

ginia. Coles had carefully arranged his affairs, making two exploratory trips to the western country, selling his Virginia property, and obtaining an appointment as registrar of the United States land office at Edwardsville, Illinois. In the spring of 1819 he made his move. Two of his slaves were old women whom he left behind after he had provided for their needs. Ten of the others he emancipated en route to Illinois, granting each of the three families involved 160 acres of land in the southern part of the state. To provide for his remaining slaves, a woman and her five small children, he purchased the woman's husband from a Virginia neighbor. They were allowed to settle in St. Louis, Missouri, where they were legally freed in 1825.[28]

In effecting an escape from a system he deplored, Coles had fully assumed his responsibilities to the human beings he had inherited as property. Jefferson could not have failed to approve of what he did for the freed blacks. Madison commended his former secretary for having provided the families in southern Illinois with land but made the realistic observation that he could not assure their enjoyment of all the rights of white Americans without changing the color of their skins.[29] Despite its illegality, slavery actually existed in that region, and the introduction of free blacks was resented by many settlers. The former slaves of Coles were ushered into an unfriendly world, and he himself suffered much unpleasantness because of his sentiments.

Into the details of his career in Illinois we cannot enter here, but we should note that he published part of Jefferson's letter of 1814 in justification of his antislavery position. This was in the course of his successful campaign for the governorship a few years after his arrival.[30] There appear to be no recorded comments of Jefferson's on the activities of Coles in Illinois, but the high regard the two men had for each other seems never to have diminished. Much as he regretted the loss that the state suffered when this promising young man left it, there is no reason to believe that he tried to discourage Coles's generous act of manumission. It released one owner and his particular slaves from a detested system,

[28] Alvord, ed., *Governor Edward Coles*, pp. 40–47, 261–263, 330–332. Initially Coles expected the husband to repay his purchase price, but when he proved unable to manage this, the payment was waived.

[29] Madison to Coles, Sept. 3, 1819 (MP).

[30] As the antislavery candidate, Coles was elected in 1822 to a four-year term as governor. Although he succeeded in 1824 in blocking a serious attempt to open Illinois to slavery, he was unable to advance his personal political career. After a devastating defeat in the congressional election in 1831, he left the state for Pennsylvania. Alvord, ed., *Governor Edward Coles*, pp. 59–63, 162–163, 346–347. Donald S. Spencer, "Edward Coles: Virginia Gentleman in Frontier Politics," *Journal of the Illinois State Historical Society* (Summer 1968), LXI, 150–163.

but no such way of escape was open to Jefferson and his slaves at Monticello and Poplar Forest. For him exile from Virginia was unthinkable, even if it had been feasible, and his unavoidable problem at this stage of drought and depression was not how to free his slaves, but how to feed them.

[XXIII]

Firebell in the Night: The Missouri Question

EARLY in 1819 Jefferson wrote Senator Nathaniel Macon that he was less interested in the modern than in the ancient world. He was reading about the Trojan War, about Athens and Sparta, Pompey and Caesar, without thought of affairs in Washington. "I slumber without fear," he said, "and review in my dreams the visions of antiquity." He acknowledged uneasiness about the monetary situation, admitting his concern over the lack of a measure of value. This jostled him at every turn, he said, and prevented him from knowing where he stood "in the scale of property."[1] His own troubles and those of his countrymen increased greatly in the course of the year. The failure of Wilson Cary Nicholas, whose notes he had endorsed, occurred in the summer.[2] At that time he was busily engaged in the affairs of the University of Virginia. He maintained remarkable imperturbability during most of this disastrous year. It took a national political crisis to terrify him. Toward the end of 1819 he told John Adams that the Missouri question was more ominous than any they had faced during the American Revolution. A few weeks later he described it as a firebell in the night.[3]

The controversy over the admission of Missouri to statehood, which depressed him so profoundly, had its beginning in the last weeks of the Fifteenth Congress. When the Missouri enabling bill was being debated in the House of Representatives, Congressman James Tallmadge, Jr., of New York proposed an amendment which seems to have taken his colleagues by surprise. There had long been slaves in the territory of Missouri, and others had been brought in by recent settlers. This amend-

[1] TJ to Nathaniel Macon, Jan. 12, 1819 (Ford, X, 119–122), replying to a letter of Jan. 4 (LC) requesting his opinion on the trend of national politics.

[2] See above, p. 310.

[3] TJ to Adams, Dec. 10, 1819 (*A.-J. Letters*, pp. 548–549); to John Holmes, Apr. 22, 1820 (Ford, X, 157).

ment provided that there should be no further importation of slaves and that all slaves born after Missouri's admission to the Union should be freed, though they might be kept in service until the age of twenty-five. Both provisions were adopted in the House by a small majority and a strictly sectional vote. In the Senate both were defeated and the enabling bill was then adopted. The House declined to concur in this action, however, and the bill died when the Fifteenth Congress adjourned on March 3, 1819.[4]

At the time, these events attracted little attention in the nation. Jefferson could have read the reports of the congressional proceedings in the *Richmond Enquirer*, but he appears to have made no reference to them. Precisely when he heard the firebell we do not know, but his first recorded expression of alarm is in his letter of December 10, 1819, to Adams. The Sixteenth Congress had convened a few days earlier, and a campaign of "anti-Missouri" meetings was still going on in the North. This crusade began with a meeting in Burlington, New Jersey, on August 30 and reached its height about the time Congress met. Shortly before that, Thomas Ritchie in the *Enquirer* expressed regret that the Missouri question had been taken up in the North in this way.[5] While these meetings were chiefly in the middle states, they must have reminded Jefferson of those in New England against the embargo during his presidency. They were largely Federalist in character.

Jefferson afterwards said that the northern people had been "fanaticized" for political reasons, and he denied that morality was at issue in what was really a struggle for power. But, while maintaining that Missouri should have the same control of her domestic institutions as any other state, he did not defend slavery itself at this time or later. In fact, strong language of his in condemnation of the institution was and continued to be cited. Before he made his first known comment on the Missouri question, the passage in the *Notes on Virginia* in which he described a raging master was quoted in a powerful attack on the slavery system in the southern states. If he did not see this in the *Edinburgh Review*, he could hardly have missed the anonymous reply to it by a Virginian which appeared in the *Richmond Enquirer* about the time that the stormy congressional session of 1819–1820 began.[6]

The attack was in a long review of a group of books by British trav-

[4] Glover Moore, *The Missouri Controversy, 1819–1821* (1966), pp. 35–59.

[5] *Richmond Enquirer*, Nov. 23, 1819. For an account of this crusade, see Moore, *Missouri Controversy*, pp. 65–83.

[6] *Edinburgh Review*, XXXI (Dec., 1818), 146–148; American edition (July, 1819). It is uncertain whether TJ had canceled his subscription by this time. Reply signed by "an American," who stated that he was a Virginian, copied by the *Richmond Enquirer*, Nov. 23, Dec. 3, 7, 1819, from *National Intelligencer*.

elers in America — one of whom, Lieutenant Francis Hall, had visited Monticello. The Scottish reviewer designated slavery as the curse of America and referred to it as an "atrocious crime." Because of it, Americans' boasts of liberty were ridiculous, and the young Republic was ranked below all European countries in wisdom and virtue. Calling slaveholders scourges and murderers, he laid great emphasis on the cruelty of the system and introduced the quotation from Jefferson in this connection. Lieutenant Hall had copied it from the *Notes*. Here Jefferson said that the master who could prevent his manners and morals from becoming depraved must be a prodigy. However, Lieutenant Hall did not charge him with depravity.

The anonymous writer in the *Enquirer* who was seeking to counter the charge of cruelty could not well ignore the quotation from the *Notes* which seemed to support the allegation.[7] In brief, his explanation of the passage was that it had been written in a mood of emotion in an era of revolution. He claimed that it was not the result of reflection and said that conditions had greatly improved in forty years anyway. For a full answer he referred the reader to the chapters on slavery in *Arator* (1813), the work of John Taylor of Caroline. Others besides Taylor regarded the passage as extravagant, and one may doubt if Jefferson would have expressed himself just this way in his seventies. After he had seen the chapters on slavery in *Arator*, however, he said that he and the author differed in opinion on the subject.[8] Taylor regarded the system as bad for agriculture but did not believe that it could or should be abolished. Far from agreeing that it was injurious to the characters of the masters, he claimed that it promoted the spirit of benevolence. He defended the institution as desirable in itself. Jefferson merely held that the system would have to be endured until an acceptable plan of emancipation, deportation, and replacement could be worked out. At this juncture he may be said to have favored a holding operation.

In his first recorded comment on the controversy over the admission of Missouri, Jefferson spoke of it, not as a threat to slavery, nor to his commonwealth, but to the Union. The question of the restriction on that prospective state had been and continued to be argued on constitutional grounds. Opposition to the growth of federal power had increased in Virginia since the end of the War of 1812, and Jefferson himself was more fearful of "consolidation" in the administration of Monroe than he had been in that of Madison. His reaction to the nationalizing decisions of the Supreme Court in this era need not concern us yet. We should

[7] He referred to it in the third and last installment of his letter (*Richmond Enquirer*, Dec. 7, 1819).

[8] TJ to the publisher, Apr. 26, 1815 (Sowerby, I, 371).

note, however, that he advocated state rights and strict construction for other reasons than the defense of slavery. He made relatively little reference to that institution in his discussion of the Missouri question.

Toward the end of the year 1819, John Adams, assuming the role of Cassandra, expressed the belief that another Hamilton or Burr might rend the vast American empire in twain. Indeed, Adams thought it not impossible that there might be as many countries in the present area of the Republic as in Europe.[9] The devotion of that old patriot to the Union, which he and Jefferson had done so much to establish, was open to no question, but the dangers he pointed out were far from unreal. Jefferson had been especially fearful of disunionist sentiment in the West, and both as secretary of state and President he tried to remove its main cause by securing the free navigation of the Mississippi River. This object was attained by the Louisiana Purchase, and the trans-Appalachian region was saved to the Republic. If he exaggerated the threat imposed by the Burr conspiracy, it was primarily because of his determination to preserve the Union. In his Farewell Address George Washington had said that this would be endangered if political parties should ever follow geographical lines. In his effort to make his party truly national Jefferson went to special pains during most of his presidency to cultivate the New England states. His success in gaining the support of the farmers was largely nullified by the embargo, which was so disastrous to the commerce of the region; and the separatist spirit was stronger in Massachusetts and Connecticut than anywhere else in the nation during the administration of Madison.

In the course of the War of 1812 Jefferson wrote a South Carolinian: "It seems to me that in proportion as commercial avarice and corruption advance on us from the North and East, the principles of free government are to retire to the agricultural states of the South and West, as their last asylum and bulwark."[10] The new states above the Ohio, besides being agricultural, were dependent on the Mississippi River as an outlet for their produce. Many of their settlers had come from Virginia, and they had strong ties of interest with the southern states. Their society of small farmers was distinctly Jeffersonian in spirit, and in politics they had been overwhelmingly Republican. The sectionalism that took form after the War of 1812 was never congenial to Jefferson, and no doubt he continued to think of himself as a Virginian rather than as a Southerner. He never crossed the boundary line between his state and

[9] To TJ, Dec. 21, 1819 (*A.-J. Letters*, p. 551).

[10] TJ to Henry Middleton, Jan. 8, 1813 (L. & B., XIII, 203). Because of his concern for national self-sufficiency, he was reconciled to manufacturing at this stage.

North Carolina, which his father had helped survey, and he had closer ties with Philadelphia than with Charleston or New Orleans. But he certainly wanted the South and West to maintain their historic alliance.[11]

Congress had been in session a couple of days when Jefferson expressed his forebodings in his letter to John Adams. The Missouri question dominated the proceedings of that body for nearly three months. Throughout this period it was referred to in virtually every number of the *Richmond Enquirer.* Thus Jefferson could easily keep up with developments. Also, he received regular reports from Hugh Nelson, the representative of his congressional district, and he got several long letters from President Monroe. In one of his letters to Nelson, he spoke of the question much as he had done to Adams two months before. "It is the most portentous one which ever yet threatened our Union. In the gloomiest moment of the revolutionary war I never had any apprehension equal to what I feel from this source."[12] Nelson took the liberty of reading this extract in the course of a speech in the House. He said he could not resist the temptation to employ Jefferson's name and influence to check "the mad career of the majority."[13] It appears to have been the only comment of Jefferson's on this subject that was made public at the time. His words may possibly have had a calming effect on some of the angry congressmen, but there is no reason to believe that he had, or tried to have, any direct influence on the course of events in the crisis. He himself was deeply affected by it, however, and he said some memorable things about it in private letters.

The determination of the northern majority in the House to impose antislavery restrictions on Missouri had been manifest throughout the session, and they had persistently rejected compromise proposals that emanated from the Senate. Since the states where slavery was legal happened to be equal in number to those where it did not exist or was in the course of extinction, there was a balance in that body, and senators from the Northwest tended to be sympathetic to the South. Early in the session a petition was presented to the House for the admission to the Union of the part of Massachusetts that went by the name of Maine. In February Jefferson was informed by Nelson that the Senate had rejected

[11] The South may have been little more than a geographical term before the Missouri crisis. A distinguished historian has said: "There was no Southern political party, no slave-state bloc in Congress, and no sentiment of Southern nationalism" (C. S. Sydnor, *The Development of Southern Sectionalism, 1819–1848*, p. 1).

[12] TJ to Hugh Nelson, Feb. 7, 1820 (Ford, X, 156), replying to a letter of Feb. 2 (*Papers, MHS*, pp. 290–291).

[13] Nelson to TJ, Feb. 29, 1820 (*ibid.*, p. 293).

by a substantial majority the restriction on Missouri that had been approved by the House, and that they had coupled the admission of Maine with that of Missouri, hoping to win a few votes for the latter in the House.[14] From President Monroe, Jefferson learned a little later that a further action had been taken by the Senate in the hope of overcoming the intransigence of the House. An amendment, introduced by Senator Jesse B. Thomas of Illinois, stipulated that in all of the Louisiana Purchase north of 36°30′, except for Missouri, slavery should be forever prohibited. The right of Congress under the Constitution to forbid slavery in the territories was generally conceded, but its right to bind future states was much disputed.[15] This compromise measure was transmitted to the House, and there, a few days before Nelson quoted Jefferson in a speech, it was rejected. The compromise that was eventually worked out, after maneuvers into which we need not enter, followed these lines. However, there were two bills and the provision for the admission of Maine was separated from the Missouri enabling bill, to which was attached the Thomas amendment.[16]

Passions ran so high in this session that Jefferson's fears for the Union were not surprising. These were shared by President Monroe, who interpreted this unexampled domestic crisis essentially as Jefferson did. So also did the other member of the Virginia dynasty, James Madison. They were agreed that this was a struggle for political power. Perhaps the most conspicuous leader of the opposition to the admission of Missouri without restriction was Senator Rufus King of New York, who had been defeated by Monroe in the presidential election of 1816 and was probably the most prominent Federalist in the nation. It was easy for Jefferson to believe that his old enemies, the Federalists who had been so discredited by their unpatriotic conduct in the War of 1812, had seized upon the slavery issue in the effort to create a new political alignment and alienate northern Republicans from their allies in the South.[17] Monroe told Jefferson that the "expedient" the power seekers had chosen was well adapted to their purpose. He said that it enlisted in their support the "best feelings" of all parts of the Union where slavery did not exist and where the people were unacquainted with the condition of their southern brethren.[18]

[14] Nelson to TJ, Feb. 2, 1820 (*ibid.*, 290–291).

[15] James Monroe to TJ, Feb. 19, 1980 (S.M.H., VI, 115–116).

[16] Moore, *Missouri Controversy*, pp. 88–111.

[17] It should be noted that the origins of this movement remain obscure. Tallmadge, who was a Republican, was no longer in Congress. De Witt Clinton of New York was charged with involvement in it, but this has never been proved. (*Ibid.*, pp. 37–40; George Dangerfield, *The Awakening of American Nationalism, 1815–1828* [New York, 1965], pp. 107–109, 119–122.)

[18] Monroe to TJ, Feb. 7, 1820 (S.M.H., VI, 114).

Madison remarked to Monroe that the prime concern of the promoters of the anti-Missouri movement was obviously not the welfare of the slaves. He inclined to the opinion that "an uncontrolled dispersion" of the slaves in the United States would be most favorable both to their emancipation and their condition in the meantime.[19] The argument for "mitigation by diffusion" was being heard in Congress, but the northern determination was to keep the vast reaches of the Northwest for free men, not slaves, and, as some put it, for white men, not black. Southerners were believed by many to have too large a part in the government anyway. According to the Constitution their representation in Congress was based on their white population and three-fifths of their slaves.

Early in March, 1820, Jefferson received from Nelson a report of the agreement the two houses of Congress had reached on the question which had agitated them throughout the session. The old patriot was not comforted. In his letter of acknowledgment he did not comment on specific details of the settlement, but he said that it was only *for the present.*[20] In fact, while Maine had become a fully recognized member of the Union, the constitution of Missouri still had to be approved by Congress. Thus the contest could be and actually was to be renewed at the next session.

ii

At no time since his retirement had Jefferson appeared so discouraged as he did in this period. He and his neighbors were in the depths of the financial depression. He told Nelson that wheat was selling for only a third of what it once brought, that farms were being sold by sheriffs at heavy loss, that a good horse could be bought for five dollars. The legislature had adjourned without doing anything to correct the banking system and by its indifference to the University was driving him to despair. Worst of all was the newly excited antagonism between North and South.

Writing William Short on his seventy-seventh birthday, he said that the old "schism" between Federalists and Republicans threatened nothing since it existed in all the states and these were drawn together by "fraternism" of party.[21] What appalled him was the emergence of an issue that tended to reduce the political conflict to geographical terms. To a northern Republican who was exposed to retribution for his support of compromise in Congress he wrote: "The idea of a geographical

[19] Madison to Monroe, Feb. 10, 23, 1820 (Hunt, IX, 21–26).

[20] Nelson to TJ, Mar. 4, 1820 (*Papers, MHS,* I, 294–295); TJ to Nelson, Mar. 12 (Ford, X, 156–157).

[21] TJ to William Short, Apr. 13, 1820 (L. & B., XV, 247–248).

line, once suggested, will brood in the minds of all those who prefer the gratification of their ungovernable passions to the peace and union of their country."[22] He seems to have regarded the debates in Congress as unworthy of men of patriotism and reason.

This particular observation was addressed to Mark Langdon Hill, one of two congressmen from Maine who had voted against the proposed restriction on Missouri and had been condemned by Federalist colleagues for that reason. Hill had asked permission to publish an old letter from Jefferson to the late Governor Langdon of New Hampshire in which the Federalists were criticized. Jefferson's opinion of them had not improved. But having no desire to rekindle old embers, he pleaded his concern for tranquillity as he so often did. His letter to Langdon remained unpublished, but he had some memorable correspondence with another Republican congressman from Maine.[23] John Holmes, who had presented the petition for the admission of Maine to the Union, and who had been a co-chairman of the conference committee from which the compromise emerged, sent Jefferson a copy of a letter to his constituents in which he had explained his course.[24] Compromise of some sort was necessary to restore tranquillity and preserve the Union, he said. Furthermore, he accepted the argument that slavery was mitigated by diffusion.

Because of its color and clairvoyance as well as the writer's historic eminence, Jefferson's private letter of April 22, 1820, to Congressman Holmes has been quoted very many times in the generations since his death.[25] In it he stated that the momentous Missouri question, "like a firebell in the night," had awakened him from repose and filled him with terror. Continuing, he said:

> I considered it at once as the knell of the Union. It is hushed, indeed, for the moment. But this is a reprieve only, not a final sentence. A geographical line, coinciding with a marked principle, moral and political, once conceived and held up to the angry passions of men, will never be obliterated; and every new irritation will mark it deeper and deeper.

He did not define the "principle" and appears to have deliberately avoided the word "slavery." He spoke here of a "heavy reproach," saying

[22] TJ to Mark Langdon Hill, Apr. 5, 1820 (*ibid.*, XV, 243), replying to a letter of Mar. 28 (LC).

[23] In a public letter of May 15, 1820, Hill did quote from TJ's reply as well as from one from James Madison (Noble E. Cunningham, Jr., ed., *Circular Letters of Congressmen to Their Constituents, 1789–1829* [1978], III, 1122–1123).

[24] John Holmes to TJ, Apr. 12, 1820, enclosing a letter to constituents, dated Apr. 10 (Cunningham, *Circular Letters of Congressmen*, III, 1109–1115).

[25] TJ to John Holmes, Apr. 22, 1820 (Ford, X, 157–158).

that no one on earth would be willing to sacrifice more than he to relieve his society of this in a *practicable* way. The loss of that sort of property, as it was misnamed, would be a bagatelle if general emancipation and *expatriation* could be brought about. He stated that this might be done "gradually and with due sacrifices." He did not sound very hopeful, however, and he described the existing situation in unforgettable language: "But as it is," he said, "we have the wolf by the ears, and we can neither hold him, nor safely let him go. Justice is in one scale, and self-preservation in the other."

In his forties when in France, he had said that the conflict in his slave-holding society would be between justice and avarice. By the term "self-preservation," which he was using now, he meant far more than the protection of economic interests. Judging from many other utterances of his, he was referring to physical security and the safeguarding of republican society. He may have laid too little emphasis on the economic difficulties that would inevitably attend general emancipation, but he spoke more often of the greed of bankers and merchants than of that of planters, and he knew that the shadow of fear hung perpetually over the Virginia countryside.

While slavery as it existed in the southern states was assailed in the course of the congressional debates, the actual question was that of the future of the institution beyond the Mississippi. Jefferson observed that the passage of slaves from one state to another did not increase their total number, which was true enough. Also, like Holmes and Madison, he claimed that dispersion would be advantageous to the slaves themselves. He repeated the claim several times in later letters when challenging the northern assumption of moral superiority. We may doubt, however, that this was more than a debater's point with him. Though he could not have been unaware that slaves were becoming embarrassingly numerous in his own state, there is no reason to suppose that he wanted to send the surplus to Missouri. He himself was extremely reluctant to sell slaves, and rarely did he do so except with the lands on which they were working. Before he died he expressed the opinion that they would be better off as serfs than in their present condition, and he would have been appalled by the domestic slave trade as it afterwards developed.[26] His idea was to expatriate the slaves after they had been prepared for freedom. He wanted to send them to the black republic of St. Domingo.

He objected to the proposed restriction on Missouri as a violation of the Constitution and a threat to self-government. He referred to it as an attempt by Congress "to regulate the conditions of the different descrip-

[26] TJ to William Short, Jan. 18, 1826 (*ibid.*, X, 362), replying to a letter of Jan. 11 (*MHS*).

tions of men composing a state." He claimed that this was the "exclusive right" of every state. No doubt he took particular pleasure in citing the example of Connecticut, where he had been so often assailed in pulpits. Under its provision for gradual emancipation there were slaves in that old Federalist stronghold. Calling these "non-freedmen," he asked if Congress could require them to be freed or forbid them to go to another state. That is, the majority in the House of Representatives had attempted to make a special case of Missouri. To his mind this would have been an unwarranted, unwise, and unworthy act of power. While he did not express himself on the subject of motivation in his famous letter to Holmes, as he did for example to President Monroe, he left no doubt of his opinion that the quarrelsome congressmen had been driven by emotion and not guided by reason. He stated here that he regarded the preservation of the Union as essential to the ultimate success of the American experiment in self-government. He said that the fruits of union should be weighed against "an abstract principle more likely to be effected by union than by scission." At this time he believed that the exploitation of sectional antagonism had already made ultimate disunion inevitable. His only consolation, he said, was that he would not live to weep over the wastage of the sacrifices and the failure of the hopes of his own generation.[27]

Speaking for himself and the friends to whom he showed Jefferson's letter, John Holmes asked permission to publish it, but this request was denied for the customary reasons. Its author insisted on remaining in retirement. His views might carry weight with those who agreed with them, he said, but would arouse the angry recollections of old political enemies. Having no desire for that to happen, he contented himself with congratulating Holmes and the new state on the election of that good Republican and devoted supporter of the Union to the Senate of the United States.[28]

In the letter he wrote William Short on his own birthday he had anticipated much that he said to Holmes, sometimes using even stronger

[27] Don. E. Fehrenbacher charges that all this despair "was poured out in response to proposals for doing nothing more than what Jefferson himself had proposed to do in 1784" (*The Dred Scott Case: Its Significance in American Law and Politics* [1978], p. 111). As a delegate to the Continental Congress, Jefferson had drafted an ordinance, one provision of which would have abolished slavery in all the territories west of the original thirteen states after 1800. This provision was eliminated by Congress (see *Jefferson the Virginian*, pp. 413–414). Jefferson seems never to have worried much about defending himself against charges of inconsistency, but Madison said that the Ordinance of 1787, which prohibited slavery in the Northwest Territory, was passed at a time when the only means possessed by Congress to check the slave trade was "the indirect one of narrowing the space open for the reception of slaves" (Madison to Monroe, Feb. 10, 1820, Hunt, IX, 22–23).

[28] Holmes to TJ, June 19, 1820; TJ to Holmes, July 8 (LC).

language. He predicted that recurrent sectional conflicts would create "such mutual and moral hatred, as to render separation preferable to eternal discord."[29] The line of separation as he foresaw it would follow the rivers — the Potomac, the Ohio, and the Missouri. He left with the North two states where slavery was still legal, Delaware and Maryland, but thought it possible that the entire Northwest would cling to the South because of its dependence on the Mississippi and its tributaries.[30]

He spoke of no future boundary line in the letter he wrote in the fall of 1820 to Richard Rush, the minister to Great Britain. Indeed, he seems to have deliberately avoided precise terms and specific references in the effort to be entirely impersonal. Without mentioning Missouri by name or using the word slavery, he stated that "a hideous evil" was dividing Americans "too angrily." He said that the magnitude of the evil was seen by one party, but only at a distance. He added that it was "more sorely felt and sincerly deplored by the other [party], from the difficulty of the cure." In plainer language what he was saying was that Northerners were chiefly aware of the evil, rather than the difficulty of getting rid of it, while with Southerners the situation was reversed. Judging from other utterances of his, he was exaggerating the interest of the southern party in the ultimate eradication of slavery, and he could hardly have expected them to concede that it was as hideous as members of the other party were making it out to be. He was indulging in wishful thinking when he said that, if time were allowed for tempers on both sides to cool and "visionary fears" to be removed, both parties would realize that it was to their common interest to devise a "practicable process" for ridding the land of this evil.

As usual, he was expecting men to be more rational and personally disinterested than they actually were. Furthermore, he predicted that, if separation should occur, it would be brief because the different parts of the nation needed each other. In expressing the belief that good sense must ultimately prevail, he may have been trying to make it easier for Rush to present American affairs in a favorable light. He emphasized the worldwide significance of the American Union in a characteristically Jeffersonian passage, one which was to be echoed by Abraham Lincoln:

> We exist . . . as standing proofs that a government, so modelled as to rest continually on the will of the whole society, is a practicable government. Were we to break to pieces, it would damp the hopes and the efforts of the good, and give triumph to those of the

[29] TJ to Short, Apr. 13, 1820 (L. & B., XV, 247–248).

[30] It should be recalled that this was before the building of the railroads which were to tie the Middle West and East together.

bad through the whole enslaved world. As members, therefore, of the universal society of mankind, . . . it is our sacred duty to suppress passion among ourselves, and not to blast the confidence . . . that a government of reason is better than one of force.[31]

This relatively optimistic letter was written before the congressional session began on November 13, and the sectional controversy was resumed. The northern majority in the House of Representatives rejected the admission of Missouri because of a provision in its constitution that called on the legislature to prevent free blacks from settling in the state. This was objected to as a violation of the provision in the federal Constitution guaranteeing that the citizens of each state were entitled to "all privileges and immunities of citizens in the several states."[32] Jefferson did not enter into a discussion of this question, but he obviously did not regard the action of Missouri as the real reason for continued opposition to its admission to the Union. As he clearly perceived, a struggle for power was still going on and angry passions had not subsided.

He did not need to be told that there were Easterners who were fearful of westward expansion and were determined that it should not redound to the advantage of his political party, but he had received a strong reminder from President Monroe. This was in the course of their correspondence some months earlier about the treaty with Spain, which had been negotiated in 1819 but had not yet been ratified by that country. Besides providing for the purchase of Florida, it drew the western boundary of the Louisiana Purchase so as to exclude Texas. Jefferson, expressing no sorrow over the failure of ratification, said that Texas would be the richest state of the Union. He believed that, since Florida was already theirs, occupation could await the proper circumstances. This inveterate expansionist, who had once hoped to annex Canada, would have liked also to acquire Cuba for strategic reasons. In response to his comments Monroe stated that, although he agreed that Spain could not prevent the United States from taking as much territory as she desired, Texas had been and must be dismissed from consideration because of fierce internal political opposition to expansion in the Southwest.[33]

Jefferson had not blamed Monroe for taking this position in his desire to maintain peace. Nor had he criticized him for accepting the supposed

[31] TJ to Richard Rush, Oct. 20, 1820 (L. & B., XV, 283–284).

[32] Article 4, Section 2. Dangerfield, *Awakening of American Nationalism*, pp. 129–134; Moore, *Missouri Controversy*, pp. 144–145, 164–167. Some southern congressmen contended that blacks could not be citizens of the United States, a position later supported in the Dred Scott case.

[33] Monroe to TJ, May 3, 20, 1820 (S.M.H., VI, 118–123); TJ to Monroe, May 14, 1820 (Ford, X, 158–159).

settlement which the Sixteenth Congress reached in its first session. That settlement was far from popular in Virginia, and the publication, in the fall of 1820, of John Taylor's *Construction Construed and Constitutions Vindicated* marked a resurgence of state-rights sentiment. Jefferson avoided public involvement in the movement, but the events of this period undoubtedly accentuated his fears of centralized national authority. He was still blaming the Missouri controversy on the Federalists. They had put up no presidential candidate against Monroe in 1820, thus allowing him to win re-election by default. They had largely given up their old name and were calling themselves Republicans, but he attributed to them unchanged aims and principles. Those whom he had once called monarchists he now called consolidationists and Tories, saying that they were seeking to regain power by claiming to be something else.

Just after Christmas in 1820, when the outcome of the conflict in Congress remained uncertain, Jefferson described and interpreted American developments in several letters to friends abroad.[34] With Albert Gallatin he discussed the deplorable financial situation and the encroachment of the federal judiciary as well as the Missouri question. To all these correspondents he said that there was only a semblance of morality in the anti-Missouri position. In 1784 he himself had recommended the exclusion of slavery from the territories, and he seems never to have questioned the constitutional authority of Congress to take such action in the present instance. But the effort had been made to impose on Missouri as a state restrictions that had not been put upon her as a territory.

In this confused situation he expressed himself strongly to Gallatin. After tracing the sectional boundary line as he envisioned it and pointing out the numerical superiority of the states above it, he said:

> With these, therefore, it is merely a question of power; but with this geographical minority it is a question of existence. For if Congress once goes out of the Constitution to arrogate a right of regulating the condition of the inhabitants of the States, its majority may, and probably will, next declare that the condition of all men within the United States shall be that of freedom; in which case all the whites south of the Potomac and Ohio must evacuate their States, and most fortunate those who can do it first.[35]

Writing John Adams early in the new year, he reported that the anxieties in his quarter were all centered on the intentions of the "Holy Alliance"

[34]Letters of Dec. 26, 1820, to D. B. Warden, Albert Gallatin, and Lafayette (Ford, X, 171–173, 175–181). As was often the case, he was unduly optimistic in writing to the Marquis de Lafayette.

[35]TJ to Gallatin, Dec. 26, 1820 (*ibid.*, X, 177).

regarding Missouri. "The real question, as seen in the states afflicted with this unfortunate population," he said, "is, are our slaves to be presented with freedom and a dagger?"[36]

Jefferson claimed that the Missouri controversy had had one good effect. He told Gallatin that it had brought to the attention of Virginians as never before "the necessity of some plan of general emancipation and deportation." In fact, their Governor had proposed one in his message to the legislature in December, 1820. He was none other than Jefferson's son-in-law, Thomas Mann Randolph, who had been in office for a year and was to serve two years more. Randolph's proposals did not go very far. Expressing alarm at the growth of the slave population, he recommended a reduction in it, coupling deportation with emancipation. This was in accord with the law of 1806, which required that manumitted slaves leave the state. As a destination he suggested St. Domingo, where it appears they would have been welcome.[37]

As Jefferson expected, the moderate proposal of the Governor was not acted on by the legislature. In fact, it excited opposition. Several months before he made it, Randolph had spoken disapprovingly of "the new morality which tolerates perpetuity of slavery, and the new doctrine of the civil benefits supposed to be derived from that system."[38] At the seat of the state government in Richmond he may have perceived the proslavery reaction sooner than his father-in-law did and moderated his proposal accordingly.

We can easily imagine what would have happened if Jefferson's own plan had been presented. As described by him to Gallatin, it still called for the emancipation, without compensation to the owners, of all slaves born after a specified date. He said that because of the closeness of St. Domingo, transportation would be feasible and would be supported by charitable contributions — especially from Europeans and New Englanders who played such a conspicuous part in the slave trade. He also said that the proceeds of the land office might be drawn upon if these should be regarded as appropriate.

Early in the new year he started the so-called autobiography he never finished. The Missouri question was still before Congress on February 8, 1821, when he wrote for the benefit of posterity the following passage:

> Nothing is more certainly written in the book of fate than that these people are to be free. Nor is it less certain that the two races,

[36] TJ to Adams, Jan. 22, 1821 (*A.-J. Letters*, p. 570).

[37] Gaines, pp. 124–126.

[38] TMR to Nicholas Trist, June 5, 1820 (Trist, UNC). He also denied the validity of the analogy, then being drawn, between the freeing of the slaves and the returning of the land to the Indians.

equally free, cannot live in the same government. Nature, habit, opinion has drawn indelible lines of distinction between them. It is still in our power to direct the process of emancipation and deportation peaceably and in such slow degree as that the evil will wear off insensibly, and their place be pari passu filled up by free white laborers. If on the contrary it is left to force itself on, human nature must shudder at the prospect held up.[39]

His hopes had to be fed by inner fire that winter. If he followed the continued wrangle over Missouri in Congress, he could have gained little comfort and no pleasure from it. At the end of February a "compromise" was finally reached under the influence of Henry Clay. The constitution of Missouri was accepted on the understanding that the objectionable clause did not in fact abridge the rights of any citizen. The Missouri legislature was required to make a statement to that effect. This it eventually did under protest, asserting the sovereignty of the state in an ill-mannered resolution. Jefferson appears to have made no specific comments on the contradictory and somewhat ludicrous settlement, but his statement to Judge Spencer Roane that the Missouri question was "smeared over" for the present was far from inexact. And his further statement that the "geographical demarcation" was indelible was appallingly accurate.[40]

Judging from the few references to the Missouri question in Jefferson's correspondence during the rest of his life, he never changed his mind about it. Late in the summer of 1821 he told his old colleague Henry Dearborn, himself a Yankee, that the only sure result of the controversy was the resurrection of the "Hartford convention men."[41] They had wriggled into seats of power "under the auspices of morality," he said. He told Dearborn he still believed that the westward extension of the "confederacy" would ensure its survival "by overruling local factions, that might shake a smaller association." He did not mention the exclusion of slavery from all of the Louisiana Purchase above 36°30′, except for Missouri. His great concern had been for the admission of that state on an equal footing with the others, and he appears to have been relatively indifferent to the price paid for this. When his friend Lafayette

[39] Autobiography, Jan.–July, 1821 (Ford, I, 68). From the manuscript of this document (LC) it is possible to determine the precise date on which this was written.

[40] TJ to Spencer Roane, Mar. 9, 1821 (Ford, X, 189). The "compromise" was approved Feb. 26, and Missouri was recognized by President Monroe as a member of the Union on Aug. 10 (Dangerfield, *Awakening of American Nationalism*, pp. 135–136; Moore, *Missouri Controversy*, pp. 154–169).

[41] TJ to Dearborn, Aug. 17, 1821 (Ford, X, 191–192).

questioned his claim that the dispersal of the slaves would facilitate emancipation, he did not take up the challenge.[42]

He continued to maintain that, while now calling themselves Republicans and masquerading as moralists, the Federalists were really Tories. As described by this ardent Whig to numerous correspondents in these years, party differences were rooted in human nature. Instead of a geographical line he wanted to draw one that was based on principle. To one inquirer he said: "I consider the party division of Whig and Tory the most wholesome which can exist in any government, and well worthy of being nourished, to keep out those of a more dangerous character."[43] At no time were his fellow citizens as rational as he wanted them to be, but for a time the sectional line was to be somewhat obscured as the result of political developments. The alignment he had done so much to create was to be essentially restored in the name of Jacksonian democracy, and the nation was again to feel the unifying force of party. He saw only the beginning of these developments and probably did not fully understand them.[44]

The fulfillment of his direful prophecy about the breakup of the Union was postponed, but the immediate effect of the bitter attacks on slavery in the North was a defensive reaction in Virginia and states to the southward. This was destined to increase greatly after Jefferson's death. He had no sympathy whatever with the proslavery philosophy, but, determined as he was to avoid controversy of any sort, he entered into no public discussion of the question. His comments on slavery and emancipation were made in private letters, nearly always in response to inquiries. These comments show that his position was unchanged. In fact, he elaborated upon his original plan. Toward the end of his life he described it in detail to Jared Sparks and other northern supporters of colonization.[45] It was a logical and humane plan, but it required enormous faith to believe that it could have been adopted and put into effect. At best it would have taken from twenty-five to fifty years and would have been an exceedingly costly operation. He himself may have doubted its practicality but could think of nothing better.

He never fully recovered his optimism after the Missouri controversy, but it was not in his nature to despair. He believed that his sentiments

[42] Lafayette to TJ, July 1, 1821; June 1, 1822; TJ to Lafayette, Nov. 4, 1823 (Chinard, *Letters of Lafayette and Jefferson*, pp. 407–409, 414–416).

[43] TJ to William T. Barry, July 2, 1822 (L. & B., XV, 388). See ch. XIV above, for a discussion of TJ's use of the terms Whig and Tory.

[44] For a most interesting interpretation of these developments, see Richard H. Brown, "The Missouri Crisis, Slavery, and the Politics of Jacksonianism," *South Atlantic Quarterly*, LXV (Winter, 1966), 55–72.

[45] TJ to Sparks, Feb. 4, 1824 (Ford, X, 289–293).

would not die with him. On reading correspondence of his that was published after his death, John Quincy Adams said: "Mr. Jefferson's love of liberty was sincere and ardent — not confined to himself, like that of most of his fellow slave-holders."[46] This consistent antislavery man added, however, that his father's old friend was no martyr. Furthermore, Jefferson was convinced that martyrdom would accomplish nothing. All he hoped to do was open the University of Virginia. He continued to view slavery as a "fatal blot" on his society. This he could not remove, but he wrote to one inquirer: "Time, which outlives all things, will outlive this evil also."[47]

[46] *The Diary of John Quincy Adams, 1794–1845*, ed. by Allan Nevins (1951), Jan. 27, 1831, p. 412.

[47] TJ to James Heaton, May 20, 1826 (LC).

[XXIV]

Republicanism, Consolidation, and State Rights

TO Jefferson's mind the crucial test to be applied to all public measures and political institutions was that of conformity to the principles of republicanism. In his judgment the proposed restrictions on the state of Missouri did not meet the test. Neither did the constitution of his own commonwealth. This had been adopted in 1776. Forty years later, speaking of that time, he said: "We had not yet penetrated to the mother principle, that 'governments are republican only in proportion as they embody the will of their people, and execute it.' "[1] He himself was the most democratic of the leading Virginians during the American Revolution, and his ardor for self-government had increased with the passing years.[2]

In his seventies he was especially desirous that this be extended in the local field, so that every citizen should have an active part in government. He described the townships of New England as "the wisest invention ever devised by the wit of man for the perfect exercise of self-government, and for its preservation."[3] As we have previously noted in connection with his unrealized program for general education, he wanted to divide the counties into wards or townships and place an elementary school in each of them. He envisaged a graduated series of republics — wards, counties, state, and nation — each of which should perform the functions for which it was best fitted, without interference from the others.[4] In the wards direct democracy, like that of New England towns and Greek city-states, was feasible. In all the other "republics," recourse must be had to the representative principle, but responsiveness to the will of the people was essential in all cases.

[1] TJ to Samuel Kercheval, July 12, 1816 (Ford, X, 37).

[2] For a discussion of his early position, see *Jefferson the Virginian*, pp. 235–239, 379–382.

[3] TJ to Kercheval, July 12, 1816 (Ford, X, 41).

[4] This series is well described in his letter to Feb. 2, 1816, to Joseph C. Cabell (L. & B., XIV, 419–423). See above, pp. 248–249.

He claimed that decentralization would make for efficiency. For example, an elementary school could be better directed by the parents in the locality than by a board of education at the state capital. The difficulties of travel and communication in that time added strength to this argument. But he was more fearful of tyranny than of inefficiency, and he was mainly concerned with safeguarding the rights and opportunities of individual human beings. He thought of his commonwealth and its subdivisions chiefly as people, not as governments. In one letter he quoted with approval the following stanza:

What constitutes a State?
Not high-raised battlements, or labor'd mound,
Thick wall, or moated gate;
Not cities proud, with spires and turrets crown'd;
No: men, high minded men;
Men, who their duties know;
But know their rights; and knowing, dare maintain.
These constitute a State.[5]

To another correspondent he said: "My most earnest wish is to see the republican element of popular control pushed to the maximum of its practicable exercise."[6]

During the session of the General Assembly (1815–1816), at which the establishment of Central College was approved, a proposal for a state constitutional convention was rejected. Agitation for such a convention continued through the year, however, and Jefferson's advice was asked on this question. Also, he received from learned friends writings of a theoretical nature that called for comment. From the letters he wrote at this juncture it would appear that his faith in the mass of the people and his zeal for constitutional reform exceeded that of any of his correspondents.

One of the most distinguished of these was Du Pont de Nemours, whose proposed constitution for the "Equinoctial Republics" was regarded by Jefferson as insufficiently republican.[7] To this correspondent he said: "We both consider the people as our children, and love them with parental affection. But you love them as infants whom you are afraid to trust without nurses; and I as adults whom I freely leave to self-government." In his own country he would never have recommended such property requirements for voting as Du Pont did. He

[5] TJ to John Taylor, May 28, 1816 (Ford, X, 30). The verses are from "An Ode in Imitation of Alcaeus" by Sir William Jones (1746–1794).

[6] TJ to Isaac H. Tiffany, Aug. 26, 1816 (L. & B., XV, 66).

[7] TJ to Du Pont, Apr. 24, 1816, replying to a letter of Mar. 31 (*J.-D. Correspondence*, pp. 176–187).

granted that the people in the newly established Latin American republics were not yet ready for full self-government. He set a high value on political experience, and at just this time he expressed approval of a literacy requirement for citizenship.

As an advocate of popular participation in American government, he went much further than John Taylor of Caroline, the leading political theorist of his own state. Commenting on that author's ponderous work *An Inquiry into the Principles and Policy of the Government of the United States* (1814), he said that he and Taylor could not disagree on the "fundamentals of rightful government."[8] But the two men did disagree on the question of reform at home. Besides defending slavery, Taylor supported the system of county government that Jefferson described as vicious. While recognizing that the county court had been a useful institution, Jefferson regarded it as a self-perpetuating oligarchy and an obstacle to the local self-government which he was so eager to establish.[9] He had concluded that the people had less participation in local government and less control of their agents than their rights and interests required. Therefore, he favored thoroughgoing reformation.

At this time the impelling force behind the movement for a state constitutional convention was not zeal for general reform such as animated Jefferson, but the desire to rid the representative system in the legislature of some of its gross inequities.[10] Since the region beyond the Blue Ridge was discriminated against, this was essentially a western movement. Each county had two delegates in the lower House despite disparities in population. Since there were almost as many counties in the west as in the east, the inequities in the House of Delegates provided little ground for sectional conflict.

Neither did the requirements for the suffrage, which had remained unchanged since 1785. In the country these consisted of a freehold of fifty uncleared acres with a house, while a house and lot were required in town. During and after the War of 1812 there was considerable protest in behalf of disfranchised militiamen, but their situation was probably worse in the east than in the west, where the law seems to have been more often evaded. The controversy centered on the make-up of the Senate, where the east had twenty representatives and the west only four, though its population was almost as great as that of the older re-

[8] TJ to Taylor, May 28, 1816 (Ford, X, 28).

[9] Taylor to TJ, July 10, 1816 (Mo. Hist. Soc.); TJ to Taylor, July 21 (Ford, X, 50–55). For their differences on slavery, see above, p. 330.

[10] See the monographs of J. A. C. Chandler, *Representation in Virginia* (1896), pp. 23–26; and *The History of Suffrage in Virginia* (1901), pp. 9–28; as well as J. R. Pole, "Representation and Authority in Virginia from the Revolution to Reform," *Jour. Sou. Hist.*, XXIV (1958), 16–50.

gion. This situation was uppermost in the minds of the westerners who gathered in Winchester in May, 1816, and called for a meeting in Staunton in August. Between those dates Jefferson received a pamphlet in which a constitutional convention was advocated. The author, who wrote under a fictitious name, asked his opinion of the proposal. His lengthy reply to the man, who turned out to be Samuel Kercheval, did far more than answer the particular question that had been asked him. Besides proclaiming the principles of republicanism as he understood them, he applied these to the government of Virginia more fully than anyone else had. Also, he expressed himself on the subject of political institutions so aptly that his words have been quoted until this day.[11]

Though he had not ceased to support the doctrine of strict construction and was never to do so, he stated here that he did not view constitutions with "sanctimonious reverence." Until the end of his days he advocated their periodical revision in the light of change and experience. Here he said:

> I think moderate imperfections had better be borne with; because, when once known, we accommodate ourselves to them, and find practical means of correcting their ill effects. But I know also, that laws and institutions must go hand in hand with the progress of the human mind. As that becomes more developed, more enlightened, as new discoveries are made, new truths disclosed, and manners and opinions change with the change of circumstances, institutions must advance also, and keep pace with the times. We might as well require a man to wear still the coat which fitted him when a boy, as civilized society to remain ever under the regimen of their barbarous ancestors.[12]

He believed that this "preposterous idea" had caused Europe to be recently deluged with blood. Rulers had clung to old abuses, leaving to their unfortunate subjects no recourse but to violence and revolution. He avowed his own faith in peaceful deliberation and collective wisdom.

In his *Notes on Virginia* he had put himself on record as favoring a constitutional convention and had spoken in particular of the need to correct the inequities in representation. He now favored a convention more than ever and did not mind saying so in private, but he did not want it to be limited to this single question. For the benefit of the westerner, therefore, he presented his ideas about what else should be done.

[11] TJ to Kercheval, July 12, 1816 (Ford, X, 37–45). This famous letter was actually addressed to H. Tompkinson, the name that appeared on the pamphlet and was signed to a letter to TJ of June 13 (LC).

[12] Ford, X, 42–43.

He told this stranger, as he had told John Taylor, that, while the people of their state were republican in spirit, there was hardly any republicanism in their government.[13]

No part of the state government met the test that he applied. Only the members of the General Assembly were elected, and, because of property restrictions on the suffrage, fewer than half of the free men could vote. Furthermore, because of the county-unit system, the apportionment did not correspond to the actual distribution of the population. The state was governed by a minority. Besides favoring general suffrage, fair apportionment, and direct participation of the citizenry in local affairs, Jefferson would have made virtually all officials elective.

In his opinion, the most irresponsible of the public functionaries were the judges. While fully recognizing the importance of their independence from a king, as in England, he regarded judicial independence from popular control as a solecism in a self-governing society. He believed that, if appointed, they should be named for terms of years by the governor, not chosen by the legislature, and that in any case they should be removable on concurrence of the legislature and the executive.

He capped this program for a completely self-governing society with a recommendation that provision be made for periodical revision of the constitution. He probably knew more about the history of Virginia than anybody else, and he frequently invoked the spirit of '76, but he tried to prevent his state from being ruled by the dead hand of the past. "The corporeal globe, and everything upon it, belong to its present corporeal inhabitants," he said, adding that they alone had the right to determine the laws and institutions under which they should live.[14]

A quarter of a century earlier, Madison had admonished him that frequent changes in basic law would be disturbing, but he still held that constitutions should be reviewed every twenty years.[15] Members of the ruling gentry could hardly have failed to regard his program as theoretical and drastic. Relatively few may have been aware of it at the time, but Joseph C. Cabell, one of the most enlightened of them, was. Jefferson sent him a copy of his letter to Kercheval. Cabell found all of Jefferson's views interesting but did not accept the main one. He distrusted the mass of the people and feared the consequences of a convention. Before returning the letter, however, he made a copy of it for further

[13] He summed up his desired amendments as follows: 1) General suffrage. 2) Equal representation in the legislature. 3) An executive chosen by the people. 4) Judges elective or removable. 5) Justices, jurors, and sheriffs elective. 6) Ward divisions. 7) Periodical amendments of the constitution. (Ford, X, 41.)

[14] *Ibid.*, 44.

[15] See *Jefferson and the Rights of Man*, p. 179.

perusal and took the liberty of showing this to a few discreet friends. To that action Jefferson took no exception.[16]

Kercheval, for whose benefit this letter was written in the first place, said that Jefferson's "lucid and candid exposition of republican canons" had taken "strong hold" on the minds of men who had hitherto been political opponents of his. Kercheval wanted to publish it. Jefferson denied that request, making his customary plea for anonymity, but continued to discuss the subject, laying special emphasis on the reform nearest his heart, the division of the counties into wards.[17] According to his nephew, Judge Dabney Carr, who lived in Winchester in the same county as Kercheval, his first letter to that gentleman was widely distributed, and he feared it would occasion bitter debate. It was in the hands of an editor, and Carr wanted to prevent its publication. He himself had read it and may be presumed not to have fully agreed with it, though he claimed that his motive in writing was to guard his uncle's repose.[18]

Annoyed by this abuse of his confidence, Jefferson wrote Kercheval another letter, entrusting it to Carr for delivery.[19] In this he requested that his original letter be recalled, along with any copies of it that may have been made. While he had had no objection to the recipient's making its contents known to a few trusted friends, he never expected the letter to leave Kercheval's hands. Since the question of a convention had become one of party, he would not enter into it, he said, adding that, despite the imperfections of their government, he could live under it, even if the constitution were not amended. That was just what he was fated to do the rest of his days.

The Staunton convention in August recommended that the question of calling a convention be submitted to a popular vote. This proposal was agreed to by the House of Delegates at the next session of the legislature but was rejected by the Senate. The inequitable apportionment in that chamber was partly remedied, however. Five senators were taken from the over-represented east and given to the west. Thus, instead of 20 to 4, the proportion was 15 to 9. Western discontent was temporarily allayed, but Jefferson, while quiescent, was far from satisfied. The question of a convention came up again in 1824. His attitude was well known at that time. Indeed, there were defenders of the state establishment who believed that no convention should be hazarded while he was still living.[20]

[16] TJ to Cabell, July 14, 1816; Cabell to TJ, Aug. 4 (Cabell, pp. 67–69; originals UVA). The passage in which Cabell expressed disapproval of a convention does not appear in the printed version of his letter.

[17] Kercheval to TJ, Aug. 16, 1816 (LC); TJ to Kercheval, Sept. 5, 1816 (Ford, X, 45–46).

[18] Carr to TJ, Sept. 24, 1816 (LC).

[19] TJ to Kercheval, Oct. 8, 1816 (Ford, X, 46–47), enclosed in a letter to Carr (LC).

[20] Chandler, *Representation in Virginia*, pp. 25–26. See below, pp. 441–443.

ii

Jefferson never ceased to hold that the Federalists had been a threat to true republicanism and that his own party had preserved and extended it. Shortly before the Missouri question aroused his fears for the Union he sketched, for the benefit of posterity, the history of the party conflict prior to his own presidency. This was in an explanation of three large bound volumes of confidential papers he had collected while secretary of state.[21] The explanation bears the date February 4, 1818. While it was occasioned by a re-examination of his papers, he had long intended to provide an antidote to what he regarded as the poison of John Marshall's life of George Washington.[22]

Jefferson paid tribute to his old chief here, as elsewhere, saying that the great man was too fair-minded to have written such a book and that it gave no impression of the nobility of the cause for which he fought. It was Marshall's account of the period immediately following the adoption of the Constitution which most dismayed the one-time secretary of state, party leader, and Vice President. From this partisan account, he said, one would suppose that the members of his party were mere grumblers and disorganizers, enemies of government, unprincipled seekers after the loaves and fishes of public office. Here he asserted that "the contests of that day were contests of principle, between the advocates of republican, and those of kingly government."

While his objections to John Marshall's interpretation of the party battles of the 1790's were certainly not without warrant, he himself viewed the conflict as a partisan, not as a judicious historian.[23] In his highly colored account he over-stated the case for the members of his party and against their opponents. Under his leadership the Republicans stemmed a tide of political reaction but seem to have faced no such a monarchical threat as he supposed. At any rate, monarchism was indubitably dead in the young Republic. So also, as he was saying at just this time, was the Federalist party.[24] He did not doubt that the basic struggle would continue — between those who trusted and those who distrusted the people generally. He could not have been pleased with the undemocratic struc-

[21] The exact contents of these volumes can no longer be determined. The informal notes he included have been published as his "Ana" or "Anas." See *Jefferson and the Rights of Man*, p. 497.

[22] The explanation is in Ford, I, 154–168. For a discussion of TJ and Marshall's *Life of Washington*, see *Jefferson the President: Second Term*, pp. 356–359.

[23] TJ's account of events, written long after they occurred, must of course be checked against contemporary records. For instance, see *Jefferson and the Rights of Man*, p. 507, for a reference to earlier and later versions of the "bargain" over assumption and residence.

[24] TJ to Albert Gallatin, Feb. 15, 1818 (L. & B., XIX, 259).

ture of the government in his own state, but for a time he was relatively complacent about the federal government. It was headed by James Monroe, a close friend whom he regarded as a true republican. He certainly did not so regard the head of the federal judiciary, and he privately approved of attacks on John Marshall as a consolidationist, though he did not instigate them.

Said the Chief Justice to Justice Joseph Story in Massachusetts: "Our opinion in the Bank case has roused the Sleeping Spirit of Virginia, if indeed it ever sleeps."[25] He expected it to be attacked with asperity in the papers and to be regarded there as "damnably heretical." A few weeks later Marshall's sweeping assertion of national supremacy and liberal construction in the case of McCulloch *vs.* Maryland was strongly assailed in a series of articles by HAMPDEN in the *Richmond Enquirer.*[26] Jefferson read these in Ritchie's paper and said that he did so again with redoubled approbation when he received copies of them from their author, Judge Spencer Roane.[27] He said that he subscribed to "every tittle" of them.

Jefferson entered into no discussion of the case itself. More than a quarter of a century earlier he had argued against the constitutionality of the first Bank of the United States in an opinion which President Washington rejected in favor of one by Hamilton.[28] The latter had come into Marshall's hands in the papers of Washington and was directly drawn upon in his own opinion in the case of McCulloch *vs.* Maryland, sometimes almost word for word. After Madison signed the bill creating the second Bank of the United States (1816), Jefferson appears to have refrained from expressing constitutional objections to that institution. There is no reason to suppose he had abandoned these, however, and he undoubtedly blamed the bank for much of the financial difficulty of the time. His comment on this momentous decision to his friend Roane was brief and couched in general terms.

He praised the essays by Hampden as containing "the true principles of the revolution of 1800." This he regarded as comparable to that of 1776. His recent review of his years in opposition, when going over his papers, had served to heighten the contrast in his own mind between the parties he designated respectively as monarchist and republican. Fur-

[25] Marshall to Story, Mar. 26, 1819 ("Story–Marshall Correspondence," ed. by Charles Warren, in *W. & M.*, 2nd ser., XXI [Jan., 1941], p. 2).

[26] June 11–12, 1819. The opinion was delivered Mar. 6. The opinion and the newspaper debate over it can be seen in Gerald Gunther, ed., *John Marshall's Defense of McCulloch vs. Maryland* (1969). Gunther provides a perceptive introduction.

[27] TJ to Spencer Roane, Sept. 6, 1819 (Ford, X, 140–143).

[28] See *Jefferson and the Rights of Man*, ch. XX. It should be noted that TJ did not see this at the time.

thermore, his reflections on the structure of government in his own state had strengthened his impression that a wholly independent judiciary was an anomaly in a self-governing society. Despite the loss of Federalist control of the executive and legislative branches, he said, "we find the judiciary on every occasion, still driving us into consolidation." He described the three branches of the federal government as co-ordinate and independent, each being empowered, as he believed, to adjudge the constitutionality of its own actions. He had proceeded on that understanding as President. Then and thereafter he denied the authority of the Supreme Court to prescribe the legal obligations of the President. The Chief Justice had assumed this in the case of Marbury *vs.* Madison.[29]

The decisions in which Marshall over-ruled state legislatures and state courts (especially from 1819 to 1824) were of crucial importance in the development of nationalism. In the year 1819, however, Jefferson condemned the Supreme Court chiefly on grounds of republicanism rather than on those of state rights *per se*. In the doctrine of liberal construction that was so powerfully proclaimed in the opinion in the bank case, Spencer Roane perceived the threat of unlimited government. So unquestionably did Jefferson, but it seems to have taken the Missouri controversy to excite his acute fears for the future of Virginia, and, as was to be expected, he denied Roane's request to publish his letter.

Private comments of his on the role of the federal judiciary, made about a year later, had some currency in Massachusetts. These were in a letter to William Charles Jarvis of Pittsfield, who had sent him a work entitled *The Republican*. In this he found what he regarded as a dangerously erroneous doctrine — namely, that judges were "the ultimate arbiters" in all constitutional matters. He said that he himself knew of "no safe depository of the ultimate powers of the society but the people themselves." He expressly stated that such power did not belong to a judicial oligarchy whose members were irresponsible and irremovable. Justice Joseph Story told Chief Justice Marshall that this letter was publicly displayed in a bookstore and described it as shocking. Its obvious purpose, he said, was "to prostrate the judicial authority and annihilate all public reverence of its dignity." To his mind the old man who wrote it was attempting to destroy the government. Actually, Jefferson was arguing chiefly against what he regarded as an unwarranted assumption of authority over the executive and legislative branches of the federal government. He did not deny the validity of judicial review of congressional actions relating to the rights of individuals. Nor did he at this time

[29] TJ's constitutional position is described and discussed in *Jefferson the President: First Term*, pp. 143–156.

address himself particularly to the question of the relations between the federal judiciary and the governments of states.[30]

Marshall himself, charging Jefferson with personal ill will toward the federal judiciary, attributed this to that gentleman's resentful remembrance of the case of Marbury *vs.* Madison and even more to that of the batture case. To these painful recollections of personal discomfiture at the hands of the Chief Justice could have been added others that arose from the Burr trial and the biography of Washington. Jefferson's antipathy to the Chief Justice was fully reciprocated by the latter. In writing Story, Marshall thus described his historic antagonist:

> He is among the most ambitious, and I suspect among the most unforgiving of men. His great power is over the mass of the people, and this power is chiefly acquired by professions of democracy. Every check on the wild impulse of the moment is a check on his own power, and he is unfriendly to the source from which it flows.[31]

This passage reflects a grave misunderstanding of Jefferson's character and motives. He used vigorous, and at times extravagant, language in the advocacy of causes in which he believed and was notably persistent in the pursuit of them. He descended to personalities less often than most of his enemies did, however, and made a special point of not doing so in public. As men of great achievement go, he does not seem to have been especially ambitious. He was no seeker of power for its own sake. He profoundly distrusted power, and while he enjoyed personal popularity, he was no mere professor of democracy. His confidence in the people Marshall did not match, and the Chief Justice feared the centrifugal forces in American society as an ex-President did the centripetal trend that he perceived in the government. There is no evidence that he and Marshall met during his retirement. The distance between their minds was even greater than that between their persons.[32]

iii

A couple of months after Jefferson wrote the letter that Justice Story was to find so shocking, Thomas Ritchie of the *Richmond Enquirer* sent

[30] TJ to Jarvis, Sept. 28, 1820 (Ford, X, 160–161); Story to Marshall, June 27, 1821 ("Story-Marshall Correspondence," pp. 7–8). Warren (pp. 9–10) says Story and Marshall, as well as subsequent writers, misread TJ's position on judicial review.

[31] Marshall to Story, July 13, 1821 ("Story-Marshall Correspondence," pp. 13–14).

[32] See J. P. Boyd, "The Chasm That Separated Thomas Jefferson and John Marshall," in *Essays on the American Constitution*, ed. by Gottfried Dietze (1964), pp. 3–20.

him at Monticello a copy of a book by John Taylor of Caroline entitled *Construction Construed, and Constitutions Vindicated.* He was on a long visit to Poplar Forest at the time and had not yet read it when, on Christmas day 1820, he thanked Ritchie for it. While expressing his unwillingness to make a comment on it for publication as requested, he said he was sure that Taylor's work was "orthodox" and that he would approve of it.[33] This was neither the first nor the last time that, when referring to principles of government, he had recourse to terminology that is commonly associated with theology. Marshall did the same thing when he said that his views would be regarded as "heretical" in his own state.

There was a definite body of constitutional doctrine that could be designated as Virginian. Strictly speaking, this was the doctrine of the Republican party in the state, but it had received official sanction. The General Assembly had approved Madison's Resolutions of 1798, protesting against the Alien and Sedition Acts on principle. It also approved his classic report of 1800. This closely reasoned and carefully written document may be said to have constituted the articles of faith of Virginia Republicanism from this time forward. Madison held that the Constitution originated in compact, that a state retained all the powers not specifically delegated to the federal government, and that it could determine when its rights had been infringed upon. He recognized that the judicial branch, as well as the executive and legislative, was capable of "usurpation." The meaning of the right of "interposition" which he claimed is not clear, but it could be interpreted as the right to protest. No violent action was suggested.

Madison's exposition of state rights is much better balanced and more moderate in tone than Jefferson's assertion of them in his draft of the Kentucky Resolutions of 1798. Jefferson claimed for the states the right to judge not only the infractions of the compact but also "the mode and measure of redress." He asserted that the proper remedy for infractions of the compact was nullification. The word does not appear in the resolutions as adopted, however, and his authorship of them remained unknown to the public.[34] In the period of the Alien and Sedition Acts he was convinced that all three departments of the federal government were working in conjunction to suppress freedom of speech and eliminate po-

[33] TJ to Thomas Ritchie, Dec. 25, 1820 (Ford, X, 169–171), replying to a letter of Nov. 23 (MHS).

[34] Taylor's reference to TJ's authorship in 1814 in *An Inquiry into the Principles and Policy of the Government of the United States*, p. 649, seems to have been little noted. Madison's report, adopted in 1800, was presented in 1799 and is referred to by both dates. It can be conveniently seen in Hunt, VI, 341–406. For a fuller account of these documents and the circumstances that occasioned them, see *Jefferson and the Ordeal of Liberty*, pp. 395–409, 422–424.

litical opposition. Some of the actions of his two successors in the presidency had been criticized by old-line Republicans, and it may have been for this reason that he assured Ritchie of his entire confidence in the republicanism of Madison and Monroe. He was unsure of Congress, as his comments on the Missouri question clearly show, but took comfort in the thought that legislators had to be elected and could be defeated. The real danger, as he perceived and described it, lay in another branch of the government:

> The judiciary of the United States is the subtle corps of sappers and miners constantly working under ground to undermine the foundations of our confederated fabric. They are construing our constitution from a co-ordination of a general and special government to a general and supreme one alone. This will lay all things at their feet, and they are too well versed in English law to forget the maxim, "*boni judicis est ampliare jurisdictionem.*"[35]

In his opinion the judges, having found impeachment to be a mere scarecrow, had "skulked" their responsibility to the public.

Jefferson had said that Taylor's *Arator* was "so involved in quaint, far-fetched, affected, mystical concepts, and flimsy theories," that it was too much trouble to get at what was good in the book.[36] After reading this difficult author's latest work, *Construction Construed*, he pronounced it the best treatise on republicanism that had appeared since the adoption of the Constitution.[37] Taylor once admitted that there was in his nature "a spice of fanaticism" on the subjects of republicanism and agriculture.[38] In his letter to this kindred spirit, Jefferson manifested zeal for the rights of a state which bordered on fanaticism. The religious liberal appears here as a political dogmatist, the universal man as a localist.

Since he never discussed *Construction Construed* in detail, it is impossible to determine how much influence it had on him. Taylor integrated the grievances that Jefferson had been writing about privately and may have caused him to regard the threat to their state and his most cherished values to be even greater than he had supposed. But he himself said that the Missouri question was the firebell that awakened him. He had no need to turn to this book for constitutional doctrine, though he could

[35] TJ to Ritchie, Dec. 25, 1820 (Ford, X, 170).

[36] TJ to John Adams, Jan. 24, 1814 (*A.-J. Letters*, p. 421).

[37] TJ to Taylor, Feb. 14, 1821 (*Papers, MHS*, pp. 305–306). For a stimulating discussion of Taylor's book and its influence, see R. E. Shalhope, "Thomas Jefferson's Republicanism and Antebellum Southern Thought," *Jour. Sou. Hist.*, XLII (Nov., 1976), pp. 548–551.

[38] Taylor to TJ, May 5, 1795; see *Jefferson and the Ordeal of Liberty*, p. 264.

have found in it reminders of what he had said in the Kentucky Resolutions.[39] It can be argued that Taylor was reverting to the constitutional position Jefferson had taken in 1798.

In 1821 the attention of both men was particularly directed to the rights of their own commonwealth, which were at issue in the case of Cohens *vs.* Virginia. The Cohens had been convicted in a lower Virginia court of selling a lottery ticket in violation of state law. The lottery had been organized by the city of Washington under authority of an act of Congress. The case was not appealed to a higher state court but to the United States Supreme Court. The legislature of Virginia by resolution protested against this action as an infringement on its sovereignty and an invasion of its jurisdiction. Counsel for the state were instructed to confine themselves to the question of jurisdiction and to have no further part in the proceedings if the decision went against them on this point. This it did when Marshall made a sweeping assertion of appellate jurisdiction over state courts.[40] Soon thereafter he upheld the action of the Virginia court on the merits of the case. Thus the astute Chief Justice availed himself of the opportunity afforded by a petty case to assert vast authority. Virginians may be said to have brought humiliation on themselves by making so much of the issue of jurisdiction, but they were no less resentful for that reason.[41]

Jefferson's fears of consolidation and judicial supremacy were undoubtedly accentuated by the decision in the lottery case, but more than three months passed before he finally yielded to the continued pressure on him to give public expression to his approval of John Taylor's book. Such action was persistently urged by Spencer Roane, and a plan of procedure was worked out with the Judge. Jefferson drafted what he designated as an extract of a letter, leaving the name of the supposed correspondent blank. He sent this to Roane who gave it to Ritchie, who published it in the *Enquirer* without implying the author's consent.[42]

If Jefferson had named the actual recipient of this "self-styled extract," he would have associated himself with the most conspicuous critic of

[39] Taylor quoted the assertion that a state had a right to determine not only the occurrence of an infraction of the constitutional compact but also the mode and measure of redress (*Construction Construed*, pp. 133–134). He stated that the Kentucky Resolutions were "said" to have been written by TJ.

[40] Mar. 3, 1821. The events are well described by Charles Warren, *Supreme Court in U.S. History*, II, 7–24.

[41] The earlier decision of the court regarding the Fairfax lands had aroused much resentment in Virginia. While it troubled TJ, he did not commit himself on its validity in public. TJ to Spencer Roane, Oct. 12, 1815 (L. & B., XIV, 349–351).

[42] TJ to Roane, June 27, 1821, with self-styled extract (Ford, X, 189–190). TJ's reluctance is strongly manifested in his letters of Jan. 19, 1821, to Archibald Thweat (Ford, X, 184) and of Mar. 9 to Roane (*ibid.*, 188–189).

John Marshall in the state. This he avoided. Also, he deliberately avoided direct criticism of the Supreme Court and the Chief Justice such as he had made and was to continue to make in private letters. Furthermore, he qualified his praise of Taylor's work by saying that he did not agree with everything in it and could not be expected to. But his general assessment of the book was unchanged. Thus he said: "It is the most logical retraction of our governments to the original and true principles of the constitution creating them, which has appeared since the adoption of that instrument." On all the important questions it dealt with it contained "the true political faith, to which every catholic republican should steadfastly hold." He now made public his suggestion that this work should be in the hands of all the functionaries of the state.

Jefferson's own constitutional doctrines changed little in the course of his long life, but his emphasis varied with circumstances and reflected the mood and fears of a particular moment. In 1821 his mood and fears were more like those of 1798 than in any other year thus far. Not even in the Kentucky Resolutions did he draw as sharp a line between the state and federal governments as he did in this self-styled extract of a letter. He said they were equally supreme in their respective spheres, as distinct as different nations. Neither could prescribe for the other, and ultimate authority to settle questions at issue between them rested with the sovereign people, peaceably assembled in conventions specifically elected for that purpose. He did not go so far as to advocate nullification, as he had done in the Kentucky Resolutions, but in his desperation he made a proposal which may have been more rational than an appeal to force but was utterly impracticable. When directly involved in the conduct of public affairs, he was usually moderate and conciliatory. He now urged upon both the states and the federal government a spirit of forbearance. He said that both parties to the constitutional compact should "prudently shrink from all approach to the line of demarcation, instead of rashly overleaping it, or throwing grapples ahead to haul to hereafter."

When the "cooked-up extract" appeared in the *Enquirer*, the editor remarked that Jefferson was pursuing "the even tenor of his brilliant course, unswayed by the fashionable heresies of the times."[43] His letter was widely reprinted and occasioned some misinterpretation. Hastening to set the record straight, the *Enquirer* stated categorically that the author was condemning the opinion in the case of Cohens *vs.* Virginia. Also, Ritchie's paper asserted that the party for which he spoke was not new but the Old Republican party — that of Madison's report of 1799 and

[43] *Richmond Enquirer*, July 17, 1821.

the Kentucky Resolutions. He specifically attributed the latter to Jefferson at this time.[44]

Toward the end of the summer Marshall told Story that the tendency of things in Virginia "verges rapidly to the destruction of the government and the re-establishment of a league of sovereign states."[45] He was smarting under the powerful and, to his mind, outrageous attack on him in the Algernon Sydney essays. These, as he knew, were by the chief judicial officer of the state, who specially resented his assertion of federal jurisdiction. Marshall said that he had reason to believe that this attack had been stimulated to some degree by Jefferson.[46] That seeker after tranquillity was not responsible for it, nor did he initiate the movement in his state that Marshall deplored. But its leaders eagerly sought his support, and, under pressure, he gave their doctrines his tacit approval.

Jefferson suggested to the editor of the *American Law Journal* that Roane's argument in the Algernon Sydney articles be published along with Marshall's opinion.[47] He said more than once, however, that for Virginia to take the lead at this stage in a campaign against the judiciary would be inexpedient. He claimed that he had couched his commendation of Taylor's book in general terms, and quite clearly he wanted to be drawn into no public discussion of specific cases. As an advocate of state rights he was concerned for much more than the interests of Virginia. To one inquirer he wrote:

> When all government, domestic and foreign, in little as in great things, shall be drawn to Washington as the centre of all power, it will render powerless the checks provided of one government on another, and will become as venal and oppressive as the government from which we separated.[48]

Referring to Jefferson's writings after his death, Madison said that allowance must be made for the habit in him, "as in others of great genius, of expressing in strong and round terms, impressions of the moment."[49] Judging from the written record, the two men did not discuss the constitutional issue until a couple of years after the "cooked-up extract" appeared in the *Enquirer*. Meanwhile, Jefferson became engaged in corre-

[44] *Ibid.*, Aug. 3, 1821. TJ was also referred to in the issues of July 27 and Aug. 17 in regard to statements in the *National Intelligencer*.

[45] Marshall to Story, July 13, 1821 ("Story-Marshall Correspondence," p. 14).

[46] Marshall to Story, Sept. 18, 1821 (*ibid.*, p. 15).

[47] TJ to J. E. Hall, Aug. 8, 1821 (LC). Hall replied that he might be going out of business (Aug. 25, LC).

[48] TJ to Charles Hammond, Aug. 18, 1821 (L. & B., XV, 332).

[49] Madison to Nicholas Trist, May 15, 1832 (Trist, LC).

spondence with his own first appointee to the Supreme Court. This was illuminating and not wholly unproductive.

Replying to a letter from Justice William Johnson of South Carolina, who had sent him a copy of his life of General Nathanael Greene, he broached the subject of seriatim opinions by the members of the Court. In his desire to render the justices more responsible to the people, he had told his son-in-law that they should be appointed for six-year terms.[50] He did not go that far now, but he suggested to Johnson that they ought to give the public the reasons for their judgments and let differences of opinion become known. He deplored the current practice. Under this he said: "An opinion is huddled up in conclave, perhaps by a majority of one, delivered as if unanimous, and with the silent acquiescence of lazy or timid associates, by a crafty chief judge, who sophisticates the law to his mind, by the turn of his own reasoning."[51] In the ensuing correspondence, Johnson revealed that he had suffered much frustration on the Court. He had found it hard to resist Marshall, who insisted on a united front on the ground that the judiciary was weak and under attack. Much was said in this correspondence about parties, of which Johnson was writing a history. Eventually Jefferson set forth his views about the line between federal and state authority and the ultimate reference of disputed questions to conventions of the sovereign people.[52]

Commenting on one of Jefferson's letters to Johnson, of which he had been sent a copy, Madison took occasion to present his own views on this issue. After pointing out in patient detail the difficulties that would attend the reference of constitutional questions to popular conventions, he stated that he adhered to the position he took in number 39 of the *Federalist*. This was simply that constitutional questions had to be decided by the federal judiciary. That was the understanding at the Federal Convention, he said, and he believed that it was supported by public opinion. He had never yielded to the "ingenious reasoning" of John Taylor against that position, and he had not gone along with Judge Roane. While critical of the conduct of the federal judges, he held that the abuse of a power did not make it unrightful.[53] He strongly approved of seriatim opinions by the justices. So did William Johnson, who delivered a dissenting opinion in 1824. As things turned out, the dominance of the Court by the Chief Justice declined thereafter.

[50] TJ to JWE, Oct. 23, 1821 (LC).

[51] Ford, X, 171.

[52] This correspondence is well described by D. G. Morgan in *Justice William Johnson* (1954), chs. IX, X. Among important letters are: TJ to Johnson, Oct. 27, 1822, Mar. 4, June 12, 1823 (Ford, X, 222–232, 246–249).

[53] Madison to TJ, June 27, 1823 (Hunt, IX, 137–144), replying to a letter of June 13 (Ford, X, 259–260).

* * *

The dangers that Jefferson perceived in the growth of federal power and judicial authority were real. In the perspective of history, however, he appears to have been better at diagnosis than in his major prescriptions. The nation could hardly have endured if such an extreme doctrine of state rights as was approved by him at this stage had prevailed. Madison was more aware of that danger than Spencer Roane and John Taylor were. Beyond a doubt he was better qualified to interpret the Constitution than his old friend at Monticello was. There is no reason to believe that Jefferson ever admitted that he had carried his doctrine too far, but, as Madison well knew, he was not likely to be extreme in action. In his republicanism he was more consistent than the local leaders of the protest against centralization. He continued to advocate the extension of self-government within the state and never defended slavery. In this troubled period he was not entirely negative. With unabated zeal for public enlightenment he was struggling to create what he called "an university."

The Old Sachem

[XXV]

Foundations and Frustrations: The University

1819-1821

IT was early in the fateful year 1819 that the General Assembly of Virginia passed the University bill.[1] This provided for the location of the proposed institution at Central College in Albemarle County but made no financial provision for it beyond the annuity of $15,000, which had been previously authorized. With no more than that, as Jefferson properly concluded, they would fall miserably short of the kind of institution the Rockfish Gap Commission had recommended. To Joseph C. Cabell he wrote: "It is vain to give us the name of an university without the means of making it so." He was of the opinion that something more should be sought at this legislative session, but Cabell believed that the effort would do more harm than good. He counseled patience, saying, "We have got possession of the ground, and it will never be taken from us."[2] During the six years that passed before the University opened, its promoters must have often thought that they were merely holding their ground. Partly because he was a long-term optimist, Jefferson was a notably patient man, but the Old Sachem, as Cabell called him, knew that his sands were running out and wanted to lose no time.

The Governor appointed the new Board of Visitors promptly.[3] Four members of the old Board were included: Jefferson, Madison, Cabell, and John H. Cocke. To make the group more representative, the Governor named two men from the western region — Chapman Johnson of Staunton and General James Breckenridge of Botetourt County — and one from Tidewater, General Robert B. Taylor of Norfolk. Jefferson did

[1]Jan. 25, 1819. The reader is reminded that, later in this year, Chief Justice Marshall delivered his opinion in McCulloch *vs.* Maryland, W. C. Nicholas defaulted on the notes TJ had signed, and the Missouri question aroused TJ's fears for the Union.

[2]TJ to Cabell, Jan. 28, 1819; Cabell to TJ, Feb. 4 (Cabell, pp. 154–155).

[3]Feb. 13, 1819, reported to TJ by Cabell in a letter of Feb. 15 (*ibid.*, p. 161).

not want to wait until the first meeting of the new Board, which the Governor had set for March 29, before making arrangements for building operations.[4] He told Cabell: "I think, with you, that we must apply all our funds to building for the present year, and not open the institution until we can do it with that degree of splendor necessary to give it a prominent character."[5] The two pavilions with intervening dormitories (rooms for students) that were under construction did not constitute a fitting habitation for a college, much less a university. He thought the available funds would warrant their proceeding with two more pavilions, a hotel for "dieting" the students, and twenty or thirty dormitories.

Jefferson called a meeting of the old Board about a month before the new one would supersede it. He demonstrated the return of his health, after his disastrous trip to Warm Springs, by riding on horseback through a snowstorm to Montpelier, the designated meeting place. There he and Madison were joined by Cocke. David Watson authorized them to sign his name to the proceedings along with theirs. They adopted resolutions embodying Jefferson's recommendations about buildings but took no action on a proposal of his relating to the faculty.[6]

While chiefly concerned to proceed with construction, Jefferson had told Cabell that they were obligated to Thomas Cooper, who had been elected to a professorship in Central College, and who must be received that spring. Jefferson's idea was to set up a classical school that would serve as a feeder to the University. The teaching at the lower level would be done by a person yet to be selected who would have no affiliation with the University. That at the upper level would be done by Cooper, who could also open a school of law. This extraordinarily versatile scholar would undoubtedly have been up to the double assignment, but he had not been elected a professor in the University. Furthermore, it is not clear just how the payment of a salary to him could be reconciled with the policy of giving priority to buildings. Added to all these difficulties and uncertainties was the fact that this paragon of learning had been a controversial figure wherever he had previously been.

General Cocke, though greatly embarrassed to find himself in disagreement with the two ex-Presidents, strongly objected to Jefferson's proposal, which he regarded as highly injudicious. So did Cabell, as Jefferson found out when he returned to Monticello and read a letter

[4] TJ feared that, because of the difficulty of travel, Taylor and Breckenridge would be unable to attend regularly. In fact, Taylor resigned in 1821 and was succeeded by George Loyall, also of Norfolk. All the other appointees of 1819 remained on the Board during the rest of TJ's lifetime.

[5] TJ to Cabell, Feb. 19, 1819 (Cabell, pp. 164–165).

[6] Minutes of meeting of Feb. 26, 1819 (*ibid.*, pp. 451–452). J. H. Cocke to J. C. Cabell, Mar. 1, 1819 (Cabell Papers, UVA).

Thomas Cooper

From a steel engraving taken from his *Lectures on Political Economy*, London, 1829

that had been written but not received before he left for the meeting.[7] Cabell did not think they were under any obligation to Cooper and was dubious about him anyway, believing him to be unpopular with the enlightened part of society. Cabell said that if half a dozen professors came at the same time, one obnoxious character might be overlooked, but that the enemies of the University would sharply criticize his appointment if he should come alone. In any case, he believed action on Cooper should be deferred until the meeting of the new Board. Cooper had not committed himself, but as soon as Jefferson became convinced that the University bill would pass, he virtually promised him an appointment. After Cabell learned of this, he wrote Cocke that their old friend had gone a little too far.[8]

Writing Cabell, Jefferson said: "Cooper is acknowledged by every enlightened man who knows him to be the greatest man in America in the powers of mind and in acquired information, and that without a single exception."[9] This transplanted Englishman was esteemed by Jefferson as an associate of Joseph Priestley, from whom no doubt he acquired some of his chemical lore, and as a victim of the Sedition Act. Originally a lawyer by profession, he served as a physician, and about 1817 received the honorary degree of Doctor of Medicine from the University of New York. At this time he was in Philadelphia, where he lectured on chemistry at the University of Pennsylvania, but did not get the professorship he sought in the medical school.

Jefferson's extravagant praise of him was matched by that of Correa de Serra, the eminent botanist who knew him well, and who said that he was without American equal "in point of science and zeal to spread it."[10] Correa attributed the opposition to him to the jealousy of mediocre men and rejoiced that the University of Virginia would begin with such a distinguished appointment. Jefferson was determined to attain distinction in the faculty and valued Cooper for just that reason. Within the Board of Visitors there appears to have been no criticism of Cooper's religious views at this stage, but something was said about his alleged intemperance. Jefferson secured testimony that refuted these charges and in due course presented this to his colleagues on the new Board.[11]

All of the Visitors of the University of Virginia were present at the meeting of March 29, 1819. To nobody's surprise Jefferson was

[7] Cabell to TJ, Feb. 22, 1819 (Cabell, pp. 165–166).

[8] Cabell to Cocke, Mar. 6, 1819 (Cabell Papers, UVA).

[9] TJ to Cabell, Mar. 1, 1819 (Cabell, pp. 167–169). My account of him in *The Public Life of Thomas Cooper* (1926) is summarized in the article in *D.A.B.*

[10] Correa to TJ, Mar. 22, 1819 (Davis, *Abbé Correa in America*, p. 169).

[11] TJ to Correa, Mar. 2, 1819 (*ibid.*, pp. 167–168). Cocke secured testimony independently (William Short to Cocke, Mar. 16, 1819, Cocke Papers, UVA).

promptly elected Rector. A secretary was named, but the minutes of this and nearly all of the later meetings of the Board in Jefferson's lifetime have come down to us in his handwriting.[12] According to the custom already established in connection with the old Board, Jefferson was host to his colleagues at Monticello the day before the official meeting. Major decisions were reached in informal conference after dinner. If he had not already given up the idea of having Thomas Cooper come to the University that spring, his guests must have talked him out of it. He did get them to agree to a proposal which he himself afterwards described as more generous than was necessary.

At the formal meeting Cooper was elected to a professorship of chemistry, mineralogy, and natural philosophy, and temporarily, to one of law. Besides a fixed salary he, like other future professors, was to receive a share of the fees paid by his students. He was assured a total annual income of $3,500, which was more than the Board expected to pay anybody else. Provision was also made for the cost of transporting his philosophical apparatus and for the ultimate purchase of his collection of minerals. It was agreed that Cooper should begin his duties on the first Monday in April, 1820. The new Board affirmed the resolutions of the old one regarding additional buildings. But it could hardly have been supposed that these could be completed by that time, and there was no assurance that the University could then assume responsibility for Cooper's salary. Jefferson had let his eagerness for excellence get the better of his practical judgment. The unwisdom of this commitment was less obvious, however, than it became when the financial situation worsened, and there was no storm of clerical protest until the appointment was made public toward the end of the year.

ii

Two years earlier, when Jefferson surveyed the site for Central College, he laid off three terraces, and then planned to have six pavilions with connecting dormitories, along with a monumental building for a library and other general purposes. Ten pavilions would be required for the ten professors recommended by the Rockfish Gap Commission, and provision had to be made for the "hotels" where the students would take their meals. Just when he conceived the plan of four parallel rows of buildings instead of two is uncertain, but at the first meeting of the Visitors of the University he showed his colleagues a preliminary drawing of what came to be known as West Lawn and West Range. The former contained more pavilions and fewer dormitories than originally envis-

[12] Minutes of the Board of Visitors (UVA), printed in Cabell, pp. 452–455.

aged, and the latter consisted of only hotels and dormitories. At this stage these faced the back of the pavilions, and the gardens lay behind them. At Cabell's suggestion Jefferson placed the gardens between the two rows of buildings and turned the second row of buildings on the West Range around so that they faced outward.

According to General Taylor, Jefferson was to be commended for the cheerfulness with which he abandoned his plans and accepted suggestions.[13] In this case he recognized that the change represented a definite improvement. He was by no means hospitable to other suggestions that were made at this time. These came to him chiefly from Cabell and from Cocke. The latter had been named with him to a committee of superintendency to oversee all operations between meetings of the Board. There was some doubt about the adequacy of the large rooms in the pavilions that were designed to serve both educational and domestic purposes. Most of the Visitors were afraid that the flat roofs which Jefferson favored would leak, even when covered with tin, as in fact they did. Of greater importance were the criticisms of his plans for hotels and dormitories on the West Range. Several members of the Board expressed fears that the students' rooms would be hot and uncomfortable, and believed that they should be combined with the hotels in buildings of more than one story. Cocke in particular advocated this arrangement and actually made drawings of such structures.[14]

Jefferson probably had no thought of abandoning his plan for one-story buildings on the West Range and never did so, but he yielded to the doubts of his colleagues to the extent of postponing a decision in this particular matter to the next meeting of the Board. Therefore, he ordered that excavations be begun on East Lawn instead of West Range. Anticipating that the entire annuity of $15,000 for 1820 could be had on January 1, he and Cocke concluded that they could begin work on three pavilions besides the four already authorized. Toward the end of June he completed plans for the buildings on the East Lawn and turned them over to Arthur S. Brockenbrough, the new Proctor. This experienced builder was to relieve him greatly by overseeing construction.[15]

Writing Madison a few days later, shortly before he set out for Poplar Forest to be gone two months, Jefferson complained of the miserable slowness of building operations.[16] Not a brick had been laid that season,

[13]R. B. Taylor to J. H. Cocke, June, 1819 (Cocke Papers, UVA). Rather than completely redraw his study of West Lawn, West Range, and the Rotunda, TJ cut out the Range portion and redrew only that. At some point he discarded this too, and in a third draft added the serpentine walls for the gardens. Architectural Drawings N366, 306, 305, 369 (UVA).

[14]J. C. Cabell to J. H. Cocke, Apr. 15, 1819 (Cabell Papers, UVA); Cabell to TJ, Apr. 17 (Cabell, pp. 174–176); Cocke to TJ, May 3 (UVA).

[15]TJ to Brockenbrough, May 17, June 27, 1819 (LC).

[16]TJ to Madison, July 17, 1819 (LC).

he said. A contingent of workmen from Philadelphia was on the way, however, and a couple of stonecutters had arrived from Italy. The former would be employed on the East Lawn, while local workmen would be engaged on the West Lawn. The Italians were expected to carve the Ionic and Corinthian capitals, which were beyond the skill of local craftsmen. By the time the Visitors met in October, it had been found that the local stone was unsuitable for work of this delicacy, and the capitals were ultimately procured from Italy. Also, it had become obvious that instruction could not begin in the spring of 1820. Reaffirming the resolution that buildings should have priority, the Visitors put themselves on record in support of Jefferson's over-all plan. As described by him at the time, this called for three more pavilions, five hotels, and connecting dormitories. They authorized him and Cocke to work things out with Thomas Cooper and adopted the report in which he discussed the future needs of the University.[17]

iii

Before he left Albemarle County for Bedford, Jefferson established a classical grammar school in Charlottesville with a faculty of one. He procured the services of Gerald Stack, who was recommended by Cooper as the best teacher of the classics in America and was thus described by Jefferson to prospective patrons. Besides Greek and Latin he taught French. Hoping to encourage the use of that important language, Jefferson induced a Frenchman named Laporte to set up a boardinghouse. Tuition was to be thirty dollars a year and board $120.[18]

Jefferson had a special interest in this private enterprise because of his concern for the education of his grandson Francis Eppes. The boy's father, John W. Eppes, now a member of the United States Senate, had kept away from Monticello for eight years, believing Thomas Mann Randolph to be unfriendly to him. The visit he made at this time, presumably to bring Francis to the school, was memorable. He afterwards told Jefferson in moving terms how much it meant to him to restore old ties.[19]

Another student at the school, of about the same age and educational advancement as Francis, was Browse Trist, who had found a home at Monticello when he arrived there with his elder brother Nicholas shortly after Christmas, 1817. Their grandmother, Mrs. Elizabeth Trist, had

[17] Minutes of the Meeting of Oct. 4, 1819 (Cabell, pp. 456–460). Ultimately six hotels were built.

[18] TJ to Wilson J. Cary, May 4, 1819 ("Some Family Letters of Thomas Jefferson," p. 583).

[19] JWE to TJ, May 15, 1819 (UVA).

been an intimate friend of Jefferson's ever since he boarded with her mother in Philadelphia when a member of the Continental Congress. At this stage, friends and family connections had drawn her to Jefferson's neighborhood, and she was often his guest. Her son, the father of these boys, had died in the Deep South during the presidency of her friend Jefferson, and his widow was twice remarried. After she acquired her third husband, the two boys came from New Orleans to Monticello. There they were promptly accepted as members of the family. Nicholas wanted to marry Virginia Randolph and eventually did, but the girl's mother said that they were both too young as yet. He accepted an appointment to West Point, while Browse remained at Monticello.[20] Wayles Baker, a cousin of Francis Eppes, and James Madison Randolph, aged thirteen, also attended Stack's school. For a time the boys walked from Monticello to Charlottesville and back, but when Laporte's boarding-house got under way they stayed there except on weekends. The little school started off well, and this seems to have been an unusually gay time at Monticello. Browse Trist wrote Nicholas that they danced regularly in the South Pavilion and that never in his life had he been happier.[21]

The euphoria of this effervescent youth lessened considerably during the summer that he and his companions spent in Laporte's establishment. Shortly after Jefferson's return from Poplar Forest in mid-September, a group of the Frenchman's boarders, including Browse, Francis Eppes, and Wayles Baker, vented their dissatisfaction with him and the food he provided by staging what Browse called a "feat." Jefferson had been consulted about the food in the first place, as in fact he was about virtually everything. His recommendations reflected the taste and appetite of an elderly man rather than those of growing boys. For both breakfast and supper he suggested bread and milk (or *café au lait*) with no meat whatsoever. For dinner he stipulated both salted and fresh meat, along with an abundance of the vegetables of which his own diet mainly consisted, but he made no mention of dessert. General Cocke's son described the fare as sparse, while others seem to have found it unpalatable.[22] Also, if young Trist is to be believed, Laporte was not a man of high character or pleasing personality. He "invited" Browse out of his

[20] Gerald Morgan, Jr., "Nicholas Philip and Virginia Jefferson Randolph Trist," in G. G. Shackelford, ed., *Collected Papers of the Monticello Association*, pp. 100–103.

[21] H. B. Trist to Nicholas Trist, May 13, 1819 (Trist, LC). TJ summed up developments about the school and the boarding-house in his letter of July 7, 1819, to Madison (LC).

[22] TJ to Laporte, June 4, 1819 (A. Koch and W. Peden, *The Life and Selected Writings of Thomas Jefferson* [1944], pp. 692–693); Alexander Garrett to J. H. Cocke, June 4, 1819 (Cocke Papers, UVA).

house because the boy complained of a maggot in his food, and it was from this action apparently that the "feat" resulted.[23]

Jefferson had expressly stated that no alcoholic drinks of any sort should be provided and that no games of chance should be permitted in the boarding-house. He expected the boys to spend their time studying Greek and Latin and speaking French. In this particular instance, after freely imbibing a mixture of wine and whiskey, about seven of them paraded around the town and through the tavern with their jackets turned inside out, scandalizing the villagers by their antics. They even stoned the house Laporte had rented — an action which Browse afterwards described as cowardly. The Frenchman rushed to Monticello to complain to Jefferson. Greatly displeased by the disorderly conduct of the three boarders who were under his particular charge, the patriarch informed them that they had made themselves unwelcome at Monticello. His daughter interceded for them, however, and after a few days the ban was lifted.

Some time after this escapade Jefferson had a brief but dangerous illness. This caused his daughter and his granddaughter Ellen to postpone a visit to Mrs. Madison at Montpelier. Ellen said her dear grandfather's complaint was a "violent and obstinate cholic," which lasted thirty hours. Judging from Browse Trist's account, he suffered from an intestinal impediment. That chastened and grateful youth waxed eloquent in praise of the old gentleman who set such rigorous standards for the young and was so quick to forgive their lapses. According to this admirer, he deserved to live half a dozen ages of men.[24]

Jefferson does not appear to have resumed his daily ride until the end of November. Meanwhile, the problems of the classical academy with which he concerned himself were related to the teacher rather than the food at the boarding-house. Gerald Stack, who had received his higher education at Trinity College, Dublin, was an excellent scholar but a painfully indecisive character. His shyness was so great that he declined an invitation to dinner at Monticello. He did summon up enough courage to ascend the little mountain to consult his major patron, who argued him out of resigning. Jefferson gave him a personal letter of commendation to help him get more pupils. He had grave disciplinary difficulties before many months had passed, but for the present the little private school carried on.[25]

[23] My account of this episode is based on the one Browse Trist gave Nicholas, Oct. 19, 1819 (Trist, LC).

[24] To Nicholas, cited above. Ellen's account is in a letter of Oct. 15, 1819, to Mrs. Madison (Madison Papers Files).

[25] Stack to TJ, Nov. 21, 24, 1819 (MHS): TJ to Stack, Nov. 25 (LC).

iv

On December 1, 1819, the Rector dispatched to Richmond the first of his annual reports on the affairs of the University of Virginia. It was addressed to the president and directors of the Literary Fund. In due course this paper, along with accompanying documents, was transmitted to the General Assembly and printed by order of that body.[26] The report was largely drafted at Poplar Forest in the late summer and was adopted at the meeting of the Visitors on October 4, 1819. Besides endeavoring to give a faithful account of developments to that time, Jefferson was trying to present the cause of the institution effectively to the legislature and the public.

In his account of the official actions of the Board, the Rector reported the appointment of Thomas Cooper to a professorship in the University. With this announcement was coupled the statement that the date of the beginning of Cooper's service was uncertain and that no other professors would be appointed until after housing had been provided for them and their students. During the fall, building operations had not proceeded as rapidly as Jefferson had anticipated in his report, but he stated in his covering letter of December 1 that the walls of seven pavilions and thirty-seven dormitories had been erected. Accompanying his report was an estimate by the Proctor of the cost of completing the buildings already under way and also that of the remaining structures on the Lawn and in the Ranges. Allowing for the probable return from subscriptions and the annuity for 1820, the Bursar afterwards calculated that the total amount actually needed was $80,000.[27] Later events proved that considerably more was required, but for a time it looked as though nothing beyond the annuity of $15,000 would be available.

As governor, Thomas Mann Randolph received Jefferson's report and transmitted it to the General Assembly.[28] During his first year in this office Randolph, who was a devoted friend of the University, was able to render it some service as president of the Literary Fund, but his powers as governor were sharply limited by the state constitution. Lacking the right of veto, he could do little to influence legislation.

[26] *Journal of the House of Delegates*, Jan 5, 1820. *Report and Documents Respecting the University of Virginia* (1820). The report, without documents, is in Cabell, pp. 457–460.

[27] Estimate of Alexander Garrett, Feb. 7, 1820 (Cabell, pp. 179–180). The Rotunda was not included in any of these estimates.

[28] Cabell described the circumstances of the election in a letter to Cocke, Dec. 12, 1819 (Cocke Papers, UVA). Randolph's interest in public affairs was stimulated by his activities in connection with the Albemarle Agricultural Society, which was organized in 1817 and was regional in membership and scope. TJ was a charter member but seems to have been inactive. In the spring of 1819 Randolph was elected to the House of Delegates. (See Gaines, ch. 8, for details.)

Besides his official report, Jefferson made a direct contribution to the legislative "campaign" for the University by means of a letter to Cabell in which he expressed his concern more vehemently. Cabell published almost the whole of this in the *Enquirer* without giving the author's name but leaving no doubt of his identity.[29] This letter reflected the fears that were aroused in his mind that winter by the Missouri controversy — fears not only for the ultimate survival of the Union but also for the future of his state. Sending Cabell a clipping about higher education in Kentucky, he said that Virginia's daughter state had a university (Transylvania) with fourteen professors and more than two hundred students. If young Virginians could not be educated at home, he would like them to go to Kentucky, since that state had "more of the flavor of the old cask." He appealed to local pride throughout the final phase of his crusade for enlightenment. Others may have been equally aware that the state was losing ground in the struggle for power, but it is doubtful that any other leader was equally disposed to attribute this to backwardness in education. "The efforts now generally making through the States to advance their science is for power," he said, "while we are sinking into the barbarism of our Indian aborigines, and expect, like them, to oppose by ignorance the overwhelming mass of light and science by which we shall be surrounded."

Jefferson realized that the economic situation in the state had worsened since he wrote his report late in the summer. Also, he knew of the recent disclosure of a serious embezzlement committed by the state treasurer.[30] But he pointed out that they had an educational fund of a million and a half dollars. He said they were higgling over this, "without the heart to let it go to its use." Only the income from the Literary Fund had been drawn upon thus far, and much of the appropriation from it for the education of the poor had not been utilized. Cabell believed that the best hope for the University lay in the surpluses of that fund. Jefferson would not have hesitated to draw on the principle, believing that no investment could be more profitable than one in education at any level.

All that the friends of the institution could get for it at this session was a law authorizing the Visitors to borrow up to $60,000 at an interest rate of not more than six per cent. In due course they secured this from the Literary Fund through the good offices of Governor Randolph.[31] At

[29] TJ to Cabell, Jan. 22, 1820; Cabell to TJ, Feb. 3, 17 (Cabell, pp. 178, 180, 182); *Richmond Enquirer*, Feb. 15, 1820. Cabell returned to the Assembly Feb. 1, after an absence occasioned by the illness of his wife. He left out of TJ's letter only the final sentences, which related to Thomas Cooper.

[30] The state treasurer's confession was made public Jan. 13, 1820, and printed in the *Richmond Enquirer*, Jan. 15. The first report was that over $80,000 was missing.

[31] The passage of the University loan act was reported to TJ by Cabell, Feb. 24, 1820

a special meeting on April 3 the Visitors, while recognizing uncertainties, adopted a tentative order of procedure. After completing the buildings under construction, they would erect three more pavilions with adjoining dormitories. Then they would turn to the "back street" on the east, and finally to the "back street" on the west.[32]

Cabell told Jefferson that the University was popular in the Senate but unpopular in the House of Delegates. That body contained more representatives from the transmontane region, where sectional hostility to the institution persisted. The claims of the University were challenged by supporters of the College of William and Mary, but Jefferson did not regard this threat as serious. More serious at this juncture was the alarm that was sounded by sentinels of religious orthodoxy.

Early in the new year General Cocke received from his friend John H. Rice a letter in which that Presbyterian clergyman deplored the appointment of Thomas Cooper to the faculty of the University. Of all the sects, the Presbyterians laid greatest emphasis on education, and Rice was no foe of learning. A year earlier he had congratulated Cocke on the chartering of the University and said that he wished it well. At that time, however, he observed that knowledge alone could not make a people virtuous and happy.[33] To his mind religion was essential and this he identified with doctrines which had been derided by Cooper.

Rice attacked Cooper's appointment in two articles in the *Virginia Evangelical and Literary Magazine*, which he edited.[34] An outraged individual in the western part of the state had sent him a copy of the *Memoirs of Dr. Joseph Priestley* (1806), to which Cooper had contributed.[35] From this work the Presbyterian editor drew numerous quotations that demonstrated Cooper's heterodoxy. Among them was the following: "The time seems to have arrived, when the separate existence of the human soul, the freedom of the will, and the eternal duration of future punishment, like the doctrines of the Trinity and transubstantiation, may no longer be entitled to public discussion." Rice did not want students to be exposed to a man who disseminated heretical ideas with such intrepidity and displayed liberality only to those who agreed with him.

At their meeting of October 4, 1819, the Visitors had decided that Cooper's services could not begin in the spring of 1820 but must be

(Cabell, pp. 182–183). Chapman Johnson gave an account of events on Feb. 28 (*Papers, MHS*, pp. 291–293).

32 Minutes of Apr. 3, 1820 (UVA).

33 These two letters from John H. Rice to John H. Cocke were dated respectively Jan. 28, 1819, and Jan. 6, 1820 (Cocke Papers, UVA).

34 Vol. III, Jan., Feb., 1820.

35 Cooper contributed Appendix 3. For a discussion of this entire episode, see Malone, *Cooper*, pp. 239–246.

postponed for a year. Jefferson and Cocke agreed to an advance of $1500 to compensate him for the derangement of his plans. Before Rice's attack appeared he had obtained a one-year appointment as professor of chemistry at South Carolina College in Columbia. He was well received in that institution and community, but his affairs were still in an uncertain state in March, 1820, when he sent Jefferson an extract from the *Virginia Evangelical and Literary Magazine*, which he himself had just received in a letter from Richmond.[36]

Having seen only a quotation from Rice's first article, Cooper may not have been aware of the full force of the attack on him, but, as he told his patron, his "feeling of security" at Charlottesville was shaken. He had curbed his temperamental belligerency in South Carolina and claimed that he wanted to avoid religious controversy in his old age. He had no doubt that he would be defended by Jefferson and Madison if he should deserve to be but was unsure of later Boards of Visitors and expected bigotry in the public. He did not resign but said he was willing to do so in order to avoid embarrassment to himself and his friends. He wanted Jefferson to tell him frankly how he stood and what the prospects of his acceptability in the state actually were.

Jefferson replied that he had only heard of this diatribe a day or two before and that few people would read it in what he described as an obscure periodical.[37] He brushed off Rice's protest as a matter of no consequence, saying that it would soon be forgotten if ignored. He claimed that, of all the religious denominations in the state, only the Presbyterians were unfriendly to the University and that among them hostility was largely confined to their "priesthood." In his effort to be reassuring he minimized the influence of the clergy and exaggerated the tolerance of the people of the state. In fact the climate of opinion in Virginia was less favorable to religious liberalism in this period than it had been when the Assembly adopted the statutes of religious freedom of which he was so proud.

At the meeting of the Visitors in early April, Jefferson learned that younger colleagues of his took the situation much more seriously than he had done. Cabell's misgivings must have been increased by a letter he received from his brother William just before the meeting. That former governor of the state regarded Cooper's views as damnable and his ap-

[36] Cooper to TJ, Mar. 1, 1820 (UVA). Regarding Cooper's appointment numerous letters were exchanged, the majority of which are at UVA.

[37] TJ to Cooper, Mar. 13, 1820 (UVA). On Mar. 8, replying to an earlier letter (Feb. 10) in which Cooper had said he did not know whether to remove his family from Philadelphia to Virginia or South Carolina, TJ had said that a pavilion could be available to them. He expressed doubt, however, that the University would open in the spring of 1821 (UVA).

pointment as calamitous. "We shall have every religious man in Virginia against us," he said.[38] There is no evidence that Jefferson was shown this letter, but he could not have failed to learn that Cooper's appointment was being denounced in pulpits, and he appears to have been subjected to pressure by Cocke. Shortly after the meeting, with Cocke's approval, he informed Cooper of the objections to him. In effect, the question of Cooper's resignation was referred to Cooper himself.[39]

A few weeks later Cooper reported that the Board of Trustees at South Carolina College had unanimously recommended to the legislature the establishment of another professorship to be added to the one he already held, bringing his total salary to $3000. While unsure of the action of the legislature, he believed himself to be relatively safe. He did not resign his position in Virginia in so many words, but he said that the $1500 already promised him would be sufficient compensation.[40] He regretted the storm he had aroused and appreciated the liberality of the Board. He was proud to have earned the respect and to have received the attention of the "first man" in the nation. Reporting these developments to General Robert B. Taylor, who had been unable to attend the meeting of the Visitors, Jefferson attributed the protests to Cooper's presumed Unitarianism, saying that the clergy would have liked to burn him at the stake as Calvin did Servetus. He said that he deeply lamented the loss of this professor, whom he had looked upon as the cornerstone of their edifice.[41]

Jefferson told Correa that the priests of the various sects dreaded the advance of science as witches do the approach of day.[42] He did not denounce them in public, however. To him religion was a private matter, like one's domestic relations. His concern was for complete religious freedom. In private he sometimes manifested impatience with what he regarded as credulity and irrationality but held that men should be judged on their conduct, not their opinions. In the *Notes on Virginia* he asserted that it did him no injury for his neighbor to say there were twenty gods or no god. "It neither picks my pocket nor breaks my leg," he said.[43] This degree of tolerance was hardly to be expected of the clerical profession. Nor is it at all surprising that clergymen should have feared the secular spirit that Jefferson exemplified.

[38] W. H. Cabell to J. C. Cabell, Mar. 21, 1820 (Cabell Papers, UVA).

[39] TJ to J. H. Cocke, Apr. 9, 1820 (UVA). Only a fragment of TJ's letter to Cooper of Apr. 8 survives (UVA).

[40] Cooper to TJ, May 3, 1820. He was more uncertain when he wrote on Apr. 24 (UVA).

[41] TJ to Taylor, May 16, 1820 (L. & B., XV, 252–256). In this letter the Rector gave an excellent account of the meeting of the Visitors, as well as of the Cooper episode.

[42] TJ to Correa, Apr. 11, 1820 (Davis, *Abbé Correa in America*, p. 178).

[43] *Notes on Virginia*, Peden edn., p. 159.

Word that the agreement between the Visitors and Thomas Cooper had been canceled may have been passed on, but no formal announcement was made, and Jefferson did not regard the matter as closed. Writing Cooper in his private capacity, he said that he had not been disturbed by the bellowing of "our pulpit mountebanks" but went along with his more troubled colleagues for another reason. In view of the uncertainties about the opening of the University he wanted to free Cooper to avail himself of his opportunities in South Carolina. In case the prospects of opening the University should improve, he hoped Cooper's engagement would not make him unavailable.[44]

Stack's disorderly school closed in the summer of 1820. Although Jefferson had already dissociated himself from its affairs, its demise, together with that of Laporte's boarding-house, must have been a relief to their original sponsor.[45] On the other hand, his hopes for the establishment of a school that would prepare students for the University were disappointed, and he was faced with the problem of providing for the further education of Francis Eppes. Under these circumstances Jefferson turned his eyes to South Carolina College as a place of instruction for his grandson. The boy's father was distrustful of Easterners and did not want Francis to be exposed to the alien influence of one of their institutions of learning. Fully agreeing with him in this, Jefferson told John W. Eppes that in South Carolina, Francis would find a society similar to their own. Furthermore, he would be under the tutelage of a man who had more science in a single head than was contained in all the colleges of New England and New Jersey, and in those of Virginia for that matter.[46] In the fall Francis entered South Carolina College. Though doubtful that the institution came up to Harvard, he was entirely complimentary of Cooper, saying that he was greatly beloved by the students and one of the most popular teachers the college ever had.[47]

The professor's popularity in South Carolina was not matched in Virginia. Early in the legislative session of 1820–1821 Cabell reported to Jefferson that "the affair of the payment to Dr. Cooper" was known to the enemies of the University.[48] After the session was over, Cabell told

[44] TJ to Cooper, July 4, 1820 (UVA).

[45] Stack had brought in a teacher of mathematics as a reinforcement and named the short-lived school the Charlottesville Academy. Its affairs are referred to in many letters of the period before it fell. The reasons for the failure of both school and boarding-house were set forth by Browse Trist in an amusing letter to Nicholas (Oct. 13, 1820; Trist, LC).

[46] TJ to JWE, June 30, 1820 (UVA). The education of Francis was discussed by TJ and Cooper in several letters during the summer (TJ to Cooper, July 4, 1820, UVA, and Aug. 14, 1820, LC; Cooper to TJ, July 12, UVA).

[47] FWE to TJ, Oct. 31, 1820 (*Family Letters*, pp. 435–436). TJ was afterwards rather critical of the course of study, which he regarded as too rigid.

[48] Cabell to TJ, Dec. 20, 1820 (UVA).

Madison that Cooper's appointment had united the religious people of the state against the University. He believed that, if they had the chance, ninety-nine per cent of the citizens would vote against him. Cabell believed that Cooper would get the votes of none of the Visitors except Madison, Jefferson, and Cabell himself. Fearing the continued championship of Cooper by the Old Sachem, he wanted to put Madison on guard.[49]

Before the spring meeting of the Visitors, Jefferson received from Columbia, South Carolina, a letter in which Cooper said that he must now regard himself as "fixed" in that place.[50] The legislature had adopted all the recommendations of the trustees regarding his salary and the purchase of his minerals. Also, he was now president *pro tem* of the College. He reported that his responsibilities in that position had forced him to discontinue reading Horace with Jefferson's grandson. Cooper did not think he would have to relinquish these responsibilities and, in fact, was elected president toward the end of the year. He was now formally renouncing any claim he might have on the Visitors. No doubt the news was received with many sighs of relief. Madison, in a gracious letter, expressed regret at a loss which he was accepting as final. In the letter Jefferson wrote the next day there was not the same tone of finality. "Although we relinquish claim," he said, "we are not without all hope."[51]

He maintained friendly relations with Cooper during the rest of his life and fully sympathized with that redoubtable controversialist when he became embroiled with the Presbyterians in South Carolina.[52] The University of Virginia did not need professors soon, however, and no favorable opportunity to reopen its door to Cooper ever came. Jefferson had told him that he wanted the University to be the "bulwark of the human mind" in the western hemisphere.[53] He also wanted it to be approved by the people, as a public institution in a self-governing society is supposed to be. In this particular instance he greatly underestimated the depth and strength of the religious opposition. He claimed that he did not yield to it, but most of the Visitors certainly did so. It would appear, therefore, that the Cooper episode increased popular mistrust of the struggling institution without advancing the cause of freedom. Cabell seems to have been right when he said that in this matter the Old Sachem went too far.

[49] Cabell to Madison, Mar. 10, 1821 (MP). In his letter of the same date to TJ he made no reference to Cooper (Cabell, pp. 210–212).

[50] Cooper to TJ, Mar. 12, 1821 (LC). He wrote Madison to the same effect on the same day.

[51] Madison to Cooper, Apr. 6, 1821 (MP); TJ to Cooper, Apr. 7 (LC).

[52] I have described their relations in *The Public Life of Thomas Cooper*.

[53] TJ to Cooper, Aug. 14, 1820 (L. & B., XV, p. 269).

[XXVI]

The Empty Village

1820-1824

WITH characteristic diligence the Rector had sent his annual report for 1820 to the Governor ahead of time, hoping that the affairs of the University would receive prompt consideration. But Thomas Mann Randolph aroused a storm at the opening of the session, with the result that he and his tangled affairs became the center of attention. In his message to the General Assembly, Governor Randolph prescribed a dose of reform that was much too strong for his apathetic countrymen. His father-in-law was encouraged by his recommendation that masters free some of their slaves. His proposals were moderate, but they were received with disfavor by his fellow planters.[1] Furthermore, he affronted many by gratuitous remarks about religion. His public avowal of faith in the God of Nature and his declaration of indifference to ceremony and doctrines caused him to be charged with impiety. Despite attacks on his character which Cabell described as scandalous, he was re-elected governor.[2] His conduct had gained for the University no friends in the quarters where it most needed them. It would be unfair to say that he became a liability to his father-in-law's most cherished project, but the value of his support lessened as his governorship continued. Resentful of the constitutional limitations of his powers, and especially of his subordination to the Council of State, he launched an attack on that body. This was by no means undeserved, but it was marred by his excess and proved to be futile. While keeping up the feud, the hapless Governor conscientiously performed routine tasks in moody loneliness.

Until almost the end of his first year in office Randolph had lived alone in what his wife called the government house. He usually spent

[1] For TJ's reaction, see above, ch. XXIII, p. 341.

[2] Gaines, ch. 9, gives a good account of TMR's governorship; on this message and election, see pp. 123–127. Cabell wrote TJ about the attack, Dec. 20, 1820 (UVA).

Sundays with the family in Albemarle. Martha had remained at Monticello, taking care of the young children and her aged father. In December, 1820, when the latter was at Poplar Forest with Ellen and Virginia, she made one of her rare visits to the Governor, staying until after his re-election and giving his living quarters the attention they sorely needed. She wrote her daughter Mary that the windows had not been washed nor had the rugs been shaken since his predecessor departed.[3] After the election he got an advance on his salary which enabled her to purchase needed articles. He was a strange man — strong, brave, intelligent, reckless, unconventional, and quick-tempered. He commands sympathy as a victim of successive misfortunes and had staunch friends, but he was not successful in his limited role as governor.

In his official report Jefferson stated that the University could not be opened for eight years if the loan was to be repaid and if they had nothing to rely on but an annuity of $15,000 from which the annual interest on the loan must be deducted. He left no doubt of his belief that sufficient funds for the full establishment contemplated by the Rockfish Gap Commission ought to be provided. He said this would require about $40,000 for a central building for the library and other uses, a remission of the loan, and an increase in the annuity to support the faculty.[4]

In advance of the legislative session he wrote Cabell at length, supplying him with facts, figures, and arguments to buttress their cause.[5] Denying that the buildings were costing too much, he emphasized the backwardness of his state in facilities for education and the modesty of his own proposals in comparison with the expenditures of other commonwealths. He told Cabell that Virginia must be rescued "from the degradation of becoming the Barbary of the Union." By contrast he pointed to "the gigantic efforts of New York" to elevate its citizens.[6] Citing a recent speech of Governor De Witt Clinton, he said that the state had six thousand common schools, forty academies, and five colleges with 718 students. He stated that its total appropriations for education were two and a half million dollars. Regarding the population and resources of the two states as roughly comparable, he saw no sufficient reason for one to be a giant and the other a pygmy in matters of education.

In public Jefferson was deferential to the all-powerful legislature. In

[3] Mary Randolph repeated these comments in a letter to Virginia Randolph, Dec. 7, 1820 (Trist, UNC).

[4] Report of Oct. 3, 1820 (Cabell, pp. 461–464); TJ's covering letter to TMR, Nov. 20, 1820 (MHS).

[5] TJ to Cabell, Nov. 28, 1820 (Cabell, pp. 184–189). He included estimates of expenses and additional needs.

[6] A year earlier he had compared Virginia to her daughter state, Kentucky. See above, ch. XXV, p. 375.

this private communication, however, he said that the "rulers" of his state had been insufficiently aware of the value of knowledge. Also he charged them with unwise use of financial resources that were already available — that is, the Literary Fund. Like many others, including the Governor, he regarded the provisions for the education of poor children as ineffectual and wasteful. He believed that, if properly directed, this fund could provide adequately for both elementary and higher education. Well aware that indifference to the former was alleged against the friends of the University, he wanted them "to take in hand the whole subject."

This suggestion came to naught. Cabell and those he consulted believed that they would be unsuccessful in any attempt they might make for a general system of schools at this session. The best hope, as they saw it, was to get enough money to complete the buildings of the University without raising the question of the remission of the loan. Repeatedly Cabell said that the difficulties would be great, and midway in the session he reported that they did not expect to get anything.[7] These successive blows were followed by a heavier one. The key representative of the University in the General Assembly announced to the anxious Rector that he had decided to retire at the end of the current session for reasons of health.

Cabell, who had what he called "pulmonary affections," had spent thirteen winters as a member of the General Assembly. He now feared that his re-election would be contested and did not want to expose his weak lungs to the rigors of a campaign. Saying that his feelings and attitudes were unchanged, he expressed his intention of doing everything he could for the University as a private citizen.[8] Jefferson was plunged into gloom by these letters, especially the last one. Brushing aside the question of health, he told Cabell that his withdrawal would really be the desertion of a sacred cause.[9] If the prospects of the University were dim now, he said, they would be much dimmer if its best friends were to abandon it. "What object of our lives," he said, "can we propose so important? What interest of our own which ought not be postponed to this? Health, time, labor, on what in the single life which nature has given us, can these be better bestowed than on this immortal boon to our country?" If any member of the Board would be warranted in withdrawing from this sacred duty, he said that it would be himself. While claiming to be physically and mentally unfit to keep the field, the indomitable old warrior declared that he would die in the last ditch.

[7] Cabell to TJ, Dec. 20, 22, 1820; Jan. 14, 18, 1821 (Cabell, pp. 189–192, 194–197).

[8] Cabell to TJ, Jan. 25, 1821 (Cabell, pp. 197–199). This letter was received by TJ the same day as that of Jan. 18.

[9] TJ to Cabell, Jan. 31, 1821 (*ibid.*, pp. 201–203).

Responding to this moving letter, Cabell said that it was not in his nature to resist such an appeal.[10] He had given notice that he would stand for re-election. He showed the letter to the other Visitors in the Assembly, Breckenridge and Johnson, as no doubt Jefferson had expected he would. They were much affected by it, especially the former. It "kindled great zeal" in him, according to his colleague. Cabell asked Jefferson to write a special letter to Breckenridge, saying that he would make powerful use of it.

In his long and eloquent response to this request Jefferson may have fanned the sectionalist spirit which was manifested in the Missouri controversy.[11] He told Breckenridge that five hundred young Virginians were in northern institutions of learning, where they were imbibing principles that were discordant with those of their own state. He would hardly have made such an assertion to John Adams or George Ticknor, and it was not in the spirit of universality that he usually displayed in intellectual matters. He had said much the same thing to Cabell, however, and he did so to John Taylor of Caroline. To that exponent of state sovereignty he wrote: "These [northern] seminaries are no longer proper for Southern or Western students. The signs of the times admonish us to call them home."[12]

Jefferson expected his University to do far more for his state than guard its youth against alien influences, but at this stage his fears of consolidation and commercialization were obsessive. Furthermore, the appeal of this lover of the land to local patriotism was well calculated to gain favor for the struggling institution. Patrick Henry's reputed saying that Jefferson "abjured his native victuals" suggests that as a cosmopolite he was viewed with a degree of suspicion by some of his countrymen. His personal devotion to Virginia and his adherence to the doctrine of state rights are equally unquestionable. Perhaps it was more than a coincidence, however, that the latter should have been so strongly asserted by him at a time when he was desperately seeking support for the University.

Cabell gave Breckenridge the major credit for the passage of the second loan bill.[13] At just this time he informed Madison of the continued opposition of religious groups and issued the warning against Thomas Cooper to which we referred in the last chapter. He told Jefferson that in southern Virginia it was the fashion to electioneer by crying down the

[10] Cabell to TJ, Feb. 8, 1821 (*ibid.*, p. 203).

[11] TJ to Breckenridge, Feb. 15, 1821 (L. & B., XV, 314–318). In a letter of the same date to Cabell, TJ said that no copy of this should be allowed to get out of the state (Cabell, p. 204).

[12] TJ to John Taylor, Feb. 14, 1821 (*Papers, MHS*, pp. 305–306).

[13] Cabell reported it to TJ on Feb. 25, 1821 (Cabell, pp. 208–209) and commented on it in his letters of March 10 to TJ (*ibid.*, pp. 210–212) and to Madison (MP).

University. Early in the session he had reported that friends of other institutions of learning were urging their claims. He tried to counter their efforts by arguing that, if they should receive aid from the state, their charters must be amended so as to provide for legislative control such as was exercised over the University. His colleague Chapman Johnson did not approve of this line of argument, and the campaign for the University actually stimulated private activity in behalf of institutions associated with churches.[14]

The most outspoken criticism of the University in the General Assembly related to the buildings. They had been seen by relatively few of the legislators, but a common impression, as reported by Cabell and others, was that they were too ornate and that the general plan was extravagant. Replying to such criticisms and also to charges that Jefferson was theoretical and visionary in his notions, the writer of an article in the *Enquirer* said: "He supposes them [the legislators] capable of a liberality and grandness of design, correctness of reasoning, and a degree of perfection in which I regret to say he is sometimes mistaken in his calculations."[15] Until the end of his days Jefferson was accused of setting his sights too high, and he was charged more than once with underestimating costs. He was informed that the legislators expected the physical plant to be finished by this second loan and was warned by his friends not to start any building that he could not finish. Cabell, who presented these and other warnings in long letters to Jefferson and Madison before the meeting of the Visitors on April 2, was prevented by illness from attending. Both Breckenridge and Chapman Johnson were there. With the two ex-Presidents they constituted a bare quorum.

The Visitors resolved that it was "expedient" to proceed with the construction of the library according to Jefferson's plan, but imposed certain conditions. The available funds must be sufficient not only to finish the buildings already authorized, but also to complete this one to the point that it was secure and fit for use.[16] Jefferson and Cocke were instructed to obtain an accurate account of outstanding obligations along with estimates of the costs of future construction. Until they were fully convinced that all these costs could be met, no contracts for the library should be made.

On their way home, Johnson and Breckenridge expressed themselves freely in a joint letter to Cocke, who had been unable to attend the

[14] Hampden Sydney College provides a particular example. (*Richmond Enquirer*, July 3, 1821).

[15] *Richmond Enquirer*, Feb. 10, 1821, article by ACADEMUS.

[16] Minutes, Apr. 2, 1821 (UVA).

meeting.[17] It is clear that they were dissatisfied with the financial reports and estimates that had been presented and believed that the two elder statesmen were not giving sufficient heed to the criticisms of the building operations by members of the Assembly. Johnson and Breckenridge told Cocke that, in their opinion, the hotels on the West Range should be two-story structures. Cocke agreed with them in this, as he did in the deferment of all contracts for the library. That building was to be modeled on the Pantheon in Rome, which Jefferson regarded as the finest example of spherical architecture, and it was called by that name at this stage.

At Bremo in late summer, Cocke heard that Jefferson was about to order the beginning of work on the Pantheon. He wrote Cabell in dismay, apparently fearing that the Old Sachem had let his eagerness run away with him and was exceeding his authority.[18] Cocke's fears were wholly unwarranted. Jefferson had promptly set Brockenbrough to work on the financial records and estimates. Believing that the desired figures would not all be ready by the designated time for the next meeting of the Visitors, he postponed this until the eve of the legislative session in November. Considerably before that date he reported to his colleagues that the Proctor had estimated that the final cost of grounds and buildings, exclusive of the library, would be about $195,000.[19] This figure exceeded the previous estimate, as might have been expected. Jefferson regarded the difference as moderate but recognized that more funds would be needed for the library.

In his annual report, which was approved by the Visitors on November 30, 1821, Jefferson stated that six pavilions, eighty-two dormitories, and two hotels had been completed. His prediction that all of the "buildings of accommodation" would be finished the next summer proved to be somewhat too optimistic, but the academical village was becoming a physical reality. Its creator was pleased with it. Writing William Short the week before the meeting, he said: "It will be a splendid establishment, would be thought so in Europe, and for the chastity of its architecture and classical taste leaves everything in America far behind it." He added that the library was essential "to give it unity and consolidation as a single object." He said that this structure was to be a sphere within a cylinder, seventy feet in diameter, which was half that of its prototype, the Pantheon.[20]

[17] Johnson and Breckenridge to Cocke, Apr. 5, 1821 (Cocke Papers, UVA). The letter was written at Staunton, presumably in Johnson's home.

[18] Cocke to Cabell, Sept. 20, 1821 (Cabell Papers, UVA).

[19] TJ to Visitors, Aug. 15, Sept. 30, 1821 (Cabell, pp. 216–217, 219–221).

[20] TJ to Short, Nov. 24, 1821 (*Papers, MHS*, p. 308).

The Visitors voted that an engraving of the ground plan of the buildings be made. This was not available at the legislative session of 1821–1822, but with his report Jefferson sent a copy of the drawing.[21] Well aware that there had been unfavorable comments on the buildings, he said that universal approval of their style and scope was not to be expected. He claimed here, however, as he did elsewhere, that the plan he and his colleagues were pursuing was the one that had been recommended by the Rockfish Gap Commission. He believed that it was "proportioned to the respectability, the means, and the wants" of their state and would stand the test of time. They were obligated to do, not what would perish with themselves, but "what would remain, be respected and preserved through other ages."

The returns from the census of 1820, of which Virginians were now becoming aware, showed that their state, hitherto the most populous in the nation, had fallen behind both New York and Pennsylvania. About a week before the meeting of the Visitors, the editor of *Niles' Weekly Register* declared that the Old Dominion had fallen even further behind in wealth than in population. In explanation of the relative decline of Virginia he said that her accomplished and learned men had been more concerned "to discuss and settle abstract questions of right than to accomplish positive benefits." Answering him in the *Enquirer*, Ritchie claimed that the state was doing more than it was given credit for and spoke particularly of its large fund for schools. A few days later the editor of *Niles' Register* said that Virginia was building a great university, but he feared that it would look better on paper than in practice unless there should be a change in legislative policy.[22]

The next year was only a few days old when Ritchie published under the masthead of the *Enquirer* a powerful plea for support of the University. He referred to this as a noble institution and asserted that the state sorely needed it. "She must make up by the intelligence of her sons what she is losing in her census," he said. "Her moral force must supply the place of numbers."[23] Jefferson himself once remarked that Massachusetts, though a small state, was the most influential in the Union. That influence he attributed to her emphasis on education.[24] Several weeks before he got the copy of the *Enquirer* in which Ritchie's plea appeared, he received a letter from George Ticknor in which his young friend said that Harvard would not be the institution it could and ought to be until it had a rival. Saying that the only prospective rival he could see was

[21] Minutes of Nov. 30, 1821, with Report (Cabell, pp. 465–470).

[22] *Niles' Weekly Register*, Nov. 24, Dec. 8, 1821; *Richmond Enquirer*, Nov. 27, 1821.

[23] Jan. 3, 1822.

[24] TJ to Cabell, Dec. 25, 1820 (Cabell, p. 193).

Jefferson's University, he wished it great success.[25] These words were comforting, no doubt, but the legislature of 1821–1822 was not cooperative in the effort to create an institution of national distinction.

Cabell soon reported that the Senate was well disposed to the University but that the House of Delegates was hostile.[26] Despite the urging of his fellow Visitors, Breckenridge had declined to stand for re-election to the House. His influence on the western delegation was greatly missed. Chapman Johnson was back in the Senate with Cabell, but these two were not in full agreement about immediate objectives and desirable procedure. Every proposal made in behalf of the University failed at this session. Cabell, in desperation, had yielded to Johnson and supported a bill which suspended the annual interest on their loans, on condition that the construction of the Rotunda be postponed. Johnson had advocated this in a strong speech during which he made the unfortunate admission that he would have preferred a different architectural plan. Cabell must have been relieved when the proposal was defeated. He told Jefferson afterwards that he was more concerned than ever that the University should not be opened until all the buildings were completed. This was Jefferson's position.[27] Johnson afterwards explained his position in a letter to Jefferson. While recognizing that the Rotunda must be built ultimately, he did not regard it as indispensable. He feared that the public would be exasperated if the present policy was adhered to. He believed that, if all the other buildings were finished by the next session of the Assembly, the loans would probably be remitted.[28]

The Rotunda had become a symbol of extravagance. Jefferson reported to Madison that a staunch supporter had declared his unwillingness to vote another cent for the University if anything was to go to that building. He himself had no intention of yielding on this point, but referring to Johnson as "our dissenting brother," he said they should treat him softly because they could not spare this strong and useful man.[29] He remarked to another about this time that there was some flaw in the system of representation, since it failed to bring the wisdom of the country into its councils.[30] The immediate task of the Visitors was to complete the four rows of "buildings of accommodation" with their appendages. For the Rotunda they must bide their time.

[25] Ticknor to TJ, Dec. 8, 1821 (*Papers, MHS*, p. 310).

[26] Cabell to TJ, Jan. 3, 4, 1822 (Cabell, pp. 223–227).

[27] Cabell summed up the complicated maneuvers of the session in his letters of Mar. 6 and 10, 1822 (*ibid.*, pp. 245–254).

[28] Johnson to TJ, Mar. 29, 1822 (*Papers, MHS*, pp. 311–312).

[29] TJ to Madison, Apr. 7, 1822 (LC).

[30] TJ to Thos. Cooper, Mar. 9, 1822 (LC).

ii

Thomas Mann Randolph was in his third and last year as governor. He fared no better than hitherto in his continuing conflict with the Council of State, but his personal situation was improved during the winter by the presence of daughters in his household. Martha remained at Monticello, enduring the noise and dirt of the boys. Writing her daughter Virginia in Richmond, she referred to them as "four rowdies" and stated that their manners left much to be desired.[31] Their grandfather had assumed the direction and expense of the education of the three older boys after their father went to Richmond as governor. The oldest of them, James, aged sixteen, studied Greek with him.[32] During most of this period James, Ben, and Lewis attended a school in Charlottesville conducted by the Episcopal minister, the Reverend Frederick Hatch. He communicated with Jefferson from time to time about the progress of these pupils.[33]

The higher education of Francis Eppes at South Carolina College was not proceeding as Jefferson would have liked. He told Thomas Cooper, as he also told George Ticknor of Harvard, that he disapproved of a fixed curriculum but believed that at this stage of education a student should be free to choose the subjects of chief value to him.[34] Jefferson's specific suggestions could not be carried out. In one letter he said that because of the miserable facilities in Virginia, his efforts to promote the education of his grandson had been baffled to a most unfortunate degree.[35] By all accounts Francis, who was now twenty, was a likable person, and he appears to have been a good student. According to his Aunt Martha, he had once been an "arrant rowdy." Dr. Cooper did not charge him with participation in the unusually violent student riot that took place early in 1822, but the discouraged president said that Wayles Baker was a ringleader. On this occasion the insurgent youths shaved off the mane and tail of Cooper's horse and rode him around the streets until the poor creature was exhausted.[36]

Shortly after Jefferson exchanged comments with Cooper on the insubordination and self-will of young Southerners, he learned that Fran-

[31] Martha Randolph to Virginia Randolph, Feb. 24, 1822 (Trist, UNC). Ellen was visiting in Washington at the time.

[32] See TJ to TMR, Oct. 8, 1820 (LC); June 27, 1821 (UVA). The names and birth dates of the boys can be found in Appendix I.

[33] See for instance a later report, Hatch to TJ, May 9, 1823 (MHS).

[34] TJ to Cooper, Sept. 16, 1821 (LC).

[35] TJ to Francis Eppes, Nov. 17, 1821 (*Family Letters*, pp. 440–441).

[36] Cooper to TJ, Feb. 14, 1822 (LC). This colorful letter is commented on more fully in Malone, *Cooper*, pp. 256–258. TJ replied Mar. 9, 1822 (LC).

cis had left the College because of shortage of funds. His father, who was in very bad health and had suffered serious reverses, could do nothing further for him. Jefferson advised Francis to begin the study of law, sending him a lengthy list of books and saying that he could read them at Monticello if not at Millbrook. He told his grandson that two years' study would provide him with a superficial knowledge of the law, but that three would be required for profundity.[37]

Francis had something in mind besides the study of law. In the summer his grandfather learned that he was to be married. Jefferson regretted that this momentous step was to be taken so soon. But, as he told John W. Eppes, the case was not "under the jurisdiction of reason" and the decision must be acquiesced in. On November 28, 1822, shortly after he became twenty-one, Francis was married to Mary Elizabeth Cleland Randolph. Her father, Thomas Eston Randolph, an Englishman by birth, was a brother-in-law of Thomas Mann Randolph. At this time he was the lessee of Jefferson's mill and in considerable financial difficulty. The children of the two Randolph families were intimate, and the bride's mother had been a close friend of Maria Jefferson Eppes, mother of Francis. There is abundant testimony to Elizabeth's beauty and amiability.[38]

Jefferson was confined at Monticello with a broken left arm at the time of the wedding, but he gave the bridegroom a handsome present. The house at Poplar Forest along with one thousand acres of land were placed at his grandson's disposal. He could not deed the property to Francis as long as the obligation for the notes of Wilson Cary Nicholas hung over his head, but to all practical purposes the place belonged henceforth to the person for whom he had long intended it.[39] He visited it only once after Francis entered upon the matrimonial phase of higher education.

iii

About a month before the marriage of Francis Eppes, Jefferson wrote an affectionate letter to Maria Cosway, now retired to a convent at Lodi. In this letter he spoke with pride of the academical village he had designed, assuring this artist that "it would be thought a handsome and

[37] Francis Eppes to TJ, Mar. 22, 1822; TJ to Francis, Apr. 9; also Francis to TJ, May 13 (*Family Letters*, pp. 442–445).

[38] George G. Shackelford, "Francis Eppes, VII" in *Collected Papers of the Monticello Association*, p. 172.

[39] TJ to JWE, July 28, 1822 ("Some Family Letters of Thomas Jefferson," *Scribner's Magazine*, XXXVI, 586); Martha Randolph to Nicholas Trist, Nov. 22, 1822 (Trist, UNC). Virginia Randolph wrote Nicholas Trist (Nov. 12, 1822, Trist, LC) that her grandfather fell down the flight of steps leading from the terrace and broke his left arm near the wrist. He made little of it at the time, but his arm was in a sling for months thereafter.

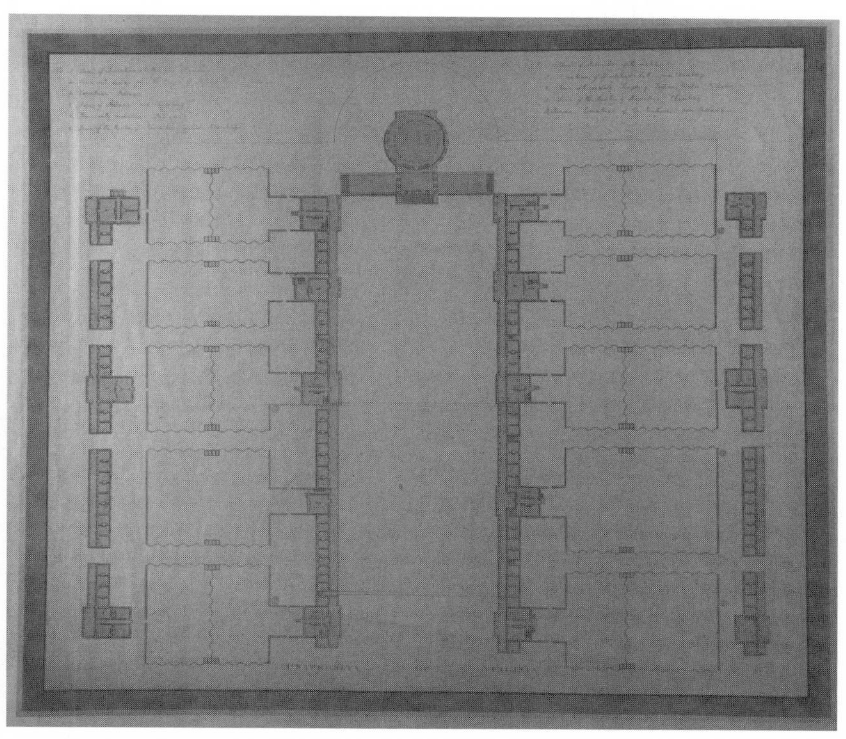

University of Virginia: The Maverick Plan

His second engraving, 1825, in which the pavilions and dormitory rooms are numbered.
(Courtesy of the University of Virginia Library, Prints File, Special Collections)

portions of the Rotunda. The Proctor was also to inquire into the time requirements of the different operations.[41]

During the summer Jefferson had made arrangements for the engraving of the ground plan of the village that had been authorized late in the previous year. He received proof from Peter Maverick in November, and copies were available early in the session of the General Assembly of 1822–1823. Jefferson had Bernard Peyton, his factor in Richmond, distribute copies among the legislators. This engraving showed the Rotunda along with the four rows of constructed buildings. It was an effective advertisement of the University and was in considerable demand by purchasers.[42]

In his report for 1822 Jefferson said that the pavilions, dormitories, and hotels were all finished except for a little plastering and a few columns that were awaiting their capitals from Italy.[43] Gardens and their walls were unfinished, but the buildings of accommodation were ready for occupancy. Without using the words Rotunda or Pantheon, he said that the "remaining building" had not been begun because of lack of funds. He strongly affirmed the policy of completing the physical plant before opening the University and the determination of the Visitors to create an institution of genuine distinction. The structure that was represented by a circle on the Maverick engraving symbolized the excellence its designer was seeking.

Admiration for Jefferson's architectural creation as a whole was destined to grow with the passing months and years. One visitor in the summer of 1822 had adjudged it to be unsurpassed in the country, perhaps unequaled in elegance, convenience, comfort, and utility. He regarded the destiny of the University as sure if properly conducted. In his opinion it would be anathema if it should cause youths to disregard religion and become dissolute, but he was confident that Jefferson could be relied on to prevent this.[44] His confidence was not shared by everybody. Jefferson himself concluded that he should give the church people of the state some reassurance.

In his report for 1822 the Rector suggested that sectarian schools of divinity be established "on the confines" of the University and have the benefit of its facilities and instruction. In view of his private comments

[41] Minutes of meeting of Oct. 7, 1822 (Cabell, pp. 470–476). Everybody was present except Chapman Johnson and George Loyall, recently appointed to succeed Robert Taylor.

[42] Peter Maverick to TJ, Nov. 12, 1822; TJ to Bernard Peyton, Dec. 12; Peyton to TJ, Dec. 23 (MHS). Edwin M. Betts discusses the engraving in "Ground Plans and Prints of the University of Virginia, 1822–1826," in *Proceedings of the American Philosophical Society*, XC, 1946.

[43] Cabell, pp. 471–476.

[44] ARGUS in *Richmond Enquirer*, July 12, 1822.

on the clergy he could hardly have been expected to welcome them as academic neighbors. No doubt his invitation represented a concession to expediency and may be regarded as a political gesture. However, it was not inconsistent with his philosophical position with respect to religion. Since these denominational schools were to be wholly independent of the University and of each other, their establishment would have been in conformity with the principles of religious freedom and the separation of church and state. Out of respect for these principles, he said, the Rockfish Gap Commission had proposed no professorship of divinity for the University. Because of the diversity of doctrine and the impropriety of giving preference to one sect over another in a public institution, the Commission believed that instruction in particular tenets must be left to the sects themselves.

This explanation was drawn from the report which he himself wrote in 1818. He now said that it did not mean that religious instruction was precluded by public authority. He declared that no subject was so important to every human being, or so incumbent on him to study and investigate, as his relations with his Maker and the duties arising from them. As he put it, the lack of instruction in the creeds of the various religious faiths in the state had created "a chasm" in the field of learning. Since he was exceedingly critical of all creeds, this statement is rather mystifying. But he believed the University could help the schools of divinity and that, if religion could be studied as other subjects were, it would round out the circle of useful sciences. Jefferson's forward-looking suggestion was not taken up by any religious group in the state, but, according to Cabell, it had a favorable effect on legislative opinion. Writing Jefferson toward the end of the session, he said: "It is the Franklin that had drawn the lightning from the cloud of opposition."[45]

In fact the skies had begun to clear before Jefferson's report reached the General Assembly.[46] Cabell told him that the quality of the members of the House of Delegates had improved and that they were well disposed to the University, as the senators continued to be.[47] The neglect of the institution by the previous legislature had been followed by a reaction in its favor. Much was said in the newspapers about its needs. In a series of letters one writer considered the question "What shall be done for the University?" Another contributor reproachfully remarked that the unfinished University was attended only by swallows, and *Niles' Register* again chided the Virginians for talking instead of acting.[48] The

[45] Cabell to TJ, Feb. 3, 1823 (Cabell, pp. 272–273).

[46] It was dispatched Dec. 23, 1822, and appeared in the *Richmond Enquirer* Jan. 7, 1823. TJ held it back in order to procure further financial information.

[47] Cabell to TJ, Dec. 19, 1822 (Cabell, pp. 255–257).

[48] *Richmond Enquirer*, Dec. 10–27, 1822; *Niles' Weekly Register*, Dec. 28, 1822.

Maverick engraving did not placate all critics, but it won friends for Jefferson's architectural design. Also, the careful accounting of expenditures tended to mitigate the charges of extravagance.

Early in the session, when asked directly whether he would prefer a remission of the debt of the institution to the Literary Fund ($120,000) or provision for the completion of its buildings, he stated that at this stage he strongly preferred the latter, since the former was sure to come in time.[49] What they actually got was authorization to borrow $60,000 more. It was stipulated in the third loan act, as it had been in each of the previous measures, that this debt was to be repaid.[50] The requirement did not disturb Jefferson perceptibly at the moment. The Bursar reported that on receipt of the news, he manifested the joy of a father on the birth of a first and long-awaited son.[51] Cabell had warned him that they could expect nothing more for buildings, but they were now warranted in proceeding with the Rotunda. A month before his eightieth birthday, Jefferson informed all the Visitors that he had instructed Brockenbrough to make the necessary arrangements and to have work begun immediately.[52] He had his way about the order of procedure and could now count on the ultimate completion of his academical village according to plan.[53]

By the fall of 1823 the circular walls of the Rotunda were finished, but, as Jefferson stated in his annual report, they were being left to settle and harden until another warm season.[54] Since the roof was of "hemispherical form" and pressed outwardly in all directions, he thought it unwise to place this on the walls while they were in a green state. He did not think that the interior of the building would be finished within a year. Since all the other buildings were ready for occupancy, he believed that the University could be opened as soon as a faculty was assembled. He figured, however, that, if the University was not relieved of its present burden of debt, its opening might be delayed a quarter of a century.

The Visitors had gone to great lengths in their efforts to collect the unpaid subscriptions. They had offered to accept payment in wheat,

[49] TJ to Cabell, Dec. 28, 1822 (Cabell, p. 260).

[50] *Supplement to the Revised Code of the Laws of Virginia* (Richmond, 1833), pp. 44–46.

[51] Alexander Garrett to John H. Cocke, Feb. 18, 1823 (Cocke Papers, UVA). Cabell informed TJ on Feb. 5 (Cabell, p. 274).

[52] TJ to Cabell, Mar. 12, 1823 (*ibid.*, pp. 278–279); see also TJ to Madison, Feb. 16, 1823 (UVA).

[53] Apparently nobody objected at the meeting of the Board on Apr. 7. Chapman Johnson, whom TJ once described as a dissenter, was present.

[54] Minutes of the Visitors, Oct. 6, 1823 (UVA).

corn, oats, or rye, or in short-term notes. They had appointed a collector and at their last meeting had authorized him to bring suit against delinquent subscribers. Little more than a small contingency fund could be expected from this source, and only the annuity of $15,000 could be relied on.[55]

During the legislative session of 1823–1824 Jefferson flatly rejected a proposal that the University be relieved of interest charges for a specified period of years. "Once you get the professors and students here," he said, "you cannot turn them adrift."[56] He favored the remission of back interest as well as the entire principal. What the University got from the legislature was described by him as a "Scotch gift."[57] He could not close his eyes the night after he read about the proposal in the *Enquirer*, he said. The measure relieved the University not only of the payment of interest but also of the pledge to repay the principal. What Jefferson objected to was the assertion in it of the right of the legislature to reimpose these obligations.

Cabell assured him that this would never happen. He said the proviso was a meaningless concession that had won over some waverers. Also he reminded Jefferson that the University, by its charter, was subject at all times to the will of the legislature, and that denial of ultimate legislative authority would have been inconsistent with the democratic character on which they had prided themselves.[58] They could not have it both ways. Jefferson had no choice but to agree. They could not hope to gain complete security but they had won a great victory, as Cabell said.

Toward the end of the session, after much maneuvering, they were promised $50,000 from the claim against the federal government for interest on expenditures during the War of 1812. Jefferson himself had suggested this resource a couple of years earlier.[59] Cabell went to Washington to press the claim, but the prospect of obtaining this money, which was earmarked for books and equipment, was uncertain when the Visitors met in April. Cabell reported that they had "exhausted the favor" of the legislators, but they could get a temporary loan from the state if necessary. Therefore, they believed that the time had come to acquire a faculty.

[55] Out of the annuity they were now paying $10,800 for interest, and they would be put to some expense merely to care for the buildings. Only the small amount that would be left could be applied to the reduction of the principal of $180,000.

[56] TJ to Cabell, Jan. 19, 1824 (UVA).

[57] TJ to Cabell, Jan. 23, 1824 (*ibid.*).

[58] Cabell to TJ, Jan. 26, 29, 1824 (Cabell, pp. 287–290).

[59] Cabell to TJ, Mar. 7, 17, 1824 (*ibid.*, pp. 294–298). See also Cabell to TJ, Jan. 14, 1822 (*ibid.*, pp. 231–232).

Francis Walker Gilmer

Portrait by an unknown artist. (Courtesy of the University of Virginia Library, Prints File, Special Collections)

[XXVII]

A Bold Mission and a Memorable Visit

WRITING Madison before the legislative session of 1823–1824, Jefferson said he believed that the Visitors were all agreed that they should send an agent to Great Britain to procure professors.[1] The most traveled of them, Joseph C. Cabell, had seriously considered undertaking the projected mission but concluded that he would be unable to do so. On learning this, Jefferson turned his attention to Francis Walker Gilmer, son of his old friend Dr. George Gilmer of Pen Park near Charlottesville, and, in Jefferson's opinion, the best-educated Virginian of his generation. Gilmer, who had just turned thirty-three, was beginning a promising career at the bar. After consulting Madison, Jefferson approached this brilliant and amiable young man, making him a provisional offer of the mission and of the professorship of law in the University. Gilmer asked for time to consider the latter but agreed to undertake the trip abroad.[2] This was a novel and precarious venture of which full local approval was not to be expected. Jefferson intended it to be secret until it could be presented as a *fait accompli* and be justified by its fruits.

The minutes of the Visitors' spring meeting state that they were "of opinion that to obtain professors of the first order of science in their respective lines, they must resort principally to Europe."[3] Such efforts as Jefferson himself had made until this time to recruit academic personnel in the United States had been wholly unsuccessful. Not only had he lost Thomas Cooper. His advances to George Ticknor and Nathaniel Bowditch of Massachusetts had been politely but decisively rebuffed. In his formal report for 1824, which he transmitted late in the year, he went to some pains to explain the resort to the Old World. He then said

[1] TJ to Madison, Nov. 6, 1823 (LC); Madison replied Nov. 11 (MP).

[2] Gilmer to TJ, Dec. 3, 1823 (*Correspondence of Thomas Jefferson and Francis Walker Gilmer, 1814–1826*, ed. by Richard Beale Davis [1946], pp. 81–82).

[3] Minutes of the meeting of Apr. 5–7, 1824 (UVA).

that competent professors might have been found in American seminaries, but that it was not probable that they would have been willing to leave their posts and that it would not have been honorable to "seduce" them from their positions anyway. He said that "to advance in science we must avail ourselves of the lights of the countries already advanced before us."[4]

To make the best use of the funds available, the Visitors agreed that at first the faculty would consist of eight professors, instead of the ten for whom that number of pavilions had been built.[5] Besides being provided with a rent-free residence, each professor was to receive a fixed salary of not less than $1000 nor more than $1500 per annum, along with the fees paid by the students enrolled in his particular "school." He might be guaranteed an annual income of $2500 for five years and was to be under contract for that period. By American standards these provisions were generous.[6] It was expressly stipulated that no professor should engage in remunerative activity beyond his academic services without the consent of the Visitors.[7] Jefferson and his colleagues intended to have a full-time faculty. They hoped to open the University on February 1, 1825, and expected to keep it in continuous session until December 15.

The reduction in the size of the faculty was not matched by a corresponding reduction in the number of subjects of instruction. The "useful sciences" that Jefferson had originally arranged in ten professorships were now distributed among eight schools. In the first place the division of ancient languages contained Greek, Latin, and Hebrew. To these were now added rhetoric, belles-lettres, ancient history, and ancient geography. Similarly, government, political economy, and the law of nature and nations were included in the school of law. Additions were also made to other schools. Jefferson recognized that the professors would be over-taxed and said that some adjustments were to be expected.[8]

It was deemed expedient that the professorships of moral philosophy and law should be held by American citizens. The Visitors appointed Gilmer to one of these, leaving the choice between them to him. Also,

[4] TJ to the president and directors of the Literary Fund, Oct. 5, 1824 (Cabell, p. 482).

[5] Minutes, Apr. 5–7, 1824 (UVA).

[6] American professors of this era seem to have earned from $600 to $1200 a year, except at Harvard, South Carolina, and Virginia. At this time a Harvard professor received an annual salary of $1700, but this was reduced to $1500 in 1826. A Yale professor made $1100 a year (Brooks Mather Kelley, *Yale: A History* [1974], p. 143).

[7] The professor of medicine was allowed to practice within the university community (Minutes, meeting of Mar. 5, 1825, UVA).

[8] For TJ's distribution of subjects in the Rockfish Gap report, see Cabell, pp. 437–438. This may be compared with the distribution in 1824 (*ibid.*, pp. 481–482). The term "school" continued to be used rather than "department" at the University of Virginia into the twentieth century.

they voted to defer the appointment of the anatomical professor for a time. Financial uncertainties were assigned as the reason for the delay, but there was sentiment favorable to the selection of an American for this post. Cabell and Cocke had a "scheme" to attain balance in the faculty, which the Old Sachem upset. Shortly after the meeting broke up, Jefferson reviewed the financial situation and concluded that they could afford eight professors. He promptly wrote a circular to his colleagues, saying that he proposed to authorize Gilmer to engage a professor of anatomy and medicine along with the five others. He asked that they express their opinions without delay. Expostulating to Cabell, Cocke said: "Do save us from this inundation of foreigners if it is possible."[9]

Cabell talked about the circular with Cocke at Bremo and replied to it from that place. At the meeting he had taken the position that there should be as many Americans as foreigners on the faculty. He still believed that his arguments had merit but saw no need to repeat them. Instead, he yielded his consent to Jefferson's proposal. He deferred to what he recognized as superior academic judgment. Also he made the revealing statement that it was his greatest happiness to give Jefferson pleasure "upon any and all occasions." Cocke added a postscript to this affectionate letter, saying that he concurred in its judgment. So did Madison.[10]

Toward the end of April, Gilmer made a visit to Monticello where he received a full briefing from his host, who seems to have thought of everything. Provision was made for the envoy's expenses and for advances to professors. Their salaries were to begin October 1 or on whatever day thereafter they should set out for the New World. Gilmer was given letters of introduction to Richard Rush, the American Minister to Great Britain, whose aid was specially requested; to Samuel Parr, who was described by Jefferson as the "purest classic" alive; and to the philosopher Dugald Stewart of Edinburgh, whom he had known long ago in Paris.[11] Gilmer was instructed to avail himself of the counsel of these gentlemen and to inquire particularly into the temperament and character as well as the learning of each prospective professor. He was supplied with a copy of the Maverick engraving in order to show them where they might live and work. He was also given a letter to George Blaetter-

[9] TJ to the Visitors, Apr. 9, 1824 (Cabell, pp. 302–303). Copies of this circular were made by his granddaughters. Cocke wrote Cabell on Apr. 10 (Cabell Papers, UVA). Apparently they hoped to attain an even balance between Europeans and Americans by the time there were ten professors.

[10] Cabell to TJ, Apr. 16, 1824 (Cabell, pp. 303–304); Madison to TJ, Apr. 16, 1824 (MP).

[11] Notes, dated Apr. 26, 1824 (LC); letters of the same date to Rush (L. & B., XVI, 31–35), to Parr and to Stewart (*Papers, M.H.S.*, I, 332–336). Madison also gave Gilmer letters of introduction.

mann, to whom he was to offer the professorship of modern languages unless, upon personal observation, he should find him unsuitable. This German, now living in London, was recommended by Ticknor and had corresponded with Jefferson. He was elected by the Visitors at their meeting in April.[12] Jefferson was well aware of the prestige of the ancient universities of Oxford and Cambridge. In his opinion the former was especially notable in the classics, and the latter in mathematics, natural philosophy, and natural history. He suggested that Gilmer make headquarters at Cambridge at first and thought it most likely that he would find a professor of anatomy and medicine at Edinburgh.

On May 8, 1824, Gilmer set sail from New York. The *Enquirer* reported his departure ten days later, saying that he was commissioned to buy books and apparatus abroad. This was correct as far as it went, but the major purpose of his mission was unmentioned. A few days later the Richmond paper reprinted from the *American Farmer* a letter from John H. Cocke which stated not only that the University would open on February 1, 1825, but also that Gilmer was going to procure professors.[13] No formal announcement about the opening had yet been made and none was made now, but Jefferson drafted an informal statement. This he passed on to the Charlottesville paper, and it was duly copied in the *Enquirer*. It did not bear his signature or refer to the mission of Gilmer.[14] Cocke stated afterwards that his letter was not intended for publication and that the news was out anyway.[15] Jefferson indulged in no recrimination, but he must have been disturbed by the leak.

About a month after Gilmer's departure, Jefferson sent him some copies of the Rockfish Gap report and a letter to John Cartwright. Replying to one from that English reformer, he said, among other things, that the study of government in the University would be based on the rights of man.[16] He had instructed Gilmer to write him every two weeks but could not hope to hear from him until late summer. The only good news from him that came before the fall meeting of the Visitors was that Blaettermann had accepted appointment as professor of modern languages.[17] Apparently he was undeterred by the stipulation that he provide instruction in French, German, Spanish, and Italian, along with

[12] TJ to Blaettermann, Apr. 26, 1824 (LC). Blaettermann's first letter to TJ was Apr. 27, 1819 (UVA).

[13] *Richmond Enquirer*, May 18, 25, 1824. Cocke's letter of May 3 was addressed to John S. Skinner, editor of the *American Farmer*.

[14] TJ to Clement P. McKennie, May 25, 1824 (UVA), Charlottesville *Central Gazette*, May 28, 1824, published in *Enquirer*, June 4.

[15] Cocke to TJ, Aug. 27, 1824 (HEH).

[16] TJ to Gilmer, June 5, 1824 (*Correspondence of TJ and Gilmer*, p. 84), enclosing a letter of same date to Cartwright (L. & B., XVI, 42–52).

[17] Gilmer to TJ, June 21, 1824 (*Correspondence of TJ and Gilmer*, pp. 86–88) received Aug. 7.

modern history, but he had not studied Anglo-Saxon, which was also to be offered in his school. Jefferson informed him that he did not have to teach that subject immediately, thus giving him time to prepare himself in it. Meanwhile, books bearing on the subject were to be purchased in England.

Less than two weeks before the autumn equinox Jefferson received from Gilmer a letter largely devoted to the difficulties the envoy faced. These had put him in a pessimistic state of mind.[18] This was not because of ill treatment, for the attractive young Virginian had been well received in England, as he was to be in Scotland. But as yet he had found no competent person, except Blaettermann, who was willing to go to a distant country under the conditions Jefferson had prescribed. The German had accepted a multi-lingual assignment without demur, but others were surprised by the arrangement of subjects and appalled by the number of them assigned to each professor. The session of ten and a half months that the Visitors had approved was excessively long by English standards. Gilmer heard complaints about the lack of a summer vacation and found that the salaries of popular professors at Oxford and Cambridge were higher than he had supposed. His own health was bad and he needed more money for expenses. He now saw no prospect that he could engage professors in time for them to reach Virginia by November 15, as had been originally planned. In midsummer his hopes were low. He was to become even more depressed when subjected to "the wretched climate of Edinburgh."

Shortly after he gave final instructions to Gilmer in April, Jefferson made a ride to the University which so tired him that he wondered if he could get home. It left him in such a state of languor and fatigue that he did not expect to mount his horse again for some days. Therefore he sent a note to Brockenborough, asking the Proctor to come to Monticello if there was need to consult him about anything.[19]

During the summer of 1824 he was chiefly occupied with paperwork. He was preparing a catalogue of books for the library of the University. This task proved to be more laborious than he had expected. Early in August he told Madison that for more than two months he spent four hours a day on the project and had devoted all day to it for some time lately.[20] Shortly before the fall meeting of the Visitors, he completed his

[18] Gilmer to TJ, July 20, 1824, received Sept. 9 (*ibid.*, pp. 92–97). Gilmer's mission is described in detail by W. P. Trent in *English Culture in Virginia* (1889) and by R. B. Davis in *Francis Walker Gilmer: Life and Learning in Jefferson's Virginia* (1939).

[19] TJ to Brockenbrough, May 4, 1824 (UVA).

[20] TJ to Madison, Aug. 8, 1824 (LC). He sought help from Madison on the theological section.

catalogue. To Madison he reported that he had listed 6,860 volumes and that they would cost more than $24,000.[21] He had sold Congress a library of approximately that size for about the same amount of money. The University did not have the funds to buy these books as yet, and the shelves they were to rest on were not yet built. But Jefferson was already in touch with a firm of booksellers in Boston.[22]

On October 5 "a most unwelcome letter" came to him from the ancient capital of Scotland. He told Madison he had never received a greater damper on his hopes and spirits. Francis Walker Gilmer wrote that he was so doubtful of his ability to procure such persons as he "should choose to be associated with" that he had determined to refuse his own election as professor at the University. Fortunately, four days later a letter from him brought more hopeful news.[23] On his return to England after his unsuccessful visit to Edinburgh, Gilmer had engaged a young mathematician with the best of credentials, Thomas Key, M.A., of Cambridge, who was enthusiastic about going to America and had put him in touch with a promising young classicist from the same university. Gilmer was now making his headquarters in London and had other good prospects. Not until six weeks later did Jefferson hear what came of these. He received the news after Gilmer had arrived in New York and the Marquis de Lafayette had visited Monticello and the University. That visit was the great event of the season and for a time, no doubt, it took Jefferson's mind off the baffling problem of acquiring a faculty.

ii

When Jefferson learned that the President had invited Lafayette to visit the United States, he wrote Monroe and a couple of congressmen that they must not send the General home empty-handed.[24] There was no likelihood of that, but he warned the "nation's guest" of a real danger. The American people might kill him with kindness.[25] This very nearly happened during a triumphal tour that lasted more than a year and is without parallel in American history.[26] In the course of his journey,

[21] TJ to Madison, Sept. 24, 1824 (LC).

[22] TJ to Messrs. Cummings, Hilliard & Co., Sept. 6, 1824 (LC). His immediate concern was for the establishment of a bookstore, but in due course he dealt with this firm in acquiring books for the library.

[23] Gilmer to TJ, Aug. 13, 1824, received Oct. 5; Aug. 27, received Oct. 9 (*Correspondence of TJ and Gilmer*, pp. 92–100). TJ to Madison, Oct. 6, 1824 (LC).

[24] TJ to William Short, May 17, 1824 (LC), discussing the invitation and Lafayette's financial difficulties.

[25] TJ to Lafayette, Sept. 3, 1824 (Chinard, *Letters of Lafayette and Jefferson*, p. 421).

[26] The visit lasted from Aug. 15, 1824, to Sept. 3, 1825.

Jefferson's old friend made two memorable visits to Monticello and the University of Virginia.

After arriving in New York on August 15, 1824, Lafayette turned northward, and he first wrote Jefferson from Boston. In this characteristically effusive letter he said that he must be in Yorktown to help celebrate the anniversary of the surrender of Cornwallis in October and that he would see Jefferson during his southern journey. Jefferson's welcoming letter crossed this one in the mail. It contained an invitation from the village of Charlottesville to a dinner and one from himself to stay at Monticello.[27] Lafayette was to come when he could and remain as long as he liked.

The Marquis reported to his future host that he was accompanied by his son George Washington and a retired army officer who had lived with him for some years. The latter, Auguste Levasseur, was in fact the General's secretary, and he wrote an account of this journey upon which historians were to draw for generations.[28] Lafayette said nothing about his manservant Bastien, but he did mention the Misses Wright — Frances and Camilla — who were traveling independently and might be expected to arrive a little later than he. These young ladies had been living at Lagrange as members of his family. The elder was commonly referred to as Fanny Wright during her later years of notoriety as a reformer. She was probably best known to Americans at this time as the author of a friendly account of their country, written after a previous visit.[29] There is no reason whatsoever to suppose that Jefferson, whose hospitality was as capacious as his house, was dismayed by the prospect of providing for a party of this size. No connection can be established between his anticipation of this visit and his recourse, late in the summer, to a bank for a further loan. It is a fact, however, that his bad financial situation had worsened. In the weeks immediately preceding Lafayette's visit, furthermore, he was in poor health and seemingly more conscious than usual of the infirmities of old age.

On October 1, writing from Philadelphia, the General said that in three weeks Jefferson would see his "old affectionate friend." The three weeks stretched into five. Because of the celebrations on the way, the journey from Yorktown to Albemarle County required two weeks instead of two days. Meanwhile, invitations from the village of Charlottesville to a dinner in the Rotunda had gone out. The designer of that

[27] Lafayette to TJ, Aug. 29, 1824 (received Sept. 9); TJ to Lafayette, Sept. 3, 1824 (Chinard, *Letters of Lafayette and Jefferson*, pp. 420–421).

[28] Lafayette to TJ, Oct. 1, 1824 (*ibid.*, pp. 421–423). Levasseur's account was published in France in 1829 and then translated into English as *Lafayette in America, in 1824 and 1825* (1829).

[29] *Views of Society and Manners in America* (1821).

structure wrote Lafayette that his presence would bring all the more honor to the University because he would be its first guest.[30] During the month of October Jefferson had what he called an "impostume" (an abscess) on his jaw. This affliction required him to take nourishment through a tube and kept him at home for two or three weeks.[31] He had recovered by the day of his friend's arrival but did not accompany the welcoming party at the county line. Instead, he sent by the hand of his grandson a note to Lafayette, saying that he was well enough to embrace him.[32]

About 11 A.M. on Thursday, November 4, 1824, the General, with his party and a military escort from Fluvanna, entered the county of Albemarle, where he received a rousing welcome. After a brief ceremony and a pause for refreshment at Mrs. Boyd's tavern, he set out at noon for Monticello in the landau, drawn by four gray horses, which had been sent by the host who awaited him.[33] The long procession that wound its way through the countryside was headed by a detachment of cavalry. Next came a carriage containing a deputation from the committee of arrangements. Jeff Randolph headed this, but he rode with the General, as did William Cabell Rives, who had delivered an address of welcome. The landau was followed by two carriages bearing the party of the Marquis and a "neat wagon" carrying his luggage. Next came the Albemarle Lafayette Guards in uniforms he admired. Behind them marched a body of citizens who had come to do honor to the guest.

A goodly number of spectators had gathered on the little mountain. When a bugle announced the approach of the procession, they spontaneously formed lines on two sides of the circle before the house — ordinary citizens on one side and cavalrymen on the other. Silence fell as the carriages neared the house, and the host advanced to greet his guest. According to the local reporter, he did so with feeble steps but quickened them as he approached Lafayette. It is said that they both shed tears as they embraced. This was one of the most sentimental moments and most dramatic events in the entire lifetime of this highly disciplined and characteristically undramatic man.

The crowd had dispersed when James Madison joined the company about sunset. Writing Dolley before breakfast the next day, he said they were commencing dessert when he arrived. The General's secretary, M. Levasseur, was not present. Having been taken sick on the road, he

[30] TJ to Lafayette, Oct. 9, 1824 (Chinard, *Letters of Lafayette and Jefferson*, pp. 423–424).

[31] TJ to Joseph C. Coolidge, Oct. 24, 1824 (Ford, X, 323).

[32] TJ to Lafayette, Nov. 4, 1824 (Chinard, *Letters of Lafayette and Jefferson*, pp. 425–426).

[33] The events of Nov. 4 and 5 are described in great detail in the *Richmond Enquirer*, Nov. 16, 1824, quoting the Charlottesville *Central Gazette* of Nov. 10. While romantic and rhetorical, this account appears to be reliable with respect to facts.

had gone to bed instead of to dinner. The Misses Wright had not yet arrived, but two members of the Council of State were part of the General's entourage. Also, Joseph Coolidge, Jr., who was seeking the hand of Ellen Wayles Randolph, had recently arrived from Boston.[34] Just how these guests were distributed we do not know, but at bedtime some of them must have had to climb the narrow stairs to the second floor.

Madison found Lafayette so much increased in bulk and so changed in aspect that he would not have recognized him. The General himself found Jefferson "much aged" after thirty-five years but "marvelously well" at eighty-one and "in full possession of all the vigor of his mind and heart."[35] The ceremonies connected with this visit would have taxed the endurance of almost any octogenarian, and this one had a distaste for ceremony anyway. At 10 A.M. on Friday, he and the General and ex-President Madison set out for Charlottesville in the landau drawn by the four gray horses, and they did not get back until night. Accompanied by cavalry and followed by a large crowd, they proceeded to the Central Hotel in Charlottesville, where the General heard and responded to another address of welcome. The trio then repaired to a room that had been provided for them, and presumably Jefferson had a chance to sit down while the General was being introduced to all who desired to meet him.

Another procession was formed at noon, and this slowly made its way to the south end of the Lawn of the University. The "Hero of the Revolution with two of its Sages" ascended the Lawn to the Rotunda, while hundreds of handkerchiefs were waved by ladies on the terraces. The Honorable William F. Gordon descended from the portico of the Rotunda, which was still devoid of columns, and made another address, to which Lafayette duly responded. After a brief pause in one of the pavilions, Lafayette and his companions mingled freely with the ladies on the terraces.

Dinner began at 3 P.M. on the topmost floor of the unfinished Rotunda, beneath the dome. The tables were arranged in three concentric circles, and four hundred men are said to have been seated at them. Before the arrival of the Nation's Guest, the local paper said: "We shall be able to give the General a plain substantial dinner, and a hearty, old-fashioned Virginia welcome."[36] It must have been a laborious task to bring the food for so many people up the stairs, and we may wonder if any of it was hot. This may have been a sort of picnic.[37] No doubt the

[34] James Madison to Dolley Madison, 7 A.M., Nov. 5, 1824 (Wis. Hist. Soc.).

[35] Nov. 8, 1824, in *Memoirs* (Chinard, *Letters of Lafayette and Jefferson*, pp. 358–359).

[36] Quoted from Charlottesville *Central Gazette* in *Richmond Enquirer*, Nov. 5, 1824.

[37] Provision was made for the ladies on the terraces and in one or more of the pavilions. It is uncertain whether any of the kitchens were equipped as yet.

Dome Room of the Rotunda (restored 1976)
(Courtesy of the University of Virginia Library, Prints File, Special Collections)

food was ample, and the first public dinner at the University of Virginia was a notable affair. The meal lasted about three hours. The presiding officer, Valentine Wood Southall, had Lafayette on his right, followed by Jefferson and Madison. President Monroe had been in the county recently and had been expected to attend, but he found it necessary to return to Washington. The members of the General's party were on Southall's left.[38]

There were thirteen regular toasts, as there were that many states in the original Union. We need refer here only to the one to Jefferson. He came prepared with a response but claimed that he had neither the strength nor voice to make it. It was read in a loud voice by the presiding officer. Lafayette is said to have grasped his friend's hand in the course of it and to have sobbed aloud. It was a sort of valediction to the citizens of Albemarle, whom Jefferson was never again to see in such numbers, and could hardly have failed to reduce many of them to tears. It was also a tribute to Lafayette and, in particular, an expression of appreciation of his services to the feeble American Republic when Jefferson represented it in France. He generously said that he only held the nail while Lafayette drove it.[39] Among the many who proposed "volunteer" toasts were Jeff Randolph, Francis W. Eppes, Nicholas Trist, and Charles Bankhead, who had been banished from the community five years earlier. James Dinsmore, whose skill as a carpenter was manifest at Monticello and in this very building, also proposed a toast. It was to "Thomas Jefferson, founder of the University of Virginia."

A few days later Lafayette made a tour of the academical village under the guidance of his host, but during the remainder of his visit he had a welcome chance to rest and talk. Before he left, on the morning of November 15, the old friends reminisced about the American and the French revolutions, discussed the low state of political liberty in Europe and the problem of slavery in the United States.[40] Accompanied in the landau by Thomas Jefferson Randolph and Valentine Wood Southall, and escorted by the Albemarle Lafayette Guards, the General set out for Orange County to visit James Madison.[41] The Misses Wright remained a little longer at Monticello, where one of them was ill. The main party had enjoyed Jefferson's hospitality for ten days. He had to replenish his stock of red wine after their departure.[42]

[38] Apparently T. M. Randolph would have presided if he had been present. Presumably he was out of town.

[39] For TJ's response of Nov. 5, 1824, see *The Complete Jefferson*, ed. by S. K. Padover, pp. 447–448.

[40] Comments of Levasseur; TJ to Madison, Nov. 15, 1824 (LC).

[41] *Richmond Enquirer*, Nov. 26, 1824.

[42] TJ to Bernard Peyton, Nov. 21, 1824 (MHS).

iii

Four days after Lafayette left him, Jefferson received the welcome news that Gilmer's difficult mission had been accomplished. Following a voyage of thirty-five days on the packet *Crisis*, during the whole of which he was sick, the envoy was in New York in the care of his doctors. He brought no professors with him but reported to Jefferson that he had engaged five altogether, and that they would arrive shortly. Besides Blaettermann and Key, the list included the following: George Long, professor of ancient languages; Charles Bonnycastle, professor of natural philosophy; and Dr. Robley Dunglison, professor of anatomy and medicine. No one had been found to head the school of natural history. The return of Gilmer after a successful mission was reported in the *Richmond Enquirer* the day Jefferson got his letter from New York, but the names of the appointees were not given. Shortly thereafter a letter arrived at Monticello that had been written by Gilmer before he left England. This contained somewhat more information about the new professors. Jefferson listed them in the statement he sent the Governor, which was to be added to his annual report as Rector. He was now confident that the University could be opened about February 1, as had been anticipated, but he did not invite applications for the dormitories as yet.[43]

The announcement of Gilmer's return excited some adverse comments on the "importation" of professors. A Connecticut editor said that any patriotic American should view this mission with indignation. He believed that its purpose could have been accomplished by a trip to New England. A Philadelphia editor held that an even shorter trip would have been sufficient. After extolling the merits of his state, he said that the mission to Europe to obtain professors was an insult to the American people. Ritchie published a number of these comments, saying that Virginians had no desire to disparage the wise men of the East and the philosophers of Philadelphia. The reasons for the mission were given by Jefferson in his report, which had been published in the *Enquirer* by this time, but it is unlikely that any of the critics had read this or that the names of the foreign professors would have meant much to them.[44]

Three of the five men whom Gilmer had engaged remained in England considerably beyond his expectation, but the others got to New York about two weeks after he did. These were George Blaettermann,

[43] Gilmer to TJ, Nov. 12, 1824, received Nov. 19; Sept. 15, 1824, received Nov. 22 (*Correspondence of TJ and Gilmer*, pp. 101–103, 113); *Richmond Enquirer*, Nov. 19, Dec. 2, 1824); TJ to Gov. J. H. Pleasants, Nov. 24 (UVA).

[44] The comments were published in the *Enquirer* Dec. 11, 1824, but actually antedated the publication of TJ's report on Dec. 2.

the oldest of the group, and George Long, the youngest. Shortly after the middle of December, Bernard Peyton informed Jefferson that the former with his wife had reached Richmond.[45] His unmarried colleague got to Albemarle County before he did. Years later, Long recalled that shortly after his arrival, he walked to Monticello to see Mr. Jefferson and surprised the old gentleman by his youthful appearance. As classicists they had much in common, and if the young Cantabrigian was not invited to dinner immediately, as he remembered, he was soon thereafter, when Mr. and Mrs. George Ticknor and Daniel Webster were guests at Monticello.[46]

The pavilions were numbered on the second Maverick engraving and they were assigned by lot. Long drew Number V, which had the most impressive portico of them all. Jefferson referred to it as Ionic with modillions. Blaettermann drew Number IV on the opposite or east side of the Lawn. His portico was said to be Doric of Albano. Writing Madison, Jefferson described this man as "rather a rough-looking German," who was not fluent in English but was familiar with even more languages than had been expected and was a man of high intelligence.[47] To Cabell Jefferson said of Long: "He appears to be a most amiable man, of fine understanding, well qualified for his department, and acquiring esteem as fast as he becomes known."[48]

The two ex-Presidents were still hoping that Gilmer would accept the professorship of law. By the end of the year Jefferson had decided to offer the professorship of natural history to Dr. John Patton Emmet, the son of the noted Irish patriot Thomas Addis Emmet who was a distinguished lawyer in New York. At the suggestion of Madison, his mind had turned to George Tucker, then a member of Congress, as professor of moral philosophy. Cabell, a relative of Tucker's by marriage, had been asked to inquire into his willingness to serve.[49] Both men became members of the original faculty, but they had not been formally elected as yet. If their names had been made public at this stage, they might have added fuel to the continuing protest against foreigners. Both were American citizens, but Emmet had been born in Ireland, and Tucker in Bermuda. Apart from Gilmer, whose services were in doubt, there was no native Virginian on the list, though Tucker belonged to a family closely identified with the Old Dominion from that day to this. Jefferson did not know just where the three other professors from Great Britain were, but he had most of a faculty on paper.

[45] Peyton to TJ, Dec. 17, 1824 (MHS).

[46] Long to Henry Tutwiler, May 30, 1875, in *Letters of George Long*, ed. by T. Fitzhugh (1917), p. 23. Ticknor to W. H. Prescott, Dec. 16, 1824 (*Life, Letters and Journals*, I, 348).

[47] TJ to Madison, Dec. 26, 1824 (LC).

[48] TJ to Cabell, Dec. 22, 1824 (Cabell, p. 323).

[49] TJ to Madison, Dec. 10, 1824 (LC); TJ to Cabell, Dec. 22, 1824 (Cabell, p. 324).

[XXVIII]

Life Comes to the University

1825

EARLY in the new year Jefferson received encouraging reports regarding Virginia's claim against the federal government from which the University was to get $50,000. Before the end of the congressional session a bill allowing it was passed by both houses. Jefferson's personal exertions in behalf of this claim, and the interest of the University in it, were said to have facilitated the passage of the measure.[1] His "parental care" of the University appears to have been appreciated in congressional circles. Writing him in January, Senator James Barbour said: "While you have been the ablest champion of the rights and happiness of your own generation, you have generously devoted the evening of your life to generations yet unborn."[2]

A few days after he received this appreciative letter Jefferson wrote Cabell that it was from posterity that remuneration for their sacrifices and services must be expected. He said that his efforts to improve the "moral condition" of his native state may have increased the esteem in which he was held elsewhere, but that they had certainly diminished it in Virginia. These efforts "ran foul of so many local interests, of so many personal views, and of so much ignorance" that a great change in sentiment regarding him had ensued.[3]

Months before this, Cabell had informed him of a plan to remove the College of William and Mary to Richmond and add a medical school to

[1] TJ brought pressure to bear on members of the Virginia delegation in Congress and discussed the claim with Daniel Webster and with Henry Clay on their visits to Monticello. L. W. Tazewell informed him of the outcome Mar. 2 (misdated Mar. 1), 1825 (MHS). In his reply of Mar. 13 (LC), he reminded the Senator of their correspondence about a university twenty years before. The claim is referred to on p. 395, above.

[2] Barbour to TJ, Jan. 3, 1825 (LC), replying to a letter of Dec. 26 (LC).

[3] TJ to Cabell, Jan. 11, 1825, referring to remarks in Cabell's letters of Dec. 31, 1824, and Jan. 6, 1825 (Cabell, pp. 324–332).

it. A petition asking that the Board of Visitors of that institution be authorized to change its site was presented to the legislature in the session of 1824–1825. Cabell was actively combating this and was charged with doing so on Jefferson's orders. In fact, Jefferson had advised Cabell to take no public stand on the question of moving the College from Williamsburg. In private he blamed the sad plight of his venerable alma mater on its poor management, and he charged the Richmonders with greed for its endowment of $100,000. He wanted the institution to stay where it was. As he told Cabell, however, he did not doubt the authority of the legislature over it as "a public institution, endowed from the public property . . . for public purposes."[4]

Several weeks after the legislative session began, while still believing that Cabell should not enter into the conflict over the removal of the College, Jefferson outlined a proposal which might enable his troubled colleague to counter the plan to set up a potential rival to their own University.[5] This proposal harked back to an earlier remark of Cabell's that they might be able to do something for the academies. Jefferson suggested that the endowment of the College could be used to establish a system of intermediate institutions such as had been recommended by the Rockfish Gap Commission. One of them could be in Williamsburg and one in Richmond, thus providing openings for the present faculty of William and Mary.

On receipt of this proposal, Cabell stated that it was too bold for the public mind at present, but he showed the letter to a few friends. Several weeks later, when his fears had increased, he asked Jefferson to put this counterplan into a bill and thus enable them to vanquish their enemies. Jefferson promptly responded to this request, saying that the effort had exhausted him. The paper he drafted was entitled "A bill for the discontinuance of the College of William and Mary, and the establishment of other colleges in convenient distribution over the state."[6]

While awaiting developments in the lower house, Cabell kept the bill private. On the strength of Jefferson's earlier letter, however, the rumor got out that he had ordered the plundering of the College and the bribery of various parts of the state. According to Cabell, Jefferson's view of legislative authority over a chartered institution was rejected by most of the lawyers. They found it difficult to reconcile this view with the recent

[4] TJ to Cabell, May 16, 1824, replying to a letter of May 5 (*ibid.*, pp. 305–313). At this time TJ suggested that the College might be combined with the University — i.e., that its endowment might be acquired. Cabell rejected the suggestion as utterly impracticable.

[5] TJ to Cabell, Dec. 22, 1824, replying to a letter of Dec. 17 (*ibid.*, pp. 316–318, 320–323).

[6] Cabell to TJ, Dec. 31, 1824, Jan. 6, Jan. 16, 1825; TJ to Cabell, Jan. 22 (*ibid.*, pp. 324–329, 332–333, 335); text of bill (*ibid.*, pp. 499–501). There were to be ten districts.

decision of John Marshall in the Dartmouth College case.[7] In an article Cabell published under the signature of "A Friend of Science," he drew heavily from letters of Jefferson written in 1817 and 1818 advocating the establishment of intermediate institutions.[8] There can be no doubt that these were more needed than a second university, and few will deny that it was to the interest of posterity to leave the ancient and honorable College of William and Mary in the old colonial capital. To what extent Jefferson influenced that decision we cannot say. At any rate, Cabell informed him that a resolution approving the petition had been defeated in the House of Delegates and that he might set his mind at rest.[9]

During the winter the Rector and Visitors of the University were troubled and embarrassed by the non-arrival of the rest of the professors who had been engaged by Gilmer. They had embarked at London in October, but were delayed over six weeks in the English Channel. Late in January Cabell, who had feared that they were lost in the October gales, was immensely relieved to learn that their vessel, the *Competitor*, was still at Plymouth on Dec. 5.[10] Dr. Dunglison reported their arrival at Norfolk to Jefferson more than two months later. On receipt of this welcome news, he drafted an announcement that the University would open on Monday, March 7.[11]

The newcomers made up a party of five. Dunglison and Key brought their wives with them; Bonnycastle was unmarried. After spending several days in Richmond, where they made a good impression, they proceeded to Charlottesville by stage. Jefferson sent them for their perusal the rules and regulations that the Visitors had adopted in October, along with some notes about the use of the library, and said that he would come down from the mountain to see them as soon as he could.[12] He may not have met them before the meeting of the Visitors on March 4, but presumably Brockenbrough took them in charge. They drew the three pavilions below the one already occupied by the Blaettermanns on

[7] Cabell to TJ, Jan. 30, 1825 (*ibid.*, pp. 336–337).

[8] Cabell wrote TJ the day the article appeared in the *Richmond Enquirer*, Feb. 3, 1825, that he had used TJ's name and letters (*ibid.*, pp. 337–338).

[9] Cabell to TJ, Feb. 7, 1825 (*ibid.*, pp. 341–342). In my opinion, the treatment of this episode by P. A. Bruce (*History of the University of Virginia*, I, 308–321) is based on an inadequate understanding of the complicated circumstances, and I regard his judgment of TJ and Cabell as harsh and unwarranted.

[10] Cabell to TJ, Jan. 30, 1825 (Cabell, pp. 336–337).

[11] Robley Dunglison to TJ, Feb. 10, 1825 (*The Jefferson-Dunglison Letters*, ed. by John M. Dorsey [1960], p. 11): announcement of Feb. 16, signed by Brockenbrough (*Richmond Enquirer*, Feb. 22). Their arrival was reported in that paper Feb. 17, and Cabell wrote TJ on Feb. 18 that he had visited them in Richmond (Cabell, pp. 346–347).

[12] TJ to the Professors of the University, Feb. 26, 1825 (LC).

University of Virginia

Engraving by B. Tanner, 1826. Published in Böÿe map, 1827. (Courtesy of the University of Virginia Library, Prints File, Special Collections)

East Lawn, leaving George Long the only resident of West Lawn for the moment. Something further may be said at this point about them and their new quarters.

Charles Bonnycastle, professor of natural philosophy, was educated by his father, a noted mathematician at the Royal Military Academy, Woolwich.[13] He drew Pavilion VI, which was described by its architect as "Ionic of the theatre of Marcellus."

Thomas Hewett Key, professor of mathematics, besides being the holder of the Master of Arts degree from Cambridge, and an alumnus of Trinity College, had studied medicine at Guy's Hospital, London.[14] He and his wife were in Pavilion VIII, which was "Corinthian of Diocletian's baths."

Robley Dunglison, next door in Pavilion X, had Doric columns. The professor of anatomy and medicine was a Scot who had picked up medical degrees in London and Germany and had a diploma from the Society of Apothecaries.[15]

At their meeting on March 4, the Visitors ratified the actions of Jefferson and Madison by formally electing two other professors: John P. Emmet, natural history; and George Tucker, moral philosophy. The former had attended West Point and had received the M.D. degree from the College of Physicians and Surgeons in New York.[16] When he arrived he was assigned Pavilion II, but he afterwards moved across the Lawn to Pavilion I, exchanging Ionic columns for Doric. George Tucker was a graduate of William and Mary and an author of some note.[17] On his arrival in April he drew Pavilion IX, the last on the West. It was modeled on the temple of Fortuna Virilis in Rome and is supposed to have reflected the influence of Benjamin H. Latrobe. Since the faculty was incomplete, not all of the pavilions were occupied; Number VII served as a library until the dome room in the Rotunda was finished. Number III was reserved for the law professor, if one could ever be found.

From the time he learned of Gilmer's firm decision not to accept the professorship of law, Jefferson was driven to desperation by his successive failures to fill this position. He sought a man of legal learning. Gilmer could have become one, if he was not one already. Jefferson said he could have ruled out the late Spencer Roane, because the judge was too limited in scholarship.[18] Chancellor James Kent, with whom Gilmer had talked in New York, would have been unacceptable for quite a different

[13] See *Appleton's Cyclopaedia of American Biography* (1887).
[14] See *Dictionary of National Biography*.
[15] See *D.A.B.* and *Dictionary of National Biography*.
[16] See *Appleton's Cyclopaedia*.
[17] See *D.A.B.*
[18] TJ to Cabell, Feb. 3, 1824 (UVA).

reason. This distinguished jurist was an upholder of what Jefferson called consolidation. "An angel from heaven who should inculcate such principles in our school of government should be rejected by me," said that vigilant republican.[19]

Writing Madison, he expressed concern that a "Richmond lawyer," or someone infected with the doctrines of consolidation, might be proposed. He thought it his duty to guard against this danger by prescribing the textbooks in government which should be used. Although textbooks were often chosen by governing boards at this time, he said that in most fields the professors would be more competent to judge than the Board of Visitors. He believed, however, that the latter were the best judges in this particular field. He suggested the writings of Locke and Sydney, the Declaration of Independence, the Federalist papers, and the Virginia Resolutions of 1799.[20]

Madison agreed that the "true doctrines of liberty" as exemplified in the American government should be inculcated in those who were to sustain and administer the system, but he recognized the difficulty of finding books that would serve as both guides and guards. He commented sagaciously on the merits and limitations of all the texts and documents suggested by Jefferson, being most dubious about the Virginia Resolutions of 1799, which in fact he had written. He took the position that the Board should refer to accepted standards "without requiring an unqualified conformity to them." With these sensible qualifications he agreed to Jefferson's list, adding to it Washington's inaugural speech and Farewell Address.[21]

Jefferson accepted these suggestions gratefully. The resolution adopted by the Visitors at their next meeting reflected Madison's judgment both in form and substance. Washington's brief inaugural speech was dropped, but his Farewell Address was on a list which, viewed as a whole, was well balanced.[22] Madison, like Jefferson, used language normally associated with theology. He said that the best safeguard against "heretical intrusions" in the school of government would be "an able and orthodox professor."

Five years before this, Jefferson had said: "This institution will be based on the illimitable freedom of the human mind. For here we are not afraid to follow truth wherever it may lead, nor to tolerate any error

[19] TJ to Gilmer, Jan. 20, 1825 (LC).

[20] TJ to Madison, Feb. 1, 1825 (Madison, LC). He wrote along the same lines to Cabell, Feb. 3, 1825 (Cabell, pp. 339–340), enclosing a proposed resolution on the subject (UVA). For other treatments of this topic see Arthur Bestor, "Thomas Jefferson and the Freedom of Books," in *Three Presidents and Their Books*, pp. 24–44; and L. Levy, *Jefferson and Civil Liberties*, pp. 151–157.

[21] Madison to TJ, Feb. 8, 1825 (MP).

[22] TJ to Madison, Feb. 12, 1825 (LC); minutes of the meeting of Mar. 4 (UVA).

so long as reason is left free to combat it."[23] This private saying came to be regarded by later generations as a classic statement of the principle of academic freedom. We may properly ask if the position he took in 1825 concerning the teaching of government can be reconciled with it. The resolution that the Visitors adopted just before the official opening of the University was carefully worded. As here stated, it was the duty of the Board to ensure that no doctrines incompatible with the basic principles of the state and federal constitutions should be inculcated. It might be necessary, therefore, to point out where these principles could be found.

The reason for the choice of each of the texts or documents was briefly stated. The Virginia Resolutions of 1799 were designated as a response to the Alien and Sedition Acts, rather than as an exposition of a philosophy of government. Since all of the approved writings antedated the pronouncements of John Marshall as chief justice, perhaps it may be said that the Visitors begged the question of their acceptability. Of Jefferson's intense disapproval of the trend of these there can be no doubt whatsoever, but the main ground of his opposition to "consolidation" was his belief that it would be inimical not merely to local self-government but also to individual liberty. The concept of academic freedom as an absolute was not in vogue at the time, if in fact it ever has been, and he may have thought of himself as faced with a practical problem rather than a philosophical dilemma. Complete consistency cannot be rightly claimed for him, but it seems safe to say that no other American of his generation did more to remove shackles from the mind. And, judged by contemporary standards, the institution he had planned was to be one of notable liberality.

The distinction of the University he was seeking to create lay not only in its architectural design but also in its academic structure. This was best described in the rules and regulations that were adopted by the Visitors at their meeting in the fall of 1824.[24] Before drafting these Jefferson had gone to great pains to inform himself of the practices in other institutions in the Old World as well as the New. From his grandson and Thomas Cooper he had learned about the ways and troubles of South Carolina College. From George Ticknor he received information not only about Harvard but also about the German and to some extent the British universities. He consulted books dealing with the latter.[25]

The system described in the rules and regulations that Jefferson sent

[23] TJ to William Roscoe, Dec. 27, 1820 (L. & B., XV, 303).

[24] Minutes, Oct. 4–5, 1824 (UVA).

[25] Probably the most important was Michael Russel, *View of the System of Education at Present Pursued in the Schools and Universities of Scotland* (Edinburgh, 1813).

the professors shortly before the opening day was necessarily theoretical, and in important respects it differed from that in other American institutions of higher learning. Instead of a fixed curriculum Jefferson set up a system of free election, and he organized instruction vertically in schools rather than horizontally in classes. A student could enroll in more than one school but was not required to do so. He must register and pay for a year but was subject to no other requirements regarding the length of residence. He might receive a diploma, following a public examination in one of the oval rooms in the Rotunda. This could be in any school, but the candidate must also demonstrate his ability to read the highest Latin classics with ease and would gain further distinction if he had a like proficiency in Greek. As Jefferson put it, the reputation of the University should be committed only to those who had attained "eminence" in one or more of the sciences taught in it, along with a proficiency in those languages "which constitute the basis of good education." Jefferson viewed degrees with indifference and he made no provision for that of Bachelor of Arts. Diplomas were to be of two grades, doctor and graduate.[26]

He drew up a schedule of classes before there was a faculty to conduct them. Even though the professors were overburdened with subjects, they were assigned only six hours of teaching a week.[27] While wisely refraining from any prescription of classroom procedure, he shared Ticknor's dissatisfaction with the recitation system as practiced at Harvard and elsewhere. Under this the major if not the sole function of the teacher was to ascertain whether or not the students had learned their lessons from their textbooks. Lectures were not then customary in America, but he expected them to be given in his University. He did not think that any professor should be asked to "bawl daily to multitudes," but he realized that some of the student audiences would be too large for the rooms that were provided for class use in the pavilions. These classes were to be transferred to the Rotunda.[28] When finished, that building would consist of a basement, where the chemistry laboratory was to be located, and two upper stories. The top story was to house the library, while lectures and public exercises were to take place in one of the oval rooms on the first floor.[29] He rejected the suggestion that one of these rooms be built in the form of an amphitheater, such as

[26] TJ also provided for lesser awards. The actual practice proved slightly different.

[27] Classes of two hours each were to be held Monday, Wednesday, and Friday or Tuesday, Thursday, and Saturday. The school day began at 7:30 A.M. and ended at 3:30 P.M.

[28] TJ to Madison, Apr. 30, 1823 (MP).

[29] These arrangements can be readily understood by visitors to the Rotunda since its restoration, which was completed in 1976. The interior of the building had been remodeled after the great fire of 1895.

The Rotunda from the Lawn
(Courtesy of the University of Virginia Library, Prints File, Special Collections)

Cabell had seen at Bologna, with ascending tiers of seats. He said that only in the case of anatomy, for which he planned a separate building, and the natural sciences was this desirable.[30]

The opening of the University on March 7, 1825, appears to have been entirely unceremonious and could not have been impressive. About thirty students were on hand. The Visitors had relaxed the regulations for the present year so as to permit enrollment at any time. Students continued to drop in by twos and threes, despite a long spell of rainy weather during which the Richmond and Fredericksburg stages stopped running. Writing Madison a couple of weeks after the opening, Jefferson reported that between fifty and sixty students were then in attendance and that more were coming.

A major difficulty had already appeared. They were "so defectively prepared" that it had been found necessary to relax for the first year the admission requirements he had specified for the several schools.[31] Another difficulty, which was exceedingly vexatious during the weeks it lasted, was the non-arrival of the textbooks he had ordered from Boston.[32] Whatever reservations he may have had about the students, Jefferson seems to have had none whatever about the professors. Since the two Americans who were elected on March 4 did not arrive until more than a month later, the faculty consisted at the outset of the five foreigners. He told Thomas Cooper that they were all "highly qualified, full of zeal, disposed to meet cheerfully all novelties and difficulties, and pleased with their accommodations and prospects."[33]

No provision was made for a president in Jefferson's academic design, but the professors were authorized to elect a chairman for a one-year term. The faculty did not meet and carry out this injunction until April 12, when they chose George Tucker, the only member from Virginia. He did not arrive until a few days later, but Emmet, the only other American citizen, served for him in the meantime.[34] The Visitors had elected two men to the professorship of law, having virtually no hope that one would accept and being far from sure of the other. Judge Henry St. George Tucker declined as was expected. So did Judge Philip Pendelton Barbour, despite the exercise of Jefferson's great persuasive power in a conversation of two hours at Monticello and also a visit from Madi-

[30] Joseph C. Cabell to Madison, Apr. 16, 1823 (MP); TJ to Madison, Apr. 30, 1823 (*ibid.*).

[31] TJ to Madison, Mar. 22, 1825; TJ to L. W. Tazewell, Mar. 13, (LC).

[32] TJ to Wm. Hilliard, Aug. 31, 1825 (UVA).

[33] TJ to Cooper, Apr. 4, 1825 (*ibid.*).

[34] Faculty minutes, UVA.

son.[35] Several weeks later Jefferson yielded to the pressure of his colleagues and approached Judge Dabney Carr, but his nephew declined on the ground that he lacked the necessary learning.[36] For more than a year longer the young institution was to be without a school of law, and the school of medicine could not amount to much until the anatomical building was constructed and Dr. Dunglison could perform dissections.[37] Without these schools Jefferson could not have a real university. Otherwise, in the spring of 1825, it seemed that the child of his old age had made a good start. John Adams disapproved of the idea of foreign professors, but the men themselves exceeded Jefferson's own highest expectations and created a distinctly favorable impression on others.[38] The report got out that Easterners in Congress were fearful that the new University would draw students from their region, accustom them to southern ways, and reconcile them to slavery.[39]

Professor George Ticknor of Harvard continued to wish it well. Shortly before Christmas, when visiting Monticello with his wife and Daniel Webster, he described the buildings of the University as "more beautiful than anything architectural in New England, and more appropriate to an university than can be found, perhaps, in the world." He also reported the salary scale without saying that the professors would receive more than he got at Harvard. On that visit he wrote his friend William H. Prescott that the "system" his host proposed to put into operation was more practical than he had feared, but not sufficiently practical for him to be sure that it would be successful.[40] Writing Jefferson after the University opened, he complained that his own institution had remained essentially unchanged for one hundred and fifty years. Therefore, he wished all success to Jefferson's "experiment."[41]

In the letter Jefferson wrote this sympathetic friend he reported, as he had previously to Senator Tazewell, that the students were "wretchedly prepared."[42] He had expected more of them than he was likely to get. The need for an adequate system of elementary and intermediate education in the state was obvious. While the professors well deserved his

[35] TJ to Madison, Mar. 22, 1825 (LC); Madison to TJ, Mar. 26, 28 (MP). Barbour weakened but was unwilling to give up his judicial post.

[36] TJ to Carr, Apr. 3, 1825; Carr to TJ, Apr. 30 (LC).

[37] This building was not finished in TJ's lifetime, and his plan to send medical students to the naval hospital in Norfolk for clinical experience was never carried out. John Tayloe Lomax, the first professor of law, arrived a few days after TJ's death.

[38] Adams to TJ, Jan. 22, 1825 (*A.-J. Letters*, p. 607); TJ to Horace Holly, Apr. 15, 1825 (UVA).

[39] B. Peyton to TJ, Mar. 20, 1825 (MHS).

[40] Ticknor to W. H. Prescott, Dec. 16, 1824 (*Life, Letters, and Journals*, I, 348).

[41] Ticknor to TJ, Mar. 28, 1825 (LC).

[42] TJ to Ticknor, Apr. 7, 1825 (LC).

Serpentine Wall on the Grounds of the University of Virginia
(Courtesy of the University of Virginia Library, Prints File, Special Collections)

admiration as men and scholars, no one of them, except for Blaettermann, had had any previous experience as a teacher. Jefferson seems to have made no mention of this fact, but he was undoubtedly aware that they might have disciplinary problems. He told Ticknor that the elective system appeared to be working well. A month was too short a time to prove that, and it remained to be seen whether or not the rules and regulations regarding student conduct were effective.

Besides being free to choose their subjects of instruction, the students could make their own "dieting" (boarding) arrangements. The hotels were leased to individuals. No spiritous liquors or wines were permissible, and all games of chance were forbidden in dormitories as well as in hotels. So also was the use of tobacco. No student could have a servant, a horse, a dog, or a gun. Dueling was punishable by immediate and irrevocable expulsion. If a professor knocked on a student's door, this must be opened and, if necessary, it could be broken down. Offenses cognizable by the law were subject to the civil authorities. No immunity was claimed for the precincts of the University. Provision was made for a board of censors, chosen by the faculty from the most "discreet" students, which would deal with minor offenses and make recommendations to the faculty. Apparently this board was not set up, however, and the problem of discipline was left to the professors. Student testimony was to be voluntary. The germ of the honor system may be perceived in these provisions, but by present-day standards the rules were strict. Jefferson, who was far from unaware of the rebelliousness of youth, sought to guard against it.

The election of a chairman of the faculty did not in itself relieve the Rector of his responsibilities to the extent that might have been supposed, but Jefferson's health took a turn for the worse before summer and for months his activities were greatly reduced. Before entering upon that sad story we should say a few final words about public affairs as viewed from Monticello in his last years.

[XXIX]

A Last Look at Public Affairs

DURING his last years Jefferson often said that he knew little of public affairs, but his letters show that he kept up with major developments on both sides of the Atlantic. He was well aware that the settlement of 1815 marked the beginning of an era of general repression on the Continent of Europe. He knew that revolts against this system were put down in the name of legitimacy and order. He deplored the actions of "the alliance of tyrants, blasphemously calling themselves the Holy Alliance."[1] Also, his heart, like that of very many Americans, was with the heroic Greeks, who were in revolt against their Turkish rulers. But he was convinced that Americans must content themselves with expressions of sympathy for those struggling for self-government and national independence in the Old World. He had long believed that the Republic he had done so much to create must sedulously avoid involvement in the quarrels of Europe. By the same token he wanted to rid the New World of any and all interference in its affairs from abroad. Thus he was gratified by the revolt of the Spanish colonies in Central and South America, which began during the Napoleonic Wars and was expanded thereafter. He thoroughly approved of the recognition of the new nations in Latin America by President Monroe early in 1822 and was glad that the United States was the first to grant this.[2]

In the late spring of 1823 he received from Monroe a detailed account of the state of international affairs, along with a request for his opinion regarding American policy. Specifically, the President asked if they should do anything bolder in support of the cause of liberty than to provide an example.[3] The immediate threat to liberty at this juncture was in Spain. There the monarch, who had been returned to power by

[1] TJ to Dr. John F. Oliveira Fernandes, May 28, 1821 (LC).

[2] TJ to Destutt de Tracy, Dec. 26, 1820 (Ford, X, 174–175); TJ to Monroe, Mar. 19, 1822 (*ibid.*, 208*n*).

[3] Monroe to TJ, June 2, 1823 (S.M.H., VI, 308–310).

the victorious allies after Napoleon's downfall, had been forced to reinstate the relatively liberal constitution which had been granted by that conquerer. The French, with the sanction of the Holy Alliance, had invaded the country in order to crush the liberal movement and restore Ferdinand VII to his old authority.

Jefferson said that the attempt to dictate to the Spanish the form of their own government was so presumptuous, so arrogant, so atrocious, as to arouse indignation and execration. Beyond expressing sympathy for the Spanish, however, he saw nothing that his own government could or should do. Speaking of the European nations, he said: "Their political interests are entirely distinct from ours. Their mutual jealousies, their balance of power, their complicated alliances, their forms and principles of government, are all foreign to us." He saw no reason to become involved in the conflict in Europe or in that between Spain and her revolting American colonies. "Peace and neutrality seem to be our duty and interest," he said.[4]

Toward the end of the summer of 1823 the French troops put down the liberal movement in Spain. Jefferson, who was disposed to take a long view of the prospects of mankind, would not admit discouragement because of the ascendancy of the counter-revolutionary forces in Europe. In a memorable letter to John Adams he reflected on the half century of revolution and reaction through which they had passed.[5] He stated that the light shed by the art of printing had actually reached only the middling class of people as yet. He considered the rulers and rabble as equally ignorant. But he was sure that light would spread and believed that the spirit of freedom had already touched all of the European countries except Russia.[6] He predicted that there would be other revolutions, that rivers of blood would flow, and that ultimately there would be some degree of representative government on most of the Continent. He told his generally less optimistic friend that they would look down from Heaven on these "glorious achievements."

Of more immediate concern were the affairs of the former colonies of Spain. Late in the summer Monroe reported to Jefferson that they were facing great difficulties in establishing governments because of the ignorance of their peoples. Also, their independence was threatened by the Holy Alliance, which opposed revolution anywhere. The British, who had drawn away from their former allies, scented the danger of interposition by them, and George Canning, the British Foreign Secretary,

[4] TJ to Monroe, June 11, 1823 (Ford, X, 257–258).

[5] TJ to Adams, Sept. 4, 1823 (*A.-J. Letters*, pp. 596–597).

[6] TJ must have been greatly disappointed by Tsar Alexander II. For their correspondence and the high hopes TJ once held of him, see *Jefferson the President: Second Term*, ch. XXIV.

thought that something should be done to forestall it. Through Richard Rush, the American Minister to St. James's, he made a proposal to the government of the United States which President Monroe communicated to ex-President Jefferson and through him to ex-President Madison. Replying to Monroe after a few days, Jefferson said: "The question presented by the letters you have sent me is the most momentous which has ever been offered to my contemplation since that of Independence."[7]

The specific question was whether the government of the United States should cooperate with that of Great Britain in an effort to prevent the intervention of the Holy Alliance in Latin America. All that the British Foreign Secretary sought at the moment was a declaration, but he believed that would be sufficient to deter the European powers from an overt act. He stated that his government had no thought of interfering with any amicable arrangement that Spain might make with her old colonies. Although he denied that they were seeking any territory in the western world, it was clearly to the commercial advantage of Canning's country that the liberated provinces remain independent. Monroe labored under no illusions about British motives, but his inclination was to accede to Canning's proposal.

Jefferson's response to the President's request for his opinion has been cited many times in accounts of events leading to the formulation of the Monroe Doctrine. In this he stated the fundamental maxims of American policy: not to become entangled in the broils of Europe and not to suffer Europe to intermeddle in the affairs of the Western Hemisphere. He was actually repeating himself and saying what Monroe may be presumed to have fully agreed with already.[8] Until this time, however, the United States government had been in no position to carry the second maxim into effect. Jefferson promptly concluded that Canning's proposal provided an opportunity to protect the entire Western Hemisphere and believed that his government should seize upon this opportunity. One nation only could now disturb them in their attempt to make South America as well as North the domicile of freedom.

> She now offers to lead, aid, and accompany us in it. By acceding to her proposition, we detach her from the bands, bring her mighty weight into the scale of free government, and emancipate a continent at one stroke, which might otherwise linger long in doubt and

[7] TJ to Monroe, Oct. 24, 1823 (Ford, X, 277–279), replying to a letter of Oct. 17 (S.M.H., VI, 323–325). Monroe enclosed two dispatches from Rush.

[8] Three years earlier TJ had expressed similar sentiments in a letter to William Short, an extract of which he had shown to Monroe. TJ to Short, Aug. 4, 1820 (L. & B., XV, 262–264); Monroe to TJ, Aug. 23, 1820 (S.M.H., VI, 151–152). See also TJ to the Abbé Correa de Serra, Oct. 24, 1820 (Ford, X, 163–165).

difficulty. Great Britain is the nation which can do us the most harm of any one, or all on earth; and with her on our side we need not fear the whole world. With her then, we should most sedulously cherish a cordial friendship; and nothing would tend more to knit our affections than to be fighting once more, side by side, in the same cause.

Coming from one who had been anti-British in policy throughout almost his entire public life, these comments may seem surprising. But he had consistently opposed the power or powers which he regarded as most threatening to the interests of his own country. Britain was no longer that power. He was pleased with Canning's assurance that she was not seeking territory in Latin America, but he wondered for a time if the United States should make a similar promise. He had long coveted Cuba for strategic reasons and was particularly anxious that the island should not fall into British hands. He was willing to give up his thought of it if it could be independent or remain under the feeble rule of Spain. Therefore, he recommended that Monroe encourage Canning and join him in such a declaration as he proposed.

Madison took essentially the same position and went somewhat further in recommending expressions of sympathy for the Spanish and the Greeks.[9] Apparently the President kept these communications wholly to himself until after it had been decided not to issue a joint declaration. He then showed them to the Secretary of State, John Quincy Adams, and presumably to nobody else.[10] Nevertheless, the pronouncements regarding foreign policy that Monroe made in his message of December 2, 1823, were in full accord with the principles Jefferson had set forth and reflected his very language. He received from the President a lengthy explanation of the reasons for the decision to follow an independent course. After describing recent diplomatic developments and communications, Monroe stated that the independent course was more conciliatory and respectful to Russia and the other powers than one of concert with the British would have been. Also, he believed it would be more creditable to the United States in the eyes of the revolting colonists.[11]

Jefferson seems to have made no response to Monroe's explanations and may be presumed to have dismissed this question of foreign policy

[9] Madison to Monroe, Oct. 30, 1823 (Hunt, IX, 157–160).

[10] Harry Ammon, *James Monroe*, p. 480. This biographer says that Monroe showed them to Adams after the Cabinet meeting of Nov. 19.

[11] Monroe sent a copy of the message with his letter of Dec. 4, 1823, and gave his explanations in an undated letter, received Dec. 11 (S.M.H., VI, 325–345). Monroe said nothing about domestic political considerations. For a detailed account of the formulation of the Monroe Doctrine, see Dexter Perkins, *The Monroe Doctrine, 1823–1826* (1932). A revisionist approach is taken by Ernest R. May, *The Making of the Monroe Doctrine* (1975).

from his mind. In the summer of 1824, Monroe, who had become uncertain about the attitude of the British, asked his advice about what to do if the whole burden of protecting Latin America should fall on the United States. In his reply Jefferson said that they could not defend the former Spanish colonies against the combined fleets of Russia and France. With almost brutal frankness he said that their own first concern must be self-preservation. It was not to the interest of the new republics in the South that the Republic of the North should be blotted out, and they must look to the British for protection.[12] Though he did not say that the government of the United States ought to have accepted Canning's proposal, he no doubt perceived that the effectiveness of the Monroe Doctrine was contingent on the concurrence of the British. He had believed that they would act in accordance with their own commercial interest, as in fact they were to do. There was to be no Anglo-American alliance in his century, but he anticipated the longtime trend. In his own mind he had come to terms with his ancient enemy.

Jefferson's personal relations with Monroe were probably not affected by their communications regarding foreign policy, but they unquestionably worsened as a result of the failure of the President to grant one of his rare personal requests. This was that he appoint Bernard Peyton to the postmastership in Richmond in 1824.[13] At this stage there was much harsh criticism of the President in Virginia by the ardent advocates of state rights with whom Jefferson had let himself become identified. But he frequently expressed confidence in Monroe's republicanism and was reluctant to criticize him even in private. However, Jefferson believed that, so far as he was concerned, the ground in Washington had changed and that recommendations from him were no longer welcome.[14]

ii

If Jefferson's influence at Washington had declined, as he believed, his name had not lost its magic in the nation. Such must have been the judgment of those who sought to invoke it in behalf of their favored candidate for the presidency in succession to Monroe. Since the demise of the Federalist party every one of the numerous candidates called himself a Republican, and any one of them would have welcomed a nod of approval from the old party chieftain. He nodded only in private, but he

[12] TJ to Monroe, July 18, 1824 (Ford, X, 316–317), replying to a letter of July 12 (S.M.H., VII, 29–30).

[13] See below, pp. 449–451.

[14] TJ to William Duane, Oct. 24, 1824 (LC). TJ told him to burn the letter. Also, TJ to Thomas Leiper, Oct. 27 (Ford, X, 297*n*.).

was unwittingly involved in the presidential campaign to some degree. A few days after the year 1822 began, the *Enquirer* reprinted a dispatch in which his name was coupled with that of William Lowndes, who was nominated for the presidency by a legislative caucus in South Carolina. It was stated that a letter from Jefferson was read at this meeting. Saying that he did not intermeddle in matters of this sort, he asked Thomas Ritchie to publish a denial that he ever wrote such a letter. This the editor promptly did.[15] Nothing came of the candidacy of Lowndes, who died before the election of 1824 occurred, but there were other aspirants for the highest office and a Jeffersonian blessing.

By the time the electors actually cast their ballots the field of presidential candidates was reduced to four: the Secretary of State, John Quincy Adams of Massachusetts; the Secretary of the Treasury, William H. Crawford of Georgia; the Speaker of the House of Representatives, Henry Clay of Kentucky; and General Andrew Jackson of Tennessee. Until almost the end of the race Jefferson believed that the choice would be between the northernmost and the southernmost of these candidates, Adams and Crawford. His private letters leave no doubt that, while respecting both, he preferred the latter. The election of Crawford, a native Virginian who had shown himself to be a competent public servant, would have meant, in effect, the continuation of the Virginia Dynasty. Writing Lafayette in the fall of 1822, Jefferson said that Adams was supposed to be a consolidationist while Crawford was a republican of the old school.[16]

Adams had broken with the dominant party in his own locality during Jefferson's presidency in support of the embargo and was now conducting foreign affairs in a Republican administration. But Jefferson was chiefly concerned about the course of domestic affairs at this time and was generally suspicious of former Federalists who had assumed the Republican label. He likened them to a fox, pursued by dogs, who found shelter in the midst of the sheep. He did not specifically apply this rather unpleasant metaphor to Adams in this letter to a distant friend, and he guarded his pen closely in domestic correspondence. During the next few months he was actually reported to favor the northern candidate. It was also rumored that he supported Henry Clay and positively disliked Crawford.[17]

Jefferson reiterated his determination not to meddle in this contest and permitted the publication of statements of his to that effect. Replying

[15] *Richmond Enquirer*, Jan. 3, 10, 1822. TJ wrote Ritchie Jan. 7 (Ford, X, 203).

[16] TJ to Lafayette, Oct. 28, 1822 (*ibid.*, 233–234). He described the presidential campaign in similar language to Gallatin in France, Oct. 29, and to Henry Dearborn in Portugal, Oct. 31 (*ibid.*, 235–237).

[17] Many rumors were reported in the *Richmond Enquirer* in July and Aug., 1823.

privately to a letter in which Samuel Harrison Smith, former publisher of the *National Intelligencer*, had tried to draw him out, he stated that the line of demarcation between state and federal authority must be maintained. "The true old republicans stand to the line, and will I hope die on it if necessary," he said.[18] He claimed he was in no position to choose between the candidates, but he provided a sufficient clue to his preference between the supposed leaders. He said he had long acquaintance and little political unison with one, a shorter acquaintance and complete unison with the other.

If events had occurred as scheduled, he would have become better acquainted with Crawford, and no doubt their names would have been coupled to that candidate's advantage. In mid-September of 1823 it was reported in Albemarle County that Mr. Jefferson expected Crawford to arrive for a visit any day.[19] It was understood that the Secretary of the Treasury would come by way of Montpelier and proceed to Monticello in the company of James Madison. He got no closer than Barboursville, where he was visiting Senator James Barbour. Precisely what happened to him there is still unclear, but the *Enquirer* reported on October 14 that he was very ill. The air was filled with rumors but nobody knew what to believe.[20]

Jefferson seems to have made no allowance whatsoever for changed circumstances. Writing Lafayette in November, he described the political situation much as he had done previously and clearly expressed his continued preference for the southernmost candidate. He was unwilling for this to be made public in America, however; he refused the request of Samuel H. Smith for permission to publish the letter in which he had given himself away. He told this supporter of Crawford not to let the letter be copied or get out of his hands.[21] Meanwhile, by foiling an attempt to create a rift between John Adams and himself, he helped the cause of the northernmost candidate to some degree.

Shortly before this happened, John Adams had become involved in an attempt to minimize the value of Jefferson's services as the author of the Declaration of Independence. On July 4, 1823, at Salem, Massachusetts, Timothy Pickering delivered an address in which he quoted extensively from a letter he had elicited the year before from the Old Patriot at Quincy. Pickering may have been aware, and his correspondent may have been unaware, of efforts that were being made about this time to

[18] TJ to S. H. Smith, Aug. 2, 1823 (Ford, X, 263).

[19] Conway Robinson to John Robinson, Sept. 12, 1823 (Va. Hist. Soc.).

[20] Historians generally say he suffered a paralytic stroke.

[21] TJ to Lafayette, Nov. 4, 1823 (Ford, X, 280–282); TJ to S. H. Smith, Dec. 19, 1823 (*ibid.*, 264*n*).

denigrate Jefferson in behalf of Richard Henry Lee, who presented the resolution for independence in the Continental Congress.[22] In response to Pickering, a man he had abundant reason to distrust, Adams sent him an account of events relating to the drafting and adoption of the Declaration.[23] This letter contains generous references to his fellow committeeman from Virginia which have been often quoted by historians, along with factual statements that have been much disputed. From it, however, one gains the impression that the New Englander regarded the prominence of Jefferson in this connection as fortuitous and believed that the famous document was over-rated. He agreed with Pickering that all the ideas in it had been "hackneyed" in Congress for two years. In essence, he said, it had been anticipated by a pamphlet that James Otis wrote and Samuel Adams edited. He was never loath to claim primacy in the American Revolution for his own province.

An account of the celebration at Salem on July 4 was reprinted from a local paper by the *Enquirer* two weeks later. Jefferson saw the entire speech before the end of the summer. He made no public response, but he wrote an informative letter to Madison about it.[24] He was suspicious of Pickering and blamed Adams for a faulty memory. After consulting notes that he had made in 1776 he gave a more accurate account of events than his comrade of that year had done.[25] He recognized the invaluable support that Adams gave the Declaration in Congress and expressed surprise rather than resentment at the comments on its lack of originality. He saw no need to defend the most notable product of his pen, but he did not think that originality should have been expected of him.

Fully agreeing with him, Madison said: "The object was to assert not to discover truths, and to make them the basis of the Revolutionary Act." Jefferson blended Madison's ideas with his own when replying more than a year later to an inquiry about the Declaration. In a private letter, he made a masterful statement about his purpose as its draftsman. This was not to find out things that had never been said or thought of, but "to place before mankind the common sense of the subject, in terms so plain and firm as to command their assent," and to justify the rebels

[22] A number of articles on the Declaration were published in the *Richmond Enquirer*, Aug. 6–20, 1822. In a letter to Ritchie, Aug. 13 (MP), Madison commended him for exposing attempts "to pervert the historical circumstances" relating to the drafting of that document.

[23] Adams to Pickering, Aug. 6, 1822 (*Works*, II, 512–514).

[24] TJ to Madison, Aug. 30, 1823 (Ford, X, 267–269); Madison to TJ, Oct. 6 (Hunt, IX, 155–156).

[25] TJ may also have referred to the section in his autobiography dealing with these events. While not without error, this is recognized as an invaluable source. He began his autobiography Jan. 6, 1821.

in the independent stand they were forced to take.[26] This statement has been quoted repeatedly by historians, but it was not available to John Adams. Neither was Jefferson's letter to Madison. It is a pity Adams did not see this, but only a few weeks after it was written he received ample proof that its author would not let past utterances come between him and the comrade of 1776.

While they were in hostile camps, Adams had made some highly uncomplimentary remarks about Jefferson in letters to one William Cunningham. He had asked the recipient not to publish these in his lifetime, but, after Cunningham's death, they were published by his son.[27] The latter was said to have been a supporter of Jackson's and to have done this with the design of injuring John Quincy Adams. Excerpts appeared in the *Enquirer* in September. Included among these was a statement of Adams's in 1804 that Jefferson had "a thirst for popularity, an inordinate ambition, and a want of sincerity." The *Enquirer* said: "A fine character this of one of the best benefactors of the country and the age!"[28]

Jefferson wrote Adams a couple of weeks later, saying he had not seen the book containing the Cunningham letters, but had heard rumors of them and seen extracts from them. After saying that he regarded this publication of private correspondence as an outrageous betrayal of confidence, he assured Adams that he was incapable of being impressed by this effort "to plant thorns on the pillow of age" and "sow tares" between friends of half a century. He asked the octogenarian to treat this wicked attempt as something that had never happened.[29] His letter was received by Adams at breakfast, where it was read aloud by one of the younger members of the family. Adams reported to its author that it was greeted with exclamations of admiration as it was passed around the table. "How generous! how noble! how magnanimous!" He himself described it as the best letter ever written.[30] He saluted the fireside of his friend with cordial esteem and affection, adding that, in his eighty-ninth year, he was too fat to last much longer.

A leading supporter of John Quincy Adams, who was also the son of Jefferson's old Secretary of War, asked permission to publish his magnanimous letter. It appeared in the *Boston Patriot* the day before Christ-

[26] TJ to Henry Lee, May 8, 1825 (Ford, X, 343); quoted at greater length in *Jefferson the Virginian*, pp. 220–221.

[27] *Correspondence Between the Hon. John Adams, Late President of the United States, and the Late Wm. Cunningham, Esq. Beginning in 1803, and Ending in 1812* (Boston, Published by E. M. Cunningham, 1823).

[28] *Richmond Enquirer*, Sept. 28, 1823.

[29] TJ to Adams, Oct. 12, 1823 (*A.-J. Letters*, p. 600).

[30] Adams to TJ, Nov. 10, 1823 (*ibid.*, pp. 601–602).

mas.[31] John Adams told Jefferson that it was received with universal approval, but he did not allow sufficiently for the animus of Timothy Pickering.[32] That High Federalist published a pamphlet in which he reviewed the Cunningham correspondence to the discredit of both Adams and Jefferson.[33] The latter learned of it in the spring from Martin Van Buren, who was visiting him and who sent him a copy of it afterwards. Designating it as an "elaborate philippic," Jefferson expressed amazement that Pickering had for so many years harbored such violent passions and that he had gone to such labor to collect materials for purposes of vituperation. He claimed that he himself had never had any personal animosity for Pickering.[34] In the account of the visit, which Van Buren wrote years afterwards, he said that he was particularly impressed with the freedom of his host from personal prejudice against old political foes.[35] This impression was not recorded at the time and some of this visitor's later comments may sound too good to be true, but Jefferson undoubtedly tried to keep politics and personal relations in separate compartments and to remain on good terms with everybody. It was for just this reason that he was charged with insincerity.

He told Van Buren that the purpose of his letter to John Adams, which had so annoyed Pickering, was to soothe the feelings of a friend. It had no reference to the political ambitions of John Quincy Adams, but Jefferson's manner toward that high official was one of politeness and entire respect. As a signer of the Declaration of Independence, he received from the Secretary of State two copies of the lithograph facsimile of the historic document. In his gracious reply he not only referred to its sacred principles but expressed confidence in the zeal of Adams to maintain them.[36]

While Jefferson recognized that the electoral vote might be so divided that no presidential candidate would receive a majority, he continued to believe that Crawford had the best chance.[37] Despite his physical condition, the Secretary of the Treasury was nominated by a sparsely attended congressional caucus, and by a more representative legislative caucus in Virginia. In the fall of 1824 a visitor who saw both him and

[31] H. A. S. Dearborn to TJ, Nov. 24, 1823 (LC); TJ to Dearborn, Dec. 9 (LC); *Boston Patriot*, Dec. 24; *Richmond Enquirer*, Dec. 30.

[32] Adams to TJ, Dec. 29, 1823 (*A.-J. Letters*, p. 602).

[33] Pickering, *A Review of the Correspondence* (1824).

[34] TJ to Van Buren, June 29, 1824 (Ford, X, 305–316).

[35] *Autobiography of Martin Van Buren*, p. 183.

[36] TJ to Adams, July 18, 1824 (L. & B., XIX, 278).

[37] TJ to Richard Rush, Oct. 13, 1824 (Ford, X, 322).

Jefferson remarked that his infirmities were greater than Jefferson's.[38] Nevertheless, he carried Virginia easily and received nearly all of the votes cast in Albemarle County. The Georgians remained loyal to him, but he fell behind Jackson and Adams in the count.

Shortly after Jefferson learned of the election of the latter by the House of Representatives, he wrote two letters on the same day. In one he expressed to Crawford his regret that things had not turned out as they had hoped. In the other he congratulated John Adams on the election of his son.[39] At first glance these letters may seem to be contradictory, but they may be presumed to reflect his actual feeling. He had clung to Crawford considerably longer than the circumstances warranted, but there is no reason to question the genuineness of his hopes. His congratulations to the elder Adams can be sufficiently explained as an act of friendship. Writing him while the issue of the election was still uncertain, Adams referred to the Secretary of State as "our John," saying that when they were together in Paris he had seemed almost as much Jefferson's son as his own.[40] Failure to congratulate the old man would have been unforgivable.

The election of the younger Adams was not well received in Virginia. The *Enquirer* stated that he was neither the candidate best qualified for the position nor the choice of a plurality of the people.[41] Jefferson voiced his fear of consolidation and told Crawford that his confidence in the discretion of his fellow citizens was dampened. But it does not follow that he would have been pleased by the accession of Andrew Jackson to the highest office in the land.

His attitude toward the General was to be much disputed during the next four years and is still uncertain. He was on the best of personal terms with the national hero, whose victory over the British at New Orleans had delighted him and whose more recent operations in Florida, while high-handed, were regarded by him as warranted under the circumstances. But he is reported to have told Daniel Webster and George Ticknor, during their visit to Monticello in December, that Jackson was unfit for the presidency, being a man of violent passions who had shown little regard for laws and institutions and was merely a military chief-

[38] Said by Horace Holley, as reported by Henry Clay to Josiah S. Johnston, Oct. 2, 1824 (*The Papers of Henry Clay*, III, 854).

[39] TJ to Crawford, Feb. 15, 1825 (L. & B., XIX, 282–283), replying to letters of Jan. 31 & Feb. 4; TJ to John Adams, Feb. 15 (*A.-J. Letters*, p. 609).

[40] Adams to TJ, Jan. 22, 1825 (*A.-J. Letters*, pp. 606–607).

[41] *Richmond Enquirer*, Feb. 12, 1825.

tain.[42] According to this report he said that Jackson's passions had cooled but that he was still a dangerous man.

Actually, Jefferson had no perceptible influence on the outcome of this presidential election. But Jackson's supporters, looking to the next one and clearly recognizing the immense value of Jefferson's benediction, sought to associate his name with that of their idol on grounds of political doctrine. At a dinner for the General in Nashville on the eighty-second birthday of the Sage, the latter was toasted in these words: "Thomas Jefferson — His wisdom brought us back to true republican principles — let us go no more astray." Another toast was this: "Virginia — Unshaken in her principles, she admits no compromise in defeat."[43] The campaign of 1828 was under way and the process of merging Jeffersonian republicanism with Jacksonian democracy had begun.

iii

Jefferson's opinion of the General may not have changed, but in his last winter his latent fears of consolidation were aroused by John Quincy Adams. In his first annual message Adams asserted, as none of his predecessors had done, that the federal government was obligated to promote the welfare of the people by positive action, and he outdid all of them in his recommendations.[44] Not only did he favor the construction of roads and the digging of canals under federal authority; he advocated the establishment of a national university and the erection of an astronomical observatory. His expression "light-houses of the sky" was much derided. Jefferson himself looked to the heavens and loved the light. He could hardly have welcomed the establishment of a rival university, but that danger seemed remote. Jefferson would have been inconsistent if he had objected to the recommendations of Adams on the ground that the proposed improvements were undesirable in themselves. In fact, he did not do so. But he believed that the President was claiming for the general government authority that had not been conferred on it by the Constitution.

A few days after the President's message was published and sharply attacked in the *Enquirer*, Jefferson received from William Fitzhugh Gor-

[42] It should be noted that Webster and Ticknor were Adams men. "Notes of Mr. Jefferson's Conversation 1824 at Monticello," in *Papers of Daniel Webster, Correspondence*, I, 375–376.

[43] Both toasts in *Richmond Enquirer*, May 10, 1825.

[44] The message and criticism of it are in the *Richmond Enquirer*, Dec. 8, 10, 1825.

don, one of the two delegates from Albemarle County in the General Assembly, a request for suggestions about the desirable course to pursue in what was described as a constitutional crisis.[45] Jefferson's attempt to answer the question that Gordon propounded was made in a long paper that he sent James Madison for perusal.[46] This was entitled "The Solemn Declaration and Protest of the Commonwealth of Virginia on the Principles of the Constitution of the U. S. of America and on the Violations of Them."

In the paper he set forth the doctrine of strict construction and declared that the assumption by the federal government of the authority to build roads and canals within the boundaries of a state was an infringement on its constitutional rights. This Virginians could not concede. After avowing complete devotion to principle, however, he denied that they were raising "the banner of disaffection or of separation from their sister states." He said that they would consider the disruption of the Union one of the greatest calamities that could befall them, but not as the greatest. That would be "submission to a government of unlimited powers." They would accept measures of internal improvement if authorized by a constitutional amendment and if the costs and benefits were equitably distributed. In fact, such an amendment had been proposed by Congressman John Bailey of Massachusetts, and the *Enquirer* had said that they might still save the Constitution from false construction.[47] Jefferson knew this by the time he wrote Madison, but not when he wrote the paper in which he made so much of principles. In it he did say that even in the absence of an amendment his state should not forcibly resist measures for the building of roads and canals. He went so far as to say that the citizens should be instructed to acquiesce in these just as if they had been enacted by their own legislature. Thus he was tentatively proposing that his countrymen voice protest and promise compliance at one and the same time.

Madison saw no sufficient reason for them to do either. In his reply he took the position that their state should not be the leader of a movement against national roads and canals. Jefferson himself afterwards remarked that Virginians had come to be regarded as habitual complainers. Madison doubted that their constitutional scruples would carry much weight against the popular clamor for material benefits from governmental action. However, he pointed out that internal improvements such as were being sought by Westerners would be of questionable advantage to

[45] W. F. Gordon to TJ, Dec. 10, 1825 (LC).
[46] TJ to Madison, Dec. 24, 1825, with enclosure (Ford, X, 348–352).
[47] *Richmond Enquirer*, Dec. 20, 1825.

New York and New England, and tried to show that the situation was not so desperate as his dispirited friend supposed. He had discussed it at length in response to a request for counsel from Thomas Ritchie. His conclusion was that the legislature should do no more than instruct the representatives of the state in Congress to be on guard against unconstitutional measures. Along with his reply to Jefferson he sent a copy of his letter to Ritchie. Jefferson promptly reported that he accepted Madison's views and would suppress his own paper.[48]

Replying on the first day of the new year to William F. Gordon, he expressed the opinion that the best thing for the legislators to do at this juncture was to rest on their oars and await developments.[49] He fully agreed that they faced a constitutional crisis. He said that the three branches of the federal government were working in conjunction to usurp the domestic powers of the states and set up a government of unlimited authority. This, in his opinion, was the one thing worse than disunion. At just this time the state of Georgia was in conflict with the executive branch in Washington over lands occupied by the Indians within the borders of that commonwealth.[50] Jefferson said the Virginians should not take up arms as the fiery Georgians were doing, but that they should never give up the ship. At the time of the Missouri controversy he declared that the firebell in the night had sounded the knell of the Union. He now stated that he saw little hope of stopping the torrent of consolidation and bemoaned "the degeneracy of public opinion from our original and free principles."[51] He counseled patience nonetheless.

For reasons of bad health, physical infirmity, family troubles, and financial difficulties, Jefferson's spirits were unusually low.[52] If his fears outweighed his hopes, that should not be surprising. The legislators of his state appear to have been even more fearful than he was. In the resolutions they adopted they denied the authority of Congress in the matter of tariffs as well as that of internal improvements.[53] His private advice may have reached only a few of them, and he seems to have had little influence on the course of public affairs at the time.

[48] Madison to TJ, Dec. 28, 1825 (Hunt, IX, 236–240), enclosing a copy of his letter of Dec. 18 to Ritchie (*ibid.*, 231–236); TJ to Madison, Jan. 2. 1926 (Ford, X, 359–360). I cannot do justice here to Madison's wise and patient letters.

[49] TJ to W. F. Gordon, Jan. 1, 1826 (*ibid.*, 358–359).

[50] A compact that had been negotiated in Jefferson's own administration was involved. See the discussions in Charles S. Sydnor, *The Development of Southern Sectionalism*, pp. 182–184; and Bernard Sheehan, *Seeds of Extinction: Jeffersonian Philanthropy and the American Indian* (Chapel Hill, 1973), pp. 256 ff.

[51] TJ to C. W. Gooch, Jan. 9, 1826 (L. & B., XVI, 152).

[52] See ch. XXI, below.

[53] See the account of the "Virginia Resolutions Concerning the Powers of the Federal Government" in *Richmond Enquirer*, Mar. 2–11, 1826.

* * *

Two letters he wrote William Branch Giles in the last December of his life were published for political reasons during the next presidential campaign. Thus he unwittingly became a posthumous participant in that. About a week before Christmas the weary old man received from Giles, now in retirement, an inquiry about an interview he had when President with Senator John Quincy Adams. This was at the time of the embargo. Giles, who was then in the Senate, claimed that he had arranged the meeting. The purpose of his inquiry was to procure information for "Political Disquisitions" he was writing for the *Enquirer*. As he stated to Jefferson confidentially, he intended to show that Adams abandoned the Federalists and joined the Republicans to promote his own interests and not for patriotic reasons as had been alleged.[54] Giles was one of the bitterest and most bellicose partisans of the era. The University of Virginia and Jefferson himself had been objects of his attack during his years of retirement. He had not been reproached by the Old Sachem, however, and he presumed that his political sentiments were shared by that elder statesman in this time of crisis.

Though Jefferson did not remember that Giles had been connected with the interview with Adams, he did not question the former Senator's account of the circumstances. He could not recall the precise words that were spoken, but he said he could not forget the interview itself. The essential fact, as he remembered, was that Adams informed him of a conspiracy between the British and opponents of the embargo in New England. He also said that, as a result, he was compelled to abandon that policy. Jefferson's memory seems to have been somewhat confused here.[55] He would have been wiser not to have relied on it and to have dismissed the request of Giles altogether. But he believed he was "doing justice to Mr. Adams by repeating this proof of his fidelity to his country and of his superiority over all ordinary considerations when the safety of that was brought into question." Since this was the opposite of what Giles wanted to do and he made no use of the letter although told that he might publish it, Jefferson may be said to have outwitted him. When published on Adams's behalf in 1828, however, while vindicating his

[54] W. B. Giles to TJ, Dec. 15, 1825 (LC). Two letters of the same date, apparently one to be made public and the other to be kept confidential.

[55] Adams visited TJ on Feb. 4, 1809, when Congress was debating the repeal of the embargo, but his statement that Adams convinced him of the necessity of abandoning the measure to save the Union is in direct conflict with his letter to TMR, Feb. 7 (Ford, X, 244). Adams himself believed TJ was thinking of their meeting of Mar. 15, 1808. For what might have been said at that meeting, see J. Q. Adams, Diary, Feb. 1, 2, Mar. 4, 12, 15, 1808 (microfilm, UVA). Samuel Flagg Bemis discusses the letter in an appendix in *John Quincy Adams and the Foundations of American Foreign Policy* (1949), pp. 575–576; also see pp. 144–151.

national patriotism, it greatly injured him in his own region and was much resented by him.[56]

The letter regarding Adams and the embargo was written on Christmas. The next day Jefferson wrote Giles another letter which, as he expressly stated, contained materials not intended for the public eye.[57] While he continued to hold the President in full respect as a man and a patriot, he wanted to assure Giles that he disapproved of the trend of current domestic policy. In writing this pugnacious partisan he used stronger language than he had addressed to his judicious friend Madison and appeared more agitated than he was when he wrote Gordon, but he took the same constitutional position and prescribed the same policy of patience. He told Giles, who was an extremely impatient man, that if every infraction of the constitutional compact was resisted at once the federal government would not last a year. He told this excited warrior that, although there could be no doubt of their preference, they were under no present necessity to choose between submission to unlimited power and disruption of the Union.

His dominant concern was that his countrymen should guard the principle of a limited federal government. From the modern point of view he may appear to have been unduly fearful, but he sincerely believed that only by the maintenance of that principle could union and liberty be reconciled. After Jefferson's death Giles published the letter, omitting the statement at the beginning that it was not intended for the public. Viewed out of context it may have given and may still give a false impression.

iv

Jefferson's fears of consolidation, which were accentuated in his last years, were matched by his concern for local self-government, in which his faith never waned. He favored the periodical revision of constitutions as well as their strict construction. Therefore he was pleased when the movement for a constitutional convention in Virginia was revived in the spring of 1824.[58] The specific proposal at this time was that the question of calling a convention should be submitted to popular vote. This was strongly supported by the *Enquirer*.[59] It aroused fear in the minds of

[56] TJ to Giles, Dec. 25, 1825 (Ford, X, 350–354). On the circumstances and effects of the publication of this letter, see M. D. Peterson, *The Jefferson Image in the American Mind*, pp. 27–28. I take a more favorable view of TJ's action, though I regard his explanation of it to Monroe, Jan. 21, 1826 (L. & B., XVI, 153–155), as equivocal.

[57] TJ to Giles, Dec. 26, 1825 (Ford, X, 354–357).

[58] For the earlier movement and TJ's relations with it, see above, pp. 346–350.

[59] *Richmond Enquirer*, Mar. 30, 1824.

some leading citizens. Judge Philip Norborne Nicholas described it as a "subversion" of the constitution, while Benjamin Watkins Leigh, a prominent Richmond lawyer, said that such action would be "nothing short of high treason."[60] Into the fierce controversy that ensued Jefferson had no desire to enter, but he expressed his candid opinion of the state constitution in a letter he permitted to be published. This was in response to a request from John Hampden Pleasants, who told him that his opinions would have a "decisive effect."[61]

In the public letter he wrote a few days after he became eighty-one, he said that the constitution of Virginia could not be expected to be perfect since it was the first of its kind not only in America but everywhere else. In no other country, as far as he knew, had a frame of government been adopted after free deliberations and put in writing for every citizen to see. In his *Notes on Virginia* he had taken the position that a constitution should not be the work of a legislative assembly, as this one was, but of a convention specially chosen for that purpose. He now said that the twenty-three other states had all followed the proper procedure. Besides this basic defect, the Virginia constitution violated the principle of equal political rights and equitable representation. More than half of the free men could not vote, and counties were equally represented in the House of Delegates even though one had twenty times the population of another.

He had pointed out these faults in private letters in the past. In this public one he said that, if these fundamental principles were not important, no principles were. He said nothing here about the reform of county government, which was so dear to his heart, nor did he enter into a detailed discussion of defects as he had done in his letter to Samuel Kerchevel in 1816. In fact he declined the renewed request of its recipient to print that letter.[62] While his son-in-law and eldest grandson were actively involved in the movement to call a convention, Jefferson stuck to principles, disclaiming any desire to meddle in current affairs.

In the legislative session of 1824–1825, the House of Delegates approved a measure calling for the submission of the question to a popular vote, but this was defeated in the Senate by a very narrow margin.[63] Among the opponents of the referendum was Joseph C. Cabell, who did not agree with the Old Sachem in all things. Cabell's action aroused the

[60] Account of the public meeting of the citizens of Richmond on Apr. 10, 1824 (*ibid.*, Apr. 13).

[61] J. H. Pleasants to TJ, Apr. 12, 1824 (MHS). TJ's reply of Apr. 19 (Ford, X, 302–304) was published in the *Enquirer*, Apr. 27, over his name but without that of Pleasants.

[62] TJ to Samuel Kercheval, Sept. 5, 1824 (Ford, X, 319–320), replying to Kercheval's of Aug. 25 (LC).

[63] *Richmond Enquirer*, Jan. 18, Feb. 8, 10, 1825.

ire of Thomas Mann Randolph with results to which we shall refer hereafter.[64] At the next session of the General Assembly a similar proposal was defeated by a larger vote.[65] Jefferson's opinions must have been well known, but they certainly were not decisive.

The course of public affairs in the last years of his life could not have failed to be disappointing to him. But he sounded a note of hope in many of his letters. One of the most characteristic of these was delivered by Francis Walker Gilmer to Major John Cartwright in England in the summer of 1824.[66] In this he presented principles which he regarded as timeless and by which he sought to guide his own feet in any weather. He held that all government must rest on the will of the majority, because there is no acceptable alternative. He also believed that no generation can rightly bind another. "Nothing then is unchangeable," he said, "but the inherent and unalienable rights of man."

[64] J. C. Cabell to I. A. Coles, Feb 20, 1825 (Cabell Papers, UVA). See below, pp. 454–455.

[65] *Richmond Enquirer*, Jan. 28, 1826.

[66] TJ to John Cartwright, June 5, 1824 (L. & B., XVI, 42–52), replying to a letter of Feb. 29 (LC).

Finishing the Course

[XXX]

The Changing Family Scene

MR. J's health is rather better than it has been for some weeks past. Yet his spirits are much worse than I have ever known them. Indeed, it is wonderful that he retains any under the many distressing circumstances under which he now labors." Thus the Bursar of the University wrote General Cocke three months after that institution finally got under way.[1] The cares of the Rector were not at an end, but his chief troubles at this stage were those of a paterfamilias, not of the Father of the University. Some of them had become a matter of common knowledge, no doubt, but he was so reticent about personal matters that few may have known how extensive and how devastating they were, if in fact anybody did besides himself.

His health had taken a decided turn for the worse that spring. He said many times that he was never entirely well after his disastrous trip to Warm Springs following the meeting of the Rockfish Gap Commission in the fall of 1818. But he had outgrown the migraine headaches that had afflicted him in times past, he hardly ever had a cold or suffered from indigestion, and except when recovering from minor accidents he had lived an unusually active physical life. Though he often referred to the wrist that had been broken at Paris and complained of his age-stiffened fingers, he did a vast amount of writing. He said that his hearing had become too dull for him to take in the chatter at the table, but visitor after visitor attested to the interest of his conversation and the vigor of his mind. Not until he was entering his eighty-third year did he gravely decline.

On May 11, 1825, he received a memorandum from the physician who had been attending him but was about to leave the locality. In this he was told that he was suffering from dysuria, a stricture and inflammation of the urinary canal apparently brought on by the enlargement

[1] Alexander Garrett to J. H. Cocke, June 18, 1825 (Cocke-Shields Papers, UVA).

of the prostate gland. Dr. Watkins prescribed castor oil, warm water fomentations, rest, a mild diet, and, if there should be no improvement, a half grain of opium with one grain of calomel at night.[2] He commended his patient to Dr. Dunglison. The professor of anatomy and medicine attended Jefferson at Monticello several times a week all summer.[3]

While the state of Jefferson's health may have been of itself a sufficient cause for his depressed spirits, the troubles that were most on his mind that summer were probably those connected with his son-in-law Thomas Mann Randolph. Before entering upon that story of frustration, however, we should bring the account of his own finances up to date. His affairs had not improved along with those of the University. The latter undoubtedly provided him with a welcome escape, and he was glad to turn over as much of his own business as he could to Jeff Randolph and Bernard Peyton, but the financial distress of his last years was chiefly owing to circumstances beyond his control rather than to his negligence or indifference.

In the spring of 1823, shortly before his eightieth birthday, Jefferson drew up a statement of his liabilities and resources.[4] He calculated that his debts amounted to somewhat more than $40,000. In addition he was responsible for $20,000 on the two notes he had endorsed for Wilson Cary Nicholas. He does not appear to have been pressed to pay off the principal of the latter obligation, but he was meeting interest charges of $1200 a year. On paper he worked out a plan whereby he could pay off these debts by 1830 and still have an adequate living. This required the sale of eighty of his Negroes. He calculated that by such a transaction he could keep all his lands and 150 slaves. Actually he soon changed this plan. In the summer he wrote a creditor that he was determined to arrange a large sale of his lands in Bedford.[5]

These plans, like others he had made, erred on the side of optimism. As in times past he did not allow sufficiently for poor crops, low prices, and inability to collect from his own debtors. He minimized the decline in land values in his region and the sluggishness of the market. He soon learned that the lands in Bedford County that he had hoped to sell would bring only a half or a third of what he estimated them to be worth.[6] Therefore, he gave up the plan to dispose of them. He did send to New Orleans for sale four young men who had attacked an overseer. This

[2] T. G. Watkins to TJ, May 11, 1825 (LC).
[3] Dunglison prescribed the use of bougies. See his *Ana*, p. 26.
[4] Apr. 1, 1823 (UVA).
[5] TJ to S. Garland, Aug. 4, 1823 (LC).
[6] TJ to Joel Yancey, Apr. 1, 1824 (MHS).

disciplinary measure, which was in full accord with the custom of this society, was expected to be profitable. The four prime Negroes were thought to be worth $2000 or $2500.[7] Two of them died, however; one was reported to be very sick, and one was sold for only $400.[8]

This may have been the most distressing of Jefferson's futile attempts to raise money, but he was subjected to embarrassment as both a creditor and a debtor. He could not collect the rent for his mill from Thomas E. Randolph, father-in-law of Francis Eppes, because that harassed operator could not collect from Thomas Mann Randolph.[9] A tobacco warehouse of his in Bedford burned down with all its contents. In Albemarle in 1823–1824, his flour was stored for months because of low water in the Rivanna and the faithlessness of boatmen. As a result he was needlessly behind in his account with Bernard Peyton.[10] He was in debt to Edmund Bacon and Joel Yancey when they left his service as overseers. He largely paid off the former before the summer of 1823 ended, and Bacon afterwards went so far as to say that Jefferson was prompter in meeting his obligations than any gentleman he knew.[11] It would appear that the gentlemen of Virginia were very slow. Though this one certainly wanted to be prompt, he still had not paid off Yancey by the spring of 1824, and he never got out of debt to David Higginbotham. While that patient merchant would not accept his bond for interest, Jefferson said that henceforth he would be responsible not only for interest on principal, but also for interest on interest.[12]

He had other embarrassing obligations and suffered more misfortunes than we have mentioned here. Summing up the latter toward the end of the summer of 1824, he said that he had failed to receive a total of $5000 which he had expected. Therefore, he was compelled to ask Bernard Peyton to negotiate another bank loan and to allow his considerable account with him to lie unpaid.[13] This was what had come of his plan to pay off all his debts by the sale of property.

At this juncture the situation was peculiarly painful for both the long-suffering agent and his harassed client because of the failure of Peyton to receive the appointment to the postmastership in Richmond which Jefferson had asked of Monroe as a personal favor. He claimed that it was the first and only one he asked of that friend while President.[14] To

[7] TJ to Peyton, Jan. 5, 1824 (*ibid.*).
[8] R. C. Nicholas to TJR, Jan. 15, May 26, 1824 (Randolph Papers, UVA).
[9] T. E. Randolph to TJ, May 26, 1824 (MHS).
[10] TJ to Peyton, Dec. 28, 1823; Jan. 5, 1824, replying to a letter of Jan. 1 (all MHS).
[11] TJ to Bacon, Aug. 18, 1823; Bacon to TJ, May 4, 1824 (*ibid.*).
[12] Memorandum of July 15, 1824, made after a conversation (*ibid.*).
[13] TJ to Peyton, Aug. 28, 1824 (*ibid.*).
[14] TJ to Peyton, Sept. 3, 1824 (*ibid.*).

his mind this was a very special case. Peyton had rendered him invaluable service as a factor and was trusted by him much as his grandson was. He knew of no one better qualified for the post on grounds of character, industry, and public standing.

This episode had its beginning in the fall of 1819. In that time of general financial distress in Virginia he was requested by Peyton to recommend the latter's appointment to either the postmastership or the collectorship of the port of Richmond, whichever should first become vacant. The former post was then held by Dr. William Foushee, who was in failing health.[15] Jefferson spoke to Monroe in Peyton's behalf when the President was in Albemarle in the spring. Reporting this meeting to Peyton, he said: "I could not ask a promise certainly, but he said that it should be as I pleased."[16]

Dr. Foushee, who was an esteemed local character, hung on four years longer, but early in 1824 it seemed unlikely that he would ever arise from his bed. At Peyton's request, Jefferson wrote Monroe in February. In this letter he said that he entered into this case with his whole heart and soul, as he would in no other, and spoke as if for himself.[17] In his reply the President made no reference to Jefferson's earlier conversation with him on this subject. He observed that Dr. Foushee was still alive and reported that some years before he had given former Governor James P. Preston some hope of obtaining the postmastership if a vacancy should occur while he (Monroe) was in Washington. However, he earnestly hoped that things would work out in such a way that he could meet Jefferson's wishes. Peyton, reporting a few weeks later that Colonel Preston was in Richmond, no doubt to secure the position, said he himself was almost in despair.[18]

Dr. Foushee died on August 21. Reporting the event to Jefferson that day, Peyton said that the applicants for the vacant place were "immeasurable." Nevertheless, he was headed for the Capital to see Monroe. Jefferson promptly wrote a strong letter in his behalf. Sending a copy of this to Peyton, he said: "You will see that I place the request on ground which must prevail if I am anything at Washington."[19] Before this letter reached the White House the President, wasting no time, appointed Colonel Preston to the coveted office. On his return to Richmond, Peyton said in a letter to Jefferson that he would have to content himself

[15] TJ to Peyton, Nov. 26, 1819 (*ibid.*), replying of a letter of Nov. 11.

[16] TJ to Peyton, Aug. 1, 1820 (*ibid.*).

[17] TJ to Monroe, Feb. 20, 1824 (Ford, X, 296–297). The letter was written at Peyton's request of Feb. 16 (MHS).

[18] Monroe to TJ, Mar. 22, 1824 (S.M.H., VII, 11–12); Peyton to TJ, May 27, 1824 (MHS).

[19] TJ to Peyton, Aug. 25, 1824, with copy of his letter of that date to Monroe; Peyton to TJ, Aug. 21, reporting the death of Foushee (all MHS).

with poverty. In his response Jefferson stated that he had miscalculated his influence with Monroe but said that he would know his place thereafter.[20]

In his explanatory letter to Jefferson, Monroe said in effect that he had made promises to Preston which he could not disregard.[21] The disappointed elder statesman at Monticello intimated to Peyton that the President had not been entirely frank with him. He believed that Monroe had been insufficiently mindful of his lifetime of public service and their long and affectionate association. It is certainly not surprising that he was "sorely and deeply wounded" by Monroe's rejection of the request he made as for himself, but he seems to have been wholly unaware of one complicating factor in the situation. Monroe stated in strict confidence that there was another important applicant who could not be discussed with Jefferson. This was no less a person than ex-Governor Thomas Mann Randolph, who had kept his desperate candidacy secret from his father-in-law. The appointment of Preston may have seemed the best way out of this quandary.[22]

Bernard Peyton took to a sick bed after his disappointment. When he received news of Jefferson's financial distress, however, he arose, discounted a note for $2000 in Jefferson's name at the Farmer's Bank, and informed his anxious client that the settlement of his overdue account could be deferred to the first of the year, when he himself would be faced with an imperative obligation. Jeff Randolph made a remittance at an opportune time, much to his friend's great relief.[23] Jefferson's basic financial situation did not improve during the spring of 1825, when the University got under way and he entered upon his eighty-third year. But there were other causes for the depression of spirit that Alexander Garrett noted. His state of mind cannot be understood without reference to happenings in his family.

ii

As we noted in an earlier chapter, Jefferson made his last visit to Poplar Forest in the spring after the marriage of Francis Eppes. According to Virginia Randolph, who accompanied him, it was a very pleasant

[20] Peyton to TJ, Aug. 30, 1824; TJ to Peyton, Sept. 3 (both MHS).

[21] Monroe to TJ, Aug. 26, 1824 (S.M.H., VII, 34–35).

[22] Nothing came of TJ's commendation of Peyton to the next Secretary of the Treasury for appointment to the collectorship of the Port of Richmond if there should be a vacancy, but a dozen years after his own pen was stilled, his friend and helper was actually appointed postmaster at Richmond and served from 1838 to 1844. TJ to Richard Rush, Sept. 14, 1825 (Ford, X, 296*n.*–297*n.*).

[23] Peyton to TJ, Sept. 2, 1824; Feb. 4, 1825 (MHS).

visit. Her grandfather stood the rigors of the journey well.[24] Summer had not yet given way to autumn when he was informed of the death of John W. Eppes at the age of fifty.[25] In view of the long and affectionate association of Maria Jefferson's former husband with her father, it was unfortunate that their last letters dealt with money that the older man owed the younger. It will be recalled that Eppes had made Jefferson a loan on the understanding that he was to be repaid in slaves who were ultimately to go to Francis and thus remain in the family. The arrangement called for the payment of interest by Jefferson and, to his chagrin, he had fallen behind with this. In an undated and badly written letter Eppes said he was forced to ask for payment. Unable to get his flour to market, Jefferson could not make it before Eppes died. In fact, he had not done so a year and a half later, when he received a reminder from the executor of the Eppes estate.[26]

In the meantime, Mother Nature compensated to some degree for the loss of one life by the gift of another. On November 9, 1823, Francis and Elizabeth became the parents of a daughter. There was some disappointment with Jane Cary Eppes since girls already predominated in the family.[27] Jeff Randolph, who then had four (one daughter had died), acquired a fifth three weeks later in the person of Ellen Wayles Randolph. He was destined to get two more before he got a son. Francis got one on July 4, 1825, when John Wayles Eppes II was born.[28]

Francis and Elizabeth were not entirely content at Poplar Forest. She missed her friends in Albemarle, and, while he did not find the role of a small planter wholly congenial, he appears to have lagged somewhat in his study of law. Early in 1825 their roof caught fire from a chimney. Manifesting great concern, Jefferson promised to send John Hemings to repair the damage and recommended that the shingles be replaced with tin.[29] The roof at Poplar Forest was destined to cause further trouble, but the trials of the Eppes family were only a minor cause of Jefferson's disquietude in the spring the University opened. The misfortunes of his son-in-law Thomas Mann Randolph were undoubtedly a major cause.

[24] May 12–27, 1823. Virginia Randolph wrote Nicholas Trist about a visit, June 5, 1823 (Trist, LC).

[25] Jerman Baker to TJ, Sept. 16, 1823 (MHS). John W. Eppes died Sept. 15, after a public career of distinction. See the article in *D.A.B.* Many tributes were paid him at the time.

[26] JWE to TJ, undated letter received Sept. 4, 1823 (UVA); TJ to JWE, Sept. 9, 1823; J. C. Page to TJ, Feb. 10, 1825 (both MHS).

[27] Virginia Randolph to Nicholas Trist, Nov. 27, 1823 (Trist, LC).

[28] See the Family Table in G. G. Shackelford, ed., *Collected Papers of the Monticello Association*.

[29] TJ to Francis, Feb. 17, Apr., 1825; Francis to TJ, Feb. 25 (*Family Letters*, pp. 451–454).

* * *

After retiring from the governorship in December, 1822, Colonel Randolph returned to Albemarle in relatively good spirits and was honored by his county neighbors in the spring by his election as one of their two delegates in the General Assembly. On contemplating the state of his financial affairs, however, he concluded that he must make a large sale of property or procure a substantial loan. In the fall of 1823 he had recourse to the money market of New York. He bore a letter of introduction from his father-in-law to Henry Remsen, who had been the department clerk when Jefferson was secretary of state.[30] Remsen, now a banker, helped Randolph make provisional arrangements for a loan of $10,000. Presumably this was to be secured by Varina, though that plantation south of Richmond on the James River was already mortgaged to the amount of $6,000–$7,000. After his return to Virginia, Randolph concluded that he needed $15,000.[31]

It would appear that his negotiations with New York bankers stalled at this point and that his creditors would wait no longer. In desperation he turned to his son Jeff and Samuel Carr. The arrangement into which he entered amounted to the assumption of responsibility for his debts by them, and especially by Jeff Randolph. In order to protect them a deed of trust to Varina, Edgehill, and forty-nine slaves was executed on April 1, 1824.[32] Although the settlement of Thomas Mann Randolph's affairs was to require nearly two years more, it was clear to those who were informed of his situation that he had lost virtually all the property he had.

Like her father, Martha may have been ignorant of her husband's desperate efforts during the next few months to procure the postmastership in Richmond. She had long been aware of the increasing "derangement" of her husband's affairs, but not until a few months before the deed of trust was signed did she realize the full extent of the ruin that awaited them. The letter to Nicholas Trist in which she said this was marked by neither self-reproach nor recrimination.[33] She did not blame herself or the family for extravagance. If her daughter Ellen is to be believed, her entire married life was one of painful economy and self-denial. She herself claimed that they had always lived within the income from her husband's farms. Her explanation of their difficulties was that he had ruined himself by standing security for others. While an admirable farmer, he

[30] Gaines, pp. 140–142; TJ to Remsen, Oct. 26, 1823 (MHS).

[31] Remsen to TJ, Nov. 25, 1823; TJ to Remsen, Dec. 19 (*ibid.*); TMR to Remsen, Feb. 16, 1824 (Letter Collection, UVA).

[32] Albemarle County Deed Book (UVA). The trustees were F. W. Gilmer and V. W. Southall.

[33] Martha Randolph to Nicholas Trist, Apr. 4, 1824 (Trist, UNC).

had serious faults as a man of business. His daughter was to say years later that there was a fatality in his character that doomed him to financial failure. She agreed with her mother about his inability to say no to importunate pleaders. Thus he became the victim of his own generosity.[34]

Nicholas Trist, with whom Martha Randolph discussed impending disaster so candidly, had never ceased to be regarded as a member of her family during his years of absence. She loved him and wrote to him as to a son, and her husband seems to have shared her feeling. At this time Nicholas had been engaged to Virginia Randolph for several years. Recently he had been in Louisiana, where he had property. Apparently Virginia was reluctant to leave her mother and join him there. At any rate, a plan was devised for him to return to Monticello and study law under her grandfather's direction. The news that the family was facing ruin, which he got from Virginia as well as from her mother, did not deter him. In the summer of 1824 he returned to Monticello, where on September 11 he and Virginia were married. It is said that they lived thenceforth in the North Pavilion, though that may have been merely the place where Nicholas studied law.[35] This devoted young couple radiated warmth and happiness wherever they were. These qualities were to be needed at Monticello.

The voters of Albemarle County had signified their continued confidence in Thomas Mann Randolph by re-electing him as a delegate to the General Assembly. This was in the spring of 1824, when the state of his affairs was not generally known. He served as a Crawford elector in the fall and duly attended the legislative session of 1824–1825. At that session this passionate man was involved in violent controversy. As a supporter of the movement for a state constitutional convention he was incensed with Joseph C. Cabell for that senator's opposition to this. In his zeal for constitutional reform he was upholding the best Jeffersonian tradition, but he over-reached himself in his rage against the most active champion of the University next to Jefferson himself. On his return home from Richmond the irate Colonel sought to encompass Cabell's defeat for re-election. The outcome of the election in April need not be attributed solely to Randolph's excesses or to public awareness of his

[34] Randall, III, 327*n*.–328*n*., quoting from a letter of Ellen Randolph Coolidge, Jan. 26, 1856 (Coolidge Letterbook, UVA).

[35] Virginia Randolph wrote Nicholas Trist on Apr. 23, 1824 (Trist, LC). Earlier letters of special interest are Martha Randolph to Nicholas Trist, Mar. 7, Sept. 1, Nov. 22, 1822 (Trist, UNC). See the account of the Trists in G. G. Shackelford, ed., *Collected Papers of the Monticello Association*, pp. 103–104.

financial plight. For one thing, a constitutional convention was disapproved by many of his constituents. The results were humiliating, nonetheless. Cabell was easily re-elected while Randolph himself was decisively defeated.[36]

In May a note of his was protested at one of the banks in Richmond. His son Jeff, who had assumed responsibility for his debts, was striving to realize on the property covered by the deed of trust. If he could not sell this property, he said, he would have to sell his own.[37] He managed to sell Varina, a plantation his father did not like, but by this means he could cover less than half of the debt. The balance could be met only by the sale of the slaves and Edgehill. Father and son were in sharp disagreement with regard to this. Under these circumstances, toward the end of spring, Colonel Randolph removed himself from the society of his family at Monticello. As he himself stated afterwards, he continued to sleep there but left before breakfast and did not return until after dark. He also said that he did this in order to avoid the supercilious glances of his father-in-law's guests.[38]

A few weeks after Jefferson's illness was diagnosed by Dr. Watkins and he came under the care of Dr. Dunglison, he wrote a letter to Thomas Mann Randolph urging him to return to the bosom of his family and friends and resume his place in society.[39] The patriarch assured his unhappy son-in-law that his financial situation, while painful, was by no means unusual in their region. He attributed Randolph's distress to circumstances which no man could have been expected to anticipate — making characteristic reference to speculators, usurers, and the uncertain state of the circulating medium. His effort to restore Randolph's self-esteem and to convince him that he could find useful employment were without immediate effect, but in midsummer he got a letter from the exile which gave him the opportunity to make an even stronger appeal.[40]

The purpose of this letter was to inform Jefferson of the recent use of his name by Randolph in connection with the movement for a constitutional convention and to counteract the "misrepresentations" of his own conduct, words, and feelings which, he claimed, had been made to his father-in-law for a number of years. He stated that they had become increasingly estranged since 1815 and had virtually ceased to communicate with each other. While recognizing that his ruin was inevitable, he asserted that he was the victim of "the avarice of one, encouraged and

[36] Gaines, pp. 146–154; J. C. Cabell to I. A. Coles, Feb. 20, 1825 (Cabell Papers, UVA).

[37] TJR to Jane Nicholas Randolph, Feb. 11, 1824 (Edgehill-Randolph Papers, UVA).

[38] Statement made in 1827 in connection with his publication of letters to TJ to him (*Richmond Enquirer*, Sept. 14, 1827).

[39] TJ to TMR, June 5, 1825 (LC).

[40] TMR to TJ, July 8, 1825; TJ to TMR, July 9 (both UVA).

supported by the vengeance of many." He did not mention Jeff by name, but from other sources it is clear that he believed his son was trying to get hold of Edgehill for his own selfish reasons. He had much to say about Thomas Eston Randolph, to whom he was considerably indebted but for whose troubles he believed himself to be unjustly blamed. In his misery he thought everybody was against him.

The many corrections on the draft of Jefferson's reply to this letter attest to the pains he took with it. He made no references to the differences between father and son. He denied that there had been any estrangement between the Colonel and himself. He realized that his son-in-law may have been disappointed by his failure to come to his aid but stated that he had deliberately kept their affairs separate for the better protection of the family. Also, he said that he may have seemed reserved because of his deafness. He assured Randolph that he retained the full respect of his fellows but laid greatest stress on domestic relations, urging his return to those who loved and honored him most. There was nothing extraordinary about his financial difficulties, according to his father-in-law; his separation from the family was a grief of a more distressing kind. The recipient of this appeal responded to it by returning to the table at Monticello for a time, but the rift between him and his eldest son was not closed and he again withdrew when the sale of Edgehill became imminent.

On May 27, 1825, Ellen Wayles Randolph was married in the drawing room at Monticello to Joseph Coolidge, Jr., of Boston. Now twenty-eight, Ellen had long been the belle and pride of the family. Several years before this she had rejected a proposal from Francis Walker Gilmer, much to his chagrin. He called her "the cold mountain nymph."[41] She showed no lack of warmth toward the members of her own family, however, and she attracted much attention when visiting in Richmond, Washington, and Baltimore. A guest of her grandfather, the President of Transylvania University, who described the family as one of the most intelligent and agreeable in America, said that Ellen while not handsome was good-looking enough and one of the best talkers among women that he had ever heard.[42] Her grandfather is reputed to have said that if she had been a man she would have been a great one. She may have chafed under the limitations imposed upon her as a woman in that rural society, and the troubles she had observed may have depressed her despite her youth. Considerably before her marriage she said in a private letter that her former confidence in the supremacy of mind over matter had been

[41] Quoted in Davis, *Francis Walker Gilmer*, p. 135.

[42] Horace Holley to O. L. Holley, Sept. 6, 1824 (typescript, UVA).

Ellen Randolph Coolidge
Portrait by an unidentified artist. (Courtesy of Mrs. Charles B. Eddy, Jr.)

weakened by the experiences of recent years.[43] This highly articulate young woman was of great help to her grandfather and her over-burdened mother in entertaining their many guests, especially the most intelligent ones.

Joseph Coolidge, Jr., who had recently visited John Quincy Adams in Washington, first arrived at Monticello in May, 1824, bearing a letter of introduction from George Ticknor. This fellow Bostonian was described by Ticknor as "a young gentleman of education and fortune," possessing an "amiable and excellent character," who had spent several years in Europe.[44] Coolidge, seven years out of Harvard, had made the Grand Tour of Europe, visiting Lord Byron among other celebrities. He brought a bust of the poet home with him.[45] He and Jefferson took to each other from the start. What was more to the point, he was captivated by Ellen.

In the letter he wrote to his host in the fall, asking if he might make another visit, he said sedately that "the many valuable qualities of Miss Randolph" had made an impression on him. In fact, he said as much to Mrs. Randolph at the time. In turn she apprised her father of the "attachment that was forming" between his granddaughter and the visiting stranger he liked so much. "No two minds could be formed, better compounded to make each other happy," he said. Thus he welcomed the prospective visit and approved of its object. He frankly stated that no dowry could be offered by Ellen's father or by himself, much as they would have liked to provide one. He could offer distinguished company at any rate. He invited Ellen's suitor to be a guest, along with ex-President Madison, at the dinner in honor of Lafayette in the Rotunda of the University of Virginia.[46]

The second visit of the young Bostonian to Albemarle County overlapped that of the Marquis, but his private negotiations do not appear to have suffered any hindrance on that account. Their success was gratifying to the members of Ellen's family, who recognized that she was making a good match and could not have been expected to realize as yet how much they themselves would be losing.[47]

[43] Ellen Randolph to Nicholas Trist, Jan. 20, 1823 (Trist, LC).

[44] Ticknor to TJ, March 27, 1824; received May 23 (LC).

[45] See Walter Muir Whitehill on the Coolidges in G. G. Shackelford ed., *Collected Papers of the Monticello Association*, pp. 89–90. Joseph C. Coolidge, Jr., was a nephew of Charles Bullfinch.

[46] Joseph C. Coolidge, Jr., to TJ, Oct. 13, 1824 (MHS); TJ to Coolidge, Oct. 24 (Ford, X, 323–324).

[47] Ellen's cousin Wilson Miles Cary, writing his mother from Charlottesville in Jan. 1825, said that Mr. Coolidge was recognized in the family as "a very desirable connexion" (Carr-Cary Papers, UVA). He gave specific figures about Coolidge's fortune, saying that this was ample, though less than had been supposed.

In the months preceding the wedding, Jefferson continued to avail himself of the good offices of his future grandson-in-law in connection with the University. Coolidge, who had already put Jefferson in touch with a bookseller in Boston, made a contribution of books to the library on his own account. When acknowledging this, Jefferson made inquiries of him about a bell. He wanted one that could be heard at least as far away as Charlottesville. Coolidge replied that a bell weighing four hundred pounds could be heard for a mile and would cost about $150. One was ordered afterwards.[48]

The parents of the bridegroom did not attend the wedding, though cordially invited to do so. The state of his mother's health would not permit so long a journey. It is uncertain whether or not the father of the bride was present. If he had not yet begun to absent himself from Monticello in the daytime, he did so soon thereafter. No account of the occasion or of Jefferson's parting with the bride has been discovered, but it is easy to imagine his feelings when Ellen, who had so often accompanied him to Poplar Forest, set out on her long journey to a northern home. While he was devoted to all the others, he had acknowledged a special affection for this "particularly valued" granddaughter. Because of her relative maturity, her unusual intelligence and responsiveness, she was the most companionable of them all. Her escape from the ruin the rest of them were facing was an occasion for rejoicing, but the tired old man may have sensed that he would never see her again. After her departure one of her sisters reported that whenever they saw their grandfather looking at her empty chair, somebody hastened to sit in it, though nobody could hope to fill her place.[49]

Dr. Robley Dunglison, preferring the teaching of medicine to its practice, took few patients, but he was assiduous in his attentions to the distinguished one he acquired ten days before Ellen Randolph's marriage. During the next six weeks he rode on horseback from the University to Monticello a score of times. At the end of that period Jefferson reported to him that his health was now probably as good as it ever would be. Being relatively relieved in body, he wanted to ease his mind by compensating Dunglison for his helpful services. The doctor replied that the pleasure of contributing even a little to the comfort of one whose existence was so valuable was compensation enough and that he would accept nothing more. The net result of the polite dialogue that ensued was what Jefferson called a compromise. He would not enter into con-

[48] TJ to J. C. Coolidge, Jr., Jan. 15, Apr. 12, 1825 (*Papers, MHS*, pp. 340–342, 343–345); Coolidge to TJ, Apr. 25 (*ibid.*, pp. 347–348).

[49] Virginia Trist to Ellen Coolidge, June 27, 1825 (Coolidge Papers, UVA).

troversy regarding the past but would insist on compensating Dunglison in the future.[50]

He had to call on the good doctor again sooner than he expected. In less than a week he wrote that he had been too sanguine in reporting that his complaint was wearing off. Dunglison prescribed fifty drops of laudanum at night to relieve his pain.[51] He did not get any worse but he was housebound at Monticello during practically the entire summer. Though he may not have seen all the visitors with whom the place was thronged, their presence must have been disturbing. Cornelia reported to Ellen that they had fourteen or fifteen in the morning and ten or twelve in the evening. At one of their student dinners there were nine uninvited guests, and before they arose from the table twelve members of the Staunton convention arrived.[52] Lafayette made a parting visit to his old friend in August, but Jefferson was unable to attend the dinner the students gave him at the University.[53]

Jefferson had no part in the protracted negotiations and maneuvers that attended the settlement of the affairs of Thomas Mann Randolph, but he was aware of the widening breach between his son-in-law and his grandson. The former prevented the public sale of Edgehill, which had been scheduled to occur in August, by procuring an injuction. Jeff afterwards got this lifted, but the sale was delayed until the beginning of the next year. In the meantime some of the Colonel's slaves were being sold. Among these were the domestics who had served his daughters. Speaking of the sale of Susan, Virginia's maid, Martha Randolph said in a letter to Ellen: "The discomfort of slavery I have borne all my life, but its sorrows in all their bitterness I never before perceived." The major ill of their native society was very forcibly impressed on the family at this juncture. "Nothing can prosper under such a system of injustice," said this troubled wife and mother.[54]

Except for one brief visit to Philadelphia, Ellen Randolph Coolidge had never been outside the domain of slavery until she again crossed the boundary line of Pennsylvania on her journey northward. On leaving New York she and her husband proceeded up the Hudson, visited Lake George and Lake Champlain, crossed to the Connecticut, followed that

[50] TJ to Dunglison, July 2, 1825; Dunglison to TJ, July 2; TJ to Dunglison, July 4 (*Jefferson-Dunglison Letters*, pp. 34–36). Other letters between the two men in this collection will be referred to by date only. TJ kept memoranda of Dunglison's visits from May 17 to Sept. 20, 1825. Dunglison did not bother to do so.

[51] TJ to Dunglison, July 8, 1825; Dunglison to TJ, July 18.

[52] Cornelia to Ellen, Aug. 3, 1825 (Coolidge Papers, UVA). The convention in Staunton was designed to advance the cause of constitutional reform.

[53] Account in *Richmond Enquirer*, Sept. 6, 1825.

[54] Martha Randolph to Ellen Coolidge, Aug. 2, 1825 (Coolidge Papers, UVA).

river to Springfield, and traveled thence across Massachusetts to Boston. In the letter she wrote her grandfather on her arrival she spoke particularly of the New England villages and countryside, doing full justice to their charm. Of this scene she said: "It has given me an idea of prosperity and improvement such as I fear our Southern states cannot hope for whilst the canker of slavery eats into their hearts and diseases the whole body by this ulcer at the core."[55] She was grieved by the relative backwardness of her native region, despite its advantages in soil and climate. Jefferson's granddaughter, who had been inside only one factory as yet, was not reconciled to the burgeoning industry that was contributing so much to the prosperity of the region she had entered. She had been barely introduced to the mercantile community with which her husband and his family were connected. That community had been bitterly critical of her grandfather, and its standards and values were not identical with his. He had a high opinion of the man to whom her happiness was committed, however, and he deeply respected Boston as a center of learning.[56]

In his reply to her letter he said he had no doubt that she would find that society more congenial with her mind than the rustic scenes she had left, though these were not without their points of endearment. He entirely agreed with her about slavery, saying that "one fatal stain" deformed the fair gifts Nature had bestowed upon their region. The prosperity she had seen on her delightful trip showed what could be done by human labor under free government.[57]

From her many letters to her mother and sisters it is clear that, despite the kindness of her new relations, Ellen's adjustment to a community so different from the one in which she had grown up was attended with some difficulties.[58] Her grandfather may not have been fully informed of these, but he became aware of one misfortune that befell her. The ship conveying her baggage to Boston was lost at sea. Writing her about this loss her grandfather said that it was not to be measured by its pecuniary value, but by the value it held in her affections. "The documents of your childhood, your letters, correspondencies, notes, books, &c, &c, all gone! And your life cut in two, as it were, and a new one to begin, without any records of the former."[59]

Included in the ill-fated shipment was a lady's writing desk which had been made for her by John Hemings. He was deeply pained by its loss,

[55] Ellen to TJ, Aug. 1 1825 (*Family Letters*, pp. 454–457).

[56] See TJ to Edward Everett, July 21, 1825 (L. & B., XIX, 285).

[57] TJ to Ellen, Aug. 27, 1825 (*Family Letters*, pp. 457–458). He had covered much the same ground on a trip with Madison thirty-four years before.

[58] Coolidge Papers, UVA. The many letters to her from members of the family are full of what TJ called "small news."

[59] TJ to Ellen, Nov. 14, 1825 (*Family Letters*, pp. 460–463).

saying sadly that he could not make another like it. Ellen's grandfather thought of something that might replace it — the portable writing box on which he had drafted the Declaration of Independence. Though he had found it useful through the years, he claimed for it no great intrinsic worth. Its value, as he believed, was, or one day would be, symbolic. It reached Boston in due course, along with some articles her mother and sisters hoped would make up in part for those that had been lost. It was not destined to be borne in patriotic procession, as its original owner thought it might be, but years later it was given by the Coolidge family to the United States government and has been viewed as a sacred relic from that day to this.[60] The main impression one gains from this letter and others of his to the granddaughter whose place could not be filled is one of deep and abiding affection. Furthermore, he was reminding her of the historic bond between Virginia and Massachusetts. She did not need to be reminded of John Adams. Before this letter reached her, she and her husband visited him at Quincy and were warmly welcomed by that old patriot.[61]

[60] At this writing it is on display at the Smithsonian Institution in Washington.

[61] TJ's letter was dispatched with the packages for Ellen on Nov. 26 (*Family Letters*, p. 463). John Adams described the visit in a letter to TJ on Dec. 1 (*A.-J. Letters*, p. 611).

[XXXI]

A Troubled Twilight

THE more Jefferson saw of Dr. Dunglison the better he liked him, both as a man and as a physician. No other member of the University faculty came to Monticello as often as he did, but all of them may be presumed to have been there as dinner guests by midsummer of their first year. Writing her sister Ellen at that time, Cornelia Randolph commented favorably on the professors and their wives with one exception: she described Mrs. Blaettermann as "a vulgar virago," adding that the old Doctor was popular.[1] The old Rector had sufficient reason to be pleased with the faculty on personal as well as on professional grounds.

While the faculty came up to expectations with regard to scholarship and may even have exceeded these, the same could not be said for the students, of whom there were now more than a hundred. Because of the inadequacy of their preparation the admission requirements were relaxed, and by this time Jefferson was aware that a good many of them were less than eager to pursue learning. He divided them into three parts: one third were hard-working students and one third reasonably diligent, while the other third consisted of "idle ramblers incapable of application."[2] "We receive and treat our students as gentlemen and friends," he said. He usually had some of them for dinner on Sunday. On these occasions, as George Tucker stated afterwards, he sat at a little table in the tea room, an alcove off the dining room, instead of at the big table where he would have been unable to enter into the general conversation because of his deafness.[3] He could converse with them as individuals, however, and probably treated them as peers.

The antics of insubordinate students at South Carolina College were

[1] Cornelia Randolph to Ellen Randolph Coolidge, Aug. 3, 1835 (Coolidge Papers, UVA). Years later the "old Doctor" was required to leave the University because he had beaten his wife in public.

[2] TJ to Robert Greenhow, July 24, 1825 (LC). He said almost the same thing to others.

[3] George Tucker, *Life of Thomas Jefferson* (1827), II, 477.

well known to him. He could hardly have forgotten that stones were thrown through President Cooper's window and that grave liberties had been taken with Cooper's unfortunate horse. Jefferson was not unaware of the likelihood of disorder. The rules and regulations that were drafted by him before the University had either faculty or students were strict. While he recognized that these rules would need to be revised in the light of experience, he expected them to be observed as long as they were on the books. But he undoubtedly hoped that the members of this academic community would enjoy more freedom than was generally granted elsewhere. He wanted no more government than was necessary. He was not so unrealistic as to believe that the rules would enforce themselves, but he did believe that, if trusted, students would be responsive and act like gentlemen.

Early in August he wrote William Short that the University was as quiet as a convent. Toward the end of the month he told Ellen that there had been no occasion for the exercise of authority.[4] In fact, there had been some minor disturbances, but apparently no disciplinary action had been taken. The professors were reluctant disciplinarians. Rumors of laxity on their part reached Jefferson a few weeks later. He was then informed that they were not enforcing rules they did not like, that roll call was being dispensed with, and that absences from class — including those of James and Benjamin Randolph — were not being reported.[5]

About this time General Cocke spent a couple of days at the University. Writing Cabell from Staunton on September 20 he said that something should be done about the government of the institution. Students should not be left to their own devices without roll calls or examinations. He hoped that the Visitors could correct the situation at their next meeting.[6] This was scheduled for Monday, October 3. In a circular letter to his colleagues on September 10, Jefferson said he was certain that his health would not permit him to attend the meeting at the University. Therefore, his invitation to them to gather at Monticello on Sunday was more urgent than usual. He believed that a morning session on Monday at Monticello would be sufficient to complete their business. A formal session at the University afterwards would be necessary to meet the legal requirements, but this he would not need to attend.[7] As things turned out, his health improved to the point that he could ride to the University in a carriage, but their business was not finished on Monday.

The Rector and all the Visitors met on five successive days, seeking

[4] TJ to Short, Aug. 9, 1825 (MHS); TJ to Ellen, Aug. 27 (*Family Letters*, 458).

[5] Nicholas Trist to TJ, Sept. 18, 1825 (LC).

[6] Cocke to Cabell, Sept. 20, 1825 (Cabell Papers, UVA).

[7] TJ to the Visitors, Sept. 10, 1825 (Cabell, pp. 356–357).

to deal with a domestic crisis that had developed on the Lawn. They were officially informed by a letter from Dr. Robley Dunglison, secretary of the faculty, dated October 1. Presumably this was received at the meeting on October 3, along with resolutions that had been adopted by the faculty the day before.[8] In the letter Dr. Dunglison stated that the appointment of "an efficient police" had become a necessity. In the resolutions the language was stronger: unless some provision was made for the protection of the professors and their families from insult and injury, they could not continue in office. These utterances were occasioned by acts of violence on Friday and Saturday nights, but the conflict between students and faculty was of somewhat longer standing.

A couple of weeks earlier there had been a boisterous party in one of the dormitories. No permission for this gathering had been obtained, as the rules required, and the regulation forbidding the bringing of spiritous liquor into a dormitory had been violated. Though the professors may have been lax up to this time, they now manifested their intention to enforce the rules by suspending the two students whom they held most responsible for this noisy party. They restored them to good standing, however, when petitioned to do so. Although there was no special disturbance during the next few days, the proceedings of the faculty leave no doubt of their growing concern over the problem of student misconduct. Dr. Dunglison called these proceedings to the attention of the Visitors.[9]

The incidents of the nights of Friday, September 30, and Saturday, October 1, were much more serious than a noisy party. On the first night a student, who was afterwards described by Jefferson's daughter as "a rich fool," threw a bottle and pack of cards through a window of the pavilion occupied by Professor Long. According to Martha Randolph he cursed the foreign professors and threatened to take them to the pump.[10] Since his identity was unknown to the authorities at the time, this particular episode did not receive the attention of the Visitors at their meeting.[11] Their attention was focused on the events of Saturday night, when there was forcible resistance to authority. On that night fourteen masked students created a disturbance on the Lawn. Jefferson afterwards said that they were merely having fun.[12]

Professors Tucker and Emmet, who occupied pavilions at the opposite

[8] Both papers, UVA.

[9] Minutes of the faculty, Sept. 20–Oct. 1, 1825, UVA.

[10] Martha Randolph to Ellen, Oct. 13, 1825 (Coolidge Papers, UVA).

[11] This student was expelled by the faculty on Oct. 14 (minutes of the faculty, UVA). TJ did not mention him in his account of these events.

[12] TJ gave a full account of the affair to Joseph Coolidge, Oct. 13, 1825 (*Papers, M.H.S.*, pp. 356–359).

ends of the Lawn, thought the situation should be investigated. They were met by insults and at some stage a stone was hurled at them. Each of them seized a masked student. Tucker's man got away; Emmet's struck him. The masqueraders stubbornly refused to reveal their names. At a meeting with the entire body of students the next day, the faculty tried to elicit these, addressing the youths in a paper which Jefferson described as harsh. The effort was entirely unsuccessful. A paper that went so far as to question the veracity of the faculty was signed by sixty-five students the next day. The situation was complicated further when George Long and Thomas Key resigned from the faculty.

At their meeting on Monday the Visitors agreed that the professors should be requested to enforce the rules and regulations, to call the class rolls regularly, and to report absences to parents and guardians periodically. While administering a mild rebuke to the faculty, they tried to promote order by tightening procedure. But the great difficulty facing the authorities at this time was the unwillingness of students to violate their code of honor by testifying against their fellows. In the minutes of this meeting it is stated, presumably in Jefferson's words, that "this loose principle in the ethics of schoolboy combinations, is unworthy of mature and regulated minds." But the minds of the students were not as mature and well regulated as this apostle of rationality had expected; they were not yet ready to assume the full responsibilities of citizenship in a self-governing society as they were being admonished to do. Voluntary admission of misconduct by individuals was another matter, as the events of Tuesday made clear.

On the next day the entire body of students appeared before the governing board. It was reported that they were addressed by Jefferson and Chapman Johnson. According to one account, the older man was so overcome with emotion that he soon gave up the attempt to speak. The major speaker was undoubtedly Chapman Johnson, who, as a leader of the bar, was equal to this occasion. In response to his exhortation the fourteen masqueraders arose and admitted their part in the events of Saturday night. They afterwards appeared before the faculty. The net result of these proceedings was that the professors recommended and the Visitors approved the expulsion of three major offenders and that the faculty imposed lesser punishment on the eleven others.[13]

In the course of the week the Visitors, availing themselves of recommendations from the faculty, made a number of changes in the rules and regulations, relaxing these in some respects and tightening them in oth-

[13]Minutes of the Visitors, Oct. 3–7, 1825, minutes of the faculty, Oct 1–14 (UVA): Tucker, *Life of Jefferson*, II, 479–481; account of Henry Tutwiler, quoted in Bruce, II, 299–300; Dunglison, *Ana*, pp. 29–30.

ers. By dropping extreme penalties and unenforceable requirements they made the laws more realistic. While reminding the professors of their disciplinary functions, the governing board tried to free them, as well as the students, from unreasonable requirements.

The ostensible cause of the resignation of the two scholars from Cambridge, Long and Key, was that they could not put up with this particular group of young Americans. There were rumors that they had a chance to go to Princeton, where the problem of student conduct might not be so great, but these inexperienced professors wanted to be spared disciplinary duties altogether.[14] Cornelia Randolph had reported to Ellen in the summer that Key was greatly beloved, but that he had been ill, that he hated the climate, and that he believed himself to be overworked.[15] It was Long's window into which a bottle had been thrown. The Visitors, holding them to their contracts, refused to accept their resignations. Martha Randolph, contrasting their conduct with the loyalty of their British colleagues, said they had put themselves in an uncomfortable situation.[16] Jefferson himself expressed regret that there was a division in the faculty.

Writing Joseph Coolidge, Jr., in Boston about a week after the adjournment of the Board of Visitors, he characterized the recent incident as serious. But it was his opinion that the University had been strengthened by the firmness shown by the authorities. He reported that the students were now convinced, as they had not been previously, that the rules would be enforced. He believed that "the vigilance of the faculty and energy of the civil power" would prevent the recurrence of grave disorder.[17]

The effects on the public mind of the painful events that Jefferson described to Joseph Coolidge cannot be precisely measured, but they could hardly have been favorable to the struggling young University. He himself said there would be a thousand accounts, all of them inaccurate. Human nature being what it is, exaggeration was to be expected. The spirited defense of the institution in the *Enquirer* and the appeals in that paper for its support lead one to suppose that there was much unfavorable comment.[18] It was easy for foes and doubters to add the charge of

[14] Francis Walker Gilmer to TJ, Oct. 23, 1825 (*Jefferson–Gilmer Correspondence*, p. 150).

[15] Cornelia to Ellen, July 13, 1825 (Coolidge Papers, UVA).

[16] Martha to Ellen, Oct. 13, 1825 (*ibid.*).

[17] TJ to Joseph Coolidge, Jr., Oct. 13, 1825 (*Papers, M.H.S.*, pp. 356–359). He said much the same thing to William Short, Oct. 14, 1825 (LC). The accounts of the "serious incident" in these two letters came as near to being official as any that are available. It should be noted that the Visitors made the Proctor especially responsible for the observance of the laws of the state and for cooperation with the civil authorities.

[18] *Richmond Enquirer*, Oct. 11, 14, 18, 1825.

immorality to that of impiety. It was easy to cite this episode as a demonstration of Jefferson's impracticality. Actually the disorder could have been attributed to other causes: the proximity of students and faculty in the academical village, the inexperience of the professors, the lack of tradition, the restlessness of youths after close confinement during a long summer.

The affair appears to have been no worse than others that occurred elsewhere. Since later commentators like George Tucker and Dr. Dunglison agreed with Jefferson that there had been too much reliance on reason and too little resort to force, such must have been the case. While attesting to the generous spirit of most of the students, Dunglison took the position that, because of their unwillingness to testify against one another, a student court for the trial of minor offenses such as Jefferson had in mind was quite impractical. In another generation, however, a considerable degree of student self-government was attained in this University under the Honor System. Jefferson was ahead of his time in this as in other academic matters.

The disciplinary action of the faculty and Visitors was particularly painful to the Rector and his family because the chief disturber of the peace and the first person to be expelled was a close relative. Wilson Miles Cary was the son of Thomas Mann Randolph's sister and was a great-great-nephew of Jefferson's on the paternal side. By common consent this ungovernable youth richly deserved expulsion, but Martha Randolph gave him an invitation (which he did not accept) to stay at Monticello until he went home. General Cocke made a special trip to Carysbrook to inform Wilson's widowed mother of her son's expulsion. Cornelia visited her for a time.[19]

Successive rides over rough roads to the University had a bad effect on Jefferson's health. Because of the pain he suffered, his daughter increased his daily dose of laudanum from eighty-five to a hundred drops. He told William Short that because of his age, infirmity, loss of memory, and increasing deafness, he was no longer able to perform the duties incumbent on him.[20] In the confrontation with students Chapman Johnson had played the commanding role, but the actions of the Board had been taken with Jefferson's approval. During the summer, when largely confined to the house, he had attended to important University business.

[19] Cocke to Cabell Oct. 13, 1825 (Cabell Papers, UVA); Virginia Trist to Ellen Coolidge, Oct. 16 (Coolidge Papers, UVA).

[20] TJ to Short, Oct. 14, 1825 (LC). Details about his health are given in various letters to Ellen and Joseph Coolidge from her mother and sisters.

After the declination of the professorship of law by Judge Dade, he reopened negotiations with Francis Walker Gilmer, whose health seemed to have improved and who was now willing to accept the position. Gilmer was duly elected by the Board of Visitors in October, although he was not expected to begin his services until the next session.

After consulting with his colleagues Jefferson had purchased a tract of 132 acres of land lying between the two parcels that already belonged to the University and containing the pipelines through which the water for the academical community flowed. Because of this purchase, which increased the total acreage to 392.8, the funds available for the completion of the Rotunda were reduced, but work was proceeding on the dome room, which was to house the library, and on the anatomy building which was so necessary for Dr. Dunglison.[21]

The arrival at New York and Boston of the marble bases and capitals for the ten columns of the Rotunda created a minor financial problem because of the increase in the import duties since these were ordered from Carrara several years earlier. As a result of Jefferson's protests, a measure was introduced in Congress at the next session for the remission of all the duties on this shipment to an institution of learning.[22] While the measure was pending, he held up the negotiations he was conducting through Joseph Coolidge, Jr., for a clock as well as a bell. He assured Simon Willard of Boston that he should proceed with the clock as soon as they had the money.[23]

ii

Jefferson's health had not recovered in early October, when he had an alarming experience at Monticello. This was at the hands of an itinerant sculptor, John H. I. Browere, who was supposed to be adept at making life masks but was described by Jefferson's granddaughter Virginia as a "vile plasterer." In the process of making a life mask of that amiable but elderly gentleman, Browere, after covering his head and neck with plaster, left it there for an hour instead of the twenty minutes that had been expected. The plaster became so hard that a chisel and mallet were required for its removal. Though the victim afterwards made light of the danger and suffering, he emitted groans in the course of this operation, and his daughter and granddaughters feared that he would suffocate. Since the girls expressed themselves indignantly to others as well as to

[21] Minutes of the meetings of Oct. 3–7.

[22] TJ to Henry Dearborn, Sept. 13, 1825 (UVA), William Cabell Rives to TJ, Nov. 30, 1825 (LC), Mar. 13, 1826 (UVA).

[23] TJ to Ellen Coolidge, Nov. 14, 1825 (*Family Letters*, p. 462).

the sculptor, the story got out, to the injury of his reputation. To offset this Jefferson afterwards gave him a testimonial.[24]

James Madison described the bust of Jefferson as a faithful likeness. No doubt it was at this particular time, when he was withered by age and weakened by illness, but it conveyed no adequate impression of the vigor of mind and power of personality which visitors had not ceased to observe. He told Madison after this experience that he was bidding adieu to busts and portraits. It might have been well if he had done so sooner. A good stopping point could have been found in the year 1821, after Thomas Sully visited Monticello to put him on canvas, and at long last he received from Gilbert Stuart what came to be known as the Edgehill portrait.

The visit of Sully to Monticello was occasioned by the desire of the faculty of the United States Military Academy at West Point to obtain a portrait of Jefferson, during whose presidency that institution had been established. Responding to the request of Professor Jared Mansfield that he receive the artist, he quoted a remark of Voltaire's in an analogous situation. When asked that a sculptor be permitted to make his bust, Voltaire replied that what he had left at seventy-six could hardly be called a face. Jefferson was nearing seventy-eight when he said, as Voltaire had done, that what remained of him was at the service of the artist.[25] No doubt the pencil and brush of Sully were active during his entire visit of twelve days in March, but the life portrait of his host was not wholly finished in that time. Thus Jefferson did not see in its completed form the fine portrait that has looked down from the walls of the American Philosophical Society in Philadelphia for a century and a half. Nor did he ever see the full-length portrait by Sully which has attracted so much admiration through the generations at West Point.[26]

The portrait by Gilbert Stuart that arrived at Monticello in the late summer of 1821 was one Jefferson had sat for and paid for while he was President of the United States. The artist had kept it in his studio in an unfinished state and painted a number of other portraits from it. Acting in Jefferson's name, Henry Dearborn, his old Secretary of War, finally

[24] The episode was described by Virginia to her sister Ellen, Oct. 16, 1825 (Coolidge Papers, UVA), and by TJ to Madison, Oct. 18 (L. & B., XIX, 287). It was mentioned in the *Richmond Enquirer*, Nov. 15 and Dec. 13, 1825. Browere (May 20, 1826, LC) elicited a testimonial from TJ (June 6, LC). This appeared in the *Enquirer*, June 23. The mask and a bronze bust made from it are preserved at Cooperstown, N.Y.

[25] TJ to Jared Mansfield, Feb. 13, 1821 (L. & B., XV, 313–314). For TJ's previous connection with the Academy, see *Jefferson the President: Second Term*, pp. 510–511.

[26] On these paintings, see the studies of the life portraits of Jefferson by Kimball, pp. 527–531, and Bush, pp. 90–93. A replica of Sully's life portrait is the frontispiece of this volume. His portrait of Martha Jefferson Randolph (see p. 152) was painted only a few months before her death, but the artist drew upon his memories of his earlier visit and deliberately depicted her as a younger woman.

persuaded Stuart to complete it and send it to its owner. During the rest of his life it hung on a wall in the drawing room at Monticello. Not until after his death was it moved to Edgehill. Though the family preferred Stuart's medallion profile to this stylized portrait, it was a familiar sight and a cherished possession.[27]

Despite the forebodings of Martha and the girls, the episode of the life mask had no apparent effect on Jefferson's health. During the rest of the year, in fact, it improved. He continued to have paroxysms of pain followed by intervals of ease, but the latter became somewhat longer. While he left the house only for an occasional ride and still depended on laudanum, he concluded by the middle of November that he had arrived at what might be called an habitual state. Therefore, he thought this to be a good time to extract from Dunglison the bill which, as he claimed, had been promised. The doctor, denying that he had made any such promise, said that he had kept no record of his visits to this patient. In reply Jefferson issued a polite ultimatum. Though his health was much improved at the moment, he recognized the likelihood that the "fragment of life" remaining to him would be passed in sickness and suffering. Being unwilling to trust himself to inexperienced physicians, he would have to rely on nature if deprived of the services of Dr. Dunglison. He could not accept these services without making some return for them. He enclosed an order for fifty dollars, hoping it would be acceptable. It must have been, for the doctor he trusted served him to the very end.[28]

About this time Jefferson stated to one of his correspondents that the University, the main business of his life, was going on with all the success he could expect. A special meeting of the Visitors, to consider matters of government and order, was scheduled for December, but the attendance fell short of a quorum. There was no crisis at the moment; Cabell reported from Richmond that the adoption of the revised rules and regulations had enhanced the character of the University in the public estimation.[29] Nevertheless, things were not to go well for the institution at this session of the legislature, and it was to become obvious that Gilmer's desperate health would prevent him from ever assuming the professorship of law. As we have seen, Jefferson was much perturbed that winter by the state of the Union and the trend toward consolidation he perceived. For more than one reason it was an unhappy

[27] Besides the works of Kimball, pp. 512–523, and Bush, pp 71–73, see *Jefferson the President: Second Term*, pp. 30–31.

[28] TJ to Dunglison, Nov. 17, 1825; Dunglison to TJ, Nov. 18, TJ to Dunglison, Nov. 26 (*Jefferson-Dunglison Letters*, pp. 41–46).

[29] TJ to F. A. Van der Kemp, Nov 30, 1825 (LC); Cabell to TJ, Dec. 7 (Cabell, p. 358); TJ to Arthur Brockenbrough, Dec. 13 (UVA).

winter, but the troubles within his family and the precarious condition of his own finances distressed him most.

The public sale of Edgehill and the slaves of Thomas Mann Randolph on January 2, 1826, marked the settlement of his affairs to the apparent satisfaction of his creditors. Through months of bickering and confusion they had relied on Jeff Randolph, who had assumed responsibility for most of his father's debts. Jeff himself was the highest bidder for the plantation. Thus he kept Edgehill in the family while laying himself open to the charge that he was taking advantage of his own father. Into the complexities of the financial operations of this over-burdened young man we need not enter here. It can be said, however, that he sold land and slaves of his own to raise the purchase price and that he remained in considerable debt on his father's account.[30] There is no evidence that his grandfather questioned the propriety of his conduct in this matter, and there is abundant evidence that his mother and sisters strongly approved of it.[31]

About a week after the sale, in a letter to Randolph, his father-in-law expressed the hope that he would cease to look back on his affairs now that they had been wound up, and for the third time urged him to rejoin the family table and fireside.[32] This the unhappy man did not do. He still had a house in North Milton where he had long kept his books and papers. In the daytime he made it his home. At nightfall he crossed the Rivanna and joined his long-suffering wife at Monticello. He did not stop sleeping there until after Jefferson's death. This violent man does not appear ever to have quarreled with his father-in-law. Ellen attributed the lack of contention to the older man's endless patience and unconquerable good will. Toward his own son Colonel Randolph was bitterly resentful. Some months after these events he ordered his wife not to let the younger boys visit their brother at Tufton, threatening to take them from her if she disobeyed.[33] The realization that he had legal authority over them as minors did not contribute to her peace of mind.

[30] See accounts of debts of TJ and TJR, July 4, 1826 (UVA).

[31] Martha discussed the matter at length in a letter of Apr. 5, 1826, to Ellen, who took Jeff's side without question (Coolidge Papers, UVA). Ellen analyzed her father's character relentlessly in letters to H. S. Randall in later years (Jan. 26, Feb. 13, Mar. 13, 27, 1856, in Letterbook, Coolidge Papers, UVA). She said that, while considerate of his daughters, he was harsh toward his sons, especially Jeff.

[32] TJ to TMR, Jan. 8, 1826 (Ford, X, 360–361).

[33] Jane Margaret Carr to Dabney S. Carr, Feb. 27, 1826 (Carr-Cary Papers, UVA).

iii

Jefferson's own financial difficulties were increased by what he charitably termed the misfortunes of his son-in-law. He now became responsible for all the expenses of the family, including the clothing of his daughter and her unmarried children. In itself the addition to the burdens he was already bearing was insufficient to provoke a crisis, but Jeff Randolph must have convinced him that it was an absolute necessity for him to make a renewed effort to pay his debts, if he himself did not already realize this. Before the middle of January in what proved to be his last winter, he conceived a plan to solve his problems, and throughout the remaining months of his life his grandson was trying to put it into effect. His idea was to resort to a lottery.

According to his daughter, he was "lying awake one night from painful thoughts," when the idea came to him "like an inspiration from the realms of bliss."[34] At dawn he summoned Jeff, who promptly recognized the advantages of the plan his grandfather was suggesting. They were looking for a way to sell land in large quantity in a period when there were virtually no bidders in their region and prices were abysmally low. In their judgment there would be a ready sale throughout the Union for lottery tickets of small denomination. They assumed that these could be issued in sufficient number to assure a fair return for the land that was to be offered as a prize.

In times past lotteries had often been employed in Virginia to raise money for institutions and public causes. They had also been used, though less often, in sales of private property. The legislature had to authorize all lotteries, and in recent years there was more opposition to them than formerly on moral grounds. Among the most outspoken opponents of lotteries as a form of gambling were devoted followers of Jefferson, and he himself had been a foe of speculation all his life. Accordingly, there were questions that must be answered, as well as legislative operations that must be carried on.

In a letter of January 20, 1826, to Senator Joseph C. Cabell, Jefferson stated that his grandson was attending the legislature "on a subject of ultimate importance" to his future happiness and referred him to Jeff Randolph for particulars.[35] He spoke of his debts and of his proposal to the legislature in general terms. He sent no formal application for a lot-

[34] Martha Randolph to Ellen, Apr. 5, 1826 (Coolidge Papers, UVA). Presumably she learned this from TJ himself in this or similar language.

[35] TJ to Cabell, Jan. 20, 1826 (Cabell, p. 359). Letters of this date to the two other Visitors in the Assembly and the two delegates from Albemarle are listed in his record of correspondence.

tery but left that to his friends. In effect he asked this trusted colleague to do whatever might be necessary to present the case, saying that to him it was almost a matter of life or death.

While he believed that his friends could speak more effectively for him than he could for himself, he realized that they might need arguments and would certainly need further information. Therefore, he drafted a paper entitled "Thoughts on Lotteries, and on that particularly which is now asked." The paper was not intended for publication and did not appear in print in his lifetime. Presumably he wrote it in January and sent it to Richmond by Jeff Randolph with the letter to Cabell.[36]

In this private paper Jefferson tried to dissociate lotteries from games of chance that were harmful in themselves, such as cards and dice. While recognizing that lotteries could be abused and were properly subject to regulation by the government, he asserted that they could be and often had been useful in raising money for worthy causes. He cited a number of examples from the history of the state. In his opinion a lottery such as he had in mind would harm nobody, and he was convinced that under existing circumstances his property could be disposed of at its fair value in no other way.

He also believed that he was entitled to some degree of special consideration because of his public services. These he listed in what may appear to have been unnecessary detail, emphasizing those rendered to the state. He perceived no danger that the granting of the favor he asked would create an embarrassing precedent, since it was unlikely that any future applicant could offer a record comparable to his sixty years of service. In his desperation he was over-pleading his case.

The proposal he was supporting by these arguments caused consternation among his friends in Richmond. Jeff wrote his wife Jane that they were all opposed to it at first.[37] He made less of the difficulties in his letter to his anxious grandfather the next day. He then said that the leaders had taken up the matter with zeal. He attended a secret conference with Cabell, Cocke, Chapman Johnson, William F. Gordon, and most of the judges of the state's highest court. They determined that the bill should provide for the appointment of appraisers and should stipulate that the money to be received should not exceed the appraised value of the property. It was thought that any impression that this was a money-making scheme would thus be avoided. (Jefferson approved of this provision and believed the appraisal would be fair.) The supporters of the plan were said to be confident. At any rate, they were deeply

[36] The date February 1826 attached to the printed version in Ford, X, 362–372, does not appear on the original draft (LC). A reference in TJ's letter of Feb. 4 to TJR suggests that he (Jeff) had it from the first (*Family Letters*, p. 468).

[37] TJR to Jane, Jan. 30, 1826 (Edgehill-Randolph Papers, UVA).

devoted to Jefferson personally and anxious to relieve him from distress.[38]

Things did not proceed as expected. According to Jeff, when word got out that an application would be made in his grandfather's behalf, a panic seized upon his more timid supporters. They feared that the action would have a bad effect on Jefferson's reputation. He could be charged with seeking special privilege and condoning immorality. His supporters were rallied, however.[39] There was another conference, attended again by sympathetic judges. At this Cabell took the position that much more should be done for Jefferson than had been asked. His recommendation that they seek a loan of $80,000 without interest for the rest of Jefferson's life was rejected as impracticable, but the final vote of the group to support the lottery was unanimous. They were agreed that this was a very special case.

Their proposal first came into public view on February 8. On that day, as the *Enquirer* reported, Mr. Loyall of Norfolk introduced into the House of Delegates "a most interesting and touching subject." He asked leave to bring in a bill authorizing Thomas Jefferson to dispose of his property by lottery. The *Enquirer* believed it "utterly impossible" for the legislature to refuse to sanction this, but in fact Loyall's resolution was tabled by a majority of one. It was adopted the next day by a majority of four. Cabell assured Jefferson that these votes did not reflect the sentiments of the House regarding the bill itself. He was confident that it would pass but expected the opposition to be considerable. As reported on February 10, the bill provided for managers to direct the lottery as well as for commissioners to appraise the property. It contained a preamble in which reference was made to the distinguished public services of Jefferson. To Cabell it seemed that a surprising number of their countrymen were unmindful of these services. Meanwhile, the man who had rendered them may be said to have reached the lowest point of his private life.[40]

A week before Loyall offered his resolution Hetty Carr, the widow of Peter Carr, reported from Albemarle County to her son in Baltimore that his great-uncle was "very unwell." She believed that if the lottery was refused him he would die.[41] Jefferson admitted that he had underestimated the obstacles to the acceptance of his request by the legislature and acknowledged his mortification at having over-estimated his standing with that body.[42] The failure of his hopes would be more than a blow

[38] TJR to TJ, Jan. 31, 1826 (*Family Letters*, p. 466); TJ to TJR, Feb. 4 (*ibid.*, p. 468).

[39] TJR to TJ, Feb. 3, 1826 (*ibid.*, p. 467); Cabell to TJ, Feb. 3 (Cabell, p. 362).

[40] The legislative events are described in *Richmond Enquirer*, Feb. 9, 11, 1826. Loyall's speech is in the Feb. 11 issue. Cabell reported to TJ Feb. 8, 10 (Cabell, pp. 369–370).

[41] Hetty Carr to Dabney S. Carr, Feb. 1, 1826 (Carr–Cary Papers, UVA).

[42] TJ to TJR, Feb, 8, 1826 (*Family Letters*, pp. 469–470).

to his pride, he said. It would be a deadly blast to his peace of mind during all his remaining days. Since there would not be many of these, he had little reason to be concerned for himself, but he was overwhelmed with fears for the future of his daughter and her children.

He counted the affection of the family as the greatest of the many blessings life afforded him and claimed that their conduct had brought him not a moment of pain. He paid particular tribute to Jeff, whom he described as the greatest of the godsends that Heaven had granted to him. In his present difficulties he would have been helpless without this grandson, for whom he expressed "unmeasured affection." Jeff, who was managing the affairs of his dead father-in-law, along with those of his father and grandfather, could have been termed the Atlas of the family. His wife's sister and widowed mother lived with him at Tufton, and Jane bore him another daughter while he was in Richmond.

Jefferson's gloom deepened when he learned of the happenings in the House of Delegates. He wrote Cabell: "I count on nothing now."[43] His spirits were low for another reason. Jane Randolph and her latest daughter were doing well, but such was not the case with Anne Cary Bankhead, who had prematurely given birth to a son a few weeks earlier. Her death on February 11 at the age of thirty-five closed the sad story of the eldest and most unfortunate of Martha Randolph's children. Her grandfather, who had been prevented by his own physical weakness from visiting her at Carlton, found her unconscious when he finally did so. On the day she died he wrote her brother Jeff: "Heaven seems to be overwhelming us with every form of misfortune, and I expect your next will give me the *coup de grâce*."[44]

Jeff was deeply grieved by the untimely death of his sister, who had suffered so much from her drunken husband. His immediate concern, however, was to give his grandfather the encouragement that dispirited old gentleman sorely needed. Far from delivering the *coup de grâce*, he reported that the bill was daily gaining support and would surely pass. He said that if the worst should happen, which he did not expect, neither his mother nor his grandfather should ever want for comfort. It would always be his pride and happiness to watch over them both and to guard them against the shafts of adversity. Under any circumstances they would be rich enough, he said, and, when the bill passed, their ills would vanish like smoke.[45]

On the very day that this heartening letter reached Monticello, Jeff

[43] TJ to Cabell, Feb. 14, 1826 (Cabell, p. 374).

[44] TJ to TJR, Feb. 11, 1826 (*Family Letters*, p. 470).

[45] TJR to TJ, received Feb. 17 and probably written Feb. 14. Incorrectly dated in *Family Letters*, p. 472.

wrote his wife Jane that "the noblest enthusiasm" had arisen upon the subject of his dear grandfather's application.[46] A few days later Jefferson learned that the bill George Loyall had introduced was passed by a vote of more than two to one in the House and by a larger majority in the Senate.[47] According to Thomas Ritchie, the "malignant opposition" of Jefferson's determined enemies did not take place, and he did not doubt that the "distinguished services" of "this illustrious individual" to his state, the nation, and the cause of freedom throughout the world were properly extolled. Loyall and Gordon spoke eloquently in his behalf. Said the *Enquirer:* "His name was identified with every thing glorious in the history of our Republic."

Soon after he got the good news from Richmond, Jefferson told Bernard Peyton that he had been suffering from a kind of uneasiness that he had never known before.[48] This was not merely because he realized that his last hope of solvency lay with the legislature. In view of his services to the state he did not expect that body to be so reluctant to consider his application. While Cabell and Cocke regarded this reluctance as a shameful case of public ingratitude, the latter friend was fully aware of the moral objections that had to be overcome or disregarded.[49] Jefferson himself believed that the crusade for the University of Virginia had lost him friends. His application for a lottery may have injured his reputation as his supporters had feared. He was never a prophet without honor in his own country, however; and, as his plight became a matter of public knowledge, it occasioned many expressions of sympathy. One of the most interesting of these was from former President James Monroe, who was facing similar financial difficulties. He also was eaten up with interest on long-standing debts and had neglected his private affairs when absorbed in public duties.[50] He had no difficulty in understanding his friend's situation.

Jefferson had been spared the embarrassment of disclosing his assets and liabilities to the Assembly. He did not do that even to his intimate friends, but he discussed his situation with several of them in considerable detail. He told Cabell that if the lottery should fail he would have to sell his most valuable property, including Monticello and his mills, for whatever it would bring and move to Bedford, where he had lands

[46] TJR to Jane, Feb. 17, 1826 (Edgehill–Randolph Papers, UVA). His letter of the same date to TJ has not been discovered.

[47] Cabell to TJ, Feb. 20, 1826 (Cabell, pp. 375–376); Ritchie to TJ, Feb. 20 (LC); account of events and speeches in *Richmond Enquirer*, Feb. 21.

[48] TJ to Peyton, Feb. 21, 1826 (M.H.S.).

[49] Cabell to TJ, Feb. 10, 1826 (Cabell, p. 370); Cocke to Cabell, Feb. 15 (Cabell Papers, UVA).

[50] Monroe to TJ, Feb. 13; postscript, Feb. 14 (S.M.H., VII, 67–69). TJ got this letter Feb. 21 and replied the next day (Ford, X, 379).

but no place to lay his head. Some days later Francis Eppes offered to return Poplar Forest to him. This offer he declined.[51]

The passage of the lottery bill did not immediately dispel the gloom within the family at Monticello. Writing her sister Ellen, Cornelia said: "Fortune has persecuted us so unrelentingly that even though at last she seems to give us one smile to excite hope, not one of us has spirits to feel it a promise of future good."[52] Several weeks later Martha Randolph expressed some anxiety about their having enough left to live on after the lottery had taken place.[53] She was reasonably confident, however, that her father could be taken care of. He himself was gratified by the turn of events. He told Loyall that, while he could never repay his friends for what they had done for him, he could pay all his monetary debts and would be left at ease. He told this colleague that at the spring meeting of the Visitors he was expected to be a guest at Monticello as usual.[54]

[51] TJ to Cabell, Feb. 7, 1826 (Cabell, p. 365); FWE to TJ, Feb. 23 (*Family Letters*, pp. 470–472); TJ to FWE, Mar. 9 (UVA).

[52] Cornelia Randolph to Ellen Coolidge, Feb. 3, 1826 (Coolidge Papers, UVA).

[53] Martha Randolph to Ellen Coolidge, Apr. 5, 1826 (*ibid.*).

[54] TJ to George Loyall, Feb. 22, 1826 (Ford, X, 379–380). This optimistic letter contains one of TJ's fullest accounts of his financial difficulties.

XXXII

The End of the Day

THE bill authorizing the lottery named the managers and appraisers but did not specify what part or parts of Jefferson's property were to be disposed of.[1] He had believed for a time that he need give up only his mills and a thousand acres of land, and is said to have turned white when he learned that Monticello must be included in the plan.[2] This was after Jeff returned from Richmond. No doubt his grandson softened the blow by telling him that only the reversion of Monticello was at stake; the place would be his for life. Furthermore, it would remain in the possession of his beloved daughter for a decent interval after his death.[3] Jefferson had no real choice in this matter, but he is reported to have asked for time to reflect and to consult Martha before assenting to the proposal. She was well aware of the difficulty of keeping up the place and appears to have been reconciled to leaving it. Like the father whom she so closely resembled, she was disposed to make a virtue of necessity.[4]

Jefferson stated that he did not meddle with the scheme and management of the lottery but left everything to his trusted grandson.[5] Though he did his best to keep out of sight, he became involved in an important question of procedure. Among the many sympathetic letters he received after the news of his financial difficulties spread was one from North Carolina. The spokesman of a group of his admirers in that state informed him that they would gladly make monetary contributions to him if these would be acceptable, or they would buy tickets to the lottery if

[1] *Richmond Enquirer*, Feb. 21, 1826.

[2] Hetty Carr to D. S. Carr, Mar. 13, 1826 (Carr–Cary Papers, UVA).

[3] In the final formulation of the plan the period was two years. The reasons for the inclusion of Monticello were stated in the *Richmond Enquirer*, Apr. 4, 1826.

[4] Her attitude is shown in her letters of Mar. 1, 1826, to Joseph Cooolidge and Apr. 5 to Ellen (Coolidge Papers, UVA).

[5] TJ to FWE, Mar. 9, 1826 (UVA).

that procedure was preferred. Jefferson told Thomas Ritchie that this inquiry forced him to take "decided ground," since the pursuit of two plans might cause the defeat of both. He said it was not for him to prescribe the form that the manifestations of kindness by his fellow citizens should take. He was writing the North Carolinian that the lottery was preferred because it relieved him of the fear that he was imposing on his friends. In effect he was saying that contributions would be more embarrassing. He implied, however, that if offered voluntarily they would be acceptable. He would regard them as marks of appreciation of his public service.[6]

He had told his friends that he was entirely satisfied with the remuneration he had received as an official and had declared that he was now seeking no money from the legislature. Apparently they created the impression that he would not accept any gifts of money. Following his suggestions, Ritchie stated in the *Enquirer* that, while many plans had been proposed, the best way to help him was to promote the lottery.[7] But gifts of money had not been completely ruled out by Jefferson himself, and they were vigorously sought by some of his supporters.

On the very day that he wrote Ritchie, Hetty Carr, in a letter to her son Dabney Smith Carr in Baltimore, urged him to promote a campaign in that city for contributions to his great-uncle.[8] According to her, Jeff Randolph approved of this, saying that gifts of money would be accepted if offered, though he and his grandfather should not be questioned about them in advance. Some of the women in the family circle charged the Virginians with an apathetic spirit and an ungenerous attitude toward Jefferson in his distress.[9] Near neighbors of his continued to oppose the lottery on moral grounds, and there was little disposition in Richmond to launch a campaign for contributions. As Philip Norborne Nicholas, one of the managers of the lottery, told Dabney S. Carr, it would be much easier and better to start such a campaign elsewhere.[10] Since times were hard and money even scarcer than usual, contributions were likely to be small and discouraging. Virginians were committed to the lottery and to this he believed they must stick.

These considerations may not have satisfied Jefferson's feminine relations but his grandson, recognizing that he could not ignore them, de-

[6] TJ to Ritchie, Mar. 13, 1826 (Ford, X, 382*n*.), enclosing a copy of his letter of that date to Dr. Thomas Jefferson Ward (Mo. Hist. Soc.).

[7] *Richmond Enquirer*, Mar. 24, 1826.

[8] Hetty to D. S. Carr, Mar. 13, 1826 (Carr–Cary Papers, UVA). Besides being the widow of Peter Carr she was a close relative of Jeff Randolph's wife Jane. She had much to say about family matters in her letters of this period.

[9] Jane Randolph to Sarah E. Nicholas, Mar. 12, 1826 (Edgehill–Randolph Papers); S. E. Nicholas to Jane Randolph, Mar. 30 (*ibid.*).

[10] P. N. Nicholas to D. S. Carr, Mar. 25, 1826 (Carr–Cary Papers, UVA).

vised an ingenious plan whereby cash benefits could be gained in conjunction with the lottery. Tickets would be purchased by community groups on Jefferson's birthday and publicly burned on July 4, when the money would be presented to him. It was thought that, if this could be put into effect throughout the nation, there might be no need to sacrifice Monticello. The idea of purchasing tickets on April 13 was given up because they could not be printed in time, but the rest of the plan was presented to Ritchie by Jeff Randolph and duly described in the *Enquirer*. It had previously been noted in a Baltimore paper and his name was not mentioned. It made its public appearance as a suggestion, not an official announcement.[11] On that very day Jeff set out on a trip to the eastern cities. Presumably he intended to present the idea to his grandfather's supporters wherever he went, but this was an exploratory trip and precise procedure had to be determined in the light of circumstances.

From the time Jeff began to plan his trip Cornelia had looked forward to accompanying him as far as Boston and visiting her sister Ellen, who was expecting her first baby. Jeff's wife did not think Cornelia could be spared from Monticello since Martha Randolph, who had been in bad health all winter, was already over-burdened. Virginia could not be of much help since she, like Ellen, was in an advanced state of pregnancy. After Anne Cary's death her two youngest children — a little girl and the baby boy — were brought to Monticello. Cornelia was teaching the little girl, along with several other small children, and shared the care of the baby, who was struggling to stay alive. Jeff had hastened to make up with the father of these motherless children, and Martha told Joseph Coolidge that Charles Bankhead had remained sober and was behaving himself. The same could not be said of her own husband, who absented himself in the daytime but had to be put up with at night. Ellen's letters were almost her only pleasure in this "most afflicting winter," she said. The thought of her distant daughter's comfort and security brought her great satisfaction. She wanted Cornelia to be with Ellen during her confinement, as the Coolidges themselves did.[12]

Since Jeff's departure was delayed, Cornelia did not get to Boston until after the birth of the baby girl but she was there for the baptism. Before they set out, Jeff wrote his grandfather from Richmond.[13] Al-

[11] *Richmond Enquirer*, Apr. 4, 1826. The plan was described by Hetty Carr to D. S. Carr on Mar. 29 (Carr–Cary Papers, UVA). It was regarded by Joseph C. Cabell as the best idea that had been proposed (Cabell to Cocke, Apr. 6, 1826 (Cabell Papers, UVA).

[12] Cornelia Randolph to Ellen Coolidge, Feb. 23, 1826; Martha Randolph to Joseph Coolidge, Jr., Mar. 1; to Ellen Coolidge, Apr. 5 (Coolidge Papers, UVA).

[13] TJR to TJ, Apr. 3, 1826 (*Family Letters*, p. 476).

though he reported that times were hard, he said that John Randolph wanted to spend $500 on tickets and that Chief Justice Marshall had asked to be kept informed so that he might purchase some. Expressions of sympathy and appreciation by friends and former foes were a balm to Jefferson's spirit. His health appeared to have improved and his dose of laudanum was decreased. Several weeks before this, a pianoforte that had been purchased for Virginia in Boston arrived at Monticello. Jeff had protested against the extravagance, but his music-loving grandfather had favored the purchase and must have liked the instrument. He remarked that if the lottery turned out well he would like to get another one.[14] He gave letters of introduction to persons whom Jeff expected to visit on his journey. These ranged from President John Quincy Adams in Washington to ex-President John Adams in Quincy, and the list included Governor De Witt Clinton of New York. He received letters from his grandson during the next two months but he left arrangements for the lottery wholly in Jeff's hands.

ii

The meeting of the Visitors on April 3–4, which was to be Jefferson's last, occurred at a fortunate time for him, since both his health and his spirits had improved. His chief troubles during the winter had been personal; they were the tribulations of a paterfamilias rather than those of the Rector of the University. It was not a particularly good time, however, for the institution he had fathered. Before his request for a lottery was presented to the House of Delegates, that body rejected the University bill by a large majority. That is, it refused to grant the young institution any more money. Soon thereafter General Cocke remarked to Cabell that "the temper of the House ought to be an admonition to the Old Sachem that the state has enough of his buildings." The venerable Rector had already received and heeded the message; he had instructed Brockenbrough to engage in no construction they could do without. Specifically, they were to concentrate on the dome room of the Rotunda, where the library was to be housed, and the anatomical building. These could be finished with the available funds.[15]

Before the Visitors assembled, the death of Francis Walker Gilmer destroyed the last hope that he would assume the professorship of law. General Cocke expressed the opinion that the future of the University hinged on the choice of his successor. It was generally agreed that the

[14] Martha to Ellen, Apr. 5, 1826 (Coolidge Papers, UVA). The dispute over the piano is described by Helen Cripe in *Thomas Jefferson and Music*, pp. 58–60.

[15] TJ to Cabell, Feb. 4, 1826 (Cabell, pp. 363–364); Cocke to Cabell, Feb. 6 (Cabell Papers, UVA). TJ described his action to Madison, Feb. 17 (Ford, X, 375–376).

lack of a school of law had had an adverse effect on the enrollment. Jefferson had predicted that the dormitories would be filled and might overflow into the village of Charlottesville. In fact, the enrollment was disappointing. General Cocke, who visited the University soon after the opening of its second session on February 1, reported that from a half to two-thirds of last year's students had not returned.[16] There were 135 on the rolls at that time and 163 when the Visitors met.

The problem of disorder had by no means vanished. The troubled faculty asked the Visitors to provide police, saying that they themselves should not be expected to serve as such. The compact academical village could be disturbed by a single student, and the offender could easily elude and embarrass an irate professor. The request of the faculty was referred to the committee already appointed to consider the whole question of government. At this session the Visitors instructed the Proctor to make "vigilant inquiry" into the recent violence against the house of Professor Emmet and the wall of Professor Blaettermann and to bring the offender or offenders before the civil magistrates. While recognizing that the Visitors were imposing painful duties on Brockenbrough, Jefferson told him that he was the right arm of the institution and that he must be firm and fearless. The poor Proctor assumed these painful duties with good grace.[17]

Far from cooperating with the faculty in disciplinary matters, the hotelkeepers were acting in collusion with their boarders. They were often intimidated by students who threatened to leave them if not pleased. The Visitors tried to correct the situation by forbidding students to change hotels before the end of the session. Also, they delivered a moral exhortation to the hapless hotelkeepers.[18]

A few days after the meeting adjourned, Jefferson said they had a fine body of youths, but that they were "much obstructed by about a dozen of vicious and worthless scape-graces whom we shall endeavor to ferret out and get rid of as soon as we can."[19] President Thomas Cooper of South Carolina College told Jefferson in May that he was so tired of coping with obstreperous youths that he would quit if he had an alternative. Judging from his report, students in that institution were more destructive than those at the University of Virginia.[20] Writing Joseph Coolidge, Jr., a few weeks later, Jefferson said: "Our University is going on well. The students have sensibly improved since the last year in habits of order and industry." He stated that, because of some acts of in-

[16] Cocke to Cabell, Feb. 15, 1826 (Cabell Papers, UVA).
[17] TJ to Brockenbrough, Apr. 7, 1826 (LC); Brockenbrough to TJ, Apr. 12 (HEH).
[18] Minutes of the meeting of Apr. 3–4, 1826 (UVA).
[19] TJ to the booksellers Cummings & Hilliard, Apr. 9, 1826 (LC).
[20] Cooper to TJ, May 18, 1826 (LC).

subordination, the rules had been strengthened but added that the most effective instrument they had found was the civil authority.[21] He may have made too favorable a report, and he and his colleagues had certainly not arrived at a lasting solution of the perennial problem of controlling restless and rebellious youths, but they had made genuine progress.

At their spring meeting the Visitors grappled with the crucial question of obtaining a suitable professor of law. Their first choice was William Wirt, the Attorney General of the United States, but they recognized that special inducement would have to be offered this distinguished man. Before the meeting Cocke told Cabell that the University would never have effective government without a head. Chapman Johnson had taken the same position earlier, but he and his colleagues deferred to Jefferson in the matter. The Board now created the office of president on the understanding that it would be offered to Wirt, along with the professorship of law. If he should decline the offer, the resolution creating the presidential office would be invalidated and the professorship would be offered to John T. Lomax, of Fredericksburg. That was just what happened, and the outcome may have been generally anticipated. Nonetheless, Jefferson put himself on record by filing a dissenting opinion on the question of the presidency.

Although he did not say so, he was undoubtedly fearful of the concentration of power in anybody's hands and favored dispersal whenever possible. He did say that all of the functions assigned the president could be performed by the faculty. He also raised financial objections and said this action had not been taken by a full board. The main point he tried to make was that the law creating the Board of Visitors, while specifying minor officers whom it might appoint, did not authorize it to appoint a president. He was applying to a legislative act the principle of strict construction that he had applied to the federal Constitution. One may doubt that many of the legislators themselves would have required this degree of consistency, and there may be some significance in the fact that Madison did not concur in his dissenting opinion.

On learning of Wirt's declination, Cabell wrote Cocke: Mr. Jefferson's "favorite system" would continue. It was destined to do so for three-quarters of a century.[22] Cabell did not think they should pursue the question of the presidency any further, saying that there was no member of the faculty to whom the office could be prudently committed and that the necessary powers could be given the chairman. He was pleased with the prospects of the University. He was telling everybody that never had he been so confident of its ultimate success.

[21] TJ to Joseph Coolidge, Jr., June 4, 1826 (*Papers, MHS*, p. 376).

[22] Cabell to Cocke, Apr. 6, 1826 (Cabell Papers, UVA). The system continued until 1904, when Edwin A. Alderman became the first president of the University of Virginia.

Lomax, who had been suggested in the first place by Madison and whose constitutional principles may be assumed to have been satisfactory to him and Jefferson, accepted the professorship of law. The appointment was well received and was fully justified by his subsequent career. He visited the University promptly and said he would assume his duties in July.[23] Jefferson believed that, with the establishment of a school of law, all the dormitories would be filled, and with good reason he could congratulate himself on the completion of the faculty.

Before the meeting of the Visitors, Cocke expressed the opinion that Key and Long could never "fraternize freely" with their colleagues. It seemed that their conduct at the time of the riot had drawn a "line of separation" between them and the other professors.[24] They were the first members of the original faculty to depart, but they did not do so in Jefferson's lifetime. Their later achievements attested to their professional competence.[25]

The professors were at a disadvantage because of the shortage of books. The collection that was housed in Pavilion VII while the dome room of the Rotunda was unfinished represented only the beginnings of the library. At their meeting in April the Visitors had appointed William Wertenbaker student librarian, but the boxes of books that were arriving from London, Paris, and other cities remained unopened, or at least unpacked, while a place was being prepared for them. In an effort to remedy the shortage of textbooks Jefferson wrote a strong letter to the booksellers in Boston who were supposed to supply them.[26]

He was not merely concerned for book learning as life was being renewed out of doors that spring. In April his thoughts turned to the physical world and the aspects of nature that he liked best. Late in the month he wrote Professor Emmet that the time had come to consider the introduction of botany in the scheme of instruction. In his opinion the subject should be taught when nature was in general bloom in April or May and would require a botanical garden. He sent Emmet a copy of a paper given him by the Abbé Correa which summarized the actions they must take to prepare for instruction at the next session. The first of these was to select a site of about six acres for a botanical garden. He described one possibility and gave a number of specific suggestions about what should be done with it. A list of plants and trees should be made and steps be taken to procure them. He submitted his plans to the consider-

[23] TJ to Visitors, Apr. 21, 1826 (Cabell, p. 377). Lomax was to arrive on July 5, the day after Jefferson died (Lomax to TJ, June 21, MHS).

[24] Cocke to Cabell, Feb. 15, 1826 (Cabell Papers, UVA).

[25] Key left after two years and Long after three. Both became professors in the newly established University of London (Bruce, II, 144–149). For their later careers see the *DNB*.

[26] TJ to Cummings & Hilliard, Apr. 8, 1826 (LC).

ation of the professor but made it clear that he wanted to begin operations. Emmet was appalled by the letter, saying that the school of natural history contained too many subjects. This chemist did not want to teach botany.[27]

In his reply Jefferson said that he would like to relieve Emmet of some of the subjects assigned to him but made it clear that under existing circumstances the professor would be held responsible not only for chemistry but for botany, zoology, geology, and mineralogy. He did not prescribe the proportion of time that should be allotted each, but he left no doubt that he himself thought botany more important than geology and preferred the study of plants to that of rocks.

The Rector availed himself of this opportunity to describe the policy of the institution for the benefit of all the professors. No one of them should expect to confine himself to his field of special interest. Each of them must do the best he could with all the subjects assigned to his school. While no one familiar with his own habits of study could have rightly charged him with condoning superficiality, he recognized that they were subject to necessary limitations. Thus he said:

> We do not expect our schools to turn out their alumni already enthroned on the pinnacles of their respective sciences; but only so far advanced in each as to be able to pursue them by themselves, and to become Newtons and Laplaces by energies and perseverance to be continued through life.[28]

He had not given up the eighteenth-century idea of a well-rounded man, and he regarded formal schooling as merely the beginning of an educational process which everyone must continue for himself. Emmet had no choice in this matter. Late in May Jefferson told Cocke that they had selected a site for a botanical garden.[29] It was not to be established, however, and after Jefferson's death Emmet was relieved of the task of teaching botany.

There were other plans of the Old Sachem's that miscarried or could not be put into full effect. Although the enrollment had not come up to expectations, some of the classes were crowding the quarters that had been assigned them in the pavilions, and it might have been predicted that faculty wives would prefer that lectures be given elsewhere than in their living rooms. His policies and principles were maintained to a re-

[27] TJ to J. P. Emmet, Apr. 27, 1826 (L. & B., XVI, 163–167); Emmet to TJ, Apr. 28 (HEH).

[28] TJ to Emmet, May 2, 1826 (L. & B., XVI, 168–172).

[29] TJ to J. H. Cocke, May 20, 1826 (UVA).

Thomas Jefferson
Statue by Carl Bitter, 1915 (on the Lawn at the University of Virginia).
(Photo by Robert Llewellyn)

markable degree, however; and his parental authority was fully recognized as long as he had the strength to exercise it.

iii

On March 16, 1826, Jefferson drafted and signed his will; he added a codicil the next day. This was four weeks before his eighty-third birthday. Both documents are in his strong, clear handwriting. In the will proper, after describing in precise detail the land he was giving Francis Eppes at Poplar Forest, he bequeathed his residual estate in trust to his daughter Martha.[30] That is, he left it to three trustees: his grandson Jeff, his grandson-in-law Nicholas Trist, and Alexander Garrett, bursar of the University. The purpose of this procedure, as he stated specifically, was to avoid all possible danger that the property would fall into the hands of the creditors of his insolvent son-in-law. After the death of Thomas Mann Randolph the property could come into Martha's legal possession. Jeff Randolph was named the sole executor.

The will contained the customary injunction about the payment of the testator's debts. An indication of how much they amounted to was given to the public about this time. In the first official announcement of the lottery, which was made three weeks after Jeff set out on his journey to the eastern cities, it was stated that there would be 11,480 tickets at ten dollars each. Some allowance should be made for the expenses of the lottery but these were expected to be small. All the rest of the money would be applied to Jefferson's relief.[31]

In the codicil provision was made for specific bequests — a walking staff to James Madison, watches to all the grandchildren, his books to the University, freedom to certain slaves.[32] These were Burwell, who might have been called the maître d'hôtel but was by trade a glazier; John Hemings, the carpenter; Joe Fosset, the blacksmith; and Madison and Eston Hemings, apprentices of John, who were to be freed on attaining maturity. Each of these valued servants had a trade by which he could be supported. Apparently Burwell had not been actively pursuing his. He was left $300 with which to buy tools or use in some other way. John Hemings and Joe Fosset were to keep their tools. Their owner directed that these workmen be provided with houses that were located at a convenient distance from the probable scene of their future labors.

[30] Jefferson's will (Ford, X, 392–396). Francis Eppes, though living at Poplar Forest, was not yet in legal possession.

[31] *Richmond Enquirer*, Apr. 25, 1826. His debts on July 4, 1826, were calculated to be $107,273.63. See Appendix II, Section E, below.

[32] TJ's library was actually sold to help pay his debts.

He hoped they could be employed at the University. Since the law required that emancipated slaves leave the state within a year, he asked the legislature to grant them permission to remain, as in fact it did.[33] These freedmen could take care of themselves. The same could not have been said of the large body of his slaves. To have turned them loose in a society in which they would have been unwelcome would have been no kindness to them, and, in view of his indebtedness may have been illegal as well as impracticable.

The papers dealing with business went to Jeff as executor and all the others were left to him as his personal possession. These papers were kept in wooden presses. Apparently there were eight of them, and most if not all of them stood under the windows in Jefferson's cabinet.[34] He kept remarkable records and filed his voluminous papers systematically.[35] He did not regard everything he wrote as his personal property. He had left numerous official documents in Richmond and Washington, believing them to belong to the state and federal governments. Thus the collection at Monticello was smaller than the entire body of the Jefferson Papers as known today. But many writings of great public interest and historical importance — such, for example, as the one that came to be known as his autobiography — were there. Written in 1821, this is essentially an account of public affairs during the American Revolution and his stay in France, as participated in and observed by him. It is not an especially self-revealing document.[36]

His bequest to his grandson included everything that was personal — not merely his Farm Book and Account Books but his vast correspondence. Jeff said in later years that the collection consisted of forty thousand letters. Throughout most of his mature life Jefferson kept copies of nearly all of the letters that he wrote; these he filed chronologically. Those he received were filed alphabetically in three series. His family letters were kept separate.[37] A man who guarded his private life as closely as he did could hardly have wanted these to be exposed to public view, but he almost certainly expected the rest of his papers to be made available, as they have been in repositories and, increasingly, in print. Thus his grandson's heritage became a priceless gift to posterity. His

[33] *Richmond Enquirer*, Jan. 6, 1827.

[34] One of these presses can be seen at Monticello, and four others have been located. Often called pedestal cases, they had doors, shelves, and sometimes drawers, and were about three feet high.

[35] A partial list of the presses with tables of their contents, in the writing of Nicholas Trist, provides an idea of TJ's system of classification (Coolidge Papers, UVA).

[36] TJ described this writing as "some memoranda," and TJR called it a "memoir." It is misleadingly printed as an "Autobiography" in Ford, I, 1–153.

[37] TJR to H. A. Washington, Aug. 6, 1850, quoted in the introduction of *Index to the Jefferson Papers* (LC, 1976), pp. ix–x.

literary legacy has been aptly described by a distinguished scholar as "the richest treasure house of information ever left by a single man."[38]

Jefferson left more than his gold-mounted walking stick to James Madison, his intimate friend and close associate for nearly half a century. In a letter written a month before he drafted his will, he included a valedictory passage. After referring to their long and harmonious association, he committed to Madison's special care the University he had fathered and the cause of pure republicanism to which their lives had been devoted. "To myself you have been a pillar of support through life," he said. "Take care of me when dead and be assured that I shall leave with you my last affections."[39] In his reply Madison said that Jefferson did not over-rate his interest in the University but that he could not hope to replace the "tutelary genius" of the institution. He also said that if his old friend valued their long and harmonious association, how much more must he prize it.[40]

Jefferson was in his mid-seventies when he told Abigail Adams about an old man who said that he was tired of pulling off his shoes and stockings at night and putting them on again in the morning. He did not say as much for himself but he observed that among human beings the desire to remain on earth was gradually extinguished.[41] The good lady to whom he was writing died of typhoid fever before two years had passed. To her bereaved husband he said that, having been tried in "the school of affliction," he was well aware of what his friend had suffered. He had learned that time and silence were the only medicine for immeasurable ills. Meanwhile, they could take comfort from the thought of an afterlife and their "ecstatic meeting" with those whom they had loved and lost but would never lose again.[42]

Jefferson once said that he rarely discussed religion and did so only in reasonable company. In response to one query from Adams he said that his religion was known only to himself and God and that its evidence must be sought in his life. "If that has been *honest and dutiful to society*," he said, "the religion which has regulated it cannot be a bad one."[43] In fact, his views on religion were almost as harmonious with those of Adams as were his political views with those of Madison. Eventually, for the benefit of this friend he stated at considerable length his reasons for

[38] Gilbert Chinard, *Thomas Jefferson: The Apostle of Americanism* (Boston, 1929), p. xvi.

[39] TJ to Madison, Feb. 17, 1826 (LC; all but first paragraph in Ford, X, 375–378).

[40] Madison to TJ, Feb. 24, 1826 (Hunt, IX, 243–246). On Madison's services to Jefferson after his death, see Adrienne Koch, *Jefferson and Madison: The Great Collaboration*, ch. IX.

[41] TJ to Abigail Adams, Jan. 11, 1817 (*A.-J. Letters*, II, 504).

[42] TJ to Adams, Nov. 13, 1818 (*ibid.*, 529).

[43] TJ to Adams, Jan. 11, 1817 (*ibid.*, 506).

believing in God.[44] He rejected as false John Calvin's God, whom he regarded as cruel. The God that he and Adams adored was "the Creator and benevolent governor of the world." To his mind it was impossible to view the Universe without perceiving in it a designing mind and a guiding hand. He did not need revelation; to him the evidence was irresistible.

Apparently he gave no explanation of his belief in immortality, of which no proof was available, but he continued to speak of his reunion with his wife and daughter. Toward the very end of his life he sent word to his old schoolmate James Maury that he looked forward to the reassembly of their class. John Adams shared his faith but could not resist making a humorous reference to it. He said he hoped and believed that he and Jefferson would meet in another world, but that if they did not they would never know it.[45]

Adams was well aware of his friend's anticlericalism and dissatisfaction with traditional Christian doctrine. He knew that Jefferson had his own version of the Gospels, although he never saw it. In final form this was called "The Life and Morals of Jesus of Nazareth." After deleting the miraculous passages Jefferson arranged the text in four columns — in Greek, Latin, English, and French. Thus he tried to present the ethical teachings of Jesus in all their purity. He began the work in his presidency and elaborated upon it some time after 1819, when he wrote William Short about it.[46] Whether anybody besides himself saw it in his lifetime is uncertain. He stated that the ethical teachings of Jesus far surpassed all others, and there can be no possible doubt that he sought to guide his conduct by them. In theology he was a Unitarian, but he was no sectarian, and this lifelong advocate of religious freedom practiced what he preached. He drew the plans of the little Episcopal church in Charlottesville, which was consecrated a few weeks before he died. He contributed to it as he did to the Presbyterian and Baptist churches in the same community.[47]

Although he believed in God and immortality, Jefferson was in no sense otherworldly. When Ellen Coolidge made her first visit to John

44 TJ to Adams, Apr. 11, 1823 (*ibid.*, 591–594).

45 TJ to Thomas Walker Maury, Mar. 3, 1826 (UVA); Adams to TJ, Feb. 25, 1825 (*A.-J. Letters*, II, 610).

46 TJ to Short, Oct. 31, 1819 (Ford, X, 144–145). On the presidential compilation see *Jefferson the President: First Term*, pp. 204–205. In the twentieth century "The Life and Morals" has appeared in many editions. A facsimile with an introduction by Cyrus Adler is bound at the back of L. & B., XX. An attractive printed version was edited by Henry Wilder Foote (1951).

47 Account Book, Mar. 8, 1824. On his church, which was torn down about 1895, see Fiske Kimball, "A Church Designed by Jefferson," *Architectural Record*, LIII (Feb., 1923), 184–186.

John Adams in his Ninety-first Year

Portrait by Gilbert Stuart, 1826. (Courtesy of the Smithsonian American Art Museum, Adams-Clement Collection; gift of Mary Louisa Adams Clement in memory of her mother, Louisa Catherine Adams Clement)

Adams, that veteran gained the impression from her report of her grandfather that he was willing to live his life over again. Adams disagreed, saying that he had lost father and mother, wife, children, and friends, and could not go through these griefs again. In response to this expostulation Jefferson stated that, although he did not actually desire to do so, he would not be unwilling to go over the scenes of the past. He had had a larger share of good health than most people, he said, and his spirits had never failed him except in paroxysms of grief. He would be glad to give up the last seven years, during which he had never been entirely well, but believed that, with good health and good spirits, the pleasures of life would surely outweigh its pains.[48]

iv

Jefferson's last letter to John Adams was the one in which he introduced Jeff Randolph. In it he said that if his grandson did not meet Adams on his New England trip he would think he had seen nothing. Joseph Coolidge, Jr., accompanied him to Quincy, and their visit was duly reported by their host.[49] Thus Jeff met a notable survivor of an age which his grandfather referred to as heroic. The old patriot was pleased with the manners of the young Virginian and much impressed with his stature. As for the letter Jeff brought with him, Adams described it as one of the most beautiful and delightful he had ever received. This was not the first time he complimented one of his letters from Monticello, but it was the last time, for he never wrote his comrade of 1776 again.

After the meeting of the Visitors in early April the Rector made only a few visits to the University, but he did something to expedite the lagging building program. Following a visit on May 4, he gave Brockenbrough precise instructions about the columns of the Rotunda.[50] During the next two weeks the Italian marble bases and capitals were hauled from the Rivanna River the final miles to the building site.[51] It was probably in early June that one of the capitals was placed on the southwest column on the portico of the Rotunda. It was on this occasion that Jefferson made what was probably his last visit to the academical village he had created. The story was told in the first place by William Werten-

[48] Adams to TJ, Dec. 1, 1825; TJ to Adams, Dec. 18 (*A.-J. Letters*, II, 611–613). For their earlier discussion of the same question see pp. 167–168 above.

[49] TJ to Adams, Mar. 25, 1826; Adams to TJ, Apr. 17 (*A.-J. Letters*, II, 613–614).

[50] TJ to Brockenbrough, May 5, 1826 (UVA).

[51] TJ may have made another trip to the grounds about this time; he reported to Cocke on May 20 (UVA) that he and Emmet had selected a site for the botanical garden.

baker. It was not recorded at the time, but it has an established and honored place in local tradition.[52]

According to one version, Jefferson viewed the operation from the balcony of Pavilion VII, after inspecting the provisional library there.[53] Since no trees had been planted as yet, his view would not have been obstructed. According to another account, he surveyed the scene through a window in the dome room of the Rotunda.[54] It is agreed that the student librarian provided the old man with a chair and that he occupied it for one hour. It is said that on this occasion he made the journey to the University and back on his horse Eagle. Before he rode away he must have inspected the work in the dome room, which had been delayed by the shortage of skilled craftsmen. Also, his bad luck with roofs continued, for this one leaked.

In the middle of May he had received the good news that the bill relieving the University of the import duties on the marble from Italy had passed both houses of Congress.[55] With the money to be refunded by the government he would be able to pay for the clock and bell about which he had corresponded with Joseph Coolidge. Therefore he instructed that obliging gentleman to close the deal with Simon Willard for the clock for the Rotunda. He sent him specifications, saying that they could easily take care of the aperture. If Willard could not provide the bell, someone else should be asked to do so.[56] Jefferson had previously stated that he wanted one that could be heard as far away as Charlottesville. Apparently this was the last business of any consequence that he transacted for the University.

With this letter he sent one to Ellen. He was expecting a visit from her and her husband in the near future. To this and the return of Cornelia he was looking forward with joyful anticipation, he said, and he reported that his health was tolerable.[57] His appetite for reading had not diminished; several weeks earlier he had ordered three books and he afterwards bought another. Nor had he lost his zest for measurement. In his Farm Book he had made this entry, not knowing that it would be his last:

[52] A bibliographical note on the various versions of this story of William Wertenbaker is given by Harry Clemons in the footnoted manuscript (Clemons Papers, UVA) of his *University of Virginia Library, 1825–1950* (1954). Wertenbaker (1797–1882) apparently repeated the story to many generations of students.

[53] Bernard Mayo, *Another Peppercorn for Mr. Jefferson* (Charlottesville, 1977), p. 26.

[54] David M. R. Culbreth, *The University of Virginia: Memories of Her Student-Life and Professors* (New York, 1908), pp. 140–141.

[55] L. W. Tazewell to TJ, May 11, 1826 (LC), received May 16.

[56] TJ to Coolidge, June 4, 1826 (*Papers, MHS*, pp. 374–377).

[57] TJ to Ellen, June 5, 1826 (*Family Letters*, pp. 477–478).

May 22, 1826. a gallon of lamp oil, costing $1.25 has lighted my chamber highly 25 nights, for 6 hours a night which is 5 cents & 150 hours[58]

As usual, Monticello was flooded with visiting relatives that spring. Early in May the feminine contingent in the family was increased: Virginia gave birth to a baby daughter. A letter of advice and encouragement from her somewhat more experienced sister in Boston arrived after the event.[59] On June 2 Jefferson gave to each of his grandsons Ben and Lewis his customary monthly allowance of two dollars. Soon thereafter Mary saw her first elephant at a circus in Charlottesville. It is possible that her grandfather also saw the creature since he made one of his rare visits to town that day.[60] He complained to Madison about the letters he had to answer but did not adopt that friend's suggestion that these be merely acknowledged in notes which members of his family could write.[61]

Jeff did not get home until June. His wife Jane had joined him in Baltimore, where they visited relatives. She afterwards expressed regret that tickets for the lottery were not put on sale at that time.[62] Jeff was awaiting word from New York, where the prospects of a large subscription were encouraging. On May 12 an account of what was now called the New York plan appeared in the *Enquirer*. This was a formalized version of the one that had been suggested in that paper a month earlier. It called for the purchase of lottery tickets by the community and their destruction on July 4. At the end of the month a caucus of Jefferson's friends was held in Richmond. This was followed by a public meeting on June 5, at which Governor John Tyler presided, Thomas Ritchie served as secretary, and several prominent citizens made speeches. It was decided to seek subscriptions that were limited to five dollars each so that they would be within the reach of nearly everybody.[63] One may doubt if much money could have been raised under this plan even in normal times, and, if Bernard Peyton is to be believed, the depression in Virginia was greater than it had been in 1819 and 1820. Just how this plan was to be reconciled with that of the lottery is not clear; nor is it

[58] *Farm Book*, Fuel and light section, p. 71.

[59] Martha Jefferson Trist was born May 8, 1826. Ellen wrote Virginia on May 9 (Coolidge Papers, UVA).

[60] Mary Randolph to Ellen, June 6, 1826 (*ibid.*).

[61] TJ to Madison, May 3, 1826; Madison to TJ, May 6 (MP). This was their last exchange of letters.

[62] Jane Randolph to Cary Ann Smith, June 27, 1826 (Edgehill–Randolph Papers, UVA).

[63] Peyton to TJR, May 31, 1826 (Randolph Papers, UVA); *Richmond Enquirer*, June 6.

clear just what came of the many meetings that were held in Virginia and elsewhere. Though he was discouraged by the unresponsiveness of Albemarle County, Joseph C. Cabell expressed confidence that the united exertions of Jefferson's friends would result in his deliverance from all his debts.[64] That would have pleased him greatly but it was destined not to happen.

When this devoted friend of the Old Sachem made his hopeful forecast on July 1, he must have been unaware of the state of affairs at Monticello. No lottery tickets were destroyed on July 4 because none had yet been sold. Before Jeff got the long-awaited message from New York, his grandfather had entered upon his final illness. Jefferson is said to have been conscious when $7500 arrived from admirers in New York. His grandson reported his death in a gracious letter in which he acknowledged this generous gift. A metropolitan newspaper printed the letter, saying that the gift had smoothed the patriot's way to the grave.[65] Jeff said that it was a comfort to his grandfather. No doubt it was if he was really aware of it, but the contributions to him from all sources fell far short of what was needed to pay his debts. The day after his death Bernard Peyton, who could not have heard of it as yet, said that a great deal was staked on his life just then.[66] The future of his daughter was staked on the success of the lottery, and, as Jeff was to find out, his death was a fatal blow to that.

Whatever Jefferson himself may have thought in his last days about the prospects of the lottery, he made a further effort to safeguard Martha. When Jeff got home he found his grandfather much disturbed about her. He said that she was sinking every day under the sufferings she was enduring and was literally dying before his eyes. He asked Jeff to promise never to leave her, and this his grandson did without hesitation.[67]

In the summer of 1825 Jefferson had said with grim humor that he had one foot in the grave and that the other was uplifted to follow it.[68] The date which marked the beginning of his last illness was June 24, 1826, when he summoned his trusted physician.[69] Dr. Dunglison had visited him earlier in the month, when he became troubled with diarrhea. His small reserve of strength was being depleted. His physician now had no hope of his recovery, and he himself seems to have had

[64] Cabell to Cocke, July 1, 1826 (Cabell Papers, UVA).

[65] TJR's letter of July 4, 1826, and an explanation from the *New York Commercial Advertiser* were reprinted in the *Richmond Enquirer*, July 18.

[66] Peyton to TJR, July 5, 1826 (Randolph Papers, UVA).

[67] Jane Randolph to Cary Ann Smith, June 27, 1826 (Edgehill–Randolph Papers, UVA).

[68] TJ to Frances Wright, Aug. 7, 1825 (Ford, X, 344).

[69] Dunglison, *Ana*, p. 32. TJ's letter to Dunglison is missing.

none. During the last week of his patient's life Dr. Dunglison remained at Monticello and was always on call. The members of the family in Boston were urged by Virginia to hasten their journey southward. To Cornelia she said: "Oh! How I wish you were all here."[70] Martha was usually at her father's bedside in the daytime. Jeff or Nicholas Trist was on watch at night. By all accounts Jefferson was lucid until the last two or three days and never lost his habitual serenity.

The events on July 3 are of special interest and have become familiar for that reason. The patriarch had lapsed into unconsciousness the night of July 2 and he awakened only a few times thereafter. On one or more of these occasions he inquired if this was the Fourth. Dr. Dunglison's response was that it soon would be; Nicholas Trist nodded his head before he had a right to do so. As midnight neared, he and Jeff kept their eyes glued to the slow-moving minute hand of the clock. When the hands reached twelve they knew that the old patriot's wish to live until the day he had done so much to make glorious had been granted.[71] The end came at fifty minutes past noon. It was remarked afterwards that the Declaration of Independence was presented to the Continental Congress at approximately that time.

There were many references to Jefferson in the papers on July 4, before the news of his death got out. In a sense the day already belonged to him as to no other. A letter of his appeared in the *National Intelligencer* that morning. Written on the very day he summoned Dunglison, it was his response to an invitation from the citizens of Washington to attend a celebration of the fiftieth anniversary of the Declaration of Independence.[72] He acknowledged the invitation with characteristic grace and declined it with deep regret. He did far more than that. He expressed the hope and belief that the bold action that he and his colleagues took half a century earlier would be a signal to the world. He hoped and believed that it would arouse men everywhere to throw off the shackles of tyranny and superstition and assume the blessings of self-government. "All eyes are opened, or opening, to the rights of man," he said. "The general spread of the light of science has already laid open to every view the palpable truth, that the mass of mankind has not been born with saddles on their backs, nor a favored few booted and spurred ready to ride them legitimately, by the grace of God."[73] This spirited expression of his own

[70] Virginia Trist to Cornelia Randolph, June 30, July 1, 1826 (Coolidge Papers, UVA).

[71] Accounts of TJ's last illness are in Dunglison, *Ana*, pp. 32–33; Randall, III, 543–548.

[72] TJ to Roger C. Weightman, June 24, 1826 (Ford, X, 390–392), replying to a letter of June 14 (LC), received June 21. The other living signers and presidents were also invited and responded.

[73] A source of the imagery of this letter is described by Douglass Adair in "Rumbold's Dying Speech, 1685, and Jefferson's last Words on Democracy, 1826" (*Fame and the Founding Fathers*, pp. 192–202).

undying faith may be regarded as his farewell message to his fellow Americans. It was reprinted many times after his death and was destined to be quoted by votaries of freedom from that day to this.

In his own community bells began tolling for its most distinguished citizen the afternoon he died. The next day both the faculty and the students of the University adopted resolutions. The latter assembled in the Rotunda. One of them said: "I never saw young men so deeply affected by any circumstance in my life."[74] They and their teachers were the more deeply grieved because they had known him personally. They afterwards wore black crepe on their left arms, as many local citizens did. All business in Charlottesville was suspended for a day. On July 7 the columns of the *Enquirer* were bordered in black, as they were again on July 11, after news of the death of John Adams on the same day as that of his fellow signer had reached Virginia. His last words, "Thomas Jefferson still survives," may have proved to be his most famous. The coincidence of the deaths of these two on the fiftieth anniversary of the founding of the Republic electrified its people. No less a person than President John Quincy Adams saw the hand of God in it.[75]

Jefferson was buried at Monticello on July 5. His gardener Wormley dug the grave, and John Hemings may be presumed to have made the coffin. It was borne to its resting place by his family and servants. The funeral services were performed by the Reverend Frederick Hatch, rector of the church Jefferson had designed and the teacher of his grandsons. The weather was bad, but the great body of the students and many of his Charlottesville and Albemarle neighbors were in attendance.[76] Ellen and Cornelia were not there; neither were James Madison and William Short, though they afterwards wrote impressive letters about their old friend. Immediately after her father's death Martha was so overcome with grief that she could not cry. Years later Dr. Dunglison said that he had an exalted opinion of his former patient. Jeff Randolph said that he died a pure and good man, but that comments on his greatness must be left to others.

There were enough tributes at the time to fill a volume. At the end of this volume it can be said that this man of many parts and great generosity offers something of interest to everybody. Not only was he an intensely devoted family man; he was a friend to mankind. Although rooted in his native soil he never ceased to contemplate the universe. No

[74] Henry Horace Worthington to Reuben B. Hicks, July 6, 1826 (University files, UVA).

[75] For the reaction of the nation to TJ's death, see Merrill D. Peterson, *Jefferson Image in the American Mind*, pp. 3–8. He describes the sources on p. 460.

[76] *Richmond Enquirer*, July 11, 14, 1826.

one can sum up his claims to remembrance better than he himself did. As the well-known inscription on his tombstone says, he wanted to be remembered as the author of the Declaration of American Independence and the statute of Virginia for religious freedom, and as father of the University of Virginia.[77] In these pages he has been viewed in his own time and circumstances. He was limited by these, and he made concessions to the society in which he lived. But he perceived eternal values and supported timeless causes. Thus he became one of the most notable champions of freedom and enlightenment in recorded history.

[77] It is uncertain just when TJ drafted the instructions for his tombstone. The original monument was erected by the "architects and builders" of the University. They requested the privilege of doing this on July 28, 1826. TJR agreed to it Aug. 4 (*Richmond Enquirer*, Feb. 3, 1827).

[APPENDIX I]

Descendants of Thomas Jefferson

THE following charts are based chiefly on the family table compiled by Olivia Taylor for *The Collected Papers of the Monticello Association of the Descendants of Thomas Jefferson*, edited by G. G. Shackleford (1965). Much additional information on the descendants is available in that book and in the annual reports of the association. Another source is *Burke's Presidential Families of the United States of America* (London, 1975).

A. *Children of Martha Jefferson (Sept. 27, 1772 – Oct. 10, 1836) and Thomas Mann Randolph (May 17, 1768 – June 20, 1828)*

NAME	BIRTH	MARRIAGE	CHILDREN THROUGH 1826	CHILDREN AFTER 1826	DEATH
1. Anne Cary	23 Jan. 1791	19 Sept. 1808 to Charles Lewis Bankhead	4	0	11 Feb. 1826
2. Thomas Jefferson	12 Sept. 1792	10 Mar. 1815 to Jane Hollins Nicholas	7[a]	6	8 Oct. 1875
3. Ellen Wayles	30 Aug. 1794				26 July 1795
4. Ellen Wayles	13 Oct. 1796	27 May 1825 to Joseph Coolidge, Jr.	1	5	21 Apr. 1876
5. Cornelia Jefferson	26 July 1799				24 Feb. 1871
6. Virginia Jefferson	22 Aug. 1801	11 Sept. 1824 to Nicholas Philip Trist	1	2	26 Apr. 1882
7. Mary Jefferson	2 Nov. 1803				29 Mar. 1876
8. James Madison	17 Jan. 1806				23 Jan. 1834
9. Benjamin Franklin	14 July 1808	13 Nov. 1834 to Sarah Champe Carter	0	3	18 Feb. 1871

12. George Wythe	10 Mar. 1818	Meikleham 20 Apr. 1852 to Mary E. (Adams) Pope			13 Apr. 1867

B. *Children of Maria Jefferson (Aug. 1, 1778 – Apr. 17, 1804) and John Wayles Eppes (Apr. 7, 1773 – Sept. 15, 1823)*[b]

NAME	BIRTH	MARRIAGE	CHILDREN THROUGH 1826	CHILDREN AFTER 1826	DEATH
1. Infant	31 Dec. 1799[c]				25 Jan. 1800[c]
2. Francis[d]	20 Sept. 1801	28 Nov. 1822 to Mary Elizabeth Cleland Randolph	2	4	30 May 1881
		15 Mar. 1837 to Susan Margaret (Ware) Couch		7	
3. Maria	15 Feb. 1804				July 1807

[a] The third child died in 1821 in her third year.
[b] Eppes's dates are from his biography in *D.A.B.*
[c] Probable date determined from letters and index of correspondence. See TJ to Martha Randolph, Jan. 21, 1800, and to Maria Eppes, Feb. 12 (*Family Letters*, pp. 181–185).
[d] Sometimes called Francis Wayles Eppes (FWE).

[APPENDIX II]

Jefferson's Financial Affairs

A. *The Milton Lands*

A few weeks before Jefferson's inauguration as President, his attention was called by Craven Peyton, then the lessee of Shadwell, to the possibility of purchasing lands from the heirs of Bennett Henderson, one of the founders of the village of Milton, who had died intestate in 1793. These lands, surrounding and in part including the village, lay south of the Rivanna and abutted Jefferson's on the east. Following court action in the fall of 1801, Henderson's estate was divided into relatively small parcels among his widow and ten children. Meanwhile, Jefferson had authorized Peyton to become a purchaser for him, negotiating in his own name.[1] Mrs. Henderson, who moved to Kentucky with most of the children, was a cousin of Jefferson's, but relations between the two families do not appear ever to have been intimate and in recent years they had become strained. Bennett Henderson had built a mill at Mountain Falls on the Rivanna below Jefferson's property, but this had long been inoperative. When the Hendersons sought to build a new dam, Jefferson obtained an injunction on the ground that this would infringe on his rights by raising the water level of the Rivanna, thereby affecting the operation of his mill. A court ruling in his favor was handed down in the fall of 1799. His actions in this connection appear to have been resented by the Hendersons.

During Jefferson's presidency, Peyton bought up nearly all of the Henderson holdings at Milton, going to Kentucky to negotiate regarding those of the minor children. These purchases were listed in Jefferson's land roll of 1810 but were not legally conveyed to him by Peyton until

[1] Peyton to TJ, Feb. 6, 1801; TJ to Peyton, Feb. 15, 18, 1801 (UVA). Numerous letters and documents bearing on this topic are in the Jefferson Papers at the University of Virginia. For the location of Milton, see map, p. 254, above.

August 11, 1811. The cost to him, which he met as he went along, was a little short of $8000.[2] He made some purchases in his own name after his retirement.[3] Title to some of these lands was later disputed. Three of the children, having come of age, refused their consent to sales made to Peyton in their behalf by their brother James. It came to light that he was not their legal guardian, and their mother professed ignorance of these negotiations. Furthermore, the land that James had put in bond as a safeguard proved to be of little value and not wholly his. The final outcome of the legal proceedings in this case in 1817 was that Jefferson's ownership of at least three parcels was denied, and that he was required to pay rent on them for the period of his occupancy and repurchase them.[4] He did not question Peyton's integrity in this matter, but appears to have had considerable doubt of that of the Hendersons.

Other legal difficulties arose from the Henderson properties. The eldest son, John, whom Peyton described as a man of "base principles," remained in Albemarle and threatened to rebuild the mill at Mountain Falls. He did not do so, but he did dig a canal across lands formerly belonging to his mother that had been purchased for Jefferson by Peyton. Henderson claimed that his mother had granted him the right to do this before she sold the land. Peyton went to court against him but lost his case in the early stages. Before it came up again on appeal Henderson, who was in desperate straits, sold the mill site. After Peyton bought these former holdings the case was dropped. But hardly had this happened (January 7, 1812), when a new contender appeared in the person of David Michie, who claimed that he had prior rights to the mill site, based on an agreement of 1804 with Henderson. Peyton tried but failed to engage Michie in a duel, and that claimant forcibly entered the property. Jefferson regained it by warrant, however, and Michie first promised, and then refused, to settle the dispute out of court.

This was in 1813 and the matter dragged on at least four more years, during which Jefferson under authorization of the county court took depositions in the case. As late as 1817, Michie was threatening further legal action, but he seems to have taken none.[5] The episode is chiefly significant as an illustration of the litigious character of the society in

[2] Statement of account with Peyton on Jan. 7, 1811 (LC) shows a total of $7844.50, to which no doubt some legal expense was added.

[3] In his Account Book, May 7, 1810, he notes that the purchase of a share from Joseph Brand in the warehouse at Milton consolidated his title to the Henderson property there.

[4] See below, ch. XXI. Afterwards a fourth child objected to the sale of his inheritance, but what came of this is unclear (Bennett Henderson to TJ, May 15, 1818, UVA).

[5] Michie to TJ, Mar. 20, 1817; TJ to Michie, Mar. 22, 1817 (MHS).

which the ex-President lived, and of the annoyances he suffered as a landowner and millowner in his last years.[6]

B. *Foreign Debts upon Retirement*

The subject of Jefferson's pre-Revolutionary debts to British creditors, particularly those connected with the Wayles inheritance, is dealt with in *Jefferson the Virginian*, especially pp. 441–444, and in *Jefferson and the Ordeal of Liberty*, pp. 176–179 and 529–530, references being given to the sources. During his presidency, Jefferson made a final payment on his share of the Wayles debt to Farell & Jones of Bristol.[7] Upon retirement he was still obligated to two British firms, although he had made payments to both. In a letter of July 13, 1810, he stated that he owed Cary & Co. of London a total of £684 6s. 3d.[8] This was primarily a debt of the Wayles estate. His debt to Henderson, McCaul, & Co. of Glasgow, represented by James Lyle in Virginia, amounted to £877 as of May 14, 1808.[9] A small portion of this was on his mother's account.

A post-Revolutionary foreign debt was owed to Van Staphorsts & Hubbard of Amsterdam. This was based on an outright loan of $2000 made in 1796, and on money advanced for him in Europe amounting to $1120 in 1797. By December 31, 1815, when Jefferson refinanced the debt with the company, he owed $6249.60.[10] The representatives of the Van Staphorsts in the United States were Leroy and Bayard of New York until September 1823, and after that Ludlow of the same city. Although Jefferson made further payments on his foreign debts during his retirement, at his death he still owed money for at least two of them and probably all three.[11]

[6] Boynton Merrill, Jr., presents an interesting and somewhat more detailed account of these affairs (*Jefferson's Nephews*, pp. 55–70). I was privileged to see this in advance of publication. Unfortunately, a number of relevant letters were unavailable when he conducted his research and this led him to attribute to TJ a grander scheme than is warranted.

[7] Mar. 7, 8, 1807, Account Book.

[8] To L. W. Tazewell (MHS).

[9] Account of that date, UVA.

[10] Account of that date, LC.

[11] See below, Section E. The records are unclear concerning the Cary & Co. debt. The last mention of it found is in a March, 1823, statement of his debts in his Account Book.

C. *Dealings with William Short*

While William Short was abroad, Jefferson looked after his interests in Virginia along with some of his investments and appears to have had a very free hand.[12] In the years between his retirement from the secretaryship of state and his accession to the presidency, being in need of cash to buy nailrod, he availed himself of interest payments of Short's which were at his disposal. He treated these as a temporary loan against ample assets. Writing his old secretary in complete candor and some dismay on his own fifty-seventh birthday, he reported that his total indebtedness on this account amounted to $9000 with interest.[13] He executed mortgages on lands and slaves to cover this. He may have revealed a weakness in his accounting system when he said that, although he had duly recorded every item in his memorandum book (referred to in this work as Account Book), he had neglected to sum up the items. It would seem that, while he kept in his current Account Book a full record of his financial transactions day by day, he had no ledger and thus was not always aware of just where he stood.

Short, who revered Jefferson and trusted him implicitly, was rarely if ever disposed to criticize any of his actions and did not do so in this instance. By the middle of Jefferson's second term he was fully repaid.[14] In the first year of the War of 1812 Jefferson again became indebted to Short, but this was as a result of a transaction that appears to have been to the latter's advantage. In 1795 Jefferson had purchased for him, from Charles Carter of Blenheim, the estate then known as Indian Camp.[15] This contained somewhat more than thirteen hundred acres, adjoining James Monroe's lands, and had no mansion as yet. Preferring to remain in Europe, Short did not build one and settle there, as Jefferson had hoped he would, and on his return to America in 1810 he chose to live in Philadelphia. So far as Albemarle County was concerned, he was content to be a guest at Monticello. Jefferson found a purchaser for his lands in David Higginbotham, the Milton merchant to whom he was always indebted. Late in 1812 he negotiated and early in 1813 he put into effect a plan whereby Higginbotham got Short's estate in return for the cancellation of Jefferson's debt to him as of August 1, 1812. Short got from Jefferson three bonds totaling $10,000.

[12] Of special interest on this topic are "Some Letters of Jefferson," in *Southern Bivouac* of Louisville, Ky., new series, II (1887).

[13] TJ to Short, Apr. 13, 1800 (*ibid.*, pp. 633–634).

[14] TJ recorded in his Account Book, July 6, 1807, that with the remittance of that day of $797.11 his debt to Short was paid in full.

[15] G. G. Shackelford, "William Short and Albemarle," in *Magazine of Albemarle County History*, XV, 1955–56, p. 21.

If this was precisely the same tract that was purchased for him in 1795 for $4700, Short made a considerable profit on the deal. No doubt he found Jefferson's bonds fully as acceptable as those of Higginbotham would have been, and they were wholly paid off in only a little more than two years. From the money Jefferson got in 1815 for the library he sold to Congress, he took $10,500 to repay Short with interest. At the same time he paid $1000 on his current account with Higginbotham.[16]

D. *Jefferson's Debt to Mazzei*

From the time of their first meeting in 1773, Jefferson often found himself called upon to assist Philip Mazzei with his financial affairs.[17] While both were in France, this assistance extended to personal loans of a substantial sum of money. After Jefferson returned to America and Mazzei stayed in Europe, Jefferson ended up looking after Mazzei's American property and attempting to settle his affairs.[18] These numerous services all were done purely as a matter of friendship.

The last and most difficult part of Mazzei's Virginia estate to be settled consisted of a house and lot in Richmond. Jefferson in 1805 recommended that he be empowered to sell the property, to which Mazzei agreed, but it proved necessary to recover it through proceedings in the courts, and no satisfactory sale could be arranged until 1813.[19]

At that time the war with Great Britain was in progress and the enemy was blockading Chesapeake Bay. Fears of inflation and bank insolvency had driven up the price of real estate so the sale was quite favorable ($6342.21), but the remittance of this sum to Mazzei in Italy was impracticable. Unwilling to trust the banks with the proceeds, and believing that it was undesirable to tie up the money in long-term government loans, Jefferson determined to retain the money himself at the legal interest rate of six per cent per annum. He promised to remit the interest annually if desired and to repay the principal within two years after a

[16] TJ to Short, Oct. 17, 1812, and Feb. 10, 1813 (*Southern Bivouac*, new ser., II, 752–753); Account Book, Feb. 10, 1813, and Apr. 29, 1815, noting bonds to Short and their payment; TJ to Higginbotham, Nov. 5, 1812, and documents dated Jan. 31, Feb. 27, 1813 (UVA).

[17] *Jefferson the Virginian*, pp. 164–165; *Jefferson and the Rights of Man*, pp. 109–110.

[18] Much material on these affairs has been published by Howard R. Marraro: "Jefferson Letters Concerning the Settlement of Mazzei's Virginia Estate," *Miss. Valley Hist. Review* (Sept., 1943), pp. 235–242; "Unpublished Mazzei Letters to Jefferson," *W. & M.* (Oct., 1944), pp. 374–396, and (Jan., 1945), pp. 71–100; "The Settlement of Philip Mazzei's Virginia Estate: Unpublished Correspondence and Other Documents," *Va. Mag.* (July, 1955), pp. 306–331.

[19] Mazzei to TJ, Feb. 15, 1811, *W. & M.* (Jan., 1945), pp. 94–95; TJ to Giovanni Carmignani, July 18, 1816 (misdated 1817), *Va. Mag.* (July, 1955), pp. 312–313.

call. As he told Mazzei, with American commerce blockaded, the use of this money was certainly a convenience to him.[20]

Although upon learning of the sale Mazzei requested immediate remittance of the proceeds, Jefferson was informed by Thomas Appleton, American consul at Leghorn, that his aged friend was no longer to be trusted to manage his own affairs and that his family wished Jefferson to hold onto the money.[21] Circumstances changed after March 20, 1816, when Mazzei died. Informed of this by the executor of the estate, Jefferson proposed in a letter of July 1816 to repay the principal and interest in three annual installments, beginning the next spring.[22] But the harvests of 1816 and 1817 turned out disastrously for Jefferson. He was forced to ask that the money be allowed to remain in his hands, though he promised to make an annual payment of the interest owed, and to repay the principal as soon as he could.[23] Andrea Pini, the husband of Mazzei's daughter, acceded to Jefferson's request, thanking him for his "infinite kindness," and saying that they were unable to invest the money to better advantage.[24]

Jefferson sent his first interest payment in August, 1817, and faithfully remitted a similar payment every year following until the end of his life. After he settled up the back interest in April, 1818, the new principal amounted to $7400 and his annual interest payments to $444 plus exchange expenses.[25] Though the Pinis began calling for payment of a portion of the principal after 1820, Jefferson was never able to manage it. On his deathbed he drew Jeff Randolph's attention particularly to the debt and Jeff, as executor, promised to pay it.[26] He began payments in 1828 but held up after Mazzei's stepdaughter contested the right of the Italian heirs to the money. It was not until 1840 that he settled the account. Altogether he seems to have paid $13,082.69 to the Pinis, which covered the interest to August 1, 1841.[27]

[20] TJ to Mazzei, Dec. 29, 1813 (Ford, IX, 440–443).
[21] Appleton to TJ, Oct. 25, 1815, *Va. Mag.* (July, 1955), pp. 309–310.
[22] TJ to Giovanni Carmignani, July 18, 1816 (*ibid.*, pp. 313–314).
[23] TJ to A. Pini, Aug. 19, 1817, *Miss. Valley Hist. Review* (Sept., 1943), pp. 237–240.
[24] A. Pini to TJ, Nov. 15, 1817, *Va. Mag.* (July, 1955), p. 314.
[25] Account and Bond, Apr. 5, 1818, *W. & M.* (Jan., 1945), p. 98. See also Account Books.
[26] TJR to Henry Pratt, *Va. Mag.* (July, 1955), pp. 320–321.
[27] Thomas Green to TJR, Nov. 22, 1840, Randolph Papers, UVA.

E. *The Final Estate of Thomas Jefferson*

No record has been found that completely describes the settlement of Jefferson's estate. A list of his debts as of July 4, 1826, is available.[28] These are stated as:

James Lyle (Henderson, McCaul, & Co.)	$ 7,095.00
Opie Norris, assignee of David Higginbotham	5,026.00
Andrea Pini, heir of Mazzei	8,066.00
Hiram Saunders	344.90
A. Robertson, Lynchburg	6,164.33
James Leitch	2,807.40
Ludlow of New York (Van Staphorsts, Hubbard, & Co.)	1,120.00
Banks in Richmond	16,540.00
Th. J. Randolph	60,110.00
Total	$107,273.63

All of these accounts, except for that of Hiram Saunders, who provided groceries, have been discussed previously. Exactly what was encompassed in the debt to Jeff Randolph is unclear, but it certainly included the obligation for Wilson Cary Nicholas, as well as various expenses he paid for his grandfather out of his own funds and those of his father's estate. Jeff Randolph calculated that the debts in his own name amounted to $61,064.25. Unfortunately for anyone who wants to understand Jefferson's financial situation, his affairs were entangled with those of Nicholas and the two Randolphs.

As for Jefferson's assets, while there are inventories and appraisals of his property, these are incomplete. In his will he dispensed with any inventory of his belongings within the house at Monticello. The appraisers for the lottery valued Monticello and 409 acres surrounding it at $71,000, the Shadwell Mills at $30,000, and the Milton property at $11,500.[29] If these amounts had been realized, Jefferson's liabilities would have been more than covered; and half the real estate and all the slaves would have remained.

It is said that Jefferson's debts were not completely paid off until 1878, after Jeff Randolph's death.[30] To determine what actually happened will take far more study, if it is possible at all. The answer is unclear to as

[28] Edgehill–Randolph Papers, UVA.

[29] *Richmond Enquirer*, July 28, 1826.

[30] G. G. Shackelford on TJR in *Collected Papers of the Monticello Association*, p. 79. Joseph Vance, in his dissertation on TJR, devoted a chapter to his role as executor (pp. 107–124), but he did not work out the details.

basic a question as how many slaves Jefferson possessed at the end of his life. According to the Farm Book, by 1822 he seems to have had upwards of 260. Yet in a statement estimating his assets and liabilities as of April 1, 1823, he seems to indicate that he held 230.[31] The advertisement for the November 3, 1826, sale of his personal property said that about two hundred Negroes would be offered.[32] This should not have included the five he wanted to set free. However, the inventories of his slaves in the Albemarle County Will Book add up to only 150. Another puzzle is how much money was raised to assist Jefferson in 1826. What it is possible to say is that most of Jefferson's properties were sold by his descendants and that ultimately all his known debts were paid.

[31] UVA.
[32] *Richmond Enquirer*.

[APPENDIX III]

The Hemings Family

DURING the years covered in this volume, the descendants of Betty Hemings, who had died in 1807, continued to play a prominent part in the daily lives of Jefferson and his descendants.[1] These mulatto slaves tended to be singled out for the jobs requiring skill and responsibility: butler, painter, cook, seamstress, carpenter, children's nurse, blacksmith. All five of the slaves freed under Jefferson's will were members of this family; others of them previously had been freed or, if able to pass as white, allowed to run away. They merit study, but the record left of their lives is disappointingly small.[2] This is particularly true in the period of this volume with regard to Sally, the tenth of Betty's children. No evidence has been found of her except in various census and provisions lists in the plantation records.[3]

During Jefferson's presidency it had been alleged that Sally was his concubine and that he was the father of her children. He denied the story in a personal letter. Grandchildren of his later stated privately that Sally was in fact the mistress of one of his nephews. These matters were discussed in detail in *Jefferson the President: First Term*, pp. 212–214, 494–498. Additional information is presented in Dumas Malone, "Mr. Jefferson's Private Life," American Antiquarian Society, *Proceedings*, LXXXIV, Pt. 1 (Apr., 1976), 65–72.

[1] The Hemings genealogy in Bear, *Jefferson at Monticello* (opposite p. 24) identifies twelve children and nineteen grandchildren. At least eight of the family had been freed, or sold, or had died by 1809. However, there were additional grandchildren as well as great-grandchildren.

[2] James A. Bear, Jr., director of Monticello, has made a particular effort to add to our knowledge of the family. In "The Hemings Family of Monticello" (*Virginia Cavalcade*, XXIX [Autumn, 1979], 78–87) he brings to light new information on Robert, James, and John. He has published additional findings in his reports to the Board of Trustees of the Thomas Jefferson Memorial Foundation for 1977, 1978, and 1979. Another recent account is Elizabeth Langhorne, "The Other Hemings" (*Albemarle Magazine*, III [Oct./Nov., 1980], 58–66).

[3] Most of these are in the *Farm Book*.

The context in which the stories appeared has also been examined. Several articles have been published which shed new light on the politics and personalities involved in the scurrilous attacks on Jefferson at the beginning of his presidency.[4] "A Note on Evidence: The Personal History of Madison Hemings," by Dumas Malone and Steven H. Hochman (*Journal of Southern History*, XLI [Nov., 1975], 523–528) discusses a controversial later statement of the legend. In *The Jefferson Scandals: A Rebuttal* (New York, Dodd, Mead, 1981), Virginius Dabney ably summarizes much of what has been written about the topic in all its aspects in the last decade.[5]

[4] Steven H. Hochman, "On the Liberty of the Press in Virginia: From Essay to Bludgeon, 1798–1803," *Va. Mag.*, LXXXIV (Oct., 1976), 431–445; V. Dennis Golladay, "Jefferson's 'Malignant Neighbor,' John Nicholas, Jr.," *Va. Mag.*, LXXXVI (July, 1978), 306–319; Charles A. Jellison, "James Thomson Callender: 'Human Nature in a hideous form,' " *Va. Cavalcade*, XXIX, 63–69.

[5] This is an expansion of his article done with John Kukla, "The Monticello Scandals: History and Fiction," *Va. Cavalcade*, XXIX, 53–61.

Acknowledgments

THROUGH all the years that have been spent on the preparation of this volume, and for almost as long a period before that, the biographical enterprise in which I have been engaged has enjoyed the support of the National Endowment for the Humanities. There have been many changes in the personnel of this great agency since I first turned to it for help. If I should attempt to name all of its officials who have befriended me and this series, I could not help leaving somebody out. Therefore, I shall content myself with thanking them as a group for their generosity, patience, and understanding. Also, I want to express my appreciation of the honor that has frequently been paid this work in the publications of the Endowment, and, in the last few years, by Chairman Joseph D. Duffey on more than one public occasion.

The Thomas Jefferson Memorial Foundation, which may be said to have assumed the guardianship of this enterprise more than a score of years ago, has continued to give it material aid and strong moral support. The resident director, James A. Bear, Jr., and his staff at Monticello have continued to be fully cooperative. I have expressed my gratitude to the Foundation in three of the previous volumes of this series, and it is my particular pleasure to do so in the last one.

While this work on the Father of the University of Virginia is in no sense an official biography, it has received much help from the officers of the institution at all stages. An episode that occurred when this volume was half done calls for special mention. The University librarian, Ray W. Frantz, Jr., always a solicitous landlord, procured a magnifying machine which enabled me to read and write well enough to finish the book. Professor Raymond C. Bice, Jr., on whom I rely in electronic matters, installed it. Soon thereafter President Frank L. Hereford, Jr., caused a second machine to be procured for my use at home. The funds for this were provided by the Thomas Jefferson Memorial Foundation. For these invaluable services I am profoundly grateful.

The resources of the Alderman Library, where this enterprise has long been housed, have been of greater value for the study of the last period of Jefferson's life than for any other. While obligated to the entire staff from Ray Frantz downward, I am specially indebted to the staff of the Division of Manuscripts, with whom we have been in contact every week. Therefore, our special thanks to Edmund Berkeley, Jr., Douglas W. Tanner, and Michael F. Plunkett.

The study of the founding of the University has been greatly facilitated by copies of the minutes of the Board of Visitors during Jefferson's rectorship, which were generously provided by C. Waller Barrett. The editor of the Papers of James Madison, Robert A. Rutland, by making his files available, has made it unnecessary for us to consult the manuscripts of Jefferson's most intimate colleague.

There are two reasons for the use of the term "we" instead of "I" in many of these references. Since September, 1967, Katherine M. Sargeant has been my half-time secretary. The papers she has to keep in order have greatly increased in number during this period. In recent years, besides typing and retyping my interminable writings, she has read and reread them to me, helping me edit them in the process. A year after she entered upon her secretarial responsibilities, Steven H. Hochman began work as my part-time research assistant. He went on full time in July, 1973. Not only has he provided me with materials in abundance; he has helped me understand them by talking with me about them. He has made himself useful in so many ways that I rarely use the word "research" in speaking of him but refer to him without qualification as my assistant. The services of these two highly competent fellow workers, always great, have been indispensable in the years since my eyesight became dim. I salute them here, and elsewhere I am dedicating this book to them.

The help given me in connection with particular episodes and topics is gratefully acknowledged in the notes. If I have missed anybody, I hope I may be forgiven.

Because of the untimely death of Larned G. Bradford, my editor for many years, I cannot thank him for his many acts of kindness. I greatly appreciate the interest in this volume that has been shown by his successor, Roger Donald, and by Arthur H. Thornhill, Jr., president of Little, Brown and Company. I am grateful for their patience and have benefited from their counsel. Also, I am deeply indebted to Jean L. Whitnack for her invaluable services as copyeditor.

During the last few years nearly all of my writing has been done at home. Therefore, I owe my wife a special measure of thanks for putting up with me while I was working on this volume.

List of Symbols and Short Titles[1] Most Frequently Used in Footnotes

Account Book	Jefferson's informal account books, in various repositories. Cited by date only.
A.H.R.	*American Historical Review.*
A.-J. Letters	*Adams-Jefferson Letters*, ed. by L. J. Cappon.
Annals	*Annals of Congress.*
A.S.P.	*American State Papers*, ed. by Lowrie & Clarke. (Volumes entitled Foreign Relations are referred to as *A.S.P.F.R.*)
Beveridge	*Life of John Marshall*, by A. J. Beveridge.
Boyd	*Papers of Thomas Jefferson*, ed. by Julian P. Boyd.
Brant	*James Madison*, by Irving Brant.
Bruce	*History of the University of Virginia*, by P. A. Bruce.
Butterfield	*Letters of Benjamin Rush*, ed. by L. H. Butterfield.
Cabell	*Early History of the University of Virginia, as Contained in the Letters of Thomas Jefferson and Joseph C. Cabell*, ed. by N. F. Cabell.
Conant	*Thomas Jefferson and the Development of American Public Education*, by J. B. Conant.
D.A.B.	*Dictionary of American Biography.*
Domestic Life	*Domestic Life of Thomas Jefferson*, by Sarah N. Randolph.

[1] Repositories are designated by roman capitals run together, the names of editors and authors are in roman type, and the abbreviated titles of printed works are in italics. Further details about these works, and about others frequently used but more easily identified from the references in the notes, are in the Select Critical Bibliography which follows. To avoid excess of italics in the lists, long titles are printed there in roman except in cases where a magazine or other work is italicized to distinguish it from an article in it.

Family Letters	*The Family Letters of Thomas Jefferson*, ed. by E. M. Betts and J. A. Bear, Jr.
Farm Book	*Thomas Jefferson's Farm Book*, ed. by E. M. Betts.
Ford	*Writings of Thomas Jefferson*, ed. by P. L. Ford (10 volumes).
FWE	Francis Wayles Eppes, grandson of Jefferson.
Gaines	*Thomas Mann Randolph*, by William H. Gaines, Jr.
Garden Book	*Thomas Jefferson's Garden Book*, annotated by E. M. Betts.
HEH	Jefferson Manuscripts at the Henry E. Huntington Library, San Marino, California.
Honeywell	*The Educational Work of Thomas Jefferson*, by R. J. Honeywell.
Hunt	*Writings of James Madison*, ed. by Gaillard Hunt.
I.B.M.	*Instructions to the British Ministers to the U.S., 1791–1812*, ed. by Bernard Mayo.
J.-D. Correspondence	*Correspondence between Thomas Jefferson and Pierre Samuel du Pont de Nemours*, ed. by Dumas Malone.
JWE	John Wayles Eppes, son-in-law of Jefferson.
L. & B.	*Writings of Thomas Jefferson*, ed. by Lipscomb and Bergh.
LC	Library of Congress. Unless otherwise indicated, the references are to the Jefferson Papers there.
MHS	Massachusetts Historical Society. Unless otherwise indicated, the references are to the Jefferson Papers in the Coolidge Collection. See *Papers, MHS* below.
MP	Papers of James Madison, Library of Congress.
NA	National Archives, Washington, D.C.
Papers, MHS	*Jefferson Papers, Collections Massachusetts Historical Society*, 7 ser., I.
Pierson	*Jefferson at Monticello*, by H. W. Pierson.
Randall	*Life of Thomas Jefferson*, by H. S. Randall (3 vols.).
S.M.H.	*Writings of James Monroe*, ed. by S. M. Hamilton.
Sowerby	*Catalogue of the Library of Thomas Jefferson*, compiled by E. M. Sowerby (5 vols.).
TJ	Thomas Jefferson.
TJR	Thomas Jefferson Randolph.
TMR	Thomas Mann Randolph, Jr., son-in-law of Jefferson.
Trist, LC	Nicholas P. Trist Papers, Library of Congress.

Trist, UNC	Nicholas P. Trist Papers, University of North Carolina.
UVA	Alderman Library, University of Virginia. Unless otherwise indicated, the references are to the Jefferson manuscripts.
Va. Mag.	*Virginia Magazine of History and Biography.*
W. & M.	*William and Mary Quarterly.*

Select Critical Bibliography

A. *Manuscripts*

After Jefferson left the presidency his annual correspondence was reduced by more than half, but it remained extensive. In fact, for the seventeen years covered in this volume, more of his papers were available and studied than for any of its five predecessors. These manuscripts were drawn, with a few exceptions, from the following repositories:

University of Virginia, Charlottesville (UVA)
Massachusetts Historical Society, Boston (MHS)
Library of Congress, Washington (LC)
Henry E. Huntington Library, San Marino, CA (HEH)
Missouri Historical Society, St. Louis (Mo. Hist. Soc.)

All have published microfilm editions of their Jefferson collections, and these have been used at the Alderman Library of the University of Virginia in the research for this book.

While the research and writing were in progress, both the University of Virginia and the Library of Congress rearranged their collections in a more chronological fashion for new microfilm. To a fine calendar of the UVA collection (1950, reprinted with a supplement in 1973) was added a guide to the microfilm (1977), edited by Douglas W. Tanner. This includes much valuable information on other Jefferson collections and bibliography. An index to the papers at LC was also published (1976), with an essay by Paul G. Sifton on provenance. Therefore, the practice in earlier volumes of listing in footnotes the folio numbers of the previous arrangement has been discontinued. The strength of the LC collection is in public affairs but is hardly limited to that. The papers in the other repositories are more often of a private nature. The University itself is the subject of many manuscripts at UVA. However, the smaller HEH collection also includes much on the topic.

The letters of Jefferson's family were a particularly rich resource for this volume. Far more are available for this period than for earlier years.

They include at UVA various Randolph and Edgehill–Randolph collections, Carr–Cary papers, Coolidge papers, Carlton papers, Meikleham papers, and Nicholas papers. Much use was made of two large Nicholas Trist collections, one at LC and the other in the Southern Historical Collection, University of North Carolina, Chapel Hill.

The most important of Jefferson's associates was James Madison. Fortunately, his papers are being edited at the Alderman Library. Virtually all of his papers cited in this volume were seen as copies in the files of this project, though most originated at LC and are cited as MP. For James Monroe the LC microfilm of his papers was consulted. The papers at UVA of the Cabell family and of the Cocke family were of great value. Also useful were University records, particularly the Faculty Minutes, and various Albemarle County records, available on microfilm. Other manuscript collections and repositories drawn on for an item or two are mentioned in the footnotes.

B. *Jefferson's Published Papers*

For this volume as for its predecessors the most important printed sources are:

The Writings of Thomas Jefferson. Paul Leicester Ford, ed., 10 vols. (New York, 1892–1899). Referred to as Ford.
The Writings of Thomas Jefferson. A. A. Lipscomb and A. E. Bergh, eds., 20 vols. (New York, 1903). Referred to as L. & B.

L. & B. is more comprehensive, but its transcriptions are often unreliable. Ford is far more accurate. The culmination of Jeffersonian editorial scholarship is anticipated in

The Papers of Thomas Jefferson. Julian P. Boyd, ed. (Princeton University Press, 1950–). Referred to as Boyd.

For as far as it goes, currently to March 31, 1791, in nineteen volumes, it supersedes all previous work. Meanwhile, the researcher must use a wide variety of sources, many of which offer far more than the documents themselves.

The works of Gilbert Chinard, published by the Johns Hopkins Press in Baltimore, deserve special recognition. Those used for this volume include:

The Correspondence of Jefferson and Du Pont de Nemours (1931).
Jefferson et les Idéologues, d'après sa correspondance inédite avec Destutt de Tracy, Cabinis, J. B. Say et Auguste Comte (1925).

The Letters of Lafayette and Jefferson. With an introduction and notes (1929).

The Literary Bible of Thomas Jefferson: His Commonplace Book of Philosophers and Poets (1928).

Volney et l'Amérique, d'après des documents inédits et sa correspondance avec Jefferson (1923).

The Family Letters of Thomas Jefferson (E. M. Betts and J. A. Bear, Jr., eds., Columbia, University of Missouri Press, 1966. Referred to as *Family Letters*) actually includes only his correspondence with his children and grandchildren. This may be supplemented by:

"Poplar Forest: Jefferson's Legacy to His Grandson." By Norma B. Cuthbert. In *Huntington Library Quarterly*, VI (May, 1943), 333–356.

"Some Family Letters of Thomas Jefferson." Wilson Miles Cary, ed. In *Scribner's Magazine*, XXXVI (November, 1904), 573–586.

Thomas Jefferson and His Unknown Brother Randolph. Bernard Mayo, ed. (Charlottesville, Tracy W. McGregor Library, University of Virginia, 1942).

Also valuable, now more as sources of family traditions and letters than as secondary works, are:

The Life of Thomas Jefferson. By Henry S. Randall. 3 vols. (New York, 1858). Referred to as Randall.

The Domestic Life of Thomas Jefferson. By Sarah N. Randolph (New York, 1871). Referred to as *Domestic Life.*

The Life of Thomas Jefferson. By George Tucker. 2 vols. (Philadelphia, 1837).

Correspondence with other major figures includes:

The Adams–Jefferson Letters: The Complete Correspondence Between Thomas Jefferson and John and Abigail Adams. Lester J. Cappon, ed., 2 vols. (Chapel Hill, University of North Carolina Press, for the Institute of Early American History and Culture at Williamsburg, 1959). Referred to as *A.-J. Letters.*

Correspondence between Thomas Jefferson and Pierre Samuel du Pont de Nemours, 1798–1817. Dumas Malone, ed., translations by Linwood Lehman (Boston, Houghton Mifflin Co., 1930). Referred to as *J.-D. Correspondence.*

Correspondence of Thomas Jefferson and Francis Walker Gilmer, 1814–1826. Richard Beale Davis, ed. (Columbia, University of South Carolina Press, 1946).

Early History of the University of Virginia, as Contained in the Letters of Thomas Jefferson and Joseph C. Cabell. Nathaniel Francis

Cabell, ed. (Richmond, 1856). Referred to as Cabell. There are deletions from a number of the letters.

The Jefferson–Dunglison Letters. John M. Dorsey, ed. (Charlottesville, University of Virginia Press, 1960).

Minor collections of miscellaneous letters are:

Glimpses of the Past: Correspondence of Thomas Jefferson, 1788–1826 (St. Louis, Missouri Historical Society, 1936).

The Jefferson Papers. Collections of the Massachusetts Historical Society, 7 ser., I (Boston, 1900). Referred to as *Papers, MHS*.

Thomas Jefferson Correspondence. Printed from the Originals in the Collections of William K. Bixby. With Notes by W. C. Ford (Boston, 1916).

"Some Jefferson Letters," Sigmund Diamond, ed. In *Mississippi Valley Historical Review*, XXVIII (September, 1941), 225–242. Primarily letters to David Bailie Warden.

Writings other than correspondence include:

The Complete Jefferson. Containing His Major Writings, Published and Unpublished, Except His Letters. Saul K. Padover, ed. (New York, Duell, Sloan & Pearce, 1943).

The Life and Morals of Jesus of Nazareth. Henry Wilder Foote, ed. (Boston, Beacon, 1951).

Notes on the State of Virginia. William Peden, ed. (Chapel Hill, University of North Carolina Press, published for the Institute of Early American History and Culture at Williamsburg, 1955).

Thomas Jefferson's Farm Book, with Commentary and Relevant Extracts from Other Writings. Edwin M. Betts, ed. (Princeton University Press, for the American Philosophical Society, 1953). Referred to as *Farm Book*.

Thomas Jefferson's Garden Book, 1766–1824, with relevant extracts from his other writings. Edwin M. Betts, ed. (Philadelphia, American Philosophical Society, 1944). Referred to as *Garden Book*.

On his works in architecture and in other arts there are:

The Eye of Thomas Jefferson. William Howard Adams, ed. (Washington, D.C., National Gallery of Art, 1976). Catalogue of the Bicentennial Exhibition.

Thomas Jefferson Architect. Original Designs in the Collection of Thomas Jefferson Coolidge, Jr. With an essay and notes by Fiske Kimball (Boston, printed for private distribution, 1916). The classic work.

The same, with a new introduction by Frederick D. Nichols (New York, DaCapo Press, 1968).

Thomas Jefferson's Architectural Drawings. Compiled and with commentary and a check list by Frederick D. Nichols. Revised and enlarged 2nd edn. (Boston, Massachusetts Historical Society; Charlottesville, Thomas Jefferson Memorial Foundation and University Press of Virginia, 1961).

A most unusual work, compiled and annotated by E. Millicent Sowerby, is the *Catalogue of the Library of Thomas Jefferson*. 5 vols. (Washington, Library of Congress, 1952–1959). Referred to as Sowerby. It describes the library TJ sold to Congress in 1815 and includes comments of his on many of its contents. A supplement to this, compiled by William B. O'Neal, is:

Jefferson's Fine Arts Library: His Selections for the University of Virginia Together with His Own Architectural Books (Charlottesville, University Press of Virginia, 1976).

C. *Official and Semi-official Collections*

American State Papers. Documents, Legislative and Executive. Selected and edited, under the authority of Congress, by Walter Lowrie and Matthew St. Clair Clarke. 38 vols. (Washington, 1832–1861). Referred to as *A.S.P.*

Foreign Relations. Vol. III. Referred to as *A.S.P.F.R.*

Annals of Congress, 1789–1824. 42 vols. (Washington, 1849–1856). Referred to as *Annals*.

Calendar of Virginia State Papers and Other Manuscripts. H. W. Flournoy, ed., Vol. X (Richmond, 1892).

Circular Letters of Congressmen to Their Constituents, 1789–1829. Noble E. Cunningham, Jr., ed., 3 vols. (Chapel Hill, University of North Carolina Press, for the Institute of Early American History and Culture, 1978).

Instructions to the British Ministers to the United States, 1791–1813. Bernard Mayo, ed. In *Annual Report of the American Historical Association for the Year 1936*, Vol. III (Washington, 1941). Referred to as I.B.M.

Journals of the Senate and House of Delegates of Virginia. (Richmond, 1817, 1820).

Manual of the Board of Visitors of the University of Virginia. (Charlottesville, 1975).

Report and Documents Respecting the University of Virginia. (Richmond, 1820).

Reports of Cases Decided by the Honorable John Marshall, in the Circuit Court of the United States for the District of Virginia and North Carolina, from 1802–1833, by John W. Brockenbrough (Philadelphia, 1837).

The Statutes at Large; being a Collection of all the Laws of Virginia. William Waller Hening, ed., 13 vols. (Richmond, 1809–1823).

The Statutes at Large of Virginia . . . being a Continuation of Hening. Samuel Shepherd, ed., Vol. III (Richmond, 1836).

Sundry Documents on the Subject of a System of Public Education for the State of Virginia (Richmond, 1817).

Supplement, Containing the Acts of the General Assembly (Richmond, 1812).

Supplement to the Revised Code of the Laws of Virginia (Richmond, 1833).

D. *Contemporary Writings*

1. CORRESPONDENCE AND OTHER PAPERS

ADAMS, JOHN. Correspondence between the Hon. John Adams . . . and the Late Wm. Cunningham (Boston, 1823).

———. The Spur of Fame: Dialogues of John Adams and Benjamin Rush, 1805–1813. John A. Schutz and Douglass Adair, eds. (San Marino, Calif., Huntington Library, 1966).

———. Statesman and Friend: Correspondence of John Adams with Benjamin Waterhouse, 1784–1832. W. C. Ford, ed. (Boston, Little Brown, 1927).

———. Works. C. F. Adams, ed., 10 vols. (Boston, 1856).

ADAMS, JOHN QUINCY. Diary, 1794–1845. Allan Nevins, ed. (New York, Scribner's, 1951).

CORREA DA SERRA. The Abbé Correa in America, 1812–1820. Richard Beale Davis, ed. In *Transactions of the American Philosophical Society*, Vol. 45, Part 2 (1955).

DUNGLISON, ROBLEY. The Autobiographical Ana. Samuel X. Radbill, ed. In *Transactions of the American Philosophical Society*, Vol. 53, Part 8 (1963).

GALLATIN, ALBERT. Writings. Henry Adams, ed. Vol. I (Philadelphia, 1879).

LONG, GEORGE. *Letters.* Thomas Fitzhugh, ed. (University of Virginia Library, 1917).

MADISON, JAMES. Papers. Robert A. Rutland et al., eds. Vol. 8 (University of Chicago Press, 1973).

———. Writings. Gaillard Hunt, ed. 9 vols. (New York, 1900–1910). Referred to as Hunt.

MONROE, JAMES. Writings. S. M. Hamilton, ed. 7 vols. (New York, 1898–1903). Referred to as S.M.H.

RUSH, BENJAMIN. Letters. L. H. Butterfield, ed. Vol. II (Princeton University Press, for the American Philosophical Society, 1951). Referred to as Butterfield.

———. The Spur of Fame. *See* Adams, John.

SMITH, MARGARET BAYARD. The First Forty Years of Washington Society. Gaillard Hunt, ed. (New York, 1906).

STORY, JOSEPH. "The Story–Marshall Correspondence (1819–1831)," Charles Warren, ed. In *William and Mary Quarterly*, 2 ser., XXI (January, 1941), 1–26.

TICKNOR, GEORGE. Life, Letters, and Journals. George S. Hillard et al., eds. 2 vols. (Boston, 1876).

VAN BUREN, MARTIN. Autobiography. John C. Fitzpatrick, ed. In *Annual Report of the American Historical Association for the Year 1918*, II (Washington, 1920).

WEBSTER, DANIEL. Papers: Correspondence. Vol. I. Charles M. Wiltse, ed. (Hanover, N.H., University Press of New England, for Dartmouth College, 1974).

II. TRAVELS AND REMINISCENCES

BACON, EDMUND. Jefferson at Monticello. *See* Pierson, Hamilton W.

FOSTER, SIR AUGUSTUS JOHN. Jeffersonian America. Notes . . . Collected in the Years 1805–6–7 and 11–12. Edited with an introduction by Richard Beale Davis (San Marino, Calif., Huntington Library, 1954).

JEFFERSON, ISAAC. Memoirs of a Monticello Slave. As Dictated to Charles Campbell in the 1840's by Isaac, one of Thomas Jefferson's Slaves. Rayford W. Logan, ed. (Charlottesville, University of Virginia Press, for Tracy W. McGregor Library, 1951). This and Pierson, below, have been reprinted together under the title *Jefferson at Monticello.* James A. Bear, Jr., ed. (Charlottesville, University Press of Virginia, 1967).

PIERSON, HAMILTON W. Jefferson at Monticello: The Private Life of Thomas Jefferson (New York, 1862). Referred to as Pierson. This presents the reminiscences of Edmund Bacon.

III. MISCELLANEOUS WORKS

BURK, JOHN DALY. The History of Virginia. Vol. I (Petersburg, 1804).

[CARPENTER, STEPHEN CULLEN]. Memoirs of the Hon. Thomas Jefferson. 2 vols. (New York, 1809).

[DESTUTT DE TRACY, COMTE ANTOINE LOUIS CLAUDE]. A Commentary and Review of Montesquieu's Spirit of Laws (Philadelphia, 1811).

DESTUTT DE TRACY, COMTE ANTOINE LOUIS CLAUDE. A Treatise on Political Economy (Georgetown, 1817). Reprinted in John M. Dorsey, *Psychology of Political Science* (Detroit, Center for Health Education, 1973).

IRVING, WASHINGTON. A History of New York. Edwin T. Bowden, ed. (New Haven, College & University Press, 1964).

MERCER, CHARLES FENTON. A Discourse on Popular Education (Princeton, 1826).

PICKERING, TIMOTHY. A Review of the Correspondence Between . . . John Adams and Wm. Cunningham. . . . 2nd edn. (Salem, 1824).

[SMITH, MARGARET BAYARD]. A Winter in Washington; or, Memoirs of the Seymour Family (New York, 1824).

[TAYLOR, JOHN]. Arator, being a Series of Agricultural Essays, Practical and Political (Georgetown, 1813).

TAYLOR, JOHN. Construction Construed, and Constitutions Vindicated (Richmond, 1820).

———. An Inquiry into the Principles and Policy of the Government of the United States (Fredericksburg, 1814).

TUCKER, ST. GEORGE. Blackstone's Commentaries: With Notes of Reference, to the Constitution and Laws of the Federal Government of the United States; and of the Commonwealth of Virginia. 5 vols. (Philadelphia, 1803).

WIRT, WILLIAM. Sketches of the Life and Character of Patrick Henry (Philadelphia, 1817).

E. *Newspapers and Periodicals*

"I read but a single newspaper, Ritchie's *Enquirer*, the best that is published or ever has been published in America." Jefferson's statement to William Short, September 8, 1823 (L. & B., XV, 468–469) suggests the importance of the *Richmond Enquirer* (before Sept. 20, 1815, simply *The Enquirer*) to this biography. It represented his primary source of news and generally reflected his point of view. To Thomas Ritchie, its editor and publisher (Claiborne W. Gooch became a partner March 3, 1820), Jefferson turned when he wanted his opinion made known. The *Enquirer* took a more rigid position on state rights than did Jefferson, but he himself lost flexibility in his last years.

Jefferson did not actually limit himself to a single news vehicle. Not until December 1818 did he cancel his subscriptions to the *National Intelligencer* (Washington, D.C.) and the *Aurora* (Philadelphia, Pa.). He maintained his subscription to *Niles' Weekly Register*, a news magazine that began publication in Baltimore, Md., in 1811, and when a paper was founded in Charlottesville, the *Central Gazette*, in January 1820, he subscribed to it. Other papers were also sent to him at times. In varying degrees all these were consulted for this volume. Unfortunately, relatively few issues of the *Central Gazette* have survived. Other newspapers used for research include the *Boston Patriot* (Mass.), the *Charleston Courier*

(S.C.), the *Virginia Gazette* (Richmond), and *Poulson's American Daily Advertiser* (Philadelphia, Pa.).

Periodicals that Jefferson received were consulted. These include the *Edinburgh Review* (published in Scotland but reprinted in the U.S.), the *North American Review* (Boston) and John E. Hall's *American Law Journal* (Baltimore).

All publications were read at UVA, mostly in the original but occasionally in microform.

F. *Maps*

The maps in this volume are included to help its readers understand the setting. They are not intended to be definitive in terms of scientific cartography. Nevertheless they are based on research. The "Jefferson Country" map drawn for the endpapers of the Betts edition of the *Farm Book* provided a starting point.

The best sources found regarding Jefferson's properties and those of the University were the maps and plats in his own papers at UVA. He drew many of these himself. Also in his papers were itineraries, one including the mileages between the stops on his routes from Monticello to Poplar Forest.

Two printed maps of Virginia with which Jefferson was connected were used: the 1818 edition of Bishop James Madison's map and the 1827 Wood–Böÿe nine-sheet map. Jefferson contributed corrections to the first, suggested guidelines and a surveyor for the second (see TJ to Bishop Madison, Dec. 29, 1811, L. & B., XIX, 183–184; and TJ to W. C. Nicholas, April 19, 1816, L. & B., XIV, 471–487). Green Peyton's 1875 map of Albemarle County provided many locations for old estates.

Current highway and geological survey maps were also of assistance. Nathaniel Mason Pawlett of the Virginia Highway and Transportation Research Council offered suggestions, as did several residents of Buckingham County. A relatively successful attempt to follow Jefferson's travel routes provided other valuable insights.

G. *Secondary Works and Articles**

Adams, Henry. The Life of Albert Gallatin (Philadelphia, 1879).

Adams, Randolph G. Three Americanists (Philadelphia, University of Pennsylvania Press, 1939).

*This very select list contains the titles of indispensable works and others to which I am specially indebted.

Alexander, Edward P. "Jefferson and Kosciuszko: Friends of Liberty and of Man," in *Pennsylvania Magazine of History and Biography*, XCII (January, 1968), 87–103.

Alvord, Clarence W., ed. Governor Edward Coles (Springfield, Ill., 1920).

Ambler, Charles Henry. Thomas Ritchie: A Study in Virginia Politics (Richmond, 1913).

Ammon, Harry. James Monroe: The Quest for National Identity (New York, McGraw-Hill, 1971).

Anderson, Dice R. William Branch Giles: A Study in the Politics of Virginia and the Nation from 1790 to 1830 (Menasha, Wis., 1914).

Bemis, Samuel Flagg. John Quincy Adams and the Foundations of American Foreign Policy (New York, Knopf, 1949).

Bestor, Arthur. "Thomas Jefferson and the Freedom of Books," in *Three Presidents and Their Books* (Urbana, University of Illinois Press, 1955).

Betts, Edwin M. "Ground Plan and Prints of the University of Virginia, 1822–1826," in American Philosophical Society, *Proceedings*, XC (April, 1946).

———, and Hazlehurst Bolton Perkins. Thomas Jefferson's Flower Garden at Monticello. 2nd edn. (Charlottesville, University Press of Virginia, 1971).

Beveridge, Albert J. The Life of John Marshall. Vol. IV (Boston, 1919). Referred to as Beveridge.

Boorstin, Daniel J. The Lost World of Thomas Jefferson (New York, Holt, 1948).

Boyd, Julian P. "The Chasm That Separated Thomas Jefferson and John Marshall," in *Essays on the American Constitution*, Gottfried Dietze, ed. (Englewood Cliffs, N.J., Prentice-Hall, 1964).

Brant, Irving. James Madison: The President, 1809–1812 (Indianapolis, Bobbs-Merrill, 1956). Referred to as Brant, V.

———. James Madison: Commander in Chief, 1812–1836 (Indianapolis, Bobbs-Merrill, 1961). Referred to as Brant, VI.

Brown, Richard H. "The Missouri Crisis, Slavery, and the Politics of Jacksonianism," in *South Atlantic Quarterly*, LXV (Winter, 1966), 55–72.

Bruce, Philip Alexander. History of the University of Virginia, 1819–1919. 5 vols. (New York, 1920).

Bruce, William Cabell. John Randolph of Roanoke. 2nd edn., 2 vols. in one (New York, 1922).

Burns, Francis P. "The Graviers and the Faubourg Ste. Marie," in *Louisiana Historical Quarterly*, XXII (April, 1939), 385–427.

Burns, James MacGregor. The Deadlock of Democracy; Four-Party Politics in America (Englewood Cliffs, N.J., Prentice-Hall, 1963).

Bush, Alfred L. The Life Portraits of Thomas Jefferson. Catalogue of an exhibition at the University of Virginia Museum of Fine Arts,

April 12–26, 1962 (Charlottesville, Thomas Jefferson Memorial Foundation, 1962).

BUTTERFIELD, LYMAN H. "The Dream of Benjamin Rush: The Reconciliation of John Adams and Thomas Jefferson," in *Yale Review*, XL (December, 1950), 297–319.

CHANDLER, JULIAN A. C. The History of Suffrage in Virginia (Baltimore, 1901).

———. Representation in Virginia (Baltimore, 1896).

CHINARD, GILBERT. *See* pp. 522–523 for works by this author.

COLBOURN, H. TREVOR. The Lamp of Experience: Whig History and the Intellectual Origins of the American Revolution (Chapel Hill, University of North Carolina Press, for the Institute of Early American History and Culture at Williamsburg, 1965).

COLES, HARRY L. The War of 1812 (University of Chicago Press, 1965).

CONANT, JAMES B. Thomas Jefferson and the Development of American Public Education (Berkeley, University of California Press, 1962).

CORWIN, EDWARD S. John Marshall and the Constitution (New Haven, 1919).

CRIPE, HELEN. Thomas Jefferson and Music (Charlottesville, University Press of Virginia, 1974).

DANGERFIELD, GEORGE. The Awakening of American Nationalism, 1815–1828 (New York, Harper & Row, 1965).

DARGO, GEORGE. Jefferson's Louisiana: Politics and the Clash of Legal Traditions (Cambridge, Harvard University Press, 1975).

DAVIS, DAVID BRION. The Problem of Slavery in the Age of Revolution, 1770–1823 (Ithaca, Cornell University Press, 1975).

DAVIS, RICHARD BEALE. Francis Walker Gilmer: Life and Learning in Jefferson's Virginia (Richmond, Dietz, 1939).

———. Intellectual Life in Jefferson's Virginia, 1790–1830 (Chapel Hill, University of North Carolina Press, 1964).

———. *See also* Correa da Serra, p. 526.

DORFMAN, JOSEPH. The Economic Mind in American Civilization, 1606–1865. Vol. I (New York, Viking, 1946).

DUMBAULD, EDWARD. "A Manuscript from Monticello: Jefferson's Library in Legal History," in *American Bar Association Journal*, XXXVIII (May, 1952), 389–392, 446–447.

———. Thomas Jefferson and the Law (Norman, University of Oklahoma Press, 1978).

FEHRENBACHER, DON E. The Dred Scott Case: Its Significance in American Law and Politics (New York, Oxford University Press, 1978).

FISCHER, DAVID H. The Revolution of American Conservatism: The Federalist Party in the Era of Jeffersonian Democracy (New York, Harper & Row, 1965).

FREDRICKSON, GEORGE M. The Black Image in the White Mind: The Debate on Afro-American Character and Destiny, 1817–1914 (New York, Harper & Row, 1971).

FUSSELL, PAUL, JR. Theory of Prosody in Eighteenth-Century England (New London, Connecticut College Press, 1954).

GAINES, WILLIAM H., JR. Thomas Mann Randolph, Jefferson's Son-in-Law (Baton Rouge, Louisiana State University Press, 1966). Referred to as Gaines.

GOFF, FREDERICK R. "Jefferson the Book Collector," in *Quarterly Journal of the Library of Congress*, XXIX (January, 1972), 32–47.

GRAMPP, WILLIAM D. "A Re-examination of Jeffersonian Economics," in *Southern Economic Journal*, XII (January, 1946), 263–282. Reprinted in M. D. Peterson, *Thomas Jefferson, A Profile* (see below).

GRAY, LEWIS CECIL. History of Agriculture in the Southern United States to 1860. 2 vols. (The Carnegie Institution of Washington, 1933).

GUNTHER, GERALD, ed. John Marshall's Defense of McCulloch v. Maryland (Stanford University Press, 1969).

HAMMOND, BRAY. Banks and Politics in America, from the Revolution to the Civil War (Princeton University Press, 1957).

HATCHER, WILLIAM B. Edward Livingston: Jeffersonian Republican and Jacksonian Democrat (Baton Rouge, Louisiana State University Press, 1940).

HOFSTADTER, RICHARD. The Idea of a Party System: The Rise of Legitimate Opposition in the United States, 1780–1840 (Berkeley, University of California Press, 1969).

HONEYWELL, ROY J. The Educational Work of Thomas Jefferson (Cambridge, Harvard University Press, 1931).

———. "President Jefferson and His Successor," in *American Historical Review*, XLVI (October, 1940), 64–75.

JOHNSTON, WILLIAM DAWSON. History of the Library of Congress, Vol. I, 1800–1864 (Washington, Government Printing Office, 1904).

KAPLAN, LAWRENCE S. "Jefferson, the Napoleonic Wars, and the Balance of Power," in *William and Mary Quarterly*, 3 ser., XIV (April, 1957), 196–217.

KENNEDY, JOHN P. Memoirs of the Life of William Wirt. 2 vols. (Philadelphia, 1850).

KIMBALL, FISKE. *See* p. 524 for this author.

KOCH, ADRIENNE. Jefferson and Madison: The Great Collaboration (New York, Knopf, 1950).

———. The Philosophy of Thomas Jefferson (New York, Columbia University Press, 1943).

LAMBETH, WILLIAM A. and WARREN H. MANNING. Jefferson as an Architect and a Designer of Landscapes (Boston, 1913).

LAMONTAGNE, LEO E. American Library Classification, with Special Reference to the Library of Congress (Hamden, Conn., Shoe String Press, 1961).

LEHMANN, KARL. Thomas Jefferson, American Humanist. 2nd impression (University of Chicago Press, 1965).

LEVY, LEONARD W. Jefferson and Civil Liberties: The Darker Side (Cambridge, Harvard University Press, 1963).

LONG, ORIE WILLIAM. Literary Pioneers: Early American Explorers of European Culture (Cambridge, Harvard University Press, 1935).

MADDOX, WILLIAM A. The Free School Idea in Virginia Before the Civil War: A Phase of Political and Social Evolution (New York, 1918).

MALONE, DUMAS. The Public Life of Thomas Cooper, 1783–1839 (New Haven, Yale University Press, 1926. Reprint, Columbia, University of South Carolina Press, 1961).

———. Jefferson the Virginian (Boston, Little, Brown, 1948).

———. Jefferson and the Rights of Man (Boston, Little, Brown, 1951).

———. Jefferson and the Ordeal of Liberty (Boston, Little, Brown, 1962).

———. Jefferson the President: First Term, 1801–1805 (Boston, Little, Brown, 1970).

———. Jefferson the President: Second Term, 1805–1809 (Boston, Little, Brown, 1974).

MARTIN, EDWIN T. Thomas Jefferson: Scientist (New York, Henry Schuman, 1952).

MEARNS, DAVID C. The Story Up to Now: The Library of Congress, 1800–1946 (Washington, Library of Congress, 1947).

MERRILL, BOYNTON, JR. Jefferson's Nephews: A Frontier Tragedy (Princeton University Press, 1976).

MILLER, JOHN CHESTER. The Wolf by the Ears: Thomas Jefferson and Slavery (New York, Free Press, 1977).

MOORE, GLOVER. The Missouri Controversy, 1819–1821 (Lexington, University of Kentucky Press, 1953).

MORGAN, DONALD G. Justice William Johnson: The First Dissenter (Columbia, University of South Carolina Press, 1954).

NADEL, GEORGE H. Studies in the Philosophy of History: Selected Essays from *History and Theory* (New York, Harper & Row, 1965).

NICHOLS, FREDERICK D. and JAMES A. BEAR, JR. Monticello (Charlottesville, Thomas Jefferson Memorial Foundation, 1967).

NORFLEET, FILLMORE. Saint-Mémin in Virginia: Portraits and Biographies (Richmond, Dietz, 1942).

O'NEAL, WILLIAM B. "Michele and Giacomo Raggi at the University of Virginia." With Notes and Documents. In *The Magazine of Albemarle County History*, XVIII (1959–1960), 5–31.

———. Pictorial History of the University of Virginia. 2nd edn. (Charlottesville, University Press of Virginia, 1970).

———. "The Workmen at the University of Virginia, 1817–1826." With Notes and Documents. In *The Magazine of Albemarle County History*, XVII (1958–1959), 5–48.

———, and FREDERICK D. NICHOLS, "An Architectural History of the First University Pavilion," in *The Magazine of Albemarle County History*, XV (1955–1956), 36–43.

PEARDON, T. P. The Transition in English Historical Writing, 1760–1830 (New York, Columbia University Press, 1933).

PEDEN, WILLIAM H. "Some Notes Concerning Thomas Jefferson's Libraries," in *William and Mary Quarterly*, 3 ser., I (July, 1944), 27.

———. "Thomas Jefferson, Book-Collector" (doctoral dissertation, University of Virginia, 1947).

PERKINS, BRADFORD. Prologue to War: England and the United States, 1805–1812 (Berkeley, University of California Press, 1963).

PETERSON, MERRILL D. The Jefferson Image in the American Mind (New York, Oxford University Press, 1960).

———. Thomas Jefferson, A Profile (New York, Hill and Wang, 1967).

———. "Thomas Jefferson and Commercial Policy, 1783–1793," in *William and Mary Quarterly*, 3 ser., XXII (October, 1965), 584–610.

———. Thomas Jefferson and the New Nation: A Biography (New York, Oxford University Press, 1970).

POLE, J. R. "Representation and Authority in Virginia from the Revolution to Reform," in *Journal of Southern History*, XXIV (February, 1958), 16–50.

RISJORD, NORMAN K. The Old Republicans: Southern Conservatism in the Age of Jefferson (New York, Columbia University Press, 1965).

ROBERT, JOSEPH C. "William Wirt, Virginian," in *Virginia Magazine of History and Biography*, LXXX (October, 1972), 386–441.

ROSENBERGER, FRANCIS COLEMAN, ed. Jefferson Reader: A Treasury of Writings about Thomas Jefferson (New York, Dutton, 1953).

ROTHBARD, MURRAY N. The Panic of 1819: Reactions and Policies (New York, Columbia University Press, 1962).

SARICKS, AMBROSE. Pierre Samuel du Pont de Nemours (Lawrence, University of Kansas Press, 1965).

SHACKELFORD, GEORGE G., ed. Collected Papers to Commemorate Fifty Years of the Monticello Association of the Descendants of Thomas Jefferson (published by the association, Princeton University Press, 1965).

SHALHOPE, ROBERT E. "Thomas Jefferson's Republicanism and Antebellum Southern Thought," in *Journal of Southern History*, XLII (November, 1976), 529–556.

SNAVELY, TIPTON R. George Tucker as Political Economist (Charlottesville, University Press of Virginia, 1964).

SPENCER, DONALD S. "Edward Coles: Virginia Gentleman in Frontier Politics," in *Journal of the Illinois State Historical Society* (Summer, 1968), LXI, 150–163.

STAUDENRAUS, P. J. The African Colonization Movement, 1816–1865 (New York, Columbia University Press, 1961).

SYDNOR, CHARLES S. The Development of Southern Sectionalism, 1819–1848 (Baton Rouge, Louisiana State University Press, 1948).

TAYLOR, WILLIAM R. Cavalier and Yankee: The Old South and American National Character (New York, Braziller, 1961).

TYLER, LYON G. Letters and Times of the Tylers. 2 vols. (Richmond, 1884–1885).

VANCE, JOSEPH C. "Knives, Whips and Randolphs on the Court House Lawn," in *The Magazine of Albemarle County History*, XV (1955–1956), 28–35.

———. "Thomas Jefferson Randolph" (doctoral dissertation, University of Virginia, 1957).

WALTERS, RAYMOND, JR. Albert Gallatin: Jeffersonian Financier and Diplomat (New York, Macmillan, 1957).

WARREN, CHARLES. The Supreme Court in United States History. 3 vols. (Boston, 1922).

WASHBURNE, ELIHU BENJAMIN. Sketch of Edward Coles, Second Governor of Illinois, and of the Slavery Struggle of 1823–4 (Chicago, 1882), reprinted in Clarence W. Alvord, ed., *Governor Edward Coles* (Springfield, Ill., 1920).

WRIGHT, LOUIS B. "Thomas Jefferson and the Classics," in American Philosophical Society, *Proceedings*, LXXXVII (November, 1943).

Index